MORPHEUS SPEAKS

THE ENCYCLOPEDIA OF DREAM INTERPRETING

R. J. COLE, MS, LEP

iUniverse

MORPHEUS SPEAKS
THE ENCYCLOPEDIA OF DREAM INTERPRETING

iUniverse books may be ordered through booksellers or by contacting:

iUniverse
1663 Liberty Drive
Bloomington, IN 47403
www.iuniverse.com
1-800-Authors (1-800-288-4677)

ISBN: 978-1-5320-7006-8 (sc)
ISBN: 978-1-5320-7007-5 (e)

Library of Congress Control Number: 2019942698

Print information available on the last page.

iUniverse rev. date: 07/26/2019

Contents

Acknowledgments

I would like to acknowledge all those who have shared the images of their dreams with me over the last thirty or so years. There have also been many teachers who have shown me how to read the enigmatic narratives of the dream world, some who have left their wisdom behind them through their books and lectures, such as Carl Jung and James Hillman, and some whom I have worked with directly, such as Jeremy Taylor and Stephen Aizenstat. I also thank my wife and children, who opened their hearts and dreams to me over the years and helped me to refine my craft.

Finally, I wish to thank the deep wisdom of the psyche and the playful way it has revealed itself through my own dreams and visions. This journey of self-discovery has opened new worlds, perspectives, realities, and understanding, making the world I live in so much richer than I ever imagined it to be.

Preface

My first memory of a dream happened when I was four. I dreamed of something trying to hurt me, and I couldn't scream or turn on the light. Sometimes I would wake clawing at the walls, bloodying my fingers, and watching the room pulsate around me.

At eight years old, I watched balls of light flitting about my room from my bed. At eleven, creatures and comic book characters flew through the sky as I lay on the grass during a summer evening.

As I grew older, the dreams grew more sophisticated and complex but continued to delight and haunt me across the next few decades of my life here on earth. I didn't always know how to read their enigmatic narrative, and I am still learning how to probe into their deeper meaning and how their symbolism applies to the days of my life.

Over time the symbolic world in dreams has transformed my relationship with the waking world. I now see the collective psyche of humankind playing out a fantastical mythology that I didn't know existed up until the last half of my life.

What have I learned? I've learned that we are much more than we seem. We are not just "skin encapsulated egos" as the late philosopher Alan Watts once said during one of his radio shows. In fact, these *egos* and bodies with whom we identify may very well be the tools through which our true selves interact with and create reality.

Be Gentle with Your Dreams

Be careful as you walk through the hidden forests of your dreams. They compose the unprotected essence of who and what you are. They are the messengers of your soul and your deeper self.

They harbor all your worries and fears, your dislikes and rejected aspects, your hopes and desires laid bare. They are born of the irrational, the imaginative, and the intuitive—a world of being as real and as informative as the rational world of science.

Both the outer masks that we all present to the world and the masks turned inward so that we don't look too deeply at the mysterious inner self are stripped away during our sleep, allowing us to see our most beautiful faces and darkest shadows.

Through our dreams we get a glimpse of what God sees in each and every one of us without judgment or condemnation. Dreams are a grace unearned and a gift to those who learn to accept and interpret them.

Treat them with care, respect, and compassion, for they reveal the best of us and the worst of us. They represent our guide through life and the equilibrium and balance that all living creatures need in order to survive in what is often a chaotic world. Our dreams are our inner saviors.

Dreams reveal a truth about our emotional state of mind, our physical well-being, our psychological health, and our sense of the spiritual. They are our deepest connection with everything, one another, and God or the universal spirit.

Dreams create a nightly map to the experience of being human, and if read properly, they can guide us to worlds not dreamed of through the conscious mind.

And they do all this uniquely for the dreamer who has them. Interpreters can hold our hands briefly and point to the way of the psyche, but the individual needs to walk this path alone. It is about the person's story and life narrative, and only he or she can know the true meaning of dreams.

In a way, how we interpret our dreams may be about how we interpret ourselves and how we think and imagine ourselves into being.

Introduction

Who looks outside, dreams. Who looks inside, awakens.
—C. G. Jung (*Memories, Dreams, Reflections*, 1961)

Is all that we see or seem is but a dream within a dream?
—Edgar Allan Poe, "A Dream within a Dream"

First of all, here's a little background on what qualifies me to write such a book. As part of my graduate school training in educational psychology, I learned the technique of using children's dreams as part of a therapeutic and diagnostic workup early on. I honed these skills through work with such dream analysts as Jeremy Taylor, James Hillman, and Stephen Aizenstat, as well as working the dreams of several hundred children assigned to me over twenty-eight years in working with the Santa Clara County Office of Education, special education, and alternative schools divisions.

I have also helped to decipher the dreams of more than three thousand individuals who sent me their dreams through my website and blogs this past decade. In addition, I have journalized and interpreted more than four thousand of my own dreams and presented several workshops on dreams, meditation, and dream interpretation.

I have authored two books on dreams titled *The Dragon's Treasure: A Dreamer's Guide to Inner Discovery* (2009) and *The Archipelago of Dreams* (2011).

Though I have written books on the subject, one of the complaints by those who have read them is that I have not provided enough detail for the process of interpretation or a broad enough list of possible dream image interpretations to help the beginning analyst (recreational or professional). I hope that this book will correct those oversights.

To be clear, I draw a distinction between dreams and dream interpretation, the former being the phenomena of dreaming and sleeping that is a scientifically studied, valid inquiry but tends to reduce dreams to objects of mere mechanistic interest, something our egos are already pretty good at, while the latter is an art, an intuitive expression of the psyche. They are the poetry of existence and an expression of our greater selves.

Fundamentally there are no hard-and-fast answers to the question "What does my dream mean?" And as with any art or expression of the self, it takes practice to perfect and to set it free.

You may, then, want to think of this book as an art class that will expose you to techniques and ideas that will help you to explore this expression of yourself.

Scattered throughout this encyclopedia, you will find **insights** attached to various dream image definitions. These are designed to help readers understand the history or etiology of some images, explain how I developed image interpretations and how one can contemplate broader meanings, and aid dreamers in going deeper into their own psyches, their inner selves.

The Primeval Mind

You and I think in symbols, language, or image-based symbols. Everything we see, every image and experience, is a symbolic representation of the people we are beneath the surface.

Some dream images are very personal and unique to an individual, and because of this uniqueness, there is no compendium of symbols that will apply to all people. Some are provided by our cultures and subcultures, but others come to us from our primeval minds, a shared human symbolic architecture that we call the *archetype*.

It is these *archetypes* of the symbolic mind that roam the forest primeval, the deep inner self, the unconscious, the ancestral underworld of the human *psyche*.

This part of our psyche leads us, guides us, and informs the essence of our being. It's what the soul draws on to manifest into the world and mingle with our dreams. It is our connection with all other humans and part of our shared patterns of thought. These archetypes of the unconscious are the universal images in our dreams and myths.

Among their vast number reside the symbols of the shadow, the anima/animus, great wisdom, and the divine. The trickster, the monk, the father, the queen, the devil, and death itself are also characters of this universal inner theater of the mind.

Here dream images of the budding flower, egg, and the phoenix bring forth a message of rebirth and resurrection and the idea that our being needs to continuously die to make room for something new. In other words, growth requires death.

Typically, we humans deny that ultimate conflict within us. All too often we project the conflict onto the world outside. This doesn't work, because that's not where the conflict resides.

It is in this world of the dream that the conflict between opposites is confronted, where Armageddon is played out as the metaphorical reconciliation of the conscious and unconscious mind.

Though we imagine a final battle between good and evil as though they were something outside ourselves, there is no real win or lose here, for it is not about dominance but about balance.

It is in these nether reaches that humankind can learn to accept both sides of our nature and become whole again. Until we sit down with both sides of ourselves and reconcile the differences, there can be no inner peace and therefore no peace on earth.

Without this ongoing negotiation, humans cannot see or hear one another genuinely. We only engage in dialogue with some unrecognized part of ourselves projected upon others.

While in the unrecognized shadow of the internal self, the world's problems seem to be outside ourselves, so we try to manipulate this outside world with limited success. But this results in less and not more personal control, which then leads to even greater attempts to control others.

Those who reject their shadows through either the rejection of others or their rejection of themselves shackle their opposite personalities (e.g., the extrovert to the introvert, the thinker to the emotional, the sensing to the intuitive). Note that in the evil person, the shadow is its good side, its compassionate side.

For some of us, this rejection hinders the expression of what has been called the oversoul, the Christ, the symbol of the true self, or the pneuma of humankind.

When we demonize other beings, we lay on them our shadow selves in order to punish or kill them. For many the rejection of the shadow is equal to the rejection of sin. But the sin is not in having a shadow. It is in refusing to recognize it and deal with it.

When we call another person arrogant, who is actually being arrogant? When we label people as being greedy, whose greed are we rejecting or refusing to see? When we accuse someone of being incompetent, have we acknowledged our own contribution to that legion of dishonor?

Contrary to the commonsense quote that suggests that what we don't know won't hurt us, the hidden parts of ourselves (i.e., that which we don't know) *can* hurt us and others.

We should not run from taking walks in the forests of our unconscious minds through the portals of our dreams. These are journeys toward healing and toward bringing balance to our chaotic lives.[*]

Do You Dream?

Dreams are a natural part of how the brain deals with all the information that is thrown at us on a day-to-day basis. Basically, this process happens during the second of three stages in our sleep cycle (called REM sleep), and it takes up 20 to 25 percent of our sleep time.

Everyone dreams all the time, whether they remember their dreams or not. Dreams are a way to peer into what is going on in the body, life, and the deepest and most closely held self, and intuition.

---

[*] Cole, R. J., "Dream Symbol Archetypes," http://thedreamingwizard.com/dream-symbol-archetypes_296.html (2016).

Through dreams one can lift the veil that seems to shroud reality. They can help one see through life's illusions—those created by the individual as well as the collective.

Thomas Moore calls dreams "the royal road to the soul" and claimed that "it is impossible to care for the soul and live at the same time in unconsciousness."[1] James Hillman thought of the dream as the psyche doing soul work.[2]

Through dreams people can learn what is necessary to create the world they envision. The answers are there if you can only learn to read the signs and interpret the language.

The ancient Greeks used to send their sick to temples called asclepeion to be cured. In these temples dreams would be incubated and used as part of the healing process. These dreams were also used to predict the future. The idea that dreams could be used to predict the future was very much a part of both the Greek and Roman religion. To predict the future through dream interpretation is sometimes called oneiromancy (from the Greek word *oneiros*, meaning to dream) and is a form of divination. The Oneiroi, those gods that ruled over dreams and nightmares, were said to be the brothers of Hypnos, the god of sleep, and of Morpheus, the god of dreams and the leader of the Oneiroi.

In ancient Egypt, the priests were dream interpreters, and these interpretations can still be seen in the hieroglyphics on some temple walls.

One of the earliest written dream interpretation records came from Egypt around 1350 BCE. In it the god Bes was said to be responsible for people's dreams.

However, the earliest may have been on a clay tablet from the Sumerian Epic of Gilgamesh around 2100 BCE.

The Welsh wizard Myrddin (Merlin) was a prophet, but he also interpreted dreams. A story by a sixteenth-century writer tells how Myrddin interpreted the dreams of his sister, Gwenddydd.[3]

In both the Old and New Testament, dreams were often referred to as a way in which mortals communicated with God or as omens. For example, in Genesis 37:5 of the Revised Standard Version of the Bible, Joseph dreamed an omen of his future success, and Jacob dreamed of a ladder to heaven where God spoke to him from the top (Genesis 28:12–17).

In the New Testament, the magi were warned to avoid King Herod (Matthew 2:12), and Paul was directed to travel to Macedonia (Acts 16:9–10) through a dream.

Though modern men have trouble understanding the influences of their unconscious especially in reading their dreams, the indigenous native peoples from all over the world, have through time shown remarkable ability to better understand the guidance that comes from their internal selves.

From the Australian Aborigine to the Hawaiian kahunas, Navajo, Lakota Sioux and Azteca shaman the waking and dreaming selves have always been a seamless whole.

> But if the vision was true and mighty, as I know, it is true and mighty yet; for such things are of the spirit, and it is in the darkness of their eyes that men get lost.
>
> *–Black Elk*

If you look carefully at your own dreams, you can see your own mythology, gather information about your emotional and spiritual development, and also gain insight into the events and people around you.

What Are Dreams?

There is experimental evidence that dreams are how the mind integrates the waking day's events into the overall experience of the brain. For example, it solidifies what is learned.

However, I also see dreams as revealing patterns within one's life that are unconscious to the waking mind. Because the mind has so much input during the waking hours that it needs to respond to just to survive, it has little time to observe objectively what is going on. Dreams provide this insight. Dreams can be the conscious mind's communication with the unconscious.

There is also some evidence that dreams may create some of our experiences in the waking world by revealing patterns in the every day that we ordinarily wouldn't see.

There is evidence that excessive dreaming or more specifically, excessive REM sleep can actually cause disorders such as depression. Why? We're not sure, but if you think of dreaming as part of the brain's regulatory system, continuous ruminations about negative material and intense emotions on behalf of the waking person can overload the conscious mind's ability to deal.

If the housekeeping aspect of the dream becomes overloaded as well, then it, too, has too much to deal with. This may result in anywhere from three to four times as much REM sleep in those who are suffering from depression, and indeed, some research has shown an increase in dreams from those who suffer depression. No wonder they wake up still tired.

The deeper effects of psyche overload can be found in the Nightmare section of this book.

Guided imagery, active imagining, cognitive behavior therapy,

and relaxation therapy have all been known to help.

For some patients with PTSD, a prescription drug used to decrease nightmare activity has also proven useful. However, a caution should be applied here. Until we know more about the functions of dreams, we should not attempt to end all dreaming as a means of *curing* the symptoms of too much dreaming!

Others claim that dreams have a problem-solving function. In the age of computers, some use the analogy that dreams are a "cleaning out of the software," sort of an off-line dumping of what is useless. Still others suggest that dreams serve no function and are just throwaway material. Consider the following perspectives about dreams:

The quote from Edgar Allan Poe at this chapter's beginning is not unlike the Australian Aborigine's belief in the dreaming of creation. Are we dreaming ourselves into existence?

Chuang Tzu, a Taoist philosopher from the fourth century BC, suggested that one could realize that life is no more than a dream as well. In his butterfly story, he seems to be making the same statement. In this example he dreams of being a butterfly, and upon awakening, he asks whether he is Chuang Tzu dreaming he was a butterfly or a butterfly dreaming he was Chuang Tzu.[4]

Philosopher Bertrand Russell (1872–1970) said, "I do not believe that I am now dreaming, but I cannot prove that I am not."

The Austrian psychiatrist Sigmund Freud claimed that dreams were wish fulfillment, though this might not at first be evident. He also thought that dreams might be a projection of one's fears based on past conditioning. (See Freud in the following sections.)

Is it possible that dreams can bring themselves into reality, that dream images, especially fearful images, can be brought into existence in the waking world?

Carl Jung, a Swiss psychiatrist and contemporary of Freud, believed that dreams have a self-regulatory aspect in that they maintain the individual's balance and harmony. He believed that dreams integrated the conscious with the unconscious. (See Jung in the following sections.)

Another psychologist named James Hillman was against the traditional theory that dreams tell people what to do. He thought that they were more for telling us where we are and that the images of the dream should not be broken down and analyzed for what they may say about the waking world but for what they may say about the psyche (i.e., the inner world). To Hillman, dream work was soul work. I think that Jung would agree. (See Hillman in the following sections.)

There is also some research that dreams have a mood regulator role.[5]

Tools for Interpreting Dreams

Searchers who want to understand the why of the world beyond its mechanics—most of all, the why of themselves—have to look inward for the answers.

I used dream interpretation to help develop a reliable psychological and emotional portrait of the children I worked with, and you can do this for yourself as well.

Getting Started

I've tried a number of techniques to both recall my dreams upon waking and then to interpret their meaning. Certain techniques seem to work for me more often than not, and I'll share them here in hopes that they will help you get started.

First, it takes a real commitment to do this because recalling dreams doesn't usually start right away. You may not recall a dream for days or weeks, and then if you remember anything, it sometimes seems like just a fragment. But fragments are good. Write them down. This practice reinforces the system. Besides, fragments can have meaning if taken in the right context.

Insight: There are times when I have a devil of a time remembering my dreams. I know that I've dreamed, but the memory has just melted away before I can get ahold of it. This is when I have to get in touch with my intention to recall a dream.

Sometimes a couple of days will pass; however, eventually, a snippet will remain, and I'll grab a pen and jot it down. These snippets or fragments may come to me for several days, but the stalled cycle has been broken. Eventually, I'll recall a full dream with all the bells and whistles.

Dream work takes patience, and that is something in short supply these days. Most of us have been programmed to want everything right now. Even our smartphones, tablets, faxes, internet contacts, social, and news media reinforce (or reflect) this.

But that whisper of the spirit within can't be heard above the noise and bustle of the modern world unless you take the time to quiet both the outer and inner worlds in order to hear the wisdom. And hear it we must, for it is our only reliable guide through the maze that is life.

For me, this is what has been the arduous work of interpreting the dreams that I have written down. This difficulty has sometimes acted as a deterrent.

Why are dreams so hard to interpret? With dreams, everything can have multiple meanings.

I have found that though multiple meanings can be discovered in my dreams, I can become obsessed with finding them. This can become quite tedious, and for me, it's discouraging. But over time I have learned that I don't have to go looking for every possible meaning and can still get value.

Insight: There is a cautionary note here in that one can stop too soon while interpreting meaning. This is called premature closure. It's when you stop considering other possibilities prematurely, and it's one of the two big sins in dream work (e.g., premature closure and excessive judgment).

People also need to be careful that they aren't closing off the most important aspect of dreams. Their preconceptions and expectations also add biases to interpretations.

In short, everyday cognitive errors can limit meaning, and that is why I recommend working with others on dream meaning. I also go back at a later time to review some dreams so as to limit situational bias (referring to my mood) in an interpretation.

Your personality type can influence interpretation as well. Are you the type that likes closure and certainty but abhors ambiguity, or are you the type who likes to look at all sides and has difficulty settling on a single issue? Knowing your personality style can help you make more meaningful interpretations.

There are also all kinds of cognitive illusions that can lead you to see patterns where there are none or significance where there isn't any. In short, greater self-awareness can come from dream work, but dream work requires greater self-awareness. They're mutually supportive.

Keeping a Journal

I always keep a journal or even just a piece of paper with a pen or pencil beside the bed. Whatever I recall in the morning, I write down. In the beginning of this work, I found myself waking several times during the night to jot down things. This obsession* can upset sleep patterns. But don't worry. It will probably pass. If it doesn't, then stop reaching for the pen during the night. Reinforce only normal morning dream recall, and the obsessive behavior will extinguish itself.

When I start to settle in, I remind myself that I want to remember my dream. This seems to help program the system.

When you wake in the morning, don't move from your waking position. If you've awakened during the dream, your position is connected to it, and moving will make the recall more difficult. I've also found that taking vitamin B6 before going to sleep can be very beneficial to dream intensity and to dream recall.

---

* Note that *obsession* is a theme in my life, especially when I take on anything new. There is always the danger that I will overwork something, burn out, and then drop the thing altogether. "Everything in moderation," my grandmother used to say.

Some dreamers prefer to just write down the images recalled from the dream without trying to figure out what they mean. All too often when we jump too quickly into meaning analysis, our ego-selves begin a revision of what was seen before the actual images are listed.

We want to make sense of the dream as soon as we begin to recall it, but this drive to know can affect the material that the unconscious has served up and frequently not in a helpful way.

With your journal in hand, try to remember the *main emotion* within the dream and jot it down. This will help you interpret the meaning of the overall theme.

Because dream symbols are nearly always connected to events of the previous day, some analysts suggest keeping your dream journal embedded in your regular journal. The results for interpreting everyday issues or ongoing issues are phenomenal.

Because I don't normally journal my waking life (e.g., write in a diary), I often write down what's going on in my waking life in the margins of my dream journal. This can help with the direction my analysis will take and give me some context when I go back and read the dream at a later date.

When you recall a fragment or full dream, write it exactly as you remember it. Don't worry about spelling or punctuation. The subconscious mind doesn't care. Don't judge it, edit it, or try to figure it out at this point. Just get it down on paper.

I usually assign a title to my dream to recall it or summarize its content. I've found that this can aid in the process of interpretation.

I also write the date and where I am when I have the dream. If I have time—that is, if I'm not pressed for work or some appointment—I begin the process of interpreting or analyzing.

When interpreting, I always write down the salient points, themes, and symbols (e.g., animals, people, numbers, buildings, death, falling, etc.) in an outline.

Using this format seems to naturally separate the different parts and characters of the dream and allows me to interpret the pieces in isolation and then look for patterns when reviewing the whole.

My first go at their meaning is usually some form of what they mean to me. I ask myself, "What thoughts about George or Betty do I have that may give me a clue as to what they represent in my dream?"

Remember that one person's symbols are not necessarily the same as another's. In Derek and Julia Parker's book *Dreaming: Remembering, Interpreting and Benefitting,*[6] Carl Jung is quoted as saying, "No dream symbol can be separated from the individual who dreams it, and there is no definite or straightforward interpretation of any dream."

There are, however, certain *themes*, *patterns*, or *concepts* that seem to show up universally, so a good dream dictionary can be helpful. Even a practiced dream analyst will get stuck, but I'll let you in on a little secret. When I draw a blank on the meaning of an image, I'll go to the online thesaurus and type in "synonyms and antonyms for _____ (whatever the image is)." This often provides me with a broader definition that I can then use to interpret its meaning. It really works to unstick me.

Ultimately, to determine if any interpretation to a symbol or theme is accurate, you must feel whether or not it resonates with you. Do you feel the light turn on, that "ah yes, that's it" moment? If so, then you can use the assigned meaning.

Sometimes there's also more than one image buried within an image. For example, a bicycle is a symbol of needed balance, but it is also a vehicle, wheel, circle, and mandala, all of which have their contributing meanings.

I also look for the *main action*. What is the overall activity of the dream, such as running, flying, hiding, fighting, etc.? Who you are in the dream should be noted because it can speak to how you play your role in your waking life. I also note feelings and reasons for actions. For example, I might ask why I didn't go into that dark room in the dream.

Another very important aspect to dream analysis for me has been to assume that *most everything pertains to me*. "Yes, Virginia, it is all about me!" In your dream, most every character is you. Every being, event, or image is about you or your personality, behavior, wishes, fears, hidden desires, or what you admire or reject.

I use the caveat *most* because dreams can also reflect environmental cues regarding other people (e.g., how they are feeling), and on some occasions, some precognitive events may be detected through the subconscious.

I will, however, be placing more emphasis on the personal projection of the psyche and what it may say about you, the dreamer.

A personality placed on some character in the dream from someone you know in the waking world is a personality trait that you recognize in yourself or fear that you lack. You even have the traits that you don't like to some degree, whether you are conscious of them or not. This fact can be quite useful for those who wish to make changes in their lives but aren't sure where to start.

Actually, you can only see in others what is already in you, like it or not. It's amazing what things about yourself you can discover through dream work.

Whoa, back up a moment! I just said that you only see what is already in you. This is a hard concept for those of us who are proud that we don't have certain traits in us.

I find a sense of solace, peace, and pride in the fact that I wouldn't hurt a fly, as the saying goes. But I can see the murderous evil in some other people. Am I saying that is in me? Not exactly. Negatives that you see in others are usually traits that strongly conflict with a value in you that you admire. It's not that the negative trait isn't in the other person. It's the contrast that is being *projected* onto the other person.

You may have this trait as well, but it may be that deep down, you fear that weakness or vulnerability that you judge to be in the other who does have the trait. There is also the possibility that you are not always true to your value. You may have a hidden trait that is in conflict with your value.

For example, when I succumb to my fear associated with wanton murder, my internal reaction is to want to destroy the threat, obliterate the perpetrator, grind the person into dust, and spill the blood of his or her worthless being. Of course, this reaction scares me, and I want to purge it from myself. I find myself making extreme statements about the other person. When I do this, I am *projecting* my fear of my reaction away from me and onto the other individual.

> What you meet in another being is the projection of your own level of evolution.
>
> —Ramdass.org/quotes

This is where strong judgments in both the sleeping and waking dreams can help you become conscious of inner motivations. Awareness then allows you to take action if you choose to do so.

For me, the awareness of my dark side allows me some control over its expression. And instead of resisting it, which seems to only serve to strengthen it, I can now work on accepting its presence.

Your individual personality traits may affect whether or not you are able to see a theme or pattern. Whether you are perfectionistic, possessive, image-conscious, self-absorbed, secretive, anxious, engaging, scattered, self-confident, willful, easygoing, or self-effacing, these traits are at some level going to affect your interpretation of dream themes and patterns.

The more you know about your traits, the more you can spot what the pallet you're using to create your dream picture looks like.

Knowing Your Personality Type

Knowing something about your emotional makeup is also going to help in understanding your waking world behaviors as well as your dreams.

There are several personality-type indicators with each focusing on different foundational philosophies of personality and personality development. For the purpose of this book, I'm highlighting two that I have the most experience with—the Myers-Briggs Type Indicator and the Enneagram Type Indicator. Both will provide the user with rough though usable information.

I've taken the liberty of sharing these links to sites that I believe to be useful:

- Myers-Briggs: http://www.PersonalityPathways.com/
- Enneagram: http://www.enneagraminstitute.com/

Both these sites can be quite useful at an entry level, and they can help you get a handle on how you respond to the symbols, circumstances, and events of your life and make the process and results of dream interpretation all that much richer and more meaningful.

Jung's original *personality types* are briefly explained in the codex of this book.

In the book *The Dragon's Treasure*,[7] I discuss in some depth some of the variables that affect our relationship to both the sleeping and waking consciousness.

Not only does your personality determine the symbols and the interpretation of those symbols, but so does the extent to which you have immersed yourself in the beliefs of a religion and the values of a culture.

The Quran, the Christian and Jewish Bible, the Vedas and other books of religion are used to interpret one's life and to attempt the understanding of God, so why would they not influence your dreams? The danger in this is that rigidly narrow interpretations can sometimes only give you information about what you know and not what you don't know.

I'm not sure that the *self* of the unconscious adheres to any religion, though it may use your belief as a way of communicating to you. This may add yet another layer of complexity to be unpeeled before getting at the small kernel of truth hidden within.

Dream Work after You Wake Up

The first part of dealing with a dream's meaning after having written it down is to separate out the various images and symbols and then look for themes and connections between these images.

Underlining the words, phrases, or images that seem important can be a useful way to get started. Make special note of any image that captures your main interest (e.g., that woman, man, place, or event in the dream).

Symbols in a dream also carry their opposites, so even if a symbol seems straightforward, one should look for its opposite. (If the symbol is one of happiness and contentment, one should also look for where he or she is unhappy and not content.)

This process of considering the built-in opposites of a dream's symbols also allows for one to move beyond one-sidedness.

For many of the symbols in the codex, I've not designated whether it's the dreamer or another person displaying the action or feeling. This is because all dreams relate to you, the dreamer, either in that the symbols describe some part of you or your relationship with others, but you are the central character in all cases. Everyone in the dream is an aspect of you and/or represents a part of your life.

When I interpret my dreams, I always do so in the context of the rest of my life, especially in what's happening in the here and now. It helps to write a short explanation about what's happening in the margins. That way, if you don't get back to the dream for a few days, you can remember context.

I'll also go back and rework a dream when other ideas come up, and any notes about what was happening in the waking world are always helpful.

As I said earlier, I begin with titling my dreams upon waking to help me remember them. I started doing this sometime during the early '90s. Titling also helped me in the interpretive phase.

As I looked through old dreams to use in this book, I was struck by the variety of titles and how often they told a story all their own. Though just fragments, they seem to have their own poetry.

I've also found that remaining in the physical position I was in when I woke up also helps with remembering my dreams.

Sometimes it will be necessary to look for several words in order to decipher a dream image. For example, if you see a severed head or hand in a dream, you would have to look under *body terms* for the head or hand and the word *cut*, *sword*, or *knife* for the action.

When you can't find an image in a dream dictionary such as this one and have no idea about its meaning in your own life, you might research the meaning of the word. (I look up synonyms and antonyms for the word or phrase.) For example, a periscope may show up in your dream. Ask yourself, "What is a periscope, and what does a periscope do?" It enables you to see over obstacles, to achieve another perspective. It may be that the dream is suggesting that you need to change your perspective on something.

A periscope is also a device that is curved so that you can see over obstacles. Consequently, perhaps you need to be less linear in the way you think. (A doesn't always have to lead to B.)

Depending on the emotion being displayed or felt in the dream, then you may also have to go to *emotions* or a specific emotion such as *anger*. But sometimes an emotion like *anger* is covering up another emotion such as *hurt*, or an emotion such as *happy* may refer to its opposite (sadness).

When you don't feel an emotion in a dream, you may see a dominating color such as *red* for anger or *blue* for depression or sadness. Emotions can also be symbolized by bodies of *water* and the state of the water (e.g., calm, stormy, drowning, raining, tidal waves, etc.).

In short, all parts and images of the dream should be considered when attempting to interpret.

Insight: In this book such things as animals, body parts, clothing, colors, furniture, numbers, and parts of a house will be grouped under these headings and not alphabetically.

Group Dream Work

I have also found it useful to become part of a dream group from time to time. The points of view from others regarding your dreams can be quite enlightening as can listening to and interpreting the dreams of others.

Dream work can be done alone, but I recommend that you do it in the company of others, especially those who have experience with the techniques.

Sharing my dreams with family or trusted friends has been very useful in that it helps to formulate my ideas, and their feedback is often quite useful. You can find more formal groups online or through formal classwork or workshops that are presented by various local dream instructors and gurus.

It takes a little personal experience and persistence to find a group that feels right, a group where you share similar temperaments and interests. I have also found groups where I felt totally out of my element, but even so, the group often turned out to be quite uplifting though uncomfortable. Perhaps if I had stayed with the discomfort longer, I might have discovered something valuable.

The technique of active imagining proved most enlightening with regard to unlocking the mystery of the unconscious material hidden within a dream.

There is a caution here in that this kind of group gestalt dream work, though useful for enhancing individual insight, can give the dreamers permission to not go deeper into material that they may resist. I found that sometimes if the group skirted around a certain embarrassing issue that I was dealing with through a dream, I would let it stay hidden. This, in effect, kept the issue unresolved.

When you share a dream with another person, you are taking on the responsibility of sharing something quite personal. Clarity is most important, so be prepared for the person analyzing the dream to ask you questions. What will ensue is a dialogue that eventually inserts a little of both people into the meaning of the dream.

Dreams reflect current concerns, and when they are shared, the analyst and the dreamer can develop relational meanings. Both can lend their individual experiences to the meaning. Ultimately, however, *meaning* is the dreamer's responsibility. The analyst can help point toward perhaps an unrealized meaning, but the dreamer has to go with what *resonates* or seems right.

Jung thought that dream work was essentially a theater in which the dreamer was the scene, actor, producer, author, and audience.[8]

Other forms of dream work might include dream poetry, hypnosis to aid in recall and/ or symbol amplification (e.g., asking the symbol, "Why are you in my dream?"), active imagining (dialoguing with the dream elements of the unconscious as detailed in the "intuitive interactive approach" section), or Gestalt dream work (becoming part of the dream and taking on different characters within the dream to take on different perspectives).

Intuitive Interactive Approach

One can also use what I call the intuitive interactive approach to dream interpretation. I don't always have the time to do this, but if the dream is powerful enough, if it contains a recurrent theme, or if it's a nightmare, I'll take the extra time.

- After you have written the dream down in your journal, recall your dream by closing your eyes and replaying the entire scene. Notice such things as feelings, and jot them down. Don't edit anything, and keep writing until you sense there's nothing more to write. Note any clues to meaning that may have been revealed during this process. Jot down the characters and objects of the dream.

- Write down the waking world context for the dream. What's happening in your life is what often stimulates the dream. Your unconscious mind will use images and events from the day to symbolically represent your emotions and hidden bits of information. I usually write these notes in the margins. This aids me in applying the dream messages to my life. After all, this is the point of dream analysis.

- Bring a prominent object or character into your consciousness by using the process described in the "active imagining" section in this book. By tapping into the same source as the dream, these characters can reveal a great deal of meaning and lead to waking life applications.

- Drawings of the characters and symbols can also add substance to the overall dream material. Try drawing a key character or symbol that stood out, and notice what you get (feelings, thoughts, etc.) about their identity and/or messages they're bringing that may be related to you. Drawing how you were feeling at any stage of the dream that you are depicting is also quite useful.

- Sometimes you can graph a time line or order sequence for your dream. Add anything to this diagram associated with the events and characters that may come up for you.

- Find people to share and discuss your dream with. Be open to any additional info that they may offer. One of the best ways I've found to add meaning to other people's dreams is to preface my input by saying, "If this were my dream …" In this way, I'm not making them wrong for their interpretation, just adding another perspective.

As with any dream interpretation, it has to resonate with you in order to be of use to you. When I am interpreting the dreams of others, I always add this caveat:

> Please note that the interpretation(s) that I provide are not the ultimate meaning of the dream. Every interpretation is but a hypothesis and an attempt to read what is often an enigmatic narrative. You, the dreamer, will know what meaning(s) would be your own truth by what you feel in your heart. If it resonates as true, then go with it. Otherwise, discard it in part or in its entirety. I can only offer what the dream would mean for me if it were mine.

Another technique for determining the meaning of the dream is to notice what your body does with input from you or others. In other words, be mindful of what your body is doing as you ponder the dream or the dream's interpretation.

Until that fuzzy and vague feeling about the dream's meaning crystalizes and you feel a physical release from the "that's not quite it" feeling, you probably haven't gone deep enough.

Try to focus on the vague, indefinable feeling sense without thinking about it or trying to work on it by trying out different possibilities. Just focus your attention on the sense of it. Sometimes that will offer a breakthrough.

A breakthrough is usually a physical sensation of an energy release before the thought, *Yes, that's it!*

In short, listen to the thoughts of others, but only use what touches you.

Carl Jung, the famous dream analyst, had this to say about interpretation: "Every interpretation is a hypothesis, an attempt to read an unknown text. An obscure dream, taken in isolation, can hardly ever be interpreted with any certainty."

He also went on to say that no one dream can really do justice to one's story.

> For this reason I attach less importance to the interpretation of single dreams. A relative degree of certainty is reached only in the interpretation of a series of dreams, where the later dreams correct the mistakes we have made in handling those that went before. Also, the basic ideas and themes can be recognized much better in a dream-series.[9]

A Few More Helpful Hints

As said earlier, all objects and all people represent aspects of yourself. Those aspects can be ones that we reject, embrace, have neglected. The dream is all about us. It only appears as though the other objects are different from us. Eventually, we wake up, and the dream bodies return to their sources, namely us. Perhaps this is a metaphor for who we are in our waking lives as well.

Remember that to be meaningful, these symbols need to resonate for you and should not be taken verbatim. These are symbols that appear frequently in my dreams or the dreams that others have shared with me over the years and are not by any means all the possible symbols available to the dreamer.

Insight: Dream Books have been around for centuries. For example, Almoli's *Pitron Halomot* or *Interpretation of Dreams* was a book first published in 1515 by Eastern European Jews. The last edition of this book was published in New York as late as 1902.[10]

Earlier versions of dream books tended to reflect a folk etymology. With earlier Sumerians and Jews, if one dreamed of an olive tree, the interpretation would depend on whether the fruit was still on the tree (meaning that one would advance in the world) or it had been harvested (meaning one would be beaten down). The idea came from the manner in which olives are harvested. (The tree is shaken or beaten until all the fruit has fallen to the ground.)

Acknowledgment of the value of dreams can be found in all three of the great religions—Judaism, Christianity, and Islam. All see dreams as communiqués from God. For example, in Islam, there is a quote that says, "Dreams of the prophets are divine inspirations." One can also find 121 references to dreams in the Bible, seven of them being in the New Testament.

Depending on the sect of each religion, the interpretation of dreams is either encouraged or discouraged. There are sections of the Bible that discourage dream interpretation, considering it a vanity to do so. (For example Ecclesiastes 5 says, "Dreams give wings to fools.") However, there are many modern denominations that provide interpretative counseling regarding dreams and encourage the practice as a means of growing deeper in their faith and understanding of God.

The following list of images, variations, events, and symbols are from a large number of dreams of my own as well as those I've collected from more than three thousand other people from more than 144 countries.

All these symbols have been strongly affected by culture and subculture and include religious and regional meanings. Where appropriate I've included some of the culturally influenced meanings.

Though there are more than five thousand dream images and variations on images interpreted in this book, it is beyond its scope here to list all the possible meanings of all the variations of each symbol or all the possible images that we create in our dreams, so feel free to add your own; however, you can use this collection as a guide to how you might interpret the symbols.

There are, however, several archetypal dream images that all cultures seem to share by virtue of our common humanity. For an overview of these shared dream images, you might want to jump to the "archetypes" section.

Most importantly, signs and symbols mean nothing in and of themselves. Until a person with beliefs comes along and gives a meaning to the symbol, it has no power. If the person decides it's evil, then it *means* evil for that person. By itself, it is not evil. The evil is only in the mind of the person giving it the meaning.

Remember that symbols are only representations of what's in the mind of the observer. The symbol itself is nothing without your thoughts about it. Do you want a symbol to be positive? That's easy. Imbue it with a positive thought. It doesn't matter what anyone else thinks of it. All the agreement in the world that a symbol is evil doesn't make it evil. Only you do.

In short, symbols *only* take on evil actions when the observer uses them to make evil actions.

People not only do this with symbols but with everything else as well. We all give meaning to what we see, and that meaning is not necessarily reality.

This Book

The book is divided into two sections, the introduction, which includes the tools for interpretation, and the codex. In turn, the codex is divided into four sections, an encyclopedia of images, archetype meanings, nightmare meanings, and an endnotes section.

But do you really need a codex (i.e., a dream dictionary or encyclopedia) in order to interpret your dreams?

Some dream analysts insist that a dream dictionary is of little help in decoding dreams because it is the meaning that the dreamer brings to the symbols that makes the difference.

This is only partially true. What I've found to be true amongst the thousands of people's dreams that I've worked with is when I provide initial meanings that I can gather from a good dictionary or my own intuition, it begins the process of personal interpretation. It's sort of like priming the pump. When stumped, I, too, will thumb through a dream dictionary to get another insight to the symbols of my dreams.

For those who are just getting started in interpreting their dreams and for those who don't have a dream analyst or dream group handy, a well-thought-out codex of dream symbols can be quite useful.

Overall, this book of dreams is designed to help dreamers look deeper into the realm of their dreams and to extract meaning through that part of the everyday that makes up roughly one-third of their lives—the sleep part.

It has also been said that more than 70 percent of our life experience is bound up within our unconscious mind and that this material affects everything we do, say, think, or feel. This unconscious material lies within our dreams and can be accessed by using some rudimentary tools, some of which are presented in this book.

Section 1

The Encyclopedia of Images

Before entering this codex, there's one word of advice that will add perspective to the images contained within. Though I have provided meanings based upon the general implications of the words and concepts that many people assign to these images, they are only a part of the true picture.

Each of you who use this book has your own personal meaning and experience of every image and every word contained herein. These you must mix with the general definitions to decode the overall message(s) of the dream.

Just remember that every person or thing in the dream relates to you. Dreams really are all about you. As you interpret the symbology, keep asking yourself, "How am I this? What does this say about me?"

Ultimately, the definitions in this book are *suggestions* that may help to guide you toward deciphering your dream.

It is up to you to create a meaningful narrative that applies to your waking world life, for what would be the point beyond just curiosity of interpreting a dream if you couldn't apply its message to your life?

As you decode your dreams, you may wish to review the introductory section of this book and pay particular attention to the section titled "Keeping a Journal."

I also recommend treating each interpretation as a hypothesis. Be willing to go back more than once over time to test your interpretation or to see if anything has changed in the interim.

Sharing the dream with others to gain another perspective can also yield valuable information. Just the process of sharing aloud can stimulate your insight into the dream's meaning.

My wife and I share our dreams with each other every morning as part of our new day ritual of coffee, newspaper, and crossword puzzles.

With all that said, enjoy!

A

a: To see the letter A might symbolize the beginning of something, but it can also be a way of grading or judging something or someone.

abacus: This could mean an outdated or old-fashioned perspective. Is this a way of counting something?

abandoned: This could be an abandoned building or city or road that may represent isolation, a feeling of being unwanted, anxiety about losing someone (e.g., a loved one or a friend), or a part of you being left behind (see also *cheat/cheating*).

To dream that you are abandoned or left behind suggests that it may be time to leave behind past feelings and characteristics that are hindering your growth. Let go of your old attitudes. It might also reflect some impending and perhaps worrisome change.

A more direct interpretation of this dream may be that you have a fear of being deserted or abandoned.

It may stem from a recent loss or a fear of losing someone. The fear of abandonment may come into your dream as part of the healing process and dealing with losing a loved one. It may also stem from unresolved feelings or problems from your childhood.

Alternatively, the dream may indicate that you are feeling neglected or that your feelings are being overlooked.

Have you abandoned reason or your moral core? This can also show up as indifference.

There may be some issue that only you can deal with effectively.

Perhaps the dream is a metaphor that you need to approach life with *reckless abandon* and live more freely. To abandon others in your dream may suggest that you are overwhelmed by the problems and decisions in your life.

To abandon or leave the path you're walking on could suggest that you are deviating from your goals or values.

Have you abandoned some aspect of yourself or some value that used to be important? See also *alone, dropping, letting go,* and *lost*.

Insight: Some mystics have suggested that one needs to abandon their attachments to things, beliefs, and ideas in order to see their true selves and see reality as it really is.

abbey: This could represent spirituality or contentment. If the abbey is in ruins, then it may suggest feelings of hopelessness (see *church*).

abbreviation: This could be someone's or some organization's initials. It could also suggest an abbreviated or truncated process (i.e., something ending before its time).

abdomen: Is there something you can't stomach? See also *body* under *stomach*.

abduction: When it happens to you, you may be feeling influenced, manipulated, or controlled by another person or event. When you abduct others, it could be your desire to control them. Perhaps you need to let go of something (such as a feeling, relationship, grudge, or something from the past).

abhor: Do you have a waking hatred for the person or thing in your dream? If others hate you in the dream, perhaps you are forcing your beliefs, opinions, or values on others?

Everything that irritates us about others can lead us to an understanding of ourselves.

—Carl Jung

abnormal: If you are feeling abnormal in a dream or someone is acting in an abnormal way or if some event seems unexpectedly different, are you or others deviating from some norm or in an odd or atypical manner? See also *surprise* and *unexpected*.

abominable snowman: See *yeti*.

aborigine or any native: This could possibly represent the intuitive or primordial wisdom self (i.e., the untamed self). Do you need to be more in touch with your intuitive self?

Insight: The Australian Aborigines have lived in the vast land of the Australs[*] for some twenty-two thousand generations. Before the arrival of the Europeans, some two hundred different language groups existed. Though there are now only seventy groups remaining, each calling their land something different, they all tell a similar story of the creation of the world—the story of the dreamtime.

From the Dreamtime, Rainbow Snake and others *dreamed* the world into being. Areas in the tribal lands of the Aboriginal world are named for the "Dreaming" into existence of that part of creation that took place there. For example, "Kangaroo Dreaming" is where the creation of the kangaroo took place.

----

[*] Variously known as Australische by the Dutch and Terra Australis Incognita (The Southern Unknown Land) and colloquially as Oz since the early twentieth century.

The word *Dreaming* symbolizes another aspect in that it represents the individual tribal beliefs and spiritual understanding. For example, one tribe might refer to themselves as having kangaroo dreaming while another calls itself honey ant dreaming.

All that comes into the world, including paintings, other objects, or even ideas, is still dreamed and is claimed by the person or group that has produced it. To them, everything comes from the dreamtime. Individual lives come from those of the dreamtime as well, and they return to it when their bodies die. In all people there is an eternal part born through the mother in time from the originals of the dreamtime.

The visions of the early Aborigine—and to some extent today—do not differentiate between men or their surroundings. They experience an undifferentiated state of mind that makes separation much less common among them than with modern man.

There was no separation between their daily living, eating, working, sexual, and religious lives. All were either dreams or waking visions. And all come from the *all-at-once time* and are born into a *life in time*. In a way, the Aborigine lives in a dream within a dream.

Through the waking dream (awake state) and the sleeping dream and various altered states, Aborigines interact with their reality—indeed with their souls. To them, everything is connected.

See also *insight* under *Native American*.

abortion: This possibly signals the loss of something new or something that has died, such as a relationship.

Perhaps you're blocking your own growth and development.

If someone else in the dream is having an abortion, then perhaps the relationship isn't growing. Some people see this as a form of murder. What in yourself are you killing off? Do you need to abort or bring to an end some project or activity?

above: If something is hovering above you, perhaps you need to set your goals higher. Could you be feeling inferior to something or someone?

abroad: Do you need a change in scenery or need to escape something or someone?

abscond: Perhaps you feel insecure about achievements. Maybe you aren't feeling good enough or trying to fill a void with something that isn't yours. See also *stealing*.

absence: If something or someone is absent in the dream, this might suggest that you are looking for something you've already lost. Are you trying to fill a void in your life?

Insight: To me, a dream of blank spaces that give presence by their absence is the place where the ineffable soul meets us in the bounded world of the material and where what can't be described describes what is, was, and is yet to be.

I am always excited by the blank sheet of paper or blank document of the word processor, for in these is present the beauty of the infinite potential of the soul's creativity. I'm never sure what's going to happen when I begin to write. Each filled blankness is a journey never taken before.

The artist's use of what is not there to hint at what is has always fascinated me and helped me realize that often reality is defined more by the abstract and the potential than the concrete and fixed.

abundance: Perhaps you need to conserve your resources. Perhaps you're lacking something?

abuse: If you're doing the abusing, perhaps your past is coming back to haunt you. If you're being abused, then perhaps you feel victimized by someone or something.

Animal abuse can suggest your own primal desires are being suppressed. Child abuse might suggest that you are lacking a voice in some situation or life in general. Do you

need to speak up for yourself (i.e., defend yourself)?

Being verbally abused can be about being bullied, or it could mean that you yourself are bad-mouthing someone.

Are you abusing someone or something (drugs, alcohol, sex, etc.)?

See also *bully*.

Standing at the edge of an abyss or cliff might suggest impending change as in the end of something, or emotional emptiness.

abyss: This is a symbol of great depth, often signaling the profound and infinite. If you fear it or if you are about to fall or are falling into it, it might signal the fear of losing control or failure or death. It can also represent the unconscious mind or where the shadows of your personality lay. An abyss could also be a synonym for depression (see *cliff*, *pit*, and *void*).

accelerator: If you're pushing down on the accelerator in the car, you may need to advance in your life through personal effort. Perhaps you need to hurry with something and step on the gas.

If it's broken or doesn't work, perhaps you've lost or are losing the ability to move forward with some aspect of your life (see *car*).

accent: If you speak with an accent that you don't use, perhaps you're having difficulty communicating your thoughts.

Does the accent make you stand out? Are you trying to hide it so that you don't look different?

Is the person with the accent difficult to understand? Perhaps you are having difficulty understanding something that is foreign to you or different from what you're used to. What are your judgments about not being able to understand the person? Where are you judging others?

acceptance: Are you having difficulty with self-esteem? Are you not measuring up? See *award*.

access: See *door* or *entry*.

accident: This may represent anxiousness or unexpected change. This is most likely not a harbinger of doom as in a precognizant dream. Where might you be avoiding change? See crashes under *car* and/or *crash*.

If someone you care about is killed in an accident, perhaps there is something in you that has died. Has your relationship with that person come to an end, or do you fear it will?

Accidents in dreams can be a reflection of your worries and anxieties.

If someone else has caused the accident because of his or her own actions, the dream may be reminding you that you have no control over the actions of others.

Are you or is someone else being reckless?

accomplice: If you are an accomplice to a crime, is someone having a negative influence on you or enabling you toward some bad habit? Are you experiencing some guilt with something you've done (see also *accuse*)?

accounts: Are you having financial problems? Do you need to take a step back and check out the facts of something?

accusing: If someone is accusing you of something, perhaps you are experiencing extreme guilt or doubts about something.

Is someone questioning your actions or the choices you're making? Are you questioning yourself?

If there are people accusing one another in the dream, it may suggest you're in an environment where there is much dissension and disagreement. What's that all about?

ace: To see the ace in cards could be a metaphor for being the best. The ace of hearts could refer to love while the ace of spades could be about scandal. The ace of diamonds could be about your reputation while the ace of clubs could be about some legal matter. Consider also that you may be an *ace* at what you do (i.e., the best at what you do or at least would like to be thought of in that way).

Insight: The ace of clubs has also been known as the God card because it is both the Alpha and Omega (first and last card depending on the game) as well as the trinity (reflected in its three lobes).

acid: This might be about hateful language (as in an acid tongue) or hate and revenge in general. Acid can also suggest someone or something that is having a negative influence on your life. Acid rain might suggest that you are letting something take you over and poison your mind.

acquit: To be acquitted or found not guilty of a crime might suggest that you have learned a valuable lesson or that there is one to be learned.

Do you feel vindicated or want to be vindicated?

acrobat: This may reflect a need to find better balance in your life. If associated with sex, it may be about better, different, or more sex.

acting: Are you putting up a false front? Are you living your own life or living from a script someone else wrote?

active imagining: This is a mental method that uses the imagination and can be used to reanimate the images of a dream and interact with them while influencing them as little as possible in the process. It's a way of tapping into the unconscious mind to deepen the experience of a dream.

One can tap into the imaginal realm of the unconscious through both the dream and various forms of meditation.

In this technique the ego remains fully conscious. The ego gets to observe and even feel unconscious content, but it also gives up critical content so as to be open to what might be available.

Once the unconscious has downloaded its content with respect to certain dream images, the ego can then elaborate (activate its imagination). After doing so as completely as possible, it then determines the meaning. This last part is critical. Just enjoying the elaboration isn't enough.

The key to this technique is to not allow the ego to manipulate the process. To do so would cause a degeneration of the outcome. That is why I would recommend doing it with a qualified therapist who's adept with this kind of in-depth dream work.

Some dream groups can also be helpful if they understand the parameters and possible outcomes of this kind of self-exploration technique.

Note, however, that beliefs can determine the material that comes from the unconscious.

If done properly, the process can lead to a transcendent experience. Ibn Arabi, a thirteenth-century Sufi mystic and Islamic scholar, suggested, "Spirits embody themselves through the power of imagination." He thought that form was related to spirit in a significant way, and he also believed that relating to the forms within the imagination can lead one to go beyond the boundaries of the psyche.

If there is no difference between spirit and the imaginal form, then this technique may actually lead one to the divine. We all have this potential within the latent self.

To some degree we are all putting on an act and hiding our less acceptable qualities. But these unwanted and undesirable qualities can be like shadows that can haunt us in our everyday lives (see shadow in *archetypes* section).

actor: This could symbolize the pursuit of pleasure. A particular actor may reflect an aspect that you would like to have or one that you reject and thus reject in yourself. Are you putting too much emphasis on how you look? Are you not being genuine but just putting on an act? Is someone else just putting on an act? Is the role you're playing in life authentic or just put on (see *acting* or *theater*)?

acupuncture: Are you in need of healing (physical, emotional, and/or spiritual)?

adolescent: This could represent intense social and sexual issues. Where is your growth and development most intense? See also *teen*.

advertisement: This could be a way of the dream bringing attention to something or you bringing attention to yourself.

adder: This may represent a sly or cunning person who cannot be trusted. See also *snake*.

addict or addiction: To be an addict may suggest that you are no longer in control of some situation. Perhaps you are obsessed with something or someone, or maybe something is taking control of you. Are you being a fanatic about something (see also *obsessed* and *possession*)?

Insight: All addictions are not in your best interest—whether physical addictions like alcohol or drugs; psychological ones like gambling, idealism, porn; or emotional ones like anger or fear. To be addicted is to no longer be free. Frequently, they are there because of some void in your life that your psyche is attempting to fill or a wound that it is attempting to heal. This is not the way to do it.

addition: You may need to add something into your life. Something may be straightforward, and you shouldn't read too much into it. Is it possible you're feeling less than?

address: If you see an old address, perhaps you need to look back. Do you need to address (deal with) an old issue?

Adler, Alfred: Adler was a contemporary of Freud but diverged with him over the idea that sexual impulses were the most important of human behaviors. He believed that humans were goal-oriented and always moving toward wholeness.

He believed that in our dreams we see what we think of ourselves and our strategies to deal with and succeed in the world.

admiral: Perhaps you are or need to tackle some issue with decisiveness and confidence? Are you acting all bossy or controlling?

adobe: An adobe is a house and therefore may represent you, perhaps the traditional and simple you.

adopt: Are you taking on something new? This could include a change in a way of being or behavior.

Adopting something or someone may be like taking the qualities of the thing adopted into yourself or becoming more of that.

adult: If you are a child or teen, perhaps you need to act more mature. If you are an adult, perhaps you have some growing up to do.

adultery: This could signal sexual desire longing to be expressed. Perhaps you are entangled in something that isn't in your best interest. If your significant other is the adulterer, then perhaps you are feeling cheated or taken for granted. This could also suggest your insecurities around abandonment or betrayal.

Another meaning may be about being disloyal or unfaithful. Do you need to keep the faith in something or someone (see also *cheating*)?

adventure: Perhaps you are lacking adventure in your life. Maybe you need some variety.

affair: Surrendering, as in "What do you need to give in to?" It could also mean you are falling in love or be a statement about betrayal (see *betrayal* and *cheating*).

afterlife: See *heaven*.

age: There are three stages here, each with their separate symbolism. *Youth* could symbolize immaturity or part of you that is opening up. *Middle age* could symbolize maturity or where you are headed now. And *old age* could symbolize wisdom.

There are archetypes of the old man, old woman, and the child that give meaning to age as well (see *archetypes*).

Insight: These age symbols show up in Wiccan as phases of the moon (e.g., waxing crescent pointing left, full in the center, and waning pointing to the right) and represent the phases of life.

air: This is one of the four ancient elements—earth, air, fire, and water. It is often associated with wisdom and otherworldly concerns.

Cold air could be symbolic of discordance while hot air could be about being pretentious or prone to exaggeration and/or insincerity. Hot air might also represent an argument or anger. See also *breath* and *wind*.

airplane: This could symbolize the rapid movement across distance, perhaps leaving things or people behind. It can also be about rapid change or taking a risk. What kind of change are you in a hurry for? A crashing plane might indicate your concern about failure or loss. A near crash might represent near failure with a sense of recovery and moving forward.

To add further meaning, note if you are just boarding the plane, which might indicate the desire for change. On the other hand, being on the plane might mean you are in the process of change.

Note your feelings here because they will tell you something about what is going on with you regarding the meaning (e.g., fear of flying, loss of trust, failure, panic, escape, awe, freedom, anticipation, etc.).

See also *jet plane*.

airport: This could symbolize making changes or having a desire for something different. It could also be a departure point for something new. A canceled flight might suggest that you are feeling trapped in some situation and feeling helpless.

alarm: Are you experiencing some conflict that is creating anxiety and alarm? Have you made some bad decisions? Is there something that you need to pay attention to immediately? An alarm clock may be about deadlines, or it could signal that it's time to get started with something or that you're late for something. Perhaps you don't have enough time for something or someone.

albatross: This may be about bad luck. Are you worried about something going wrong?

album: This could be a metaphor for true friends, or it could signal that you aren't willing to let go of the memories from the past. Are you idealizing something from the past?

See also *library*.

alchemist: This may be an agent of change or magical messenger. He or she may be a conjurer of new things, transformation, and the crucible for rendering the common into the divine.

Insight: On the surface the alchemists seemed to be looking for a means of transmuting base metals into precious metals (e.g., lead into gold). I think that they were trying, among other things, to make sense of this world of opposites and dichotomies in order to find an underlying unity. Why?

Part of the human condition seems to be that we are all separate from one another and the environment that we find ourselves in. This experience of separation breeds, I believe, various levels of fear ranging from discomfort to all-out panic.

We want to protect ourselves from what is *not us*, whether that be on the personal or communal (meaning the tribe, state, or nation) level. Of course, this is the basis for personal and social conflict. Finding a resolution to the conflict that arises from opposition has been key to the history of alchemy and politics (which is a kind of alchemy itself).

Alchemy has been likened by depth psychologists to the recovery of the soul.

Carl Jung thought of it as representing the individuation process, where human beings wrestled with and integrated their varied and opposing aspects so as to develop into fully actuated beings. In short, this was the process of people aligning their outer natures with their inner natures—the quest for wholeness.

To Jung, it was the promise of our *becoming*. He thought that the images of the alchemical process mirrored a person's inner psychic state of being and thus gave guidance to what was needed to achieve this inner/outer balance where the body, soul, and spirit are consciously reunited with the world soul—the *unus mundus*. See also the *collective unconscious*.

Jung suggested that the alchemists were most likely not trying to turn base metals into gold but exploring how to turn our basic instincts into *philosophical gold* (i.e., to transform our materialistic thinking into something much more spiritual).

Christianity created an unsolvable dilemma by separating humankind from their shadow, which would make it impossible for them to ever become whole again. In Jung's view of the alchemists, he saw how one might overcome the dilemma through the alchemical-like process of psychotherapy.

This is an image of the Alchemist Airmeith from the book *The Archipelago of Dreams, R. J. Cole* (2011). Though an experimenter in the alchemical arts, she was also a healer of souls. Symbolically, she represented a number of archetypal aspects (i.e., the anima, goddess, Great Mother, warrior, and magician).

alcohol: Drinking in moderation could signal contentment, but if you are heavily drinking, it could symbolize feelings of inadequacy or regrets. If you are having alcohol problems in your waking life, this could be a reflection of that too.

Recovering alcoholics can have these dreams of drinking as a means of compensating for what they've given up or because it brings up the guilt associated with their alcoholism.

If you are not an alcoholic in your waking life but you are in the dream, you may be desperately looking for some outlet to express yourself. Perhaps you are asking for help (see *drunk*).

alien: You may have the feeling that you are an outsider or that others might think some part of you is strange or different. Sometimes it may be speaking to some potential in you (i.e., some heretofore undiscovered part of you). You add the judgment of whether the potential is good or bad. Are you alienating others? The alien in a dream can also represent the unconscious mind (see *collective unconscious*).

Sometimes embracing what is alien to you and what may seem dark and perhaps a little chaotic is the soul reaching out to the conscious mind. It is part of the process of becoming whole. To shun the alien is to shut out a part of yourself, thus leaving yourself not quite fulfilled or feeling complete.

The alien can represent any part of you that has yet to be accepted or integrated into your personality. It is what is chasing you and what you, in turn, chase after.

An alien can also represent an unexplored relationship or a situation that's unknown or foreign to you.

If the alien is a little green man or a Martian, see *green man*.

alienated: There may be some issue that only you can deal with effectively. See also *abandoned*, *alone*, or *ignoring*.

Allah: See *god and goddess* and the *archetypes* section.

alone: Are you feeling isolated or left out or unsupported? Are you feeling rejected? Are you not getting enough alone time? What part of you is isolated? Are you feeling as though you don't belong?

There may be some issue that only you can deal with effectively.

See also *abandoned*, *alienated*, or *ignoring*.

alphabet: Individual letters may represent any number of themes. For example, **A** might be for a new stage of something. **B** might be for "let it be." **C** might be for seeing or a reference to something average. **D** might represent the mediocre or the roman numeral for five hundred. (Note that other letters represent numbers in the Roman system.) **F** might stand for failure. **K** could be digital-speak for okay or represent one thousand.

At the other end of the alphabet, the letter **X** could be the roman numeral for ten or signal that something is forbidden. It could symbolize a kiss or reference the X that marks the spot where you could find something. **Y** would be a question or the point on your life's path where you need to make a decision, and finally, **Z** might represent sleep or the end of something.

Above are three examples of altars. In dreams these can refer to ones spiritual aspect. To be kneeling before them might suggest a plea for help or a need to connect with one's spiritual self.

altar: This could symbolize a personal sacrifice or concerns about your spirituality. Perhaps you need to *alter* some personal behavior, an attitude, or a point of view.

A satanic altar might suggest that you are feeling some dark energy at work in some endeavor or in your life (see *devil or demon* in the *archetypes* section or *witches*).

The deities or icons that are displayed on or near the altar might also give you direction regarding the message of the dream.

See also *Buddha, Christ, Christian, church, Judaism, Muslim, religion, Shiva,* and/or *gods and goddesses* in the *archetypes* section.

altered state of consciousness: These are induced changes in a person's mental state. Dreams are considered altered states of consciousness because they are thought of as exhibiting significant changes from one's waking awareness.

There is also some evidence to suggest that dreams constitute, under certain conditions, a form of ESP through out-of-body and precognitive experiences. Meditation and hypnosis may also fit under this category.

Extreme stress, pain, and emotional trauma can induce an altered state. Oxygen deficiency, sleep deprivation, pharmaceutical, psychoses, and other pathological causes can also induce altered states.

Shamans often enter altered states in order to connect with the individual or collective soul or to seek guidance.

aluminum: What may seem cheap or insignificant to others may be of value to you. It could also be about "lightening up."

Alzheimer's: Perhaps you are worried about giving up, letting go of, or losing the past? If you have it in your waking life or are caring for someone who suffers with this disease, then perhaps the dream is a statement for how you're dealing with it.

amber: This can symbolize the sun. It's also said to have healing power for those who believe in the power of gems and stones.

ambulance: This could represent the need for rescue or being saved. There is an emergency quality to this symbol, especially if combined with an injury. It may also be asking you to pay attention to some illness you are experiencing in your waking life.

ambush: Is danger lurking nearby? Something may be changing or about to take a turn for the worst. If you are waiting in ambush, are you being underhanded or deceitful? This can also be a symbol of betrayal.

America: Depending on where you live and your political bent, this could represent opportunity, freedom, crass commercialism, abundance, materialism, relative safety, or gun violence. As with all countries, a nation's meaning is affected by one's political views and prejudices.

amethyst: This gemstone can be about peace of mind and contentment. It can also be about spiritual wisdom (see *violet* in *colors*).

Amish: This could signal that more important and basic necessities need your focus. Do you need to focus more on the basics of something, your life, or your job? Do you want a more simplified life?

ammunition: Are you trying to get your way negatively? Are you collecting evidence to make someone or yourself wrong? If running out of ammunition, are you finding it difficult to defend yourself? Are you about to lose something (i.e., be defeated)?

amnesia: Are you trying to block out, suppress, or forget something? Could it be some aspect of your personality that you reject? See *shadow* in the *archetypes* section for more on the effects of blocking or stuffing things down into your subconscious.

amorous: To be amorous in your dream could be about some personal temptation. Could this lead to problems? Are you flirting with some action or idea? See also *flirting*.

If others are amorous toward you or just in general in the dream, ask yourself, "Is someone trying to persuade you in some endeavor?" Amorous animals might speak to your more instinctual or animal desires (e.g., lust).

The person you are being amorous with may also represent a part of yourself that you admire or love. Though the love affair with *this* part could also mean you are compensating for a lack of love or acceptance of this aspect or of yourself in general within your waking life.

amphitheater: If it's like a Greek theater, perhaps there's some wisdom or knowledge you need to listen to. Also see *acting* and/ or *theater or play*.

amplifier: Do you need to be heard? Do you need to voice your opinion? Do you need to stand up for something or for yourself?

amputation: Perhaps there's some part of you that you've cut off? This could also be about helplessness or an inability to handle or finish something.

What is being amputated will also affect the dream's meaning (see *body*). In general, this image may be a statement of something that is limiting you.

amulet: Do you need to feel protected? Are you feeling vulnerable to something or someone? These can also represent the need for good luck, a safe journey, or help with some endeavor.

Crosses, ancient Venus figurines, scarabs, depictions of saints such as St. Christopher, satchels with the verses of the Quran, Runic symbols, rabbits' feet, coins, fetishes, or any objects used in a ritual or religious or sacred ceremony can be interpreted as amulets.

See also *charm*, *magic*, *pendant*, and *spell*.

Vegvisir amulet: Icelandic magic symbol amulet of navigation otherwise known as a "runic compass." Legend has it that if you carry this sign, you will never lose your way in stormy weather.

amusement park: Do you need to take a break for a little relaxation and fun? If the rides are breaking down or not functioning as they should, it could suggest that things aren't going as they should in some part of your life. If appropriate, see also *Ferris wheel*, *merry-go-round*, or *roller coaster*.

analyst: Perhaps you need to take a closer look at something, someone, or yourself. Do you fully understand the facts of something?

analytical psychology: This study originated from the ideas of the Swiss psychiatrist Carl G. Jung. It recognizes the value and importance of symbolism in life and how it directs the diverse aspects of human beings toward wholeness (i.e., the self). Any thwarting of this process is said to cause disharmony and can result in severe health issues.

It is the material that is stored in our unconscious mind—both the material of the human collective passed down through our psyche's DNA and our personal unconscious material.

Many in this discipline believed that dreams express beliefs, ideas, and emotions that we are not aware of. It does this by way of visual metaphor.

The realization that this material is present though hidden and that it affects virtually everything that we do is what this kind of psychological analysis is designed to get at. See also *collective unconscious, depth psychology, individuation,* and *Jung*.

ancestors: They might suggest tradition. An ancestor might also represent some part of the past you are trying or need to preserve.

anchor: This object or action could refer to stability, security, or providing a solid foundation. It could symbolize someone who keeps you grounded and in place, someone who prevents you from drifting off course. Have you lost this?

Note that it could also represent something or someone (including yourself) that is holding you back.

In old Ireland between the fourth and tenth centuries, the Celts wrote Ogham on stones with many symbols representing trees (e.g., the first five letters as depicted on the Ogham stones in the image: Beith for birch, Luis for rowan, Fearn for alder, Sail for willow, and Nion for ash). See also *tree*.

ancient writings: If you see ancient writings in your dream, perhaps there is something you need to learn from the past, something you need to record, or some old experience you must remember. Some old communication may still be affecting you today.

Are some of your ideas or beliefs out of date? Is there some message from your subconscious that you don't understand? Is there something that you can't quite put into words (see also *writing*)?

androgynous: This may reveal something in a dream that's neither male nor female but contains characteristics of both. Are you trying to integrate different parts of your life or yourself into others?

android: This image might suggest that you feel something or someone is robotic. Have you lost your vitality and aliveness? Are you moving through life without thoughtful purpose? Are you acting without thinking?

anecdote: This could symbolize some lesson to be learned. Is there a moral you need to recognize? Are you making a judgment based on hearsay or something not based on fact?

anesthesia: Are you trying to suppress some emotion or memory? Is there something you're trying to avoid but should actually confront and deal with?

anesthetic: This could mean you are shutting out some pain. You may not be willing to look at or deal with something (see also *door*). Are you suppressing some emotion or something you're trying to avoid?

Perhaps you're feeling numb in some part of your life. If the anesthesia is Novocain, perhaps you feel speechless about some situation or are unsure of how to respond.

angel: This may represent religious concepts or a guardian angel. What needs protecting? Sometimes it may be about your desire for guidance or compassion. The angel can be a guide to higher consciousness or an epiphany (e.g., transcendent knowledge). It can be the symbol for self-realization and higher consciousness.

The angel can be a messenger as was Gabriel, who foretold the coming of Jesus and gave Mohammed the Quran. Angels gave most of the prophets their responsibilities. Angels can also symbolize the arbiters between your ego-self and your true spiritual nature.

They can represent the connection between heaven and earth or the unconscious and the conscious, and they can symbolize some revelation (see also *Jacob's ladder*).

The Angel of Death is also known as the Grim Reaper. It can also symbolize a psychopomp as in the guide of the soul as it crosses over after death. He or she severs the ties that the ego self has with any part of themselves or the world around them.

angel of death: Frequently, they come as messengers from your unconscious mind. This figure can represent an aspect of yourself that you are rejecting or suppressing, though you may be better off dealing with it openly.

They can also represent the ends to relationships, hopes, careers, etc.

anger: Anger in a dream can represent that you are repressing your anger about something or that your unacknowledged anger is causing health problems.

Sometimes in your waking life, you may have the belief that it is not appropriate or safe to express anger. In dreams, you can allow its expression. This can help make you become more assertive in your waking life. Perhaps the anger in the dream is suggesting that you stand your ground and become more confident. It can also provide relief for pent-up feelings.

Anger can also show up in a dream when people are shouting at one another or when people or animals are fighting.

Another image might include an angry face (see *face* or *frown*) or many angry faces as in a *mob*.

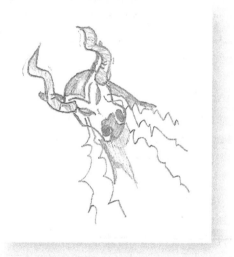

Anger in a dream can present itself as a feeling or as an event (e.g., war, killing, or violent conflict) or as an object. This dream image of a raging bull with lightning coming from its eyes is also a symbol for anger.

Insight: C. G. Jung looked at people as though they had two distinctly different spirits—spirit of the times (that which you live in culturally and subculturally) and the spirit of the depths (the soul or essence of who you are).

Both the *sleeping dream* and the *waking dream* present emotional data that speaks to an imbalance in one's life. For example, anger that one has not transcended and dealt with appropriately in his or her waking life can turn inward and create a feeling of depression. And sometimes this feeling of depression is a call from the Spirit of the Depths that one is becoming too dependent on the Spirit of the Times.

One may need to trust more in the quietness of his or her soul than the sound and fury of the outer world.

The first step when you find that anger has reared its ugly head is to not respond to the provocation (i.e., not responding to anger with anger). Try delaying your response for several seconds. (This is like the old "count to ten" method.) This will help you establish self-control and give you some time to engage the brain.

Another important step in reducing anger is to treat others with kindness and compassion. This includes those who are not like you or don't believe what you believe. This also includes those from a different tribe (i.e., family, neighborhood, village, gang, school, team, city, state, or country).

We are all humans who are trying to survive, feel safe, love, and be happy. With few exceptions, mostly by those who have psychological, spiritual, brain, or psychosocial damage, we all make mistakes, want to make a difference, and want to feel and be seen as good people.

We also share another common trait. We don't always know the right way to go about it. This is probably due to the fact that none of us came with an instruction manual, although many have written down a number of rules and laws designed to give us guidance in this area.

animal terms: This is a huge category, and I will only be naming the few that I have come across. Animals in general can speak to your drives and feelings about events and people with the usual social controls lifted.

As images, they also speak to our attitudes about and experiences with them. For example, a love for horses or dogs can represent feelings of love whereas a fear of these animals can symbolize our fears and anxieties. The dreamer needs to include these personal relationships with the images in their interpretations.

I have had dreams with animals nurturing their young, and I have interpreted this to mean something about my parenting role or relationship with my children.

Native Americans assigned totem spirits to a variety of animals with the nature of the animal representing the nature of the spirit. These totems would watch out over a person or group of people such as a family or tribe, sometimes for generations. Some people think that totems, spirit guides, and witches' familiars are very similar in nature.

The word totem is a Native American word for a sign or signifying mark. This is what an animal in a dream is to the dreamer. It represents a part of the dreamer. See *totem*.

Basically, animals in dreams represent our instinctual feelings or behaviors (see *instinct*). This extends to waking life as well. In fact, some therapists have dogs in the therapy room and watch the dogs' reactions to the patients entering the rooms or during their sessions in order to get clues as to the patients' emotional states.

Some dream therapists think that animals come to us in our dreams almost as spirit guides, each one bringing their own gifts, voice, symbolic energies, and usefulness to the dream. Other therapists have suggested that animals will attack or even befriend us in our dreams as a means of bringing our attention to those instincts we've ignored or neglected.

Consider that every animal in a dream is a reflection of your own personality.

I've included insects and fantasy creatures in this section as well.

Animals in dreams are depictions of ourselves stripped of our social controls and often present us with our unedited feelings. They depict our drives and urges for procreation, love, caring, and nurturing. Their skins were once thought by early native tribes to impart the power, personality, and wisdom of the animals they once belonged to. Animals continue to give their power in our dreams.

alligator or crocodile: Alligators in dreams often reflect our animal nature—the reactive, instinctual, and irrational side to our nature.

They can represent feelings of being attacked or overwhelmed. Who or what else is in the dream may give some clue as to who or what is attacking.

They might also represent the devious or hidden emotions or memories that can attack without warning.

These animals also seem to reflect our primitive and elemental fears.

ants: These may represent small irritations or stinging remarks and/or small anxieties, including times when you feel antsy. They also represent industriousness while their anthills could represent teeming hoards in which the individual makes little difference.

ass or donkey: This is a beast of burden. I have experienced it as a metaphor for how I have been behaving (i.e., as a jerk or being stubborn).

bat: This animal symbolizes intuition. Some, like the Australian Aborigines, see the bat as the spirit of death.

Its black color often is seen as suggesting evil, the unknown, or the unconscious.

Are you becoming nocturnal or going blind? Or perhaps there's something you're refusing to see.

bear: This represents the danger of the unpredictable. It symbolizes the reclusive or something to do with hibernating, withdrawing, or being solitary. It could also be a pun on something you need to bear or cannot bear (i.e., something you must live with or cannot live with).

In Native American culture, they are often seen as magical or medicine images and are associated with healing, though they can also be seen as aggressive and violent.

beast: An animal of no particular type. When it is threatening, it could be a fear or a hurt or even a person that is causing us pain. Sometimes beasts cause nightmares and we awaken. In this case, the fear may be so great that we cannot face it. If the nightmares are recurring, you might want to seek professional help in confronting what is hidden but perhaps wants to be known through the dream. Are you being beastly to someone?

beaver: This animal may represent the need to be productive. It may also be a symbol of ambitiousness. Do you need to work harder at something?

bee: A collective and cooperative activity, self-sacrificing for the good of the whole. A stinging bee can be about a painful and "stinging" remark, criticism or judgments made by either yourself or others. If buzzing you perhaps something threatening you. Perhaps you are being too busy and need to take a break or alternatively need to get busy with some project.

See also *carpenter bee.*

bird: Freedom, to move beyond your limitations (self-imposed or from others) or the limitation of the job or relationship. It can also represent your imagination, such as a "flight of fancy." Birds can represent the idea of flying high to another level of consciousness or rising above something, as in "taking the higher ground" or as in escaping.

A dead bird can be like a threat to your freedom or your ideals while an attacking bird can be a threat to your opinions from others or from yourself.

Sometimes birds can symbolize aspects of oneself or represent people in one's life.

Insight: In Celtic mythology, birds could symbolize omens and either the message or the messenger. In a Celtic legend the goddess Deirdre dreams of the three great birds. They arrived bearing honey and left

with blood, symbolizing treachery on the part of King Conchobar.

In the Christian tradition, and especially through the early Christian Celts, the bird was seen as symbolizing the Holy Spirit.

o *blackbird:* This bird can represent the unconscious and its urges that are trying to come to consciousness.

o *buzzard:* This may symbolize death and decay. This bird can symbolize an ugly side to yourself or the practice of being too opportunistic.

o *cardinal:* Cardinals can represent happiness or the need for it. They can also represent being first. A cardinal number is any whole number, such as one, two, three, and so on. See *numbers* for further meaning if any bird in the dream comes in a specific number.

o *chicken:* This bird is often linked to being chicken or afraid to do something. The male (rooster) can represent strutting arrogance.

o *crow or raven:* These birds are often linked with death or bad news. If one of these were in my dream, I might recreate the image and experience of the crow in my mind in a meditation and ask it what it wants or what it wants me to know. See **Insight.**

o *cuckoo:* This is seen by Australian Aborigines as a guide into the afterworld (see *psychopomp*).

This image could also be a commentary on someone's mental state.

o *dove:* This bird represents peace and the renewal of life in many mythologies.

In Christian myths, it is often seen as the Holy Spirit, one of the tripartite expressions of God. It also represents a love interest, as in a turtledove or lovebirds.

In southwest Africa, some tribes believed the dove to be the host for the ancestor spirit of gentleness, laughter, and song.

o *duck:* These can represent amusement, floating as in buoyancy, or the ability to swim through or over feelings.

The phrase, "water off a duck's back" suggests an ability to just let things go.

Black ducks can represent your darker or negative emotions.

o *eagle or hawk:* They can represent the dominant male figure, power, majesty, or nobility.

In the Celtic tradition, the eagle or hawk has stood for wisdom, a visionary's ability, and royal dignity.

In the Book of Kells, the eagle represents St. John and stands for the ascension to heaven and keeping its unwavering gaze upon the truth. Carl Jung thought of the eagle as an image of the "liberated soul," referring to what happens during the union of opposites (the integration of our opposing natures, namely the masculine and feminine attributes). See also *syzygy*.

Native American's saw the eagle as a bridge between the Great Spirit, humanity, and Mother Earth. They also saw the eagle as representing one's ability to see the big picture.

By flying high, the image of the eagle may suggest you want to see something from a different perspective. In short, the eagle can be interpreted as a symbol of the spirit.

The hawk is also seen as a symbol for a spiritual messenger and guide.

o *heron:* This is a stately bird that could symbolize pride. Perhaps you need to hold your head up high. Are you acting too arrogantly or prideful? Do you need to be more self-confident and stand tall?

o *hummingbird:* This bird could represent the soul but also your flightiness or hyperactive nature.

o *jay:* Perhaps you're being too confident. Are you being too arrogant?

o *ostrich:* The ostrich often refers to burying one's head in the sand and not wanting to face up to something or some situation you're not yet ready to accept.

o *owl:* They can symbolize wisdom, protection, messengers, and advisors. It has the ability to see into the dark, the night, and the hidden worlds of your unconscious. European Celts saw the owl as representing the Great Mother.

Owls are also night predators, and they may represent that which stalks you from your unconscious dark side and threatens the status quo.

Seeing an owl perched upon your head might indicate wisdom.

o *peacock:* This could represent pride and vanity or a desire to look better.

o *pigeon:* Are you being someone's pigeon? Is someone taking advantage of you? This could also be about gossip, or it could represent a nuisance.

This is a depiction of the raven from Edgar Allen Poe's poem *The Raven.* In the poem it sat upon the bust of Pallus. In a dream a bird sitting on or near one's head can suggest wisdom or trying to bring something unconscious into consciousness.

o *raven:* These are mystical messengers in some Native American cultures that help show the way and give warnings. They are natural opportunists, stealing anything they fancy. Ravens are often seen as tricksters, magicians, shamans, guides to our deeper selves, and cultural heroes.

Ravens and crows were also seen as psychopomps—guides to the underworld after death or guides to the inner and unconscious self.

Some cultures claimed that man communicated with nature through animals such as birds (trees and other animals as well).

Sometimes ravens will act as though they are trying to protect their mates or nests. This can suggest that there may be something in you that you need to protect.

o *sparrow:* This could symbolize your inner dignity, and it could tell you not to underestimate something that seems small or weak. It can also be a symbol for solitude or being alone.

o *swan:* This could symbolize dignity, grace, prestige, and beauty. Legend has it that the song of a pair of swans could heal the sick. There is also the metaphor of the swan song, which signifies one's last act before the end of something. There's also the idea of the ugly duckling, referring to times when something on the surface isn't so attractive but is quite beautiful inside (see *geode*).

o *vulture:* This could symbolize the act of waiting for something or someone to die so that you can take something that used to be the other person's (e.g., money, job, relationship, etc.).

Insight: The natives of the North American Pacific coast saw the raven as a hero, messenger, thief, trickster, and creator of the world. There's an Inuit story about how the raven brought the light into the world of darkness.

The raven is a symbol for solitude and an attribute of many saints whom the ravens fed in the wilderness (e.g., St. Anthony Abbot, St. Paul the Hermit, and St. Benedict). God sent ravens to feed Elijah the Tishbite by the brook Cherith during a long drought (1 Kings 17:6; Leviticus 11:15; Deuteronomy 14:14).

And the raven has long been a symbol of divine providence (Psalm 147:9; Job 38:41; 1 Kings 12:16–17). Though many may remember the Lord's command to consider the sparrow and the lilies, the following words are seldom revealed: "Consider the Ravens, for they neither sow nor reap, which have neither storehouse nor barn; and God feeds them" (Luke 12:24).

In the Song of Solomon, the beloved's locks are "black as a raven" (Song 5:11).

The raven symbolizes wisdom, hope, brother-sister gratitude and affection, longevity, fertility, and death. It is still used as a symbol in modern magic, witchcraft, and mystery.

In alchemy, it represents change and the advanced soul dying to this world. It is also considered the symbol of intuition.

The symbolic crow is associated with the sun, longevity, beginnings, endings, change, bad luck, prophecy, Christian solitude, and death. As with the raven, it also is considered a messenger of the gods. Among ancient Greeks and Romans, there were some who considered the crow a bad omen and the raven a good one.

In the telling of myths and legends, the crow frequently took the place of the raven. The Irish war goddess Badb often took on the shape of a crow. In classical mythology, this bird is an attribute of Cronus or Saturn and Athena, the goddess of wisdom, victory, and the arts.

Finally, the crow is associated with motherly love and spiritual strength. It was believed that fairies turned into crows in order to cause trouble. In heraldry, a crow was used to indicate a dark person such as a Moor or a Saracen. In Egypt, two crows, like two doves, were the sign of monogamy.

Among the Celts, the white crow was the emblem of the heroine Branwen. Her heroic brother Bran was pictured as a raven. In North America, the Kiowa Indians taught that the white crow turned black from eating snake eyes.

Early Christians gave a more sinister meaning to white ravens, suggesting that God turned them black because they were selfish.

bug: Is something annoying you? Is there something wrong that is negatively affecting some outcome (i.e., a *bug* in the system)? Is someone eavesdropping on conversations? See specific insects for more meaning.

bull: This might include a bison, buffalo, or ox. It could represent passion, instinctual response, and basic drives.

Insight: The bull can also present itself as a minotaur, the mythological character with the head of a bull and the body of a man. If this form appears in your dream, you may be wrestling with the instinctual, aggressive, or violent side of your nature.

Within the beast may be deep unconscious hurts that may be driving you to lash out at others. This creature can also represent someone you're dealing with in your life who has a scary beast-like nature. Where the minotaur is located and what he is doing will give you some idea.

If it is in a labyrinth (where he's found in Greek mythology), he might be symbolic of the fears you're experiencing in a life with seemingly never-ending twists and turns that aren't getting you anywhere. In this case, you feel lost and threatened.

butterfly: This could symbolize transformation, change, freedom, or independence. The ancient Greeks used the word soul for butterfly because the butterfly represents rebirth and resurrection.

If the butterfly lands on you, what part its landing on will have some significance. Perhaps it's this area that needs to change or be set free (see *body*).

If you experience butterflies in your stomach, it could be a metaphor for nervousness and anxiety.

cat: This may represent the feminine aspect, the soft, and the yielding. It could also signal the compassionate side to one's nature and the need to express it more. It can also represent a sense of independence.

It could also be symbolic of the negative feminine or a shadow aspect of yourself (see the *archetypes* section). It may represent cattiness (i.e., being bitter, tart, or hostile). Do you need to be more civil or diplomatic?

A black cat might be a symbol of fear or intuition, or you could have a sense of something being evil or bad luck.

If it's biting you, then it may be trying to get your attention.

If it's killing something, it may reflect your desire to kill off or control some dominating basal aspect of yourself. For some insight, look to see what it is killing.

In general, cats tend to be introverted as opposed to dogs, which often seem more extroverted. When you are forced to live your life contrary to your nature, an animal may angrily attack you in your dreams.

A sick or injured cat could represent your own need to return to your neglected cat nature and heal yourself.

A cat escaping from some confinement, such as a car, a box, or a house, may reflect your need to be set free and be independent.

A cat curling up in your lap and purring may reflect your own needs to relax and back away from the stresses of your life.

Cats can also reflect holding in secrets. In a man's dream, a cat can actually refer to a woman or women in general, or it can represent the intuitive side to his nature that is yet manifested.

caterpillar: This image might represent life changes. It could also suggest that you are getting ready to emerge as the new you or the desire to stay the same.

chameleon: Are you trying to look like something you're not? Are you hiding your real self? It's also possible that you feel overlooked.

chicken: See *bird*.

cockroach: This could represent a nuisance and disorder. It could be a symbol of something dirty and impoverished, and it frequently symbolizes regression. It can represent our primordial instincts, and it is also a symbol of darkness and our shadow self.

The cockroach can slip under and between some of the tiniest cracks, thus symbolizing the breaching of our defenses.

In our dreams, they can signal an impending psychological and emotional regression.

They also represent the chthonic, the underworld of the psyche.

cow: This could represent your docile or passive nature. Perhaps you obey others with too little questioning. It could also represent your desire to be cared for, or if you are in a herd, then perhaps it symbolizes your desire to belong.

It could also represent a mother figure or motherhood itself. Note that the cow is seen as a spiritual creature in some cultures. If this is so for you, then the cow may make you look at the spiritual side of your nature.

coyote: This is the trickster as in the Navajo tradition. The trickster is one of the human archetypes as well (see the *archetypes* section).

In the context of human trafficking, he's (spelled *coyotaje*) the one who takes someone's money and spirits them across the border. If unsuccessful, the illegal immigrant sometimes dies. This makes the coyote a sneaky and clandestine symbol as well. Are you being sneaky? Coyotes are also firefighters in the context of a forest.

crocodile: This could represent hidden danger and aggressiveness. Are you being lulled into a bad decision?

These creatures may represent the conscious and subconscious mind, the instinctive and the rational. If it's coming to the surface, perhaps something from your unconscious mind is trying to get your attention. A crocodile may represent some painful and *biting* aspect of your own inner self.

deer: The deer is gentle, harmless, vulnerable, and easily hurt. Sometimes it represents the soul. They can also represent your instinctual self that's ready to run at any sign of threat or danger.

Killing a deer can represent a gentle part of yourself being harmed by some aggressive or cynical act.

dinosaur: This could symbolize basic urges, the old brain, or an outmoded way of doing or thinking about something.

dog: This could represent aggression, loyalty, faithfulness, friendship, companionship, or unconditional love. The Celts saw dogs as protection animals, guardians, and animals of the hunt. If one bites you, perhaps someone is being disloyal or has betrayed you, or maybe you have done so to someone else.

Biting can also represent *biting* remarks (i.e., criticisms or judgments). Attacking can be an euphemism for bullying (see *bully*).

A black dog could signal something hidden—the unaccepted side of yourself. (This is similar to the shadow archetype and may very well be the shadow, especially if the dog is a male in a male's dream or female in a female's dream.) A white dog paired with a black dog could be about confronting your opposite natures or the clash between an obvious part of yourself and a hidden part.

Winston Churchill called his depression "the black dog." It was this dog that he could sometimes master, but it could also turn on him and bite him.

If the dog is biting you, see *bite*.

Dogs can also be symbols of poverty or being treated.

dolphin: This may be a spiritual message from the deeper part of yourself. Dolphins in dreams can often reflect spiritual guidance and emotional trust. This dream may be encouraging trust in the link between your conscious and subconscious self.

The dream might also suggest that you should become or are becoming more willing to explore your emotions and inner self.

donkey: This can represent foolishness, stubbornness, entrenched habits, or plodding. If you're riding, it can symbolize humility or a feeling of being less than. Perhaps you need to act less arrogant and get off your high horse.

duck(s): Ducks can be about your subconscious. It's as though they are the connection between your spiritual self and the physical world.

Ducks floating around reminds us of the phrase "sitting duck," and you might feel targeted by someone.

If a duck is biting you, it can mean that there's something you're not paying attention to, perhaps something instinctual that you are ignoring. Your subconscious may be trying to get your attention.

Insight: Visions of animals imparting hidden knowledge has been around for some time. Remember the story of the donkey in the Old Testament where the prophet Balaam ignored his donkey who thrice darted off the road because it sensed a danger that Balaam could not (Numbers 22:21–34 NIV)? The instinct of the donkey opened its eyes to what stood in the road, and its actions eventually helped to open the eyes of Balaam. In short, trust your inner animal as a guide.

dragon: See *animals as fantasy creatures*.

dragonfly: This could symbolize the unconscious mind or the fact that you are being a bit flighty.

eagle: See *birds*.

elephant: This can be an image of power and influence. Perhaps these are aspects of yourself that you need to express more. If you are being chased by an elephant, it can represent things or issues that you are not willing to face as in *an elephant in the room*.

Elephants can also represent memories or never forgetting. If the elephant is swimming in the water, perhaps there's something that you need to let go of or some memory or part of yourself you need to clean up.

In India and some parts of Asia, the elephant can symbolize burdens or wisdom. They are water symbols such as Ganesha, the bringer of rain.

ferret: The ferret might be something or someone devious or untrustworthy. It can also symbolize distrust or suspiciousness of others.

firefly: Fireflies can be about bright insights or ingenuity coming out of the subconscious.

fish: Fish can often represent feelings coming to the surface and/or thoughts, fantasies, and emotions swimming around inside us.

They can be either nourishing or threatening. You might need to allow for feelings that are being constrained. By eating them, you may need to come to some realization.

When a smaller fish eats a larger one, that could mean that you may not want to underestimate the power of the underdog or your own power to get something done.

If you're being eaten by a much larger fish, perhaps someone or some organization is overwhelming or undermining you.

Fish jumping above the surface of the water could depict chaotic emotions. Fish can also represent messages from the unconscious.

In a religious context, it could also represent Christianity. Jesus was also considered a "fisher of men." If you believe in the zodiac, you might look up some of the attributes of Pisces.

See *fish bait, fishing, fishing pole, fish pond, fishy smell,* or *seafood,* if appropriate.

fly: This could signal a desire for independence. A fly on the wall could be about curiosity. Flies can be about dirt and sickness. It can also represent some annoyance.

If it lands on your ear, ask yourself, "Is someone trying to get my attention and tell me something?" If it's flying from your mouth, ask yourself, "Have I said something I wish I hadn't, such as something foul?"

fox: This image is similar to the coyote (i.e., a shrewd and clever trickster). It can also be a symbol for wisdom gained from experience. So too, it can refer to someone who is sexy.

frog: This can represent the instinctive part of you or be a metaphor for a frog prince indicating transformation into something greater than the overt image. This creature can be archetypal in nature as in the *hero archetype.*

Do you wish to be a big frog in a small pond (i.e., to be more important)?

Frogs attacking or fighting one another might reflect some inner turmoil, struggle, or conflict. The aggressiveness may reflect an aggressive aspect of yourself.

In the North American Zuni tribe, the frog is a mystical and/or magical creature associated with water and the essence of life (see also *magic*).

They are also fertility symbols both for human reproduction and the bounty of a crop.

giraffe: Have you got your head in the clouds? Perhaps you're reaching high for some goal or desire. Maybe you need to take a broader perspective on something. Consider the phrase "sticking your neck out." Are you trying to get your head above the crowd (i.e., to think at a higher level)?

goat: This could be about a lack of judgment.

Consider the phrases "getting one's goat" (upsetting), "scapegoat" (being blamed), and "old goat" (old man). An old goat can also symbolize lechery.

This image could be a metaphor for a scapegoat. See *scapegoat* in the *archetypes* section. See also *betrayal*.

gopher: These underground creatures may be referring to your subconscious self or some normally hidden aspect of yourself that is out in the open and threatening your world.

gorilla: Gorillas might represent some overpowering influences that you would like to get rid of in yourself or in your life. Gorillas can sometimes reflect your own over-the-top behavior.

They can represent the primitive impulses that can result in your expression of negative energy (even sexual energy).

guinea pig: This could symbolize something being tested or tried out. It could also represent the feeling of being used.

horse: This could symbolize exuberance, energy, sexual drive, or a loss of any of these things as in "falling off the horse" or a "dead horse."

It is also a symbol for freedom, and it's one of the twelve celestial creatures in the Chinese zodiac.

The horseshoe is seen as a symbol of good luck. Where do you need your luck to change?

If the horse is galloping fast, perhaps you are moving too fast with something.

The color of the horse might also give you information (see *color*). Consider the phrase "the horse of a different color." This might suggest that you've found an alternative to something or some issue or problem isn't what you thought it was.

Mythological horses include the centaur, the genus Hippocampus (seahorse), Pegasus, and the unicorn. See *animals as fantasy creatures*.

It was said that Mohamed flew to heaven and returned on a white horse named Al Borak (Lightning). White horses carried St. George into battle. Tir, who battled for rain in Persian folklore, also rode a white horse. This might then imply that the white horse can come into a dream as a spiritual symbol.

Insight: The Tibetan symbol for the human soul is the wind horse. It flies in the wind and carries the prayers of humankind to heaven, thus connecting one with his or her divine nature.

Mara, a mare of the night (from which the word nightmare is derived), is an Anglo-Saxon and Norse mythological creature that would sit on the chests of sleeping individuals and cause them to have bad dreams.

hummingbird: See *birds.*

jackal or hyena: This represents the wild aspect of the dog, or it could symbolize a trickster like the coyote or fox. It is sometimes associated with death. Perhaps you feel you are feeding off others.

When we are self-critical and judgmental, we are *eating* or devouring our own innocence.

jaguar: This could be about your agility, power, speed, and/or mobility.

kitten: Kittens may indicate a transitional phase in your development where you are ready to explore new things. This dream may also represent innocence. If they are injured or dying, it may reflect a loss of innocence.

The koala is an Australian marsupial. They inhabit the Eucalyptus woodlands. In an Australian Aborigine "Dreaming" story the Lyre bird is said to have taken the tail of this arboreal creature as punishment for hoarding water. This story also explains the koala as a native symbol for lack and not having enough.

koala: This may be about nurturance, or it could represent the spirit world. It could also represent laziness. This may also be a feminine image and represent maternal nurturing.

Perhaps you are being too docile. These animals also live isolated from one another. Do you need to connect with others more? Are you trying to escape from the harshness of everyday life?

Seeing a stuffed koala may be about the desire to regress and become childlike again and free from adult responsibilities. They can also represent calmness, protection, and contentment.

By living high in trees, they achieve different perspectives on life.

To the Australian Aborigine, the name means dryness or a lack of water. This name was given to them because they didn't seem to drink water.

lamb: This could symbolize the traits childlike, dependent, vulnerable, and innocence. It could also be symbolic of being peaceful.

As a religious symbol, it could refer to sacrificing oneself.

This image may also represent the Agnus Dei, the symbol of Christ. See *Christ* in the *archetypes* section. See also *totem* or *totem pole*.

See also *sheep*.

leopard: This could reflect you thinking about who or what you are. You can't change your spots, but you may feel you need to. It also signifies power and strength.

lion: This represents physical strength, strong emotions (especially temper), and power. The lion can also represent one's father or God.

In the Celtic tradition, it was seen in warrior gatherings, and in the Christian tradition, the Celts used it to represent St. Mark, power, and royal dignity. Lions can also represent the emotion of pride.

If wearing a lion's skin, perhaps you are trying to assume the power, strength, or other attributes of the lion, or you may just be trying to look powerful.

Allowing yourself to be chased and then caught by a lion might also be an attempt to assume the power and strength of the lion.

If a lion is situated around something as though guarding it, you may feel that you need to protect some aspect of yourself. It could also mean that you may need to be more guarded about some aspect of yourself or someone else.

lizard or gecko: These could refer to the basal quality of our actions and natures—instinctive and reactive (as opposed to thinking or thoughtful). These are also cold-blooded animals and can represent someone without feelings. As such, they can also help you deal with difficult situations or people.

If the lizard darted out near you, did this surprise you? If so, has something caught you off guard?

If it's just lazing about, perhaps you are not being fully engaged in your life.

See also *dinosaur, dragon,* or *snake.*

Insight: That ancient part of us that I call the lizard brain (i.e., the reptilian brain structure at the base of the mammalian forebrain called the basal ganglia) was originally dominant in the reptile brain but built on and mitigated by the newer mammalian complexes such as the neocortex.

Lizard brain activity is evident when one person tries to conquer, control, and dominate others (e.g., Putin in the Crimea). It's also apparent in the reactive response to that situation when the minority attempts to dominate the majority (e.g., Tea Party enthusiasts, Muslim militants, sadists, Christian militants, dictators, bigots, killers, rapists, or groups that advocate for the violent physical, mental, spiritual, or financial control of anyone). Moreover, it's evident when the ego tries to dominate the individual through the use of addictions, self-mutilation, masochism, and/or depression or when the person continuously sabotages him or herself and thus falls short of success.

The lizard in our brain is often the archetypal demon we all have to wrestle with.

mole (or badger): Animals such as moles or badgers that burrow underground could represent you digging into your unconscious self to get down to the essence of who you are.

monkey: This could represent foolishness, mischievousness, or allowing oneself to be ruled by impulse. Monkeys can suggest immature attitudes or playfulness. A dead monkey might mean it's time to get serious.

A monkey can also reflect deceit and the feeling that there are others working against you for their own interest.

In India, the monkey could represent Hanuman—a Hindu deity and devotee of Rama. His story can represent a similar waking life allegory for the dreamer. This is true for all cultural and religious images.

moose: This animal can symbolize being both the powerful and the gentle. Use your power sparingly and only when necessary.

moth: Moths can often refer to compulsive urges. They can represent the hidden side of yourself. They are also symbolic of being flighty, and they may represent your character flaws.

Moths and butterflies have also been likened to souls reborn. Both are attracted to the light of the psyche's desire—the libido pursuing the promise of desire but also being self-destructive in nature.

mouse: This can symbolize timidity, small fears, irritations, shyness, or worries. If you're reaching out to capture a mouse, you may need to conquer some shyness by reaching out.

owl: This can be a spirit bird and thus represent a spiritual aspect of your life. It is also a symbol of wisdom and inner knowledge, and as a symbol of darkness, it can bring information from the dark side of yourself, the unconscious.

As a creature of darkness, it can also represent stirrings of fear. As a symbol for the night, an owl might also be affiliated with the moon and may perhaps serve as a messenger. See *moon*.

If the moon is the ruler of the night, might the owl be her knight? See *knight*.

The owl is often seen as a mystical creature or can also be seen as a witch's fetch or familiar that is able to cross between different planes of being. Sometimes these can be demons in hiding. See *demon*.

As a totem animal, it can be emblematic of deep intuitive knowledge. If present in a dream, it may be announcing the need for or the presence of change or transition (i.e., the death of a way of being).

As a spirit guide, the owl can be a means of looking behind an illusion or deception to see what is hidden. Its wisdom can help with discernment and decision-making. The owl can represent your own inner wisdom. See *birds*.

peacock: A peacock can be about pride or glory, and in some cultures, it may represent immortality. The colors have often been associated with the spiritual.

phoenix: See *animals as fantasy creatures*.

pig: This can symbolize dirty, basal drives. Pigs can refer to something dirty, greedy, gluttonous, or selfish. If you normally like pigs, then your dream may be telling you that you've been mistaken about something or someone. This image may be a metaphor for someone in your life (typically a man) who may be acting chauvinistic.

If chasing a pig out of your house or yard (i.e., out of your life), you may be looking for an answer to your problem. However, *chasing* can also be a metaphor for avoidance, and avoidance might be better confronted than avoided. Either way, you want to get rid of this negativity.

possum: Is something not what it appears to be? Is there some hidden meaning?

puppy: This image could be about playfulness, innocence, or dependence.

rabbit: This could symbolize sexuality, luck, or insecurity. It can represent gentle and passive idealism (or foolishly passive) and can be used as a sacrificial image like a lamb.

Sometimes the presence of a rabbit can represent fertility, especially if it's hopping around.

White rabbits can be about faithfulness in some love relationship, and black rabbits may be about your fears of being intimate.

The Celts associated the rabbit with performing magic and doing something considered impossible as in pulling a rabbit out of a hat.

raccoon: This critter can represent something or someone (even yourself) as a nuisance.

ram: This could symbolize aggression, energy, and/or impulsivity.

rat: This is often a negative symbol that can reference sickness, fear, frightening urges, sexual repulsiveness, sex for personal gain, squalor, or something gnawing away at you. Black rats can be about deceitfulness. Some interpret white rats as positive images in dreams.

To rat people out is to tell on them or to squeal (see *snitch*).

Consider also the term *rat race*, especially if the rat is trying to bite your feet or legs.

rooster: See *chicken*.

scarab: This was a symbol of rebirth and resurrection to the ancient Egyptians. That is why it is represented in so many ancient Egyptian tombs. Moreover, it is a symbol of adaptation but also one of death. Something (such as a behavior, a way of being, or a habit) may need to die or end in order for something else to be born.

Egyptian scarab, found in hieroglyphs, also known as a dung beetle.

Insight: In C. G. Jung's 1969 book *Synchronicity: An Acausal Connecting Principle* (Princeton Press), he tells the story of a female client who is relating a recent dream that starred an image of a golden scarab.

Prior to this dream, this woman was apparently trapped in a world of intellectual rationalization that prevented her from moving on in her therapy and kept her fixed in a negative worldview. While listening, Jung heard and then let in a golden beetle through the window of his study, captured it, and presented it to the woman, exclaiming, "Here is your scarab."

The event helped to break through the woman's intellectual resistance, and it opened her to a whole new reality. It was a rebirth or resurrection.

scorpion: This can represent the sting of death. It's the poison of murderous ambitions as with Macbeth. "Oh, full of scorpions is my mind, dear wife" (Shakespeare, act 3, scene 2, p. 43).

It can reflect murderous thoughts and self-criticisms that tend to kill one's serenity and ability to think straight.

Note that this is a creature that shuns the light and hides in darkness in order to attack. In a dream, consider also the zodiac symbol Scorpio (in reference to self-control, tenacity, healing, and sometimes transformation). See also *Scorpio.*

seahorse: This may represent the power of your unconscious mind. Seahorses may also reflect emotional issues or the feeling of being afloat within deep emotions. See also *Hippocampus* in *animals and fantasy creatures.*

sea serpent: This might be about a transformation regarding emotional issues or the need for a change. A two-headed sea serpent could reflect being emotionally torn between two issues or people.

shark: This can be about anger, or you may feel that someone is stalking you or that you or someone is being hostile and threatening. It can also represent fierceness and hostility. A shark attack might suggest a struggle with irrational urges. They can also represent dangerous emotions and inner conflict.

The shark can be symbolic of the greedy and unscrupulous within you or in others. It can also be a metaphor for going after what it is you want and being undeterred in regards to your goal.

A group of circling sharks can suggest people lurking and ready to take advantage of your vulnerability in some struggle.

sheep: This could refer to conformity, being a follower and not a leader, acting as just one of the herd. Consider the phrase "the blind sheep." The presence of a sheep, especially if it's attacking or threatening someone, may be encouraging you to step outside your comfort zone and start to exercise your leadership in some situation.

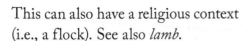

This can also have a religious context (i.e., a flock). See also *lamb.*

snail: Are you feeling slow? This may be a metaphor for slow and steady progress toward some goal or the need to slow down with regard to your goals.

If you are spitting out snails in your dream, ask yourself, "Are you being overly sensitive or saying disgusting things?" (See also *vomiting.*)

snake: This can be a very complex image. It can represent one's blind, impulsive urges. It can also be a symbol for fear or a hidden threat, or if the snake is attacking from someplace hidden, it can be symbolic of betrayal.

In many cases, a snake can represent one's ego (e.g., temptation, lying, and cajoling). It can be the constant voice in one's head that's judging and criticizing anything and everything.

As with all animals in dreams, it can also represent your instinctive animal nature. If the snake is attacking, this can mean that at some level this part of you is wanting to reconnect with the rest of you and restore balance.

It can represent the power of the Kundalini, sexuality (dangerous or overwhelming), energy, and the symbol of awakening as in higher self-realization. In the Celtic tradition, the snake's ability to shed its skin made it a symbol of rebirth. They could also stand for fertility because of their large number of progeny.

The snake was also seen as a *symbol for healing.* Hence, its use on the iconic staff of the medical profession, the caduceus. In this form, it can represent worries about your health. Even a snake's bite can represent healing in some positive ways.

If the image is more about *snake oil,* you might want to do more research into what might be healing (see also *used car dealer*).

It can be a symbol of transformation, change, or renewal. The *color of the snake* might also provide information as to its meaning. For example, yellow might represent being cautious about someone or perhaps a cowardly act on someone's part (see *colors*).

The snake can also represent someone who is *being deceitful* or tempting you toward something that may go against your better judgment or may not be in your best interest.

Insight: In the Victorian era, the snake often symbolized everlasting or eternal love. Queen Victoria of England had a ring shaped like a snake—an *ouroboros* or snake biting its tail and forming a circle that symbolized wholeness and the eternal (i.e., perfection with no end). See ouroboros.

A snake with a head on each end might suggest that you are being pulled in multiple directions. Seeing the beheading of a snake might suggest that there's an issue you're not confronting.

If snakes are all around you but none are threatening you, perhaps this is an invitation to explore your deeper self since it won't hurt you.

Being attacked or bitten by a snake can be about inner aggression or poisoning.

You may be attacking yourself and causing illness in the process. If you were bitten on the foot or leg, it may suggest something about the balance that is lost when you attack yourself. This kind of dream may be revealing a fundamental (foundational) issue in this person's life.

Biting might also reflect your subconscious worries about your health or your frustrated sexual impulses or experiences.

If the snakes are threatening, they may represent your fears and worries about something bad happening or something overpowering taking place. This can also represent the feeling that someone in particular cannot be trusted.

Pulling a snake from your vagina has obvious sexual connotations but may also reflect pulling something out of yourself (e.g., deceit, frustration, or problems). Perhaps you are rejecting some part of your sexuality.

You may also be dealing with a poisonous person in your life.

Being *swallowed by a snake* may also suggest that something or someone is swallowing you up (i.e., consuming you).

Snakes are also cold-blooded, so they may also signify a lack of compassion in your actions. They also shed their skin, so they may also serve as symbols of change (i.e., shedding the old to make room for the new).

Being chased by snakes may be about avoiding some issue or some deceit, or you may not be facing your own deceit. Perhaps you have some memory, feeling, desire, or action that you're not willing or ready to deal with.

Cutting off the head of the snake can be about an issue that you are not dealing with or confronting (i.e., something you are refusing to face). Maybe there's something you're not seeing here (see also *ouroboros* and *boa constrictor*).

Insight: In ancient times, serpents were revered as symbols of renewal in that they shed their skins each year, beginning anew.

In the Bible, the seraphim (meaning "the burning ones") were like snakes or flying serpents. Their job was to maintain the divinity in perfect order.

Later Christians morphed the seraphim into humanlike angels with six wings and relegated the serpent to a more basal position of deceit and the dragon to symbolize Satan as a means of discrediting pagan religions so as to reinforce the new religious worldview.

Often snakes found underground and in the water (rivers, lakes, and oceans) represent hidden emotions in dreams. In China, people used to hide their money and treasure underground so that it would be protected by the snakes. A snake in the water can represent a strong emotion attacking you when you look too deeply into your unconscious.

The people of the Zambezie Valley in Zimbabwe, Africa, believed that they were protected by the river snake Nayaminyami. This snake was the ruler of the sacred water, and his symbol is still worn to protect against the forces of darkness and to attract good fortune.

In Greek mythology, Medusa is the prettiest of three Gorgon sisters. Her hair was made of writhing snakes, and her eyes could turn you to stone if you looked at them. Naturally, she has a number of symbolic meanings.

To be turned to stone might indicate becoming incapacitated or rigid in thinking, deed, or response.

With another interpretation, this visage might be considered a dangerous and seductive force in your life (look to see what it might be referring to in the dream) or a controlling, subversive feminine power.

Medusa was one of three sisters known as the Gorgons. In psychoanalysis, she represents incapacitating fear and castration because one look at her would turn a person to stone.

The ancient Greek god Asclepius, originally a mortal healer, would appear to the practitioners of his medical arts as a snake.

The healer god Amphiaraos would become a snake and then lick and suck the poison from the bodies of those who came to the dream clinic to be healed. For this reason, snakes were allowed to run freely through the dream incubation centers, which were called asclepeions.

In alchemy, the *quadricornutus serpens* (four-horned serpent) was a symbol for the liquid metal mercury.

In Hindu mythology, the serpent Karkotaka denotes eternal wisdom. (Snakes are considered to be long-lived or even immortal because they continuously renew themselves by shedding their skins.) In Hinduism, Vishnu used a snake to churn the ocean. Nag is the king of snakes in the Hindu tradition. She is a female deity in India, and she is called "the mother of all that moves."

In both Hinduism and Buddhism, Tantric sages consider her (the snake) the inner power of the Kundalini and what they try to awaken through their meditations.

The color of the snake may also add meaning (see *color*).

spider: This could symbolize the dark feminine force. It can also mean organization and patience. So too, it's possible that a mother figure (or family member) may be dominating you.

Spiders can also represent conflicts that you may feel caught in and any emotions that you may not want to get caught up in or deal with. The phrase "Oh, what a tangled web we weave" reflects lies or deceptions that either we or others have woven.

If they're crawling on your face, perhaps they represent some problems you're facing, or perhaps something is bugging you. See also *web*.

squirrel: This may be a trickster symbol (see the *archetypes* section). It may be a distractor, or it may represent something or someone who is being devious.

swan: The swan can be about purity. It can also be about grace, beauty, and dignity, especially if it's white. If it's black, it can be about the unknown and perhaps something forbidden though alluring.

Because swans are often seen as being graceful creatures, perhaps you need to handle something with grace or something more gracefully.

tiger: This can represent the power and leadership you exert. It can also be symbolic of female power (e.g., seduction, assertiveness or aggressiveness, and sexuality).

Being attacked or threatened by one could be about some repressed emotions, while a caged tiger might imply repressed emotions that are about to surface.

A tiger can also represent one's mother as either a protector or destroyer. Consider the term *tiger mom*, meaning a fierce protector.

toad: This could mean that something is hidden in you. Sometimes this image represents the deep unconscious or the ugly part of ourselves or someone else.

Consider also the term *toady* (or sycophant), referring to a disingenuous flatterer. (This symbol may be heightened if you or someone has turned into a toad in the dream.) Do you need your ego stroked? Are you praising or complimenting (or kissing up to) someone for personal gain?

To the Chinese, this symbol represented longevity, wealth, and money-making, and the toad is also a goddess of transformation and immortality.

turkey: This might be about your foolishness. Perhaps you are not thinking clearly. Note that this bird is also symbolic of Thanksgiving.

turtle: This animal can represent self-protection (i.e., a defensive shell). These creatures can also represent longevity and deep wisdom. Sea turtles can be messengers from one's subconscious or deeper, more spiritual self.

wasp: This might represent negative feelings and/or anger. If stung by a wasp, perhaps someone is turning his or her anger toward you as with a stinging comment or harsh criticism. To kill a wasp might indicate your willingness to stand up for yourself or to push back against the negative.

It can also represent a Caucasian person (white Anglo-Saxon person).

weasel: Do you have trouble trusting others? Are you being untrustworthy or deceitful?

whale: At one time seafarers thought of the whale as a dragon. In your dream it may represent intuition and rising awareness. It can also be a spiritual symbol.

A beached whale might suggest a lost sense of spirituality. If it's dead, it may suggest that something deep within you has died (e.g., a belief or a hope). It can also be something that is overwhelming you. Perhaps a project or activity that's way too big?

wolf: A wolf can represent fear or powerful male sexuality, instinct, and threat. The wolf can be the wildness in ourselves. It can represent and even inspire freedom and independence. In my dreams the wolf is always white, indicating clarity or purity.

The wolf is a loyal guardian in my dreams and is usually depicted as an alpha or lead wolf. Some would say that the wolf is one of my spirit animals. (The eagle and dragon are two more.)

To the Zuni tribe in the Southwest of the United States, the wolf is a pathfinder and trailblazer. Symbolically, the wolf represents working together as a team. The Zuni fetish on the lower left is a spirit guide, a totem protector. Note the arrow pointing from the mouth to the center of the fetish. This is known as the heart line (i.e., the life force or soul leading to one's greatest power). The object on its back is known as a prayer bundle.

In some Native American tribes, the wolf is the teacher animal that teaches us about our inner nature and our intuitive sense, and we learn how to listen to the still, small voice within. The wolf can be both family/group-oriented and a loner.

Consider the phrase "the wolf at the door" as symbolizing survival or poverty.

worm: Are you being degraded, or do you feel weak? This symbol is generally thought of negatively and may relate to your self-image. Sometimes a worm in your dream can be a metaphor for some unscrupulous person.

Insight: The worm, toad, frog, turtle, snake, and crocodile are all symbolic of the primordial nature that lies within the human psyche.

animals as fantasy creatures: There are also fantasy creatures in our dreams that impart meaning. Here are just a few to get you started.

At the top of my list of fantastic dream fauna is the *unicorn*. They're not only horses that conjure expressions of power and sexuality, but these particular equines also symbolize high ideals, insight, hope, gentleness, and purity.

The unicorn was sometimes a symbol for the Virgin Mary and even for the Christ, and it represented the one spirit. In the Jewish tradition, it represented the unity of spirit.

The presence of its form heralded peace, self-confidence, and prosperity in the Japanese and Chinese traditions.

In Wicca, these creatures can act as spiritual guides to light and love, and they belong to the angelic (see *angel*).

Dragons are sometimes associated with the vast foreboding unconscious and/or wisdom. In the Celtic tradition, a dragon was the protector of treasure and a powerful presence.

A dragon coming up from the deep sea or ocean may represent a threatening aspect of yourself or an emotion that threatens to overwhelm you.

Sometimes when two dragons are fighting, it can signal a struggle for power. Overcoming a dragon can mean that you desire to overcome your fears.

A multiheaded dragon, such as a hydra, might represent huge obstacles in the way of some goal. You may need to overcome these obstacles in some way.

In medieval Europe, people who secured a coat of arms from the king often used animals to represent qualities in themselves. For example, the dragon represented a brave defender and protector. In the East, a dragon motif on a family banner meant good luck and fortune.

Turning into a dragon might suggest that you get carried away with your passion, whether it be your emotions, competitive spirit, self-control, leadership, or strong will. If you are breathing fire, you may feel you use your anger or aggression to get your own way. Do you need to control yourself better?

However, if the dragon is a spiritual creature for you, then it may be symbolic of that which protects your soul and may even represent the nature of that soul. When morphing into a dragon (or any animal), you might be aware of your transformation into something new.

A paper dragon can represent a false power. In the Chinese tradition, dragons bring wisdom. (Note the pearl of wisdom many Chinese dragons offer.)

The dragon is actually the major symbol of good fortune in Chinese astrology. The Dragon constellation, for example, is accorded the honor of being the guardian of the Eastern sky. Traditionally, the dragon brings in the four blessings of the East—wealth, virtue, harmony, and longevity.

Of the twelve signs of the Chinese zodiac, the dragon is the most special as it is a mystical being rather than an earthly animal.

According to Chinese astrology, it's a karmic sign, and we can expect grand things from the year dedicated to this beast.

In both Chinese and Japanese mythology, the dragon is seen as a symbol of wisdom and good fortune.

Dragon

Interestingly enough, the root word for dragon in ancient Greek was *drakon*, which translates as "to see clearly" or "that which sees." This might be interpreted as wisdom.

Ancient dragons in Japanese mythology seem to be mostly water gods and thus associated with one's emotions and the spirit of life (i.e., what refreshes life).

The color of the dragon may also provide insight as to its meaning (see *colors*).

Giants are archetypal images in children's dreams because in their worldview most everyone towers over them. Because adults are dominating figures in their lives, they will often show up in dreams when children are trying to deal with independence issues.

Confronting these figures in dreams helps children deal with the emotional aspects of their waking world struggles.

In an adult dream, they can represent huge problems or an inflated sense of self.

In dreams, the *griffon* (part lion or leopard with the head and wings of an eagle) is often seen as a symbol for the positive aspects of change, representing the physical power and stability of the lion as well as the clear vision and spirit of the eagle.

In mythology, the griffon is the herald of change. For Christians, it sometimes appeared along with the dragon, and it was considered a symbol for Satan.

The *Hippocampus* is a horse of the sea (see *seahorse*). Note that this is also the name of an area of the brain that is involved with emotions, memories, and the automatic (autonomic) nervous system.

Werewolves in dreams can suggest that something in your life is not what it seems. It is a symbol for anger, repressed violence, and fear. Perhaps you or someone else is being hurtful to others or to you. Alternatively, it can be a symbol for repressed instincts.

A Chimera is any creature composed of more than one animal (in this case lion, goat, snake). They can symbolize the disparate parts of oneself or as something implausible. They were often seen as bad omens. The Sphinx in Egypt would be considered a Chimeric symbol. See also *beast* and *monster*.

Chimeras can be about feelings of confusion and the need to sort out your thoughts and feelings.

Centaurs in dreams can represent the dualities in human nature, and thus, one of these can mean that you are trying to balance your intellectual side with your animal side (i.e., the body/mind conflict). The centaur can also represent compassion and wisdom.

If a *cyclops* (a creature with a single eye) shows up in your dream, it could refer to singular vision or restricted perception. Do you need to broaden your perspective?

Satyrs are symbols of sexual freedom and masculine sexual power. Perhaps you need to be more in tune with your environment. Perhaps you're being too serious and need to be more carefree.

Though not an animal per se, the *fairy* or *faery* in a dream is often a symbol for the soul and the feminine aspects of oneself (e.g., intuitiveness, compassion, or acceptance), though an evil fairy can represent the negative feminine (e.g., controlling or indecisiveness) or even suggest that some part of yourself needs to be set free.

An injury to a fairy in the dream might reveal a hurt that you suffered in the past or one you are experiencing in the present.

A *minotaur* or any human and beast combination (frequently a human body with the head of an animal, such as a bull) might suggest that you're acting on blind impulse somewhere in your life. A minotaur could represent the animal or instinctual aspect of your nature that you are either ignoring or that may be overwhelming the rest of you. See also *labyrinth*.

To see a *nymph* (male elf-like characters) in a dream can be about the mystery of the feminine aspect. It can be about grace and innocence as well.

In general, fairy-tale dreams symbolize a need to be rescued or to leave the pain of the ordinary world, but they may also be a means of highlighting what is normal or be a way of telling you to expand your imagination and creativity (i.e., to explore all options).

An *ogre* may represent self-criticism or something acting in an overbearing way.

The *phoenix* or firebird (the bird that goes up in flames only to be reborn again and again) can be about renewal, new growth, new beginnings, transformation, resurrection, death, and rebirth. Jesus has often been symbolized by a phoenix.

Insight: Animals—whether of the ordinary earthly kind or the fanciful kind—are usually messengers from the unconscious and speak to our primitive desires, which we often repress to some extent and which can devour us if we don't pay enough attention to them.

They are also wisdom guides and even spiritual messengers from the soul. In short, when animals show up in your dream, pay attention. They are only there to help you.

animus/anima: Male within a woman's dream *or* female within a man's dream (see the *archetypes* section; see also *Eros* and *Logos*).

The root, *anima*, means soul or animating principle in Latin. It is also the Latin translation of the Greek word psyche.

It is believed that the soul of a man is feminine while the soul of a woman is masculine, and it is the process of integrating the two into one that can bring about wholeness (see also *spirit*).

See *Sophia* as an example of an anima image.

ankh: This symbolized empowerment. It's seen as a symbol of eternity and eternal life. It is a symbol of divine power. See also *cross*.

Ankh

Insight: In ancient Egypt, the ankh was a hieroglyphic character symbolizing *life* as in the concept of life. It was most often found near or in the hands of the Egyptian pantheon of gods, as well as depictions of pharaohs.

anorexia: If anorexia shows up in a dream, you may be experiencing low self-acceptance or self-esteem. You may not be accepting yourself as you are. You may be punishing yourself, and you may also be failing to nurture yourself.

Your sense of self, well-being, and happiness may depend on how you look, and you may never be satisfied with that look. You may need to confront these feelings and seek assistance in dealing with them.

If you are purging or vomiting up a meal, you may be trying to get rid of some part of yourself with which you are dissatisfied.

See also *vomiting*.

answers: If you are calling out to people in your dream but no one is answering, perhaps you have feelings about those most important questions in life that you are searching for. Perhaps you are listening to the wrong things.

Antarctic: See *Artic* and also *south*.

antiques: Certain things from the past may be worth holding on to. This image can symbolize aging or wisdom as well.

antivenom: Antivenom could be about restoring your sense of self or reputation. See also *poison*.

ants: See *animal*.

anxiety: This kind of dream could just be reflecting your overall waking anxiety or some worry over a specific issue.

Dreams about missing classes or taking an important exam that you haven't studied for often reflect your waking anxieties and worries. But they could also refer to the need to learn something that you've not given enough attention to.

See *confusion*, *fear*, *scared*, *uncertainty*, and/ or *worry*. See also *class* or *school*.

apartment (or flat): This may be the same as a house if that is what you typically live in. What are the feeling states in this apartment? Did you live alone, and what was that like?

apocalypse: You may have a worry or sense of impending doom or catastrophe. Perhaps you're being too fatalistic and negative about something. Apocalyptic thinking can bring on even more apocalyptic thinking. One can become consumed by this view of reality and thus view most of reality in a negative way.

This can also be an escape from the everyday pain of life. Many "end of the world" believers find it too hard to deal with life, so they fantasize about the rapture (being taken to heaven during the end days).

This kind of dream may actually be a healing dream in that it is making conscious your inner turmoil and response pattern to stress.

See also *end of the world*, *Armageddon*, or *apocalypse* in the *archetypes* section.

Insight: Once caught in this kind of self-reinforcing cyclical thought pattern, it can take a concentrated effort to escape. Healing this pattern can be done through various therapeutic means. Chief among them are various forms of cognitive behavioral therapy as well as relaxation techniques (see the therapies reviewed in the nightmares section).

apologize: If you or someone else is apologizing in a dream, it may be about creating harmony. Are you feeling guilty about something? It can also be a symbol of some wrongdoing that you are not paying attention to. Do you need to forgive someone?

See also *forgiveness*.

appendicitis: If you or someone else is experiencing appendicitis in your dream, it might refer to some need to heal a certain pain (emotional, psychological, spiritual, or physical). Because the appendix is in the stomach, it may represent a gut-wrenching pain (perhaps one that is emotional in nature).

It may also suggest that you need to pay attention to your gut (i.e., your intuitive sense) about some situation.

apple: Apples have meanings associated with temptation, sexuality, and love. The presence of it might suggest that you want some more attention and love. To eat one might be telling you something about fertility and/or harmony or your desire for this.

Apples can also be about health or the computer.

Note that this can represent any number of digital machines manufactured by the company with the same name and symbolize your particular positive or negative relationship with said company and/or their products.

A rotten apple can represent someone who is dishonest, hurtful, and/or harmful. Green or unripe apples may represent something that is ripening but not quite mature.

Apple juice or cider can be symbolic of the need for more energy and vitality.

appointment: Perhaps you need to be more goal-oriented. If you've missed an appointment, you may need to pay more attention to the details in your life or in some project.

Aquarius: This sign is symbolic of originality and independent attitudes and outlooks. It can also represent unconventional relationships and freethinking attitudes.

Are you feeling a little smothered or bound up by something or someone? Do you need more space or greater freedom?

Sometimes people born under this sign are seen as people who exist outside of the box, but they can often become space cadets and lose their grounding to reality with too much and imbalanced thinking. See also *zodiac*.

archery: Are you setting goals? Are you on or off target?

architect: This could symbolize your creativity and the building or designing of something new in your life. If architecture shows up in the dream, it could be symbolic of buildings in general or specific ones that might have meaning (e.g., police stations, halls of justice, museums, libraries, etc.). These might also be symbolic of houses, which often refer to your sense of self and your body.

archetypes: Deep within all of us is a universal thought form that influences virtually everything we do, believe, or think we know. This form, feeling, or image is expressed in a myriad of ways at our most unconscious level. These universal forms are called archetypes, and they reside in an ethereal realm called the *collective unconscious.*

They are most often accessed through our dreams or other trance states. But the images are expressed in more than just our dreams. We can see them in our myths and our fairy tales, and they shape the relationships that matter in our lives.

Carl Jung used this word to express something that he observed in human nature in terms of common themes and patterns in dreams that are universally expressed across all cultures. He perceived them as something in the psyche not personally created but more a genetic inheritance as in something from the collective unconscious. See the *archetypes* section.

Arctic: This symbol could be about your emotional state (e.g., cold, rigid, and isolated). (See also *ice* and *north*).

arena: Do you need to be in a place where you can completely express yourself? Is there some issue that you need to bring out into the open?

arguing: This could represent verbal conflict. Where do you hope for a resolution? If you and another person are arguing in your dream, it could also represent an internal conflict that you are having and your attempt to resolve it (see *quarrel*).

Look to see who is doing the arguing. If the argument is between your parents, this may represent their negative voice in you.

Aries: This sign often symbolizes new beginnings and/or growth. It can be about courage or enthusiasm. Maybe you need to approach something head-on as a ram would.

arithmetic: Is there some situation or decision that requires that you be more rational in your thinking and less emotional? If you're having trouble solving some arithmetic problem, you might look to where in your life some issue seems unsolvable. Perhaps you need to take another approach.

An arithmetic test might suggest that you are being confronted with problems to be solved.

arm: See *body*.

Armageddon: Are you feeling out of control and helpless? This may also represent your general anxiety. Something in your waking life may make you feel very stressed and hopeless.

This is also an archetypal theme similar to conflict of opposites (see *apocalypse* and the *archetypes* section, as well as *death* and *resurrection*.

A theme of death and resurrection in this dream might mean that something may not be working for you and may need to die in order for something new to happen.

armor: If you or someone else in a dream is wearing armor, it may symbolize what you use to protect yourself emotionally. Are you being overly defensive? Do you need more self-confidence?

Armor may say something about your energy reserve or lack thereof.

army/military: This can refer to either internal or external conflict. Are you gathering your forces? In some cases, this image could be symbolic for control and domination (see *attack* and *soldier/warrior*).

arrest: This could perhaps refer to the fear of being caught or restrained in some way. Consider the phrase "arrested development," which means being stuck emotionally or psychologically. You may also feel guilty about something.

arrow: This could symbolize the targets or goals that you're shooting for. Broken arrows might be about disappointments, failures, and/or broken relationships. If you are shot by an arrow, it could represent being struck by love (as with Cupid's arrow) or overcome by some tension or stress.

A flaming arrow may be symbolic of anger or an angry voice or action.

See *Cupid*.

arson: This could represent destructive and perhaps unexpressed rage. It could also symbolize the clearing away of anger.

art: Art generally refers to one's self-expression. Do you need to express yourself more? Do you need to be more creative?

artery: If clogged, it might mean that some aspect of yourself is hindering the successful flow of your life. This could also signal a health issue that you don't want to ignore.

artifact: Could this refer to some part of your former self or life that you have not let go of? This could also represent a memory.

artist: This often represents the irrational and creative aspect of the self. What part of you is ready to be expressed?

ascending: This could mean rising feelings, finding a different perspective, or trying to get to your higher self. Perhaps you need to broaden your outlook on life.

ascetic or monk: This invokes the image of the loner. See *monk* under the *archetypes* section.

ashes: This can refer to the remains of an experience, perhaps negative. What is finished for you?

Breathing out ash or putting ashes into an ashtray could also be a metaphor for getting rid of or letting go of past issues.

Ashes in a dream could represent your disappointments, regrets, or losses (i.e., things that disrupt). They could also represent failed projects or relationships.

Ashes may also indicate the past. Are you focusing too much on the past?

ashram: This could be about the need for spiritual renewal and healing. See also *yoga* and *church*.

Asian: See *Chinese*.

asking: If you are asking someone a question, it could reflect your need to know or your desire for an answer to some question in your life. It could also be a rehearsal for engaging with others (see *query or question*).

asleep: If you or someone is asleep in your dream, it may mean that you need to wake up and become conscious of something.

Are you being unconscious about something or someone? Do you need to pay more attention to something?

See *dreaming*.

Asclepeion: This is an ancient type of healing temple like those found along the Aegean around the era of Hippocrates. These were health clinics where priests used dreams to diagnose and treat people with various diseases.

It was said that the doctor-demigod Asclepius or an assistant would come to the patients in their dreams, and then the patients would share this information with the priests who were present.

Modern-day medicine now sees some value in what they believe is the body's natural self-healing ability, which can be accessed through the dreams of their patients in some cases. See also *Cadeuseus*.

Ruins of an ancient Asclepeion found along the shores of modern-day Greece.

ass: This could symbolize a lack of understanding or insensitivity on your or someone else's part. If it's carrying burdens in the dream, something may be burdening you. Maybe you need to lighten the load.

assisting: See *help*.

assault: You may be feeling vulnerable or criticized. (This is especially true if the assault is verbal.) If rape is involved, it could reflect a feeling that you've been victimized or violated in some way (see *rape*).

Are you reliving an actual assault (verbal or physical)? If so, you may want to seek the help of a professional to assist you in working through the resulting emotions.

assassin: This might imply that you are trying to kill off a part of yourself (i.e., a behavior, way of being, or habit). This can also relate to an attempt to lose weight.

Are you trying to end a relationship or trying to attack and destroy someone's character?

asteroid: This can be a message from your spiritual aspect. This can also portend some kind of enlightenment. See also *meteor*.

Astral Projection aka Astral Travel can also be like an Out of Body Experience or OBE (see *out-of-body experience*).

Some say that they have experienced this through induced hypnosis or during an hallucinogenic episode. Rosicrucians, Hermetics, and Theosophists thought of what they call the astral body as an intermediary between one's soul and body.

As a dream symbol, it can also be referring to the spiritual aspect of oneself.

astral projection: Perhaps you are looking at things from a totally new perspective. It is also possible that you have disconnected yourself from those around you both physically and emotionally. It could also be symbolic of your desire to escape your circumstances. See also *out-of-body experience*.

Insight: This is also known as astral travel. It's a type of out-of-body experience (OBE). It happens when the so-called astral body leaves the physical body and journeys outside. Though this has been known to happen when one is dreaming, it's generally induced through hypnosis or hallucinogenic substances or through some form of trance state. Many world religions have made reference to it as a ritual for attaining enlightenment, and they often describe a different level or plane of existence.

The Theosophists, who were popular in the 1920s, thought of it as a way to journey to other worlds through the medium of the dream.

astrologist: This may represent your intuitive self or some worries about your future. Is something or someone influencing you beyond your will? This symbol may also represent your goals in life.

See also *zodiac*. See also any specific sign of the zodiac if present in the dream.

astronaut: Perhaps you need to or are already expanding your awareness. Are you reaching for the stars (see also *outer space* or *spaceship*)?

astronomer: You may need to be more thorough or methodical in your approach, or you may already take such an approach. Perhaps you need to look at the bigger picture. It may also suggest that you need to look at something from a greater perspective.

atheist: If you are an atheist or see an atheist in a dream, you may be questioning your beliefs about God or the hereafter.

Do you need to look again at your spiritual aspect?

See *god and goddess*, *godhead*, and *three views on god* in the *archetypes* section.

athlete: This could symbolize strength and skill. You may feel you need to work on your physical energy and performance. You may have a competitive nature. Who are you competing with?

ATM: See *money*.

attack: This could represent violent change. You may feel attacked by your own basal impulses (e.g., anger). You may be attacked by your beliefs or point of view too. This could also represent self-criticism. (See *soldier/warrior* for information regarding PTSD and the effects and treatment for continuous trauma.) A biting dog or snake can also symbolize this (see *animals*).

Whether fair or unfair, accusations can be a form of attack and can either reflect the criticisms of others or yourself. Being attacked by a mob can often refer to overwhelming feelings of being treated poorly or unfairly. Sometimes these dream attacks can reflect self-punishments regarding some guilt (see also the *nightmares* section).

attic: This could represent the higher consciousness, intellect, or stored memories and/or feelings. What's in the attic? What do you feel while in there? Was the door leading into it locked or open? If locked, perhaps you are hiding something or trying to forget something (see *door*).

attorney: See *lawyer*.

audience: This may represent the need for appreciation, or if you're in the audience, you may want to appreciate yourself or look at some emotion or some aspect of your life. Are you ready to make something public?

aum or om: This is the sound of the universe and perhaps a symbol of spiritual peace or the need to calm the mind. See *insight* under *music*.

aura: To see an aura around you or someone else might suggest that some important information is being given to you in the dream. You may need to pay close attention to the message, or you may need to draw on this energy for strength.

Some say auras or light hallucinations in dreams can warn of oncoming migraines. These auras can also indicate an oncoming nightmare.

See also *glow* or *light*.

authority: This image could take the form of a policeman, boss, teacher, or parent. All may reflect your own inner authority or your relationship/attitude with and about authority figures. Where did you acquire that bias? Does it continue to serve you?

See also *boss*, *domination*, *father*, *mother*, *police*, and *teacher*.

Insight: Authorities that are sensitive to only their self-developed rules rather than the human beings they owe their existence to in the first place is not unlike how the ego trumps the expression of the soul. For example, the soul has no rules, it is the ego that makes up the rules and then uses those to control the expression of the soul.

autopsy: Are you looking at something in you that has died or something inside you that is hidden? Are you trying to figure something out or what happened or what something means? You can think of dream analysis as an autopsy of a dream.

autumn: See *fall*.

auto shop: This may be a healing symbol. Some part of you or your life may feel broken and in need of repair (healing).

See also *building* or *houses*.

avalanche: This is a catastrophic and perhaps overwhelming release of emotion. It may trigger some barely controlled feelings.

It can also refer to frozen feelings overwhelming you. If it covers the road you're on, perhaps something is frustrating your progress toward some goal (see also *tidal wave*).

Note that avalanches don't need to be made of rocks or snow but can be composed of almost any overwhelming number of objects (e.g., clothing, toys, garbage, or people). Look at these images to get further information about the dream.

avatar: Are you putting up a front to protect yourself emotionally. Is the person you're being around others reflecting the real you?

Are you hiding the real you? Why?

Is this another layer between you and other people?

awakening: This is a symbol for spiritual rebirth or actualizing your full potential. You may be open to some new idea.

An awakening in a dream without realizing that you're still dreaming is probably not lucid dreaming, but it does represent a need to become more conscious of something you may be ignoring.

awake while in a dream: Do you wake up in a dream and know you are dreaming (see *lucid dreaming*)?

award: Are you looking for some acknowledgment?

ax: What are you ready to chop away at? This image can be a hostile symbol or be about revenge if you have an ax to grind with someone (see *knife* and *sword*).

B

baby (animal cubs): This could represent rebirth or the infant self. What is being born in you? A baby can represent new beginnings, new development, or something being developed. It can also represent feelings such as joy, curiosity, innocent love, vulnerability, and dependence. See *stillborn* if the baby is born dead or dies shortly after birth.

A baby near birth but as yet unborn in a dream may be an image about your future, perhaps something hoped for or anticipated. See *future*.

Babies may be the part of your self-expression or soul expression that you have resisted or rejected and therefore have not fully developed.

What do you need to develop or create?

If you are protecting a baby, perhaps you are protecting this part of your own childhood or your own vulnerability that you may be protecting.

If someone in your dream is acting like a baby, perhaps you are not acting responsibly about something.

If you or someone drops a baby, it may reflect carelessness or a lack of responsibility. Are you ready to take on such a big, new endeavor? You may also be worried about your ability to bring something to fruition.

babysitting: Babies or young children can signal new beginnings that you may need to nurture for a while. The symbol can also be about caring for someone, or it can be about mentoring and helping someone or something develop.

It can also refer to your inner child, which may also need nurturing.

Consider also the negative symbolism of doing something of minimal importance or something you consider less important than something else. For example, a teacher may not feel as though he or she is teaching anything. The person may just felt like he or she is just babysitting.

back or behind: This could be about privacy, a barrier, or repressed urges. Being pushed or pushing back could mean being restrained or fighting back. The back of your body could represent the unconscious. What is happening that you cannot see? Is there something happening behind your back?

backward: Are you moving backward (i.e., going in the opposite direction of your goals)? Are you feeling backward or less than?

See also *head on backward*.

backyard or back porch: This could represent a private place. It could also be a place where you hide your secrets. This can also be about new memories and/or childhood ones.

The condition of the yard might also add meaning.

See also *yard*.

bag: This might represent small burdens, things that we carry around with us in a psychological way. A handbag (see *purse*) might have something to do with your identity just as with a wallet.

It could also represent a reference to a *fait accompli* as when someone says, "It's in the bag," referring to something accomplished before anyone knows about it.

See also *luggage* or *suitcase*.

baggage: This could be about your past or your opinions and attitudes.

It can also be about your possessions or responsibilities. Too many bags might suggest the many burdens you are carrying. See also *luggage* or *suitcase*.

baking: This may be about your ability to make something happen. It may also reflect your creative self.

If the ingredients seem to be incompatible, you might want to check if there is something in your life that you need to work on.

See also *food*.

balaclava or hood: This could be about hiding a dark and sinister secret that may be burdening you. It could also be about your desire to be anonymous or signal that you are hiding yourself.

It may very well be your shadow aspect, the things that you've suppressed and rejected in yourself (see *shadow* in the *archetypes* section).

balance: If you're losing your balance, that could be about making mistakes. It could also be about losing or compromising some of your value (see *falling*). You may be trying to balance conflicting responsibilities.

If you are walking a balance beam or a tightrope, perhaps you are trying to negotiate a tricky situation in your life and need to give it your full attention. See also *tightrope*.

See *yin/yang* and *enantiodromia*.

balcony: If you see a balcony or you are standing on one, you may want to be noticed. Do you wish others looked up to you? Do you wish you were higher on the social ladder or above it all?

bald: Going bald could be about a loss of self-esteem or age-related worries. If you feel okay with it, perhaps you're at a stage where you are ready to reveal more of yourself (see also *hair* under *body*).

balls: If these balls refer to testicles, the image could mean you're being gutsy (i.e., making a statement about your courage). See also *sphere* under *shapes* and *testicle*.

balloon: Balloons can be about the need for freedom.

They can also represent the containers of what we breathe into them (e.g., our emotions, desires, motivations, and imagination).

This could be about your playful side. Are you all puffed up with yourself? Are you full of hot air and don't know what you're talking about? Are you holding tightly to the balloon so that it won't fly away? Perhaps you are holding too tightly to something and need to let it go.

Are you like the balloon and want to soar but something is holding you back? The color of the balloon might also give some insight (see *color*).

bamboo: This is a symbol that usually has local meaning. For example, in China, it can be a symbol of hardiness, tranquility, and/or simplicity, or when it bends in the wind, it can symbolize being flexible.

Dead or dying bamboo in India can represent death or funerals (see *death* in the *archetypes* section and *funeral*). It can also mean friendship in certain Indian cultures. It is also part of many creation stories, such as those in Malaysia or the Philippines.

If it appears as a construction material, it might be about doing some work on yourself or building something new in your life (see *construction*).

Local, cultural, or subcultural meanings will affect the interpretation of this dream image.

banana: This image has sexual connotations and may represent repressed sexual desires as it is a phallic symbol. If you see peels on the ground, you might want to be careful that you don't make a mistake, slip up, and fail in something. Also see *fruit*.

band: This image might mean teamwork or camaraderie, or it may symbolize being in harmony with something. Are you out of harmony?

bandage: This may be an image of protection or hurt feelings in need of healing. It could also be about covering up an emotional wound.

Band-Aid: This may represent a healing of small hurts. It could also suggest that your solution to a problem isn't adequate and that it won't really fix the issue over the long haul.

bandit: This could signal the threat of loss. What are you afraid to give up?

bang: See *explosion or eruption*.

bank: This could refer to anything that has to do with money, financial issues, social power, or something you can count on. What can you count on? What do you want to keep safe?

Banks may also have some meaning based upon certain behavioral aspects or that banks in the current environment possess and also contributed to financial meltdown (e.g., deceitfulness, greed, and usury). These meanings are situation-specific and tend to wax and wane over time.

If you were to suffer a loss from a bank in a dream, the meaning for this image could then reflect that. If you don't trust banks, then this symbol could present that lack of trust.

Banks are also places where we store things of value (e.g., ideas, memories, beliefs, values, feelings, etc.).

See *money* and *gold*.

bank robbery: Perhaps someone has stolen your love or betrayed your trust. It could also be a metaphor for betrayal. Perhaps someone stole what you originally could bank on.

banner: To see a banner in your dream may symbolize your subconscious trying to get your attention.

A banner can also suggest something exceptional or outstanding has happened and you need to take notice.

Banners can also reflect special moments in life that you may want or need to hold onto.

It can also reflect a call to arms.

See also *flags*.

banquet: This can symbolize recognition or a need for acknowledgment. It can also signify abundance (see *audience*).

baptism: This can be about purification or an emotional trial, or it can be an event or series of events that makes you a part of something. It can be a symbol for inclusion, initiation, or induction. Are you feeling left out or not included?

This can also symbolize your relationship with your spiritual aspect. If it's about your sins being washed away, what are you feeling guilty about? Are you seeking forgiveness for something?

Do you need to let go of some old part of yourself so as to make room for or reveal something new?

See also *water*.

barbarian: This could refer to a less controlled part of yourself, less refined aspect of yourself. See also *savage*.

barbed wire: Barbed wire can be about obstacles and/or feeling confined or trapped in something. It can also indicate the need to protect/defend yourself or to keep something out.

barber: See *haircut*.

Barbie doll: You may be acting inauthentic (i.e., not showing your real self).

Are you trying to live up to an unattainable standard?

See also *dolls* and/or *ego*.

barefoot: This could represent your playful side, or it could be a metaphor for poverty or restricted mobility in a physical or social sense.

bargain or bargaining: Are you feeling undervalued? Are you putting less than your best into some endeavor? Are you cheapening something?

barn: This can represent the home to your animal nature and/or a place to store memories.

barometer: How are you coping emotionally? Are you weathering a storm?

barracks: This can often refer to a restrictive situation in life. Perhaps a change is in order.

barricade: This can signal some obstacle to growth. Perhaps something, someone, or you yourself have cut you off from your potential and your ability to fully express yourself.

bartender: Are you trying to escape from your daily life? If you drink a lot, what are the feelings that lead to your drinking? The sex of the bartender can affect this image's meaning (see *anima/animus* in the *archetypes* section).

bar mitzvah or bat mitzvah: This ceremony could represent a transition you may be going through. It may also be about some social or moral responsibilities.

barracks: You may be feeling restricted or overly regimented/controlled in some way. Perhaps you need a change.

barrette: See *hair barrette*.

baseball: If you are playing baseball, perhaps you need to set goals. You may also consider it as a pun for sexual foreplay (e.g., getting to first base, hitting a home run, etc.). It can also be a metaphor for competitiveness, teamwork, and/or cooperation.

If you're playing with a hardball, perhaps you are being too harsh. If you are playing with a softball, perhaps you are not being assertive enough.

baseball bat: This could represent your driving forces.

basement: This can represent the unconscious and intuitive mind. A basement is similar to a cave. It can represent the instinctual you.

If it's cluttered, perhaps you're confused. If it's flooded, perhaps you're overwhelmed by some emotions you're hiding or suppressing.

The basement is also where you store what you don't want to look at (e.g., your faults, emotions, memories, problems, and parts of yourself you're not happy with).

basket: This could represent the womb or things you're holding on to. Consider the pun basket case, which can refer to someone who's a little crazy or exhausted.

basketball: This may reflect cooperation and teamwork. Perhaps there's some situation where you need to show more of this. This can also be about your competitive spirit or some inner or outer conflict.

bath or bathing: This could be about a cleansing or releasing (emotional, psychological, spiritual, behavioral, attitudinal, or social). What do you want to wash away?

It may also have something to do with forgiveness or the need to forgive.

What you're trying to wash off may give some insight into the meaning of the dream (see also *dirt*, *feces*, *insects*, *mud*, or *color*).

Consider also the phrase "taking a bath," which refers to losing big time.

bathed in light: You may see a figure bathed in light or surrounded by light. A halo may represent divine energy.

If you see someone glowing, that can also suggest that you are looking at this person in a new light from a new perspective.

They may also represent spirit guides. This light can also be a metaphor for happiness.

This may also be a metaphor for enlightenment, or it may suggest that a new light has been shed on something. See also *aura*, *divine child*, and *divine mother* in the *archetypes* section. See *light* and/or *mountaintop*.

bathing suit: Are you feeling a little exposed or vulnerable? If you are feeling uncomfortable in the dream as you're wearing your suit, this image could refer to your sense of self-confidence or lack thereof.

bathroom: This image can relate to your instinctual urges. It can represent the place of cleansing or getting rid of something. It's a place where emotions can flow freely.

What burdens, habits, behaviors, and/or feelings are you ready to let go of (see *defecation*, *feces*, *toilet*, or *urinate*)?

If you find you're in the wrong bathroom for your gender, perhaps you've overstepped your boundaries, or it's possible you are feeling conflicted about your gender. This could also be a metaphor for the *union of opposites*.

If it's a public bathroom and there are no stalls or no doors on the stalls, it could have something to do with a lack of privacy and/or a feeling of vulnerability or of being exposed.

If you are having trouble finding a bathroom, perhaps you're having difficulties in expressing or releasing your emotions. Perhaps you're looking for professional help.

A bathroom cabinet might be where you are hiding personal secrets.

If the bathroom is dirty, that might suggest that some situation or relationship that you are trying to let go of or get rid of might get messy.

bathtub: This can be about emotional self-renewal and the escape from the stresses of everyday life. This image can also be about pleasure and relaxation.

battery: This may represent a source of energy and vitality. If there are problems with the battery, it could be referring to health issues known or as yet unknown.

battle: This could symbolize a conflict or struggle with something or someone. Are you at war with something, someone else, or yourself (see *enemy*, *fighting*, and/or *soldier/warrior*)?

bay: Suggesting shelter. This could also symbolize calmness or the need for a protected area.

BDSM: If you are practicing some form of bondage, you may be feeling restricted in some way, or you may feel out of control and at the mercy of others.

This may also reflect some sexual frustration or anger at yourself or at another.

This could also be symbolic of extreme self-criticism, a desire to hurt yourself because of some misplaced guilt, or self-condemnation.

See also *domination* or *tied up*.

beach: Being at the beach can be about standing between two ways of being or two worlds. It is also a metaphor for intuition and the opening to one's emotions.

If you're not entering or can't enter the water, the image may be suggesting that you need to trust your intuition rather than hold back from it and not enter.

Longing to get to the other side of a great body of water can be about our barriers, limits, ambitions, and goals, while tides can be about the ups and downs of our lives.

The beach could represent where the conscious and unconscious meet. It could also represent the body and soul—the physical self and the spiritual self (i.e., the transition between the two or even integration of the two). This may be especially so if you are swimming toward the beach.

beans: This could be about your connection with your roots. As with all vegetables, it could also be related to your soul and the nourishment of your spiritual side. Beans could refer to your need for a healthier diet. Beans can also be about frugality.

bear: A bear can be about independence, strength, and power. The bear can also represent the cycle of life or the need to step back and hibernate. It could also be about reawakening to something.

Bears can also be dominating figures. It could be about *bearing* (putting up with) something or *baring* your soul or feelings about something.

beard: This could be suggestive of masculine traits, or if it's part of a bearded lady, it could symbolize the union of masculine and feminine traits (see *anima/animus* in the *archetypes* section).

If it's a particularly long one, it could be about old age or a symbol of covering up hidden aspects of the self (see also *mask*).

A long white beard could be about old age or wisdom. If you don't wear one but dream that you do, perhaps you are trying to hide something.

If you or someone else shaves off your beard in the dream, perhaps there's something that you need to reveal. If you're a woman and you have a beard in your dream, you could need to embrace some part of your masculine nature (see *animus* in the *archetypes* section).

beast: This image suggests ignorance, fear, insecurity, and possibly brutishness. Are you being a bully? This could represent parts of yourself that you reject and aren't dealing with (see *shadow* in the *archetypes* section).

For any image where the beast is part human, you might also want to look at the *minotaur* entry.

beating: If you are being beaten, perhaps you need to make some basic changes in your life. It could also suggest that you are being pushed beyond your limits. Is someone trying to *beat* some sense into you?

If you're beating up someone, are you trying to shove your point of view onto someone else?

beautiful: Seeing someone or something that's beautiful may represent aspects of yourself or someone else that you admire. Perhaps you may want to incorporate these into yourself.

beauty mask: If you are wearing one, perhaps you're trying to hide your imperfections.

beauty and the beast: This duo might symbolize the need to integrate all parts of yourself in order to feel whole and fully accepted as a human being. See *shadow* in the *archetypes* section.

beauty contest: Are you feeling a little insecure about your looks? Do you feel that you don't measure up to expectations?

beaver: See *animals*.

bed: This may be your intimate self. If you're searching for your bed, you may feel inhibited, or you may be having trouble expressing your sexuality. If you're in someone else's bed, it may represent the consequences of some decision you've made.

Floating above your bed could represent feelings of helplessness, or you may feel disconnected from your deeper self or from others.

See also *furniture*.

bed-wetting: This could reflect a loss of control, high anxieties, feelings of unacceptance, or even problems with sexual situations.

Insight: The same symbolism exists for those who actually experience bed-wetting. Reactions to stress, anxiety, and a sense of helplessness and social insecurity can cause enuresis or bed-wetting. Most children outgrow the condition by their teens.

Children need a lot of positive support during this time. Bladder training, moisture alarms, and rewards are some of the techniques that parents or guardians use to help children through this problem. Medications are available but tend to be less effective once the children have discontinued their usage. As with any physical issue, you should always consult a physician.

bee: Though bees can be a symbol of wealth and good luck, they also suggest hard work. Your life can be *buzzing* with activity. If stung, you may have been wronged or criticized unjustly. If they were chasing you, you might be avoiding some painful situation or feeling.

beekeeper: You may want to take caution with some endeavor that could result in harm if you don't handle it correctly.

beer: This could symbolize happiness, relaxation, and your social life (see also *drunk*). In general, any alcohol means conviviality. Where do you need to relax in your life? Your judgments about alcohol could also color the meaning of this image.

beg: Begging may symbolize your unhappiness with your waking situation. Perhaps you're afraid of or too embarrassed to admit that you need help?

beggar: This could symbolize insecurity and poor self-esteem. Consider the phrase "Beggars can't be choosers." Maybe you shouldn't be so picky about something. If you're giving a handout to a beggar, perhaps you need to work on overcoming your hardships or inadequacies.

begin: If something is just starting or beginning, you need to stop procrastinating.

behead: This could represent poor judgment or a bad decision. Maybe you are not thinking clearly. You may need to confront some negative situation even though it's uncomfortable.

Have you lost your mind?

Alternatively, do you tend to act before you think? Do you need to think something over before taking an action?

behind: To be behind someone could mean that you need to support someone or something.

This could also be a metaphor for your subconscious thoughts and feelings. However, if you've been left behind, perhaps you feel rejected or abandoned. You may also be worried about not being able to keep up or not being up to the task at hand.

Leaving someone else behind might suggest that it's time to let go of something and move on.

Something coming from or happening behind your back could be about a lack of trust or be symbolic of some deceit.

believing: Are you trying to say something but no one believes you? Perhaps you're losing your self-confidence and questioning your judgment or decisions.

bell: This could represent a warning or a signal for the beginning of something. It could also be your subconscious trying to get your attention. A gold bell might signal that you have something important to say or that someone else has something important to say that you need to listen to.

bellhop: Are you carrying the burdens of others? Perhaps you're burdened by others' problems.

belonging: Are you feeling left out or alienated and not part of the group? Are you trying to be accepted, trying to develop a rapport with someone, or longing for a relationship? Do you feel loyal to something or someone? Are you being inclusive or exclusive?

If you are standing alone or have been left behind by other people, you may feel alone and left out. You may also feel that you don't belong (see also *homeless*).

below: If you're looking at someone below you, perhaps you're acting too high and mighty and looking down on others. It can also suggest that you need to look into your unconscious self.

bench: This could symbolize procrastination. You may also feel that you've been *benched* and placed on the sidelines. Are you being too passive and not showing enough initiative?

It can also be about taking a break from something.

bending: Are you being flexible or not flexible enough in some situation?

bereavement: Perhaps you're repressing your sadness or grief. Is something bothering you more than you're willing to admit?

You may also be expressing what you haven't been expressing in your waking life because it's safer in the dream. It's also possible that the dream is just reflecting what you are feeling in your waking life.

best man: This could represent self-confidence or that you are the best for the job. Perhaps you need to become a better person.

bestiality: This may be about your animal nature or raw sexuality and lust. It's possible that you may be uncomfortable with some part of your nature.

betrayal: This can show up when you are feeling insecure in some relationship (e.g., familial, romantic, or work-related). You may feel left out or that something is hidden. See *double-cross* or *snitch*. See also *scapegoat* in the *archetypes* section.

betting: Are you taking risks somewhere in your life? See also *cards*, *gambling*, or *lottery*.

bewildered: If you're feeling bewildered, perhaps you are stuck between opposing points of view (see *confusion*).

bewitched: Maybe you are being influenced or manipulated without being aware.

Insight: Our own fantasies about ourselves or about others can charm us as well. This is similar to how the shadow aspects of our own personalities affect what we do or don't do and lead us into making bad decisions (see *shadow* in *archetypes* section).

Bible: This image may be about truth, belief, comfort, or inspiration. Perhaps you're in need of guidance. It could also reflect that you need to be more attuned to your spiritual aspect(s).

If some specific part of the Bible is referenced, look to see what it is because this can also help with the interpretation of dreams. For example, did your dream show the Old Testament or the New, implying old or new ways of thinking? Parables are similar to Zen Koan and may suggest the need for deeper spiritual thought and exploration while psalms may be about a way of connecting with God on a deeper level (see *Psalm 23* as an example).

See also *holy book* under *book*.

bicycle: This could suggest a personal effort toward one's goals. This image could also be a metaphor for balancing all aspects of your life or just certain aspects.

If you're in a race, note your position because it could be a statement about how you feel about yourself in comparison to others. In other words, it could be a comment on self-worth.

If you fall off the bike or crash, you could be losing confidence in yourself. That same could be true if a bike is stolen in your dream. Riding the bike recklessly, downhill, or without hands could be about taking risks or facing some risk.

Fixing a bike could be about fixing some part of yourself so that you can continue on to some goal. Whatever is broken could be keeping you from going forward. What needs fixing?

Insight: Note also that a bicycle image has wheels or circles that are like mandalas. The bicycle is also a vehicle. Exploring these aspects of a bicycle might reveal other meanings for the dream (see *circle*, *mandala*, *vehicle*, and *wheel*).

bikini: This can be about revealing something or about your vulnerability. It can also be about the need to be more open.

big: Size can represent how important we see ourselves or want to be seen by others. It can also reflect how small we feel next to someone. Do you have an inflated image of yourself (see *giant* under *animals*)?

bigot: Are you unaccepting of differences? Are you trying to make yourself important at the expense of others?

bindi: This is often depicted as a dot just above and between the eyes by some Hindu sects. This is a symbol of unity and where creation begins. It is also a symbol of the potential or unmanifested universe. So too, it is related to the third-eye chakra of inner wisdom (see *chakra*).

In Sanskrit it is known as Bindú, the point in the Hindu religion where creation begins. It is also analogous to the third-eye chakra (see *chakra*) or the place of concealed wisdom.

Note also that the Bindú is the point at which the mandala is formed (see *mandala*).

binge eating: Overeating may be a way of stuffing something down or trying to fill a void in your life.

birds: Birds are an extremely important dream image. Birds in our dreams often speak of and to our higher selves, goals, ideals, and spirituality. They release us from our earthbound limitations.

They can represent freedom, liberation, independence, imagination, intuitive messages, and heightened awareness.

They also speak to a need to broaden our horizons. This may be especially true for falcons and eagles.

Eagles are also great metaphors for focus, vision, and determination. Many of the masculine traits attributed to the animus can be found in both the falcon and the eagle. In fact, these birds can represent the animus archetype in the dreams of women.

Dead or dying birds can speak to disappointments and worries. Attacking birds can represent internal conflicts and/or spiritual conflict. There's also the possibility that someone is fooling around with your life, invading your peace of mind, and fouling up your plans. Nesting birds can be about security, comfort, or the need for it. A nest can also be a metaphor for a nest egg (e.g., savings or a plan B).

A bird in a cage can represent a loss of freedom or limiting expression. It can reflect domination and control too. Birdseed can be about nourishing your higher self.

When visited by a flying bird in a dream, you might ask yourself, "What part of me wants to fly? What am I wanting to rise above?"

Various birds such as the whip-poor-will, raven, sparrow, owl, or cuckoo have been thought of as *psychopomps* (e.g., guides to the afterworld).

See *bird* in *animal terms* for a list of meanings attributed to different kinds of birds.

There is an ancient belief that after death the soul leaves the body in the form of a bird. Many religions give various symbols of divine spirits with wings (e.g., angels, seraphim, and cherubs). As a symbol of the sun, royalty, and the gods, the eagle is a yang or masculine symbol of power, strength, keen vision, and fearlessness. Birds in dreams often represent messengers from the soul.

But the raven, sitting lonely on the placid bust, spoke only that one word, as if his soul in that one word he did outpour.

Nothing further then he uttered—not a feather then he fluttered till I scarcely more than muttered, "Other friends have flown before

On the morrow he will leave me, as my hopes have flown before."

Then the bird said, "Nevermore."

—Edgar Allan Poe ("The Raven," 1845)

birth: This could suggest a new way of being or a new idea or attitude. It could be about new beginnings for life skills, projects, attitudes, or points of view.

These may represent huge changes in your life and the death of old ways.

This image may be calling your attention to the inner child that you have kept hidden but need to let out. If the mother dies during birthing, it could signify transformation (i.e., one thing is ending while another begins). If the baby dies during birthing, it could be about a new project or idea dying before it really comes to life (see *abortion*).

If you are currently pregnant and you dream of a nonhuman baby being born, this could reflect your fears about birth defects in your own baby.

Birth dreams for expectant mothers may chronicle the changes going on in them physically, psychologically, and emotionally. This may be true for their husbands as well because many men seem to have sympathetic physical experiences and frequently have their own issues regarding parenthood and the changes that their wives are going through (see *baby*).

birthday: Do you need to celebrate yourself or some part of yourself? If you dream of missing your birthday, are you feeling underappreciated, or are you feeling old and want to deny the aging process?

See also *happy birthday*.

birthday cake: Perhaps your wishes will come true.

bit part: Are you playing a role that's beneath you?

Consider the phrase "There are no small roles, just small actors." See also *small*.

bite: If you're being bitten, perhaps you feel vulnerable to someone or some issue that you haven't dealt with. Have you been making *biting* and hurtful remarks? Consider also criticisms, including self-criticisms.

bizarre: See *surprise* and *unexpected*.

black: See *color*.

black angels: See *angels of death*.

blackboard: See *class*. If you hear a squeaking sound on a blackboard, see *dissonance* or *disharmony*.

black cat: See *cat* in *animals*.

black dreams: Black dreams can be metaphors for depression or even reflect a waking life full of anxieties. I also believe that there are black dreams in the waking world that bring to consciousness what a society is ignoring or repressing in the collective psyche.

Insight: Wars and mass murders can also reflect the psychological health of a society or community. As with individuals who seem to self-punish (or unconsciously create real-world issues for themselves) for problems, feelings, or behaviors they haven't or poorly dealt with, societies seem to have an equivalent consciousness raising process.

In the waking dream, the black dream comes in the form of war, oppression, financial, political meltdown, and singular and mass murders. This may be the world psyche offering a wake-up call to our folly.

Ours is a culture of personal independence taken to an extreme. I believe that this has caused the culture to become overprotective, overly reactionary, defensive, and punitive. It seems to be in a constant and high state of anxiety and this unprocessed anxiety can lead to inappropriate actions on a collective level.

Killers shooting at us and our children (most recently at a Connecticut elementary school) naturally makes us want to defend against the unknown and causes us to irrationally buy more and more weaponry, create more and more indefensible laws, and manufacture devices to protect ourselves, but one can easily see that such action has only heightened the anxiety and that we are no safer, perhaps actually much less so.

Easy access to guns and a propensity to violence as a viable solution to what threatens us is not a very effective protection strategy in the modern world.

The archetypal animal responses of either run or fight have their place in dire emergencies, but they shouldn't be incorporated into our everyday functioning, whether on an individual or corporate level. We pay a lot of lip service and money trying to suppress or restrict our animal nature.

We also act as though we are helpless victims to our rejected and hidden animal natures. But the fact is that we are not. First, we need to acknowledge them and then deal with them in a humane and effective way. Locking our shadows up or trying to kill them off does not and will not work either on the personal or collective level. And how about restricting the number of guns? That train left the station long ago. There are more than 250,000,000 guns in the United States! And yet I don't see any evidence that we feel safer.

black hole: Have your hopes for the future disappeared from your sight? Do all your efforts seem fruitless? Has the light in your life disappeared? This image can reflect depression. See also *abyss, color, dark matter, dark night of the soul, darkness or night,* or *depression.*

blackmail: Do you feel you've been coerced into doing something you don't want to do? What are you trying to hush up? Are you trying to get your own way through coercion?

If you're blackmailing someone, perhaps you're engaged in a power struggle and are trying to dominate the situation.

This could also be symbolic of your helplessness or lack of confidence.

Consider also the pun black male.

blackout: This could be about ignorance, poor perspective, failure, or a fear of the unknown.

black (dark) person or creature: If you are not black, then this could represent a shadow aspect of yourself (i.e., a rejected

personality trait) (see *shadow* in the *archetypes* section). A white person in a black person's dream could represent the shadow aspect.

Insight: Opposites in dreams often reflect inner conflicts or unresolved shadow aspects of the dreamer. Over the years of helping people work through their dreams, I have noticed that nonwhite people will sometimes have white people as negative or shadow aspect images while those with light complexions will sometimes have their shadow aspects show up as black, dark, or swarthy. Though this may or may not reflect some racial bias, I believe it does often symbolically reflect the shadow archetype.

blacksmith: This could be about strength and endurance (i.e., the need to be strong or to strengthen something).

blame: If you're being blamed in your dream, this may be about feeling guilty or not wanting to take responsibility for some behavior. Perhaps you're trying to deflect your responsibility.

Are you taking on guilt that doesn't belong to you?

You may also be feeling powerless in some situation. See also *blaming.*

Insight: As humans, we don't really want to be responsible for what isn't working in the world around us. It's too much of a burden. And besides, what can one person do? But what if I were to tell you that you are responsible for it all? I didn't say that you were to blame or that you had to take on the whole world. What I said was that you are responsible.

Simply put, it's *your* world, *your* nation, *your* community, and *your* family. But we often act as though something outside of us is responsible (i.e., God, the president, bankers, corporate CEOs, politicians, Mom, Dad, and the ubiquitous *they*).

But nothing outside of yourself can really save your butt just as nothing outside the dream is the cause of the dream or its focus. Both inside and out of the sleeping dream, we use our images and our constructs of people, events, and things to establish meaning, *our* meaning.

In short, there is no *they* out there.

blaming: What are you blaming? What are you blaming someone else for? Do you feel guilty, or do you feel like a failure? Are you feeling blamed?

blank: If anything is blank or you see nothing at all, this might suggest that there's something missing in your life. There may be an emotional void.

Perhaps it's a metaphor for potential (i.e., a space for some future experience or goal).

It can also be a metaphor for loneliness. It can also refer to being zoned, spaced out, or drunk.

Insight: I am always excited by the blank sheet of paper or blank document of the word processor, for in these is present the beauty of the infinite potential of the soul's creativity. I'm never sure what's going to happen when I begin to write. Each blankness filled is a journey never taken before.

The artist's use of what is not there to hint at what is there has always fascinated me, and that idea helped me realize that often reality is defined more by the abstract and the potential than the concrete and fixed.

I also feel the experience of something that becomes more present by its absence every time I am stirred by some event or object and then recall a close friend or loved one. In some ways, these people have become closer through their not being than they were when they were here. I am more frequently reminded of them as I travel about in the haunts of our shared past.

See also *empty* or *emptiness*.

blanket: This could be a desire for warmth, security, and shelter. Alternatively, it can be symbolic of a cover-up (i.e., something to hide).

Wrapping yourself in a blanket may suggest that you're protecting yourself, but wrapping others in a blanket might suggest that you want to take care of them or some aspect of yourself that they may represent.

bleach: Bleach can represent cleansing and healing. Do you feel dirty for something said or done?

bleeding: See *blood*.

blessing: If you are receiving or giving a blessing in a dream, this image might be a message that you can now move ahead with some endeavor.

Are you or others giving their approval of something or someone?

Is there something that you need to give thanks for? Is there someone you need to thank?

blimp: This could symbolize your goals and ambitions. You may feel you are too fat, or it could represent your inflated sense of self.

blind: You may have lost sight of something or someone. You may not be looking at some aspect of yourself or others, or you may be concealing something from yourself or others. It may be symbolic of something that you do not understand, something you cannot see, or something

you are unaware or unconscious of. See also *fog* or *blurry*.

To be blind or to experience someone who is blind in a dream might relate to being *blind* to something in particular (i.e., some behavior, attitude, or situation). It could also be symbolic of being in denial.

A blind date might represent some aspect of yourself that you may want to get to know.

blindfold: Maybe you or someone else is trying to deceive you. It could also mean that you are blinding yourself to what's going on in the world or refusing to see something for what it really is. Are you being dishonest?

bling: This can signify ostentation and wanting to stand out. See *gold* under *colors* and *sparkling*.

blizzard: Perhaps you're feeling emotionally cold or experiencing the absence of warmth in some relationship. Are you feeling left out?

You may feel unloved.

blood: Blood is the universal life within us, our essence, life itself, and all people's shared experience.

To lose blood is to lose energy and aliveness. Are you feeling exhausted? Bleeding can also be a symbol for depression.

If you have blood on your hands it may be a metaphor for having someone's death on your hands or being responsible for some problem or situation.

Women sometimes dream of blood before their periods. Blood pressure might suggest too much stress or some health concern.

To drink blood can sometimes mean you are taking in the essence of the animal or person whose blood you are drinking. It can also suggest a fresh infusion of vitality and/or power.

By donating or giving blood to others, you might be trying to enliven them. If you are receiving blood through a transfusion, it might indicate that you need to revitalize yourself.

If something is written in blood, perhaps you have put a great deal of energy into some project (as in the fact that you have given your blood, sweat, and tears).

Note that blood can refer to one's children, descendants, family, kin, lineage, parentage, or pedigree. With this in mind, a lack of blood in a scenario where there should be blood might be related to family in some way.

blossom: To see a blossom or some flower blossoming might be symbolic of your own inner beauty that needs to be outwardly expressed.

blow-up doll: This can possibly suggest a one-sided relationship.

blueprint: This could be about attention to details or the need to pay attention to them. Do you want to change and need a map or a schematic to help navigate that change?

blurry: If you have a blurry dream or if you're looking through something that's blurry there may be something you're refusing to see clearly, perhaps even something in you. See also *blind, clouds, confusion*, and/or *fog*.

boa constrictor: Are you feeling constrained or suffocating in some situation or relationship? See also *snake*.

boarding pass: The boarding pass (or ticket) may represent permission to seek or accept change. It represents the start of something new—a new endeavor, a new life, a new direction, or a new way of being.

boats or ships: These may represent your journey through life with all the rough and smooth places. Boats can represent the movement across deep emotions. They can also symbolize emotions that you are navigating. Note the roughness of the seas and the condition of the boat, for this may give you an indication of how you are doing on your journey at the moment.

Missing a boat might suggest a missed opportunity. A sinking boat could signal a sense of loss or failure. This can be another symbol for depression (see *blood*).

bodiless: Are you feeling unnoticed or unrecognized? Are you feeling cut off from your body? If the lower half of your body is missing, it could suggest some issue with your sexuality or the instinctual part of yourself. See also *faceless*.

body terms: This generally reflects your image of yourself and how you feel about that. Different body parts have different meanings. Cutting off any part of the body suggests a loss of that aspect or expression.

Interestingly, the body will often communicate what's happening within it (e.g., health issues, pregnancies, or feelings picked up from others) through our dreams. Carefully listening to your body can be very useful.

> **abdomen:** This part of the body could symbolize natural instincts or repressed emotions. Could it be a symbol for instinct as with a gut feeling? Is there something that you can't stomach? If swollen (or pregnant), then perhaps you have

some new project in the works (see also *stomach*).

ankle: This could symbolize support. If broken, something may be throwing you off balance.

anus: What do you want to get rid of? Or what are you holding on to? See also *feces* and *buttocks*.

arm: This could symbolize strength, that which gives and receives. If an arm is held between you and another person or object, perhaps you are keeping someone or something separated from you, keeping it *at arm's length*. Are you trying to protect yourself from something?

back: This could symbolize the unconscious, what you can't see, or what's behind you. (This can be a metaphor for the past as well.)

bone: This could symbolize strength. If the bone is broken, then it could reflect a loss of strength or a fundamental weakness. Burying a bone could refer to hiding something. It can also refer to the essence of something. Bare bones can be about poverty or being reduced to the minimal.

Bones are the tangible reminder of what once was. It can represent your innermost being and life support structure. When you feel something in your bones, it can mean that you feel something viscerally, intuitively, authentically, and at your core.

brain: This could symbolize reason, the intellect, and understanding.

breast: This could symbolize nurturing, motherhood, love, or what needs loving, nursing, or nurturing. Depending on what's happening, it could also mean lust. If your own breasts are showing, that could be about vulnerability and being exposed.

If there are three breasts present on one person, the image can be about balance. This could also be a metaphor for abundance or an allegory for scarcity. It could reflect the need for love or be a symbol for lust.

breath: If you're out of breath, you might be experiencing some kind of tension or anxiety. If you are holding your breath, you may be stubborn about something. Should you be more open to the opinions and desires of others? To catch one's breath is to take a time-out from something.

buttocks: This could symbolize humility. Are you being an ass? Do you need forgiveness? If your butt hurts, are you or someone else being a pain in the ass?

chest/lungs: This could symbolize the breath of life or a readiness to expand. Pains in the chest could symbolize a health issue in waking life. If your chest is prominent in the dream and it seems as though you're sticking it out, it could be about confidence or pride. Consider the phrase "Getting something off your chest."

chin: Because the chin is sometimes symbolic of one's character or resolve, it could reflect a presence or lack of either in you or someone else regarding some situation or way of being.

ear: This could symbolize receptiveness or openness. What are you ready to listen to? If your ear is injured, what are you not hearing, or are you not ready to hear something?

Big ears might represent the importance of what you need to listen to. Big ears can also be linked to the expression "You've got big ears," meaning that you need to stop eavesdropping.

elbow: Perhaps you need to make space for yourself or put some elbow grease (effort) into some endeavor. If your elbow is wounded, you may be having difficulty functioning in some situation.

eye: This could symbolize vision, clarity, awareness, the soul or psyche. If your eyes are shut or you can't see in the dream, see *blind* and *shutter*.

The eye with which I see God is the same with which God sees me.[11]

—Meister Eckhart, theologian and mystic

Insight: This quote reminds me of a time when I left work just after sunset and headed down the hill to the parking lot. I had been worrying all day about how I was going to deal with some very upsetting events when I passed a young man and happened to catch his eye. His eyes shone like stars, and I had the distinct impression that I was looking at myself through his eyes! I was really taken aback, and I was going to say something when I noticed the eyes of the people in the cars passing by. They all shone with that same light! It was as though God were looking at me through their eyes. I began to cry when I realized that we were all looking at one another through God's eyes.

The eye in the triangle above a pyramid found on the US dollar is called the eye of providence, and that image could mean that the eye of God is watching.

Eyes are often painted on things or worn as a talisman to ward off the *evil eye* or evil spirits. This was an exaggerated apotropaic eye, and it was painted on Greek drinking vessels in the sixth century BC to ward off evil spirits while drinking.

Today these eyes are like blue beads with a white center and black pupil. Fishing boats in some parts of the Mediterranean region still have stylized eyes painted on the bows. A Turkish budget airline has adopted the symbol (known as *Nazar Bonjuk*) as a motif for the tail fin of its airplanes.

To see your own eyes in your dream might represent enlightenment, knowledge, comprehension, understanding, or intellectual awareness. Unconscious thoughts may be coming to the surface. According to the ancient Egyptians, the left eye was symbolic of the moon, while the right eye represented the sun. The eye can also represent the word *I* or the self.

If you dream that your eyes have turned inward and that you can see the inside of your head, then it might symbolize insight and something that you need to be aware of. This dream may be literally telling you that you need to look within yourself. Trust your intuition and instincts.

Insight: The psychiatrist Carl Jung likened the eye to a mandala when it's viewed in a dream. Because the eye is that which sees the light, it can symbolize consciousness. It takes in the light of the universe and then gives it to the inner self, acting as a gateway between the universe and our spirits (see *mandala* in the *archetypes* section).

If you dream of having something *in your eye* and you believe in the biblical admonition "Why do you look at the speck of sawdust in your brother's eye and pay no attention to the plank in your own eye?" then the symbol might indicate that you are judging others without noting your own frailties. It might also mean that something is obstructing your vision and clarity.

To dream that you have *one eye* may indicate your refusal to accept another viewpoint. It suggests that you may be one-sided in your way of thinking.

To dream that you have a *third eye* may symbolize inner vision, insight, or instinct. Perhaps you are seeing what others cannot. Or perhaps you should start looking within yourself and trust your instincts.

To dream that your eyes are *injured or closed* might suggest your refusal to see the truth about something or your avoidance of intimacy. You may be expressing feelings of sympathy, pain, or hurt.

If your eyes are bleeding, it might suggest a loss of vitality and/or energy. It may also symbolize the loss of hope. So too, it may suggest a lack or loss of perspective.

Bleeding eyes can also be symbolic of sacrifices you've made and/or deep pain you have endured.

The image of a *black eye* might be about unresolved conflict.

Seeing *red eyes* can be about great fatigue or the aftereffect of grieving.

If you or someone in the dream has *no eyes*, you may be blind to a point of view or aspect of yourself. See also *blind*.

Insight: Any obstruction to the eye (e.g., a hood, closed eyes, sunglasses, an eye patch, hiding your head under a pillow, an ostrich with its head in the ground, looking through a keyhole, etc.) can be about you restricting your vision or acceptance of something.

To have or give a *black eye* might signify disgrace, dishonor, or shame. It can also mean that one is casting dispersions (see also *slander*).

If someone won't look you in the eye, that person or you may be lying about something. So too, people who won't make eye contact with you may be hiding something. Are you afraid someone will see who you really are or who you fear you really are?

Try another way of looking. Try you looking and the whole universe seeing.

—Rumi

Insight: The Horus eye symbol is worn for protection and used to ward off evil spirits. Horus's left eye, which has been torn out (or so the myth goes), relates to the waxing and waning phases of the moon during which the moon appears to have been torn out of the sky before being restored every lunar month.

There is also the third eye of the chakra, that which leads to the inner realms of higher consciousness. It is the symbol of enlightenment in both Hinduism and Buddhism.

From the top and clockwise: third-eye chakra, eye of providence, evil eye, eye of Horus

face: This could symbolize your self-image, ego, reputation, and identity. If you're hiding it, you may feel shame or guilt.

Other emotions can be read from the face as well. If your face has been injured, you may be suffering from some public injury or an attack on your reputation.

If your or someone else's face has been painted red, perhaps you are embarrassed about something.

Someone with two faces could mean that either you or someone else is being untrustworthy and pretending to be something false.

A burnt face might suggest an emotional hurt and may leave a scar.

Something eating a face or your face could reflect someone attacking your self-image or reputation (see also *faceless*).

If something is not quite right with the face, perhaps you are feeling inadequate.

See also *angry, frown, happy, makeup, mask, sad,* or *smile.*

fingers: This could symbolize sensitivity, the ability to manipulate something, physical and mental dexterity, and/or communication.

If fingers are damaged or cut off, it can suggest some anxiety about your ability to accomplish some task. Are you losing your grip?

The *ring finger* can represent unity, and the *index finger* can point to something you need to attend. It can also signal an accusation. Perhaps you've either been unjustly accused or you've unjustly accused someone else in actuality or in mind.

If pointing straight up, it could be a sign that you want to be the best or that you actually think you're the last.

The *middle finger* can be symbolic of an obscenity (e.g., something said that's crude and hurtful).

The *little finger* can be about power or intellect, a promise made, or putting on airs when it's held up.

A thumb could signal that something is either okay (up) or not okay (down). If you're sticking it out, you might be asking for help. See also *finger* and *fingernails.*

foot or feet: This could symbolize your grounding or footing, your balance, or your contact with reality. The loss of your feet may have something to do with a loss of independence or mobility.

Dirty feet could reflect an issue with your self-image and some behavior. In India, the feet are the holiest part of the body.

forehead: One's forehead can signify judgment and intellectual ability. If something is popping into or puncturing the forehead it could represent ideas, thoughts, or even actions that you may need to take.

hair: This could symbolize another part of your self-image, your sensuality, and how you look to others.

If the hair is all different colors, it may reflect all the different aspects of your self-image. Note that projected self-image (what you want others to think of you) can often be about the need for acceptance or even the need for self-acceptance.

Cutting any hair could have something to do with change or loss of power.

A loss of hair could be about losing your mind or the loss of self-esteem.

Brushing other people's hair could represent you trying to reconnect with them and/or their memories and what they meant to you, perhaps even on a spiritual level. This can also be seen as an act of love and the need to express it.

Dark or black hair may reflect dark thoughts whereas *red hair* may reflect incendiary, destructive, or flamboyant thoughts. Red hair could also reflect your fiery personality and passion.

White or *gray* hair or a beard could mean wisdom or experience. If your hair is *turning gray*, some situation may be making you age prematurely. You may also have concerns about growing older.

Blonde hair could suggest that you need to have more fun in your life (see also *bald*).

If your hair is on fire, perhaps you are being a hothead (one who is quick to anger).

If you're brushing or combing someone's hair or someone is brushing yours, this may be about clarifying your thoughts or trying to smooth out your mental confusion.

Well-quaffed hair may refer to the quality of your self-image or perhaps a desire for an enhanced image (see also *shampoo*).

Pulling your hair out can be about frustration or vexing problems.

A rather drastic change to your hair might signal a need for some drastic change or new approach to some situation.

A *toupee or wig* could symbolize some kind of deception or false impression.

hand: This can mean your self-expression or your grasp of situations. It can mean what you are ready to handle, whereas dirty hands can mean participating in some unclean activity or doing some dirty work.

To soil one's hands is to do something that you are not proud of.

To lose a hand can affect your self-expression. Look at *right* or *left* for more information. It could also suggest the need to be less dominant or to let some part of you be less dominant. Alternatively, it could be that you want to allow some part to be more dominant.

Hands are often used to hold tools, draw, or write. They can be symbols for creativity or the need to change something or some part of the self.

The palm of your hand can be about your openness to something (an idea or person). To see a light in your palm can also suggest that you hold your personal light or your own enlightened awareness within the palm of your hand. (It is within you and not the words of others, though they can stimulate your awakening.)

See also *fingers*.

head: This can symbolize the intellect, thoughts, intentions, the rational self (as opposed to the irrational, emotional, and intuitive heart), or understanding.

Because the Celts thought of the soul as residing in the head it was thought that owning the head of someone was akin to inheriting his or her abilities. Thus, heads could ward off evil and were also collected as trophies from battle.

To see an owl on your head might suggest you use some wisdom in some decision.

A snake on the head, especially one that attacks, might be a metaphor for self-criticism. This can be a poison to your self-image. It being on the head might also suggest that something or someone is being a powerful seductive force that may not have your best interests at heart. See also *snake* in *animals*.

If you see a rock on the head, this might be a stand-in for the phrase "You've got rocks in your head," meaning that you are acting foolish or crazy. To see two heads might mean you are conflicted or ambivalent about something (i.e., that you are of two minds).

Consider the phrase "Two heads are better than one." This means that you need to work together and cooperate with others. Consider also the phrase "Use your head." That might suggest that you should try being more rational about something.

Two heads might also represent how you are of two minds regarding something. If they are in disagreement, then this may reflect an inner conflict that you are having over some issue.

To be headless might be a metaphor for being thoughtless. See also *decapitation* and/or *headless*.

See also *head on backward*.

heart: This can symbolize love and/or emotions. Any damage to the heart may indicate you've been hurt or something physical that should be investigated.

If someone is eating your heart, it could symbolize criticism, even self-criticism. A broken heart could reflect a physical problem or a loss of compassion. See also *broken*.

Hiding your heart can be like hiding your sorrow when only its openness can heal.

This image is sometimes seen as one's soul—the spiritual, intuitive, and irrational self—in contrast to the head, which represents the intellectual and rational self. Sometimes leading with one's heart instead of one's head is the best policy. The heart can forgive where the head cannot.

There are Chinese proverbs that speak of a small heart (handling something with care), a thin heart (cautious perfectionist), or a thick heart (if you're clumsy or careless).

In the Western tradition, a small heart could reflect someone who is stingy and needs to be more compassionate. A thick heart might mean someone who is hard-hearted.

Different cultures can often provide different meanings for some images.

However, it should be noted that in both China and the West, having a black heart refers to being evil.

Insight: In the Zuni tribe of North America, there are what are known as heart lines. They are often drawn as arrows leading from the mouth of an animal to its heart. They signify the life force of the animal, and they point to its soul or spirit.

It represents their centers of energy and their spiritual places.

You might also refer to *chakras* (specifically, the heart chakra).

If you or someone else is coding and being shocked back to life, it may suggest that you need some sort of revitalization (i.e., emotional or motivational rejuvenation). See also *shapes*.

intestines: This could be about being gutsy or having courage. It could also be about a gut instinct (intuitiveness).

To have one's guts spill out could reflect a loss of courage, resolve, or self-confidence. See also *guts*.

jaw: Is someone or something taking a large bite out of your time? A broken or dislocated jaw may suggest that you are compromising your principles. A jaw may be stubbornness or determination, but a tightly clenched one might indicate anger or unexpressed strong feelings.

knee: This can symbolize flexibility or the ability to bend. If you are on your knees, you may be experiencing defeat in some situation.

left side: This side the of body may refer to the unconscious mind.

leg: This can be about support and motivation. It can also symbolize confidence and independence as in "standing on one's own legs." See also *feet*.

When people have their legs knocked out from under them, that may indicate a loss of confidence.

A wounded or broken leg could suggest that you have lost balance or autonomy in your life (see *snakebite* under *snake* in *animals*).

If your leg is bitten, you may want to be cautious, for someone may be trying to throw you off balance.

If you have a prosthetic and have both your legs, then perhaps it's symbolic that you need to restore some balance or independence in your life.

lips: This could be about sensuality, love, and/or romance. Lips are associated with communication. Consider the phrase "Giving someone lip," referring to talking back or being uncivil (see also *lipstick*).

lungs: This could be an image invoking tension, or it could represent the feeling of suffocation in a situation. As it relates to breath, it might represent catching your breath or not holding your breath. Consider how a child who screams a lot has a "good set of lungs."

mouth: This can symbolize nourishment as well as a means of expressing or communicating. If it's full of something, perhaps you are having difficulty saying something or expressing yourself.

If you're trying to catch something in your mouth, perhaps you are trying to take in, absorb, understand, or believe something. If you're having trouble catching it, then perhaps you are having difficulty accepting or understanding something.

If you're having difficulty expressing something and everything you say seems to miss the mark, you might want to look closer at what is happening.

If you've ingested something that you're trying to spit out, perhaps you've experienced something distasteful that you want to reject (see *oily*).

neck or throat: This can symbolize a connection between body and mind or intellect and feeling. Up to your neck in something means that you are in trouble but still okay. The throat may represent vulnerability.

To cut or break someone's neck is to cause a separation from one's feelings. Perhaps you're in your head too much. It could also be a metaphor for severing some relationship.

nose: This can symbolize instinctive knowledge, intuition, and curiosity. It can also represent wisdom or getting involved in something that may be

none of your business (nosy). See also *nosebleed*.

palm: See *hand*.

penis: For males, this represents their drive in life, their yang power, and their potency of expression (see *snake* and *impotency*).

For females, it may have sexual connotations or symbolize power.

Consider also that either you or someone is behaving badly (i.e., being a dick).

right side: This side of the body might refer to the conscious mind.

shoulders: This can symbolize burden and how strong you are to carry what life presents. Have you taken on any blame or responsibility?

If something is sitting on your shoulder, it might reflect inner conflicts you're trying to deal with.

If you're placing something on someone else's shoulders, you may be blaming them for something you may be at least partially responsible for.

skin: This may represent protection of the inner self. Perhaps you're being too superficial? If your skin is covered in sores or a rash, perhaps you fear facing the harsh reality of something.

If the skin is new or if the old skin is stripped away to reveal new skin beneath it, this might mean renewal or being renewed.

If your skin has been removed, you may be feeling vulnerable, exposed, and defenseless. If your skin is of a different color, you may not be true to yourself. Are you worried how you look to others?

Consider the term *thin-skinned* if you feel overly sensitive to criticism.

stomach: Are you having trouble putting up with some situation? Sometimes the stomach can represent your emotional or instinctual center, so how it's feeling can give you hints as to the image's meaning.

See *indigestion, butterfly, abdomen,* or *appendicitis.*

The stomach can also represent your intuition about something (i.e., your gut feeling).

The loss of teeth can seem nightmarish and symbolize impending disaster. Loss can also signify a lack of self-confidence. Perhaps you have misspoken or said something you should not have.

teeth: These can refer to power and/ or independence. To lose teeth is to be weakened and to lose power. Broken, decayed, or missing teeth could also imply a problem with your self-image.

If you are grinding your teeth, perhaps you are in resistance to something or resenting something or someone. It could also be about repressed anger.

If the tooth grows back, that might refer to your need to regain that power through personal growth and development.

93

If you're biting or being bitten, consider the phrase "Bite off more than you can chew," which means you've taken on more than you can handle.

Insight: Frequently, psychologists use projective tests where children draw certain standard objects and unconsciously *projects* their emotional patterns into the drawings. These projections, generally speaking, come from the same place as dream material. An effective reading of dreams can enhance the material gained by the use of the more formalized projective tests.

See also *dream body*.

body bag: If you see a body bag or you are inside one, this might suggest that something has died in you. Perhaps you are feeling disconnected or are losing touch.

body odor: Are you being offensive to others? Perhaps there's some issue that needs to be confronted. Do you need to adjust your attitude?

body snatcher: If something is taking over your body or someone else's body, you may be feeling invaded in some way, or you may be feeling disconnected from your body (i.e., not in touch with its needs).

If aliens are taking over people's bodies or yours, it may represent some unfamiliar part of yourself that you feel is taking you over. (This could also reflect a habit or something becoming a habit.)

bomb or atom bomb: This could symbolize an explosive situation or something that may cause fear or that seems totally unexpected. An atom bomb is just more so in that the situation may be devastating. See *explosion or eruption* and/or *shrapnel*.

bondage: This can signal the feeling of being taken over by something or someone. It can suggest feelings of helplessness and a loss of self-control. It can also suggest feelings of being trapped or possessed (see *possessed*).

book: This could represent guidance, information, and/or memory storage. It can represent your life story up to the present, or it could signal the announcement of a new chapter or new story that's needed or emerging.

Books can also reflect a narrative or an inner dialogue. Is yours positive or negative?

A holy book could be about your beliefs and what inspires you spiritually. It can also represent advice or help that you must seek out. See also *Bible*.

If the book is underwater or has been dropped into the water, it may represent you being submerged in your own emotions or overwhelmed in your own thoughts right now (see *underwater*).

Books can also represent one's attitudes toward learning. The type of book will give more information (e.g., fantasy, nonfiction, fiction, etc.). See *library* and *story*.

boomerang: This could mean that power returns when it is given. See also *weapons*.

In the aboriginal *dreaming*, rainbow snake created the world that we live in. This world is the *Dreaming* (i.e., the spirit world or what the Christian might call heaven). To the Australian Aborigine, we are already in heaven. The dreams are not the product of human dreams but that of the "spirits of place." For example, the spirit of the kangaroo was created at a specific place in the land known by its inhabitants as the Kangaroo Dreaming. Waking from a sleeping dream into the waking reality is an act of creation in itself.

bordering sleep or wakefulness: See *hypnagogia* or *daydreaming*.

born again: If you're dreaming you've been born again, it may symbolize the need for change or transformation. Perhaps you need to let go of an old way of thinking in order to make room for a new way of being.

Your biases regarding those who claim to be religiously born again may also add meaning to this image.

boss: Though this could represent your waking world boss or someone *bossing* you around, it can also represent your own inner authority. It can also be about your relationship with authority in general.

bowl: This could symbolize a container for one's life. What's in it? See also *cup*.

box: What are you hiding from yourself? This could contain something. This could symbolize a way of keeping something safe or making sure something doesn't get out, such as an emotion or a secret.

Opening it can be about you revealing some part of yourself. Boxes can also be about social conformity.

Being trapped in a box or a boxlike room may also be about rigid thinking. Do you need to see outside your box or the box others have put you in?

If you're giving it as a gift, perhaps you are giving something of yourself to others. See also *gift*.

boy: This could be a symbol of developing yang power. It could also represent your inner child or you at that age. What the boy is doing or who he is can also provide meaning.

Boys could also represent immaturity and/or represent recent experiences with immature masculine figures.

boyfriend: This image could be about feelings, attachments, and sexuality associated with boyfriends. It could also represent the hopes or dissatisfaction connected with this person. This image can be a symbol of the longing for love too.

In a female's dream, the boyfriend could represent her animus (i.e., the masculine traits such as decisiveness, assertiveness, and orientation toward action). See *anima/animus* in the *archetypes* section.

Boy Scout: This may be about your commitment toward some task or goal.

Are there some good behaviors that you need to model more in your life (e.g., honor, truthfulness, helpfulness, caring, dedication, and/or loyalty)?

On the negative side, are you being too naïve? Do you feel like a do-gooder?

bracelet: This might be about passion or the need to reach out. It can be about friendships, and if it's lost, it can be about a lost friendship or possible impending loss. Who was the bracelet from?

If the bracelet gets broken, it might reflect a tendency to sacrifice yourself for the happiness of others. See also *charm*.

bragging: This might suggest insecurities. Perhaps you're not acknowledged enough, or you're trying to get too much acknowledgment?

brambles: If you've fallen into some brambles, it could suggest that something may very well be annoying you. It could be something that you reject in this case (e.g., some annoying thoughts, reactions, beliefs, attitudes, or some emotions).

The spines of a bramble might suggest something very prickly in nature (e.g., something nettlesome, annoying, bothersome, bristling, or even bad-tempered).

Getting caught up in a bramble bush might also be a metaphor for unwanted emotional or physical entanglements or dependencies.

branches: This may have some meaning rooted in family relationships. Note the condition of the branches (e.g., broken, dying, or dead). Perhaps they're threatening you with injury because of proximity.

If caught up in the branches, the image can also reflect entanglements or dependencies, good or bad. See also *limb* or *trees*.

brass: This is a common image, and it is often not highly valued. All that shines is not necessarily gold. (Something may look good but be less so in reality.)

breaching: If a baby is being born feet-first, perhaps things are coming out all wrong or topsy-turvy. It could also be a pun for some kind of breach in trust. See also *baby* or *birth*.

bread: Symbolic of nourishment (bodily, psychological, emotional, or spiritual). If you are breaking bread, it can be about friendship and cooperation.

Bread can also symbolize money. For Christians, it can be the body of Christ, that which nourishes the soul. See also *foods*.

breaking up: If a breakup occurs on the phone, perhaps there's something that you're not communicating or receiving clearly. If you're breaking up with a significant other, perhaps there's something that you need to let go of, or you may be moving onto another level in your relationship.

This can also be an symbol about endings, suggesting that you leave behind the past and move on to something new. Have

you not been able to accept whatever the ending is? See also *static*.

breakdown: If a car or vehicle breaks down, this could suggest that you're pushing yourself too hard and in danger of injuring your health and well-being.

breakfast: This could symbolize the start of something new. You could be nourishing some new endeavor, goal, or way of being.

breastfeeding: This could be about nurturing something or feeding an aspect of yourself. If there's breastfeeding in public, it could reflect a feeling of being exposed and/or vulnerable. If a breast is injured or missing, you could be worried about being undesirable or imbalanced in your life.

breastplate: Do you need to protect yourself emotionally? Are you shutting something or someone out?

breath: Breath can represent the spirit and the measure of life. You can take in something with breath, or you can breathe a sigh of relief. If you can't catch your breath, perhaps you're working too hard and need to take some time for yourself.

Someone breathing air into you may suggest the need to be enlivened in some way. If someone is forcing you to breathe, it may reflect that you have to do something you don't wish to do (i.e., take in something you're resisting).

If you're holding your breath, perhaps you are being willful or repressing some emotion.

Hyperventilating might suggest that you are taking in too much and not taking time to process. Perhaps you need to slow down. See also *vent or ventilate*.

Not being able to breathe might suggest that you are feeling suffocated or strangled by someone or some situation. See also *breath* in *body* and *air*.

Sometimes breathing issues in a dream can reveal health issues such as sleep apnea (a breathing issue that you might want to talk to a doctor about, especially if you are a snorer or have been told that you snore).

breathing down your neck: If someone or something is breathing down your neck, it may be a metaphor for someone keeping a close watch on you. You may also feel you need to keep a close watch on certain others. Some kind of deadline may be threatening you.

bribe: If you bribe someone or you witness a bribe, perhaps you are too willing to compromise your ethics to get what you want.

Are you easily influenced? Are you about to do something that you know you should not? Are you being too demanding of yourself or others?

brick: A pile of bricks might indicate that something is tearing you down.

Consider also the phrase "As dumb as a brick," meaning that someone is very unintelligent or not thinking smartly.

Has something hardened you? If you're building a brick wall, perhaps you are shutting someone in particular or people in general out in order to protect yourself emotionally. If someone is breaking up the wall, perhaps you need to tear down the wall that separates you from others.

Someone throwing a brick through a window could reflect your anger and rage or your desire to break through some obstruction.

Bridges damaged in any way can suggest difficulty in getting to the other side of something or gaining a different perspective. Do you need to mend some relationship?

bridge: This might represent the transition from one phase of your life to another. Bridges can be the connection between you and someone or something else. Have you burned your bridge (i.e., created an unfixable situation)?

If you are building a bridge, you may be trying to find a way to deal with something or someone. It can also symbolize a connection with your inner and/or outer self or perhaps a connection with your emotional and/or spiritual self.

Note that the neck can be seen as a bridge between the intellect and feeling. Thus, the symbol of the bridge can point out a need for unity with things that are actually complementary in nature.

A bridge in music could symbolize a transitional period in your life.

On a ship it could be about the need to control some situation or person.

brochure: If you see a brochure in your dream, perhaps you need to be more open-minded about differing points of view. Maybe you need to get an overview of something, or perhaps you are searching for answers to some issue.

Are you thinking about getting away from the stresses of your life (see *vacation*)?

broken: If something is broken in the dream, this might signify a loss of trust or faith, a disappointment, a broken relationship or self-image. Are you trying to fix it, or is it beyond repair?

If your *glasses are broken*, perhaps you are having trouble seeing the truth of something.

If some part of a body is broken, then perhaps the ability associated with that body part has been compromised. For example, a *broken hand* might signify an inability to express oneself in some situation. A *broken leg* might be symbolic of something limiting your mobility and independence.

A *broken heart* might reflect a loss of livelihood and vitality or a broken relationship. Perhaps you have been emotionally hurt. See parts of the body in *body* for more insight.

broom: See *sweeping*.

brother: If you are female, he could represent your aggressive or assertive self. You may feel dominated by someone, or he may represent a number of personality traits that you either admire and desire for yourself or reject (see *anima/animus* in the *archetypes* section).

bucket: A bucket is a receptacle. Perhaps you are ready for change. It can be a receptacle for both good and bad things (e.g., good feelings and bad feelings).

If the bucket is empty, it can be about feeling empty, but it could also imply that it is ready to be filled with something good.

Buddha: Buddha appearing in a dream could remind you about your spiritual aspects in life. It is also a reminder that truth comes from within and not without. Perhaps you need to find the stillness at your center.

See also *lotus position*.

If you notice the position of the Buddha's hands, take note because that can communicate many things.

If you are trying to find one of the Buddha's hands, this might be about trying to find your spiritual voice or your spiritual expression. Are you looking in the wrong place?

See also *Christ* and *Shiva*.

building: Are you setting some goal and building toward it?

If the building is incomplete or only partially done, you may ask yourself, "Do I feel incomplete regarding some goal?"

The condition of the building can add more information (e.g., *construction*, *destruction*, *dirty*, or *ruin*).

Like houses, buildings can also represent you, the dreamer. The type of building might add more meaning (e.g., apartment, castle, hospital, library, mall, mansion, museum, ruin, penthouse, school, slums, store, warehouse, etc.).

bully: Do you or someone else tend to dominate the conversation or relationship? To see or act as a bully in a dream can represent your repressed rage or misguided sense of self-importance.

Are you or someone else being overbearing or pushy? Are you thinking only of yourself or being narcissistic? Are you being a tyrant?

You might also look at *terrorist* for a bully is often equated with a terrorist. Some people bully or terrorize themselves with a constant litany of putdowns and self-criticisms.

This image is most likely your shadow self (see *shadow* in the *archetypes* section).

You may liken someone or some animal biting you to certain *biting* remarks that can also be like criticisms or bullying.

bum: You may feel like an outcast and/or a failure. This image can also suggest that you are being lazy and that you need to work harder.

bureaucracy: If you're dealing with one in your dream, it may signify a lack of emotion and compassion on your part. It may also reflect your rigidity. Have things become too routine, and do you have to shake things up?

burglar or intruder: This could be about something unpleasant coming up from the unconscious or someone actually intruding into your life or stealing something precious from you. A burglary might suggest that you feel violated in some way and that you are feeling helpless (see *invasion*).

buried: This could be a symbol for something put to rest or something from the past. It could signify something dead and gone or not visible on an everyday basis. If you are being buried alive, it might suggest that you are feeling stifled or trapped.

Burying a body could symbolize some rejected part of yourself you're trying to hide. Are you trying to cover up something? See *cemetery* and *zombie* for additional meanings.

burning: Seeing something burning could represent something that you can't ignore.

If you or someone else is burning, perhaps you are *burned out*, or maybe you are sacrificing yourself or well-being.

Being burned in a dream may be about being emotionally injured, betrayed, or angry. Are you being consumed by something?

The object, place, animal, or person who is being burned may give you more meaning.

burning bush: This is a symbol related to spirituality. Through the burning bush, Moses was told by God to lead the Israelites out of Egypt. Theologically, it is often seen as being symbolic of being burned (suffering) but still alive and flourishing (a symbol of hope when all seems lost).

If you are witnessing the burning bush, you are meeting the spirit of God head-on and are probably standing on holy ground (i.e., a spiritual place).

After Moses asked who he was, God says to him, "I am that I am," meaning "I will be who I will be." This may be the message within your dream—that you should be who and what you are and that you are bigger than your image of yourself.

burning flag: See *flags*.

burning house: This might refer to big changes in your life. Perhaps you're leaving parts of you or your life behind. Things that are burning can sometimes suggest that you are feeling intense emotions.

Perhaps there's something that you need to confront because it is just burning you up. Being burned alive may be symbolic of being obsessed by some ambition. Consider also your *burning desire*. You also may have been *burned* as in betrayed, and you may feel angry as a result (see also *ruins* and *fire*).

burst: If you see something burst, you may be under intense pressure and about to burst. See also *explosion or eruption*.

bus: This could symbolize a shared journey or you trying to get somewhere with the help of others. It can also refer to you giving up responsibility for the direction of your life. If you are waiting at a bus stop, that could be a metaphor for waiting for something to happen in your life rather than taking charge of it. (However, if this is your only form of transportation, then the aspect of this *shared journey* may be more appropriate.) The bus stop could also suggest that you must make some decision.

bush: If you are hiding behind a bush, it might suggest that you are trying to hide something. Perhaps you aren't being open and are protecting yourself.

business: If you own a business or work for one, this dream might give information regarding your business. It might be about some project you are working on or problem areas.

butcher: Your emotions may be raw, or you are ruining something. There may be suppressed anger for something or someone.

butterfly: This creature could be about transformation, a life change, or a sense of freedom. It can also signify a *flighty* personality instead of someone who is down to earth. Other aspects of the dream should help you discern the meaning (also see *butterfly* in the *animal* section).

butter: Are you buttering up someone? Melting butter might suggest that you may need to soften up a bit. It's also a food, so it may also be symbolic of the need to nourish or pamper yourself.

buttons: Are you being too restrained, rigid, or closed off?

A shirt with no buttons might suggest you're closed off. Unbuttoning a shirt or garment might suggest the need or the act of opening yourself up to others.

Losing a button might be a metaphor for the loss of self-confidence.

A jar full of buttons might reflect your energy reserves or your playfulness.

buying: If you or anyone in the dream is buying something, it could signify your acceptance or need for acceptance of something, perhaps of yourself.

If you're not buying something, that could reflect that you're rejecting some part of yourself or that you don't believe something you're being told or are telling yourself.

It is also possible that it signifies a lack of something in your life. What you are buying will help clarify the symbolism. For example, if you are a doughnut maker in your waking life and are asked to buy doughnuts in your dream, this may be symbolic of self-acceptance.

All inner journeys begin with self-acceptance, for you can't go any further if there are parts of yourself that you aren't willing to accept.

buzz: This could be slang for getting a *buzz* on. Are you trying to become unconscious about something (see *drunk*)? Are you trying to take the edge off some negative feelings?

This could also reflect the need to have some fun and relax.

A buzzing sound may also indicate something or someone who's annoying or trying to get your attention.

Consider also the phrase "The buzz around the office/town/neighborhood" as another reference to gossip.

buzzer: Hearing a buzzer in your dream might reflect a feeling of being wrong. Perhaps someone has judged you wrongly, or maybe you have taken the wrong turn on some project.

You might pay close attention to the part of the dream where the buzzer shows up.

buzzard: See *animals*.

C

cab: Is someone taking advantage of you or taking you for a ride? Or do you just need help to get where you want to go? Are you letting someone other than yourself determine the direction your life takes?

cabbage: This can represent something petty. Do you need to rethink some decision?

cabin: Do you feel or want to be self-reliant? Do you want to simplify and enjoy the simpler things in life?

cabinet: This could be symbolic of the female body or be a place where you hide some personal or family secret. What's in the cabinet can help with the interpretation. If there's food in the cabinet, it could be about nourishment (e.g., emotional, spiritual, or psychological). (See also *kitchen* in *house*.)

cable: This could be about strength. If the cable is broken or frayed, then it could signify a loss of that strength.

caboose: Do you feel as though you are always at the end of the line with something or someone?

Do you need to take the lead?

cactus: Feeling a little prickly (i.e., agitated or cross)? Is someone trying to stick it to you? Are you acting too self-protective by being prickly?

cadaver: If you're cutting into it, perhaps you are ready to expose or need to expose something about yourself. It could also symbolize that something inside you is dead or is dying.

Cadillac (or any high-end car): Perhaps you are driven to be successful? This may be a symbol of your ambition(s) in life.

caduceus: The staff with wings at the top and two entwining snakes might symbolize possible health concerns (see *doctor, hospital,* and *nurse*).

Insight: According to myth, Asclepius, son of Apollo, was taught medicine by the centaur Chiron. He also learned how to bring the dead back to life using a Gorgon's blood.

Asclepius's symbol was one serpent entwined around a staff and called the rod of Asclepius—the caduceus (or kerukeion) is the symbol of medicine today.

Originally, it was considered a symbol of commerce and negotiators.

It was a also a type of wand that could bring the dead back to life.

The caduceus was originally the rod of Asclepius, and it resembled a wand with one snake curled around and no wings. The winged rod with two snakes that's often attributed to the healing profession today was actually a symbol for the Greek god Hermes and the element mercury. Therefore, it was regarded as an alchemist's symbol.

See also *Asklepian, doctor, healing or any health-related issues, hospital, medicine*, and/ or *nurse*.

Caesar: See *king* in the *archetypes* section.

café: This symbol seems to be about a meeting with friends or socializing. This could be about the need to socialize. Are you alienating yourself from others?

Because it's associated with food, it is also a symbol for physical and emotional nourishment, the soul, and the spirit.

cafeteria: Are a lot of issues eating you up? You may have a choice of things that can nurture you.

cage: Something may be suppressing your expression or limiting your freedom. Perhaps you're feeling powerless or inhibited. You might be caught in some relationship. What feelings are imprisoning you? It could also represent resentment or anger (see *trapped* or *fence*).

cake: That might represent a celebration, an indulgence, or sensual enjoyment. Maybe you need to share more. Maybe you're not getting your fair share.

Note the phrase "having your cake and eating it too." Perhaps you're being too greedy or asking for too much.

A piece of cake might be a pun and representative of something that's really easy to accomplish.

calendar: This could be about the passage of time or a reminder of something. Some people's lives seem to be run or controlled by the calendar.

calling for help: This can look like prayers. You could be calling out to God, Jesus, or another religious figure, or you could be calling for a parent or some authority figure. At a subconscious level, you may know that you cannot handle something alone.

See also *help*.

camel: This can represent emotional or physical endurance or survival. This animal is often associated with the desert, so it could symbolize loneliness, bareness, or burdensomeness in life.

camera: This may refer to recording something or taking notice of something. How does something look to you? It may also be similar to the eye in that it can represent points of view (see also *photographs*). Being out of focus may suggest you need to clear something up.

If you've lost your camera, perhaps you have lost your focus on some issue. If it's broken, perhaps your ignoring some issue or problem. If it's stolen, perhaps someone has stolen your idea, or you have done the same to someone else.

Are you fixated on the past? Do you need to live more in the moment?

camouflage: You may be hiding your true feelings. Are you hiding your true self? Are you trying to blend into some situation and not be noticed?

camping: Perhaps you need to take a break and move into a more simple lifestyle. Do you need to become more self-sufficient? See also *tent*.

cancel: Canceling something might suggest that you fear dealing with something (i.e., that you don't want to face the facts).

cancer: This could symbolize destructive growth or something in your personality that is out of step with the image you have of yourself.

This image may depict something that may be eating away at your self-confidence or a loss of personal control. It can also be a symbol of fear or a part of yourself that's in discord with other parts or the community you live or work in.

Consider also the *zodiac* sign. As a sign, it might represent your tendency to hold on to everything. It could also suggest that you are being moody and emotional.

Because dreams can come to you in the interest of your own health and well-being, you might also consider a health-related message that the body is trying to communicate through the dream (see also *disease*).

candle: This can come in the form of a single candle, a candelabra, or a menorah, and it can represent illumination, enlightenment, or understanding. It can represent the soul of one's being.

It's an archetype for divine energy.

Insight: The flame of the candle can represent life itself. Is the flame sputtering? Has it gone out? Going out or sputtering may indicate depression or impending failure. If it's blown out, it could suggest that you are giving up on or letting go of something. If you blow out candles on a cake, it could reflect your wish for something.

An unlit candle might symbolize feelings of rejection or disappointments, or it could mean that you are not utilizing your potential. If you try to light the candle and it won't light, then it may represent grief or denial about something, or it may mean that you feel powerless over something.

If it has melted down, it might suggest impending change or a softening of a position, belief, or point of view. A brightly burning candle may represent passion. There are also old flames (your exes). You may also be *burning the candle at both ends* (i.e., overdoing or overextending something). For some Christians, the candle can represent a prayer.

Unlit candles might represent disappointments or rejection, especially if they're lying on the floor.

A candle burning down to nothing might reflect life coming to an end or you getting older.

Red candles can represent passion, especially if they are also lit. If they've been blown out or they aren't lit, that can represent a lack of passion.

A candle might also represent a penis.

candy: To see or eat candy may symbolize the joys and the special treats in life. It can also represent indulgence, sensuality, and/or forbidden pleasure. Are you devoting too much time to unimportant issues?

candy cane: You may be hungering for some childhood memory. Do you long to be indulged? Are you denying some pleasure or some temptation?

A candy cane for some people can represent the shepherd's crook, and thus, it may have something to say about humility or spiritual surprise.

cane: Do you need someone to lean on? Do you need some advice? Are you feeling crippled by something? See also *walking stick*.

caned: Do you feel forced into submission, or do you feel guilty and a desire for punishment in order to reconcile this guilt? If you are hitting someone with a cane, it could be about repressed aggression.

canopy: Are you trying to protect something or hide something? Are you covering something up to make it look more presentable? If a large area is covered, are you trying to deal with too much?

Do you need to uncover or reveal something? See also *tarp*.

cannibal: Are you sacrificing some part of yourself for the good of the rest? What part of you is consuming you. What in particular is eating you up?

This image can also be about some destructive obsession or forbidden desire. Do you feel as though you are being eaten alive or consumed by some situation, guilt, or relationship?

cannon: Is there some drastic action that needs to take place? Are you feeling anger toward someone or something?

Consider also it being a pun for doctrine, dogma, or collection of precepts (as in canon).

canoe: See *boat* and *kayak*.

canyon: This is similar to a passageway. Are you letting your feelings pass through to your consciousness, or are you blocking them? If you are at the top of a canyon and looking down, you may be looking into your subconscious self. If you are dangling above the canyon or at its edge, this may

reflect a fear of failure. Hanging onto the side of a canyon wall and falling can reflect a fear of losing your grip (i.e., going crazy).

cap and gown: Perhaps you are transitioning to a higher level in something? You could be graduating from one stage and moving onto the next stage.

Capricorn: This could be about self-doubt and fears of inadequacy (i.e., feeling that you're not measuring up). It can also be symbolic of ambition and drive. See also *zodiac*.

capsize: If a boat capsizes, then perhaps you're avoiding some unpleasant feelings, or maybe some feeling has *upended* you (see *boat, sinking, water,* and *drowning*).

captain: This possibly refers to taking charge of your life and emotions, or it could reflect how you need to take charge. You may also be a powerful influence on something or someone. Consider how you can be *the captain of your fate*.

captive: Perhaps you're feeling trapped by someone or some circumstance (career, relationship, or life in general). Are you trapped in your own denial of something? You may be held captive by your own beliefs, prejudice, or ignorance?

car: This could symbolize personal power, your motivating drives, ambition, personal mobility, and/or the power to direct your life. It can be symbolic of your ego (i.e., your personality). It may represent where you're going in life and/or where you want to get to.

If someone else is driving, then you may feel as if that person may be driving your life or that you aren't taking responsibility for this direction. Basically, if you're not in the driver's seat, you are not making your own decisions. Do you need to get back in the driver's seat?

If someone is trying to break in, perhaps someone is invading your personal space, usurping your power, or trying to steal your dreams and ambitions for life.

A *crashed car* may indicate failure or self-destructiveness, or it could signal reckless behavior if you are driving the car. If someone else is driving, you may be letting someone other than yourself direct your life while you are negatively affected.

Looking in the mirror could remind you about what you left behind.

The *car going in reverse* could represent how your life seems to be going in reverse instead of forward. Perhaps you are going the wrong way in life or with some activity.

Crashing into a lake or body of water could represent something that's emotionally overwhelming and affecting your progress toward your goals.

Running *out of fuel* could indicate weakening motivation. If you're driving with your headlights off, you may lack an awareness of what is happening in your life.

A *parked car* might suggest that you need to turn your energies elsewhere or put your life in drive and get on with it (whatever *it* is). Does it feel like your life is on hold or stuck in park?

The *trunk of a car* is where you store or hide things. The trunk may store old memories you haven't yet dealt with and some that might come back to bite you.

If you are stopped at a railroad crossing, it could mean that you are experiencing a temporary hiatus or setback in achieving your goals.

The type of car can also aid in the interpretation. If it's an old jalopy, you may be feeling old and broken down. If it's a Cadillac, BMW, Mercedes, or other high-end auto, then perhaps you are driven to succeed or want to impress others. If it's a race car, it may suggest that you are moving too fast in your life, taking too many risks, being competitive, or treating something as a contest.

A toy car may reflect a lack of seriousness or some childish attitudes, though it can also reflect your playfulness.

The person in the car with you or the people you're racing against will provide information. A race car could also reflect your sexual drive (see also *passenger*).

car keys: Car keys may represent what can turn your life on. If you've lost them or someone has stolen them, perhaps the answer to getting your life started and moving forward has been lost or taken away.

Keys can represent control and the forward movement of your life. Keys can also be sexual in nature, and if they are lost or stolen, that could be symbolic of impotence.

cardinal: Cardinals can represent happiness or the need for it. They can also represent being first. A cardinal number is any whole number—one, two, three, and so on. See *numbers* for further meaning if anything in the dream comes in a specific number.

Consider also the pun for a religious or spiritual leader (see *priest*).

Cards have often been given meaning beyond their intended meaning. For example, the Ace of Clubs has often been called the God card. One reason for this is that Aces are both the Alpha and the Omega, the highest or lowest, depending on the game. The club suite can represent God in that each lobe of the clover symbol represents different aspects of the Christian God (e.g., the Father, Son, and Holy Ghost).

cards or gambling: Are you making a game of life and not taking it seriously? Are you taking a chance or a risk on something or someone? What do you hope to win?

Cards can be about the games people play or sometimes about old and new ways of being if the deck is used or new. You have to work with the hand you were dealt in life. An old deck might reflect the past, while a new deck might refer to a new life, a new way of being, or a new hand to play.

Is there an image on the front of the card? This can add meaning as well.

Playing cards can be about pleasure and socializing or the need for this in your life.

See also *gambling* or *tarot*.

caring: If you are caring for someone or if someone is taking care of you, ask yourself, "Do I need to be more compassionate or to take care of someone?" Are you being indifferent as a means of protecting yourself?

Do you need to be loved and cared for?

Do you need to be more responsible for the outcome of something (e.g., relationship, situation, or project)?

See also *indifference*.

carnival: This could symbolize freedom from restraint and a desire to cut loose.

carousel: Perhaps you're reliving something, maybe your childhood. Do you feel as if you're going nowhere in life or stuck in some job or relationship (see also *Ferris wheel* and/or *fair*).

carpenter: This could represent the practical side of creativity but doing so with old ideas or principles that are tried and true. What are you trying to build in your life or in yourself?

carpenter bee: Carpenter bees could be like termites. If that's so and they're eating

wood to create a space for themselves, that could represent something attacking your soul or your sense of being.

These things bore into wood like something can bore into and weaken one's psyche or sense of self.

Alternatively, the carpenter aspect could also reinforce the hardworking or creative aspect of the bee symbol. See also *bee* in *animals*.

carpet: This could symbolize protection and/or luxury beyond your basic needs. It may also be a symbol for a cover-up (e.g., something you're hiding).

carrot: In a woman's dream, this image may represent thoughts about sex.

A carrot may also represent someone trying to influence you, or it could have something to do with rewards or punishments as with *a carrot on a stick*.

carrying something on your back: This could symbolize a problem, a burden, or a habit.

cartoon: If you see your life as a cartoon or if you are watching cartoons, that may mean you are not taking life seriously. This can also be a suggestion that you be more lighthearted and laugh at yourself a little. It can also be an escape from stress.

Specific cartoon characters have certain personality aspects or qualities assigned to them that you either admire or reject. You could also find them endearing or amusing. A particular character may reflect an aspect of yourself that you may need to learn to accept. Seeing yourself in a cartoon character can enlighten you and make it easier to accept.

cash: See *money.*

cash register: This could symbolize your concerns about money. A missing register may reflect a loss of esteem, love, or place in the world.

casino: Are you a risk taker? Should you take a risk on something or someone? Perhaps you need to be more informed and thorough in your decision-making process.

casket: This can reflect your fears of death. This image can also represent ideas, beliefs, hopes, and/or habits that are no longer useful and need to be put away.

Bodies in caskets can be about depression or feeling trapped or restricted in freedom (especially if you find yourself buried in one). Maybe there's something that you need to end so that you can move on.

See also *coffin.*

castaway: See *abandoned* or *lost.*

castle: This can symbolize the noble self and hiding behind fortifications and emotional walls to protect one from hurt. Basically, a castle is a metaphor for your experience of security or defensive attitudes (i.e., how you defend against *attacks* such as criticisms).

If the castle is in ruins, it could mean that your defenses are in shambles and you feel vulnerable or that some defensive posture is no longer needed and it's time to let it go.

Pen and ink by John M. Cole, 1941.

Castles can signify the protected and noble self. The high walls are put up to keep us separate from our fears and the *others* we fear. They can come into our dreams and signify a need for refuge.

cast-off: Perhaps you need to let go of something.

You may feel neglected, or you may feel you are neglecting someone or thing. Are you feeling shabby? Are you feeling alienated or abandoned?

castration: This may represent limits to your creativity, a denial of your power, or your sexuality. It can reflect a fear regarding your sexual drive or rejection, especially by the opposite sex.

cat: That can represent the feminine aspect and/or the independent self. See *cat* in the *animal* section.

catacombs: Walking through dark catacombs can be like walking through your subconscious, where dislikes and fears reside. Perhaps you need to face some fear.

See also *maze*.

catalyst: Something may be causing some action in your life but is not part of the change. Are you forcing some changes without being a part of it or being responsible for it? Do you need to make something happen and become more than a bystander?

catastrophe: This could be about a sudden instability or a violent upheaval in your life. You may be feeling anxious about what's unknown. See also *destruction* and/or *ruins*.

caterpillar: See *animals*.

cauldron: A cauldron in your dream may imply that you are undergoing some transformation. It could also indicate destiny or some magical, spiritual force. Consider the symbolism of what is in the cauldron and its importance (see *witch* or *witchcraft*).

cave: This may suggest hidden issues or things from the past. It has also been interpreted as female sexuality.

A cave is an entrance to the shadows of the unconscious mind that is inside you and beckoning you to explore it.

It can also be considered a place of refuge (see also *basement, cellar, hole, rabbit hole*, or *tunnel*).

Insight: In Plato's allegory of the cave, he imagined a group of prisoners chained in a cave and facing a wall, unable to turn around. Behind them was an eternally burning flame, and between the flame and the prisoners, there was a parade of objects and people that cast their shadows upon the wall.

To the prisoners, their reality was this two-dimensional movement of shadows before them. Unknown to them was a reality of immense multidimensional complexity. If they had known of this complexity, it would have totally explained their universe.

In a lot of ways, Plato's shadow world is a reflection of what the unconscious shadow mind that resides in each of us does to our experience of reality.

The cave you live in is the one of your conscious mind and its three-dimensional way of seeing things. Like the prisoners in Plato's allegory, we cannot see the reality behind us when all we have is the wall of our conscious minds to perceive with.

But there is an inestimable reservoir of creativity that resides in the shadow world of the unconscious mind. (Both that which is labeled positive and that which is labeled negative contribute significantly to what is created in the conscious world.)

Next time you have a dream where something or someone dark shows up and threatens your dream self, don't run from it. Instead, engage it. Perhaps start a conversation with it. You may find that such a conversation actually illuminates what's going on in your life.

The shadow often has information to enlighten even though it seems to come from the darkness. Using your dreams to unlock the chains that have kept you staring at only one dimension of reality can be immensely rewarding.

caveman: This can symbolize the primordial aspect of the self (i.e., what is basic to your nature) (see *animals*).

ceiling: See *ceiling* under *house*.

celebrity: This could represent the desire for fame and recognition and perhaps your high aspirations. The exact celebrity will have personality traits that you either wish for yourself or reject. See also *famous person*.

cellar: If you are in a cellar in your dream, that might represent a part of your subconscious where you have kept your fears and problems hidden. If you dream that you are going down into the cellar, that might signify that you're digging deep into your own past and your unconscious memories in order to face your fears (see also *basement* in *house*).

cell phone: This could symbolize accessibility and vital communication. However, it could also represent distraction, rudeness, or a nuisance, depending on other aspects of the dream.

Is there a part of yourself that you need to connect or consult?

Also see *telephone*.

Celtic knot: This image may represent continuity, longevity, or immortality. It could also refer to no beginning or ending (i.e., the eternal). Sometimes this could represent a love knot or the intertwining of souls or spirits.

The shape of the knot may add more information (e.g., *square*, *triangle*, or *circle*).

The triquetra or trinity knot is a type of Celtic knot, and it represents the Father, Son, and Holy Ghost to Christians; however, for the ancient Celts, Druids, and modern Wiccans, it refers to the natural forces of earth, air, and water. On a more spiritual level, it can represent life, death, and rebirth.

cemetery: A cemetery is a place of endings. It's where things from the past are put to rest. Note any emotions associated with the dream cemetery. During Halloween, many see the cemetery as the place where the dead and the living can come together (see *buried*).

censoring: Is someone preventing or putting up obstacles to you expressing yourself? Are you censoring yourself?

center: If you are at the center of a group or a circle, is it because you act as though you are the center of everything, or are you searching for your center, your spiritual self? See also *mandala*.

ceremony: A ceremony in a dream or something that seems ceremonial can refer to the need for some sacrifice or devotion on your part in order to achieve some goal.

Perhaps there's some commitment and self-discovery and/or inner change that you want or need.

certificate: This can represent a formalized confirmation of something. It could also be symbolic of the end of something. It can also represent the fact that you are qualified to do something in particular. It can also be a document that certifies the authenticity or truth of something.

A certificate can also be about acknowledgment. Do you need to be acknowledged for something? Do you need to acknowledge someone or be more acknowledging? Do you need to praise more or to be praised?

cesspool: This suggests stored-up or concealed negativity. It could also be a negative judgment about something.

chain: Chains can bind, restrict, or limit you. This is especially true if you or someone is chained up in some way. It can also be what connects you with other people.

A broken chain could reflect an end to some tyranny by others or yourself. (Self-criticism and negative judgments can be tyrannical.) A broken chain can also reflect a broken habit or way of being or thinking or the need to break it.

chainsaw: What do you need to cut down? This may also refer to a horror or massacre.

chair: See *furniture*.

The seven chakras of the human body

chakra: If you see a chakra in a dream, it might suggest a blockage to your spiritual energy. If it's violet (V), it may represent your crown chakra and reflect wisdom or intellect. As the eye chakra, indigo (I) may be about intuition (see also *eye* under *body*).

Blue (B) might be about your ability to express yourself verbally, while green (G) might symbolize the heart chakra and suggest divine love. See also *heart* or heart in *body*.

Yellow (Y) is often symbolic of the solar plexus and can be about relationships,

whether good or bad. It is also said to be where energies such as intuition, personal power, and emotions are integrated into the self.

Orange (O) can be about your sexual aspect, while the root chakra, which is red (R), can be about your rootedness or lack of it.

See also *colors*.

chameleon: See *animals*.

change: Perhaps this reflects the need for change or impending change (see *transition dreams*).

Consider the term *short-changed* as in not getting your due acknowledgment. To be short-changed could also refer to some issues with low self-esteem. Getting more change than what you are due might refer to your sense of entitlement and/or an inflated ego. See also *coins*.

changing clothes: Changing clothes can be about changing a way of being.

This can be about dying to the way you are now so as to become something new. Some mystics think that the death of the body is a way the soul changes clothes. (The corporeal body is just a set of clothes or a garment for the spirit.)

chanting: Are you trying to or need to connect with your spiritual aspect? It may also be a way of honoring this spiritual source.

chaos: This suggests a lack of order or predictability in your life or some situation. Have you noticed any recurrent drama that shows up in your waking life? What might this show you about your unconscious desires and motives?

charm: Casting a charm may reflect a need for protection. Charm bracelets can also be symbols of protection. A specific charm on the bracelet might give more information about the meaning. See also *amulet, bracelet, magic,* or *spell.*

chased: This could mean avoidance. What we avoid chases us down. Emotional pain, guilt, responsibility, love, desire, and/or failure will pursue us until we deal with them or until we integrate them if we are missing them.

Does the same problem keep coming up again and again? What seems to be after you? Is there some part of yourself that's trying to get your attention or some negative that keeps recurring and won't leave you alone?

Are you being bullied?

If you are being chased by an unseen pursuer, is there some aspect of yourself that needs to be integrated into your consciousness? If you are chasing something, what are you pursuing? See also *ghost, haunted house,* or *stalker or stalking.*

chasing: Could this be an unachieved goal? Are you chasing after something but not able to get it?

If something is chasing you, is there some part of yourself or your life that you are not acknowledging? See also the *nightmares* section.

If you are chasing something, could you actually be avoiding that thing? What are you running away from?

Is there something that you need to get ahold of and integrate into yourself? Do you need to be more like the personality of the person or thing that's chasing you?

See also *stalker or stalking.*

cheat/cheating/cheated: Are you being dishonest with yourself or another person? Even if someone else is cheating or cheating on you, perhaps it is you who is cheating him or her in some way? Are you cheating yourself (i.e., selling yourself short)? Are you selling someone else short?

A cheat may be something that is not right or a betrayal of trust. It can also refer to a sense of abandonment or something you haven't attended to.

Sometimes when there isn't enough romance in a relationship, this image can show up.

check: Writing, giving, or receiving a check might be about paying off a debt. Consider also that you may need to *check* on something or prevent something from continuing or happening.

cheese: Something may be cheesy. It can also represent success or gain. Consider the phrase "Say cheese." You may need to smile more.

chef: It could mean that you have the ability and talent to guide your own life. There's a course of action you can take, and you know what it is.

This symbol can also be about nurturing, transformation, and change. It is your inner means for feeding your emotional, psychological, physical, and spiritual self.

chemistry: Dreaming of a chemist or chemistry might be about a transformation. Do you need to change some part of yourself or your life?

It can also be about manipulation (i.e., being manipulated or manipulating others).

Consider also that it may speak to the chemistry or synergy between others (i.e., how things or people work together and their connection). Do you need to change

yourself to change the chemistry between you and others?

If the dream image is about taking chemo to combat a disease, perhaps you need some kind of healing (see *medicine*).

cherub: This is a small baby-like angel with wings, and may represent childlike innocence. Are you taking life too seriously? See also *Cupid* or *Eros and Logos*.

Cheshire cat: This could represent the mischievous you. It could also represent deceitfulness or someone you're not sure you can trust.

There may be no substance behind someone's smile.

chess: Perhaps you need to carefully think something through. It's a game of strategy, so ask yourself, "Do I need to strategize about some action or response?" Have you met your match in something? To what degree are you absorbed in the game? Have you shut out everyone around you?

What's your next move?

chest: See *body*.

child: This could be about innocence, something within you developing. This may also be about your feelings or thoughts about your childhood and family relationships. See *child and divine child* in the *archetypes* section.

Insight: In many myths and religions, it is a child who reunites heaven and earth (man and God). This child is the archetype for paradise, heaven, and the ancient Tibetan city of Shambhala—a sacred place where you can cross into another world.

There seems to be an universal urge to seek paradise either in the form of spiritual growth and transformation or a physical world of perfection as in the case of Shambhala.

Seeing a child, heaven, or paradise in a dream can suggest you are seeking innocence, perfection of the spirit, or perfect happiness. You may also be trying to escape the difficulties that you're experiencing in life.

The image of the child in a dream or a meditation is a powerful one. Using a meditation to revisit a dream and thus reconnect with the power of your inner child, which stays within each of us no matter how old we are, can add significant depth to any dream.

The following is an example of a personal dream and the meditative technique that I used to answer two questions I needed to ask in order to better understand the message. I asked myself, "What's down the road?" and then I asked, "What do I want to find there?"

In a dream I experienced some time ago, a woman floating above the ground invited me to leave the world I was in and travel down a road that lead into the distant hills. (Was I going forward or backward in time?) Angels climbed up and down a staircase to and from the sky while children ran up a grassy hill.

What I wanted to find was the *powerful child*, the once competent and confident child, and its whole and undamaged soul, which I knew still resided within me. As suggested by my mentor, I put on a CD that played a shaman's drum and focused on my breath. I counted four in, held my breath, and then counted four out. I did this until my body rested and my mind began to quiet.

When I revisited the dream, I began to talk to the woman in blue, who was clearly my mother. She invited me to walk with her down the road and into the hills where I once again saw the story of my life and witnessed all those times when I had felt loss and defeat.

"You chose your meanings long before you ever experienced them and thus limited yourself, Robert," she said. Then she encouraged me to shift their meaning so as to see another side of their reality.

As I did this, each event began to transform into something new. Betrayal turned to love, and abandonment either disappeared altogether or became the prequel to an embrace. I began to see that every interpretation could have yet another hiding behind it, and even though I had chosen one meaning, I could as easily choose another.

I thought this would become easier if I were to shift the context of my life from being centered around me to being centered around us.

Farther back into the hills, I found a young boy sitting with a drum, quietly tapping out his rhythm.

As I approached, this towheaded boy turned toward me and smiled. Then he rose from the grass, crawled into the lap of a large mama bear, and nuzzled his head under her chin. Wrapped in her embrace, warm and secure, he felt loved and in her embrace had become the power of the mama, the power of the bear. Everything began to fog, and I found myself in the embrace of the bear. I had become the boy.

Soon I found myself running beside Onoma, the she wolf, breath frosting like steam as we panted and ran through the snow-covered forest.

Suddenly, I was lifted and rose above the trees as the she wolf looked up and grinned at me. Now I twirled and spun with my arms outstretched to my sides, flying higher and racing headlong through a tunnel of lightly falling snow. Then I reached for a star that was just waiting there at the tunnel's end.

With an outstretched arm, I grasped for it and pulled it into me—this light with its warmth and its power. It was finally mine.

The drum, its rhythm, my rhythm, my song, my dance, the beat of my soul was pounding out every step to show me the way back home. My soul was in the trees, the bear, the mother, the wolf, and the light, which was mine to claim once again.

Now on the ground, I looked down and to my right, and I saw the boy looking up at me with a worried look on his clear, bright face.

"Where've you been?" he said as he took my hand, and then we strolled across the mudflats of his world. "I've missed you."

"I've missed you too," I said.

"You're always welcome, you know," he said encouragingly.

"I know. Can I come any time?"

"Yeah! Any time." (See *active imagining*.)

The child in a dream can also reflect a part of the soul that has been missing since your childhood or a part that you have not attended to. To recapture, save, or embrace the child in the dream could be about regaining your energy.

Seeing the child in a dream can be about finding the pieces of ourselves that we've lost along the way.

Insight: Note that the child shows up in dreams as the nature child, the magical child, and the orphan child as well, and it is always in the service of our well-being (see the *archetypes* section).

childhood: This could represent a time when you had fewer responsibilities and worries.

It's a time of greater innocence. But it can also represent the opposite. You may have some childhood anxieties that you have yet to resolve, and the dream may be bringing them up so that you can deal with them.

childhood home: This can be about your childhood values, the security you felt during that time, and/or your desire to build a similar family experience of your own. This symbolism would probably be the same for your hometown or a former house.

Being lost and unable to find your way back might reflect a loss of confidence in yourself. Alternatively, if your home life as a child was negative or possessed some negative aspect, something in your waking life may be triggering the image in your dream.

children: These can be about your own childlike qualities or symbolize that you are regressing into an earlier state. It can also suggest that you, someone or a group is/are acting childish or irresponsibly. They can also represent growth and the future (see also *child*).

children's dreams: A child's dream tends to be about interests and emotions in the waking world. For example, from about two years of age to about twelve, girls' dreams tend to be about people and references to clothes, and boys' dreams are more about objects and implements. Girls' dreams also tend to be longer than boys'.

Because they also tend to be more animistic in their thinking, children also have more animals in their dreams than adults usually do. They also seem to have more aggressive themes in their dreams than adults. This may be due to the fact that children are trying to integrate their own powerful impulses with the expected norms of society and family.

The wild creatures of their dreams are often representative of their own barely controlled impulses. These bogeymen can also symbolize their parents and the difficulty these children have in reconciling the loving and protective aspects of the parents with the disciplinary aspects.

With any dream interpretation, one should not impose a meaning. This is especially true of children's dreams. Adults should not impose an adult meaning but help the children in developing their own symbolic associations.

Children's dreams may be full of witches, vampires, giants, and partially seen ghosts and bogeymen since they are trying to integrate the fearful and unknown forces of nature into their worldviews, but adults with the same fearful dream elements may be trying to display reality as something predictable as well. Sometimes this process is a lifelong one (see also *giant* in *animals*).

chilies: This could symbolize passion or raw emotion.

chimera: See *animals as fantasy creatures* and/or *phantom*.

chimes: This could symbolize tranquility or the need for it.

chimney: This image suggests warmth and family values. The chimney can also be a phallic symbol, and thus, a smoking chimney could be about sexual release or the need for it. A broken-down chimney could be about impotence or emotional coldness.

If you are cleaning a chimney, that might suggest you may need to clean something up (i.e., confront something negative and deal with it).

Chinese: If you are not Asian and you dream you are this ethnicity, this may be symbolic of something you don't understand or some aspect of yourself that you don't understand.

This could also be a symbol for totalitarianism. Look to your own prejudices in order to add meaning to this symbol.

Insight: The Chinese believed that the dream world was an actual dimension and thought that a person's spirit and soul left the body every night to visit other places in another world. They also believed that if they were suddenly awakened, their souls might fail to return. Some say that to this day some Chinese people won't use alarm clocks for that reason.

Zhou Gong from the Zhou dynasty of China (1046–256 BCE) wrote the book on meaning for Chinese dreams titled *The Book of Auspicious and Inauspicious Dreams*. His interpretations continue to have some importance to the Chinese people, though these interpretations are often thought of as folk interpretations weighing heavily on fortune-telling.

Chuang-tzu, another Chinese thinker and philosopher (fourth century BCE), added greatly to the world of dreams and their meaning when he posed a simple question, "How do we know when we are dreaming or when we are awake?"

Once Chuang-tzu dreamed that he was a butterfly. He fluttered about happily, quite pleased with the state that he was in, and he knew nothing about Chuang-tzu. Then he awoke and found that he was very much Chuang-tzu again.

Now, did Chuang-tzu dream that he was a butterfly, or was the butterfly now dreaming that he was Chuang-tzu? This raises the question of monitoring reality in dreams, a topic of intense interest in modern cognitive neuroscience (https://en.wikipedia.org/wiki/Dream_interpretation).

chocolate: This could be about love, sensuality, or self-reward. Alternatively, are you indulging yourself or someone else too much?

choice: If you are given a choice, you may have the ability to define what happens to you in some situation (i.e., you defining the reality rather than it defining you). You can choose to control some outcome or response. Alternatively, you may be victimized and have little or no choice.

choir: Singing can be about spiritual harmony or the need for it. It can also be about cooperation—that is, unless you're singing out of tune. Then it might suggest that you're not in tune with others.

choke: This can reflect conflict. You could be repressing some emotion or something you want to say but can't get out. Is something strangling/stifling you? What's choking you may also have significance. If you are choking someone, you might be having aggressive feelings, or you're choking off something from being said or revealed.

choking: See *strangling*.

chopping: This could be about breaking something up so that you can manage it better. If you're chopping something on a chopping block, it could be a metaphor for a loss (e.g., a job or a relationship). What are you chopping?

choreographer: This could be about unrestrained expression (see *dance*). Alternatively, it may mean that you're choreographing your life too much and thus restricting its flow and surprise.

chosen: To be chosen may be a metaphor for being special, the desire to be special, divine favor or preference, or standing out.

Perhaps you need to make a choice about something.

Christ: This could be a powerful dream symbol that's not necessarily connected to the historical Jesus. It is a powerful influence on one's personality. It can also represent one's universal connection.

A Christ figure can also represent the sacrifices you've made or that you need to make. The Christ symbol is often a metaphor for the greater self, the self beyond one's ego. Searching for this symbol in a dream is tantamount to the individuation process (see the *archetypes* section).

Christian: This image may reflect your personal beliefs about Christianity or those who practice the faith. It can also be about inner development. See also *religion*.

Christmas: This can suggest family togetherness, celebration, peace and goodwill, and a time to express generosity and to give to others.

It can also represent new beginnings. Your associations with the holiday will also give you hints to its meaning in your dream.

Christmas cards: These may be about the need to reach out to someone, perhaps family.

Christmas tree: A Christmas tree might be about family celebrations, stress, and anxiety looming. It can also be symbolic of your spirituality.

chthonic: This relates to the underworld with all the deities and spirits that lurk there.

In analytic psychology, it refers to one's spirit nature within as well as the positive and negative unconscious impulses that can motivate us. This term can also be used to refer to the archetypal material of the *collective unconscious*.

church: This is often symbolic of spiritual belief and moral codes. What is holy in your life? (A synagogue, cathedral, temple, or mosque can be similar in nature of their meaning.) See also *synagogue* or *temple*.

cigar: As Sigmund Freud suggested, this could represent a phallic symbol or an icon for someone who has some significance for you. Sometimes a cigar is just symbolic of taking a break and relaxing.

Insight: Sigmund Freud was quoted as saying, "Sometimes a good cigar is just a good cigar," meaning that we shouldn't read too much into symbols because they have their limits. Sometimes there's no hidden meaning to a symbol. It is what it is.

Cinderella: Do you feel overburdened? Do you feel you are taking on too much? Do you feel overshadowed and neglected?

circle: This could represent completeness/wholeness or coming full circle. A circle can also be a mandala (see *mandala*) that might represent the soul, your inner self, positive change, or inner peace. As with the square, the circle is said to represent the self.

Concentric circles might represent layers of your inner self, your own complexities, or the complexity of some project, situation, or relationship (see also *onion* and *wheel*).

Moving in a clockwise circular direction could represent going with the flow whereas a counterclockwise direction might indicate that you're moving or acting contrary to others and in resistance to circumstances or events.

circuit board: Do you need to take a planned and orderly approach to something?

circuit breaker: Are you feeling overloaded? Do you need to just turn it all off and take a break?

circus: Are you not taking something seriously? Are you expressing your more playful side? Does the world around you seem to be going slightly crazy or becoming chaotic?

city: This can represent culture, a civilized order, or your interaction with the society you live in. It can represent your sense of community. If you're lost in the city, you may be uncertain about your place in society, or you may feel as if you've lost your direction or purpose.

To move from one part of the city to another might be a metaphor for a shift in your point of view or the need for one (see also *ruins*).

clairvoyance: See *divination, far, mysticism, premonition*, and/or *prophecy*.

class: Is there something that you need to learn? Perhaps your behavior should be classier.

If you forget to attend a class, it may symbolize your fear of failing at something (see also *exams*).

classmates: Perhaps former associations will help with a current situation or relationship. They may also represent earlier socio-emotional lessons.

classroom: A classroom might be about an important lesson you've learned or one that you need to learn. Maybe you need to learn something about yourself.

claustrophobia: This image may be about your guilt or the feeling of being too constricted and less open. Thus, you may need to open up.

cleaning: It's possible that there is some aspect of your life or yourself that needs cleaning or that you need to remove some negative(s) from your life. You may also be moving on to some new stage of your life.

clear: The image of clear water or clear skies could signal a message for calming down so that you can see things more clearly.

clearance: If something is being sold on clearance, perhaps you are selling yourself or someone else short.

Perhaps you're undervaluing something. Do you need to clear out something such as some old habit or relationship?

cleaver: Is there something or someone you need to cut out of your life? This image can also represent anger and suggest that you look more deeply into what is angering you (see *anger*).

cliff: This could represent being on the edge of some new awareness or danger. It can also be a challenge that you wish to aspire to. Sometimes you stand at the edge of a cliff to face your fears.

You may be at the edge of conscious awareness looking into your deeper, more spiritual self. It may be time to focus more

on your inner self instead of the outer world.

For me, standing at the edge of a cliff and watching a roiling sea can be like a conversation with my soul.

To jump or leap from the cliff into an abyss or body of water could be symbolic of entering the soul. See also *abyss*.

climbing: This can be about aspiration, growth, and achievement. What are you trying to get to (or escape from)?

Climbing can also be about trying to reach new heights (emotional, spiritual, and physical) or social success.

clock: This is often symbolic of measurement or timing. Clocks or watches could also reflect a sense of urgency or plenty of time.

The ticking of a clock could represent your life passing by or the beat of your heart. A stopped clock may indicate the death of something, or if the clock is racing, it could signal a sense of urgency.

It can also be about the restrictions we place on ourselves (i.e., becoming slaves to time and thus being less creative and spontaneous).

clockwise/counterclockwise: Moving in a clockwise circular direction could represent going with the flow. A counterclockwise direction might indicate that you're moving or acting contrary to others and in resistance to circumstances or events.

closet: A closet may be about hidden things. There may be some aspects of yourself that you have hidden from others or yourself. Consider the need to reveal what is hidden and come out of the closet.

See also *wardrobe*.

closing: The closing of a door could mean you have closed yourself off to something or someone. If something has closed but reopened, perhaps an opportunity you thought had passed has reopened.

clothing terms: This often suggests the stance we take in social situations. It can represent our identities, our self-images, and what we put on for the rest of the world to see (see *face*). It is also what we put on to hide our real selves. It's also a symbol for covering up or hiding something.

The clothes you are wearing can indicate your status or desired status in life.

Dirty clothes can signal something in your way of being that you need to clean up. Perhaps you need to change some old way of thinking. Messy clothes can signal that you believe you should keep your life in better order.

Changing clothes can be about changing a way of being. This can be about dying to the way you are now in order to become something new. Some mystics think that the death of the body is a way that the soul changes clothes. (Many believe that the corporeal body is just a set of clothes.)

If you are covering up some bit of clothing, you may be trying to hide some part of yourself. If you cover up some brightly colored piece of clothing with something more sedated, you may be trying to hide a flamboyant part of yourself that perhaps you fear someone may reject.

If some piece of clothing doesn't fit, it may suggest that some part of your inner image of yourself that you've been covering up is no longer applicable. (It doesn't *fit* anymore, and you don't need to hide it anymore.)

> **bathing suits:** These may suggest vulnerability.
>
> **blouse or shirt:** This may be about the upper versus the lower body.
>
> **boots:** These might imply a statement of power or the ability to stand firm.
>
> **cloak:** This might signal magical protection. It might be a synonym for hiding.

coat: This might suggest you are covering up something. It could also represent a coating, veneer, or partition between things. To coat the truth would be to varnish the truth (i.e., cover it up).

dress: This is often related to the feminine self-image or a feminine perspective on something. If the dress is a uniform, it could be about high standards and rigid formality (see *uniform*).

If someone in the dream is wearing the same dress as you are, perhaps you need to be more creative and better express your unique self. Because people in dreams often reflect a part of your own personality that you either like or reject it's also possible that the person is a personality reflection of you. In this way each person in a dream can act as a mirror or reflection of yourself.

hat: This image might have something to do with opinions or thoughts. If the hat is in your hand, perhaps it is referring to the need to apologize for something. Perhaps you need to be more humble in some situation.

high heels: This image may be about glamour. How comfortable are you with the conventional feminine?

If there are a mix of shoes in your dream (tennis shoes and heels), it may refer to some questions you have about the type of career you've chosen. It could also suggest the need for relaxation (or balance) mixed in with the more formal parts of your life.

shirt: This may be about your feelings. It could also be about your public image. Consider also the phrases "stuffed shirt" (overly proud and arrogant) and "rolling your sleeves up" (getting down to work or business).

shoes: These indicate one's grounding and connection with the world. Shoes can be symbolic of support or independence (i.e., standing on our own two feet).

If you're only wearing one shoe, perhaps you feel unbalanced.

Two different shoes might be symbolic of needing help from some other sources, or if you're not wearing your shoes, then you may need to experience someone else's need before making a judgment about him or her.

See *balance, enantiodromia, shoes,* and *yin/yang.*

skirts or pants: These might suggest the lower passions. Pulling them off may be a metaphor for exposing something, perhaps a lie.

suit: This may suggest formality and professional identity.

tuxedo: You may be trying to look good. This could also represent the formal you. Do you feel uptight? Perhaps you need to loosen up.

underpants or underwear: This may indicate the private self and your sexual identity.

uniform: This can represent conformity. Do you want to become independent from the rules?

veil: This could represent something mysterious or suggest something hidden or something that needs to be revealed, perhaps another reality behind this reality (i.e., something you're not seeing).

vest: This may signal something you may be empowered by or have an interest in (vested).

See *veneer* or *pretending* as well.

clouds: Depending on whether it is a bright (clear) or dark (overcast) day, they could either be uplifting or depressing.

Consider also the phrase "To cloud the issue," meaning to make something less clear or to confuse an issue.

It could also be a place where you store something (i.e., the cloud of the internet). Consider also the expression "head in the clouds," which might indicate that you're not being rational about something, you're in denial, or you're being flighty and ungrounded.

Clouds can also refer to transitions or the confusion you may experience during transitions and changes. Look closely at what you are moving through as you transition.

See also *fog, blurry,* and/or *confusion.*

clown: This could suggest self-depreciation or not taking something too seriously. It may represent your childlike nature or the childish side of you.

Notice the clown's emotional expression because it probably reflects your own.

This can also reflect an image of horror. Because of the makeup and/or mask that a clown wears, it can also represent something or someone who is not what it appears to be (see also *cartoon, face paint, makeup, mask,* or the *fool* in the *archetypes* section).

Clowns can also reflect your inhibitions or things that inhibit you.

Are you or someone else being thoughtless or insincere?

club: This could be about joining together and belonging. Alternatively, it could be about not belonging or a desire to belong. This could also be a weapon (see *weapons*).

clutter: Are you feeling confused? Are you unorganized or unfocused? Perhaps you need to become more organized.

cobra: It might mean that you are mesmerized (charmed) by something or someone. See *snake* in *animals*.

cobwebs: If you see these in an attic or roof, they could refer to old ideas and beliefs that you may be caught up in. Are you neglecting some issue or your responsibilities? It is also possible that your talents are not being fully used (see also *web* and *spider* in *animals*).

cocoon: This suggests a place of safety and a place of potential transformation, rejuvenation, or healing.

coconut: This can represent perseverance or hardness. It can also be about a getaway, relaxation, and the need to go on vacation.

See also *fruit*.

code: The *code* could be about finding some way of unlocking the door/gate to a much-needed change or finding the answer to some problem.

coercion: Is someone trying to get you to do something that you don't think is right?

Do you feel out of control? See also *pushing*.

coffee: The need to gain insight before making a decision. Perhaps you need to sit back and slow down. It's also a symbol for companionship and hospitality.

Do you need to be more alert about something going on around you? Perhaps you need to get together and catch up with old friends.

coffee shop: See *café*.

coffin: This contains the end of something or someone, or it could be a reminder of your mortality. To put someone into a coffin might suggest that you want to get him or her out of your life. Sometimes it reflects the end of a relationship or the fear that it is ending.

Coffins are often symbols of the things we bury that we don't want in our lives.

If you are in the coffin, it might reflect the fact that some part of you is dying or that you wish to get rid of that part.

If a coffin is exhumed, that might represent something from the past being dredged up and coming back to consciousness.

See also *casket*.

coincidence: This may mean that something serendipitous or fortuitous may be presenting itself.

You may need to pay closer attention to what is going on around you and the opportunities and openings that are presenting themselves.

What seems like a coincidence may also represent a sign or guidepost. It may suggest that you need to reconnect with the more imaginative side of yourself. See *synchronicity*.

coins: May represent something of small value or things of little concern. Perhaps you're selling yourself short?

However, certain coins can be symbolic of something of great value (as with buried treasure or a collector's coins).

Alternatively, coins can refer to overlooked opportunity. Silver coins might be about spirituality, self-worth, or intuition while gold coins might be about high value and wealth.

Gold coins can also symbolize specific people you value. The number of coins can also help with identifying who these people are. For example, if you have two children, they may be represented by two gold coins.

Of course, the gold coin can also represent the real you—the you beneath the mask that you project to others or the negative narrative that you may tell about yourself.

If the coin is attached to a chain, perhaps the real you is being restricted or limited in some way. See also *chain*.

Coins may also be symbolic of love or finding love, especially if you pick them up from the ground.

If it's a black or dirty coin, you may be rejecting something that you know won't work for you. These dirty black coins could also suggest that you are earning money in a grubby way or that you don't want to earn it in this way.

Flipping a coin might suggest that you're not acting seriously about some decision or you're taking a chance with something or someone (see also *money*).

colander: Perhaps you can't keep your emotions contained, or maybe you need to separate your feelings in order to be objective. Consider the phrase "Mind like a sieve," meaning that you're having trouble remembering things or need to spend more time recalling certain things.

cold: This can symbolize missed warmth or holding back emotions. There is a feeling of neglect in this symbol. Consider the phrase "Left out in the cold." You may need to be more compassionate, caring, charitable, and/or responsive toward others.

cold-blooded: Perhaps you or someone else is being too callous or cruel.

cold wind: This may indicate that something may blow through your life and bring a chill or slow you down in regard to your goals or intentions. Perhaps someone is rejecting you or your idea.

Are you bitter about something, or have you made a cold and bitter remark? A feeling of doom could be giving you a chill. Sometimes it can be a metaphor for seeking warmth.

coliseum: Are you making a spectacle of yourself? Are you performing and trying to make an impression?

collapse: Are you exhausted or falling apart? Perhaps you're pushing too hard?

collapsing: The image of collapsing may be about pushing too hard or a loss of trust in your own judgment about something.

Have you lost sight of or given up on your goals?

collar: Is something too restrictive or confining?

collective unconscious: According to Freud, the unconscious can be compared by analogy to an iceberg in that significant events take place beneath the surface. Jung divided this up between the collective unconscious and the personal unconscious.

Jung went further by suggesting that there were inherited psychic materials—what he called archetypes—that we all collectively share and also reside in the unconscious mind. He called this the *collective unconscious*.

He posited that there were two components within this collective—the *instinctual* and the *archetypal*. Instinct was thought to be that which determines one's actions while the archetypes determined one's apprehension.

These archetypes both hide and reveal themselves in images. Often when they show up in a dream, they are *numinous* in nature, a charged experience that seems almost sacred.

It's as though these primal images are trying to rise out of the darkness and into the light.

In short, these images give us glimpses into our deep unconscious minds, informing our experience and actions within this arena we call reality.

The collective unconscious seems to never recognize finality, seeing only a continuous stream of change.

See also the *archetypes* section.

colors: These can represent emotions, especially when they are vibrant.

Colors can signify the vitality of something or the self. But *colors* can also symbolize a subculture or group, gang, club, country, school, or team affiliation (e.g., something one belongs to or desires to belong to).

To show your colors is to make a stand and reveal what you stand for and who you really are. To lower or strike your colors may mean that you want to give up on something (i.e., to stand down, surrender, defeat, or retreat).

The phrase "With flying colors" could be about being successful. A false color could be about deception.

Interestingly, if you have not seen the color of something in the dream before, it's new to you, or it's never been invented, it *may* speak to an aspect of yourself that you have heretofore not seen or been aware of.

> **beige:** This could mean blah, neutral, and nondescript.

> **black:** This could symbolize separation, the unconscious, evil, depression, and/or the shadow side of the self. If a person or creature is dressed in all black, this may represent a dark side to your personality (see *shadow* in the *archetypes* section).

Insight: Black in a dream can be symbolic of the unknown, the unconscious mind, and mystery. It invites the dreamer to dig deeper into the unconscious to gain a better understanding. It can also represent the spiritual and the divine.

Alternatively, it can be a symbol for danger, depression, rejection, and sadness. Black can represent death but also an ending from which something new can grow, so it can be a symbol for possibilities, transformation, and potential as well. Black can represent the darker sides to your personality (see shadow in archetypes section).

> **black and white:** Carl Jung also suggested that a black-and-white pattern might represent the unification of opposites (e.g., the conscious and unconscious forming a greater self).

> The black and white might also suggest a need to unify or bring together parts of yourself that are in conflict.

blue: This could symbolize depression if it is dark or intuitive awareness that's almost spiritual in nature if it is light blue. Blue is said to soothe illness and treat pain.

Insight: There is some evidence that colors on the blue end of the spectrum are high energy and might have some health effects. For example, the use of blue laser therapy for arthritis pain, strains, and carpal tunnel has been ADA approved.

brown: This could signify dullness, earthy aspects, or the material world.

gold: This could represent something valuable and significant or something of great worth. (This could be a moral value, an object, a goal, or a behavior.) Sometimes it symbolizes the soul.

If you see a gold nugget, this could represent a small piece of information that may be very important. Perhaps you've overlooked something.

Finding gold can also represent a bright outlook on something or the need for a brighter outlook.

gray: This is a dull, hard, officious, perhaps even an unhappy color.

green: This could symbolize serenity and healing through growth. Nature and fertility are also associated with this color.

Some research has shown that laying a transparent green sheet over reading material can increase reading speed and retention.

Green can also represent tranquility, harmony, balance, good luck, and health. Some suggest that a light green work environment can decrease upset stomachs.

Green is also a synonym for being environmentally conscious.

It is the color of the heart chakra that represents complex emotions such as compassion and tenderness. It is said that it is from here that we emotionally relate to others.

Someone who is green is someone inexperienced or childish. See *green man*.

pink: Pink can be a calming color. Pink can also represent softness and femininity along with tenderness and love.

Red or pink and gray together can suggest depression.

Pink smoke may be a metaphor for something obfuscating your ability to get clear about something or someone that looks harmless but may not be.

"In the pink" is a phrase that often refers to feeling good or being healthy.

purple: See *violet or indigo*.

rainbow: This can represent an awareness of the beauty of life in the midst of problems and difficulties, or it can be a visible blessing. It can also represent happiness, hope, and a bridge between your higher spiritual and earthly grounded self.

In some cultures, rainbows can represent redemption and forgiveness.

It is also a symbol for gay pride and acceptance in Western cultures.

red: This could symbolize passion or vigor. This can also be an aggressive color as with anger. It's also a chakra color and a base color related to one's vitality. It can be thought of as an energizing color.

To be red-faced might also symbolize embarrassment.

orange: This may represent the act of blending or bringing balance. It can also refer to warmth and be a spiritual color.

silver: This color can be about the moon, intuition, and the feminine aspects of one's self. This can also reflect understated confidence.

If something is given on a silver plate, it could be about receiving something unearned.

violet or indigo: This can be about spiritual feelings. Indigo is related to the third-eye chakra or inner eye and thus related to spiritual insight and intuition.

white: This can represent clarity and purity, or it can designate an ethnicity. It can also represent awareness or light feelings.

In some dreams, whiteness can be a harbinger of something threatening and darker.

The color white probably has special meaning for you. For me, white is elegant, pristine, and high-class. What is it for you?

yellow: This can represent lightness vitality, and hopefulness but also cowardice or caution, depending on context.

It's a cheery color, but it's also quite fatiguing to the eye. It's also about grabbing attention (i.e., grabbing the spotlight). As a chakra color, it may be related to self-worth.

Insight: Color meanings are a bit iffy. You should be especially careful to interpret their meanings based on the resonance and meaning for you. Color interpretation is also cultural in nature.

Jennifer Kyrnin (http://webdesign.about .com/od/colorcharts/l/bl_colorculture .htm) has developed a cultural color chart that you may want to refer to. The previously outlined meanings are Western in nature.

The theosophist C. W. Leadbetter also created a chart in his book *Man Visible and Invisible* (1902) that doesn't seem to follow any of the current cultural or Western definitions.

A similar color chart was used to interpret auras or what the theosophists Annie Besant and Leadbetter described as "thought forms." They believed that thoughts were things radiating vibrations and floating forms. These ideas were presented in their treatise, *Thought Forms* (1901). In all fairness, their definitions were slanted toward his understanding of the spirit world and the concept of auras. My symbol interpretations tend to be somewhat more prosaic.

Color and music also have a close relationship in dreams. Some people have shown a connection between color meaning, sound, and the zodiac.

The musical scale is an ascending chromatic scale where the frequencies range from low to high on both the visual and auditory scale. The zodiac symbols don't follow a consistent pattern, however, in that there are many zodiac color wheels and all are very different.

This attempt to coordinate color and sound to affect an emotional state is nothing new. Both Isaac Newton and Pythagoras created their own scale.

Also see *music*.

In some ancient societies, such as the Chinese and Egyptian cultures, people practiced a type of color therapy. Today we call this chromotherapy, though there is little evidence as to its lasting effectiveness.

That's not to say that colors don't affect us, but the effects don't seem to last or create any substantial changes in our overall behaviors over time. However, several holistic treatments use color in their therapies.

column: This may suggest something that supports you, something that holds you up, or that you support. See **pillar**.

Consider it being a possible pun for a newspaper column or a column (line) of people.

coma: Comas in dreams may indicate helplessness and an inability or difficulty in functioning. Perhaps you are not prepared or not coping well with some major changes.

comet: This might suggest impending change or the birth of something new. It is also a messenger from the unconscious and an awakening, or it could be something just passing through. Like shooting stars, comets can be about inspiration and ideas.

comments: This can be about communicating or a lack of communication. If the comment is *snarky*, perhaps you're being insensitive or inappropriate.

commune: Living in a commune may symbolize your search for an alternate way of being. Are you looking for a less complicated and simpler lifestyle? Perhaps you want to live life in harmony with your environment instead of in competition with it.

There is always a little stress between living in the material world and trying to stay connected with the spiritual.

This image might also indicate that you want to withdraw from society and live your life by your own rules.

By being in community, you may need to nurture your relationships with others.

communion: Are you having difficulty reconciling the spiritual and material worlds.

This can suggest that you may be experiencing some internal conflict in that you may be having some difficulty distinguishing between feelings or desires and values.

Are you trying to get some sort of acceptance from someone or some group?

community: Are you looking for something to belong to? Do you need to nurture your relationships with people more often?

compass: This may represent an attempt to find your direction in a situation or in life. People can feel lost if their inner compasses aren't working or they are broken (see *north, south, east,* and *west*).

compensation theory: Some psychologists say that dreams compensate for what the dreamers are not manifesting in their waking lives. For example, the cold, calculating pragmatist of the waking world might have dreams of feelings, compassion, and intuition to aid in the psychological balance of the individual.

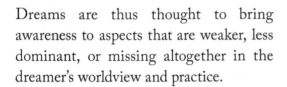

Dreams are thus thought to bring awareness to aspects that are weaker, less dominant, or missing altogether in the dreamer's worldview and practice.

competition: Do you need to grow or expand your knowledge or abilities to accomplish some goal? Do you need to be more assertive? Are you challenging yourself enough or too much?

Are you trying to prove yourself worthy? If you win, it could mean a positive self-image, but if you lose, then it might suggest a lack of self-esteem.

Insight: Note that this type of dream seems to be more frequent with males and more prevalent in adolescence than in adulthood.

complex: This could possibly reflect a pattern of emotions, perceptions, wishes, or memories in our personal unconscious. Some of these patterns can manifest themselves somatically (i.e., through the body).

Severely negative, untreated, and/or denied emotional patterns are thought by some psychologists to lead to neuroses such as obsessive-compulsive disorders but also perfectionism, poor impulse control, or extremely low feelings of self-worth.

All too often when we deny our complexes, our worries, and our repressed fears, our demons can possess us. We then allow another force and energy to take over our lives, both internally and externally.

Both Jung and Freud thought that these unconscious patterns were the most important factors influencing our waking behaviors and attitudes.

computer: This could symbolize communication or the rational, unemotional mind.

If the screen goes black, perhaps you are looking at something wrong. Perhaps you need to reevaluate some problem, issue, or decision (i.e., reboot and start over). See also *crash* and/or *internet*.

concentration camp: This could possibly refer to a fear of differences or an attempt to control what you fear or find distasteful as a means of keeping these uncomfortable feelings out of sight.

This could also be symbolic of being imprisoned by your inflexible demons, beliefs, or points of view.

concert: This could be about working in harmony with someone or something. It could also be working in harmony with yourself. See *music and/or symphony*.

confession: Are you feeling guilty about something? Is there something you need to get off your chest and reveal? Do you need to be forgiven and/or be absolved for some action, belief, or behavior? Do you need to forgive or absolve someone?

This image might also suggest the beginning or the need for some changes in your life.

If you're in a confessional, perhaps there is something that you can no longer keep hidden or keep to yourself.

conflict: This can reflect any difficulty with parts of your own personality, a decision you must make, or a problem with situations or people outside yourself.

This can also represent a conflict of opposites within one's psyche. For example, all human beings have both a feminine and masculine nature. The former reflects all the direct relational, emotional, and nonrational aspects of one's ego-self, and the latter reflecting the abstract, objective, unemotional, and rational aspects.

If there are people in the dream with whom you have conflicts in your waking life (the main figures representing people with whom you don't really get along with), this may reflect how you may be treating yourself. For example, if it means that you don't really respect them, it could also be a reflection of the lack of respect that you may be giving yourself (e.g., it's you that you aren't getting along with).

This self-critique or lack of respect for yourself may be what leads you into some of the messes and questionable choices that plague your well-being.

If there's someone in the dream or some circumstance that you don't have a conflict with but you would normally experience conflict in the situation within the waking world, this may suggest an unacknowledged conflict that you may need to attend to. It could also indicate the need for greater harmony.

See also *anima/animus* in the *archetypes* section.

See also *people.*

You might also look at *battle, dissonance, fighting,* or *soldier/warrior.*

confrontation: If you are confronting a person or you are confronted by someone in a dream, it may be about someone or some issue that you are facing in your waking life. This may be a means for you to safely deal with inner or outer conflicts.

It can also be a means for dealing with your fears.

confusion: This may represent inner discord, chagrin, embarrassment, or chaos. It could also reflect some anomaly, inconsistency, or paradox in your waking life.

Perhaps you're seeking calmness, peacefulness, order, or clarity.

Sometimes confusion can bring about greater understanding.

See also *blurry*, *fog*, and/or *paradox*.

conquer: If you've conquered or have been defeated, perhaps you need to change direction. Perhaps you need to reevaluate some situation or overcome some limitation.

You may be too competitive or not competitive enough. Are you experiencing some kind of inner or outer conflict?

You may be feeling overwhelmed.

constellation: This may be about some mental process (i.e., the way some things are coming together). It could represent a group of ideas or friends, issues, problems, or solutions.

As a group of stars in the sky, the name of the constellation may also be of some value (see *zodiac* or individual zodiac signs).

constipation: This might represent the fear of letting go of something (e.g., a memory, a hurt, a belief, etc.).

contradiction: Is someone putting you down or disputing your word? Are you in opposition to something or someone? Are you being inconsistent. Perhaps you are feeling negated.

You could also be experiencing an inner conflict.

construction: Perhaps you need to work on improving yourself or building something new in life. If a building is under construction, that may symbolize you are recreating yourself.

construction equipment: Do you have the right equipment to build or create something, or are you equipped, trained, or skilled properly to succeed?

cookie: This could be about a computer cookie. It could also be about someone sweet, a desire, or a treat. So too, it could be about needing special nourishment (i.e., being cared for and loved).

Baking cookies might indicate a need to nourish or to be more optimistic.

Buying a cookie might be about giving into a temptation.

cooking: This could be about the way one transforms the unpalatable to the palatable. See also *chef*.

copper: Unlike silver or gold, which are images we associate with high value, copper might be seen as common and mundane.

To some, this might represent the power of healing.

The healing may be something common, such as accepting one's fate, lot, or current situation. However, you may determine the gold or silver of something to be of greater value. Sometimes the greater value is in the more common object.

As a conductor of electricity and a material often used in plumbing, it could also represent the flow of ideas and your connections with others.

coral: This can be about protection and beauty. It can also symbolize the need for purification.

Because it may be a symbol for negative effects on the environment, you might also want to explore this aspect.

corn: Harvesting and corn can be about abundance or recognizing and taking advantage of abundance.

Certain foods are attached to good and/or bad memories. Some are comfort foods, but you may find others distasteful. If the corn is about to be harvested because it's ripe, it might suggest a reward of some type is due to you.

This image could also be about fertility and refer to a sense of fulfillment.

If you are going through tough times, it might be an image of sustaining or building up your strength during hard times.

corner or cornered: Perhaps you're feeling that there's no escape or that you're trapped. Where are your decisions and choices leading you?

To turn a corner might be a symbol for something about to change or a significant benchmark for change (i.e., success is within sight).

corridor: See *house, hallway,* or *tunnel.*

cottage: This could symbolize the familiar house of the self (see *house*). Look closely at the objects within the cottage, and evaluate the general *feel* of the place.

For example, if there is an old, unused altar for worship, it may be speaking to a neglected spiritual aspect of yourself.

See also *furniture.*

coughing: This could be about getting rid of or expelling something that's of no use. If you are coughing up blood, perhaps the image represents useless or wasted energy (see also *blood*). Perhaps you're doing something that's not productive.

There might also be some communication caught in your throat that you need to bring out.

counterfeit money: Is something, someone, or you yourself not being genuine? Are you being something you are not? If money is a metaphor for love, is someone's love not genuine, or are you questioning some relationship? Are you feeling unworthy or unvalued?

counting: If you are counting in a dream, perhaps you are trying to control something. Are you trying to make something count? Consider the phrase "Counting on something or someone." Can people *count* on you? If you are counting numbers, look at *numbers* for further information.

If you are counting money, you could be thinking about something that's due to you. It could be symbolic of greediness or reflect a focus on the material versus the spiritual. It could also be about the relational aspects of yourself or your life.

See also *money.*

country: If you are escaping to another country, perhaps you desire (or you are currently experiencing) some change in your life. Perhaps you are going through a transition into something new, something different than what you are currently experiencing. If you're lost in the other country, perhaps you are not ready for a change.

countryside: Are you searching for a simpler way of life? Perhaps you're too stressed and need to relax. Are things too constricted? Do you need to open up or become more independent and free from others?

couple: Seeing a couple in your dream could be about a relationship or reflect something missing in your life. What the couple is doing in the dream will provide more information.

courage: Being courageous in a dream may be about a new understanding. This might reflect the need to deal directly with some issue you have been avoiding in your waking life.

courtroom: This can be about the resolution of conflicts, though in some cases it might refer to either justice or injustice, pain or resolution, redemption or loss. If you are the defendant, you may be dealing with some fears, guilt, or the emotions associated with being judged.

coven: This is often a reference to a community of witches. The image of a coven brings to mind a group or community of like-minded people, a family of believers who may have something to offer you. These people may have answers to some questions you've had, perhaps even those you may have had about your life and the direction it's going.

See also *witches*.

cover: Covers of any kind may be about things hidden or suppressed. Are you trying to emulate someone you admire? This can sometimes lead to not being fully yourself, warts and all.

If something is covering your body, ask yourself, "Do I feel embarrassment or shame?"

If you're covering a pool, are you hiding your emotions?

cow: See *animal terms*.

coward: See *cowardly lion*.

cowardly lion: Perhaps this symbolizes a person who acts tough but misses a golden opportunity out of fear. Are you feeling inadequate? Do you need to face your fears?

Are you or someone you know wearing the mask of the tough guy, thus keeping people at bay?

Are you limiting yourself by adhering to an inner dialogue that leaves you feeling less than?

Are you being overly self-protective?

cowboy: This could be about independence and romance or perhaps the salt of the earth. It could also be a derogatory image referring to an arrogant, testosterone-filled, chauvinistic, undiplomatic, gun-toting, swaggering, foulmouthed, shoot-from-the-hip jerk. Are you being this jerk?

crane: This may represent heavy lifting, burdens, ascending to great heights, or rising above it all. A falling crane can represent crashing back to earth after you have achieved great success.

If you see one at a construction job, it can be about building something new (see also *construction*).

crap: This can symbolize junk or something worthless (see *feces*).

crash: If a *car crashes*, it might suggest the life path you are on is colliding with someone else's or with your goals. Has someone hurt your pride? If you aren't the cause of the crash, especially if you're just the passenger, are you or someone else being reckless in life?

If a *plane crashes*, perhaps you have goals that are too high and unrealistic. Both the plane and car crash could indicate a loss of confidence.

A *stock market crash* might represent a major setback to your hopes, dreams, and life goals.

A *computer crash* might signify that your life is out of control or that something has ended and is forever gone.

A *train crash* might be about chaos in your life. You may feel that nothing is going to plan, and you're worried about not reaching your goal (see also *derailment* and *train*).

crater: This may represent a memory of a past hurt.

crawling: This could possibly represent a regressive movement and/or taking your time with something.

crawlspace: This could symbolize your subconscious mind.

crayons: This could be about a childhood memory. Crayons can represent a time when you were more carefree. Do you need to think outside the lines? Do you need to be more creative?

crazy: When a crazy person appears, you might feel threatened. If you feel crazy, you might think about controlling your behaviors. There is a loss of control here and perhaps an aspect of falling apart.

cream: This possibly represents the sweeter things in your life. Consider the phrase "Cream of the crop" as a symbol. Perhaps you want to be top-notch but aren't.

creature: This could possibly reflect feelings of fear and insecurity (see also *monsters*).

credit card: This could be about your self-worth, value, and/or credibility. Alternatively, are you in debt or indebted to someone? If you've lost one of these, ask yourself, "Am I being too careless?"

credit score: Do you measure up? Is this a symbol of not measuring up or an indicator of your sense of self-worth?

creek: Are you up a creek without a paddle? If it's running freely, is everything running smoothly? If it's dried up, are you cut off from your spiritual or emotional self? If it's dry, are you emotionally dried up and/or exhausted?

cremation: This may represent an end to some way of being or some phase in life. If the person who's cremated is someone you know, then perhaps you are trying to deal with his or her loss.

crescent: This may signal the emergence of your feminine nature (see *moon*).

crib: This image is quite interesting. It may reflect your more immature dealings or relationships with some aspect of yourself or your life.

It can also refer to the creation of a new idea or way of being.

Alternatively, it can reflect your desire to have a baby. Consider also that the image can refer to the colloquialism for your house and home. See also *bed* in *furniture*.

crime: If you or someone else is committing a crime, perhaps you are experiencing guilt in your life. If you are a criminal, perhaps you're looking for too many shortcuts in life or you feel you're entitled.

cripple: This possibly represents the feeling of being limited or disabled in some way (emotionally, socially, physically, or spiritually).

critic: Are you being too judgmental of yourself or others?

crocodile: This could symbolize hidden strength and power (see *animal terms*).

cross: For millennia, the cross has been a symbol with special spiritual meaning. The cross has four points symbolizing the four cardinal directions, the four seasons, the four winds, the four archangels, and the four gospels.

The Celts saw it as representing the four quarters as follows:

- *north* for wisdom and stability, winter, and death;

- *east* for learning, knowledge, spring, beginnings, and youth;

- *south* for passion, strength, and summer; and

- *west* for intuition, inner knowledge, emotion, endings, and autumn.

This symbolism is also seen in the Native American medicine wheel. In Christian tradition, the cross can mean resurrection just as it does with the Egyptian ankh (see *ankh*).

Consider also the idiomatic phrase "A cross to bear," meaning a responsibility or unpleasantness that you have to put up with.

See also *crucify*.

Cross-dressing: Seeing someone or yourself cross-dressing may indicate that you need to attend to some part of your personality—feminine or masculine aspects. If you are a male and you dress as female, perhaps a feminine aspect such as your compassion, caring, or intuition needs to come forward in your approach to some issue.

If you are a female and you dress as a male, perhaps you need to exercise some male aspect of yourself (e.g., assertiveness, decisiveness, or action-orientation). See also *transgender*.

crossing guard: Are you trying to be careful about the risks you're taking? See also *guard*.

crossroad: This is symbolic of the point where you must make a decision. It may be a place where two ideas or people cross paths and interact. See also *intersection*.

crowd: Are you feeling crowded out or lost in the crowd? You might want to find a way to stand out in the crowd. Crowds can also be about anonymity.

crown: This is often symbolic of being chosen or recognized. It can symbolize the noble side of yourself. It can represent your inner authority, a high achievement, or a crowning achievement.

crucify: If you are being crucified or you are seeing someone crucified, perhaps you are feeling guilty. Are you punishing yourself? A crucifix may mean the same thing but may also be connecting with your inner spiritual or Christ consciousness. See *Christ* in the *archetypes* section.

See also *cross*.

cruel: If you or someone else is being cruel in a dream, perhaps there is a hidden anger and hostility in you that is being released in the dream. This may also reflect a shadow aspect of yourself.

cruise ship: This may refer to some emotional journey you are navigating. If you are just *cruising*, perhaps you're going through life with little effort. See also *ship*.

crutch: Do you feel incapacitated? Are you using something or someone to hold you up instead of standing on your own two feet? It can also be a substitute for personal support.

Using a crutch could symbolize a sense of weakness.

crying: This may signal a release of tension, joy, sorrow, or grief. Sometimes if you've held back some sadness during the day, the dream can act as a pressure release. This can be cleansing or healing. Sometimes we cry for ourselves, and sometimes we cry for others. Sometimes we cry for the whole world (see *whining*).

crypt: This may reflect feelings associated with death. A crypt could represent a place of hidden forces and perhaps a connection with the unconscious. Sometimes the image refers to things, feelings, or thoughts that you've buried (see *grave*).

crystal: This could represent a sense of the eternal or something becoming clear in our minds (i.e., crystal clear). Sometimes we're just looking for clarity.

Crystals can also represent the need for healing.

crystal ball: This object could represent one's intuition or an attempt to see what the future may bring.

It could also represent the need to look into yourself for answers.

Are you afraid to go forward for fear of the future?

cubist: This could be like a painting by Picasso. Several sides of an object could be presented simultaneously. Perhaps you are not seeing all sides to an issue, or maybe you are.

cuddle: To cuddle or to snuggle is a loving gesture. Perhaps you need to be more loving (maybe even to yourself).

You may need to get close to someone.

cup: This possibly represents the feminine aspect of nourishment. A cup, cauldron, or the Holy Grail is a ritual object of feminine gender.

Insight: The Celtic warrior Bran's life-restoring cauldron was considered a grail symbol. In physical essence, the cup in the ritual is often crescent-shaped. This symbolism links it to the moon, another feminine aspect representing the sacred vessel or the womb. There are many symbolic references to the feminine, the Holy Grail being one of them.

Though descriptions of the Last Supper of Jesus speak of a cup in which Jesus poured wine and offered it as his own blood so that his followers could drink it in remembrance, the famous painting by Leonardo da Vinci shows no cup on the table, only a plate or dish. Was the plate or dish the original grail?

Whether a dish or cup, both might represent the feminine aspect of spiritual nourishment. It has a life-restoring quality. The dish may also be seen as a sacred vessel that would have a feminine aspect—the womb. In magic the symbol for a cup or container is often a crescent, the shape of the moon, which is another feminine aspect. The cauldron is the symbol for the goddess.

The Holy Grail is the symbol of rebirth, perhaps even reincarnation—the passage from life to death and beyond.

Jung suggested that the Holy Grail (or Grael) was symbolic of the principle of individuation or the process of knitting together an individual's opposites into a whole. As a religious symbol, both individuation and the grail represent a divine guide toward wholeness. The quest for the grail in the Arthurian legends thus becomes an archetypal story of the search for humankind's true nature.

To see a cup in your dream might also represent love, nurturance, and the womb. The cup may also signify rejuvenation and healing.

Alternatively, it could indicate transcendence into a realm of higher consciousness.

Is the cup half full or half empty? Do you see life from an optimistic or pessimistic point of view.

A cup with a broken handle suggests your feelings of inadequacy and your anxieties about an inability to handle a particular situation.

A broken cup in your dream may suggest feelings of powerlessness, guilt, and/or low self-esteem. Perhaps you feel unqualified or inadequate to deal with a situation.

If the cup is a *chalice*, it could represent your need for spiritual nourishment. Perhaps you are on a search or quest for your individual self and for a more meaningful existence.

cupboard: This might be about hidden truths or personal secrets. If you're putting something into the cupboard, perhaps there's something you're trying to hide.

It's also a place to store memories.

Cupid: This might represent a love interest. It might also suggest that you may need to take a chance in some relationship. See also *arrow* as well as *Eros and Logos*.

curious or curiosity: Are you being too nosy? Are you having difficulty understanding something or trying to understand some mystery?

Has something or someone piqued your interest?

Are you trying to overcome apathy (i.e., trying to care about something)? Is someone digging into your life? How does that feel?

See also *surprise* and *unexpected*.

Insight: Alice's curiosity in Lewis Carroll's book *Alice's Adventures in Wonderland* led her deep within her unexplored self where she learned several lessons about life as well as her own behavior.

Even though curiosity can be dangerous (remember that it killed the cat), it can also be what is necessary to grow as a human being.

A person without curiosity may no longer be growing/maturing.

See also *rabbit hole*.

curtains: You can either open them to reveal something or close them to hide something.

cutting: This may mean you want to sever or cut connections with someone or some feeling or desire. It could mean you want to cut something or someone out of your life. It could also be about cutting something out of yourself (e.g., a feeling, a habit, a painful memory). See *dagger, knife, saw, self-injury,* or *sword*.

cyclone: See *tornado* or *storm*.

cyst: This is often representative of a growth or a morbid collection of memories or feelings that aren't adding to your life.

D

dagger: This is an image for aggressiveness, anger, force, or hatred. It can also represent a penis (see *sword* or *knife*).

daemon: A strong sense of otherness in a dream can suggest the presence of the daemon. This may be similar to the shadow self (see *shadow* in the *archetypes* section).

The daemon can be an inner voice urging you toward some action in the same way an angel would, though with the daemon image, one often has to wrestle with it in order to learn its secrets.

It also serves the spiritual aspect of one's nature. A person or place can often represent this in spirit. Mine is found in most forests, especially redwood forests or in the Australian Outback. Many creative people experience the daemon through the torment they experience in the creative process.

When I come out of my normally reserved shell, I become powerful in the process, and I reveal my daemon.

See also *muse* and/or *angel*.

dairy: This could symbolize the desire to be nurtured and well cared for.

dam: Perhaps this is about bottling something up or holding something back.

damage: This could perhaps symbolize an injury, a loss, or negative change.

damn: If you're damned, you might want to use caution in some situation, or maybe you're being too concerned about what others think of you.

dampen: To dampen or wet something may be about mild consequence or the slight negation of the consequence as a result of some personal action. It can also symbolize the subduing of your spirits, hopes, dreams, or behaviors.

dancing: This could be a symbol for feeling at one with someone, something, or yourself. It could also signify being in harmony with the world and ourselves. It can represent one's dance with life or the desire for intimacy. Going to a dance could be symbolic of celebration. Ritual dancing could suggest the spirit within.

Dancing around crazily as though on some kind of drug might suggest things may be getting out of hand. It may also reflect how you fear others may view you.

dance class: Perhaps you need to learn to let go or need to learn new steps to some new activity, endeavor, or way of expressing yourself.

dance floor: This possibly reflects your need to be more expressive.

dandruff: Perhaps you're misusing your power. Do you need to rethink your approach to something?

danger: Is something threatening change? Is something making you feel vulnerable or unsteady?

Danish: This could symbolize richness. It may represent something pleasant and satisfying. It could also represent something foreign that you may not be accustomed to.

dare: If you're daring someone, perhaps you're being too domineering. If you're being dared, perhaps you need to be careful that you won't be compromised or embarrassed.

daredevil: The image of a daredevil might suggest the need to be more daring.

It could also suggest that you are being irresponsible.

dark dreams: See *black dreams*.

dark-complexioned person or creature: This could symbolize the shadow aspect (see *black person* or *creature*).

dark matter: This could be symbolic of the unconscious mind.

Insight: The unconscious is a realm of all manner of magic, and one can make objects do anything without fear of failure there. For example, the dead can be resurrected, and we can breathe underwater, fly, and cause all manner of levitation.

In the mind beneath our consciousness, time itself can pass without either cause or effect, count off nonsequentially, and even run in reverse. People and animals become interchangeable and often morph into one another.

In the waking world, this world at the bottom of Alice's rabbit hole would seem irrational and chaotic, and yet there's just a hint of common sense that can lead us to make greater sense of the waking world at the top of the hole.

I believe the dream world is very much like the so-called dark matter that makes up most of the universe. Is it a coincidence that both the unconscious mind and dark matter account for approximately 85 percent or more of their respective totals (the total psyche the individual's perceived and perceivable universe in both the conscious and unconscious mind).

darkness or night: This is symbolic of the unknown, secrets hidden, mystery, potential, or a place of fear. What is hidden to you?

Darkness or the encroaching night could be a metaphor for old age or the end of one's life.

Consider also that it might reflect the death of the ego or certain aspects of oneself. It is also a symbol for the unconscious mind.

Do you need to keep some part of yourself under control? Being lost in the darkness might suggest desperation, insecurity, or depression. To be in a dark room might suggest that you are waiting for something or someone. Are you curious about what might happen?

Consider the phrase "It is always darkest before the dawn," which highlights a new beginning.

A dark heart may represent one's shadow self or what seems to be an impoverishment in one's nature (see *shadow* in the *archetypes* section).

As with many cosmological origin stories, darkness is likened to chaos and disorder that can only be dispelled through light or the *ordering* force. Note that this seems true for both theology and science as with the big bang.

Insight: Sometimes the quenching of the light of reason and consciousness allows for a connection with our source—our greater spirit. As Moses climbed and became more perfect, it was in the darkness that he was able to *see* God.

Darkness can be experienced as enshrouding or menacing (i.e., something terrifying or unpredictable). It can also mirror the ocean's abyss or the loneliness of the void.

There are hidden treasures to be found in the darkness of one's being if one can endure the enshroudment.

In alchemy the darkness is the nigredo (the first stage of the ancient alchemical process of turning lead into gold) signifying the eclipse of the ego's point of view, which needs to happen before the transformation toward wholeness can take place (see *alchemist*). Carl Jung thought of this as one of the steps toward what he called individuation or becoming a whole human being. This step was thought of as the step where one confronts their shadow so as to bring about a psychological equilibrium (see *shadow* in the *archetypes* section).

See also *void, tunnel, abyss,* and *cave*.

dark night of the soul: This is symbolic of depression. It also refers to the hidden aspects our unconscious minds. The dark night of the soul is a hidden force deep within our psyches that moves our consciousness toward the light and is part of the process of enlightenment.

I said to my soul, be still, and let the dark come upon you which shall be the darkness of God.

—T. S. Eliot, *"East Coker"* No.2 of the Four Quartets

dartboard: Are you feeling targeted by someone? Is there some goal you're shooting for? Perhaps you need to take aim at something new?

Darth Vader: This fictional person or any evil character might suggest a struggle between good and evil or may even represent your shadow aspect. Is something pulling you toward or revealing your dark side?

date: This could represent a need for self-discovery or self-awareness? Perhaps there are hidden aspects that you need to exercise? If you see a particular date in the month or a specific day, perhaps it's an inner reminder. Note the numbers for any significance (see *number*).

daughter: She may represent your ideal self. This image could be your waking relationship with your daughter or your feminine aspect.

If you're a mother, this could represent companionship, emotional bonds, yourself at that age, urges, hurts, lost opportunities, or youth.

If a daughter is in a father's dream, she could represent his feeling self or feelings and judgments about her dating, or she could represent his wife when she was younger.

dawn: This may symbolize rejuvenation, enlightenment, and vitality. It may represent an emergence into a new stage in life or a new beginning.

day: Sunny days might be about the need for clarity or a suggestion that things will get better. A day's passing may be about getting older or managing your life better. An overcast day might suggest some gloom or melancholy, or it could signal that your emotions are blocking out the sun. For dark days, see *darkness*.

daycare: This might suggest that you want to be taken care of or that you need to take care of something yourself.

daydreaming: Basically, we are a daydreaming species. A recent Harvard study suggested that we humans tend to daydream up to 47 percent of the time we're awake. But this is not useless idle time. Other studies have shown that unusual associations and pairings—counterfactuals—take place during visits to what I call Neverland (i.e., the daydream).

From our unrestricted depths come all kinds of strange and new thoughts that often turn out to be quite useful. New possibilities surface beyond what people are already exposed to in their waking lives (Baird and Schooler, 2012).

Many suggest that more creative solutions result when the mind is allowed to wander into Neverland (i.e., in general the better one is at wandering through the borderlands, the more creative they tend to be). When one allows themselves to wander outside the box that their culture has created for their way of being the more likely they are to find a new way.

See also *hypnogogia*.

day's end: See *dusk* or *sunset*.

dead people: These may represent some person or aspect in your life that has died and you are dealing with. You must deal with grief because of the death of a loved one or your own future death and its inevitability. What has ended in your life?

When people die, their physical presences disappear, but the memories of them, what they meant to us, and the lessons learned through them continue to inform our lives.

In this way, they never really leave. They just take on a new form in our lives.

All of us deal with death on a personal level when people we know die. Death usually brings a very big change in the patterns of our lives and forces us to shift our stances and points of view on many things. The unconscious may be trying to bring some of this material to consciousness through our dreams.

If you see certain people's obituaries or their graves or you are at their funerals, you may be processing your or life's dismissal of them from your life. Perhaps they left the job or the neighborhood. Maybe they fell from your affection or fell from grace in general.

If you are talking to the dead, see *necromancer*.

Death, suicide, and murder could all fit under this symbol. Suicide and murder in a dream can symbolize the need to make a change in your life, perceptions, reactions, and circumstances. It's the *active* ending of something (see *transition dreams*).

It is the symbol for actively overcoming something. You might say, "I need to symbolically kill who I am or am being in order to become what I want to be" (see *death* in the *archetypes* section).

Insight: Some dream analysts claim that thoughts of suicide in the waking state are symbolically similar to those in the sleeping state and can be analyzed in a similar manner. This may be partially true; however, if thinking of suicide progresses to frequently planning a suicide (even without acting on it), it can lead to what psychologists call *ideation*.

These thoughts of suicide don't usually lead to actual attempts, but they can lead to gestures (without the conscious intention to die). These gestures or *para-suicides* can, however, lead to accidental death or physical harm. Here's a shocking statistic. Did you know that nearly half of all suicides began with suicidal gestures?

Anyone spending too much time thinking about death should consider consulting a counselor or should be referred to a counselor.

dead end: This may represent the end to the pursuit of some goal. Need to find another way? Perhaps your efforts are leading nowhere. This could also refer to a dead-end job or relationship.

deadline: This could be a preoccupation with time. Perhaps time is running out on something.

deaf: You may need to work on communication. What do you fear

hearing? Is there something or someone you are refusing to hear?

death: This may represent an end to something, a part of you that has died (see the *archetypes* section for more detail). See also *ego death*.

Because death brings forth change, this image can represent change or the need for it. Something has to die in order for change to come.

If you dream about the death of a loved one, it can be about a very big hole that takes some time to deal with. Dreams are a way of dealing. When people we love die, they continue to inform our lives, but they do so through our emotions and memories of what they did or said.

What's amazing is that these memories often come to us when we most need them to help us through our lives or through our grief. Their bodies may be gone, but in a very real way, they are not.

Losing loved ones may also speak to our fears of losing relationships or even cherished parts of ourselves.

The death of those close to us can also alter our sense of self and our place in the world.

Dreams also bring up material we may not have noticed during our waking lives, and in this way, the images can inform and guide us in ways we've not experienced before.

Insight: When death shows up in your dreams, it is the harbinger of change, that which heralds the end to one way of being to make room for something new.

And sometimes death in a dream is an invitation to go deeper into yourself in order to find the energy and power to go after a dream, goal, or achievement in the waking world. Sometimes in order to engage life, you must let go of it.

Because resistance to evil can sometimes give energy to the evil death in a dream can symbolize the need for the active ending of the resistance on the part of the dreamer.

The fear of death is often an impediment to healing and growing. Death's dark aspect is often used to avoid dealing with scary things, and yet there is treasure hidden in the darkness of death's potential.

Death in a dream can point to your inner demons and the need to deal with them appropriately, to take personal responsibility for them, and to accept that they are parts of yourself.

Accepting without becoming and acknowledging one's dark side without judgment begins the journey toward real change. Thus, death can symbolize the need for or the beginning of real growth.

Death in this light is a transpersonal image, a means for transcending the ego-self.

The tragedy of life is not death but what we let die inside of us while we live.

—Norman Cousins

See also *dead people* and *kill or killing*.

death penalty: Perhaps you need to reevaluate your life and the direction you're going in (see also *deadline*).

debate: This may be about some inner turmoil or a need for closure on some issue.

debt: This could represent imbalance, struggle, or anxiety over some personal situation. If you feel indebted to people, it might suggest that you owe someone your loyalty.

decapitate: See *behead*.

decay: Perhaps some situation or relationship has started to fall apart. However, decay needs to happen before something new can happen.

decapitation: If you are witnessing a decapitation in a dream, it may be symbolic of losing your mind or not using your head.

If you feel nothing emotionally while watching this, there might be a disconnect between your head and your heart. Perhaps you need to reconnect with the heart or the soul.

deception: If you're deceiving someone, you may be lying to yourself. Everything may not be going the way you think it is. Are you trying to cover something up?

decline: To decline something offered might signal the rejection of some part of yourself (see also *gift*). It could also be about becoming less than what you were.

decomposing: See *decay*.

decorate: Are you trying to mask something (i.e., putting up a false front)?

decoy: Are you trying to mislead someone?

deer: This image suggests grace, gentleness, alertness, compassion, and perhaps your inner feminine attributes. It can also be a symbol for vulnerability.

defeat: Are you headed in the wrong direction? Is there a lesson to be learned? Do you feel like a failure? Are you feeling overwhelmed? Also see *conquer*.

defecate: This may represent anger (or a loss of temper or control) and hostility released, especially if it's spread everywhere. If one defecates on you, then perhaps you are feeling shit on or feeling you're not worth a shit (i.e., low self-esteem or a feeling of being or having said something dirty, negative, or undesirable).

If you're trying to defecate and can't, perhaps you are having difficulty letting go of something, or perhaps you are too controlling. To find a bathroom covered in feces might suggest that there are some messy feelings that you may need to clean up. If it's a public toilet, then perhaps you are worried about how something may look to others (see *urinate* and *feces*).

defend: Perhaps there's an unacknowledged hurt in your waking life. Sometimes defending others in a dream can suggest that you are projecting your values onto them.

The other people you are defending may also represent an aspect of yourself that you are defending.

Are you being too defensive about something? Do you feel attacked, judged, or criticized?

defibrillation: Do you need reenergizing, or does some goal or project need to be reinvigorated?

deflate: To pop a balloon or a rubber raft or dirigible may reflect your lack of self-esteem or loss of self-worth. It may also reflect impotence with regard to some situation.

Are you disappointed in something, someone, or yourself? Have you lost your interest or hope for something?

deformity: This could symbolize disappointment about yourself. This could also reflect undeveloped parts or aspects of the self. To ignore these aspects may affect not only the flow of your life but your creativity as well.

defriend or unfriend: To defriend or unfriend (as declared in the *Oxford English Dictionary*) someone on Facebook might suggest that your friendships or relationships are drifting apart or that you are feeling disconnected from others.

defiance: Are you going against your better judgment or your conscience? Are you suppressing or resisting some emotion?

Why are you resisting?

deity: See *Buddha, Christ, Christian, church, Judaism, Muslim, Shiva, religion,* and/or *gods and goddesses* in the *archetypes* section.

déjà vu: Is there some unresolved issue that you aren't dealing with? Perhaps there's a message that you need to pay attention to?

Is some personal history or event repeating itself?

delay: Some obstacle may be present. Don't let trouble or stumbling blocks discourage or defeat you.

delight: This may be a positive event or positive change. It could also be a wish for this. Are you looking for more joy in your life?

delinquent: Perhaps you are behind in some endeavor. If there's a delinquent person, it could be about him or her owing you something. Are you selling yourself short and wasting some aspect of yourself?

If you are a juvenile delinquent, are you misbehaving or resisting authority? Are you acting childish and irresponsible? Are you wasting your potential?

deliverance: *Deliverance* might be a metaphor for letting go of something. It could also be about your need to feel protected because you feel vulnerable.

Are there some negative influences that may be affecting you and/or your decisions?

Perhaps you need to be saved from someone, some problem, or yourself.

demand: If someone is demanding something from you, perhaps you are feeling dictated to or controlled. It's also possible that you are making too many demands of others or of yourself.

Are you or someone else being too authoritarian? Are you being too brusque with others?

Are you feeling overburdened by some job, project, or issue?

demeaned: See *mocking*.

dementia: Is there something that is causing you to *lose your mind* or something that is driving you crazy? This could also reflect a worry for yourself or someone else.

demolition: This could symbolize major changes in life. Are you or someone doing something that is wrecking your life?

demon: See *archetypes* section.

denial: If you're denying something in the dream, perhaps you are doing this in your waking life as well. Are you resisting some truth?

If someone is denying you something in the dream, maybe you don't measure up to some expectation. Are you using them as an excuse for not getting what you say you want?

See also *blind*.

dent: If your car has been dented, it could symbolize some self-doubt. It's also possible that something has blemished your reputation.

Have you failed to get even part of some goal accomplished?

dentist: Are you concerned with your appearance? Are you trying to repair your strength or power and/or regain your independence? See also *teeth* in *body terms*.

deported: Are you feeling abandoned or cast out and unwanted or rejected? This could also refer to some part of yourself you've rejected.

depression: To be depressed in a dream or to see someone who is depressed may be a reflection of how you're feeling in your waking life. You may not be feeling good about yourself right now (see *abyss*, *void*, and/or *dark night of the soul*).

If this feeling has gone on for an extended period of time and you feel so physically and emotionally drained that you have trouble getting up in the morning or getting anything done, you should probably seek professional help.

If you are having thoughts about suicide, you should contact one of the suicide hotlines (see *suicide* in this section).

depth psychology: This psychotherapeutic discipline states that the psyche is in part conscious, unconscious, and semiconscious and that uncovering this material can help in healing mental and emotional disorders.

Repressed material is believed to affect a person's behavior. The cast-out material creates a myth with patterns and themes that show up symbolically in one's waking life and dreams. Discovering this material is thought to help one deal with the myths or rejected material in the light of day.

This approach also aids in seeing how societal and cultural material expresses itself and affects the individual. See also *analytical psychology, Carl Jung, James Hillman*, and *Thomas Moore*.

derailment: This might suggest doing something against your own self-interest or against your conscience. It can also represent a plan or goal that has been thrown off track (see also *crash* and *train*).

descending: This could represent past traumas or just getting more down to earth and pragmatic about something. It can also mean a loss of status or importance (e.g., being demoted).

If you're going downstairs into a cellar, you may be going into your subconscious mind. If you are going down to the first floor from some upper floors, perhaps you're looking to be more grounded.

If you're falling down stairs, see *falling*.

desert: Walking across a desert may be about loss and barrenness or loneliness and isolation. Are you feeling deserted or abandoned?

Has your life become a barren wasteland? Do you feel blah and uninteresting? Do you need to add some excitement and purpose to your life?

If you're parched and without water, perhaps you are not in touch with your feelings. Are you missing some emotional expression? It can also suggest a lack of feeling loved or a lack of belonging (see *thirst*). It can also mean being deserted or feeling dry/lifeless.

For some the desert can represent the spiritual and the deeper psyche. Standing in the desert with a breeze blowing across the sands can be like communing with the soul.

desk: See *furniture*.

desperation: This could reflect your waking world feeling of being trapped and powerless and not knowing what to do.

dessert: This can be about indulgence, celebration, or reward. It can also symbolize temptation.

destruction: This might refer to chaos in your life. Are you being self-destructive in the choices you are making? See also *catastrophe, disintegration*, or *ruins*.

detained: To be detained might suggest that you have made some mistakes that you need to reflect upon.

detective or detecting: This might suggest something being searched for. This could also represent something hidden that needs to be revealed, some problem or mystery to be solved.

Are you looking for the truth of something?

If a detective is following you or trying to talk to you, are you feeling guilty about something?

This can also be about the desire for knowledge, understanding, or answers.

See also *scientist*.

determined: This can be a positive masculine trait, but it can also be a negative one too.

Are you spunky, steadfast, dogged, strong-willed, or maybe too inflexible? This can also be symbolic of being gritty or gallant, but it can also suggest that you're being dogmatic, rigid, intolerant, egotistical, hell-bent, and/or unwilling to look at other points of view. Perhaps you need to loosen up a little and be more open.

detonation: This could be a release of one's thunder. See *explosion or eruption* and *thunder*.

detour: This could suggest a change in your direction in life. You could also be avoiding dealing with something directly.

devoured: Are you losing your sense of identity? Are you being taken over or dominated, perhaps by the negative feminine?

diamond: As a jewel, it could represent something of great value. It can also suggest clarity but also vanity or an unyielding (rigid/hard) nature.

A cut diamond could suggest the many facets of your personality or some issue. To see a diamond ring might indicate love or a desire to get married. See also *diamond* under *shapes*.

Diana: See *huntress*.

diaper: This possibly symbolizes your childish nature. To change them might be a metaphor for changing your childish ways or for cleaning up your act or the messes you've made.

diary: This image can represent memories or personal insights. Perhaps you need to look deeper within yourself to know yourself better.

See also *journal*.

If someone else is reading your diary, perhaps you are feeling betrayed (see *betrayal*) or you fear some secret is about to be revealed.

diarrhea: Your life may be getting out of control emotionally, and you might be making a mess of things. It could also be a metaphor for talking too much.

dictator: Are you being too inflexible and/or too controlling, or is someone else?

dictionary: Do you rely too much on the opinions of others? Are you being a know-it-all? Are you being too rigid in your approach to something?

diet: If you're going on or off your diet, do you need more nurturing? Are you making unhealthy choices? Do you need to cut back on something (i.e., do less than or just say no to something)?

digging: This could symbolize uncovering the truth (or burying it). Consider the phrase "Do you dig it?"

dildo: Are you feeling unsatisfied or unstimulated with some part of your life?

dim: This might suggest a lack of or loss of clarity on some situation. It could also be a judgment of intelligence.

dimensionality: If it symbolizes three dimensions instead of two dimensions, this might be pointing out that you're being too shallow, that you need to look more deeply into some issue. Perhaps you're not seeing all sides to something or are not viewing reality correctly.

Seeing only a two-dimensional picture of yourself is similar to not seeing yourself for who you really are. Perhaps you need to put yourself out there more and demand to be recognized.

dining room: See *house terms*.

diner: See *café*.

dinner: The image of going to dinner may be about physical nourishment, emotional nourishment, and/or nurturing. A shared dinner is often about nurturing the soul.

dinosaur: This might reflect an outdated idea or way of being. If you are chased by one, are you feeling as if you're no longer needed?

diplomat: This may be about the need to approach someone or some situation with great care and tactfulness.

diploma: This could represent the successful completion of something. This could represent recognition for something done or done well.

directions: This could be about giving or taking criticism, or it could be about accepting or being in authority (see *north, south, east, west, left,* or *right*).

director: This could be about the need to assume more control over a situation or an indication that you already are in control. Is it enough or too much?

dirigible: This may be a symbol for ambition or an inflated sense of self. This could also represent the feeling of being free. See also *sky*.

dirty: This could represent sexual disgust. This could also suggest low self-esteem and feelings of unworthiness.

Perhaps you're exhibiting less than honorable behavior. Perhaps you need to clean something up (i.e., a social or psychological mess).

disability: This could be about low self-esteem. Have you lost your power or direction in life? What part of your body is disabled (see *body*)?

disagreement: There may be some discord in your life. You could be internally conflicted as well. Your actions or desires may conflict with your stated values.

Do you need to let go of some feud, fight, squabble, hassle, or tension?

Are you or someone else being divisive?

See also *incongruent*.

disappearing: If people or things are disappearing in your dream, this could refer to your fears and anxieties of people leaving you or dying.

These people could also represent aspects of yourself that you have ignored and that are disappearing. If you're disappearing, are you being ignored or overlooked, or are parts of your life or self disappearing? See also *disintegration* or *fading*.

disappointment: This could symbolize real-life disappointments or depression. It can also signal thwarted intentions or expectations.

disaster: This could symbolize your personal anxieties. Perhaps you're afraid of the future. See also *ruins*.

discipline: Perhaps you are not focusing or taking responsibility. You may need to organize yourself better and stick to the goal. Things may be out of control, or you might be out of control and need to become more responsible with your actions.

discovery: Have you discovered some new aspect of someone or yourself? Is there something hidden that you need to reveal and deal with?

disease: This could represent some personal fear or an indication that something physical may be wrong and you need to check it out. The part of the body that's diseased will add meaning to the dream (see also *epidemic*).

disfigured: Perhaps you've been scarred emotionally. Maybe you no longer feel like yourself.

disgrace: Are you feeling guilty about something?

disguise: Are you hiding something? Is it time to face up to something or to reveal your true self?

disgust: Is there some part of yourself you're rejecting? Is there something you're trying to protect yourself from?

disharmony: Is there some friction between you and someone else? Are you feeling some hostility toward someone or something?

See also *dissonance*.

dishes: What are you dishing out? Is there someone you're really interested in? Consider the phrase "She's a dish."

Breaking or broken dishes can signal a feeling of impoverishment, an inadequacy, or a lack of something. This sense of inadequacy might also be reflected in dreams when someone asks for dishes but they are not given or are absent.

If you throw dishes at someone, you may have anger or some internal conflict.

Dirty dishes might reflect the mess you've made of something that you may need to clean up.

dishonest: See *liar*.

disinherit: Perhaps you need to reevaluate your social status.

disinherited: Should you take a closer look at your social or work-related standing?

disinfect: Perhaps you need to cleanse, heal, or resolve hurt feelings or dishonest dealings. Perhaps it's time to clean up some deceit.

disintegrating: If something is disintegrating in your dream, do you feel as though you're losing your mind? Do you feel alienated or that you no longer belong? Do you feel weakened or helpless? Are things in your life coming apart?

Do you feel as though you are on the verge of an emotional breakdown? Does it feel as though you are losing your individuality or identity?

Is some relationship falling apart? See also *catastrophe, destruction, disappearing, dissolve, fading,* or *ruins*.

dislike: If you dislike someone or something in your dream, perhaps there's some part of yourself you dislike.

dismember: Something in your life may be falling apart, including you. Perhaps you're feeling cut off and isolated or experiencing some loss. Note which part of the body is cut off and then look up that part under *body*.

dissect: Perhaps you're trying to get to the bottom, heart, or essence of something. Dissecting a cadaver might suggest that you are trying to reveal some aspect of yourself. Are you trying to figure something or someone out?

dissolve: This can be about the end of something or the integration of different aspects of yourself. See also *disintegrating* and *divorce*.

dissonance: Does music sound disharmonious or out of tune? Does there seem to be an inconsistency between what you believe is true and what evidence is telling you is true or between what you want reality to be and what it is?

Are you ignoring some dissonance or inner conflict in your life?

See also *conflict* and/or *incongruent*.

distress: Are you experiencing unhappiness or worries in your waking life? Do you need to get rid of your emotional baggage and/or burdens?

ditch: This could be about being trapped or a means of escape. It may also reflect a means for *draining away* your emotions.

divination: Looking into a blackened mirror, a crystal ball, or a cup full of tea leaves might be symbolic of a premonition, prediction, prophecy, intuition, or insight. Perhaps you're looking for an answer to something. You may also want to get a sense of something eluding you (see *ESP*, *medium*, *Ouija board*, *premonition*, and *tea leaves*).

Sometimes divination might refer to being able to forecast an outcome and thus be similar to a prognosis (i.e., a suggestion of what might happen regarding some personal behavior or action of the dreamer).

See also *oneiromancy*.

divine child: See the *archetypes* section.

divine mother: See the *archetypes* section.

diving board: Are you about to take the plunge into some endeavor? Think carefully before you dive into it. Consider also the condition of the water (see *water*).

divorce: This may not be about leaving your spouse but separating yourself from some issue or some situation in order to get a better look at it.

Dreaming of someone else divorcing a spouse may be highlighting your inner conflicts or your desire to unite these aspects.

It can be about letting go or disconnecting emotionally from something or someone.

It might also reflect your desire to quit, let go, or give up something or someone.

Perhaps there's some part of yourself that you want to divorce yourself from.

dizzy: Are you confused about something? Are you having trouble deciding something?

Do you need to find a way to balance your life?

DNA helix: This could possibly be about renewal. This can represent a connection between the spirit and body. It also represents science and one's identity. Are you questioning your identity? See also *Jacob's ladder.*

dock: If your boat is docked or you're standing on a dock, you've either completed your task or haven't dared to leave for some reason. If you're standing on the dock and the boat has sailed, perhaps it's about a missed opportunity or something that you can't get back or do over.

doctor: This may reflect a need for healing or support (physical, emotional, spiritual, psychological, and/or relational). Something may need patching up.

The type of doctor may point to what needs to be healed. For example, a pediatrician may be about your inner child or your childlike self that has been hurt or shut down. Ask for help if you need it. It's not a sign of weakness.

Doctors may also suggest being open and vulnerable with the hidden parts of yourself.

document: Something important may be revealed soon. Something has been or is about to be discovered. If the document is hidden, perhaps you're worried about something you've been hiding.

dog: See *animals.*

dogfight: You may be rejecting some aspect of your personality or your physical self. It might also suggest that there may be a conflict between you and someone else.

doghouse: Are you in some kind of trouble?

dolls: These can be about the anima/ animus (i.e., the qualities of the opposite sex in each of us). They are also only representations of reality and therefore false in nature. Are you projecting a false nature?

A doll can also be a euphemism for a woman you're attracted to or slang for a good person.

If there's a dollhouse associated with this image, perhaps you are glorifying or idealizing some aspect of home life. Maybe everything isn't perfect. Are you in denial about family issues? Do you need to work on some issue?

See also *Barbie*.

domination: Are you feeling controlled (or overpowered), or are you trying to control others? Are you being too dominating and not allowing others the freedom to be themselves? If so, what are you trying to protect in yourself?

There's also the possibility that this image has sexual or erotic connotations (e.g., a dominatrix), and you may have urges that you may not have acknowledged before. See *authority* and *possessed*.

Insight: Note your relationship with authority or domination. Do you dominate and/or avoid domination? Do you feel controlled a lot in your waking life, or do you try to control others or the circumstances? Why is that? Remember your relationship to authority reflects the decisions you have made regarding it. You alone are responsible for these decisions. If you do not reflect on and openly deal with these biases and decisions, they will negatively affect all your relationships and dominate your thoughts and actions.

dominoes: Your actions may affect those around you. Consider the phrase "Fall like dominoes."

door: This can be a very significant dream image. You may also want to review *door* in *house*.

This image can represent a transition point. If it has a large lock, it may indicate defensiveness or some hostility.

A locked door also could mean that you are locking something or someone out of your life or closing yourself off from others. Locking something could also be about your feelings of self-worth. What are you hiding?

A locked door to something might suggest that you are having difficulty getting in touch with whatever you've locked out or up. What room is locked (see *house*)?

A very small door may be limiting access to yourself. An open door might represent accessibility and openness.

A broken-down door could be about your defenses being broken down, thus making you more vulnerable to something.

The back door could represent your private life, and the front door might represent your public self. Going through the side door could be about escaping or avoiding.

Revolving doors could be about how your life is going (i.e., around in circles).

A doorbell ringing could be like a knock at the door (i.e., an opportunity making itself known). See also *knock or knocking*.

A door left ajar might indicate that you are leaving or need to leave a part of yourself open to others. This might suggest that you allow yourself to be a little vulnerable or that you need to allow yourself access to the deeper and perhaps unknown parts of yourself.

If the door is ajar, perhaps you need to be more open to new ideas or ways of being. Doors that are slightly ajar can also symbolize the need to allow life in without being overwhelmed by being too vulnerable.

Insight: Doors can be entrances into new experiences, or they can signal boundaries and transition points between states of being.

Doors can lead to backyards that can be private places for family life, or they can lead to entrances to the soul. On the other hand, front doors can be openings or protectors of our public lives.

Doors to strange or fanciful places can be openings to new awareness.

See also *door* in *house*.

doppelganger: If you see your double, you may be seeing a reflection of your negative aspects. If you're fighting with your double, it could reflect an inner conflict between what is right and wrong, good and evil. To kill the double could suggest that you are repressing certain negative aspects of yourself.

double-cross: This is a betrayal (see *betrayal*). It's a loss of trust in something or someone. Perhaps you need to be more trustworthy.

double-dog dare: A double-dog dare may reflect something that you feel trapped in. Perhaps you can't get out of something or can't refuse something or someone.

down: Things may not look positive. It could refer to your emotional state as with being depressed or sad. See also *descending* and/or *downstairs* in house.

drafted: Is someone forcing something on you? It could also mean that your skills are needed for some project.

dragging: Are you behind on something? Are you exhausted? Are there some burdens or struggles that are dragging you down?

If you are dragged or watching someone being dragged, do you feel powerless or out of control with something?

Do you feel as though you've been dragged into something you'd rather not do or be a part of?

dragon: See *animals*.

dream body: During every dream the dreamer inhabits a body other than the one he or she has when awake. Sometimes this body is just a bystander or an observer. Sometimes it takes form amongst the forms of other selves. Sometimes it can even transform at will and become another self (e.g., a human, animal, or spirit guide).

In this waking world, we are male and female, old and young, inanimate and animate, powerful and vulnerable simultaneously. In our dreams we are our real selves living in a world of authenticity.

In the world of dreams, we inhabit the images of myth, and we become our mythology.

This is what I call the dream self or dream body, and it can do everything that the awake self can only dream of. It is the hero who is famous without the negative consequences of fame. It is the self who has great powers, can fly, and always gets the guy or girl.

The self in a dream isn't bound by time or place, and it is often able to move from the present to the past to the future back to the present with no effort at all.

In many dreams meaning doesn't follow the linear rules established in the world of the awake. In the dream there doesn't have to be hard-and-fast meaning or rules for the way things have to be. Chaos can be an acceptable way of living in the dream world.

But often the self of your dreams seems more real than the self of your everyday.

Sometimes I wonder upon awakening if the self of my dreams is the real self and if the self of my waking world is but an illusion of the mind.

Sometimes when I'm particularly conscious of my surroundings, I become acutely aware of the reality that I'm creating moment by moment. Sometimes it feels as though I've voluntarily entered a dream. When I read the news, I wonder how real it all is. Is it but a dream, a disturbing nightmare, or a wild imaginary story conjured by some insane spirit?

Some mystics think of the dream body as an aspect of the soul.

dream catcher: To see a dream catcher might suggest that you are avoiding something negative. You may be putting up protective emotional walls.

Is there something from your subconscious that you're not dealing with or avoiding?

Legends of the Ojibwa believed that the dream catcher was created by Spider Woman as a way of capturing the sun each morning. She was the protector of the children. Sometimes they could be found on the cradleboards of new babies. Good dreams would pass through the hole in the center, and bad dreams would get caught in the web.

dreaming: Dreaming of dreaming might suggest your awakening to an inner reality.

To be asleep in a dream might suggest that you need to wake up to something because you're not paying attention.

Some people have wondered if everything is but a dream—a projection of our consciousness.

What is real for you?

See also *asleep* and/or *waking dream*.

dream narrative/story: Dreams are most often bits and pieces that don't follow any linear pattern. It is when we wake up that the rational self takes over and creates a narrative, a story.

Dreams do hint, however, at patterns, major themes, or attitudes that may exist in our waking lives that we are not paying attention to.

Writing down the images of the dream after you first awaken and before your mind has a chance to create a story can be an important first step in dealing with the essence of a dream before the ego has a chance to interfere.

Sometimes dreamers can get more information from the dream narrative by using a technique called active imagination (see *active imagining*).

dreams of loved ones who have died: Sometimes a loved one who has died comes to visit in a dream. Frequently, this is the psyche trying to deal with and come to terms with the loss. Grief is a terribly painful experience, and the mind deals with it the best it can. Our dreams will often be a means of helping us to heal. Be open to the messages of these dreams.

See also *dead people*.

dress: See *clothing*.

dried up: Perhaps you are devoid of emotions. You may be withdrawn or depressed. Have you suffered a major loss recently?

drink: This could be about absorbing something into yourself or taking in a feeling. Consider the phrase "Drinking in," meaning to be aware of and focused on your surroundings. It may also reflect your needs or what you are longing for. If you are drinking with someone, it may represent that you are, need to, or want to take in the pleasure of that person. You might want to see *drunk* as well if the drink is alcohol.

driving: This could be about life's journey and your path in life. If you can't see the road ahead, perhaps you don't know where you're going in your life? Are there obstacles along the road that you are trying to avoid or get around? Roads with many curves or

potholes could reflect the difficulties in achieving your goals.

If you're not driving the car but are just a passenger, perhaps you're not taking responsibility for the direction of your life.

Driving in reverse can indicate setbacks. Driving drunk might suggest you or your life is out of control.

Driving into water might suggest you're letting your emotions control you. If you're driving too fast, perhaps you need to slow your life down, and driving recklessly might suggest that you are not treating yourself well and perhaps being unsafe.

What kind of vehicle you're driving and your attitude toward that vehicle in the waking world will also add information (also see *car* and *road*).

driving test: As with any test in a dream, your points of view, beliefs, goals, and aspirations may be put to the test. If you fear failing or are failing the test, you may be questioning whether or not you have the skills necessary to attain your goals. You may lack confidence (see *exam* or *test*).

drone: Are you being passive aggressive? Perhaps you're causing trouble but not owning up to it. Are you trying to stay uninvolved? Are you ducking direct responsibility for something?

Are you trying to gain a different vantage point or point of view?

dropping: If you or someone is dropping something in a dream, it might suggest that you need to let go of something (e.g., a relationship, project, point of view, or position). Note what you are dropping as that might have some significance.

This image could also be about your carelessness or your lack of responsibility. You may have dropped the ball and let someone down.

See also *abandoned* and *letting go*.

drought: Perhaps you are devoid of emotions or are depressed and withdrawn. It can also indicate a lack of something in your life (e.g., love, job, good ideas, or sex).

drowning: This can suggest being overwhelmed by emotion or circumstances (see *flood*, *sinking*, or *tidal wave*). Drowning can also represent a *dissolving* (i.e., the transformation or letting go of a closely held or fixed belief, a way of being, or an attitude).

Drowning could thus signify the need to wash away the old points of view. The ego doesn't like change and will often act as though it's drowning in the emotional pressure to change.

Sometimes death by drowning makes way for a new point of view or a new way of being. This idea is also symbolically embedded within the stories of Gilgamesh and in Noah and the ark where all is washed away in order to make room for a new and purified consciousness.

It's like the drowning of Pharaoh's legions in order to save or make way for the new order of being (i.e., to no longer be enslaved by the limited and limiting ego of man so as to make way for the unlimited service to God). The biblical story of the parting of the Red Sea speaks to the power of water in the psyche of humankind.

Insight: I, too, have had drowning dreams as have many of the people who have written to me about their dreams over the years. In fact, the image of water plays an important part in the state of our emotional lives.

Whether we acknowledge feelings in our waking lives or not, our dreams will often bring to consciousness how we're navigating the seas of our lives. In many ways, these symbols have a lot to say about how we relate to our feelings.

drugs: Are you looking for an escape from reality or your problems? Have you anesthetized yourself to some pain that you feel helpless to deal with?

Overdosing could imply that you don't know or are ignoring your limits. Are you on a self-destructive path? Are you trying to deal with fear by distracting yourself? Are you unwilling to take responsibility for your actions?

If you are being drugged, it might be about something unconscious, something you're not facing or dealing with but need to. This can also be about feeling as though someone is taking advantage of you.

See also *medications*.

drums: This can symbolize the rhythm of life or suggest that you're trying to *drum up* something (i.e., make something happen). You feel something deeply.

There may be something that you need to pay attention to.

Something may be reverberating in your life. Is something trying to communicate on a deeper level?

Because drumming can resonate deeply in the body as you listen to it, the sound and feel of a drum can signify power, not the force that is of the ego, but the deep-seated power of the soul.

Insight: To some tribal people, the drum has a spirit of its own. It symbolizes the heartbeat and the sound of thunder.

Drums were used by armies throughout time to build bravado in the soldiers and propel them onward into battle, and they often informed the speed of their charge too.

drunk: This could be about being out of control or shutting something painful out. You may be losing control in your life and not being responsible. Are you trying to escape or avoid some situation in the waking world?

A lack of reason or giving in to natural urges may also be implied by this image.

The bottom line is that drunkenness in a dream may be about being irresponsible or behaving irresponsibly.

duet: Are you and someone else singing the same song (in agreement)? Do you need to cooperate more? Do you need to balance the disparate parts of yourself and integrate them more fully?

dumped: This may be a metaphor for being left behind, unvalued, fired, or demeaned.

If you are being *dumped on*, perhaps you are feeling put down, harassed, or made into a scapegoat. Dumping something (an object, habit, or point of view) may mean you desire to get rid of something or someone. See also *feces* or *rejection*.

dusk: This could symbolize the evening of life or the end of some aspect of your life. This can also reflect a relinquishing or letting go of something, someone, or a chapter of life.

The image of the end of the day could also reflect your acquiescence to reality (i.e., part of your acceptance process).

Dusk can also reflect what the conscious mind is doing as it goes off to sleep and gives way to the unconscious. See also *sunset*.

dust: Dust may suggest that certain aspects of yourself have been neglected.

Something turning into dust might indicate that something is unimportant.

Have you been left in the dust (i.e., left behind)?

If dust is leaking between your fingers, perhaps you have lost or are losing something or someone.

If dust is filling the air, see *clouds*.

dustup: See *fighting*.

dust devil: This is sometimes known as a willy-willy, and it's symbolically similar to a tornado but on a much smaller scale. It can represent anger or some chaotic event. Where the dust devil is and what it's doing can also add meaning to the dream. Is it in the desert or in a forest? Is it chasing you or just threatening (see *tornado*).

dwarf: This image can suggest an undeveloped part of the personality, unconscious forces, and/or magical transformation.

dying: See *death*.

E

eagle: See *bird* under *animal terms*.

ears: Do you need to be more responsive or receptive to others? A pain in the ear can symbolize bad news. If the ears are cut off, perhaps you are tired of listening to others or to what they are saying about you or someone else.

If they're turning red, perhaps you're feeling shame, guilt, or embarrassment. Do you wonder if people are talking about you behind your back? If someone is whispering in an ear, perhaps you need to pay closer attention to something, or perhaps there's a secret that you need to tell.

A fly in the ear may represent rumors or something that you don't want to hear. Perhaps you've overheard something you shouldn't have.

earplugs: Are you refusing to hear something? Are you turning a deaf ear to something? Do you need some peace and quiet? Or are you isolating yourself from something or someone? The image of earwax can also be a metaphor for this.

earrings: Do you need to listen more carefully? If they belong to other people, could they reflect a memory of that person, or do you need to listen to them? This image can be about listening carefully or suggest that you're the only one who's getting the message. Perhaps you feel that you're not being heard, or it could be about listening to your intuitive sense.

earth: This could represent your roots or your connection with the physical world (see *trees* and *roots*).

Perhaps you're *grounded* and realistic about something. Seeing the planet might suggest wholeness and global consciousness whereas seeing its molten core might refer to some suppressed anger—the holding of negative emotions.

Insight: The earth is the mother of us all, that which gives us life and brings us into the world. It is the grounded aspect between the father, the sun, and our spiritual self (e.g., the other side of the heaven and earth or the mind/body dichotomy).

See also *Gaia*.

earthquake: This could be about soul-shaking insecurity. An earthquake could be about a breakdown of anything, such as relationships, attitudes, or points of view.

This can represent something that can literally *shake up* your world (see also *fault*).

earthworm: This can represent the need to go deep into your subconscious in order to unearth deep feelings or desires. They can also represent renewal or the restoration of some aspect of the self.

east (as a direction): This can represent ancient truths, beginnings, the mysteries of the unconscious, renewal, enlightenment, the source of life, birth, religious aspects, and inner wisdom. As with all directions, one might ask, "Where am I heading?"

Easter: This could symbolize spiritual rebirth. See also *death*.

eaten: If you are being eaten alive, perhaps something is consuming your aliveness (e.g., envy, jealousy, fear, or anger).

If you are being eaten underwater, it could be about some overwhelming emotion eating at you. If you are in a cave, cellar, or hole, it could be about your dark side, your unconscious, and unexamined demons threatening to devour you.

eating: This can signify satisfying your hunger and not necessarily with food (i.e., hunger for any of the hierarchy of needs). What are you eating? Are you overeating or starving (see *starvation*)?

eavesdropping: Is there bad news coming your way? Maybe you don't like what you're hearing, or perhaps someone is hiding something from you.

echo: Are you repeating yourself? Is a sound echoing or repeating? The impact of your words or past actions will come back on you. Perhaps you need to confront past issues?

eclipse: An eclipse of the sun can be about self-doubt, self-confidence waning, or the masculine side of your personality being hidden or suppressed. Have you been hiding your light?

If it's an eclipse *of the moon*, it could represent your feminine side (e.g., compassionate, caring, or intuitive aspects) that may be overshadowed. After it's passed, there might be new light or awareness.

Eclipses might also be symbolic of something overshadowing you or some relationship.

The moon eclipsing the sun could very well be a union of the feminine and masculine aspects of yourself (see also *moon*).

Insight: In the fifth century BCE when eclipses were not well understood, they were associated with supernatural forces. Witches from the Greek area of Thesally boasted about their ability to extinguish the moon's light and draw it down from the sky.

editor: Are you censoring yourself or trying to control your feelings? Should you be?

education: See *school*.

eel: Consider the simile "as slippery as an eel." Are you having difficulty holding on to or grasping things (e.g., money or understanding)? It can also be a phallic symbol.

eerie feeling: Are you feeling frightened? Has some situation or event left you with an uncanny or creepy feeling? Does some behavior seem bizarre? Is something you've experienced left you feeling in awe?

The feeling of eeriness can also reflect a feeling of holiness, what Jung called the numinous. It is more often than not a healing experience. This can evoke fear or amazement and a sense of blessing. This feeling often comes at the dreamer with intense energy, awe, and wonder and can lead to a resolution of intractable issues and a sense of renewal, peace, and calm.

Sometimes a spectral presence in a dream can signal the presence of an archetype (i.e., a god or goddess, divine child, divine mother, or the devil). See the *archetypes* section and *numinous*.

effigy: Perhaps you are not seeing reality for what it really is. Maybe you're only seeing a representation. Perhaps you need to look deeper into something. Maybe you're trying to find your own power. Are you trying to steal someone else's power to bolster your own? Do you wish you were like someone else because you admire their traits?

egg: This can symbolize your potential or what you may wish to develop—the seed for something new. A cracked egg may suggest a failure to achieve potential (see also *Humpty-Dumpty*). If a chicken is being born, it could suggest the beginning of something new (see *birth* and *pregnancy*).

A nest of eggs could symbolize financial gain or refer to a cache of money (i.e., a nest egg). Do you need to save or invest for some future endeavor? See also *nest*.

Insight: On a more spiritual level of the dream, the egg can also represent the divine egg (i.e., that which comes out of nothing to become something). This is similar to the Genesis story where light came out of the void as the first act or manifestation of God.

eggshells: This could represent fragility and vulnerability. Perhaps you need to break out of your shell and let your guard down.

ego: Simply put, it is the I of one's life, who you think you are, and your sense of self. It is the "Das Ich" as Freud called it (see *Sigmund Freud*).

It can be considered the center of our consciousness. Note this is not your sense of self (i.e., the inner whole of which the ego is only a part).

Another reference for the ego is the *false self*. See *mask*.

Often this ego projects its own shadow onto others (see the *archetypes* section and *psyche*), thus making *them* the problem. An individual or collective ego of a society irrationally inflated where it imagines itself to be godlike; for example, any autocrat/dictator or in the superiority belief of white supremacists can cast or project their shadow onto anything or anyone who challenges them.

Ego is an intellectual construct or model of the psyche, not a real thing, and it cannot be found in any one place in the brain. It is one of three constructs or mental life apparatus (i.e., ego, id, and superego as defined by Sigmund Freud).

ego death: This represents the loss of subjective self-identity—what Jungian psychology would call psychic death and what Joseph Campbell labeled self-surrender and transition in his book *The Hero with a Thousand Faces* (Pantheon Books, 1968).

The Sufi Muslims call it *fana* (annihilation), and the Jewish Kabbalists call it the kiss of death. In short, it's the rejection and end of the need to hold onto a self-centered existence separate from all other existence (see also *peak experience*).

Ego death can also be seen as the process of letting go of the ego as the center of one's being and thus the ultimate kenosis (a way of emptying oneself so as to be open to God, the Tao, or what exists).

Egyptian: Is this your spiritual core? It can represent a place of ancient wisdom. This symbolic meaning may be reinforced if the Egyptian is a queen as well.

Insight: The ancient Egyptian word for dreams was *rswt*, meaning "to be awake."

The priests were considered the masters of the secret things, and they considered dreams to be a time when our eyes are opened. It was said that the priest would travel consciously through their dreams, sometimes shape-shifting into the form of animals.

Dreams were a form of a mini death in a philosophy where death was a journey whose final goal was the recovery of one's true nature.

The ancient Egyptians were often considered the fathers of the dream incubation technique.

When an Egyptian man had trouble, he would sleep in a temple where he would dream, sometimes to the sleep-enhancing fragrance of lilac oils. Upon waking, the priest (or the master of the secret things) would interpret that night's dreams.

Though today we think of dreams as being relevant only to the individual who has them many dreams were considered in the past as messages from the gods and were visited upon the dreamer for the good of all and could only be interpreted by a priest.

Dream interpretation in ancient Egypt was at least as important as incubation. *Instructions for Merikare* (2070 and 2100 BCE), one of the first dream interpretation books, suggested that the true interpretation of a dream laid in the exact opposite of the symbols. In this way, a dream depicting happiness was really a portent of future disaster.

Notwithstanding the prediction quality of these interpretations, the idea of a symbol representing the opposite is still a viable tool in modern interpretation. For example, if you see people happy in a dream, that could mean you are not happy and are seeking it yourself.

Eiffel Tower: This could symbolize strength, longevity, and/or romance. See also *tower*.

eight ball: Perhaps you're leaving something to chance. Are you behind the eight ball (i.e., stuck in some hopeless situation or in trouble)? Does the number eight have any significance for you (see also *numbers*)?

ejaculation: You may have a need for emotional release.

elastic: This may represent the ability to adapt. If the elastic is snapping back, it may have something to do with *rebounding* emotionally or psychologically.

elbow: See *body*.

elderly: An old person might represent wisdom or spiritual power. Listen to what this person has to say (see *wise old man or woman* in the *archetypes* section).

election: You need to make a choice. Or this image may only reflect your judgments about elections in general.

electric chair: The sudden end to something may have jolted you, or you may need a jolt with regard to something in your life. See also *death, electricity,* or *killing*.

electric fence: Perhaps you've isolated yourself in some part of your life. Are you trying to keep something out or in? See also *fence* or *wall*.

electricity: This might represent vigor and life energy/vitality or the need for it. If it goes out, that may suggest a lack of insight on your part about something or someone.

It can also be symbolic of one's power and suggest that you are either expressing too much or too little. Are you or is someone else abusing power?

See also *energy*.

electrocution: Your current course of action/behavior could cause a shocking disaster.

elevator: If you are *ascending*, it might reflect a rise in status or signal that things are looking up. Perhaps you've risen to a new level of understanding or awareness? If it crashes through the roof or goes out of control, you may not be ready to handle it.

If you're *descending*, that could mean you're coming back to reality. It could also be a setback. Often an elevator represents the ups and downs of life. If it's out of order, perhaps your mobility has been stymied.

If it stops at a floor you hadn't planned on going to, perhaps something unexpected or unintentional has happened in your life recently.

Floors in a building can sometimes refer to your level of development. What's on that floor?

eleventh hour: Is time running out for you? Is some deadline looming? Have you waited until the last minute? It could also relate to your age. Consider when people say, "It's getting late in the day." They could also say, "You're getting old, and there isn't much time left."

elf: This creature sometimes acts like a guide for the soul. It may suggest that you need to be more carefree. It can also point to some imbalance.

As a helper to Santa, it could refer to industriousness and a hardworking nature. See also *fairy or faery* in *animals as fantasy creatures*, *psychopomp*, and/or *Santa Claus*.

elope: Are you trying to escape some problem, situation, or responsibility?

email: This may reflect your need to reach out and communicate. Are you spending too much time in front of the computer?

See also *memo* and/or *Twitter*.

embarrassment: This could symbolize hidden weakness or a lack of confidence. It might also be about insecurities or fears.

embers: This could symbolize a dying love or the last vestiges of a dream.

embryo: This could symbolize a new idea or an idea in development. Perhaps something subconscious is surfacing. Sometimes women who are pregnant see an embryo in the dream.

emerald: This could be symbolic of strength and longevity. It could also suggest faithfulness and healing (see *color*).

emergency: Something urgent may need your attention.

emergency room: Perhaps your lifestyle is causing you harm, and you need to reevaluate something.

emigration: Perhaps you're dissatisfied with a current situation and desire a change? Perhaps you need to face the problem instead of running from it.

emoticons: This can be about your range of emotions. If it's a specific emotion, then look it up under emotions or look for the specific emotion.

emotionless: This might suggest that you are closing yourself off from others. Are you neglecting your own feelings and perhaps need to start paying more attention to them?

emotions: Emotions in dreams can be a way for the dreamers to act out the feelings that they normally would not express if they were awake. The dream provides a *safe* outlet for these emotions.

However, if the dreamers feel a mix of emotions in their dreams, especially if the emotions are contradictory, then it may mean that the conscious and subconscious are in emotional conflict.

Emotions in dreams are integral to the way the brain works. (There seems to be a primitive network that links both dreams and emotions.) This is why one must focus on the prevalent emotion(s) of a dream in order to derive broader meaning.

Other than reflecting a current way of being, emotions can also signal the need for new ways of being. For example, anger can be about the need to stand up for yourself. Fear can be about being more assertive. Happiness can be about being more serious, and anxiety could suggest the need to be more cautious.

The actual emotions can also add meaning to any image (see *anger, fear, happy, mystical, sad, scared,* and *stress*).

emperor: Because all human beings have within them both feminine and masculine aspects to their personality (see *archetypes* section) the emperor image in a dream can represent the masculine archetype of leadership, assertiveness, and courage. He is the doer aspect in contrast to his feminine empress or nurturing aspect (see below).

In a dream and in his positive aspect, he can symbolize the need for action, decisiveness, completion, balance, or the need for harmony. His negative form would represent the opposites of his positive qualities—force instead of power as well as imbalance, disharmony, and destructiveness. He can represent the negative or positive father, even God or the devil. The emperor can also be represented by a priest or one's own father. Sometimes one's fatherly traits or habits can be helpful or debilitative. He often reflects our inner expectations for ourselves as both good or bad.

He can represent control by others or self-control. In a female's dream, he can represent her animus, her own inner masculine (positive or negative), the need for balance, and the manifestation of some needed trait (e.g., assertiveness or decisiveness).

See also *king*.

employee: This might represent some aspect of yourself. A new employee might be revealing a new aspect of yourself. Whether you're employed or not could be a metaphor for your own sense of self-worth (see also *job*).

empress: This may symbolize honor and pride. Also known as the Great Mother, the Virgin Mary, Isis, Hecate, Qwan Yin, the Hindu goddess Kamala, and Gnosis. This card can sometimes represent Mother Nature. She can be seen as the sustaining nurturer, a symbol of love (in her Venus form), and the mother of ideas. She represents the potential of humankind.

She can be seen as a gateway to the light and the ultimate divine nature of humankind. She is also both wisdom and folly. She can represent the bridge or connection between the ineffable, what cannot be experienced in words, and the manifest (how the divine translates into the everyday). She is essentially the mother of creation.

I have seen a form of her in my dreams where she has appeared as Sophia showing and inviting me to take the path less traveled into a higher understanding and awareness of reality.

In a dream she can represent power and honor and influence both in a positive and negative way. She can represent the influences our own mothers had and continue to have on our lives and how we perceive them.

In a male's dream, she may represent a need for independence from his own mother or a better or different interaction between his masculine and feminine personality selves/traits. Without a separation from his mother image, a male might always look for her in all his relationships, and he may project her image onto these relationships and never see the real person.

See also *queen* in the *archetypes* section.

empty or emptiness: What has gone or disappeared? This can suggest a lack of something in your life or loneliness. It can also represent the death of a loved one or the end of a relationship (see *death* or *killing*).

An empty pocket might symbolize the feeling of being impoverished and vulnerable.

If someone has picked your pocket empty, you might feel that you've been taken advantage of.

An empty canvas or blank sheet of paper can also represent potential and room for creativity.

See also *blank*.

enantiodromia: All humans exhibit an inner balancing system designed to maintain equilibrium within.

When an abundance of any psychic force, positive or negative, is exerted either through practice or resistance, its opposite comes to the fore. The psychiatrist Carl Jung labeled this process enantiodromia, which is defined as "running counter to." Basically, it's not unlike the principle of yin and yang.

When a counterforce is suppressed for long enough, it will eventually make itself known, sometimes in very dark and bizarre ways, as with a neurosis.

When any part of the whole personality of a person or group of persons (e.g., a society) is suppressed for a great length of time, the being will do whatever it takes to bring back balance. Sometimes that takes the form of war, pestilence, and famine, and in this way too much—or an extreme amount of—good can actually produce evil.

Material suppressed into the unconsciousness of both the individual and the collective can eventually breakthrough the individual's or societies conscious control and wreak havoc.

See also *union of opposites*.

enchantment: Are you being manipulated or overly influenced. An enchantress could signal some feminine power over you (also see *witch*).

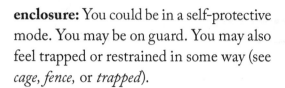

enclosure: You could be in a self-protective mode. You may be on guard. You may also feel trapped or restrained in some way (see *cage*, *fence*, or *trapped*).

encyclopedia: This could symbolize inner knowledge, collective wisdom, or the collective unconscious. Consider the reference *know-it-all* (i.e., smarty-pants or wise guy).

end of the world: This could signal big and/or threatening changes or transitions in life. This could remind you of anything that has the potential to change your life as you know it (e.g., leaving home, menopause, moving from adolescence to adulthood, having children, the loss of a job or someone you love). This can show up as an *end* to anything, such as an end to a path or road (also look at *apocalypse*, *death*, *trapped*, and *west*).

endure: Is there something you're just putting up with? Do you need to confront the issue and handle it so that you can move on?

energy: This may be a metaphor for how you're feeling about something or someone. What gives you energy, and what takes it away?

If appropriate, see *electricity*.

engagement: This could be about a relationship, sexual needs, or feelings of loneliness. Breaking an engagement could suggest that you are making a hasty and perhaps unwise decision.

engagement ring: Are you suggesting a long-term commitment to something? See also *ring*.

engine: This is symbolic of your heart. What condition is it in? An engine that won't start might suggest some obstacle that may be in your way toward some goal. If it's damaged, then perhaps it's like a broken heart. Consider also the health aspects being represented.

It could also represent the energy that drives you forward in life or toward some goal.

engineer: This may refer to creating something or manipulating something or someone. What is it you're creating? It is also a person who controls directionality or movement. Are you in charge of your own life?

If someone else is the engineer, it could mean that you have given up being charge and/or need to take charge. Are you or someone else *engineering* some aspect of your life or someone else's life?

entertainer: See *celebrity*, *famous person*, or *singer*. See also *entertainment*.

entertainment: Are you showing off? Note the type of entertainment because this could make a statement about your mood (see *actor*).

entry or entrance: This could mean that you are being led into a new or novel experience. If it's a secret entrance, perhaps it is an opening into some part of yourself you didn't know was there or some part of you that you haven't had access to (see *door*).

envelope: Perhaps this reflects a message you need to receive or send. Could you be pushing the envelope (i.e., testing the limits)?

environment: The meaning of this symbol will depend on what it's like. If it's dry, then perhaps something in your life has become dry and lifeless. If wet, then perhaps there's some emotional stress (see also *weather*).

environmental disaster: This may reflect a sense of helplessness. Perhaps you are feeling overwhelmed and out of control with something.

envy: Are you envious of someone in your waking life? Or do others envy you? Do you think too highly of yourself?

epidemic: This could represent many worries and burdens. Perhaps something

negative has infected your life. Have you taken in the negatives of others?

Eros and Logos: Often seen in dreams as Cupid (the winged baby with a bow and arrow), Eros is symbolic of our instinctive tendency toward relatedness. This runs contrary to the masculine principle of Logos, where we stand aside from experience, abstract and objectify it, and then generalize it into some universal truth.

Fundamentally, these two principles reflect the different and often competing aspects of our feminine and masculine natures.

Unfortunately, in the Western cultures, Logos is stressed beyond that of Eros and to the neglect of the feminine principles. This neglect affects religious life quite negatively in that it discriminates against women and affects people's ability to use compassion in their everyday lives and in the application of their religion.

Eros as a sexual symbol can herald the need for connection, vitality, and passion (see *sex*). To be attracted to someone sexually need not be about sex but the soul's need to be more fully expressed. In this way, Eros or Cupid becomes the psychopomp (guide) to the soul.

See *anima/animus* in the *archetypes* section. See also *Cupid* and/or *sex*.

errands: This can represent being stuck in a rut. Life may be too routine for you, but this image can also represent harmony. Errands can suggest things that you need to do.

eruption: This possibly signals a forceful and jolting outpour of emotions or urges. There may be some upheaval in your life.

escalator: This suggests movement between various levels of awareness. If you are going up, then perhaps you are addressing emotional issues or moving through your spiritual journey. If you're going down, then perhaps you are repressing something or experiencing a setback.

The image may also relate to one's transformation or need for it. Ascending might also suggest attaining a higher way of thinking or transcending the lower levels of being toward greater enlightenment (also see *elevator*).

escape: This could symbolize the avoidance of such things as feelings, certain situations, restrictions, or entrapments. Are you refusing to face your problems? A failed escape might suggest that you feel trapped or helpless.

It could also suggest a fear of being constrained, controlled, coerced, or compelled.

Some part of your personality or deeper self may want to be freed.

Insight: If you feel trapped and can't get free, are you afraid of a life with no boundaries? Are you worried about expressing yourself freely and fully?

Eskimo: This could represent some frigid/cold feelings? If you're adapting to something, then this image could be about how well you are adapting to some situation.

ESP: This may come from your deeper self (i.e., the unconscious mind). Perhaps you need to pay more attention to your intuition, hunches, and gut feelings. Do you need to act on your hunch?

espresso: Perhaps you need to act quickly on something and get moving. It could also reflect high energy.

essay: Perhaps you should think things through before acting. Be more objective in your evaluation of something or someone.

estranged: An estranged person in a dream might suggest that you may need or desire to rebuild the connection and relationship with this person, or you may want to reconnect with an aspect of yourself.

eternal: To experience the eternal or a sense of endlessness in a dream might be about the inner soul or spiritual self. It could be about something lasting forever or your desire that it could. Perhaps something is taking an eternity to happen.

I've heard that eternity dwells in the experience of a moment—in the space between words or in the emptiness between our thoughts (see *mystical*).

evacuation: Are you trying to get away from something? Are you concerned about your safety, or are you feeling insecure? Are you avoiding something and not dealing with it?

eve: Perhaps you need to be cautious with regard to the opposite sex. If it's the eve of something, perhaps you are on the cusp of some big change or event.

evening: This could represent the end of something or be age-related, or in some cases, it can represent death.

evening dress or gown: This could be about social pleasures or some image of you that you want to project to other people. Perhaps you want people to think of you as fancy and stylish.

even numbers: Even numbers may be about balance, peacefulness, or symmetry. However, odd numbers might be more aggressive in their meaning. Are you at odds with something? See also *numbers*.

evergreen tree: This could be about growth, wealth, and/or immortality. It could also be a metaphor for the need to be more environmentally conscious (see *trees*).

evil: This could relate to urges that you may think are wrong or whatever seems to threaten you. See the *shadow* and *devil* in the *archetypes* section.

When an evil figure shows up in a dream, it can reflect an inner conflict. The individual may have split off his or her negative aspects, those aspects that are in conflict with personal values or the values of the society.

But denying them does not get rid of them. They just go underground and operate in the background.

These dreams may encourage people to wrestle with their shadow aspects so as to deal with them openly, thus reducing their negative and destructive consequences.

ex: A former boyfriend/girlfriend or spouse could come up in a dream when something in your waking life reminds you of the ex (e.g., a behavior, a way of being, something you long for, or something you reject).

Is something missing in a current relationship that you had in an earlier one? If the ex misses you, turn it around and ask yourself what part of the person or that relationship you actually miss. You might also consider the term *missed* as referring to a *missed opportunity*.

If you get back together in the dream, this may have nothing to do with reality but may reflect what's going on in your current relationship. Sometimes we just miss how we felt about ourselves in the former relationship, whether good or bad. (When we're in love, we tend to love ourselves more as well.)

If the ex has died in the dream, it is possible that whatever you had with him or her has finally died in you.

Physically and intellectually, letting go of someone is not the same as emotionally letting go. The former relationship may have meant something deep to you. It may have reflected something within your soul. What he or she represented to this part of you may be more important than the actual person. It is this aspect of you that was touched deeply by the person's presence, and you want to reconnect with that experience but not necessarily him or her.

In short, when exes show up, it often reflects some aspect of their personalities, treatment of you (good or bad), or of the time when you were together that may be reflected in your current relationship. This can be about something from the past that no longer exists in the present, or it could reflect some need in the current relationship that was present in the past.

exams: This could symbolize an ordeal or test, self-criticism, or a test of self-value, or it could show that you understand something or someone.

Missed or lost exams can be about anxiety that may mirror current worries reminiscent of earlier school anxieties.

Often these are seen as anxiety dreams. Feelings of being unprepared for something, unsure of yourself, or fears of not being good enough, not being smart enough, or not knowing enough can show up in dreams with images like these.

Perhaps you are missing something or not paying attention to something important. Maybe you are missing some knowledge.

Is there something you need to learn but are failing to do so? Are you missing the point of something?

This can also represent earlier school trauma you haven't dealt with.

See also *school* or *test*.

execution: This can represent punishment. You could be trying to destroy some aspect of yourself that you don't want.

exhibitionist: If you or others are exposing themselves, it could signal that you feel overly vulnerable or publically criticized.

exit: This could be a symbol for avoidance or change in direction, or there may be an opening in something that is being presented.

An exit can mean an end to something, but alternatively, it can be an entrance to something new. This is similar to the symbol of death. An exit can also represent a gate or door (see *gate* and *door*).

exit door: This may represent a way out of something or a solution, and it may be similar to escape.

exorcism: Perhaps you're trying to regain control over some aspect(s) of your life. If you're performing it on someone else, perhaps you need to take control of some situation. You may also need to face a hidden negative aspect of yourself (i.e., a shadow aspect) and deal with it openly and responsibly.

See also *shadow* in the *archetypes* section.

expectations: If something didn't happen the way you expected it to or someone is not behaving or doing what is expected, your own expectations may be coloring your reality.

Do you expect too much of yourself or someone else? Are those expectations getting in the way of your joy and happiness?

Are you being too inflexible or rigid?

exploring: This might indicate self-discovery or the need for it. What drives or motivates you?

explosion or eruption: This suggests a sudden and violent change or an explosion of emotional material and its concomitant release of energy, such as anger or social upheaval. It could represent your repressed anger and/or rage. If you just hear the sound, then perhaps something is about to be exposed from your subconscious.

exterminator: Should you cut off ties with someone who affects you negatively? Should you stand up to your weaknesses? Should you get rid of or deal with what's *bugging* you? See also *bug* in *animals*.

extraterrestrial: This might represent your far-fetched ideas and imagination. It may also reflect your desire to escape from your daily life (see *alien*).

eye: This represents spiritual insight as in "the eyes are the windows to the soul." The eye is used to depict good and evil (i.e., the all-seeing eye). It can indicate seeing something unseen before. It could also refer to someone or something watching.

Insight: The early church in England used to place an eye above the entrance to ward off witches. Greeks created eye beads or amulets to ward off the evil eye. A closed eye or eyes could suggest that you are shutting something or someone out (see *shutters*).

If your eyes are a different color in a dream, then perhaps you need to see something from a different perspective. If you or someone else is wearing an eye patch, perhaps you are being one-sided in your view of something (i.e., refusing to see someone else's viewpoint).

If you are averting your gaze or unwilling to make eye contact, perhaps you are in denial of something and not willing to look at it (see also *eyes* under *body*).

F

fable: This could be your romantic mind or your romantic notions. There's a message in the fable, a lesson, a moral to be learned. If you are living a fable, perhaps you need to face reality more directly and face whatever situation that you need to deal with.

fabric: This could be about shaping your own experience. If it's torn, it could suggest that you need to mend or heal some situation or relationship. The fabric of your life is the thread that you are following, what your life is about, and what it's made of (see also *clothes*).

façade: This could be about the image that you put on something or what you want the world to see. (This can include the façade of a house or building.) It can represent the masks we wear to hide and protect ourselves (see *mask*).

face: This can represent one's identity and self-image (i.e., your persona). It can reflect the mask we put on for the world instead of the real you. If it's flawed, perhaps it's about erupting emotions. Perhaps you are

covering up a lie? Two faces might suggest being two-faced (i.e., you or someone else is being untrustworthy). We hide behind faces (see *face* under *body* or *clothes* and/or *mask*).

Facebook: Do you need to connect with someone or be more socially engaged? Are you looking to make friends, or do you feel *defriended*, alone, and left out (see *defriend*)?

Are you bullying or being bullied? Are you being appropriate in your communications?

Are you allowing yourself to be led astray?

Is there an issue with your privacy?

This image may also be affected by your prejudices or thoughts concerning Facebook or its users.

faceless: Perhaps you are still searching for your identity. Perhaps you aren't sure how to *read* or understand someone else.

facelift: Are you trying to change your identity or how you see yourself or how others see you? It can also suggest that you are feeling better about yourself.

face paint: This could be related to a cover-up or a need to change how you look. It could be used to hide something (e.g., make you look happy when you are not).

Are you trying to be something you're not?

Some Native American tribes used it ceremonially and in preparation for combat. In this case, the paint could serve as a magical power, protection, or means of intimidating an enemy.

Perhaps you're having trouble expressing yourself. What is painted could also reflect your mood in your waking life (see *tattoo* and *makeup*).

If your face is painted so as to hide some aspect of yourself, perhaps you are feeling guilty or ashamed (see *mask*).

facial: Are you trying to smooth over a flaw in the façade? See also *façade*.

factory: This could be about repetitive thinking. This may refer to an old way of doing things (e.g., habits and routines). Alternatively, it could be about your productivity.

An empty factory could be about leaving the meaningless monotony of your routine for something new.

fading: This could suggest a loss of energy or inspiration. Is your motivation or drive disappearing? See also *disappearing*.

failure: This could represent the fear of being inadequate or low self-esteem.

Perhaps you're managing something badly.

See *falling*.

fainting: Are you having difficulty in confronting some unconscious issues and/or feelings?

fair: Perhaps you need to let your inhibitions go. Are any of the sideshows reminiscent of parts or aspects of your personality (e.g., the daring of the knife thrower or animal tamer, the ringmaster, the tightrope walker, etc.)?

fairy: This represents a nature spirit and a realm beyond the everyday. If it's evil, then perhaps some part of yourself needs to be set free.

Insight: The Celtics included elves and fairies in their concept of the "otherworld" (the world of a new beginning and paradise).

The fairy or faery in a dream is often a symbol for the soul and the feminine aspects of yourself (e.g., intuitiveness, compassion, or acceptance), though an evil fairy can represent the negative feminine (e.g., controlling or indecisive) or even suggest that some part of yourself needs to be set free.

A fairytale might suggest that you are or need to explore your own limits.

fait accompli: Something may have already been accomplished before you've had a chance to do anything about it or to respond.

faith: If you've lost it, perhaps you've lost some trust in life or in someone.

See also *trust*.

faithless: See *cheating*.

fake: Are you or someone else pretending to be something you or they aren't? Do you need to show more of your true self?

Are you acting like you know what you're doing but don't? See *lying*, *pretending*, or *veneer* as well.

falcon: See *animals*.

fall: As a season, perhaps something is coming to an end, and maybe something new will then begin. As with the other season symbols, it could also be symbolic of the cycle of life (i.e., the gradual mellowing of middle age). Perhaps there are past ideas that have outlived their usefulness.

When falling in a dream your life may feel like it's falling apart and that you're a failure in life. You may be feeling out of control. Are you "falling" for someone? Did you fall for some lie?

falling: This could symbolize a loss of power, confidence, social standing, or control, or it could refer to the fear of failure, maybe even moral failure.

When your emotional crutches and distractions are taken away, there may be a sense of falling or losing your grip and/or emotional footing/balance.

If something or someone breaks your fall, you may be hoping for some kind of intervention. Do you need to act on something yourself and take responsibility? Do you need to not depend on something or someone else to save you?

It can also suggest a *falling out* in some relationship (see **Insight** in *hole*).

Insight: Falling into an abyss can be a metaphor for depression or a feeling of helplessness and confusion. But it can also be symbolic of change and transformation, especially at the end of the fall.

My intuitive self tells me that there's light at the end of this tunnel and a world that won't be the same as the one I left. That's a bit scary, but it's a little like Alice. While she was falling down the rabbit hole, she noticed all kinds of odd and interesting things along the way. Perhaps it's best to let it happen and see where it all takes me.

false: See *fake* or *veneer.*

false teeth: Are you not being honest with something? These can represent some kind of deception or people who aren't who they say they are.

fame: This can symbolize unrealized or unacknowledged achievement, goals, or aspirations? Perhaps you want to feel admired and are not.

family relationships: This could be about your internal value system. The *father* is the authority figure representing your ability to manage and control the external world. He can also represent the negative by being dominant and aggressive.

Your *mother* might represent your nurturing, emotional side and relationship sides, though the negative aspect of domination through emotions may also be present.

Siblings, sons, and daughters often reflect aspects of ourselves. Siblings can also represent rivalry for attention and recognition.

The son in a mother's dream can be about her ambitions or reflect the relationship with the boy's father.

Grandparents in a dream may represent the role that traditions play in your life, though they may also represent the archetypes of the wise old man, or woman. See *father, mother,* and *wise old man or woman* in the *archetypes* section. Also check out *kill or killing.*

If you're looking at a picture or posing for a picture of yourself and your family, where are you standing (close to or apart from some family member)? Who's missing? Answers to these questions might give insight to family dynamics.

famine: This could represent a negative turn in something. It can symbolize an unmet need for spiritual nourishment. It could reflect a need for love and attention and emotional support. Famine can be a metaphor for a need to nourish some part of yourself.

famous person: You may not feel noticed or important. Are you feeling unacknowledged? Are you having trouble accepting yourself as you are? The public and/or performance persona of an entertainer might give you a clue as to the image's meaning in your life.

See also *celebrity* and/or *fame*.

fan: Perhaps you need to cool down from a highly emotional situation.

fanatic: Are you being excessive or too zealous about something? Are you being stubborn and/or arrogant? Are you being too dogmatic and ignoring the opinions of others? Are you ignoring the evidence? Perhaps you're too intolerant.

Alternatively, are you being too impartial or not impartial enough? Do you need to yield a little more?

fancy: Are you or is someone else presenting a false façade? Are you putting on airs?

fangs: Have you been critical or hurtful (either to others or yourself)? This may symbolize something that was said that may have been hurtful (see *vampire*).

fantasy: Perhaps you need to be more imaginative and explore out-of-the-box options. Alternatively, it may reveal the need to be more realistic or practical.

far: To see something far away might suggest that you are being too emotionally distant or that you're feeling alone and left out. Perhaps you have a goal that you think you can't obtain or that you may have failed to achieve.

Do you need to see far in order to be more future oriented and not stuck in the past or too shallow in the present?

fare: This is the price you need to pay for something.

farewell: This is saying goodbye to something or someone and can signal an end to some relationship.

farm: This can represent the earthy and pragmatic part of one's nature and values. It could represent a need for growth.

farmer's market: This may represent spiritual, emotional, psychological enrichment.

farsighted: Are you overlooking some detail, or are you missing what's right in front of you because you're focusing too much on the big picture?

farting: Are you being passive aggressive? Perhaps you or someone else needs to be more direct.

fashion: Do you depend too much on your looks or how you look to others in order to get your way? Perhaps you need to look deeper within yourself.

fast: This could symbolize being in a hurry, impatience, or efficiency (see *running*).

fast food: This might suggest that you're not taking enough time to meet your own needs.

fast forward: Perhaps you need to slow down or look at the consequences of some planned action.

fasting: This could be about cleansing yourself for the purpose of self-renewal and/or healing. It could also reflect withholding or denying some part of yourself. Consider also that this could represent self-punishment for some guilt.

Perhaps you're experiencing a lack of emotional nourishment, nurturing, and intimacy.

fat: If you're fat in the dream but not in waking life, it may have something to do with your abundance, or you may be feeling that you are being overindulgent. Perhaps you need to be more moderate in your actions.

Are you feeling satisfied or dissatisfied with your life?

Consider the phrase "It ain't over until the fat lady sings." There's also the fear

of you gaining weight, or you may have a slanted image of yourself that's affecting your self-image.

fate: Are you unwilling to take responsibility for what's happening to you by blaming something (or someone) other than yourself? Are you depending too much on something outside yourself?

father: This image suggests an authority or protection figure.

If you are trying to get your father or stepfather to help with something, perhaps you need to tap into your own inner authority and take more responsibility for something. See the *archetypes* section. See also *patricide*.

Father Christmas: See *Santa Claus*.

fatigue: Do you feel worn out? Perhaps you're getting tired of something or someone.

faucet: This may represent the control of your emotions. Are you able to turn them on or off? If it is leaking or broken and running water is everywhere, perhaps your emotions are out of control, or you are losing control? Perhaps you are emotionally overwhelmed or drained.

fault: A fault line could represent the potential for upheaval in your life or some situation or decision. It could also be about self-blame or ducking blame or responsibility as in someone saying, "It's not my fault."

faulty structure: This may represent failings in yourself, a broken relationship, or some physical problem. See also *ruins*.

faun: If you see a half goat, half human with horns in your dream, it may reflect your carefree attitude (positive or negative). Consider also *fawning over* someone (i.e., praising excessively), which is usually seen as insincere. This may also show up as a *fawn*.

fawn: This may suggest something new and just beginning. See also *deer* in *animal*.

fax machine or fax: Perhaps some message from your subconscious is trying to get through. Are you not viewing something accurately, or are you not seeing the reality of something?

FBI: Are you experiencing some feelings of guilt? Maybe you desire to be wanted. If you're the agent, perhaps it reflects your sense of honor, integrity, and orderliness. Your own attitude about the FBI will add much meaning to this image as well.

fear: How much does it run your life? How much control of your emotions do you have? What are you afraid of? What runs you? Sometimes fear can represent unexpressed love.

Perhaps you need to learn what and what not to fear.

Insight: Anxiety or fear is probably the most common emotion in dreams. All the events of the day that have vexed you can come up as fearful elements in the dream. Remember that everything in a dream is an aspect of you. If you're being chased by some monster, it's yourself that you're trying to escape, and given that you can't escape yourself, you might as well confront this aspect and find out more about it.

Start by defining the feeling so you can get clarity on what it is you're avoiding.

Sometimes going over the events in your life that may be generating your fears in the waking world can help you defuse the emotions attached to them. When working with both adults and children, I used to have them relax into a meditative state and imagine that they were walking down a long, dark hallway. At the end of this hallway was a huge door of heavy wood that was banded in iron. I told them to imagine that behind the door there was the most frightening creature they had ever experienced, and then I said that they had to open the door and confront it head on.

I then instruct them to grab the handle, pull hard, and swing the door wide. I would ask "What's there?" I would tell them to be with it and not run. I would tell them to ask it what it wanted and have a conversation with it. This exercise worked well as a guided meditation, so having a trusted confederate lead you through it helps.

See also *scared*.

feast: This can suggest emotional needs or sexual appetite. If you're hungry during a feast, perhaps you're putting others' needs ahead of your own.

feathers: These often represent the powers or nature of the bird they came from. For example, an eagle feather may be about strength. A crow/raven feather may be about the unconscious. The peacock feather about beauty and transcendence, and an owl feather may be about wisdom.

Feathers can also represent intuition, imagination, and spiritual growth. The ancient world saw them as representing the flight between the earth and the spirit world. They can also represent transformation.

Like angels that wore them as wings, they represent spiritual messengers. Because they are subject to even the softest breezes, they can represent the psyche's ability to pick up imperceptible currents that the conscious mind may not see and thus hint at new possibilities. Consider the simile

"light as a feather" for the need to be less serious (see *birds* in *animal* section).

Insight: In alchemy there was a three-step process represented by three colored feathers, the nigredo or black feather (that which is unconscious and concrete in form); the white feather or albedo (that which is brought into the light); and the rubedo or red feather (which represented the actualization of insights).

feces: This represents aspects of yourself or your life that you may judge to be dirty/negative, repulsive, undesirable, and/or shameful.

The excrement image may be related to something that may have been useful to you at one time but is no longer needed, something you may want or need to give up.

If the feces is someone else's, it may reflect the need to let go of the negative assertions, judgments, or criticisms of others.

If the feces is everywhere, then perhaps the problem is pervasive. You may need to rid yourself of it. If you're constipated, it could be that you're being overly controlled or controlling.

If it's on your or someone else's body or face, perhaps you think that you look or feel shitty.

If you have feces on your hands, perhaps you are responsible for the negative stuff that is happening in your life.

If someone is defecating in your yard, a person may be besmirching your reputation (see *defecate* and *yard*).

feeding: This may symbolize that someone may be in need of attention or love. If you're feeding yourself, it could suggest a need to nourish yourself physically and/or spiritually.

feelings: See *emotions*.

feet: This could symbolize the stability and the foundation of your life. Can you stand on your own two feet? They can represent a sense of independence and keeping yourself grounded and practical. Consider the phrase "Putting your foot in your mouth" in reference to making a verbal blunder (e.g., misspeaking).

Washing someone's feet or having your feet washed might be about forgiveness. Following some footprints might suggest that you aren't taking your own path in life or in some activity.

female: This can reflect the mother in both a positive or negative light. If the female dominates in the dream, this might be symbolic of the role of mother in one's life.

In general, women in a man's dream can reflect his own feminine traits and/or his relationship to his own mother. A man's wife or girlfriend in a dream might also reflect the mother-son relationship.

See the *archetypes* section under *feminine*, *animus*, and *mother*.

This image will have different meanings based on whether it appears in a man's dream or a woman's dream.

fence: This may be similar to a wall. It's an obstacle or barrier in your growth path. It's a metaphor for the walls you put up to protect yourself or to keep others out. You may even be shutting yourself out.

It can also be a social barrier or what you use to segregate. It could represent feelings or attitudes about territoriality (see *trapped* and *wall*).

A crumbling fence could be about the need to take down the obstacles that you put up between yourself and others.

Falling from a fence could mean that you're in over your head and that you fear failing with some endeavor.

Fences in water can symbolize emotional barriers. (Water is often a symbol for one's emotional state.)

fencing: Are you at odds with someone or yourself? If you don't recognize the person, it could represent a conflict with yourself.

fender bender: A dent in the fender or a car accident could symbolize that someone is attacking your character. If you are the cause of the dented fender in the dream, then perhaps you need to be more tolerant and accepting (i.e., less critical of someone or something).

feng shui: Do you need more balance in your life?

fermenting: This suggests letting something develop over time. Spiritual transformation or something that you haven't dealt with will transform into something else, possibly even something that's more negative.

ferret: This could symbolize distrust or suspicion. Do you have some trust issues? Consider the verb "to ferret out," meaning to search for something.

Ferris wheel: Are you going around in circles? See *carousel* as well.

ferryboat: Are you going through some transitional issues? Perhaps you are trying to set new goals.

You may be trying to get to the other side of some problem or see someone else's side to something (see *bridge*).

fertilizer: This may represent what can lead to your personal growth. This could also be about the absorption of knowledge (food for thought).

festival: That can suggest a celebration. You may be in a good place, or you want to be. Or you may be trying to escape the everyday.

fetish: In some North American tribes (e.g., Navajo or Zuni), these can represent characteristics and/or powers of an animal that the owners would like to have for themselves. For example, these include wolf, badger, bear, mountain lion, and eagle fetishes. See *animal terms* for possible meaning of your fetish animal.

There are also certain protective fetishes (see also *statues* or *idols*).

This symbol may also represent certain obsessive traits in you. These might signal rigid behaviors, or you might be attracted to certain sexually kinky behaviors.

fetus: This may be about a developing relationship, idea, or skill (see *baby* and/ or *pregnant*).

feud: Perhaps there's some inner conflict with others or yourself. Are you not accepting of ideas or others?

fever: This may reflect anger that needs a safe way to express itself.

fictional character: perhaps you're trying to escape your reality, change identities, or absorb the qualities of the character into your own way of being.

fiction: This might be about something being unreal (i.e., a fantasy or a lie).

If you see a fictional character in your dream, he or she might represent an aspect of yourself. You might also look up the type of character (e.g., king, queen, goddess, hero, wizard, witch, etc.) in the *archetypes* section, or if it's an animal, you can look it up in *animals as fantasy creatures*.

field: This is an open area away from people where you can be with your natural self. Being out in a field can be about freedom from social pressure.

It could represent a feeling state. Are you feeling constricted, trapped, or limited? It can also represent the general career you find yourself in (i.e., your field of interest). See *landscape*.

field trip: If you are going on a field trip, this might suggest that you need to practice something you've learned or that you need to see something firsthand in order to understand it. This can be a transitional indicator between theory and application.

fiend: This often represents the need to confront your own demons. See devil in the *archetypes* section.

fighting: This can symbolize anger and frustration, a release of pent-up energy (such as fear), violent resolution, or just fighting for something such as your honor or autonomy. Sometimes it's a release of stored-up fear. Perhaps you need to confront some issue.

Insight: Basically, humans have only two forms of response to threat—flight or fight (i.e., to aggress or run away, confront or avoid, chase or be chased, stand up for something or be a bystander, get involved or be indifferent, own up to something or lie).

See also *battle, conflict, enemy*, or *soldier/ warrior*.

fig leaf: This possibly symbolizes a loss of innocence or trying to hide your vulnerability.

file: This could be a place where memories are kept, including images of yourself. Perhaps you need to revisit them. If it's in disarray, perhaps you're having difficulty organizing something.

film: If you're watching a film, perhaps you are analyzing some part of yourself or your life. It can also be about old memories looked at from a different perspective, perhaps more objectively.

If you are in the process of developing a film, perhaps you are developing or have developed some new project or relationship.

finding: This can symbolize discovery. This action in a dream can represent something lost then found or that needs to be found or reintegrated into the personality. This symbol can be about exploring or the need to explore unused potential or hidden talent (see *exploring*).

If you're trying to find something or someone you've lost, this could be about trying to reconnect with a part of yourself.

finger: If you see someone giving the finger in your dream, perhaps you are saying f—— you to those around you. Do you feel demeaned, criticized, or attacked?

If your fingers or hand is cut off, it might suggest you feel you have lost some control. Perhaps you are losing your grasp of some situation or idea.

See also *fingers* in *body terms*.

This image of a hand with fingers cut off can symbolize anxiety about one's ability to accomplish some task. Are you losing your grip? Is someone preventing you from reaching some goal?

fingernails: These can be about protection or glamour. If they are broken, it might suggest something about your self-image, or maybe you're feeling defenseless and vulnerable.

Painting and polishing your nails can also be about your self-image.

If you're chewing your nails, perhaps you are worried about something, or maybe something has become too tough to deal with.

Fake fingernails may reflect your disingenuousness toward someone.

fingerprint: If you are being fingerprinted, perhaps you're feeling guilty. It could also suggest that you are trying to find your identity.

finish line: Perhaps your goals are in sight. If you can't get to it, perhaps your goals have been put on hold or have been frustrated or blocked.

fire: This is another of the four ancient elements of earth, air, fire, and water. Like its partner and elemental opposite, water, it can represent one's emotional and temperamental aspect.

This image may suggest passion, spirit, energy, or cleansing. This may reveal a desire to destroy or to be renewed, a desire to rid yourself of something hurtful to you or others.

Insight: In the Christian period of Pentecost, it was said that the followers of Jesus had flames flickering from their heads as though they were alive with the intensity and passion of the Holy Spirit, which had descended upon the earth after Jesus was lifted into heaven.

Flames shooting from the head could also represent thoughts and passions that are changing or may signal that you need a different point of view.

Not too long ago, I had a friend share a dream where there were *walls of fire* that stood in his way on a road.

He could overcome some of these walls, but one was intractable. The *wall of fire* could be a personality trait such as a hot and quick temper that keeps others at bay or an event or a person who has become an obstruction to your forward progress. In my friend's case, it was a health issue that eventually took his life.

If you're lighting a fire, perhaps there is some project that you need to get started on. If you're lighting someone on fire, perhaps you are trying to motivate the person toward some goal.

If you are escaping a fire to safety, this could be a subconscious reassurance of your ability to overcome some difficulty or a setback regarding the achievement of some goal.

Fire can also be creative by being symbolic of forging something.

Also consider the phrase "playing with fire," meaning acting dangerously or irresponsibly. Could you get hurt from your current behavior?

Fire in dreams can be about one's temper or temperament (fiery). If you are burned in the dream, it might suggest that someone's temper is out of control and is hurting others or the dreamer.

If a house is on fire, it might suggest the need for some transformation or that some transformation is taking place that will change the very structure of the dreamer's inner being. This is the power of fire—to transform reality.

Astrologically, a fire personality can be found within Leo, Aries, and Sagittarius, which are all rather intense and fiery (i.e., the so-called *wild children* of the zodiac).

In the tarot, it shows up in the suit of wands and symbolizes conversion or passion, positive or negative, refining or destroying, new beginnings or opposition, and/or progress or oppression.

In some religions fire can be about regeneration, resurrection, and renewal, as with the phoenix bird that goes up in flames only to be reborn again and again (see *phoenix*).

Fire is often about internal change and transformation.

See also *burning* and *burning house*.

firecracker: This could represent your emotional outbursts.

fired: To be fired from your job can mean that you want or need to end some relationship or job. It can also reflect your fears and anxieties related to some activity in your waking life.

fire extinguisher: Are you trying to get your emotions under control? Has someone put out your passion? Do you need to let go of something (e.g., anger, revenge, desire, or an all-consuming thought)?

firefighter: This could be a hero symbol. Do you need to cool down some part of your personality or some situation?

fireplace: This could be about a burning desire or about the need for warmth and comfort.

Stoking a fire can be about trying to light the fire under someone or some project (i.e., to get something going).

fireworks: This could possibly symbolize an illumination, a bright idea, an insight, or a feeling of being in love. It can also represent enthusiasm, or it could mean that you are making a spectacle of yourself. Fireworks can also be about letting off steam (i.e., pent-up feelings). Consider also the phrase "playing with fire," suggesting that you might get burned or seriously hurt.

fish: This is also a Christian symbol that may speak to the spiritual side of yourself. According to Carl Jung, it could represent the creative energy of the unconscious mind.

See also *animals*.

fish bait: Are you fishing for compliments or for some attention? Are you missing some romance in your life?

fishing: Are you searching for something (e.g., yourself, companionship, life's answers, a purpose, a compliment, etc.)? Are you trying or should you be trying to bring your repressed emotions to consciousness so that you can deal with them?

fishing pole: This suggests an exploration of the subconscious mind. If the pole is bending to the point of breaking, are you being too hard on yourself or too rigid in your approach?

fishpond: This could be about subconscious material revealing itself (see also *pond*).

fishy smell: If you smell something fishy in your dream, perhaps something is not as it seems. Can you trust what someone is saying? Should you be on your guard?

fist: This could be about anger and/or aggression (see also *fight*).

fix: If you are trying to fix something, perhaps there is something you need to take another look at and reevaluate, reassess, or change (in order to repair a relationship or the effects of something you've done).

Perhaps something is not working as it should or as advertised or predicted.

What you're trying to fix will add meaning as well. If you're trying to fix a broken electrical object, it might be about rejuvenating yourself or getting back your personal power or motivation.

flags: This can be about duty, honor, patriotism, or some political or social statement (negative or positive). For example, for some people the Confederate flag is a symbol of enslavement, bigotry, and exclusion while others perceive it as symbolizing self-rule, pride, and independence.

Burning a flag can be about the destruction of pride and self-esteem or the loss or release of some emotion. The burning can also be the rejection or loss of something or some part of yourself that the flag may represent. The burning can also represent anger or the desire to rid oneself of old dependencies or viewpoints and beliefs. It can also be symbolic of something or some part of you being denigrated or of you doing the same to others.

Flags can also be warnings as in the case of a *red flag*, or they can suggest that you've done something wrong as with a flag on the play.

flame: Seeing a flame could be about purifying, an argument, an old relationship, or some commentary on someone's overt sexual predilection. Perhaps you're playing with fire and are risking the chance of getting burned/hurt.

flashlight: Are you questioning some issue about yourself or trying to shed some light on something? It could also be a metaphor for insightfulness or a flash of inspiration.

If the flashlight goes out or the lights go out and you need to use a flashlight, ask yourself, "Am I being kept in the dark about something?"

Do you need to look deeper into your subconscious for some understanding of what's going on?

flash mob: This suggests unity and cooperation or the need to coordinate something.

flat tire: Has some part of your life gone flat? Flat tires can also be about being emotionally drained and having trouble moving on in life. Driving on a flat tire could mean that you're not ready to slow down or accept defeat and that you will move on in any way possible.

See also *tires* and/or *car*.

flea market: Are you selling yourself short? Do you feel underappreciated? See also *buying*.

flirting: This can be about a need for intimacy. If a spouse or boy or girlfriend is flirting with someone else in the dream, perhaps you are feeling an emotional or physical distance, or maybe there's a communication gap between you. See *amorous* as well.

floating: This could possibly reflect a sense of freedom (like flying) or being insubstantial, light, unattached, or soaring. Do you feel unsinkable as though you're on top of everything?

Are you trying to rise above the struggles or problems that surround you?

Floating can also suggest that you've been set adrift with no clear direction or goal to shoot for. See also *flying* and *hover*.

flood: Overwhelming emotion of any kind, such as negative emotions or fear (see also *tidal wave*, *hurricane*, and *water*). One can also be overwhelmed by circumstances and dream of floods.

Consider also the idea of something being swept away that can either be positive or negative.

floor: This could be about basic security or your support system. It could also refer to your ground of being, your values foundation, and your belief system. What condition is the floor in? Does it show cracks or holes? Has it disappeared beneath you? Are you feeling insecure?

Flooring might also be a symbol of protection of things valued. If something is hidden beneath the floor, you might want to look at what you are hiding from others or from yourself.

flowerpot: This could be a metaphor for the womb. It can also be about protection. Consider the possibility that it may represent the feminine aspect of yourself. It may also be a restricted or limiting aspect affecting your growth.

flower terms: Jung saw the rose as representing the mandala, a symbol of the unconscious self. He thought that dreams with roses were very spiritual in nature (see *mandala*).

Roses can be about love and relationship, or they could suggest that people should take time out for themselves and smell the roses.

Live flowers may signify compassion, beauty, or pleasure. Withered flowers might reflect disappointments, while dead ones reflect depression or something gloomy. Has something in you died or gone to waste?

(r) rose; (l) lavender; (c) chamomile; (ww) wormwood; (v) vervain; (pf) passionflower; (g) ginseng; (lB) lemon balm

A bouquet might be about acknowledgment, reward, or admiration.

Lilies might represent the Trinity, the Virgin Mary, Easter, rebirth, or royalty (as in the *fleur-de-lis*).

The mystics used flowers for metaphysical purposes and spiritual cleansing. *Lavender* is a flower placed under a pillow to encourage dreams. To smell it in a dream can symbolize calmness and peacefulness.

Orchids may suggest that you need to give special attention to something or someone. They can also be reminders that you are surrounded by specialness.

Look to see what flowers mean to you in your daily life (love, sex, commitment, recognition, relationship, spiritual, sympathy, or celebration).

There are also medicinal plants that can aid in dream incubation, nightmare control, and sleep induction. For example, *lavender* can be used as a tea additive. It can be placed under the pillow or grown in a pot near the bed. *Chamomile* can be used as a tea or grow in a pot near the bed. *Licorice* can be infused into a tea, or it can be used as a hard candy or drop before bed. *Wormwood* can be used under your pillow or in a tea. It has also been used to calm nightmares. There are sometimes side effects (such as seizures), so if you are ingesting this plant in any form, you should be very careful. It is also found in absinthe. *Vervain* can be used in its dried form in a sachet near your pillow, and it can help with sleep. *Passionflower* can be used to treat insomnia. *Ginseng* in a tea can help induce sleep. *Sage* can be burned as a smudge during a meditation just before sleep, and *lemon balm* can be used as a tea for a soothing night's sleep.

Insight: The flower symbolism associated with poppies is beauty, magic, consolation, fertility, and eternal life. It was also the field where Dorothy of *The Wizard of Oz* fell unconscious and lost her focus on her goal to reach the Emerald City.

Tulips mean eternal life and are heralds of spring. Tulips also are symbolic of fame

and perfection. *Foxglove* flowers have both positive and negative symbolic meanings. They are said to sometimes hurt and sometimes heal. In the language of flowers, foxglove is associated with insincerity.

The *morning glory* is appropriately named because the flower blooms in the morning and dies by the afternoon.

Georgia O'Keeffe brought the *calla lily* to prominence with her series of close-up paintings of single calla lily flowers. She wanted the viewer to look closely at the fundamental form of the flower without any preconceived notions. Some consider many of her paintings to be spiritual in nature.

The concept of *seeing* something with no preconceived notions is often the Eastern way of seeing something's true nature. The idea that our judgments and expectations obscure reality is discussed in *The Dragon's Treasure*. Also, her paintings of all flowers were quite sensual in nature.

If a man could pass through Paradise in a dream, and have a flower presented to him as a pledge that his soul had really been there, and if he found that flower in his hand when he awake—Aye, what then?

—Samuel Taylor Coleridge

Flowers and their essences are often used to deal with depression (St. John's wort) as well as sleeplessness and stress reduction (passionflower and chamomile). For the incubation of dreams, mugwort, lavender, and chamomile are the most frequently employed. They can be used as an oil, in a tea, or in a fresh floral display. Often lavender is placed as a sachet under a pillow before sleep.

A poinsettia may represent the blood of the Christ, the Christ himself, and/or the giving of affection or the need to give love.

Consider also the term *flowery* as a statement of being too hyperbolic in your presentation (exaggerating or extravagant). It can also mean fancy and eloquent and something you may wish you had more of.

flute: To see or hear a flute in your dream might suggest that things are going smoothly in your life. But the flute can also be about sorrow and longing.

Sometimes flute music can highlight the feeling of something magical.

fly ball: Trying to catch a fly ball can be a metaphor for attainment. Are you trying to hit an activity or idea out of the ball park (i.e., to be successful at something)? See also *home run*.

Missing a fly ball can represent a missed opportunity.

flying: This could be about independence, which is sometimes something one fights for. This might also suggest the overcoming of obstacles.

Flying can be symbolic of freedom from being grounded in the ordinary or chaotic emotions of life.

It's also a statement about wanting to soar and do something that will be noticed. You may want to be released from what society says is acceptable behavior.

Flying can be more than a bid for independence. It can also be about doing something special and making a real difference in the moment.

If you're flying and no one notices you or seems not to care about your flying, this might be symbolic of the feeling that no one notices you or how special you are or recognizes your talents.

It's an attempt to overcome the helplessness of being stuck on the ground.

Often it's a statement about the desire to be free of your limits (i.e., those placed upon you and those you've placed upon yourself).

It can also represent the need for escape. Depending on the circumstances within the dream and your waking life, the image of flying can also depict its opposite (e.g., the need to be more grounded and less flighty).

Could flying high above it all be a desire for greater clarity and/or a higher perspective?

Flying can also represent gaining spiritual insight, the transformation of conventional thought, and eluding the limiting effects of gravity. The same could be said for helicopters and elevators. Any vertical ascent may symbolize evolving spiritual issues (see the *archetypes* section). See also *airplane, elevator, floating, helicopter,* or *hover.*

Insight: Flying has always been a magical dream experience for me that I have kept hidden from other people in the dream.

When I was going through extreme stress because of certain aspects of my job, I could not get airborne in my flying dreams, or if I did, it was a struggle to stay airborne.

When the stress came to an end because I took some actions, my dream flying became much easier.

Frequently, my flying dreams came to me when I was trying to overcome some circumstance or situation.

Often dreams reflect stresses and emotions from the waking world.

fly trap: Some plot may be afoot, or there may be some sticky situation. This might also be true for the image of flypaper. See also *trapped.*

fog: This might suggest confusion. Something may be obfuscated or hidden from sight. It may represent a lack of clarity.

Perhaps it represents something mysterious. Is the fog frightening or oppressive? Why? Is there something in your life that you can't quite see that is bothering you? See also *blurry, clouds, confused,* and/or *paradox.*

following: Something or someone *following you* might suggest that there is something you are not acknowledging. Are you being denied your power or influence? Do you need to look closer at your personal strengths?

Are you just following others and not taking responsibility for your life?

See also *chased, chasing, stalker,* or *stalking.*

foods: These can represent physical, sexual, spiritual, or emotional nourishment. Fruit may be sensual. Meat may be about animalistic desires. Vegetables could be about health (though it could also be about self-worth or feeling paralyzed).

Frozen foods can be about a cold personality. Citrus can be about a sour personality or suggest that something has *soured* you (prejudiced or caused resentment).

Oranges or apples can be about sweetness, or in the case of apples, they can also be about temptation or health.

Moldy food can be about negative energy around you or suggest that you have let something go on for too long and that it's spoiling something. Bad-tasting food can be about intense emotions.

Certain foods can be symbolic of qualities that you need to take into yourself.

If you're gorging yourself, it could symbolize a feeling that you have been denied something, or alternatively, it could reflect you're being too indulgent.

Fasting can be about denying yourself as well. It can also be seen as self-punishment because of guilt.

Certain foods are attached to good and bad memories. Some are comfort foods, but you find others distasteful. Look up specific foods for more information (see *bread, cheese, corn, dessert, egg, fish, fruit, lettuce, meat, milk, pizza, tomato,* or *vegetable*).

fool: See the *archetypes* section.

foolish: This could be about a fear or insecurity. It suggests a sense of incompetence. It may also be another word for childish or immature.

Insight: "Everything is possible, Grandpa!" said my youngest granddaughter in response to me saying, "You can't get me!" We were skipping along, and then we leaped onto the low wall framing a neighbor's garden. We walked along it while giggling and trying to be the first to push the other off onto the grass. For a brief moment, I thought about how foolish we must look.

On the way home from dropping her off at school, I thought about the idea of looking foolish and realized that the older I got, the less worried I was about looking foolish. This got me thinking about the image of the fool, one of the archetypes of the collective unconscious of the human psyche that we don't really talk about, and yet perhaps it's the most important.

What the fool shows us is that the impossible becomes possible, that life itself is full of miracles. As my wise granddaughter says, "Everything is possible, Grandpa!" See *fool* in the *archetypes* section.

foreign land: This may also be about change. If you're afraid or lost, perhaps you aren't ready for the change, but if you are happy about where you are, that might be an indication that you are ready for the change (see *alien*).

foreign language: There may be something coming up from your unconscious mind that you don't yet understand, or perhaps you aren't making yourself clear to others. Perhaps you're having difficulty expressing your thoughts, feelings, or ideas.

foreigner: Perhaps there's an aspect of yourself that is strange to you. Are you neglecting some part of yourself (see *stranger*)? Are you feeling disconnected from others or your surroundings?

forest: This can symbolize the world of the unconscious and the strange yet magical forces of your inner nature. You may be exploring a better understanding of yourself.

If you're lost in the woods, it could indicate being lost, being confused, or being without direction. Walking through it could indicate that you are changing and that you might want to follow your instincts as you go. If there are specific trees in the dream, look up those trees. You might also look up *woods*.

[A reader] does not despise real woods because he has read of enchanted woods: the reading makes all real woods a little enchanted.

—C. S. Lewis

FOREST

Forests are where we hide our natural selves, that which we want to protect from the chaos of the world we live in. In a dream, a forest symbolizes the magical world of our unconscious with all its strange forces, archetypal creatures, and the people of our souls.

forest fire: This could be about transformation or the regeneration found through hardship and struggle.

It could also reflect an out-of-control passion rising from the unconscious and wreaking havoc with your behavior in the waking world.

forgery: Perhaps you are not seeing something for what it really is. Are you lying about something? Are you being deceitful or manipulative, or is someone trying to manipulate you? Are you being something you're not?

forgetting: Perhaps you're experiencing a lot of stress that's creating a number of anxieties.

It is possible that the forgetting is a way of deliberately leaving something behind.

If others seem to be forgetting, this might be about something you've become and may not be proud of.

If you've forgotten where you live, perhaps you are experiencing some conflict at home and don't want to face it.

Forgetting can also be symbolic of too many burdens.

forgiveness: If someone asks for forgiveness in a dream, this may actually reflect some guilt and represent your need to ask for forgiveness. It's possible that you may want forgiveness for some aspect of yourself.

Forgiveness can also be about past grudges or resentments or the need to forgive (yourself or others).

Is there someone that you need to forgive? Is there something that you need to let go of?

See also *apologize.*

fort: This could symbolize defense or defending yourself. A fort can suggest the need to defend, the need to fortify (steel yourself or to nourish yourself), or the desire to add some supplement to your diet or life.

fortune cookie: Are you putting the responsibility for the direction of your life in someone else's hands?

Perhaps the *fortune* inside the cookie comes from your subconscious. What is it trying to say? You might reimagine the fortune after you wake. What does it say?

fortune-teller: Do you need to control what happens in situations? Do you have anxieties about the future or how your life is going to turn out? Are you seeking guidance in some situation?

Do you need to reevaluate your goals and ambitions?

If you don't believe in fortune-tellers in your waking life, the image in a dream might have something to do with your gullibility regarding some situation. See also *tarot.*

found: Perhaps you've found a hidden aspect to yourself. Finding something can also be about change or the need to research or look for something.

foundation: The foundation of a building can signify the stability of your life or the lack of it, as with a crumbling or cracked foundation. Foundations are the values and beliefs we build our lives upon.

foundling: See *abandoned* or *found*.

fountain: This could represent an outburst of emotions. It could also symbolize pent-up sexual urges that you need to release. If the fountain dries up, perhaps the excitement in something new is threatening to end or has come to a conclusion. Perhaps your creative juices have dried up.

foxhole: This may represent a hidden aspect of yourself. You may be trying to defend yourself from some attack or aggression.

Are you *digging in* for a rough time of it? Alternatively, do you need to get out of the hole you have dug yourself into? Do you need to stop hiding?

See also *hole*.

fragments of dreams: Even single images or seemingly unconnected images or emotions can reflect the essence of the whole.

What seems like meaningless information can yield immense insight if held in the right context. If it is true that you and I are projecting our wholly subjective meaning onto our experience of objective reality—and I believe that we do—then in everything we see (while awake or dreaming), we can glean information about our inner selves. Every event becomes a mini reflection of who we are.

frame: To see a frame in your dream without a picture in it might be about someone setting you up to take the blame for something. Do you feel unfairly judged or accused?

It can also suggest the structure for some project or idea. It can also be a metaphor for your body (i.e., your physique). Note the condition of the frame.

It could also be symbolic of a framework, map, or schematic for something. Are you having difficulty framing your thoughts (i.e., organizing your thoughts)?

It might also symbolize a new way of looking at something.

Did you feel disapproval when you were hoping for praise?

Frankenstein: If you see a Frankenstein monster in your dream, perhaps you feel rejected by society, outcast, and alone. Do you feel you are misunderstood? See also *monsters*.

fraud: Are you defrauding people (i.e., cheating them or alternatively not being real with them)? This kind of dream might also indicate guilt on your part.

Are you being too trusting?

See also *lie or lying* or *pretending*.

freeze: This could symbolize emotional coldness or rigidity. It can refer to holding something rigid in time or place.

Freud, Sigmund: In the 1890s, Sigmund Freud elevated the use of dreams to the research level of science and championed their usage as a means of understanding the individual psyche. To him, "Dreams are the royal road to the unconscious."

Sigmund S. Freud

His seminal work was written in 1899 in German and titled *Die Traumdeutung* (later translated into English in 1913 by Macmillan Press). This work introduced his theory of the unconscious as it is related to dreams. He thought of dreams as "thoughts in pictures."

Interestingly enough, he saw all dreams as attempts to resolve inner conflicts, though he thought of them as being variously connected with sex. Thus, all were seen as some form of wish fulfillment.

Perhaps his greatest contribution to psychological knowledge was that he showed that dreams were the means for consciously connecting with the unconscious mind. This led him to understand better the origins of neuroses and strategies for dealing with them.

Freud was able to show a very real connection between the unconscious mind and the actions people take in the external world.

friend: Each person in the dream reflects aspects of ourselves. A person may represent some quality or personality aspect that you admire and would like to have for yourself. Certain people may also represent past events or time periods in your life.

Fromm, Erich: Erich Fromm was an analyst from New York who talked about his ideas regarding the purpose of dreams in the 1940s and '50s. In his books *The Forgotten Language, Escape from Freedom, Man for Himself,* and *The Art of Living,* he outlined a concept of dreams that addressed the biological drives and urges postulated by Freud and the wisdom and spirituality that characterized Jung's work.

frown: If you are frowning, are you being critical of yourself or others? Are you angry about something? See *angry* and/or *smile*.

fruit: This may signify growth and even financial gain. It can also be about lust. Ripe fruit can be about fertility. Buying, selling, rejecting, or seeing fruit go missing could suggest that you are doing something that will not bear fruit (i.e., not work out to your advantage). See specific fruits for more information.

frustration: This feeling can suggest real-life frustrations. It can also reveal thwarted intentions or expectations (see *anger*).

fugitive: Are you running away from something? Are you not willing to be responsible for some action or to face up to something?

It may also reflect guilty feelings. This could depict that you are avoiding something (see *chased*).

funeral: This image can reflect feelings about death. It could also be a health warning. It could also be about the end of something or be a metaphor for burying the past.

fur: This suggests warmth and comfort. Perhaps you are coming on too hard and should use a softer approach with something.

furniture terms: Furniture can be about attitudes and beliefs from your childhood, your identity, and/or what you show to others about yourself.

Note where the piece of furniture is located or even the condition it is in because this will add to its meaning.

> **bed:** This may represent your intimate self. If you can't find it, are you having difficulties with your intimate self? If floating up from the bed, you may be feeling disconnected from those around you. Do you need to tone yourself down? If wetting the bed, you may feel out of control about some part of your life. Do you worry about being accepted?

> **chair:** If you see or sit in a chair, this can suggest that you should take time and contemplate or think about something.

> If you are in a chair off to the side, you may be feeling cast aside. If you are offered a chair, this may signify someone offering help or advice. Perhaps you should take it.

> It can also be a euphemism for the head or leader of something.

> Pulling the chair out from under someone may reflect a feeling of betrayal or a loss of support or loyalty. It may also be an act of anger and an attempt to get your attention.

A *wheeled chair* may be an euphemism for a wheelchair (see *wheelchair*).

See also *pew*.

desk: Perhaps you are working with or weighing problems. A cluttered desk may mean that you need to organize yourself better. An empty desk could be about moving on to something new. It could also mean that you're about to be laid off.

lamp: This can be about guidance and hope, inspiration and/or enlightenment. (I see the light!) If it's dim, then you may feel a little overwhelmed, and you may be having trouble finding your way. If you're having a religious dream, a dim light could refer to the dimming or loss of your faith (see *light*).

sofa or couch: This could symbolize rest, relaxation, or laziness. Like the image of the bed, this can have sexual meanings as well.

table: This could symbolize a family unity. Is it stable or wobbly? If someone is standing on the table and overlooking you, it could represent defiance or a feeling of being overpowered. Who is standing on the table, and what part of his or her personality is being expressed or may be represented in you?

As with any piece of furniture, the table can have very personal meanings. For example, the table could be the table where your grandmother served milk and cookies when you were young and thus be symbolic of being loved. In another context, it could represent the table where you were forced to sit and stare at a wall for hours as a punishment, and thus, it might not symbolize love at all. Actually, both can be a reflection for the need for love.

future: If you dream that you are in the future, you may be wondering how things will turn out. Note your emotions associated with being in the future. Are you worried, fearful, apprehensive, and/or hopeful?

Are you trying or do you want to avoid certain circumstances in the present or get away from your past?

Future-predicting dreams: There are many examples of dreams that seem to predict future events. Some may be the result of coincidence, faulty memory, or an unconscious tying together of known information. A few laboratory studies have been conducted on predictive dreams as well as clairvoyant and telepathic dreams, but the results have varied because these kinds of dreams are difficult to study in a laboratory setting.

G

gagging: You may be having trouble expressing something or how you really feel about something or someone. Is someone suppressing you in some way? Is something making you sick?

Gaia: This figure is symbolic of the Earth Mother.

This image might also represent synergy, self-regulation, and the importance of respecting the ecosystem or relationships between people and their environments.

See also *earth, goddess,* or *Great Mother* in this section and in the *archetypes* section.

gallows: Are you feeling threatened somewhere in your life? Do you feel betrayed and hung out to dry?

Consider also dark humor (i.e., gallows humor) as a means of dealing with unpleasant, frightening, and painful issues, circumstances, and/or memories.

gambling: Are you playing around with your life or counting too much on luck to achieve your goals? Perhaps you're taking too many risks with something (e.g., your health, family, career, money, etc.). See also *lottery* or *betting.*

game: If you are playing a game in your dream, are you playing around and not taking something seriously? Are you taking chances with someone else's life or with your own? See also *cards* and/or *gambling.*

Ganesha: He is often perceived as the remover of obstacles. As a god, he sometimes represents an archetype within us, one representing our spiritual aspect and perhaps the need to grow in that or some specific aspect of that.

For further symbolism regarding Ganesha, note the story and symbolic significance of this image as part of the Hindu pantheon.

Ganesha, the remover of obstacles,
the symbol of new beginnings,
and in some versions, the lord of
letters, learning, and wisdom

gangster: This is symbolic of ruling by force. This could represent the unruly part of yourself.

garage: This image takes on meaning when you explore what you feel when in your own garage both in the sleeping and waking dream.

If you're having a garage sale, it could reflect parts of yourself you're trying to get rid of. It could also be lessons you're learning that you're passing onto others.

If it is an automotive garage, perhaps there's some part of your life that needs fixing or a tuning up.

Are you storing/hiding something?

garbage: This may symbolize cleaning up and throwing away. What are you ready to give up or get rid of? Perhaps there's some negative habit or behavior you're ready to get rid of.

Garbage could also refer to how you are feeling about yourself or someone else. Do you feel useless? Do you feel like garbage? A garbage can could represent unwanted ideas, memories, or feelings—things that you reject (see *trash*).

garden: This could be symbolic of the inner self, the soul, your personal attributes, and their growth and development. If you encounter weeds, you may want to look at disagreeable parts of yourself that you need to pull out.

Dying gardens might reflect a neglect of your spiritual needs.

If you are creating a garden, it could be about the development of something new. This could reflect what is going on inside you or what you need to tend to and nurture so that it will grow healthy.

Working on a vegetable garden may be about growth, living with better health, or living more simply.

See also *landscaping* and *pruning*.

garden of Eden: Perhaps you are trying to recapture some innocence. It's also a symbol of peacefulness and abundance, a place where one's responsibilities are fewer and less burdensome.

gargoyle or grotesque: This is an ugly creature designed to scare but also to protect against evil. It is a shadow aspect, and like all shadows, it has two purposes— to scare others and to protect the sacred inner sanctum of ourselves. It teaches us the very part of our nature that we need to accept in order to become whole.

Insight: Gargoyles are like shamanic skull markers, wind demons, or a grinning multiheaded serpent called a naga.

They show up as fearsome gatekeepers at Buddhist and Hindu temples, and they are also the dark creatures of our dreams. Shadows are not really to be feared. A gargoyle in all dreams are here in the service of our health and well-being, if only to bring our rejected selves back to the fold.

Garuda: This is a creature or demigod that may symbolize balance, fierceness, power, and courageous struggles toward your highest goals and ambitions.

Because it is part animal (bird) and part human, it may also represent the need for balance between one's animal (body) and human (intellectual) natures—the instinctive and the divine.

Garuda

Because it is a significant character in the Hindu and Buddhist religions, it may also speak to the spiritual nature of the dreamer. If it flies off, perhaps you are experiencing spiritual freedom or a desire for independence.

If it is attacking, especially if it's attacking you, then perhaps you are experiencing some inner spiritual conflict.

gas or gas station: What fuels or gives you energy? Do you need to reenergize or empower yourself?

gasoline tanker: If there's a fuel tanker in your dream, it could represent a gain, loss, or need for energy depending on the circumstances of the dream.

If it blows up, this could reflect your own emotional nature and thus represent anger or rage.

gate: A gate may be a threshold between things, events, and changes in your life.

A gate or a door can represent the passage from one part of your life to another. It can signal your climb up in the levels of maturity. Often teens who are about to graduate and enter adulthood have dreams of gates or a ship that is about to leave port and embark on some journey.

Basically, gates and doors suggest the transitions or changes in our lives (see *transition dreams*).

They are also metaphors for our social, emotional, and psychological openness with others (e.g., being open or closed), and thus, they may speak to the need to be private or to hide.

Insight: Some entrances represent boundaries or limits to be overcome. In the houses of our dreams, doors are entrances to different aspects of ourselves (e.g., feelings, attitudes, and beliefs). These are the rooms of the self.

Some doors or gates lead to unknown spaces and thus represent openings to the unconscious. People knocking at our door can be a metaphor for opportunities or some new relationship or experience (see *door*).

gatekeeper: This may represent what we allow into our lives or try to keep out. Perhaps you need to be more careful about who or what you let into your life or maybe you need to be more open.

gauntlet: This may be some obstacles that you need to negotiate. Perhaps you feel picked on, or you may feel others are hazing you. Do you feel challenged (i.e., confronted or criticized)?

Does work or some other emotional issue overwhelm you? Are you being hostile or feel like you're in a hostile environment? Consider also the phrase "Trial by fire" or the word *baptism*.

gay: See *homosexual*. Note that this image could also reflect your points of view or prejudices against gays and thus be an indicator of your need to be more accepting of something. It may also indicate that you are being too prejudiced and/or rigid in your actions or thoughts.

Gemini: This represents quick thinking, versatility, and adaptability. Do you need to incorporate some of these characteristics? See also *zodiac*.

gems: These represent spiritual protection, power, riches, and ambition. What do you treasure or value?

Some examples include the following:

Amethyst represents peace of mind and satisfaction.

Jade represents spiritual aspects and soul.

Chrysacola represents healing and wisdom.

Florite represents intuition.

Aragonite represents spiritual balance.

Blue lace agate represents calm and peacefulness.

Bismuth represents the shaman's or philosopher's stone, which suggests oneness and serenity.

Opal represents the libido and passion.

Onyx represents self-confidence, spirituality, and peace of mind.

Rhodonite can be about balance and patience.

Ruby represents passion.

Emerald represents strength, longevity, fertility, and healing.

Sapphire may be symbolic of protection, heaven, divinity, getting to the truth, or an aspect of the subconscious. This may also refer to someone born in September.

Diamond represents the wholeness of the self but also vanity, conceit, self-love, and/or love for another. If fake, are you trying to be someone you're not? Are you living beyond your means?

genius: To see yourself or someone else as a genius could be about communicating with your soul. It can also imply that in seeing the genius of another it's about communicating soul to soul and thus becoming aware of the immense potential that you hold within.

To appreciate the genius of another as with a writer, performer, poet, or artist is reflective of just such a soul-to-soul communication.

To see a genius is to remind yourself of the boundlessness of your being.

genocide: This image could be about a fear of everything you value being destroyed. It could also symbolize your fear of differences and the acceptance of those differences. This could be an emotional reaction to your shadow (see *shadow* in the *archetypes* section; see *killing* as well).

ghost: This represents things that may haunt us. It can also be about something from your past trying to contact you or come to consciousness. If the ghost is a person you know, it could represent the influence they might still have over you.

It can also refer to guilty feelings. You may also be a ghost of your original self (i.e., not what you used to be).

You might feel insubstantial as though you don't belong or aren't grounded. Are you not on solid ground when it comes to some situation or relationship?

If the ghost is violent (as with a poltergeist) in any way, it could reflect your own violent nature. Perhaps it reflects an aberration in your own personality or way of being.

If you sense the ghost as an unseen presence, it might represent some part of yourself that is disturbing you. It could also represent an unarticulated threat from someone outside yourself.

Are you being transparent?

Perhaps you are somewhat detached from the reality of a situation or from life and others around you.

Consider the colloquialism *ghosted*. Are you being ignored, or are you ignoring someone? Are you being cowardly and/or rude? Do you need to communicate with someone?

It could also be unfinished business from the past. See *chimera*, *haunted house*, *phantom*, or *specters or spectral figures*.

giant: This could symbolize power or inferiority if you are small and intimidated by the giant.

gift: This could represent acknowledgment, reward, and/or acceptance.

If you didn't earn or deserve the acknowledgment, you may feel guilty because of some deceit.

If you're given a gift that you didn't expect, this may represent divine grace or divine assistance.

Receiving a gift can also indicate a reward or a recognition for your generosity.

Giving a gift can sometimes refer to giving yourself or an exchange. It can represent the gift of healing or love, which may reflect a need to forgive.

Receiving a gift might suggest that you be open to receive something.

If the gift is to you and you don't want it, perhaps you are having difficulty accepting something or someone. By rejecting a gift, you might be rejecting some aspect of yourself.

gift wrap: Gift wrapping in your dream may suggest that there is something you are trying to cover up or hide. Maybe you're trying to present something unpleasant in a more cheerful way? Consider what you are wrapping for more meaning.

girl: She can represent the yin aspect of the self as well as the receptive, nurturing quality of the self. A girlfriend in the dream might signify the feminine ideal. What qualities of the ideal are you willing to take into yourself? This image may represent your emotional self (see *daughter* and *sister*).

girlfriend: This could be about your emotional feelings about your girlfriend or your attachment to her.

This image could be about your struggles, difficulties, hopes, and dreams in and for the relationship. As a female in a male's dream, she may also represent your anima or your feminine psychological aspects (e.g., intuition, compassion, patience, and creativity). See *anima/animus* in the *archetype* section.

Girl Scout: This could be about camaraderie, strong values, and being goal-oriented. Perhaps you need to emulate more of this.

If you are buying a Girl Scout cookie, it could be about giving into a temptation or the need to nurture, to give, or to help out.

glacier: This can represent emotional coldness. There's a lot hidden beneath the surface, more than meets the eye.

gladiator: Are you fighting for your survival? What do you need to confront or deal with?

glass: This could represent invisible yet real barriers between you and something (e.g., the glass ceiling). If you see a pair of reading glasses, perhaps there's something you're not seeing or refusing to see. Are you being shortsighted?

Broken glass can reflect feelings of powerlessness and/or a part of your life that's in pieces. Suddenly shattering some

glass might reflect a breakthrough or a need for a breakthrough.

glasses: Is there something you're having trouble seeing or need to see more clearly? If you've lost them, is your judgment a bit blurry? If you're taking them off or putting them on, perhaps you need to see something from a different perspective.

If they are broken, perhaps you're seeing something from a damaged or compromised perspective.

Are you making a *spectacle* of yourself?

glass slipper: This may represent a truth and/or transformation that is needed. It may also represent some insecurity or a hope for the future.

Perhaps you are hoping to be discovered or be loved and cared for.

See also *shoe*.

glassware: Broken glass can be about feelings of inadequacy, powerlessness, guilt, or low self-esteem. Perhaps you're feeling a little fragile.

Are you worried that others can see right through you?

As with a cup, this image can also be about healing and transcendence into a higher consciousness (see *cup*).

glow: See *bathed in light*.

glowing in the dark: If you see something glowing in the dark in your dream, it could represent an unconscious and hidden aspect of yourself. This may represent some deeper and/or spiritual aspect of yourself trying to come to consciousness.

It may also represent a need to bring some light or consciousness to some matter or problem.

glue: Are you emotionally stuck (i.e., dependent)? If glued to another person, perhaps there's mutual dependence or what is called codependence.

Gluing things together could mean that you may be trying to combine different aspects of yourself. It could also suggest that you are trying to *hold yourself together* when everything seems in chaos and flying apart around you.

goal: Where are you going in life? Where are you headed? What is your goal in life?

goblin: Is someone working against you? Is it your little judgmental and self-critical demon that is sabotaging you?

God: See *god and goddess* in the *archetypes* section.

god and goddess: This represents the divine masculine and feminine (e.g.,

creation and love). Men can be the gods in their own story much as they are the heroes of their stories. For women, the goddess can represent that connection she has with all women.

See the *archetypes* section and *Gaia*.

godhead: This may be the experience of otherness (see also *numinous*). It is often reflected in the dogma of the Christian Trinity—Father, Son, and Holy Ghost.

The Trinity itself can reflect an imbalance of too much masculine power, against which the relational and intuitive aspects of the feminine are suppressed, thus creating a loss of wholeness in the individual.

See also *trinity*.

God images: These may be a group of emotional images that operate within all of us. They may represent the cores or centers of our spiritual lives.

They may be what give us meaning and a place in the universe.

gold: If you or someone else has found gold, you may feel very lucky about your success, or you may have found something or someone you think is very special. See also *colors* and/or *coins*.

golf: This may be about how you *address* your issues or problems. What obstacles

225

are in the way of your success, and how do you handle them? The golf course becomes symbolic of your life and how you're playing the game.

The golf club could represent what *drives* you and your inner power.

Being in the rough could suggest that you are going through difficult times.

Putting on the green could be about taking your best shot at something.

If you're having difficulty with a shot, do you need to take a different stance (i.e., point of view)?

gossip: Perhaps you are being counterproductive. Are you passing on information that isn't true? Are you part of a problem?

government: What governs your actions? This can also be about external control, regulation, and influence in your sense of well-being. Do you need to control your behavior?

gown: This could be about social pleasure, culture, grace, or happiness. If it's elaborate, are you living a lifestyle that's too elaborate? If it's simple, perhaps you need to live more simply. Are you trying to fit in where you don't think you belong?

A long white gown may be a reference to your spiritual aspect.

See also *dress* in *clothing*.

grade: If you see a grade on a test paper, perhaps you are worried about how you're doing on some goal or project. It could be about how you're doing in some relationship.

It's also possible that it is someone's initial.

graduation: This could symbolize the completion or the end of something. This can be like death as well. After all, it is an end making way for a new way of being.

graffiti: This may be about self-worth, low or high. It may also be about defacement or vandalism that can reflect that you're up to mischief. If the graffiti spoils the view, ask yourself, "Am I or someone else spoiling something?"

Are you feeling unacknowledged, unimportant, and/or unnoticed?

Do you need to express your creative side more?

grammar: If someone is correcting your grammar, spelling, usage of prepositions, or sentence structure, perhaps you are questioning something's foundation (maybe your own grounding). Are you questioning the bedrock or underpinnings of your beliefs, who you think you are, or what you are worth?

Are you losing your footing, faith in yourself, or sense of support?

Are you questioning your knowledge or feeling ignorant? This may be particularly stressful if you pride yourself in your intelligence and/or quality of knowledge.

Are you not following the rules?

grandchildren: Grandchildren in dreams are frequently symbolic of the renewal of life but can also be a reflection of your own past.

Grandchildren can also represent the family line or the loss of it. They can represent the cycle of life and one's legacy and connection with the future.

Granddaughters in a woman's dream can be about her own aging and loss of youth.

grandparents: These people sometimes signify warmth, unconditional love, wisdom, tradition, or values. These can also represent unconscious attitudes.

It is also possible that they represent wisdom guides. What are they trying to show you?

Both can represent tradition or old ways of thinking or being.

If they are coming to *stay* with you, perhaps there's a part of them you would like to integrate within yourself. Perhaps you wish that they were with you again.

Whether it's a grandmother or grandfather, it might represent the anima/animus (see the *archetypes* section).

grapevine: This may be about wealth and/or decadence. It can also represent wine and happiness.

Consider the phrase "I heard it on the grapevine," meaning one overheard something informally or heard it through gossip. Are you gossiping?

Do you need to keep something confidential?

grass: This is often symbolic of personal growth or overgrown thoughts and feelings. This is also a nickname for *marijuana*.

grave: Is something dead? What in you may have died?

Is there something you would like to bury or keep hidden? Is there something you want to leave in the unconscious?

If you've fallen into a pit, you may be feeling depressed or in grave danger of failing. You may at least worry that you are going to.

graveyard: See *cemetery*.

Great Mother: See *goddess* or *queen*.

greedy: This can represent unfilled desires and selfishness. Do you feel a sense of loss or emptiness? Are you desperately trying to fill some void (see also *hoarding*)?

Greek: If someone is speaking Greek in your dream, perhaps there is something that you don't understand.

In the context of a classroom, it could mean that you desire to discuss your ideas.

Insight: In the fifth century BCE, something significant occurred in Greece when the philosopher Heraclitus suggested that a person's dream world was something created within his or her own mind. This was antithetical to the other philosophers of the day who thought that dreams were the result of *outside* forces, such as the gods.

Aristotle brought the feud to an end by studying dreams in a rational way. He concluded in his book *De divinatione per somnum*, "The most skillful interpreter of dreams is he who has the faculty of absorbing resemblances. I mean that dream presentations are analogous to the forms reflected in water."

green man: A vision of a man dressed in green or a face carved in stone surrounded by foliage may represent personal growth or some developing aspect of yourself. The green man may symbolize your inner nature and spirit. See also *forest* and *green* under *color*. You might also look into alien (little green men).

The green man is found across many cultures. It can be a symbol for rebirth, fertility, and the cycle of growth within.

Insight: In Celtic tradition, this image represents the god of vegetation and is strongly connected to other folk images, such as John Barleycorn, a character who represents the fall harvest in Great Britain.

It was said the tale of Sir Gawain and the Green Knight from the Arthurian legend included a form of the green man as a knight and was a representative of the pre-Christian nature religion.

The visage shows up all over England as carvings in stone in various ancient buildings. There was a revival of its usage as an architectural element during the reign of Queen Victoria.

Some have said that Peter Pan as well as Robin Hood may have represented the green man archetype.

grimoire: Dreaming of a book of magic might suggest some mystery. Perhaps there's some hidden wisdom you need to look for. See also *alchemist, magician or conjurer, occult, witchcraft,* or *wizard.*

grim reaper: See *angel of death.*

growing: This may reflect something developing in you (e.g., an idea, talent, or way of being). It could be a new insight or some aspect of yourself.

guard: This may suggest protection. Where do you need to be vigilant or on guard? Are you being too protective? Do you need to open up more?

If a lion or some other animal is situated around something as though guarding it, it may reflect an action you need to take or a desire to protect some aspect of yourself. It could also mean that you may need to be more guarded about some aspect of yourself or someone else.

See also *crossing guard* and/or *prison guard.*

gun: Perhaps this symbolizes aggressiveness, violence, and power. It's also a phallic symbol and a symbol of male dominance.

Depending on your political views, this image is seen as either positive or negative. It could suggest defensiveness.

On some level, it is symbolic of fear. If the gun fails to fire or jams, perhaps you are feeling defenseless and helpless about something.

Being shot can mean that you're experiencing some conflict in your life or feel targeted by someone.

gunmen: Simply put, these images seem to suggest anger, fear, aggression, conflict (inner and outer), confrontation, hate, the forcing of one's views/opinions/beliefs, and/or feelings of being targeted or victimized.

Something may be killing a part of you inside—your spirit or your desire for life. Perhaps your lifestyle or way of being is killing you, or is hurting another person psychologically or emotionally (also see *killing*).

Insight: Not so coincidentally, the same actions and images in one's waking life can have the same meaning. The ultimate meaning, however, is that the perpetrator is neither expressing or feeling love or self-worth. Harassing, hurting, oppressing, enslaving, or killing someone does not enhance self-worth, importance, or godliness. Nor does trying to gain respect by bullying or killing. However, it does diminish everything else. (Forcing your ideas on another diminishes you.)

Limiting people's ability to express their divine selves diminishes you. Controlling people for your own gain or for some imagined gain of religious or political meaning also diminishes you.

The bottom line is that anything that limits the free expression of people's souls diminishes them, and no God would ever ask anyone to do this. Only a confused ego-self would attempt such an affront. Only a confused and frightened ego-self would do anything but love.

guts: If you see guts in a dream, this could reflect stamina, strength, courage, or a lack thereof.

Consider also *spilling your guts* (i.e., confessing or divulging secrets). This phrase or image could also reflect vomiting, suggesting that someone has done something that makes you sick.

See also *intestines* in *body*.

gutter: This could signal that you feel bad about yourself, especially if you or someone else is in the gutter. You may feel unhappy or depressed.

Consider also the phrase "Get your head out of the gutter," meaning that you should quit having dirty thoughts or making negative or dirty remarks.

Finding treasures in a gutter can be about finding value in the least expected places (see also *treasure*).

gym: Do you need to get more exercise?

gypsy: This may represent the need to be yourself without responsibility or any obligation to others.

Are you not following the rules or striking off on your own without regard for others?

H

habit: This may reflect your desire to rid yourself of an old habit. Is there something that you're suppressing (e.g., a behavior)?

hacking: If someone is hacking a computer, it may symbolize feelings of vulnerability. It's also possible that you need to look more closely at your self-esteem or confidence.

Hacking can also suggest that someone is overstepping his or her boundaries. If you're doing the hacking, then maybe you are the one overstepping.

hair: See *body terms*.

hair barrette: This might suggest that you're entertaining a new idea. This may also be an indicator of changing your look and inventing a new you.

haircut: This might be about a change in attitude. It can also refer to a loss of power or self-confidence. You may be cutting away some unwanted aspect of yourself. See also *hair* in *body terms*.

hair dryer: Do you need to get a new perspective on something? Could this be about something blowing your mind?

half: You may feel divided, incomplete, ambivalent, or partially aware as described in the saying "I'm half the man I used to be."

Are you not giving or sharing completely? Perhaps you're only telling half the story.

Do you need to meet someone halfway? Do you need to compromise on something?

hall or hallway: This can represent access to different parts of you. A hallway in your dream may symbolize self-exploration and/or the beginning of a path that you are taking in life.

Through the hallway or corridor, you may be going through a transition in your life and journeying into the unknown. It may suggest spiritual enlightenment, emotional growth, physical prowess, new opportunities, and mental passages in your life.

Also see *tunnel*.

Halloween: If you're at a Halloween party and/or dressed up for Halloween, it may be about death and transition. It may also represent the need to take on a new persona or the need to express yourself more freely. Are you too inhibited?

hallucination: In a dream this might represent something coming from your subconscious mind. It may also represent emotions and memories that you have repressed and may need to bring to consciousness in order to deal with them.

Note what you hallucinated. If it was a person, who was it? Or if it was an animal, what animal did you see?

halo: If this appears around your head or the head of another, ask yourself, "Am I being a perfectionist?" This image could also be speaking to some spiritual development that you want or need. See also *aura* or *light*.

hammer: Perhaps you're trying to connect something. It can also mean that you are trying to make something happen or solve something by *hammering* out a solution. Perhaps you are being overbearing if you're using a hammer to fix a small object when you should use a smaller tool.

hand: See *body terms.*

handbag: See *purse.*

handcuffs: Is someone or something holding you back? Are you having difficulty achieving some goal because someone has put some kind of restraint or limits on you?

If you are handcuffing someone, perhaps you're being too possessive or dominating.

There is also a sexual symbolism to handcuffs, especially if they are fuzzy ones.

handicapped: This can represent obstacles to achieving something. If you are physically or emotionally handicapped, it could represent a past trauma or emotional hurt.

The Hand of Fatima is also known as Hamsa.

hand of Fatima: This could speak to your spiritual aspect or be a reminder of the five pillars of Islam, which include the following: (1) the fact that there's only one true God and that Mohammad is his prophet, (2) prayer, (3) support for the needy, (4) fasting during Ramadan, and (5) pilgrimage to Makka (Mecca).

The hand can also represent the feminine aspect (see *anima/animus* in the *archetype* section).

This is an image of good luck similar to the expression "Knock on wood."

It can also represent an amulet to ward off evil and to symbolically blind the aggressor. Do you need protection? Are you feeling vulnerable or exposed? See also the evil eye under *eye* in *body*.

hand grenade: You may be experiencing repressed or hidden anger that is about to explode. Are you having trouble controlling your emotions? See also *explosion or eruption*.

hanging: This might possibly be about feelings of insecurity or some part of yourself that you want to get rid of or kill off.

You may feel guilty about something and punish yourself. If you're hanging yourself, it could be an attempt to escape some guilt or something you fear.

Perhaps you've been left hanging by something or someone. Maybe there is something left unfinished or incomplete.

Hanging something up could also be a metaphor for quitting or retiring.

Consider also the idea of *hanging* out with friends or the need to relax. See also *strangling*, *suffocate*, and/or *choke*.

hanuman: See *monkey* in *animal terms*.

happy: This could signal contentment, the acceptance of the self, or the opposite. For example, it could possess a need to be happy or desire to compensate for being sad.

See also *smile*.

Happy Birthday: If you are singing this song, it could represent the need for recognition. It could also represent celebration in general. Consider that it might represent the birth of something new.

Perhaps you need to have a little more fun in your life and not be so serious.

harbor: This suggests shelter and safety. Are you tied to home and unwilling to venture out?

Note if it's a calm harbor or stormy. This can affect the safety factor.

hardware store: The hardware store might indicate the need for some kind of self-improvement. Perhaps you need to adjust your attitude.

Does something need fixing?

See also *store* and *buying*.

harlequin: This suggests absurdity. Also see *clown*.

harpy: This may represent the devouring feminine. Is someone or something nagging at you? See also the *negative feminine* in the *archetypes* section.

harvest: This can be about abundance or reaping the benefits of something. It could also suggest that something may or may not be fully developed. If you are a farmer or you grew up on a farm, this image could reflect a simpler time or way of being.

hate: This could be about repressed aggression, a fear of confrontation, fear in general, or the forcing of views on others. Is there some resentment you're not dealing with? This is also an expression of anger and inner conflict (see *love* and *anger*).

Insight: When you hate, you lose your own self, your own soul, and your own connection with your deeper spirit regardless of what name you give to it.

hats: This could be about the roles you play in life. It could be about protection, or alternatively, it could be a symbol for hiding some part of yourself. If you are in the process of taking one hat off to replace it with another, it could mean that you are changing roles (jobs) or your thoughts and opinions (see *head* in *body*).

haunted house: This image suggests childhood or childish fears. It reflects past fears or guilty feelings.

It's also possible that the *house* of your being is haunted by something from the past (see *ghost* or *presence*).

hay: This is symbolic of hard work and may suggest that nothing in life comes easy. It can represent maternal instincts. Consider the phrase "Make hay while there's still light." It could be the subconscious trying to get your attention by saying, "Hey."

haze: This makes something hard to see. It can also represent the act of *clouding* something or causing doubt and uncertainty. See *blurry, clouds, confused, mud or muddy, paradox,* and/or *smoke.*

It can also represent an initiation rite of passage, ordeal, test of courage, or trial by fire.

hazel: This tree is often thought to be a goddess tree and is thus associated with wisdom and inspiration within certain mythologies. The Roman god Mercury was said to have carried a staff made of hazel that gave him wisdom. Gods and goddesses often reflect one's inner spirit.

head: See *head* in *body terms.*

headache: This can signal a painful self-image or a hurtful thought. Is someone or something causing you pain or anguish?

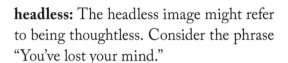

headless: The headless image might refer to being thoughtless. Consider the phrase "You've lost your mind."

If you are not able to hold your head up and it just flops over, that could be a metaphor for a loss of pride and/or self-esteem.

You may be limiting yourself intellectually or not using your head (i.e., just taking for granted something that may not be true).

headline: This might suggest something important or significant you need to become aware of.

head on backward: This may refer to the idiom "You've got your head on backward." Are you looking to the past or living too much in the past?

If it's your same-sex child who has his or her head on backward, this might reinforce the idea that you may be fixated on your past or a simpler time. It's also possible that you are not watching where you are going or that you are not thinking straight.

With the head on backward, it might also symbolize a step backward (i.e., moving in a direction contrary to your goals). This image might also reflect a worry that you are making a mistake.

Perhaps you are all turned around (i.e., confused). Or you may need to walk away from something.

See *backward* or *back or behind* as well.

headstone: This may signal a forgotten or buried aspect of yourself or your life. The condition of the stone may reflect the condition of your life right now. What was written on it?

healing or any health-related issues: This may be about the need for physical, psychological, or emotional healing.

Health-related images (see also *disease, doctor, hospital, medicine, nurse,* or any specific image like *heart attack* or *heart*) can be bringing up health issues that you may not yet be aware of or are not paying attention to. These images might get your attention and suggest a need for more awareness of what's going on with your body. See also *medication* and *medicine*.

If you are trying to decide what to eat or you're not offered what you want, this may be a metaphor for unhealthy choices. Being denied a choice can suggest that you are not being nurtured.

heart: This can represent past hurts, troubles of the heart (as in heartbreak), stored emotions, the soul, or the spirit. Contrast this with the symbol of the head (see *body*).

If you or other people are eating your heart or their own, perhaps you are being too critical of yourself.

Insight: Most of us don't really let go of past hurts. We tend to deny them, push them down, and gloss over them. We say, "What's past is past, or then was then." These in and of themselves are appropriate responses if you're actually letting go of the events and hurts, but most of us aren't letting go.

We tend to hold on to painful resentments, feelings, disappointments, grief, betrayals, guilt, and hurts by storing them in the footlockers of our unconscious minds. After many years and as many memories, we have quite a treasury of buried material built up.

These buried negatives are like cans of radioactive waste. After time, these begin to leak onto the surface of our lives or into the emotional aquifers that sustain us, thus poisoning much of what we do, think, and feel.

Most of this stuff seems to arise uninvited. It comes in our dreams or in the troubles within our waking lives.

We seem to armor ourselves against any future pains that might be perpetrated by others by walling parts of ourselves off or putting up barriers to protect ourselves. It's a slow process, and for most of us, we don't notice how much different we are as adults than we were as children.

As adults, the free expression of the self is often subdued or cut off, and the playful part of ourselves is moderated or pasted on to make it look as though we are being free spirits that are full of fun. But in the quiet of our own homes after the party, we nurse the effects of our drug-, ego-, or alcohol-induced gaiety and wonder if anyone really liked us or bought into our act. And if they did, it would be hard to accept that. After all, it was only our act that they loved.

All these stored negatives over time close our hearts to ourselves and to others, and they also weigh us down.

Many believe the heart chakra represents complex emotions such as compassion, tenderness, and well-being. Many say that we emotionally relate to other beings from this place (see *chakra*).

If you have two hearts, perhaps you are split emotionally. Maybe you're giving yourself to two loves. Do you need to choose one?

heart attack: This can be symbolic of a loss of love, support, or acceptance. It could also about your own health (see *heart*).

Sometimes a heart attack can be a metaphor for a broken heart, and at other times, a broken heart can be about a heart attack.

Insight: Eating the heart is often seen as a metaphor for self-criticism. The thirteenth-century poet and mystic Rumi had this to say about self-criticism: "Knowest thou not the beauty of thine own face? Quit this temper that leads thee to war with thyself."

heart and mind: In Western cultures, the heart and mind are seen as a conflicting dichotomy. In the West, people generally identify the mind or brain as the main instrument of thought, rationality, and intelligence, whereas the heart represents the irrational or emotional aspect of ourselves. For efficiency, decisions—if they are to be rational—must be made from the mind and not the heart.

This may have caused the West to become a culture of *doing* and *making* as well as *forcing* and *struggling* to make things happen. In short, the Western culture has become very masculine in nature.

Insight: The word for heart and mind in Hebrew is the same word, *lebh*. This is also true in Chinese (xīn 心). In these cultures, heart and mind work together as one.

heart surgery: Though this may have a personal health meaning, it might also be symbolic of what I call emotional surgery (i.e., a need for soul healing).

Sometimes what we need is to surround ourselves with a world more intimate and beautiful by tending to our wounds, ourselves, or others.

Perhaps you need to speak more from your heart and less from your head.

heaven: This could reflect your desire to find happiness or to escape the difficulties in life that you may have to face. It may also be about the need to restore your faith and hope.

To some heaven is not a place outside our mortal experience but a place that we are already in. Those people believe that we only need to get our egos out of the way to see it (see also *boomerang insight*).

heaven and earth: These images are sometimes depicted by a tree with a canopy in the sky. Oftentimes the roots are visible below ground, and there is sometimes a ladder or staircase leading from the ground to the sky as with Jacob's ladder in the Bible.

"As above, so below" is a maxim from ancient Hermeticism and modern Wicca. For me, it is a reminder that I reside between two worlds, the unconscious and the conscious.

It is also a statement that the spirit is not something separate from myself (i.e., something out there) but rather something that is within and without. It is not something that I necessarily need to go looking for because I already have it.

helicopter: Vertical flying or ascent suggests that this is a spiritual metaphor.

The helicopters may also reflect the ups and downs, successes and failures of some project or life in general.

Perhaps you or someone is hovering (i.e., looking over your shoulder and micromanaging something). Do you need to lighten up or set something free (i.e., give it some independence)? See also *floating*, *flying*, and *hover*.

hell: This suggests emotions of fear, threat, and misery. When you see hate all around, you may be projecting your hatred of yourself onto the outside world, thus creating your own hell.

help: If you help or assist someone, this may reflect your need or willingness to compromise with someone or something. It can also reflect the need to add your talents to another person's or to some group endeavor.

By helping someone you may not like, the dream may suggest that you need to come to some compromise and find some common ground of understanding.

If you are calling for help, perhaps you feel overwhelmed or lost in some way.

herd: Herding something may be about trying to control something. If you're in a herd, perhaps you are acting like a follower. Do you need to take the lead?

heretic: Perhaps you don't believe something or are saying or thinking things that don't conform to the standards of your community. If not, perhaps you need to change.

Perhaps you need to think differently than the prevailing orthodoxy. Are you disagreeing with someone or some group?

Are you being a skeptic or just a cynic? (See also *box*.)

hero or heroine: See the *archetypes* section.

heroin: See *drugs*.

hiding: This suggests secrets, withholding, withdrawal, denial, repression, avoidance, or self-protection. You may not want others to find something out, or you may feel guilty.

Insight: We hide behind masks of what we want others to think we are and sometimes turn those masks inward so that we don't look at what we are hiding from—ourselves.

high: This may be about expanding your awareness, taking on a larger view, or gaining greater understanding. You could also be *high* on something or someone.

high-tech: This might be about great potential. Do you feel advanced in something? Are you looking for some new and radical ideas? See also *computer*.

Do you feel as though you're falling behind?

Do you feel special or ordinary?

Are you being too technical (i.e., abstruse, abstract, or complicated)? Perhaps you need to get down to earth and be more comprehensible.

Maybe you're not being professional enough.

highway: Highways often reflect your goals and/or your life's path. If the highway is elevated, perhaps you are or need to take the higher road (i.e., more moral or ethical path with regard to some situation).

See also *road*.

hiking: This can represent advancement or a work in progress. Some may see this as a symbol for freedom, independence, and/or adventure (see *adventure*).

Insight: Hiking down a path can represent the *path* you are on in your life. What's happening? Do you restrict yourself to only the path, or do you venture off? Is the path straight and narrow or crooked and rocky? Does it fork into different directions? Everything about the path will help to decode its significance in the dream (see also *road*).

Hillman, James: James Hillman, an archetypal psychologist, used myth and fantasy in understanding the development of our individual and collective psychologies. Hillman's approach was more focused on the psyche, the soul of man, whereas Jung's focus was on the constituents of the self, such as the ego (*Re-Visioning Psychology*, 1975).

In Hillman's book *The Soul's Code: In Search of Character and Calling* (1997), he outlines his acorn theory of the soul. This theory suggests that individuals hold the potential for their unique possibilities within themselves much like an acorn holds the pattern for something like an oak tree.

Hindu: The use of dreams in the Hindu culture is quite complex for a non-Hindu like me, but I'll keep it simple and do my best to be accurate.

To the Hindu, dreams can be disciplinary, rewarding, and prophetic. All dreams are given to the dreamer by the supreme Brahman, the universal spirit, or the godhead.

Some dreams are read as predictions, and some are seen as punishments or rewards for certain actions. Others can be tied to various ailments.

Dreams for the Hindu are mostly seen as manifestations of evil spirits, though legend has it that some good dreams are also given by Lord Varuna, the supreme lawgiver.

It is believed that if a man leads a moral life and surrenders himself at the feet of the divine, he would be released of all evil dreams. In fact, all his dreams would become a good dream reflecting his true nature. These dreams would happen in the early morning as he became receptive to the divine nature within him. He would then experience these dreams within his waking life (another version of the waking dream or a dream within a dream).

Most of these dreams are consistent with the person's karma—a spiritual law comprising a person's total past and present actions. What you have not dealt with in the past will come around again and again until you deal with. It is not fate because humans have free will and the ability to change their actions.

At one time, the pramana (the source of accurate and valid knowledge) on dream interpretation was the Charaka Samhita, which seems to have gathered interpretations from consensus and included an interpretation style from the Valmiki Ramayana—a book on morals, generosity, and virtue somewhat like Aesop's Fables.

The Charaka Samhita is not used in the modern era, which tends to base its interpretive style on the disciplinary and rewarding aspect. Today in India dreams would be looked at in terms of what was debilitating to the dreamer, or obstructing, and what was being released as in bringing an end to the debilitating or obstructing event or action.

In modern India, dream interpretation is part of astrology. Swapna satra (the science of dream) includes *samhita* and *sakuna*, which deal with the meaning of dreams. In fact, sakuna deals with the instant recognition of natural and commonsense happenings that even the common man can understand.

The dreams of individuals are of great importance to modern interpretation, and the images envisioned are then related to gods and demons. Any Hindu astrologer will read a person's dream interpretation.

hip-hop: If you hear hip-hop or rap music in your dream, perhaps it has something to do with your popularity or lack of it. Are you trying to be one of the cool people and fit in?

Are you trying to organize your life so that it makes sense, so that it has some rhyme or reason?

Is there something you need to communicate?

Of course, your attitude about this music will affect its meaning.

See also *music* or *singer*.

history: Watching a history lesson or studying history in a dream could be about you looking at or desiring to return to an earlier time in your own history.

Perhaps you need to let go of old ways of being.

hit-and-run: Are you unwilling to take responsibility for your actions?

hitting: This could represent anger that you have not expressed. A hit-and-run could be your conscience commenting on an old guilt.

hoarding: This could represent a sense of being without. Perhaps you see the world as being limiting. Maybe there is a sense of helplessness or emptiness that you're trying to overcome. This can reflect a sense of loss or failure or a feeling of being less than (see also *greedy*).

Insight: We can become trapped by what we hoard (e.g., our ideas, points of view, or traditions). All of this can become stale and limit our growth. Hoarding can become a shadow and also become the driving force behind our lack of success.

hole: This can be symbolic for the beginning of change. This could serve as the entrance into the underground (i.e., the unconscious). A dark hole can also represent depression.

Consider also the concept of digging yourself into a hole (i.e., doing or saying something that has trapped you into something you don't want to be in or are now having difficulty getting out of).

Insight: Tunnels, holes, corridors, and hallways all make reference to the transformation from one state of being to another. Falling itself, as Alice did after following the white rabbit into a hole, can represent a quick way to the unconscious, the land of dreams.

Falling slowly as though floating gently toward the ground is akin to flying since one has independent control over the process. Following the rabbit can represent following temptation and then falling into trouble. Falling rapidly could suggest a fear of failing or the realization that you are failing. Check out your feeling level. It will give you clues as to the overall meaning (see *abyss* and *falling*).

hollow: This can be about emptiness in your life. It could also be some statement that seems to have little or no truth to it.

holly: This tree could be about Christmas holidays. It can also represent magic or a girl's name. It was also a sacred tree of the ancient Druids.

home: This can represent the center of your being, your spiritual self. It may also represent a place of fulfillment and belonging. It may also be a place of healing and safety. It can also be the opposite, depending on your experiences with the home.

See also *house* and *childhood home* if appropriate.

home improvement: Perhaps you need to make improvements in yourself. Adding to the size of the house might be about expanding yourself intellectually or spiritually. The rooms that are being improved may also add meaning (see *house*).

homeless: This could be about being spiritually deprived. It could reflect the absence of security. Are you feeling disconnected from people or yourself? It can also suggest that you are feeling ungrounded or unreal and that you don't belong (see also *belonging*).

home run: This could be about success or failure and winning or losing. It could also have a sexual meaning as in scoring a date or a sexual conquest (see also *baseball bat*).

homosexual: If you are not gay but are in the dream, it may mean that you need to better integrate different aspects of yourself. It can also symbolize self-acceptance. If this is uncomfortable, then perhaps you are uncomfortable with some aspects of yourself.

If you're in a same-sex relationship in the dream as you are in your waking life, this could be about wanting to emulate certain admired aspects of that person.

Whether you are male or female, this image can reflect how you're feeling about your own masculinity or femininity (see also *animus/anima* in the *archetypes* section).

honesty: If you or someone else is being honest, then perhaps you are seeking the truth and/or the truth of something. Alternatively, perhaps you feel that you are being misled or that someone is not being open or forthright (see *lie* or *lying*).

honeycomb: This could include bees as well. It can represent the sweetness of truth or divine wisdom. The divine honey is contained within the context of the comb much as the soul is contained within the body. Sometimes Jesus was known as the "honey within the rock." It can also represent your desire for love.

Insight: Sufi mystics used honey rituals that symbolized honey as being what would 'melt' or integrate you into the godhead.

Eros or Cupid, the god of love, was also the god of bitter honey. His arrows would both intoxicate with desire and agonize with that same desire.

honored: If you or someone else is being honored, perhaps you are craving some recognition. Maybe you're trying to get noticed. Do you feel put down or demeaned?

hood: See *balaclava or hood*.

hoodie: Are you hiding something or hiding from someone? Are you trying to cover up your feelings?

If it's a black hoodie and the person wearing it is either you or someone of the same gender as you, you might want to look up *shadow* in the *archetypes* section. See also *balaclava or hood*.

hook: To see a hook might suggest that you are caught up in something nefarious or deceitful. It can also refer to a habit.

hookah: Are you bottling up your emotions? Are you in need of some relaxation?

hookup: If you are hooking something up, it could mean you want to form a connection (e.g., get together, make an electrical connection, etc.).

Is there someone or something you wish to join? Are you courting someone's favor? Though it's symbolic for a drug dealer in urban slang, it could also be symbolic for the need for sex.

hooky: Are you playing hooky (i.e., ditching something or being absent from something)? Perhaps you are avoiding some responsibility.

Are you not showing up somewhere in your life? Are you not being genuine and/or engaged?

horizon: This could represent a new beginning or an end. It could be about the future, future goals, or future conclusions. We are all within a cycle of endings and rebirths and of constantly regenerating ourselves.

horn: If this comes from an animal, it could represent conflict or confrontation (see *ram* or *unicorn* under *animal*).

If you hear the sound of a horn, pay attention to your inner voice or intuition. Are you blowing your own horn (i.e., bragging)? Or do you need to blow your own horn more often? Consider the phrase "On the horns of a dilemma."

hornets: These can represent trouble, danger, anger, or even your temper getting the best of you. Have you been stung by stinging remarks, or have you made them yourself? A hornet's nest may be a lingering threat that you may want to avoid. Something may be bugging you.

horoscope: Do you have some concerns about your future? Is there any particular sign that stands out? What does that sign mean? This info will help you interpret the message (see also *zodiac* and specific zodiac symbols if they show up in the dream).

hose: This suggests the flow of emotions. It may indicate how well you communicate emotions.

It can also be a symbol for rejuvenation and cleansing. Hoses can wash away emotional wounds and messes.

hospital: This can symbolize the need for or the process of healing. The healing can be about emotional, psychological, spiritual, or physical. It could be about healing your body or mind healing, or it may reflect worries you may have about your health. It can also be a symbol for fear (see *doctor, illness,* or *nurse*).

Your experience with hospitals will also affect the meaning of this symbol.

hostage: Are you being prevented from doing or saying something? Are you holding someone or yourself back? Why?

Perhaps you feel imprisoned or controlled. See also *prison, prisoner,* or *trapped.*

hotel: This can reflect temporary attitudes or a short-term situation. It could refer to a work situation or a relationship that's external to one's primary relationship. Sometimes it's a symbol for a place to relax and get away from life's stresses.

It can also reflect a loss of personal identity.

hot tub: If you see a hot tub or you see yourself or someone else in a hot tub, that might signify that you are in hot water (i.e., trouble). It's also possible that you need to relax or cool down. The water might reflect warm feelings.

It's also possible that the hot tub could represent something sexual (i.e., desire).

If the tub is on fire, it could be about destruction or the desire to destroy some contained or restricted feelings.

It could also reflect anger or the need to transform your emotional relationship with something. Fire is often about internal change and transformation.

See also *fire.*

house terms: All houses in dreams tend to be representations of ourselves, the inner self where we live usually in private and away from the rest of the world.

Rooms in this house often represent aspects of ourselves—aspects that we hide and aspects that we decorate and live in openly. Not all these aspects are welcome, of course, but they are us—warts and all. It's the darker aspects that we tend to reject more often than not.

The house, its rooms, and its furniture may represent all our emotions, ideas, beliefs, politics, and creativity. Basically, the house is your identity—who you think you are.

This identity includes your body, mind, heart, and the greater community of others, both animate and inanimate.

The condition of the house will provide clues as to your current state of well-being. For example, a leaky roof may symbolize the need for better coping strategies. A house in ruins could suggest that a way of being is no longer useful to you or a certain personality structure has broken down. A house on fire could be about passion, anger, or the need for an emotional cleansing.

Are you trying to repair any damage to the house? Do you need to heal some part of yourself?

Smoke coming from the chimney could represent warm, comfortable feelings, or the desire for these feelings.

If your partner has moved to another house, perhaps he or she tends to change relationships. At least that is what you fear (see also *cheating*).

A house that appears dark and empty can represent the grief you felt when someone close to you died or relationships that have come to an end.

If the house is the same as when it was new but is located somewhere else, perhaps it's referring to you or some relationship that is in a different place than it was in the beginning (because you have grown or matured).

A row of houses may just be a reference to other people. If you go into one of these houses, it could be about you getting involved with others in some way.

A childhood house could represent an earlier you or be used to compare who you were to who you are now.

An abandoned house may represent a self, personality, or part of the past life you may have left behind.

The rooms inside a house may reflect compartmentalized aspects of yourself, whereas the type of house might also reflect aspects. (Note that all images are a reflection of yourself.)

apartment: This is just a part of the total you.

attic: This could symbolize higher consciousness (spiritual self), the stored past, and/or repressed thoughts. This can represent your intellectual self and/or your goals and aspirations.

A cluttered attic may suggest that you need to organize your thoughts better.

Sometimes old ideas, beliefs, and memories are stored here as well.

basement: This could symbolize the unconscious self and things hidden from awareness. This is the place where our psychobiological drives, such as sexual urges, are located. If the basement is flooded, perhaps you are feeling emotionally overwhelmed (see also *cellar* and *cave*).

bathroom: This could symbolize a place of cleansing, letting go, or releasing tension and other emotions. It can also be symbolic of your privacy (see also *bathing*).

bedroom: This can represent intimacy, sex, privacy, and emotional retreat.

ceiling: This could be about your upper limits (i.e., what you use to protect your identity). If it's caving in or peeling, perhaps you are having an identity crisis or feeling vulnerable to the judgments of others.

The ceiling leaking is sometimes symbolic of the loss or weakening of the beliefs you use to protect your identity (who you think you are or who you want to be). You may be losing confidence in yourself for some reason.

There's a possibility that your old way of being is breaking down and that you need new coping strategies.

dining room: This could symbolize a quest to know something (to take it in) or an important decision. If you are eating with others, it can signal your acceptance of others in your life. To eat alone might mean the opposite.

door: This can be a very significant image. Generally, it can refer to access, mobility, and a threshold to change (see also *transition dreams*). Are you being invited in or shut out?

Is the door open or locked? If the door is open, then it may be inviting you to explore or to embrace what's in the room (i.e., your inner self). What are you opening the door to? Are you or do you need to be open to someone or something (e.g., a new prospect or relationship)?

If the door is locked, then there may be something that you are shutting off or refusing to look at or something in the world that you are shutting out.

If the front door is shut, locked door, breaking down, broken, or deteriorating, then perhaps your defenses are breaking down.

If the door is shut, you might be trying to find some privacy or space for yourself. This might also indicate that you are closing yourself off emotionally or are trying to protect yourself.

Back doors can also be symbols for the need for privacy or that someone can get to you surreptitiously or through a less defended part of yourself.

A locked door may also reflect some resolve. If it's crumbling, then perhaps the resolve is crumbling.

If you've locked yourself in, perhaps you are trying to keep something from getting out (i.e., hiding it). Perhaps you are refusing to deal openly with some part of yourself or some issue.

Locking a door can also reflect a decision you have made. Unlocking the door might be about the need for being more open or transparent. If someone walks out through the unlocked door, it might mean that you are letting go of something or someone.

If you are waiting outside the door, you may be ready to enter all the potential of your life that lies behind the door. All you need do is walk through.

Is the door large or small, inviting or intimidating? These aspects of the door will help decipher its meaning.

The front door may relate to how you let others see you, whereas the back door may be about your search for an answer to a problem. If you are taking the back door to avoid something, perhaps you want to confront the way you've been portraying yourself to others. Maybe you don't want to confront the lie.

A back door can be about your private family life or secret activities.

If there are many doors, perhaps there are many or unlimited possibilities for accessing your life or something new.

If the door in a doorway is missing, you may feel vulnerable and exposed to something or someone.

A room with no doors may represent a feeling of being trapped with no way out of a situation. If you're on the outside of a room with no doors, perhaps you feel excluded.

The room that the door leads to will give you more information.

A glass door may represent invisible obstacles to your goals or a way of seeing through to the possibilities of something.

See also *door*.

fireplace: A fireplace can represent your inner fire and personal energy, perhaps the spiritual center of yourself.

A house on fire can be about huge transformation.

floor: This may represent the basic foundation of the self. What condition is it in?

The first or ground floor may be about being grounded. It's where everyday life takes place. It may also represent the practical side of yourself.

Floors in a multistory building can sometimes refer to your level of development. What's on that floor?

foundation: What have you built your life upon? How sound is it, and is it strong or crumbling?

furnishings: This suggests your personality traits. How you arrange your inner life is marked by furnishings. Is the furniture in disarray or orderly, modern or traditional? What condition are they in? See also *furniture*.

garage: If you are parked in your garage, perhaps you are being idle or are lacking drive or direction.

If opening the door and getting ready to drive out, perhaps you've made some decisions and are about to act on them.

If you are closing the door, perhaps you have put something on hold.

hallways or corridors: Hallways can be conduits to the intimate self or different aspects of the self. See also *tunnel*.

hidden room: This may represent a part of yourself (a talent, a behavior, or a personality trait) that you have neglected or rejected and may need to be revealed.

kitchen: This could symbolize nourishment, warmth, spiritual nourishment, healing, and/or the nurturing mother. It's also a place of creation and transformation.

It may also represent the soul of the house, the center of oneself. If it needs fixing up, perhaps you have been neglecting this part of yourself (see *soul*).

library: This can symbolize the mind or where memories are stored. It can represent your mental growth (see also *book*).

living room: This could represent the part of yourself that you display to others.

This room may symbolize the way you see yourself. It may be the boundary between your inner self and your public self. What condition is it in?

porch: This can represent where you meet the world, the façade that you put before the world, and your social self. Sometimes something can be hiding beneath the porch. This might be symbolic of some part of yourself you are hiding from others.

roof: This could symbolize protection. (This includes your philosophy and beliefs that you use for protection.) The roof on your home might also reflect your parenting and how you're protecting your family.

If caving in, then perhaps your world is caving in, or you don't feel safe or aren't able to keep your family safe or provide for them adequately. Perhaps you need new coping strategies (see *ruins* and *ceiling*).

If you're standing on the roof, you may have a heightened awareness of something. A roof garden may suggest mental growth, development, and/or insight.

room(s) in general: A room can represent certain feelings or aspects of yourself. For example, the bedroom could represent the intimate you.

If it's a room you haven't seen before (or an extra room), it may represent aspects of yourself (e.g., abilities, traits, or fears) that have gone unnoticed or ignored. Rooms might also symbolize the need for exploring new aspects of yourself.

Rooms without doors or windows could be about limiting access to parts of self that are shut off. (This might be true for locked doors as well.) It's also not unlike a womb.

sink: The sink can be symbolic of the need to clean up. It may also have something to do with controlling your emotions.

stairs: Stairs can be seen as a transition image (i.e., change from one aspect of the self or way of being to another).

They can reference going higher or lower. When going higher, they may represent your aspirations. The aspirations could be grand or even ostentatious if it's a wide and winding staircase. This could be about wanting to look good and important.

Going down may be where you want to be grounded. They can also represent steps toward a goal (see *Jacob's ladder*).

upstairs: This could be about your intellectual and rational self. If you're going upstairs, it could be about your aspirations or getting promoted, while going downstairs may be about being demoted.

downstairs: This may be about going deep into your subconscious to deal with repressed emotions or memories.

See also *ascending* and *descending*.

wall: This could represent a defense barrier or something you may have partitioned off from yourself or the world (see also *fence*).

window: What are you willing to see and allow others to see of you? Are your windows clear or foggy? Can you see out of them? If not, perhaps you're refusing to see something, or maybe you're rejecting some point of view. If your window is open, perhaps you're open to some point of view.

Standing outside and looking in may be about being *on the outs* with something or someone, or you may need to take a different point of view.

Adding onto a house might suggest the need for adding new aspects to yourself.

See *building* and types of houses (e.g., *auto shop, castle, church, hotel, shack, synagogue, temple,* and *warehouse*).

hover: Are you in suspense or on hold with something? Is someone *hovering* over you (i.e., keeping an eye on you in an attempt to catch you in a mistake or protect you)? Are you just *hanging around*? See also *helicopter* or *floating*.

howling: Symbolic of wounded feelings. This can be a call for help. What has hurt you?

hug: This could be symbolic of loving and caring for someone, or it could represent part of your nature. Perhaps you're holding something close to your heart.

It is possible that you may need to be more or less affectionate, depending on the circumstances of the hug.

The image can also be a metaphor for your need to heal your emotional self. If someone is hugging you, perhaps you need to let down your guard a little and connect with someone or with others.

human-beast combination: See *minotaur*.

humiliation: This suggests shame, embarrassment, betrayal, and loss of face. See also *embarrassment*.

Humpty-Dumpty: This could symbolize death without resurrection. Sometimes things cannot be fixed (i.e., cannot be put back the way they were).

This can be a cautionary image. You may be treating life too casually.

hunger: Do you have a unfulfilled feeling? Are you starving for attention, recognition, or affection?

hunt: This can suggest a quest. You may be trying to find some part of yourself or something you've lost.

Being hunted could be about some emotion such as fear that threatens failure or loss. If you're eaten, this could be about being consumed by some emotion or circumstance.

Killing an animal might suggest that you are trying to kill off some instinctual part of yourself (see also *killing*).

Hunting can also be a metaphor for sexual conquest.

If you're being hunted, perhaps you're a little overwhelmed by your life right now.

huntress: This can represent the active principle in a woman (i.e., the animus). See *animus/anima* in the *archetypes* section.

hurdle: This may symbolize the barriers and obstacles you may encounter on your way toward achieving some goal or desire. How well are you negotiating the hurdles in the dream?

hurricane: This can be a symbol of destructive emotions or chaos. Tornadoes, tidal waves, floods, and tsunamis also fit into this category.

hurt: This may refer to being either physically or emotionally hurt. See *injured*.

husband or wife: This may be the yang (husband) or yin (wife) part of yourself. It's also a reflection of your relationship (see *anima/animus* in the *archetypes* section and *wife*).

hyperventilate: See *vent or ventilate*.

hydra: See *dragon* under *animals*.

hypnagogia: This means "leaning toward sleep." This is the transitional state from wakefulness to sleep. Hypnopompia means "leading away from sleep" and refers to the transition from sleep to wakefulness.

Both are in the twilight zone at the threshold of consciousness and unconsciousness, and both can also produce intense dream images, colors, tastes, and even sounds. It's a sleep borderland where all sorts of dream phantasmata can take place.

It may feel as though you are in two worlds at the same time.

Insight: References to this type of dream state have been found in the writings of Aristotle, Charles Dickens (*Oliver Twist*), and Edgar Allan Poe. Poe called them fancies.

It was in this state that I visited the realm of *The Archipelago of Dreams: The Island of the Dream Healer* (iUniverse, 2011).

hypnosis: This is a consciousness technique that involves focused attention while shutting out as much of the peripheral stimuli as possible. During the process the individual has a heightened awareness of any focused memory. Some people believe that the individual enters an altered state while others believe it's a form of imaginative role enactment[12] (see *active imagination*).

Some people, but not all, can become very responsive to suggestions while hypnotized and be lead to alter subjective experiences.

I

ice: This can be symbolic of a restricted flow of ideas. Slipping on ice can be about self-esteem issues or insecurity. Melting ice might mean that you are or need to warm up to something, or perhaps it signals that someone is warming up to you. Falling through the ice could be about your emotions overwhelming you.

ice cream: This could be about pleasure, satisfaction, and/or playfulness. Indulging in lots of ice cream could be about trying to salve some emotional pain. Perhaps you need to cool off about something? If the ice cream doesn't taste right, perhaps it's about disappointment.

ice maker: Are you shutting others out?

ice pick: Are you suppressing your cold feelings or chipping away at something? It might also be symbolic of sexual aggression.

ice-skating: This may represent trust in yourself, but you should proceed carefully.

If you are slipping, have you made some mistake?

iceberg: Perhaps you are not taking full advantage of your potential, especially your hidden potential. Are you hiding some part of yourself? Are you looking deep enough into some situation or issue? Are you looking below the surface of something or someone? Is there an unseen danger that you're not paying attention to?

icing: You could be acting superficially. Perhaps something is extra though unexpected like *icing on the cake.* (That could be a metaphor for grace too.)

id: This is a psychological construct representing the pleasure and instinctual self.

The id is the primitive, animal, or instinctive component of your personality. It's the impulsive and unconscious part of your psyche. As a baby, you operated almost exclusively from this construct.

The id demands immediate gratification and ignores reality or the rational in the everyday world. (Does this sound like anybody you know?)

Developmentally, the id precedes the ego. See also *lizard*, *superego*, and *ego*.

ideal: If you've met the ideal person in a dream, perhaps you are being unrealistic about something or someone.

Are your expectations too high? Are you failing to meet your own expectations for yourself?

identification or ID: For example, a driver's license, passport, or someone asking you for some ID could be about your own self-confidence or your self-identity. See also *purse*.

If your ID has been changed, stolen, or lost, it could be about a loss of your identity or sense of self. Sometimes when you are changing jobs, a lost or changed ID can show up in a dream. This is often because people tend to identify with their jobs. It's part of how they see themselves.

identical twin: This may be a reflection of yourself.

idol: This could represent false values or a faulty idea. It could also symbolize the deification of something (i.e., giving something spiritual significance that it doesn't really possess). Are you mistaking an icon for the real thing?

Are you worshipping a false god (e.g., money, power, fame)? Are you making something more important than it is? See also *statue*.

ignoring: If you're ignoring someone, perhaps you are not paying attention to a part of yourself. Are you overlooking something, or are you being overlooked?

People ignoring you might also suggest feelings of hurt associated with betrayal or abandonment at a time of need. You may be feeling alienated and alone. See also *abandoned*, *alienated*, or *betrayal*.

There may be some issue that only you can deal with effectively.

illegal: Something illegal might be symbolic of some guilt associated with some part of your life. This image could be the unconscious mind imploring you to look at how you have contributed to some event, especially to the aspects that didn't work.

An illegal activity can also be symbolic of some wrong or injustice. Perhaps something has violated your sense of justice and the way the world is *supposed* to operate. It can also suggest that something is not real if it's not recognized and officially sanctioned in some way.

illness: Perhaps you need to work on your well-being. Are you holding in some anger or resentment? Are you using sickness to gain attention? What old wounds need healing?

illusion: This may be symbolic of your own illusions regarding something, someone, or some situation. Are you kidding yourself about something? Perhaps you need to see something from a different perspective.

imam: See *preacher* or *priest*. The meaning may also reflect your own prejudices.

immobile: Are you feeling terrorized? What is preventing your growth?

immortal: Do you feel all-powerful as though nothing can hurt you? Do you feel fearless? Are you adverse to change or starting something new or different?

impalement: This is symbolic of a forceful/passionate release of some repressed emotions or at least the need for it. Sometimes we are imprisoned by our repressed emotions, so this image might be symbolic of being freed from that.

Note that this is a rather aggressive action and may suggest that you need to be more assertive in confronting your hidden emotions.

impeaching: Perhaps you want to challenge some authority.

impotence: This image tends to be about the fear of losing power or the worry that you don't measure up.

Do you feel helpless or out of control when it comes to some situation? Do you feel like you don't make a difference or can't make a difference in some situation?

Occasionally, we project our impotence and its concomitant emotions (fear, anger, etc.) onto another person or object. Accusing God of being indifferent to our plight might be an example of this. Another example might include cowering before some kind of seen or unseen beast.

Alternatively, you could be dealing with sex troubles in your waking life (see also *penis* under *body*).

incest: This can be a very disturbing dream image or event and may have nothing to do with familial sex but rather be a metaphor for taboos in general. It may signal that you are contemplating something banned, forbidden, or unlawful.

Perhaps you have witnessed something or have thought of something and accepted it when heretofore it would have been anathema and disturbing.

Alternatively, this kind of dream could be about the transition from child to adult and your attempt to integrate the two. Along these same psychological lines, the image could also be suggesting the need to integrate opposites within your own personality, such as your masculine and feminine traits (see *anima/animus* in the *archetype* section).

According to Jung, the union of likes that brings forth integration with one's being (and that ultimately brings about completion or wholeness) may show up in a dream as an incestuous relationship.

It may also be possible that you feel violated in some way or that someone is manipulating, taking advantage of, or exploiting you in some way (see *rape*).

Another interpretation might be that this image reflects a feeling of being emotionally dominated by someone close or some circumstance. If you are the adult in the event, then the incestuous act within a dream can also be symbolic of trying to reclaim or steal back your innocence.

The act in a dream could also be a compensatory act in that the dream is depicting the need to be accepted and/or loved by the person with whom the dreamer is performing the act.

Of course, it's possible that the dream is a reenactment of an actual incestuous act, and if so, you should discuss it with a professional.

incompetence: The image of *incompetence* may be a projection and reflect your own feelings of incompetence regarding something. Is there something you need to learn?

incongruent: Though many dreams don't seem to follow a congruent or linear pattern, there are dreams where the image is inconsistent within itself (e.g., an American soldier wearing a kilt into battle, someone from an Asian village who isn't Asian, someone who should be speaking a different language or have a different accent but doesn't, etc.).

Incongruency can also look like an effect that doesn't align with an action (e.g., smiling while holding up your hands for someone to stop). The effect is welcoming, but the action is not.

When you notice the incongruency in the dream, you might be receiving a message that something in your life is anomalous or discordant. Perhaps you are not telling the truth about something. You might be at variance or in disagreement with some aspect of yourself or the prevailing beliefs of those around you.

See also *dissonance*.

See *conflict* or *disagreement* as well.

indifference: You could be hiding your true worries or anxieties. You may care, but perhaps you need to show it. What are you protecting by being indifferent?

What are your real intentions? What are the intentions of someone else? See also *caring*.

indigestion: This represents some suggestion or idea that doesn't agree with you and makes you sick to your stomach. It could be something you heard but didn't think anything of until now. It's also possible that this image actually reflects an upset stomach (see *stomach* and/or *abdomen*).

individuation: This is the process toward an integrated personality. It's the drive to become whole.

Carl Jung thought of it as the process where people discover the divine within themselves—their true selves and what some call the authentic self or consciousness beyond the ego.

It is the process whereby the innate personality elements, the aspects of the immature psyche, and the different experiences within one's life become integrated into a well-functioning whole. Once this is complete, you become aware of your relationship with all other things.

infect: See *epidemic* and *disease*.

inheritance: This reflects something of value from your past or something gained through a relationship.

initiation: This may be about starting something new. As an initiate, you are a beginner (see the *archetypes* section).

injection: Is something being forced on you or influencing you (e.g., opinions or social pressure)? Injections can also symbolize people's hurtful criticisms or your own self-criticisms.

injured: If you dream that you are injured, that might suggest you need to work on healing an old wound and hurt (emotional or physical).

Perhaps you need to stop and slow down. Consider where you were injured, how you were injured, or what was injured for further interpretation.

insects: These can represent irritation. What is bugging you? The attributes of certain insects can be used to represent what is going on. For example, bees, though communal, are individually self-sacrificing.

Spiders may indicate that you feel caught up in something (see *spiders*), and fireflies can indicate inspiration as in a light turning on.

inside: If you're inside something, this could be about your inner self and whether your inner feelings are acknowledged or not.

instinct: In general, animals in our dreams symbolize our instinctual selves, and the type of animal refers to what part of our natural being we have neglected. Carl Jung suggested that when we ignore or neglect our instincts, we lose or weaken our bodily wisdom.

Our instincts inform us when we're tired, when we are in need of intimate connection and expression, when we need to cooperate, or when we're hungry and need to eat, yet in many modern societies, we ignore or reject these natural mechanisms.

Eventually, this neglect catches up to us, and we start to experience all kinds of physical, psychological, spiritual, and emotional troubles.

According to Jung, this is when animals begin to show up in our dreams. They want to get our attention and drag us back into the value of our instinctual selves.

instructor: See *teacher*.

internet: This is symbolic of unbounded possibilities. Do you need to gain information or to learn something? If you're spending too much time on the internet, it could suggest that you need to get out more and interact with the real world.

Alternatively, it could be a suggestion that you need to reach out to others and interconnect. See also *computer*.

intersection: If you are at an intersection, perhaps you need to make a choice. You may also be at a crossroads where you need to make a decision in order to go forward with something.

interview: A job interview might imply that you're not satisfied with where you are or with some part of yourself.

If you are interviewing someone, are you judging that person, or are you being too judgmental about others in general? If you are interviewed, are you worried about being judged?

Being interviewed can also reflect your anxiety about being judged.

Is there some information that you need to gain about yourself, others, a situation, or a proposition?

intimate: If you are being intimate in the dream, you may be expressing your sexuality, or you may be concerned with it at least. There may be something lacking or unsatisfying in this part of your life.

Perhaps you have a problem with closeness that you need to resolve.

See also *sex*.

intruder: This may be about someone invading your privacy, vulnerability, or something unwanted (see *invaded* or *invasion*).

Insight: Intuition has sometimes been called "second sight" or extrasensory perception—something beyond the input from the traditional five senses.

It is often considered one of the aspects that dominates the feminine psyche.

Intuitive people tend to be good listeners and generally interested in understanding people. The intuitive is one of the four paired personality types outlined by C. G. Jung and explained by the Myers-Briggs Type Indicator.

intoxicated: See *drunk*.

intrusion: An intruder might represent guilt or some thought breaking into your peace of mind. It could signal an unwanted sexual interest or attention. See also *invaded* or *violation*.

intuition: Some part of you may be trying to bring something to consciousness. This may also represent something to inspire (e.g., your creative side).

This often suggests you have a hunch, a feeling, a premonition, or a suspicion. It could also symbolize a gut reaction, clairvoyance, a sixth sense, or something innate to your being.

See also *omen* and/or *premonition*.

Often our intuitive selves open us to the mysteries of life.

Perhaps you are being too rational and logical in your approach to something and need to let your deeper aspects guide you. You may need to be more open to inspiration and your intuitive self.

Don't resist this because it may reflect your spiritual nature wanting to manifest itself.

invaded: This might be a symbol indicating that you feel violated in some way. It could also reflect a feeling of being overwhelmed.

Alternatively, it could also mean that you need to be more assertive. See also *violated*.

invalid: If you see an invalid or if you are handicapped in some way in the dream, it could symbolize a feeling of weakness or vulnerability. Consider also the term *invalid* as in false or irrelevant.

Is something controlling or limiting your movement?

invasion: Perhaps this is an attack or forceful intrusion. Maybe you feel vulnerable, demeaned, and/or overwhelmed (see also *rape*).

Insight: An invasion dream can include any overwhelming circumstance, emotional or physical, that produces stress and anxiety.

People sometimes feel that their identities have become inconsequential, insignificant, and/or inferior. This can be caused by too much stimulation over too long a period or too little stimulation over too long a period.

There are those who believe certain people can magically project their ideas into your dream by entering it themselves.

Though I don't subscribe to this, TV commercials and movies are often designed to *plant* information and ideas into the subconscious that can then be processed through the dream's normal system of memory consolidation. Over time these images and suggestions begin to invade our conscious minds.

They can be particularly noticeable during dreams. In this way, advertisers and politicians have been invading our dreams for years.

invention or inventing: An invention may reflect your creative essence, perhaps even your achievements or desire to achieve. You may even be trying to raise yourself to a higher level of work or consciousness.

It's also possible that you are making stuff up (i.e., lying).

inventor: This is symbolic of your creative self and personal insights. If you are inventing something, it could also reflect that you're making something up (e.g., an untruth).

investigator: See *detective or detecting*.

investments: Do you need to plan for the future? Perhaps you need to contribute something toward some future endeavor. This could include money, time, thought, and/or energy.

It's also possible that you are taking a chance on something, or if you aren't, maybe you should.

See also *gambling*.

invincible: If you feel invincible, that could suggest its opposite. Do you also feel helpless and vulnerable? Are you being overconfident or arrogant?

See also *superhero*, *Superman*, or *Superwoman or Supergirl*.

invisibility: This could reflect the loss of the self. You may feel dispassionate and uninvolved. You may feel that no one sees you and you're having no impact. Are you feeling unimportant?

invisible man or woman: If an invisible man or woman shows up with clothing but no body, you may be putting on a false front. Perhaps you're not being the real you.

invitation: If someone is inviting you or someone else or you receive or give an invitation, perhaps there's something that you need to deal with. Is there some aspect that you need to take into yourself? Is there an issue that you need to pay attention to?

Do you need encouragement, or do you need to encourage someone?

Do you need to introduce yourself to someone or some new concept?

Perhaps some new proposition has come your way.

Do you need to turn down or deny something?

invitation: If you're receiving one, it may represent acceptance by others, or you could be compensating for not feeling accepted. Are you feeling rejected?

If you've invited others but forgot about them, are you taking something or someone for granted?

iPad: This could be about your connections or communications with others. It could also reflect your lack of connection or the need to reach out and connect. This may be especially true if the iPad is broken. See also *cell phone* and/or *computer*.

IQ test: Are you feeling insecure? Do you worry about whether you measure up? See *exams*.

irrigation: Irrigation might refer to the need for some kind of healing or spiritual enrichment. It may also reflect the need to bring some emotion or life to some situation.

iron: This is symbolic of steadfastness, strength, and endurance. It could also signify willfulness and rigidity.

irrigating: This may be about the need to heal or nurture. It may also symbolize academic, emotional, psychological, or spiritual growth.

island: This can suggest solitude or a desire to be separate. You may feeling lonely, or you may want to escape something. Sometimes it represents the inner you, real you, or the soulful you rising out of the unconscious.

You can isolate yourself by identifying too strongly with some belief or group of people. If you are on an island in a stormy sea, perhaps it represents a place of stability and strength in the middle of emotional chaos.

itchy: Maybe you have an *itch* to do something or see something. Do you have an unfulfilled desire?

Where the itch is located may give you more information about the meaning of the dream. For example, sometimes things in the eyes can symbolize something seen that bugs, irritates, or bothers you. It could be about something obstructing your vision or affecting your point of view.

If the itching seems to get worse, this might indicate that something may have started out as something minor but will only get worse if you don't attend to it.

Consider also the so-called seven-year itch, which refers to a time when a partner gets an itch to have an affair or change partners.

ivory: This may refer to endurance, purity, beauty, or strength. It can also reflect the idea of poaching and the waste of natural resources.

Because it may have negative environmental symbolism, you might also want to explore this aspect.

Consider also the *ivory tower*, which could refer to college or having your head in the clouds. You may need to get back down to earth and be more practical.

J

jackal: This represents someone who feeds off others (see *animals*).

jacket: As with all clothing, it's part of the image you want to present to the world.

It's possible that heavy jackets represent the need to protect or defend yourself or that you are being too defensive and distant and thus isolating yourself.

The color might have additional significance. If it's a "crime jacket" (slang for a criminal's file with the police), perhaps you feel guilty about something, or maybe you've done something wrong. It's also a synonym for file. Are you keeping tabs on something or someone?

jackhammer: Do you need to make some big changes in your life or in the way you're doing or thinking about something?

jack-o'-lantern: Are you trying to put on a false face (e.g., a tough-looking one)?

jackpot: Are you relying too much on fate, or do you need to take a chance on something or someone?

Jacob's ladder: This is symbolic of the path between heaven and earth as well as the connection between your physical and spiritual aspects.

It could also represent the connection between your conscious and unconscious self. Some envision the spiral of a strand of DNA as a Jacob's ladder.

Insight: I once had a dream where a blue lady visited me while angels walked up and down stairs from sky to earth much like the image seen by Jacob in his prophetic dream outlined in the Old Testament.

This staircase represented my own struggle with my polarities (i.e., those aspects of myself that I accept and those that I reject).

As the tree's roots are in the physical ground and its branches touch the heavens, the staircase in Jacob's ladder reminds me that we are bound by both soul and body. This image encourages us to accept all of ourselves (i.e., the dark as well as the light, the intellect and heart, the body and spirit).

"And Jacob went out from Beersheba, and went toward Haran. And he lighted upon a certain place, and tarried there all night, because the sun was set; and he took of the stones of that place, and put them for his pillows, and lay down in that place to sleep. And he dreamed, and behold a ladder set up on the earth, and the top of it reached to heaven: and behold the angels of God ascending and descending on it" (Genesis 28:10–12)

Jacuzzi (or hot tub): Perhaps you need to cleanse your emotions of negativity or find a way to take some time to relax.

jade: This is symbolic of good fortune. Also see the color *green*.

jail: If you're in jail, perhaps you feel restrained or censored by someone or some situation. Perhaps you feel confined. Is this a symbol for self-punishment for some perceived and unacknowledged wrong-doing?

jailbreak: This reflects the need to escape a restrictive situation or a stifling relationship. It could also mean that you may be refusing to take responsibility for some action or behavior.

jailer: This suggests anything that restricts self-expression. Guilt or self-criticism can limit one's expression of self.

jaguar: This can represent speed, agility, or power. If this is in reference to a car, then you may desire to live the high life.

Janes, Julian: In 1976, Julian Janes looked at the dichotomy of the conscious and the unconscious mind and posited a theory for the birth of the conscious mind.

In his book *The Origin of Consciousness in the Breakdown of the Bicameral Mind (1976)*, he suggested that ancient people pretty much followed or resisted the "god mind" that came from one of the unconnected brain hemispheres that spoke to them. This would later become the unconscious, that which speaks to us in our dreams.

janitor: Do you need to clean up some aspect of your life? Note that this can also be a custodian or caretaker image and thus take on those roles. Your attitude about this kind of work will also affect the image's meaning.

Janus: See *mask*.

jar (or any small container): This might symbolize the feminine womb or a place of protection. It's a place where one stores something for a rainy day. Perhaps now is the time to open it.

jasmine: See *flowers*.

jaundice: If you're turning yellow in the dream, it could be a health issue. It could also be a reaction from being prejudiced or discriminatory.

javelin: If you are stabbed by one of these, it could be symbolic of a threat to your safety. Note that it could be symbolic of a phallus.

jay: This is an arrogant and cranky bird. Its loud cry could also be your unconscious trying to get your attention.

jaywalking: Are you taking unnecessary risks? Are you breaking the rules? Do you need to think outside the lines? Are you behaving irresponsibly?

jaw: See *body*.

jealousy: This is perhaps a carryover emotion from your waking life. It could also be indicative of a fear of intimacy or the fact that you are coveting something you don't have. It could also be symbolic of a lack of trust or the need to trust more.

Jedi: This may be a symbol for your spiritual aspect. If the Jedi is fighting it may be about some inner conflict or challenges you are facing. The gender of the Jedi might help to determine what inner forces or challenges you're experiencing.

jellyfish: Are you feeling inadequate or experiencing some lack of self-esteem? Are some painful memories surfacing from your subconscious?

jester: Perhaps you're being too silly. Are you letting trivial matters distract you?

Are you embarrassing yourself? Are you pushing the limits and acting without constraint? See also the *clown, fool,* or *trickster* in the *archetypes* section.

Jesus: If you call out his name, that can represent a call for help or guidance. The Jesus image may be a part of yourself that is trying to exercise your spiritual self. See also *Christ* in the *archetypes* section and/or *religion*.

jet plane: This can be about power, freedom, or speed. It can also reflect pride. See also *airplane*.

To be on jet skis might be about traveling too fast or being on a fast and crazy journey of self-discovery.

jetty: If you see or stand on a jetty, that may mean you need to dive into your emotions.

Perhaps you need to explore your deeper or subconscious self.

jewels or jewelry: These can represent things that you or your unconscious mind might hold dear. This might include such things as your honesty, the eternal aspect of self, or your dignity.

Note the kind of jewel (see *diamond, emerald, gem, pearl,* and *ruby*).

jewelry box: This may suggest your self-worth or sense of self-value. It could also be about hidden potential and the need to unleash it.

job: If you are looking for a job, it might suggest that you're feeling unfulfilled or even frustrated with something or your current job. Alternatively, it could be your subconscious encouraging you to hang in there. Getting a job can also suggest hanging in there even if the process seems like a lot of work.

If it involves your current job, the image could be about needing to work harder, especially if you're losing your job in the dream. Losing a job can be about your insecurities as well. Do you feel overworked?

If you're changing jobs, that can be about a loss of identity or taking on a new identity.

If you're going back to work at a job you've left in the past, there may be some aspect of that job that's missing in the present. It could also suggest past accolades or a time when you felt that you contributed something more meaningful.

See also *interview.*

jogging: Maybe everything is moving along at a steady pace. Or perhaps you are not making any real progress.

joke: If you're telling a joke, ask yourself, "Are people not taking me seriously? Am I not taking something seriously? Is something just a pointless joke?"

journal: This image may come up if you're trying to rewrite the past or document something. It could also be about trying to remember something. If it's a diary, perhaps you are keeping secrets. See *diary.*

journey: This could be about how you feel about your life. It could also be about the path in your life. See also *path.*

joy: Do you need to seek some harmony in your life? Do you need to bring some harmony to some situation or group?

Judaism: The interpretation of this image might depend on your positive or negative bias regarding it and those who practice it.

It may reflect a need to get in contact with your spiritual self or to better yourself as a person.

It might also reflect your desire to incorporate some part of the religion or the way it's practiced into your own life.

See also *religion*.

juice: This can suggesting life or vitality. It could also refer to energy. Are you *juiced*?

judge: This could symbolize your inner critic or your conscience. It could be about wisdom and your decision-making process. Is there some decision that you need to make?

Are you feeling guilty about something? Are you worried about being caught or some secret being revealed?

If you are being judged, perhaps you are looking for acceptance. Are you being tested?

Judging others may actually be an impediment to your own understanding of yourself. Your judgment of another person may reveal an aspect of your own evolution or maturity. (It likely represents a part of your own shadow.)

juggle: Are you trying to do too many things at once, and as a result, are you not doing any of them well? Perhaps you're feeling a bit overwhelmed. You may need to bring more balance to your life.

jumping: Are you jumping to conclusions or not looking before you leap? Are you getting ahead of yourself or the facts by jumping the gun? What is it you're jumping into?

If you are jumping a rope, do you need to become better coordinated in your plans?

See also *leaping*.

Jung, Carl Gustav: Carl Jung was a much younger contemporary of Sigmund Freud who influenced him in his early years but later disagreed with many of Freud's theories. He did so mainly by deemphasizing Freud's focus on sexual development. Instead Jung focused on the collective unconscious.

Freud thought that dreams represented those wishes that we could not accept on a conscious level (e.g., signs of psychic illness, sexual trauma, or wish fulfillment).

Carl Gustav Jung

Jung believed that dreams were messages to oneself that helped deal with past and present dilemmas, resolve inner conflicts, and solve the most basic mysteries of one's life.

Since then, many therapists have refined the use of dreams and redefined many of the works as *soul work*.

See also *analytical psychology, collective unconscious, depth psychology,* and *individuation*.

jungle: This can suggest something coming up from the unconscious. This may have unrealized anxieties attached as well.

junk: This might symbolize the old ways of thinking, negative feelings, bad habits, and discarded attitudes or beliefs. Perhaps you need to stop dwelling on unimportant details.

junkyard: This might be about all the junk that you have repressed.

jury: This may be your conscience. A jury might indicate that you are in the process of making decisions or that you have made a decision but have not faced it yet. See also *judge* or *trial*.

Jupiter: This planet in a dream could have an astrological meaning in that it is often associated with those who are positive, generous, lucky, and honorable. (Think of the word jovial.)

See also *god* in the *archetypes* section or *planet*.

K

Kabal or Cabal: This could symbolize a connection or agreement.

Insight: During the sixteenth century, the Jewish Kabalists perceived dreams as communications from God. It was only Moses who could speak to him face-to-face. This was not unusual in that the Bible itself promoted dreams as communications from God. They were not for individuals but for mankind in general. They were more suggestions from heaven (Genesis 2:3–7; 28:12–15; 31:10–13, 24; 37:5–9; 40; 41; Judges 7:13; 1 Kings 3:5, 15; Daniel 2; 3). See the Egyptian and Hindu sections as well.

However, during the Talmudic period, dreams were also interpreted in a psychological way and seen as information from the dreamer's soul, one's innermost thoughts and feelings. Some, of course, thought them to be just vanities (see Ecclesiastes 5).

Many of the religious dream traditions of the Old Testament and Talmud have been recorded from the Chaldeans, the magicians of the ancient world, and from the early Babylonians.

In 1515, Soloman Almoli published one of the first popular works on dreams, the *Pitron Halomot*. (It was reprinted again in 1585 as well and in other Jewish dialects throughout the time.) Basically, it was a dissertation on the role and tradition of dreams in the Jewish tradition as well as a handbook for the interpretation of dreams.

kaleidoscope: If you see one of these, it might suggest that you need to be aware of the different facets that make up one's character. It could also suggest that there's a kaleidoscope of choices that may make it difficult for you to find your path in life.

Looking through a kaleidoscope can give you an enlightened perspective on something. Do you need to add some color to some part of your life?

Kali: See *Shiva*.

kangaroo: This can be about motherly protection. Note also that this image could be about aggression, or it could suggest that something is overwhelming your world.

Are you hopping mad?

karate: Do you need to direct your energy in a more focused way with regard to your goals? Do you need to defend yourself for some reason?

karma: Do you need to focus on how you're dealing with your relationships (positively or negatively)? Consider the phrase "What goes around comes around."

kayak: Are you emotionally well balanced? How are you negotiating the rough patches of your life (see *boat*)?

key: This could possibly represent a solution as in "the key to something." Or it could be what will give you access to something or someone, such as the key to someone's heart.

If you see a key maker in your dream, perhaps there is something that you need help with to uncover. If you're making a spare key, perhaps you need to look at several other approaches to solve some problem.

> To every man is given the key to the gates of heaven; the same key opens the gates of hell.
>
> —Buddhist saying

In short, beware the trickster (see the *archetypes* section and/or *keying*).

keyboard: Perhaps there's some message that you need to get out. See also *music*.

keyhole: To see a keyhole may be about looking to get a different perspective. If it's about opening a door, see *door* in *house*.

keying: Do you need to zero in on something or someone? Are you ignoring some important (key) aspect? If a car is being *keyed* (i.e., being scratched with a key), are you the one vandalizing the vehicle, or is your car being vandalized? See *vandalism*.

As a computer term, you may need to look at reprogramming something or some belief or idea. It could also be a metaphor for logging in (i.e., becoming more conscious of something or being more engaged and active in something). Are you ignoring or neglecting something that you need to pay attention to?

kicking: If you're kicking someone, it could be about some repressed aggression, anger, or frustration. This might be especially true if you're kicking a dog. If you're the one being kicked, perhaps you are being taken advantage of or victimized. Alternatively, do you need a kick start toward some goal or plan of action?

kidnapped: Perhaps negative feelings have taken you over. Confronting these feelings will help release you from their control.

kill or killing: This may suggest undermining or being undermined in your status, self-confidence, or effectiveness.

The act of killing could reflect you restricting some part of yourself or your development. (This need not always have a negative meaning. Some things are better off dead or gone.)

It can also be about ending something (e.g., a relationship, a way of being, a personality trait, etc.). The act is a symbol of inner conflict (see also *gunmen* and *violence*).

Seeing a serial killer in your dream may reflect your insecurity. If the killer is killing off friends and family members, perhaps you are cutting yourself off from them. If you're the killer, perhaps some behavior or habit is forcing you into a negative cycle that is causing you and others harm.

To kill one's father may be about the rejection of authority, rules, and a higher power. Perhaps you worry about becoming like your father and are rejecting certain power.

To kill your mother might indicate that you are rejecting your feminine aspect, your emotional side, or the influence of your intuitive sense. This may also be a symbolic attempt to become less dependent and more independent.

If you worry that you may be becoming more like your mother, the image of killing her in a dream may reflect your dislike of this possibility.

king: This could symbolize your father and his approval or disapproval. What are you ruled by (see the *archetypes* section)? It could also refer to your noble self. It can also be about power and control, especially when it comes to the parts of you that rule your thoughts and actions. See *emperor*.

kingdom: This could symbolize a level of awareness. For example, the upper kingdom might symbolize the conscious mind, while the lower kingdom may be about the unconscious. Similarly, the middle kingdom may be a union of the two. These might be about political positions as well.

It can also be about protecting one's territory (beliefs, values, point of view, or privilege).

kiosk: This can have several meanings. It can make reference to a message board, a place of business, or a temple. If it's a message board, see *newspaper or news media*. If it's a place of business, see *store* or *selling*. If it's a temple, see *church* or *temple*.

kissing: This could be about affection and intimacy—a desire to be connected (see *marriage*). It could also be a desire for romance.

If you're kissing your ex, it could be about looking back at better times or upon the better part of an earlier romance that your current one is missing.

Kissing a stranger can be about the need to accept some repressed part of yourself. This could also be a metaphor for self-discovery.

To kiss someone's foot might be about respect and/or humility. However, if you are being forced to do so, then it might be about humiliation.

If someone is forcing a kiss upon you, perhaps people are trying to force their ideas or opinions onto you.

Kissing someone else's lover could be about your desire to be in a relationship.

To break off a kiss suddenly might be acting out the verb *kiss off* (i.e., to get lost or to leave). This can express you're disinterested in something or someone.

Consider also the phrase "kissing terms," which may suggest a flirtation with someone or some idea.

kitchen: See *house terms*.

knapsack (or backpack): This could symbolize past difficulties, feelings, or

ideas about ourselves that we carry around (see *luggage*).

knife: This could symbolize cutting of something (as in cutting a thing or person out of your life) and/or the wounding of the self (self-criticism or a personal mistake). You might cut yourself off from something. Cutting a rope could be about cutting yourself free from some bondage. This image can also be similar to sword (see *sword*).

knight: This may be symbolic of the hero. It could also be a protector image. What do you need to protect? See *hero* in the *archetypes* section.

This may also be a symbol of honor and loyalty. Do you need to be more honorable or loyal?

Are you looking for someone or something to save you? Do you need to be more self-reliant?

This image could also represent assertiveness or the need for it. Are you being too assertive or aggressive?

The knight may also represent the animus or masculine aspects in a woman's dream (e.g., being assertive, decisive, or action-oriented).

A knight might also be a rescue image and might suggest that you need to take more responsibility for your own success or life in general and not depend on something or someone else taking care of you.

Be conscious of such idioms as "a knight in shining armor" (one's true love), a "white knight" (the good guy), the black knight (the bad guy or one's shadow aspect).

See also *sword* if the knight is wielding one or *dragon* in the *animals* section if the knight is fighting a dragon.

knitting: Knitting could refer to weaving different parts of the self or your life together. It's also an act of creation or making something whole. You may not feel very whole or connected right now.

knock or knocking: This can represent opportunity. Is something trying to get your attention (maybe your subconscious)? Some suggest that this knocking may be alerting the psyche to the realms of the spirit. Do you need to refocus your attention?

What's behind the door that someone is knocking on? The location of the door is also important. If it's in the front, it's the public door and may have to do with relationship. If it's in the back, it's the more private entry into ourselves and the secrets we keep. See also *door* in *house*.

It could be a reference to not dismissing something without looking into it as when someone says, "Don't knock it if you haven't tried it."

A door knocker could also be about opportunity *knocking* at your door.

knot: This could symbolize a tangle of emotions or lies, dependencies as in entanglements, or tensions as in times when one is all knotted up. Trying to untie a knot could reflect your search for a resolution. Have you failed or succeeded in untying the knot?

koala: See *animal terms*.

L

laboratory: Maybe you're exploring something, experimenting, or examining options. Perhaps you're testing an idea.

Perhaps you need to be more curious about or question something. Do you need to be more logical about something?

Perhaps there's some mystery you need to solve.

See also *scientist* and/or *science*.

Labyrinth, maze, or mandala all speak to finding your way to your inner self or soul.

labyrinth: Perhaps you are lost or hiding, or maybe you are confused about something.

This image can also represent something being more complex than you thought.

The labyrinth can also represent a map to your inner self as well as a mandala.

Insight: In the Greek myth, Theseus meets at the labyrinth's center his own brutish aspects in the symbolic form of the minotaur and defeats it. Thus, the labyrinth can be seen as symbolic of initiation and rebirth.

The Christians removed the symbol of the monster from the center and replaced it with a symbol of salvation where the twists and turns of the labyrinth symbolized the sinful entanglements of human nature.

Perhaps you are on a never-ending journey, or you've fallen into an unsolvable problem. See also *lost, mandala, map, maze,* and/or *minotaur.*

ladder: You may be reaching upward for something. Ladders can have something to do with achievement, climbing toward a promotion, or a higher perspective on something. If you are carrying a ladder, it can also be a burden (the burden of climbing the social ladder to achieve higher status).

If you are descending a ladder, perhaps you are escaping from something or losing your spiritual self. Falling from a ladder or seeing a broken ladder could be about failure or hardship.

If you walk under a ladder, consider the omen of bad luck.

A ladder can also be symbolic of the connection between your intellectual and spiritual self.

See also *Jacob's ladder.*

lagoon: This might be about stagnant emotions or being shallow.

lair: An animal's lair might symbolize your subconscious. If you're hiding, perhaps you are hiding something or hiding from something or someone.

The type of animal's lair might also give you information (see *animals*).

lake: This may reflect the unconscious or the inner world of your feelings. This symbol has a more contained quality regarding your emotions than perhaps the ocean symbol has, and perhaps it's not as deep in nature.

Lakes as well as pools can be about feeling restricted. You may feel as though you are having difficulty expressing yourself fully. Calm lakes can be about peacefulness or the need for it, though a stormy lake can reflect emotional turmoil.

Diving in can be about the need to deal with one's emotions or getting one's feet wet (i.e., getting started on some project or change). (See also *water.*)

Insight: In Celtic legend, the Lady of the Lake, as in the Arthurian tales, may represent your inner feminine power. She is a water spirit or spirit of your unconscious emotions. Like the goddess Dianna, she can be a huntress as well.

Lakshmi: See *Shiva.*

lamb: This can suggest vulnerability, gentleness, and peacefulness (see *lion and lamb*). Consider also that the lamb may represent some aspect of the Christian symbol of Jesus.

lame: Maybe you're holding back, restricting yourself, or being restricted. Perhaps you've lost confidence. What seems to have caused the lameness? Consider the reference to a lame idea (i.e., something silly, stupid, or impractical).

lament: Are you still mourning someone or something? Do you need to think more positively about something? Perhaps you need to stop feeling sorry for yourself.

lamppost: If there's a lamppost in your dream, then perhaps you need to shed some light on some dark situation. You should also consider that this could be a light to take you out of your depression.

land: This can relate to your potential, whether developed or undeveloped. It can represent what you've made of yourself. The condition of the land will also add information to this image.

See also *wilderness*.

landlord: This may have something to do with being in or out of control. It may also have something to do with controlling some part of yourself. It can reflect the rational or responsible side of yourself or the need to exercise it.

land mines: These can represent extreme stress and the fear of making mistakes. These could represent emotions (or ideas or situations) that have the potential to explode.

landscapes: These can reflect attitudes, moods, and what is beautiful within you. What attitude do you meet life with? A gray and gloomy landscape may reflect self-doubts, but a sunny landscape may reflect your optimism. It can also represent what's going on around you (i.e., the general viewpoint of the people around you).

How you present your outer self (see *house* and *clothing*). A landscape could represent your mental viewpoint. What does the landscape mean to you?

landslide: Huge obstacles may be affecting your progress toward some goal. Are there some obstacles on the path your life is on? See also *avalanche*.

language (strange or foreign to you): This may represent whatever is in you that has not yet been put into words. A strange language could indicate mysteries to be uncovered. It could also reflect frustration with not being able to understand someone or to communicate (see *choke*).

See also *speaking in tongues*.

laptop: This could possibly reflect the need to communicate or develop a social network. If your laptop is lost or stolen, then perhaps you feel lonely.

laughing: Do you need to lighten up. Is it a release from being too serious? If people are laughing at you, do you feel insecure or humiliated?

laundry: Do you need to clean up your act? Are you revealing stuff about yourself or others that is better kept to yourself? See also *naked*.

If you're sorting through your laundry, you may be trying to sort yourself out or address your problems, attitudes, or feelings.

If you're laundering money, perhaps you're trying to hide your actions.

Washing your clothes could be about cleaning up the way you are behaving.

Consider the reference "dirty laundry" in that you are trying to hide things you don't want others to see, especially things that you might think would denigrate your reputation.

Laundromat: Laundromats can be about changing attitudes or cleaning up your act/behavior.

lava: This could symbolize pent-up violence and anger (see *volcano* and *eruption*).

lavender: See *flowers*.

law: Do you need to exhibit more restraint with something? Are you abiding by or breaking the rules? Are you declaring an ultimatum as in laying down the law?

lawn: This could symbolize controlled growth.

lawyer: Do you need assistance, guidance, or someone to help you with some decision? Is some legal issue bothering you?

Do you feel guilty about something? Are your personal defenses weakening? Do you feel insecure? Do you need to defend yourself against something or someone?

This image can also refer to some resolution that needs to happen.

If the lawyer is a barrister wearing the traditional white wig, it could be a symbol

for wisdom and/or knowledge (see also *wise old man or woman* in the *archetypes* section).

The meaning of this image may also reflect your attitude about lawyers.

lead: This can represent something heavy on your mind or weighing you down, a burden.

leader: You want to be sure and confident of yourself. Is anyone following?

leaf: This is symbolic of growth. The color will tell you something about the time of year and the season, which can also add significance. Falling leaves can be about fallen hopes, dreams, or the end to a project or relationship, and they sometimes reflect a feeling of despair.

leaking: This can be about experiencing loss or disappointment. Maybe some hidden part of you or your life is being revealed even though you've tried to keep it suppressed.

See also *ceiling* under *house terms*.

leaping: Are you taking a chance (e.g., stepping outside your comfort zone or taking a leap of faith)? Are you leaping to conclusions? See also *jumping*.

leash: This could be about being controlled or controlling. If you are wearing one, perhaps you need to show more restraint in some situation.

If the leash is on a pet, it may be about controlling some aspect of yourself that the animal represents (see specific animals in *animal terms*). If the animal has broken free from the leash, perhaps it symbolizes you having broken free from some control or influence.

leather: Are you thick-skinned? Does nothing get through your defenses? This can also represent ruggedness and toughness.

Consider also that there is some sexual symbolism here.

If it's around your neck, it may have something to do with the Marine Corps or the military in general (see *soldier/warrior*).

leaving: Suggesting an end to something or a symbol for rejection.

lecture: If you're lecturing, you're being boring. If listening to a lecture, perhaps there's something you need to look into or research further before taking any action.

See also *sermon*.

ledge: If you're standing or sitting on a ledge, you may be feeling anxious, excited, or desperate. You may be at the edge of doing something. It can also reflect a cry for help.

If you're looking down, this may reflect a pessimistic view of something. Looking up may reflect a positive view, while looking straight ahead may reflect being realistic about some prospect or situation.

See also *cliff*.

left (as in direction): This could symbolize intuition, or in a political context, it could reflect inclusiveness, acceptance, and openness (or whatever your definition of the left side of the political spectrum is).

The left hand might indicate the less dominant parts of yourself or the parts that you may be hiding, while the right represents the self-confident and dominant parts of your nature.

Consider also being left out as in not belonging or feeling alone. Does the left hand know what the right is doing?

Is some problem coming out of *left field* where you didn't expect it?

For some the left is considered a symbol for the unconscious. If something is moving from left to right, perhaps it is something that is trying to come to consciousness.

LEGO blocks: Dreaming of LEGO blocks could be about expressing your creativity or your imagination. It may also be about building something new in your life.

Leo: Sometimes this is represented by a lion. It can be about pride, leadership, authority, playfulness, and generosity. Some born under this zodiac sign like to be the center of attention. See also *zodiac*.

leopard: See *animal terms*.

lesbian: If you are not a lesbian in your waking life, this image may represent a need to integrate certain aspects of yourself. It can also represent the need to love yourself more. It can be about self-acceptance.

If you abhor the thought of lesbianism in your waking life, this image can be about the rejection of certain sexual aspects within yourself. See both *gay* and *homosexual*.

letting go: If dropping something or throwing it away, perhaps you need to let something or someone go. See also *abandon, death, dropping*, and *surrender*.

letter: This can represent communication or news from someone. It might suggest an intuitive communication. Could this be a message from the unconscious?

If the letter is from someone long gone or deceased, it could suggest that the essence of that person continues to communicate and inform your life.

Tearing up or burning a letter could be about letting go of past mistakes or memories.

An unopened letter could symbolize thoughts, feelings, or opportunities that are not conscious yet.

See also *texting*.

lettuce: This could be about abundance, or if you're eating it, the image could be about spiritual nourishment. Consider also the pun *let us*. You could be seeking others' approval or desire to belong.

levitating: Perhaps you're not feeling grounded or are acting in an ungrounded way.

Consider also the phrase "Things are up in the air."

It might also be about overcoming helplessness and/sadness.

See also *flying*.

liar: See *lying*.

Libra: This symbolizes order, balance, cooperation, equality, and harmony. Libra's are said not to handle criticism very well. Are you too thin-skinned?

Do you need to bring something back into balance or be more cooperative?

library: This represents knowledge as well as the search for knowledge and understanding.

A librarian may be about a knowledgeable mind. It could also be about stored memories (see *album* or *book*).

A library may also represent the collected memories and ideas of your personal unconscious or of the collective unconscious. If you can't find a particular book, then perhaps there's some part of you that's missing or underdeveloped.

lice: Something may be bugging, distressing, or frustrating you. Lice can also be a symbol of rejection, or it could be related to a dirty or unwanted thought.

You might also feel invaded.

license: This could symbolize the amount of control you feel you have over your life or your identity. It can also represent the right or authority to do something. Are you doing something that you have the right to do or not?

lie or liar: If you are lying or someone else is lying, are you trying to deceive yourself or another person? What are you hiding or hiding from? Do you need to tell the truth about something? Are you presenting yourself falsely? See also *lying* and *mask*.

lie detector: This may suggest the loss of confidence. It could also reflect a loss of faith in someone or something? See also *faith*.

light: This can represent one's vision. It can signal being awake spiritually or consciously as opposed to being asleep. It can be about having insight, clarity, and/or guidance or finding a truth. It can also be a metaphor for the *soul*.

When it comes from a lighthouse, it may indicate a warning (see also *sunrise*).

Besides insight, light in your dream might represent illumination, clarity of mind, guidance, and plain understanding. Is the light shed on a once cloudy situation or problem?

You might also consider the color of the light (see *colors*).

Seeing a bright light in your dream might indicate that you need to move toward a higher level of awareness and feeling.

Dreams with bright lights sometimes show up for those who are near death. Death is not always a harbinger, but these dreams can suggest that death is on the person's mind at present.

Seeing soft or shadowy lighting in your dreams might indicate feelings and thoughts from the primal aspects or less developed parts of your unconscious.

Dreaming that you cannot turn on the light might suggest a lack of insight and perspective on a situation, or you may feel paralyzed when it comes to what you need to do in a worrisome situation.

Seeing something glowing in your dream might symbolize enlightenment or may indicate that something had shed new light onto a situation. You might have gained a fresh perspective and reached a welcome understanding.

Seeing an aura around you or someone else might suggest that important information is being given to you in the dream and that you need to pay close attention to the message. You may need to draw on this energy for strength.

Dreaming that you have a halo might signify that you are a perfectionist. It may also represent some significant spiritual development and supernatural energy.

Some say auras or light hallucinations in dreams can warn of an oncoming migraine. These auras can also indicate a future nightmare.

Insight: Lights are beacons to follow and indicators of the divine—the spiritual, the soul, and life itself. They can warn of dangers just as lighthouses do. Light can speak to the qualities of intellect, leadership, knowledge, and transformation. It can point to needs or solutions, give guidance and direction, and can speak to the aspects of our inner and outer selves.

Light can be about knowledge and knowing, awareness, consciousness, and self-development. It can highlight beginnings and endings, life and death, turning toward reality or away from it. It can be about new ideas and the less developed parts of the unconscious mind.

Light can focus on the primal or spiritual and that can either illuminate or go out and be in darkness. A failure to produce light can be about high anxiety and feeling paralyzed or trapped by something or someone. If the bulb burns out, you might feel ineffective or out of ideas.

Light is often a symbol for the creative point in one's awareness and bringing new light to consciousness. It is also found within the third-eye chakra, which is the *light between the eyes*. This light may be speaking to the primary force of life and creation.

In the beginning God created the heavens and the earth. Now the earth was formless and empty, darkness was over the surface of the deep, and the Spirit of God was hovering over the waters. And God said, "Let there be light," and there was light."

—Genesis 1:1–3 (NIV)

Many cultures have festivals dedicated to the light and celebrate the triumph of good over evil.

light bulb: This might refer to an idea or a revelation and insight. If it's burned out, you may be out of ideas. You may no longer be excited about something. Is it burning brightly or dimly? This might give meaning to some aspect of your life, relationship, or endeavor.

lighthouse: Lighthouses can refer to the need for guidance or a warning of danger (i.e., jagged areas ahead that may jeopardize or affect one's navigation of a situation or life in general).

lightning: This could symbolize a flash of insight, an awakening, or an epiphany. Note if you have any fears associated with this image. Light in the form of lightning can suggest sudden awareness, spiritual revelation, or even a shocking turn of events that is beyond one's control. Being struck by it might signal a permanent transformation or change taking place.

limb: As a tree limb, this could have something to do with your family relationships. Consider the condition of the limb. Is it healthy, broken, rotten, cut off, dead, threatening, etc.?

Also consider the phrase "out on a limb." Have you placed yourself in a precarious position because of something you've said or did?

See also *branch*.

lion and lamb: A lamb and a lion sitting in a field together might be a metaphor for cooperation or the concept of making peace with someone, some situation, or some circumstance.

Insight: Also note that both the lion and the lamb are symbolic of the Christ. Might the dream be making a statement about your spiritual aspect?

They also might represent two sides of your own personality. The lamb represents your peaceful, patient nature (the feminine side of yourself), while the lion can be seen as the aggressive or assertive part of your nature (the masculine side). In this vein, this image couple might suggest that you need to integrate the disparate parts of yourself.

If these two lie down together it might be the unconscious mind's way of saying that you need to reconcile or integrate your conflicting opposites.

line: Have you or someone else crossed a line (i.e., gone too far)? Also see *queue* for more info.

lips: See *body*. This image may also refer to giving lip (i.e., talking back or being rude).

Are you paying lip service to something (i.e., not really meaning what you say)?

lipstick: This draws attention to your lips, so it could be signaling that you should be careful about some communication. Are you being altogether truthful? It's also a sexual or sensual symbol.

litter: This may be about issues or ideas that you should throw away or let go of. Perhaps you're being too unorganized and need to clean up your act. See *dirty* as well.

little: This could symbolize something insignificant or vulnerable. It may reflecting how you feel about yourself.

lizard: This could symbolize being cold-blooded. Where do you need to show more warmth and compassion? See *snake* or *animal* as well.

location: This is where something is located. See *venue* or the actual location, such as *house, mall, apartment,* or *restaurant.*

locker: This might reflect aspects of yourself that you've kept hidden. What kind of things are in the locker? If you've forgotten your locker combination, perhaps you aren't sure where you stand with respect to something or someone.

If someone else is using your locker, perhaps they've seen through your façade and into what's hidden within.

locomotive: This can represent the engine that drives you forward toward your goals in life. But it could also represent the burdens of the past that you're pulling behind you (see *train*).

looking: This could be about searching for something.

lost: This is an image that signals confusion, loneliness, and encountering a new and unknown situation. It can represent being without direction and not knowing where you're going. Some part of you may be lost or missing. It can also reveal that you have lost your center. See also *abandoned.*

Losing is similar to failing or the fear of failing. It can also point to the need to regain what has been lost.

lottery or lotto: Are you relying on fate instead of taking responsibility for your finances and/or success in life? See also *betting* or *gambling.*

A ticket might also suggest that you need to leave something to fate and not always try to control the outcome.

lotus position: This is the Buddhist position where people cross their legs open their bodies to the universe. It invites peace, simplicity, and contemplation. It may also reflect the need for enlightenment or the expansion of the soul. This may be missing in your life. See also *Buddha.*

loud: Hearing loud noises or yelling in your dream could suggest that something in either your subconscious or waking life needs your immediate attention. Note that loudness can also be a way of diverting your attention so as to hide something.

love: This can represent the idealized inner self. It can also be a statement about being loved or not being loved and/or craving it. Love can be a statement about acceptance or acknowledgment (see *money*).

If you lose a loved one in your dream, perhaps it may speak to your fears of losing relationships or even cherished parts of yourself. See also *dead people*.

Insight: Love's a feeling and a longing, and it perhaps may also be an act. The practice of acceptance, forgiveness, and grace could also be part of it, but what else?

Perhaps love is not a thing as described by our conditioning but something more ethereal such as an act of being—a meditation continuously practiced instead of a set of prescriptions or proscriptions (repairs or rules). It allows another's consciousness to enter our own to show us that we are not separate.

Love is not always a feeling of being gaga over someone or something. It can be an action born of knowing that we are all connected, all one spirit, one earth but with different ways of worshipping and praying, all equal and the same in our divinity.

Anything else is not love, and anything else is not of the soul or the one spirit that enlivens us all. Anything else is *only* of the self-involved, self-serving, greedy, simpleminded, and self-centered ego-self.

The illusion of separation between us and what we love muddies the waters of our conscious minds, making it difficult for us to see our surroundings. The continuous thought patterns of our minds are what add the detritus to the clear flow of life and obscures our true selves.

Love always seems to be there in some form when I need it, not in the same location perhaps, but there nonetheless when I take the time to look. It's not tangible in that it is not an object, though it is clearly the essence of some objects. It can be sensed but never held on to.

It's as though love is a continuous meditation, as if it were water running across the land, over and around the rocks, racing headlong with abandon toward an unknown sea. As love, we *are* the stream, and to flow with it instead of against it by thrashing about and grabbing for exposed roots and debris along the edges, we become the stream. We become still, and the water around us clears.

lover: Sometimes these images are speaking to the need for some kind of adjustment in a way of thinking. It can signal a need to bring harmony to one's contrary thoughts.

Many see this image as a symbol of the need to unite the conscious and spiritual selves. See the *archetypes* section.

lucid dreaming: This is when you become aware that you are in a dream. It's a very different kind of sleep. You become aware that you are in an interior world where your senses no longer function as they do in the waking world. While in this state, you can to some degree change or consciously direct the narrative of the dream.

It can be a way of avoiding unpleasant or frightening dreams, and for this reason, one may want to be cautious because the unpleasantness of our dreams often has something important to teach us.

Psychologists suggest that continuously suppressed emotions may be at the root of a number of psychological and physical disorders. Because we often do this in our waking lives, bringing it into our dream lives could compound the problem.

Lucidity may have its place in that you can actually interpret the dream narrative while in it. This would seem to be an advantage or an additional aspect to working with an outside interpreter.

Feeling as though you have become lucid in a dream might be a metaphor and also reflect a need to become more conscious of what's going on around you or within you.

Other forms of intentional dreaming that may involve this phenomena of lucidity include *mutual dreaming* and a technique called *active imagining*, where the dreamer enters a dream in a conscious state as opposed to becoming lucid while in a dream.

See also the chapter on nightmares in section 3, where you will learn about lucid dreaming therapy.

luggage: This may represent the habits or problems that we carry around. For example, the things we carry around might be emotions, grievances, prejudices, and/or beliefs (see *bag* or *suitcase*).

lumber: This may be about what you have built your life or personality out of.

luminous: This may be similar to light, numinous, or peak experiences. This image can also speak to the qualities of one's soul or personality.

lying: If you are lying down with someone, this might be the unconscious mind's way of saying that you need to reconcile or integrate your conflicting opposites.

Or are you just lying to yourself? Are you being deceitful (see also *faking* or *pretending*)?

M

machine: Any machine may represent the automatic systems of the body that need no thought. This image could be about mechanical (or robot-like) behaviors or rigid ways of thinking that you or others may have.

mad: See *anger*. This could also be a symbol for being crazy, irresponsible, or irrational. Perhaps you need to behave? See also *crazy*.

magazine: You may be open to new ideas. The name of the magazine can also provide hints as to this image's meaning.

magic: If magic shows up in a dream or someone performs magic, this may mean that you shouldn't believe what you see.

You may be trying to solve a problem through wishes or hopes. You may want something to just go away instead of facing the problem. (This is magical thinking—irrational acts designed to solve a problem.)

Sometimes people resort to a religion, a cult, or a belief system and think that following its precepts will magically cure (rid) them of certain problems. This is how bad and incompetent people get elected to office.

Magic in a dream can also elude to a power that is stronger than you or an unconscious force (perhaps a repressed memory) trying to make itself known.

Insight: Sometimes the feeling of magic or something magical brings awe, inspiration, grandeur, majesty, or the divine. This may be the soul's presence pushing toward the sublime, your drive to create, and an urge toward transformation and transcendence of the everyday.

Magic does not come from the rational. The magical world grows from the secret orderliness of chaos. Allow yourself to be confused. Thinking that you know something about what is real can be very limiting to living what is real.

To experience the magical requires an openness and enthusiasm without preconceptions or expectations, allowing for all possibilities—a boundless, limitless, and infinite perceiving.

The rational has its place but not in the experience of magic.

The loss of a magical power in a dream could refer to a loss of *magic* in your life or just the loss of power in your life.

Is magic in a dream a symbol of a higher truth or the symbol of the charlatan? Is someone trying to pull one over (trick) on you? Are you fooling yourself or seeking to transcend the ego-self?

If you experience black magic in the dream, perhaps you feel controlled by something or someone, or maybe you are being tempted to do something against your nature (see also *witch*).

See *amulet, charm,* and/or *spell.*

magician or conjurer: This suggests the command of the inner and outer worlds (see the *archetypes* section under *wizard*). The magician can suggest the transformational part of your being. Magicians can also be masters of illusion. Are you trying to fool someone?

This symbol includes the shaman, prophet, sage, trickster, doctor, wizard, sorcerer, sorceress, magician, conjurer, and king.

This image can also symbolize the ability to change something (e.g., behavior, moods, or attitudes).

It could also mean that you are trying to fool or trick someone into thinking something is true when it isn't.

Alternatively, maybe some situation or problem is trickier to solve than you originally thought. Are you disillusioned?

In the tarot tradition, the magician or magus is the first card. It is considered by some as the symbol for transparent intelligence (i.e., perception without obstruction), and thus it represents unfettered inner wisdom. The magus represents freedom from illusions. It is the desire to know our true selves that exists in all of us.

Insight: The magician is also similar to the alchemist—the agent of change, the magical messenger and transformer (of things, ideas, and people). The alchemist can represent our ability to transform our feelings and our very nature.

By bringing things to consciousness, the alchemist aids in their transformation. After all, you can only deal with something when you are aware of it and it's out in the open (see the *shadow*). C. G. Jung saw the experimentations of the alchemists of the seventeenth century as the personification of the process of or the reconciliation of opposites in order attain self-actualization.

The magician, sorcerer, or alchemist is the magical messenger and transformer (of things, ideas, and people). As mentioned, he or she can represent our ability to transform our feelings and our nature. (The gender of the figure can tell you what part of your nature is transforming or needs to transform.)

The wizard is a father archetype and wise old man archetype—the wisdom, authority, and strength of one's life.

In the Rider-Waite Tarot deck, the wizard or magician is the male power of creation. He can make things happen by the power of the word. He can be both a healer and a snake oil salesman (i.e., a trickster).

The conjurer represents our ability to change our moods and attitudes. In some Native cosmologies, the trickster was the cocreator of the universe, and even though his exploits might seem foolish, he gradually brings about transformation. In some ways, Jesus can be viewed as the trickster.

The shaman aids in connecting with the inner world—the unconscious. The doctor is the restorer of opposites or more precisely, the restorer of balance.

Some of these symbols have dark meanings, and therefore we can look at them as the shadow—the unrecognized part(s) of ourselves. For example, the trickster can be seen as the least developed part of our personalities. It may seem crazy and unpredictable. The black magician sometimes symbolizes our selfish or negative ways too.

A witch can conjure good or evil. She can bring light or darkness with her spells.

Here are some questions to ask yourself if these symbols show up in your dreams: Are you wanting to change something or someone? Are you experiencing or have you experienced transformation? Have you obtained something through trickery or deceit? Are you trying to fool someone into thinking that something untrue is true? What mood or attitude do you need to change?

The asking questions about a dream is an effective technique designed to obtain deeper as well as more pragmatic meaning from the dream. You may want to add your answers to your journal.

maggots: These can represent a sense of illness in something or yourself. This may include unwholesome attitudes and thoughts that you may have. Because they are often associated with rotting and death, it could reflect your anxiety about death or suggest that something is rotting away (falling apart) in your life. If they're coming from your mouth, perhaps there's something bad that you've said but are not acknowledging.

magnet: This could symbolize something that you are drawn to or repelled from.

magnifier: This is something to make you clearer and more conscious. Perhaps you need to look at something more closely. Are you making something bigger than it is?

mail: This could symbolize news, guidance, or basic communication.

makeup: This could reflect your self-image, especially true with females. This involves what you show the world or use to cover up yourself. Too much makeup may suggest a desperate cover-up. Consider also the verb to *make something up* (i.e., to lie or fib).

making out: This could be about connecting intimately. You may have a desire for someone or the person with whom you're making out in the dream. You may also desire romance and intimacy. You may want to unite different parts of yourself or your life (see also *sex*).

male and female: If both are present and there seems to be some conflict, it could represent an actual waking conflict. It could also be symbolic of an inner conflict between your feminine and masculine personality traits.

See *anima/animus* in the *archetypes* section to help with the potential source of the conflict.

When there is no conflict, the dream may be highlighting the different personality aspects you might use in some situation.

mall: This represents your materialistic nature and/or fashion trendiness. It could also symbolize choices and the options available to you that will shape your life.

man: Generally, a man in a dream can reflect the father archetype as hero, protector, or authoritarian. He represents the male archetype in both its positive and negative aspects (e.g., assertive or aggressive, decisive or rigid, world-directed or totally without emotional insight).

In a woman's dream, a man may reflect the masculine side to her personality and/or her relationship, attitude, and bias toward men in general and her father specifically.

In a man's dream, it could reflect wanted or unwanted aspects of his own personality.

An old man in a dream often reflects the father image. If he is frail, it could reflect the power of one's own masculine attributes (i.e., weakened or in need of empowerment).

See *anima/animus* in the *archetypes* section and *woman*.

mandala: Perhaps this represents a map into our inner nature, leading from the conscious mind to the unconscious. Carl Jung saw it as an image representing the self and the wholeness within us.

It expresses the fully individuated person. It is said that the mandala can be read like a dream so as to get some idea of one's progress in the march toward wholeness (see the *archetypes* section on *mandalas* as well as *squaring the circle*).

Though mandalas are most often circular, they can be represented by other shapes as well, including but not limited to triangles and squares. See *shapes*.

mangy: If something seems mangy in your dream, ask yourself, "Do I feel impoverished? Is my life in tatters?"

maniac: Are you behaving inappropriately? Perhaps you need to control your temper and show more emotional restraint.

mannequin: Do you feel as though you're not taking an active enough role in something? Perhaps you feel that you're just for show.

mansion: This could represent your potential for growth. Do you have lofty goals? Are you feeling or acting better than everyone else?

A map can signify the road you're on in your life. You may also need to get directions. You might ask yourself when a map image shows up, "What do I need to know to make this journey?" or alternatively, "What might my present course be leading me into?" This map is from the book *The Archipelago of Dreams* by R. J. Cole (2011).

map: This is used to clarify your direction in life, and it's an indicator of guidance or needing guidance. Maps can also suggest how far you've come in your life or some project. If you're retracing your route, perhaps the dream is suggesting that you go back a few steps and take another direction or approach.

Maps can be metaphors for a plan of action or the benchmarks to reach your goals. Are you being too rigid in the plan for your life or some project? Perhaps you need to go off the path to find your way (see also *song lines* and/or *navigation*).

marbles: If you are trying to find them, it may be about mental health or your wits. It could also refer to your common sense. If you've spilled them or lost them, the image could be about losing your mind.

marijuana: Are you trying to escape reality? Are you trying to numb yourself to some physical, mental, or emotional pain? This could also possess past associations that may come up for you in your waking life.

marine: Are you lacking the courage to do something? Perhaps you're not being faithful to someone.

Do you need to be more organized and disciplined in your life? Do you need to be more assertive or aggressive with some activity?

See also *soldier*.

marionette: Are there *strings* attached to something? Is something not as free or positive as you thought it was? Is someone pulling your strings? (See *puppet*.)

marriage: This is symbolic of commitment. Marriage in a dream can symbolize bringing things together as one or parts coming together, such as the conscious and unconscious. It might also reflect a desire to bring together different aspects of one's life.

It can also mean the union of conflicting personal aspects or the union of the anima and animus (masculine and feminine parts of the self) as a new beginning (see also *wedding*). It may also represent the *mystical marriage*, the unification of opposites—the combining of the two into one, the transcendence of separateness.

It may also represent the transition from one way of being to another (see *transition dreams*).

Ultimately, it may reflect the deep desire to unite with something that is essentially not ourselves. We are profoundly strange to one another because we are not able to inwardly know the other. In our waking and sleeping lives, we often gravitate toward some kind of unification (e.g., marriages, weddings, and sexual experiences).

Mars: This can be a zodiac-related image of sexual attraction. It can also be related to raw energy, desire, and action.

This may be a metaphor for feeling lifeless and barren, or it could relate to a feeling of being alienated.

As the god of war, see *god* in the *archetypes* section and also *war*. See also *planet*.

marsh: This could be about a feeling of being bogged down and held back. There can be a foreboding quality to this as well (see *mud*).

martyr: This may be symbolic of punishing yourself for some guilt. What do you get out of sacrificing your well-being for someone else's? See the *archetypes* section.

Mary and Joseph: For any biblical or religious figure, consider first their meaning in the context of the religion. So too, these figures can represent certain aspects of yourself. For example, Mary and Joseph were the *caretakers* and *nurturers* of Jesus. Thus, these attributes could also be identified with you in some way.

They also were *chosen* for this task. Thus, they can represent your own *chosen* status for some task. They also represent the animus/anima archetypes, and therefore, they might represent the need for the psyche to reconcile its differences in order to become whole.

mask: This could represent the face that we put on that we want the public to see (or a mask we wear to fool ourselves), but it also covers up what we are afraid to show. Masks show up in the waking dream as well.

Masks can also provide the wearer with a new identity and a chance to try on something new or to take on the qualities of the mask (e.g., animal masks, the mask of the clown, or a mask of some celebrity).

A mask with two faces could represent Janus, the Roman deity of beginnings, gates, and transitions. It could also refer to being two-faced (i.e., being dishonest).

See also *face* and/or *makeup*.

masturbation: This could represent your unexpressed sexual desire. This is not as satisfying as you might hope, and it might be a poor substitute for the real thing. There's an intimacy that you long for but isn't being fulfilled.

match: If lighting a match, it could mean you are starting a fire (e.g., a problem or a controversy) or inflaming an issue or some emotion.

Letting the match burn out might suggest you should not intervene but rather just let the issue burn itself out.

Consider also that it may symbolize something being equal or that someone has met his or her match.

materialize: If objects or people are materializing in front of you, you may be trying to make sense of something or cause something to develop. Is there some goal you want to make happen?

Perhaps you are objectifying something and losing touch with its essence.

Perhaps you want something to manifest itself. Are you trying to express or manifest some aspect of yourself?

mathematics or maths: For some, the purity of mathematics is like poetry, while for others, it's like a foreign language coming from a place inside you that's difficult and not fully understood.

Maths can also relate to a problem you're working on where you may not want to act on your emotions. If you can't solve the problem, perhaps this relates to some situation in your waking life. Is something not adding up?

matricide: You may be trying to kill off some part of yourself that is like your mother, or you may not want to become like her in some way. Perhaps the nurturing, caring, or compassionate side of your personality has been killed off, or maybe you have ignored it.

You could also feel neglected. Perhaps your needs are not being satisfied.

mattress: This could represent a support system. It could also be like a bed and therefore represent your intimate self. It may also represent security to you. If you're crawling onto it or sleeping on it, it could also be a means for escaping some stressful situation.

See *bed*.

maze: A maze can represent confusion, being lost, or an intricate problem. A maze can also be a gauntlet to be negotiated. It can reflect the descent into the unconscious (see also *catacombs*).

Mazes can also represent one's complex defense system, especially against repressed unconscious material. Consider also the word *amazed*.

See also *labyrinth*.

meat: Perhaps you're getting to the heart of the matter, especially if you're trying to cook the meat. If it's raw, perhaps you are feeling emotionally fragile and sensitive. Are you neglecting the most important part of some issue or project?

Meat can also reflect survival needs. What might you need to do in order to survive or survive some situation?

Rotting meat could be about your psychological or physical deterioration.

mechanic: Perhaps you need to work on healing past trauma or hurts. Something may need fixing in your life right now. Or maybe you need to tune up your life or work on the mechanics of achieving some goal.

medals: Are you looking for some recognition or a reward for something you've done or achieved?

Are you trying to prove your bravery or courage? Do you want to stand out from the crowd?

Are you trying to look good or important?

Are you resting on your laurels?

A military man with a chest covered in medals may suggest boasting. Are you hogging all the recognition? Are you trying to make yourself important?

See also *military*.

medallion: This may represent an emblem of power or desire for power. It may also be about self-importance.

See also *medals*.

medicine: This represents a need for healing (emotional, spiritual, and/or physical). The situation, feeling, and other objects in the dream might give you more information about what needs to be healed or what has been healed (see *doctor* or *hospital*).

If you are taking medicine for mental reasons or if the image is related to the head in some way, it could be referring to healing the psyche or the spirit in some way. If you are taking it for the heart, it could be related to compassion, one's emotional state, or love. See also *potions* and/or *drugs*.

medication: Some medications have side effects that affect your dreams. They can cause certain distortions of reality both in your dream and waking life. Some can cause nightmares and even intensify dreams.

I still interpret the dreams as though one was not on medication and try to resolve the differences in intensity or types of distortion.

meditation: If you are meditating in the dream, perhaps you are thinking about some problem or issue and looking for a solution through the wisdom of your inner self, or perhaps you should be.

Maybe you need to be less judgmental of others and/or yourself. This could also be a message that you need to get more centered, that you're too fragmented, or that you need to un-stress your life right now.

See *mindfulness*.

Insight: In Tibet, sleep is like a mini death, a practice for the real thing. That time between death and rebirth is when the soul is in a transition state (the *bardo*), and it is similar to the state between deep sleep and dreaming (the *clear light* of sleep).

When asleep, the soul is conscious with a profound clarity, peace, and understanding. Tibetans, unlike their Western counterparts, consider sleep a conscious time, even a superconscious time.

This superconsciousness is the ideal state for meditation.

Tibetan Buddhists think that, like sleep, meditation is a form of nourishment for the body. To them, the boundaries between dreaming and meditation are blurred, and the goals and results are similar as are the brain wave patterns. Both lead one to a better understanding of the self.

And it's not just an enhancement for our own understanding. In a 2005 study on the effects of meditation, researchers found that meditation can increase one's gray matter in those parts of the brain that deal with sensory processing. This would enable us to become more conscious of our surroundings.

MRI measurements of blood flow during meditation have shown increased flow in memory areas of the brain and decreased flow in those areas related to stress and anxiety.

Meditation or deep self-reflection has been with us throughout our history and may very well have been a survival skill.

For many, meditation can be like prayer, and it may have the same calming and reassuring effect.

Meditation can also be used as a means of understanding one's dreams.

medium: This person might suggest following your intuition. It may also suggest being in contact with your unconscious mind.

medusa: See *insight* under *snake* in *animals*.

meeting: This could be about building relationships. Perhaps it represents coming together as in a *meeting* of minds.

It can also refer to your learning to accept certain aspects of yourself or some situation (see *marriage/wedding*).

megaphone: Do you need to speak up for yourself? Do you need to be more assertive? It could also suggest that you need to be more expressive.

melancholy: This could reflect depression in your waking life. It could also reflect disappointment or loss.

melt: This could be about you softening your position on something or someone, including yourself.

memo: Do you need to communicate something? Are you in or out of the loop?

See also *email*.

menstruating: This could reflect a fear of or the power of the feminine. It can also suggest the release of pent-up energy (both creative as well as emotional energy) or tension. It can also suggest the denial of your feminine aspect.

Just prior to or during their menstrual cycles, many women can have these dreams. Sometimes this image shows up if there's some worry attached to menstruation when they're awake.

For women who are menopausal, this dream image could suggest renewed vitality.

mentally ill: If there's a mentally ill person in the dream or you are mentally ill in the dream, perhaps you need assistance with some emotional issues.

If you're in a mental institution in the dream, you may need a rest from some struggle or internal conflict.

menu: Perhaps you are seeking some kind of nourishment (emotional or spiritual). What are you trying to order? See *food* and *restaurant* for more information if needed.

If you or someone is eating the menu, perhaps you are mistaking the symbolic for the real thing.

mercenary: This could represent greed, a lack of ethics, self-interest, and unscrupulousness.

A mercenary may represent a threatening aspect of yourself or an emotion that threatens to overwhelm you.

Mercury: As part of an astrological birth chart, this planet could symbolize communication, planning, and reasoning.

Also consider the word *mercurial*, meaning quick, impulsive, presenting hot and cold moods, volatile, and sometimes unpredictable.

As a god with wings on his feet, it might represent a messenger from the unconscious and/or being *fleet of foot* (i.e., quick on your feet, facile, or adept).

See also god in the *archetypes* section and/or *planet*.

mermaid: This image may reflect the feminine aspect of yourself, especially the feeling or intuitive side. It may also be the mysterious and fanciful side to your nature.

If you're a man, it might reflect your fears of being drowned by the feminine aspect within your personality. If you're a female it may reflect self-doubt about your femininity.

merry-go-round: This could represent thoughtless, boring, and meaningless repetition. You may want to get off the merry-go-round of your life (see *carousel*).

messiness: This suggests disorder and chaos. Your life or a certain project may be a mess, or you may need to clean something up (e.g., a mistake, a relationship, your life). (See also *feces*.)

Is someone messing (badgering, tormenting, teasing) with you?

metal: See *brass, copper, gold*, and *silver* in the *color* section. It may also be likened to *medal* or having one's mental ability tested.

metamorphosis (morphing): If you are morphing into someone else, it could mean that you need to incorporate some aspect of that person into your own character, or you may be in need of a major change in life.

Rapid morphing can reflect rapid change in your life (see *transition dreams*). The difficulty or ease of the morphing might shed light on how prepared you are to deal with the change.

If you're morphing into an animal, then perhaps you need to express yourself more freely. Morphing can also be about changing attitudes or perspectives. You may want to look more closely at what you're morphing into.

Morphing into an animal can also suggest that you are becoming less civilized or more instinctive in your actions, experiencing fewer boundaries. (This can be either positive or negative.)

Note that taking the form of an animal can represent unrepressed sexual urges. It's interesting that college freshmen seem to have this kind of dream (see *animal terms* for specific meaning).

Insight: At one time, it was thought that animals and mankind dreamed together, both in the waking and sleeping hours. Often the consciousness of one was also the consciousness of the other, which made it easier to integrate into being the energy and voice of the animal into that of the human. This idea still manifests itself in the skill of the shaman and continues to manifest in the rest of us through the dream.

meteor: Are you on the way to achieving goals? A shooting star might symbolize wishful thinking.

It could also be some destructive force threatening you or your way of life. A meteor shower might be about a huge psychological, spiritual, or emotional impact that threatens great change. The meteors might also be represented by falling rocks.

Perhaps it's a metaphor for the potential of a catastrophe.

microscope: This may be about the need to look at something more closely, especially something not seen or noticed, and to become more aware. Perhaps you need to see something in finer detail or print (see *magnifier*).

midnight: This might represent the end of something as well as the beginning—death and resurrection combined.

Insight: This is also considered the witching hour, the time of night when creatures like witches, demons, and ghosts were thought to appear and be at their most powerful. People also believe black magic would be most effective at this time.

midwife: Seeing or being a midwife in a dream could be about you needing to help bring some new way of being or new project into the world.

militant: Something may be threatening you. Are you being overzealous?

military: This could be about aggression, threat, and/or organized and sanctioned violence. But for some, there may be an element of protection.

The military may also be symbolic of a time when you experienced success and enhanced self-esteem, or alternatively, this could signal a time when you felt belittled or demeaned (see also *attack, enemy, explosion, fear, gun, soldier,* and *war*).

Insight: In my case, having spent time in the marines and combat in Vietnam (helicopters), military dreams often reflect my own experiences (feelings and memories) and thus symbolize something more personal in my dreams. For example, military images could represent frustrations, out-of-control aspects, the need for control, suppressed fears, pride, freedom from restrictions, mustering courage, camaraderie, loneliness, struggle, fatigue, longing, or judgments about my self-worth.

For each of us, every dream image has a personal aspect. All a dictionary can do is help to point you in a direction, especially if you haven't a clue (which is often where I find myself with some of my dreams).

See also *medals* and/or *soldier/warrior.*

milk: This can represent a mother's love, nurturance, and nourishment.

To milk something (i.e., to squeeze out from a situation, person, or circumstance all that you can) has another meaning. Many symbols can be metaphors.

If you've spilled the milk, it could symbolize not "crying over spilled milk." In other words, what's done is done. The past is the past. Consider the phrase the "milk of kindness," meaning to do something good for others.

milking: If you or someone else is milking a cow in the dream, perhaps you are trying to get as much out of some experience as you can. Someone may be *milking* you and thus taking advantage of you.

mill: This could represent something grinding at (agitating) you or something grinding to a halt. Do you need to transform something? A miller could symbolize a spiritual force in your life.

millstone: This could be representing a burden. Is something holding you back or slowing your progress toward some goal?

mindfulness: This is a form of meditation. It can also be a prayer, that which connects you with a deeper spirit and meaning. It's a way of turning a spiritual eye on the ordinary.

As a prayer, the prayer of mindfulness is a prayer of communion, observing and being with what exists. In this, we are taking care of the spirit or deity we find within us. In this way, we bring the conscious mind and the unconscious mind closer together.

Focusing on your breath, your bodily sensations, the sounds around you, and your every movement with great attention, you can quiet the incessant chatter of the mind and allow for greater communion with your inner spirit or, if so inclined, with your experience of God.

In short, this technique of being with the world can open you up to inspiration.

mine: This image could be reflecting hidden riches. It can be about hidden ideas and thoughts or your unconscious self. It can also represent the need to search your subconscious (see *cave* or *basement*).

minefield: This can suggest hidden problems that you haven't dealt with. It can also represent issues that pose unseen dangers. What you can't see will hurt you. You might want to use extreme caution.

miniatures: To see these toys or to see something or someone miniaturized might mean that you don't have much respect for them.

You may be feeling inflated or self-confident with positive self-esteem, or you may actually lack this.

minister: See *priest*.

minivan: This might be about family. Family may represent the good times but also the burdens. If this is not your usual mode of transportation and you tend more toward sporty vehicles, you may need to be more conservative with your views and/or actions.

If it is your typical humdrum vehicle, perhaps you need to be a little more outrageous and less conservative.

mink: This may be a coat, stole, or cape and may indicate value and warmth, perhaps even emotional warmth and love. They usually cost a great deal of money and therefore may also represent love (see *money*).

If the sales tags are still on it and yet you are wearing it, that may suggest there are *strings attached* to the value or warmth (i.e., that what it represents is conditional). Note that you can only return something if the tags are still on.

Because it's made from an animal, it may also represent your subconscious and its motivations.

minotaur: A minotaur or any human and beast combination might speak to you acting on blind impulse in your life. A minotaur could represent the animal or instinctual aspect of your nature that you are either ignoring or that may be overwhelming the rest of you. See also *labyrinth*.

As a centaur (a human trunk with a horse body) might be referring to your bodily desires, the minotaur may represent the more intellectual, such as greed,

selfishness, or self-protective natures (see *animals*).

miracle: You may have a great deal of confidence in some plan even in the face of hardship or evidence to the contrary. Perhaps you're hoping too much instead of doing what needs to be done to achieve some goal.

You could be relying on magical thinking about some issue.

mirage: This might be about disillusionment. Perhaps what you think is true actually isn't (i.e., what you thought was there is not or may be an illusion).

mirror: This image can represent vanity, narcissism (see also *bully* or *narcissist*), self-consciousness, the image that you present to the world, a reflection of your identity or self-image, or what's going on in your life. Some think that mirrors are entries into the soul.

Are you looking into the unconscious to see who you really are or to see what it is you're hiding from others and from yourself?

Being stuck in a mirror like Alice in *Through the Looking Glass* might suggest that you are feeling stuck in a fraudulent life or one where you do not feel satisfied. You may be looking for a different or opposite reality.

For Alice, looking and then passing through the mirror revealed another perspective on reality to her. Perhaps it means the same for you.

Your reflection in a mirror might suggest that you need to reflect on something in your life. Mirrors can also be about how God sees you behaving, especially for the very religious.

Because your reflection in a mirror reflects your opposite orientation—left is right, and right is left—perhaps you need to see the other side of something.

If the mirror fogs and makes it hard to see the reflection, you may be hiding something about yourself (good or bad).

If you or someone else is standing before a mirror and you do not see a reflection, you may have lost your sense of identity. Have you changed yourself in order to please others and now don't know who are?

Whether in our waking world or in our dreams, mirrors have always been seen as dark, mystical, and magical metaphors for what lies within us.

Insight: For thousands of years, mirrors and reflective surfaces have been used for divination and magic. They have been used for scrying, developing clairvoyance, and repelling evil, and in fact, mirrors have an ancient tradition of being associated with superstition, fear, and evil.

Prior to the thirteenth century and as far back as the third century BCE, mirrors were predominantly polished pieces of metal—likely gold, silver, and brass. These pretty much disappeared when the Christian church banned them during the medieval period because believers thought that the devil was watching from the other side of the mirror. This idea was probably reinforced by the gossip that witches used them for casting all kinds of dark spells.

Glass mirrors showed up again in Venice in the 1200s.

Those ancient black scrying (from the word descry, meaning to see or perceive) mirrors used for divination by witches and sorcerers were made black by painting asphaltum on the glass three times. These were used for foretelling the future or *seeing* what was happening from distances.

I imagine that staring at crystal balls or scrying mirrors (a black nonreflective mirror) is similar to focused meditation. Try closing your eyes in meditation, and focus on an individual, place, or event. Then *see* what you get.

Some studies have suggested the possibility that at least some individuals can see from distances beyond the physical abilities of the natural eye. Though these studies are not conclusive, they do provide tantalizing evidence for the technique of *remote viewing*.

Dreams, too, are like projections onto a darkened mirror, some of which defy an explanation of anything other than what might be called precognition or a shared viewing with someone else.

In short, meditation can often quiet the chattering mind just enough for us to see what the unconscious picked up while the conscious mind was too busy to notice.

So too, the scrying mirror may act as a focusing instrument to still the mind and lay open the secrets of the inner psyche.

Today some tribal societies believe that to expose yourself to a mirror is to render the soul vulnerable to misfortune or even death. There used to be a widespread custom—and in some areas it's still present—to remove all the mirrors from the house when a person is sick in order to prevent the mirror from stealing his or her soul.

There was also a tradition of turning the mirrors to face the wall when someone died because many believed that if they saw their reflections in a mirror after someone's death, it would cause their deaths as well. There was also a legend in the southern United States that suggested that an uncovered mirror in the house of a person who had just died would capture the soul of that person.

In the case of necromancy (communication with the deceased), the mirror represents absorption of the soul and then reflection (or its return).

There is a myth surrounding the breaking of a mirror, but did you know that many consider mirror falling on its own accord and breaking is a death omen? On the other hand, a girl who sees the reflection of the moon in a mirror will learn the date of her wedding. (Given that women generally determine the day and then tell the men when it's scheduled, this is no surprise.)

There is also an old superstition that says if you were to stare into your reflection at night, you would see the devil. Though I don't believe this, I also have an aversion to staring at my reflection in a darkened room for too long. Something creepy always seems to hover close by.

However, I have heard it said—and I have tried this myself—that if you are feeling blue or anxious with no one around to talk to, try staring into your eyes in a mirror. After a while, the negative mood will disappear.

Some Buddhists believe that if you hang a mirror on the wall directly facing the front door, evil spirits will be reflected out of the house.

In another example of how mirrors are used mystically and how they can show up in a dream are the cards used for tarot reading. For example the "mirror spread" is used to work with existing relationships. The cards are placed with the first, or querent card, placed at the top. Then three cards in descending order are placed to the left of it and three cards in descending order to the right. The 'result card' is placed at the bottom between these two rows.

In this way the reader and querent (the person for whom the reading is being done) can see the relationships in opposition (i.e., the way you see the other person in the relationship, the way the person sees him or herself, what the person represents to you, what you represent to the person, the obstacles within the relationship, and the strengths within the relationship.

I spell all this out because I think this isn't a bad way of looking at relationship symbols in dreams or in a person's waking life.

Corinthians 13:12 says, "For now we see through a glass, darkly." Some have taken that to mean that seeing something reflected in a mirror displays less of the reality of that thing than gazing upon it directly.

This happens when people look back upon their childhoods or when they try to see what the children saw of the world. They try to assign meaning to past events, or they look at God's works through their biases.

To look through a dirty window or gaze at a mirror that has been darkened by your judgments and self-criticisms makes it difficult to see your true nature. This also reminds me of the saying involving *rose-colored glasses.* To look through either does not give a true picture of the world.[*]

Maybe you should glimpse your most beautiful face … Maybe you are the bearer of hidden treasure. Maybe you always have been.

—Rumi

miscarriage: Perhaps something didn't go as planned, or maybe you feel that you've been judged or wronged badly. It may also be about loss, being ineffectual, a missed opportunity, or a failure to achieve some goal.

Consider also the phrase "a miscarriage of justice," where justice was not served because of some deceit or ineptness.

missile: Perhaps this refers to a feeling of helplessness. Are you feeling attacked? Has someone targeted you?

missing the message: This might suggest that you are missing the point of something. There may be some void that you're trying to fill but have not as yet.

missing something or someone: Perhaps there's a void you are experiencing such as a feeling of dissatisfaction or being unfulfilled. It could also represent a desire

to have something from the past become more present in your life.

mist: See *clouds.*

mistake: If you see someone making a mistake, this might suggest that you are mistaken about something or someone or that you are about to make a mistake if you continue on the path you're on.

Remember that mistakes are really the foundation for truths. Is there something you need to learn or some truth you are missing because you're avoiding making a mistake or looking foolish?

mistletoe: This is a symbol of love, and it can also indicate bearing many children. This may be seen as a symbol of peace between enemies. Certain European Celts believed that children came from the male spirits of trees.

Insight: Some Australian Aborigines believed that mistletoe contained the souls of children who could be reborn if a pregnant woman walked nearby. Mistletoe was also thought to be an energizing or healing plant.

mob: This can symbolize disarray, chaos, or rabble. It can represent being out of control or some organized criminal activity. It can also represent an overwhelming threat. See also *angry.*

---

[*] Excerpt from R. J. Cole, http://thedreamingwizard.com/magic-mirrors_302.html.

mobile home: Like a house, this may represent some aspect of yourself. The condition of the home/house and where it's located may also add meaning.

Mobile homes can also represent situations that are probably temporary, or they can represent your own mobility.

mocking: Is something or some part of yourself taunting you? Is something or someone (or you) putting you down? Are you ashamed of something? Are you experiencing low self-esteem? Are you too worried about what people think about you or what they are saying about you?

model: A fashion model might represent an image that you may want to portray to others or resemble in everyday life.

If you're building a toy model, this could represent that you are in the developmental phase of something.

To live life according to some model also suggests that you are not living your own life (see also *schematic*).

Mohammad: Calling out his name can refer to a call for help or guidance. The Mohammad image may be a part of yourself that is trying to exercise your spiritual self. See also *Christ* in the *archetypes* section and/or *religion*.

molasses: This is something that moves slowly. Perhaps you need to speed up some process (see *syrup*).

mold: Perhaps something negative is growing in your subconscious. You may need to deal with it before it gets out of control and takes over your life. You may be vulnerable to the negative energy around you.

If it's a mold for creating an object, perhaps you are molding your character and creating something new.

Consider the phrase "breaking the mold with you" because there are no others like you. You are unique, but you don't want to duplicate some mistake.

mole: If it's a blemish on the face, perhaps something is negatively affecting your self-esteem and confidence. It could also represent unseen danger. Perhaps you or someone with a contrary agenda is plotting against some project.

Because the mole is an underground creature, perhaps it is symbolic of some of your subconscious drives, especially those that may be undermining your life and your goals.

molestation: See *rape*.

monastery: Do you need to be alone? Have you become too withdrawn? Do you need to contemplate something. Monasteries can be about going deeper into your spiritual self. See also *ascetic or monk* in the *archetypes* section.

money: This may reveal what you value. Money can represent your self-worth, self-esteem, confidence, and belief in yourself.

When found, it could represent finding something valuable, and when lost, it could reflect a loss of value or a feeling of inadequacy. If you haven't been given the right change, you may have been short-changed.

When you win money, it can have something to do with success. Having little or no money or losing what you have can represent your loss of status or your feeling of low status. You may also feel you lack ambition or self-esteem. Too much money may represent an inflated ego.

If someone is giving you money, perhaps you are looking for self-worth outside yourself. It might also suggest that you give something of value to others or be open to getting it from others.

If you're borrowing money, are you living beyond your limits? If it has blood on it, perhaps you are gaining something over someone else's loss or misfortune.

Money can also be a metaphor for love or being loved. When you are giving money, you may feel the need to give love. Stealing money can be about the need to be accepted or to be loved (see *coins*).

If your money is printed on only one side of the bills, perhaps you have been betrayed by something you thought was real but was actually only real on the surface. Perhaps the love was not reciprocated. It could also suggest that you've been conned.

monitor: See *computer.*

monk: See *ascetic or monk* in the *archetypes* section. It's also a symbol of the search for God, spirit, and inner peace.

monkey: See *animal terms.*

monsters: These may represent something that you are afraid of in yourself or another person. Monsters can be the negative forces within and without. They can also represent your fears (see *birth* or *Frankenstein*).

moon: The moon is a reflection of romance and love, a reflection of the inner self, your inner soul, intuition, and even irrationality. The moon is associated with your feminine aspects (see *anima/animus* in the *archetypes* section), moods, and menstruation cycles.

If it's moving across the sky faster than usual, it might represent a woman's childbearing years moving by too quickly.

The moon may represent the inner self. It may also represent the spirit that reflects the light of God as the real moon reflects the light of the sun.

Consider the phrase "Once in a blue moon," meaning something rare that doesn't happen much. Perhaps you should take advantage of this opportunity.

The moon is often a symbol for the priestess or the goddess who may be in a man's dream. It could be about second sight (or insight), the intuitive, and a messenger guide from the unconscious mind. In a woman's dream, the presence of the goddess can also represent one's inner wisdom. See *goddess* in the *archetypes* section.

An eclipse of the moon can suggest that one's feminine side is being overshadowed or that some hidden aspect is about to be revealed. The moon eclipsing the sun could very well be a union of the feminine and masculine aspects of oneself. The new light peeking from behind the moon as the eclipse passes could be a new light, a new knowledge, or a new perspective.

Insight: Each phase of the moon can represent a phase of life. For instance, a waxing crescent could refer to youth and new beginnings. The full moon could be about adulthood, career, and family development, and the waning moon could represent old age and wisdom.

The number of moons in the sky can have significance as well. If there are two and they rise on opposites sides of the earth, that might speak to an inner tug-of-war pulling at your emotions and jockeying for dominance. This may be true for more than two moons and might also suggest chaos in your life. You may feel that you are being pulled in many directions (see numbers for the number of moons).

The moon can also represent one's moods and the cyclical nature of life or events in your life.

A red moon can be about violence, disaster, and strife, while a blue moon can represent rarity. The moon also represents the receptive and wisdom. The Virgin Mary and Sophia were likened to *the moon of the church*, the reflector of the light of the Christ (often symbolized by the sun).

moon tarot: Aside from representing the feminine, the moon also signifies mystery and nightmares—the fears that grow in the dark and secrets. The moon lights the gateway between the physical and metaphysical, the conscious and subconscious realms. The moon suggests creativity and intuition.

Moore, Thomas: Thomas Moore popularized Hillman's philosophy through such books as *Care of the Soul* (Harper Collins, 1992), making his work accessible

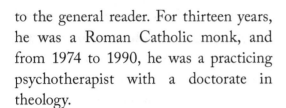

to the general reader. For thirteen years, he was a Roman Catholic monk, and from 1974 to 1990, he was a practicing psychotherapist with a doctorate in theology.

mop: This could represent the need to clean up something such as the results of a mistake or a relationship.

Consider also that it might be an aggressive symbol as in the times when one says, "I'll mop the floor with you."

morning: This represents new beginnings, fresh starts, or new or endless potential and promise. See *sunrise* or *east* as a direction.

morning star: The morning star (Venus, the goddess of persuasive feminine charm and the mother of all Romans) heralds the rise of the sun (the moon's male counterpart). This was a good sign for a new beginning and for enlightenment. However, some early Christians saw the same symbol in opposition when they determined that this star represented Lucifer, the devil, whose name means Morning Star in Latin.

Interestingly enough, the archetypal image of the devil usually refers to a dark and unwanted side of our own nature that can only be dealt with in the direct light of day through conscious awareness (see *star* and *shadow*).

morphing: In general, morphing implies turning into something new or changing from one way of being into another. If someone is morphing into another person, it might suggest that there are aspects of that other person you may want to incorporate into your own personality.

See also *transcendence*.

It is also possible that the dream is encouraging you to look at someone, something, or yourself from a different perspective. This image could suggest that you are in need of a major change in your life.

Consider also that morphing from one thing to another might be symbolic of a deception or a cover-up (e.g., hiding some secret, guilty feeling, or shameful aspect). What you or someone else is morphing into may give insight to what you or the other person may be hiding.

If you or the person is changing into an animal, it might suggest a need to express yourself more freely.

To morph into a tree might suggest a psychological change. You may need to take on the symbolic aspects of that particular tree or the strength and stature of trees in general.

Also look up the *animal* (see *tree* or *monster*) for more insight.

If what is morphing does it several times, it could indicate some indecision on your part that needs to be addressed.

This picture displays a woman morphing into a tree (or perhaps a tree morphing into a woman). Often this kind of action in a dream suggests that some kind of psychological changes may be going on in the dreamer. These images can announce changes in attitudes, points of view, or the incorporation of certain aspects of the morphed object into that which has morphed.

Even though these transformations seem to happen suddenly in a dream, they often depict what has been happening over a much longer period in one's waking life.

The legend was incorporated into the story *The Archipelago of Dreams* written by R. J. Cole (2011).

morphine: If you're taking morphine, perhaps you feel a disconnection with reality or have a desire for it, or you may want to dull your emotional pain. You may need to confront what's going on and/or what you are feeling (see *opium*).

moth: This suggests compulsive urges. Are you being lead to your destruction by the flame of something (see *fire*)? Do you feel compelled by some force?

mother: This figure can represent feelings of being looked after or dependency. On the negative side, she could represent a feeling of being dominated, a lack of bonding, or betrayal.

Your mother can also show up as other females in the dream, but their aspects will reflect her in this case.

If the son is in bed with his mother, it may reflect collusion with some behavior. If the mother's husband (or boyfriend) is also in the bed, this might suggest competition for the mother's affections (see also *son*).

See also the *archetypes* section.

mother-in-law: Are you being too dominating or controlling? This can also represent the negative feminine. See *anima/animus* in the *archetypes* section.

mountain: If you are ascending a mountain, this could symbolize aspiration, and if you are descending a mountain, this could symbolize the ending. Mountains can be places of spirits as in the Inuit (Eskimo) word *Torngat*. These mountains are said to sing when the wind passes through them, and they give people the feeling of another realm.

The specific mountain in your dream may also have significance with regard to the dream's meaning. For example, a mountain in Tibet or a mountain sacred to a tribe or ethnic group might have spiritual significance and speak to that aspect of yourself.

Other mountains may speak of mystery, death, a special place from your childhood, or some special experience uniquely yours.

See also *mountaintop*.

mountaintop: This could refer to your intellectual or spiritual aspirations as well as your achievements. It could also be a metaphor for gaining another and/or higher perspective or awareness of something. Perhaps you are at the top of your game and at the zenith of your career.

If you are standing at the top and looking fearfully at how far down the drop is, you may possess a fear of failing after having gained success. Perhaps you need to balance the heights with the depths of life.

How you struggle to the top could reflect the hard work needed to achieve success.

To the ancients and to many indigenous peoples today, the mountaintop was and is considered a sacred space.

After all, it was upon the mountaintop that Christ was transfigured into something grand and holy (i.e., spiritually changed and given a whole new perspective). See also *bathed in light*.

mouth: Perhaps a symbol for communication or something preventing it if it's full of something. If it's full of something dirty, then it might represent something you've said that you're not proud of. It's also a pleasure area (see *body*).

movie: This could signal you placidly watching your life go by without being involved in it. Life for you may feel like make-believe. Life may seem two-dimensional because you're not getting involved. Perhaps you need to participate more.

What movie are you watching? What's the plot? Who are the actors? All of this may reflect present or ongoing aspects of your life.

If you're in the movie, perhaps something about yourself is about to be revealed.

If the screen is blank, it's possible that you are distancing yourself from some situation or some feeling. It could also reflect a lack of any accomplishment with regard to some goal or in your life overall.

If you're on a movie set, it might indicate that something might not be what it appears to be. Is someone trying to manipulate reality?

movie star: See *celebrity* or *famous people*. The actual movie stars will have meaning based on your images of them or the types of characters they play.

moving: This can represent a new start or a new life.

Things moved (or moving) in a room may suggest things that have changed in your life and not necessarily for the better.

muck: This could represent your own prejudices, biases, and unwanted behaviors, feelings, and emotions. It could also symbolize the mess you've made of some situation or your life.

Are you mucking about (i.e., fooling around) with little or no purpose? Are you just wasting time?

See *mud or muddy*.

mud or muddy: This can represent messy feelings or the feeling of being stuck (see *marsh* or *muck*). Perhaps you're unclear or confused about some situation or how you feel about something or someone.

If the image is muddy water, perhaps you or someone else is compromising some situation. Are you or someone else trying to hide or destroy the truth? Are you hiding your feelings?

If the waters clear after you've gone through, then it might suggest that all will work itself out and become clear to you in good time—or at least that is likely your hope.

If there are dead animals or insects in the mud, these may represent parts of yourself that have died or that you wish would die (i.e., things that have messed up your life or have the potential to do so). (See type of animal in *animal terms*.)

If you're being careful not to get the mud or muck on you, you may be trying to save your reputation.

Avoiding the mud in life is restrictive and can undermine relationships. Avoiding blame, guilt, or anger keeps us stuck in the muck and unable to bring the light of love and forgiveness to ourselves or others.

mud-throwing: This could be about muck-raking or mud-slinging. Are you making defamatory remarks about someone?

mummy: Do you feel all tied up and trapped? Perhaps you feel all used up. Do you feel like just a dried-out shell of your former self?

311

It can also reflect how you're feeling about your appearance.

This is also a colloquialism for a mother.

See also *cemetery, coffin,* or *dead.*

murder: This can mean putting an end to an old habit or some rejected part of yourself. You could be killing off an addiction or other negative behavior. Because this is also an angry image, you may be repressing some anger or rage aimed at someone or yourself.

If you know the murdered person, perhaps you see in him or her the negative qualities that you would like to get rid of in yourself.

As a reaction to an actual murder, you may be trying to process the violence to your psyche such an act can cause. Murder upsets the status quo, the security and order of one's worldview, and dreams may be trying to help with the healing.

A murdered body could represent a time in your life or aspects of yourself that you have pushed out of your consciousness and rejected. A murdered person might also reflect your anger toward someone.

If you are the one murdered, perhaps there's some significant relationship that has been killed (see also *kill or killing*).

muse: This can represent your inner voice and can take the form of an angel, person, or animal. It can represent your inner spirit or daemon (see *daemon*).

This image might suggest that you need to come out of yourself and/or pay greater attention to some neglected part of yourself.

Muses can also be messengers trying to communicate something you're ignoring or something that you're not paying attention to. Representing intuition, the muse can also bring inspiration through the nonrational side of yourself (see *intuition*).

museum: This could be about your nontraditional past and how it may make you stand out amongst the crowd. It may also be symbolic of your own personal history. If the museum is burning down or is being toppled, perhaps you need to leave your personal history behind or turn it upside down and not let it determine your future.

To be lost in a museum could be about being trapped in the past.

Objects and/or displays in a museum can represent aspects of yourself, such as your values or talents. They may also symbolize certain events and memories.

music: This can represent harmony of expression and your creative side. Do you need more harmony in your life?

Music can also be inspiring and emotionally moving. It touches us where words cannot. How the music affects you and the lyrics will give you even more information.

According to the poet Henry Wordsworth Longfellow, music is the universal language.

Some see music as a means for connecting with the soul.

See also *symphony, drums, oboe, piano, trumpet, saxophone, tuba,* or *violin.*

Insight: There is a story that Pythagoras noted a young man bringing hot coals to the door of his lover's house so as to burn it down as retribution because she scorned him. A man playing a flute nearby was playing an energetic little song that seemed to spur the young man on.

When Pythagoras asked the flutist to play another song that was much more soothing, the young man seemed to come to his senses and removed the coals.

It is highly probable that the Greek initiates gained their knowledge of the philosophic and therapeutic aspects of music from the Egyptians.

Pythagoras realized the emotional and therapeutic aspects of both music and color.

Also see *colors.*

This is the Devanagari symbol for ohm. It is written in medieval and ancient texts, mentioned in the Upanishads, and found on temple walls. It is the sacred sound of the universe. In Hinduism, it symbolizes the Atman (i.e., the self within or soul). Some say it is the word of the creator. It is perhaps the most important symbol for Hindus, Buddhists, Sikhs, and Jains. To see this symbol or hear the sound in a dream may reflect your deeper, most spiritual nature trying to contact you.

There is music in the sound of the universe. Aum (or om) is a mystical or sacred symbol of the religions of India. It is the primordial sound at the creation of the universe— the seed symbol in Buddhism and a symbol of God in Sikh theology. It is the transcendental state of the undifferentiated I—the background for all other states of consciousness.

This symbol, according to Vedic tradition, also represents the other three states of consciousness as well—wakefulness, dreaming, and sleeping without dreams.

Note the words of the music as well as who might be singing them for any clues about the meaning of the dream. See also *song*.

Muslim: The interpretation of this image might reflect your judgments and positive or negative biases.

It might also be about bettering yourself as a person.

It might suggest that there is some part of this religion that you either want to incorporate into yourself or that you reject.

See also *religion*.

mute: This is one who is speechless or not communicating. Are you afraid to say something?

mutual dreams: This occurs when people meet within their dreams or share a mutual dream theme. This phenomenon is also known as shared dreams, collective dreams, or group dreams. This has been reported as both spontaneous and intentional.

Pregnant mothers have often reported an intuitive connection with their unborn babies. Native tribes use this sharing of dreams to help with the needs of the tribe.

The International Association for the Study of Dreams (IASD) has from time to time sponsored several websites devoted to mutual dreaming.

There are ongoing experiments to determine if people can meet and communicate within their dreams.

See also *lucid dreams*.

muzzle: A muzzle in your dream might indicate that you need to hold yourself back and be careful about what you say. Are you having difficulty expressing yourself, or do you feel as though your free expression is being suppressed?

mystery: Do you need to be on the lookout for something that doesn't seem quite right? Are you confused or unsure about an answer?

Are you trying to solve some problem or issue? Is someone or something in your life a mystery?

Do you need to be more circumspective and/or observant? Do you need to allow the unknown to be unknown? In the spiritual realm, mysteries are to ponder and not to be necessarily solved.

To be in a mystery without trying to solve it can be most uncomfortable but also most revealing, and often this allows for entry into a whole new way of being and perceiving.

mystical experience: Some people experience this when lucid dreaming while others experience it with certain archetypal images. Others see it as an out-of-body experience or the feeling of their minds being separated from their bodies.

Some see it as a light that they feel drawn to or as an experience of the presence of the divine, God, or a god or goddess.

Those who have had this kind of experience either through a dream, meditation, or just walking down the street report an overwhelming sense of unity, timelessness, and sacredness.

For most people these experiences are considered irrational in that they cannot be reached or understood through reasoning.

The Zen Buddhist word for this state of mind is *satori*.

Sometimes the mystical is an attempt of the mind to fill a void and a sense of emptiness (see *OBE, peak experience*, or *numinous*).

mysticism: According to the psychologist William James in the earlier part of the twentieth century, mysticism was defined by the presence of four states of experience.

To justify labeling an experience mystical it had to be (1) ineffable in that the experience defied expression (i.e., that there are no adequate words for describing it), (2) noetic in that there was a *knowing* that could not be plumbed by the regular intellect and that this knowing was beyond what was known before, (3) transient in that the experience didn't last for long, and (4) passive in that the effect was most often unbidden though it could be facilitated by focusing one's attention. For many, this feels as though their very ego-selves had been taken over by some greater power.

myth: Many dreams seem to have a mythic template in that gods, goddesses, heroes, other archetypal images such as beasts and tricksters, and images of the masculine and feminine aspects form a landscape of our deeper selves.

If creating a myth of your own or just reviewing a myth from old in a dream, you might ask yourself, "What kind of story about my life am I creating for myself? Is it a true story?"

Are you being delusional about something? Are you making something up and passing it off as real? Are you or someone else being deceptive?

Myths that are created by an individual instead of those created over time by a culture are often labeled mythopoeic.

Carl Jung thought of *mythopoeic imagining* as a dialogue between the fantasies of the unconscious and conscious mind as a means of bringing this material into the light and integrating it into consciousness. Through this imagining, the rational mind learns to integrate the irrational. He believed that to let the rational ego-based mind overwhelm the irrational soul was a way of courting disaster.

To him, the life of an individual, culture, or country was only as good as its imaginal life and the myths the people created.

mythology: In Greece, Morpheus, the son of Hypnos (the god of sleep), was the god of dreams. His uncle was the god of death, and his grandmother was Nyx, the deity of the night. He was the one who shaped the stories and images in one's dream.

Interestingly, he was said to sleep in a cave of poppy seeds. When grown, these seeds produce morphine (opium). The name comes from this deity.

Myth is the natural and indispensable intermediate stage between unconscious and conscious cognition.

—C. G. Jung (1989)

Note that the mythical idea of poppies as sleep inducers was used by L. Frank Baum in the book *The Wizard of Oz* (1900).

N

nagging: Is there something that you can't quite put your finger on? Is someone nagging you to do something? Are you not acting responsibly (see also *harpy*)?

nail: This represents bonding and connecting. The phrase "Hit the nail on the head" might suggest the accuracy of something or some idea.

naked: This could symbolize being vulnerable and exposed. It can be a symbol for dropping your façade. Note that clothes are often metaphors for our façades or masks, what hides the real us. Are you ready to reveal a part of yourself that you've kept private? Are you ready to show the truth about yourself?

Perhaps you need to tell the unembellished truth. Are you being real or transparent with others?

If you are trying to cover up people who are naked or they are trying to cover themselves up, are you being prudish, or are you trying to hide something like your vulnerability?

Taking off soiled clothing or washing your clothes could be about cleaning up your act or the way you are behaving.

In cultures where nakedness in public is a moral sin, it may reflect a personal scandal brewing or the fact that you've been scandalized. Maybe some misfortune will befall you.

If you're disgusted by someone's nudity in a dream, you may be disgusted for who is revealed behind the mask that has hidden his or her real self. It might also show your unwillingness to allow someone to show his or her authentic self.

As with all dream images, this image may actually reflect you and your own feelings about your hidden self. Are you ready to accept your naked self?

Consider also the reference *the naked truth*, referring to the unvarnished truth that isn't dressed up to look good.

Are you not being honest about something or with someone?

See also *laundry*.

name: If it's your name, this could represent how you see yourself. If it has been altered, there might be a change in how you see yourself.

Perhaps you need to be more aware of your own uniqueness.

If it's hanging from a display rack, it may suggest that you think of yourself as just an ordinary person, someone who comes *off the rack*.

What is the significance of the name for you?

Is someone calling you names (i.e., demeaning, belittling, or bullying you)? See also *bully*.

Being called by a different name may be about losing your identity, or perhaps you are going through an identity change.

Folklore suggests that when you name something, you make it real and can then deal with it.

In a *New York Times* article from April 2007, Thomas Friedman proclaimed, "In the world of ideas, to name something is to own it. If you can name an issue, you can own the issue." Are you trying to control or dominate some issue?

Name tag: See *tag*.

napping: You may need to relax more. Perhaps you need to reenergize yourself.

You may be *caught napping*, and thus, you may need to pay better attention to something.

narcissist: Are you being a bully? Are you thinking only about yourself? See also *bully* and *mirror*.

Insight: A true narcissist is someone who gets gratification through vanity and the admiration of his or her ego. In the *DSM-5*, it is considered a personality disorder. It was originally designated as megalomania.

If one's focus is predominately a self-focus with a strong lack of empathy, psychological awareness, a haughty and arrogant body language, and hypersensitivity to insults (both real or imagined), this person might be a narcissist.

People with this type of personality also tend to exaggerate their achievements and importance, and they also detest and demean those who do not admire them.

narcotics: See *drugs*.

narrow: This may reference a restricted point of view. It could also suggest a limited space. See *tunnel*.

native: This could symbolize the intuitive self. This can be your primordial self. The native can represent that part of you that has natural wisdom. See also *aborigine or any native*.

Native American: Perhaps it's your instinctual aspect. It may be your inner innate wisdom. Perhaps you desire greater freedom from cultural or societal restraints.

Insight: When we look at the Native American's inner relationship with themselves, we see that there is no single belief system, though once again, dreams become a common factor across all tribes. Many saw these as forms of information or reality itself.

Through dreams the tribes would gain information about hunting and solutions to social and psychological problems. Many tribes also read their dreams for prescient content, and as individuals, they read them as initiation visions that would lead one to a spirit guide who would in turn travel with them for their entire adult lives.

Through lonely vigils, fasting, and prayer, young people would alter their states of consciousness to create visions in their dreams about their destinies. This destiny was purely individual, a sacred thing between a person and the Spirit that pervades all life. This was unlike the European who could only become what his family, station, or town decreed.

As with the Aborigine, the Native Americans were heavily involved in their inner selves, and it was there that they found their calling and direction.

Whether or not the dreams had any magical influence on the lives of the Native Americans is irrelevant, for these peoples so deeply believed their dreams that the stabilities of their psyches became solid and they experienced great internal individual and tribal strength.

For the Native Americans, their dreams served a self-regulatory function. For these peoples, dreams had certain marked features. There were initiatory dreams, hunting dreams, illness-healing dreams, dreams about attracting lovers, dreams about finding and mixing a herbal medicine, dreams about diagnosing evil dreams, and dreams that offered revelations from someone who died.

Such things as the discovery and use of fire were said to have come through dreams.

For some very remote family groups that were too far apart from one another to establish social grouping at a tribal level, the people depended heavily on their internal resources, and their dreams were their primary guide in everything from the weather to the hunt.

When the Europeans came in to the Americas, they brought with them a tendency toward dependence on things external to themselves for their survival. They then forcefully changed the native belief systems, stripping them of the use of the internal such as dreams and visions.

The native peoples lost their psychological balancing mechanism. The invaders offered nothing to replace the loss.

Modern humans have trouble understanding the influences of their unconscious, especially in reading their dreams, whereas the Native American, even to some degree today, has the ability to better understand the guidance from their internal selves.

But if the vision was true and mighty, as I know, it is true and mighty yet; for such things are of the spirit, and it is in the darkness of their eyes that men get lost.

—Black Elk

nature: This can be about the need to restore or renew/reenergize yourself. It could also be about paying attention to your instincts.

nausea: Something may be making you sick to your stomach. Is something or someone disgusting you? See also *vomit*.

navel: This may represent your being and may suggest that you need to find your center or the middle ground to something. It's also a symbol for the mother-child bond or lack thereof. Do you need to reconnect with this person?

navigation: This can symbolize how one gets through life. Are you in need of guidance? Are you having trouble navigating some part of your life (see also *map* and/or *song lines*)?

navy: This can be about being organized and disciplined. Depending on the narrative that includes this image, see *boat, military, sea, ship,* and *water.*

near-death experience (NDE): If you dream of having one of these, you may be reverting back to old habits. Perhaps you're being given a chance to correct something, or maybe you're receiving a do-over.

Insight: NDE is also a real phenomenon where someone experiences impending death and detachment from the body, peace, well-being, unconditional love, the feeling of floating above everything, and the presence of a bright light.

Many who have had these claim they've had intense, otherworldly experiences, and their memories seem to last the rest of their lives—and not just the memory of having had one but the actual feelings that went along with it.

It is similar to a hallucinatory state.

Sometimes people review their lives while in this state, and when they return to consciousness, they experience profound changes in their worldview.

According to a recent study published in 2013 in the *International Journal of Behavioral Medicine*,[13] people who have had these experiences become more tolerant of differences in others and gain a greater appreciation for nature.

These people also experienced a greater understanding of themselves when compared to those who hadn't had the experience.

The reason for all this is not yet understood.

neck: This refers to the connection between the mind and body. If it's injured, it may suggest a disconnect between your mind and body (i.e., between your feelings and your thoughts).

If your neck is in a brace, perhaps you're trying to reconnect your head with your body or intellect with the heart. See also *neck or throat* under *body*.

neck brace: If you are wearing a neck brace, perhaps you are trying to reconnect your feelings and thoughts (i.e., your heart and mind).

necking: See *petting*.

necklace: This might be symbolic of an unsatisfied desire. It can also be symbolic of power or be a metaphor for the separation between bodily urges and the intellect,
the instinctual and the Logos, a division between rational and irrational thinking.

If it's broken or stolen, perhaps you need to take some action with your intuitive instincts about some situation.

necktie: This often reflects a restriction. It can also represent a feeling of being trapped by tradition, obligation, or expectation. You may be feeling tied down. How tight is the tie around your neck?

If you're supposed to wear one but are not, perhaps you are flying in the face of tradition or the status quo.

necromancer: This is someone who talks to the dead. If you have a dream with a séance, you may be dealing with the loss of a loved one. You may also be trying to get in touch with an unconscious part of yourself. Are you trying to gain some hidden knowledge?

See also *mystical experience* or *séance*.

needle: This is a piercing insight with the power to repair. It is often a means of putting things together. It may also be symbolic of mending some relationship.

If you're looking for a needle, you may be on a fool's errand or caught up in some triviality.

If you have needles stuck in you, perhaps you are being needled (i.e., teased). If you feel pain, these needles might also suggest that you're being abused in some way.

negativity: Negative feelings or experiences can show up in dreams and often reflect the outside world or your own self-criticisms. See also *shadow* in the *Archetypes* section.

Insight: Often the outside world reflects our own growth or need for growth. We tend to ignore our own flaws by projecting them onto others. By being outwardly critical, we may also be passive aggressively self-critical.

Essentially, I believe that we are not what happens to us but what we have chosen to become regardless of what happens. Furthermore, to some degree, the outside world reflects that. To varying degrees, the world we see and react to reflects some part of ourselves, whether admired or rejected. In short, we can do little to change the outside if we aren't willing or ready to change the inside.

Negativity can show up in a kind of building or landscape, such as a ruin or slum, and the image might speak to the effects of negative thinking on your self-image. See *ruins* or *slums*.

neglected: Perhaps there's some aspect of yourself that needs your attention.

You may be neglecting some part of yourself. For example, a neglected child might reflect the need to pay more attention to or nurture your own inner child and playfulness.

negligee: Are you being seductive or seduced? You might have a secret that you're afraid others might see.

Can others see right through you and see what you're hiding?

negotiate: This could be about making an arrangement. It could also be about settling something. Are you being a wheeler dealer? See also *treaty*.

neighbor: This can be about peacefulness or dissension. A neighborhood can be about connectedness and community.

If the neighborhood is poor or in ruins, you may be feeling broke, drained, needy, or ruined.

Neptune: The symbol for this is often a pitchfork, and it can represent a god, especially the god of the water. (So too, bear in mind that water often represents one's emotions.) It can also symbolize a demon. In astrology, it can symbolize dreams, psychic receptivity, confusion, and illusion.

In astrology, it represents a planet that can show up in any of the astrological signs. If this symbol shows up in your dream, you may want to research its meaning within your sign.

In astrology, it can also symbolize dreams, psychic receptivity, confusion, and illusion.

nest: This can symbolize your emotional dependence on someone. A nest can also symbolize the need to develop a family or represent the family.

An empty nest can symbolize the feeling you have when all the children have grown and left the home. For greater meaning, note the emotions in the dream associated with this image.

nets: These might be about entrapment or entanglement (see *spider*).

newness: This can apply to anything new in a dream. A new house might indicate that you need a change and/or that something new or a new way of being has developed. It can also represent something in your waking life that is unfamiliar or somehow different.

newspaper or news media: This can offer insight into some problem. Something may be trying to communicate from your subconscious mind. Perhaps you need to express yourself more about something, or maybe you need to make an announcement.

A reporter might mean that you need to report accurately on something or make some accurate observation.

Good news may be a hope for something in your waking life. Bad news may reflect your anxieties.

New Year's: This could be about anything new, or it could represent new beginnings. For example, it could be about new relationships or opportunities. It could also be about forgiveness and letting go of past grievances or problems. It can also be about change (i.e., turning over a new leaf).

The new year can also be about hope and a new outlook on something or even on your life.

Spiritually, it could represent a new understanding of something or an enlightenment.

night: This might be about mystery and the unconscious. It can also symbolize inner awareness or even danger.

nightmares: Nightmares are very common among children and fairly common among adults. Stress, traumatic experiences, emotional difficulties, drugs or medications, or illnesses can cause nightmares.

However, some people have frequent nightmares that seem unrelated to their waking lives. Recent studies suggest that these people tend to be more open, sensitive, trusting, and emotional than average.

This is a special category and can't be fully described within the context of this encyclopedia. For more details, check out the section about *nightmares*.

ninja: Are someone's intentions unclear? Are yours? Someone's motivations may not be clear. If you're the ninja, perhaps you're being passive aggressive.

no: If you're saying no to someone or some idea, perhaps you need to stand up for yourself.

nobility: Are you all show and no substance? Perhaps you're too concerned with how things look and not paying enough attention to the inside of yourself.

noetic: This can represent knowledge beyond the ordinary or beyond what has been known before. It's a transcendence of normal consciousness. See also *ineffable, intuition, nous, transcendence, mystical,* and *transformative.*

noise: To hear an odd noise might be symbolic of the unknown or something unexpected. Something from your subconscious may be trying to get your attention.

Do you need to make more noise in some situation? Do you need to get people to pay attention to you?

nomad: Do you need more direction in your life? Do you need to get motivated toward some goal instead of just wandering through your life? See *wandering* or *walkabout.*

non sequitur: When something happens in a dream that seems out of place or irrelevant to the internal theme or logic of the dream, it may reflect a deception or falsehood in your waking life.

Something another person said or did may be inconsistent, illogical, invalid, or untruthful. Perhaps you need to look closer at some situation or circumstance. See also *paradox.*

noose: If it's around your neck, it may be about feeling strangled by someone or some circumstance. If around someone else's neck, it could be about repressed anger.

north (as a direction): This can represent the place of winter, the wisdom of age, completion, teaching, and service. As with all directions, one might ask, "Where am I heading?" See also *compass* and *cross.*

North Star: This could represent your guiding light. This could also be about inner knowledge or a way home to your real self.

nose: See *body*.

nosebleed: A nosebleed can be a metaphor for worrying about something happening that doesn't go according to plan. This may suggest a feeling of being out of control in regard to something specific, and it could be affecting your vitality (i.e., your positive sense of self).

Getting a bloody nose can represent being put down, criticized, losing out, being embarrassed, or generally made to look bad or foolish.

not good enough: Have you judged someone or something not good enough? Have you judged yourself to be not good enough? Do you need to be gentler with yourself or someone else?

See *rejection*.

nous: This represents the inner self between the spirit and the soul. It's a phenomenon of the mind that is distinguished from imagination or sense perception. It is irrational in nature but allows for rationality as part of the mind's eye (i.e., the inner sight or insight). It is the basis for human understanding. Plato suggested that it was the ruling part of the soul.[14]

nude: See *naked*.

nugget: See *gold* in *colors*.

number terms: These can have personal as well as symbolic significance. A series of numbers can reflect a year, age, day, number of days, address, phone number, birth date, page of a book, etc. Patterns of numbers can have significance, especially for those who delve into numerology.

> **zero:** This represents the unconscious, the ultimate void, and the silence within us. It can be the space between all words and thoughts. If you're into tarot, it's the first card, the fool. See also letter *O*.

> **one:** This represents yourself. It can symbolize being alone or unified with everything. It is the beginning of everything—unless of course, you are referring to a time before everything when there was the nothing, and in that case, zero would be the beginning. But as zero, it is also the end. In tarot, it is the magician who pulls the fool into the world.

> The ace of clubs in a deck of cards has sometimes been called the god card. The ace is both first and last (the Alpha and Omega), while the

three lobes of the club represents the Holy Trinity (see *number three*).

two: This represents duality, partnership, and opposition. Any binary image can represent the dichotomy that is life. Its presence in a dream may represent the need for unification.

three: This represents the trinity or the balance of opposites. It is the mind, body, and spirit, as in the Father, the Son, and the Holy Spirit. It can also represent wholeness (i.e., the integration of your parts into a whole).

See also *trinity*.

Insight: The Celts saw the triad as signifying something with interlocking and inseparable views, such as life, art, gods, social order, culture, concepts, and actions. Because three represents the balance of opposites, the Celts viewed the trinity as a symbol of strength.

In the Celtic traditions, there were many mutually supporting trinities, such as the mother, the mother goddess, and the goddess of war.

Sometimes, as in the concept of the Celtic triple lunar goddess (symbolizing the maiden, mother, and crone, or the waxing, full, and waning moon), the number three can represent the three aspects of life. The

Celts also used the triskele (a pinwheel-like symbol with three conjoined spirals) to symbolize birth, death, and rebirth.

From the ancient Greeks to the Romans, the Indo-Europeans to the Celts of Gaul, England, Wales, Ireland, Spain, Saxony and Italy, the empires of China, Arabia, and the Northern Norse tribes, the triune god and goddess abound. The deity comes in the form of a trinity.

four: This represents the physical, stability and strength, the earth, and its four compass directions. It can represent the four parts of human nature (sensing, feeling, thinking, and intuition) or the four ancient elements (earth, air, fire, and water). It can represent the Christian cross (see *cross*).

See also *quarter, quaternity,* and *squaring the circle*.

five: This represents the human body. (Note the five points created by the body by spreading your arms and your legs with head on top.) It also unites all the previous numbers. (One plus four equals five, and two plus three equals five.) It speaks to the five senses, and with the Celts, it was frequently seen in the pentagram or the pentacle. It spoke to the mystical, and it was used as a magical tool to keep evil away. There are the five ancient elements of water, fire, earth, wood, and metal.

six: This represents symmetry and the unity of the body and spirit. It also represents the Star of David.

seven: This represents the days of the week and/or the seven chakras. (Note that the seventh chakra is the crown, representing one's spiritual aspect.) It can also represent the seven notes in music.

The ancient Celts claimed that this number denoted value. It was an extremely important number.

Insight: In the Otherworld, all the houses had seven doors, each leading to seven paths. Each door led to a room that contained seven cauldrons filled with meat.

Some Celtic kings took a new wife every seven years.

During the Middle Ages, there were the seven deadly sins, which include pride, greed, lust, envy, gluttony, anger, and sloth.

When most fortunate, one is said to be in seventh heaven.

There are seven wonders of the ancient world, seven visible colors in a rainbow, seven notes to a musical scale (do, re, mi, fa, so, la, ti), seven levels of heaven, seven chakras, or energy centers in the body, and seven days of the week.

Seven represents universal balance, wholeness, or even luck.

If you're into Chinese or Western numerology, seven is considered a lucky number in relationships and is thought of as an auspicious number. Any multiple of seven would also work (e.g., fourteen, twenty-one, twenty-eight, etc.). See also *colors*.

If you're a strong and devout follower of your religion, the number seven (or any number for that matter) can have specific meaning for you. For example, there are seven heavens and seven earths of the Quran. There are seven long-lived personalities in the pantheon of the Hindu religion. There are seven deadly sins in Judaism and Christianity.

eight: This represents death and resurrection, eternity, and the cosmic consciousness. In Chinese numerology, this number indicates wealth.

nine: This represents childbirth (because of the nine-month term for a fetus) and the beginning of something new.

ten: This represents a new beginning. Also consider the top ten of something or ten as the highest rating for something.

eleven: This represents the eleventh hour or the last minute.

twelve: This represents a complete cycle as in the twelve months in a year (see also *zodiac*).

thirteen: This is sometimes a symbol for bad luck. There were thirteen who attended the last supper of Jesus of Nazareth.

one million: A person can also feel like a million bucks. Is something unusual or rare (i.e., one in a million)? A million can also be about the level of something's importance.

even and odds: Even numbers may be about balance, peacefulness, or symmetry. However, odd numbers may signal that you are *at odds with something*, and thus, they might be more aggressive in their meaning.

911: This could be about emergencies. It could also be a desire for rescue (i.e., a call or plea for help).

numb: See *anesthetic* or *paralyzed*.

numinous: An odd and otherworldly feeling or presence in a dream could suggest a strong religious or spiritual experience. It is your sense of the divine or your spiritual aspect. Interestingly, this *feeling* often appears when archetypal images visit our dreams. See also *eerie feeling*.

nurse: This may represent healing, care, and compassion or the need for it. Maybe you need to nurse something in your life with special care.

If you are breast-feeding or nursing, it may reflect giving of yourself. There might be an element of infantile dependency as well.

nymph: To see a nymph in the dream can be about the mystery of the feminine aspect. It can be about grace and innocence as well.

O

o: This can be an exclamation. It can also be slang for a hug. See *xxoo*.

See also *zero* in *number*.

oak tree: This could symbolize longevity, strength, tolerance, and wisdom.

Insight: This is part of the sacred three in Celtic tradition—oak, ash, and thorn. The word *druid* is derived in part from the word for oak (*dru*). The druids made their wands from oak, yew, and applewood. In Arthurian legend, the great wizard Merlin is said to be imprisoned in an oak in a Breton forest.

oars: These could represent control over your emotions. They're a symbol for a means of navigating through life. If paddling with only one oar, you might be going around in circles, or if you've lost both oars, perhaps you're dead in the water and going nowhere.

oasis: If you're looking for one, perhaps you're looking for emotional support. Do

you need a break or vacation? Is it an image of a place where you can get away from some problem or a port in a storm?

oath: Are you taking an oath? Do you need to find the truth of something? If you or someone else is refusing to take an oath, are you hiding something?

oatmeal: Perhaps you're looking to be more grounded, or maybe you already are. It could also symbolize simplicity. If you see porridge, it might represent poverty.

obedience: Are you not voicing your opinions or beliefs loud enough? If you are being disobedient, are you also being too rebellious?

obelisk: This could be a phallic symbol. It could also be your or someone's hard and cold nature. Think of it as the number one (see *numbers*). It may also be a symbol of power.

obese: Perhaps you're being overindulgent. Do you have waking diet issues?

obituary: Is something coming to an end, or does something need to end (e.g., an attitude or habit)?

oblivious: Are you too focused and missing out what's going on around you?

oboe: The sound of an oboe may reflect the sound of loneliness. Note the emotion you feel when hearing the sound of the oboe in your waking life.

obscene: If you hear something obscene, this might represent some part of you that you reject or won't acknowledge because of its distastefulness. If you're repulsed, perhaps you regret something you said, thought, or practiced in your waking life.

observatory: This may represent lofty goals and aspirations or the need to connect with your spiritual side.

observing: Just watching without involvement could be about too much passivity. You may need to engage life more.

obsessed: Do you need time to work through something? Are you obsessed with something that threatens to take over your whole life?

obstacle(s) or obstruction: Any obstacle might represent something preventing you from achieving some goal.

Criticism can become an obstacle to you feeling good about yourself.

They may also be things to be overcome to reach some goal. Is there a solution given in the dream?

obstacle course: These may be the hardships you've been going through. This

image may be pointing to what you need to overcome in order to reach your goals.

occult: Perhaps there's something just beneath the surface you're not seeing. It may also refer to some unacknowledged wisdom.

Is someone behaving in a mysterious or scary way?

Is something clandestine or secretly going on?

Are you trying to predict the future (see *precognition*)?

ocean: This can represent vast and deep feelings and emotions. This can also symbolize overwhelming or stormy emotions, depending on the action of the ocean or sea (see also *sea*).

octopus: This can symbolize an entanglement that may cause you a problem in judgment. Perhaps you're being too clingy, or maybe you're in a codependent arrangement that isn't healthy (also see the *number eight*).

odd: If something or someone seems odd in a dream, are you behaving in a strange manner? See also *surprise* and *unexpected*.

odd numbers: Seeing odd numbers in the dream could be about unresolved or aggressive issues. See *number terms*.

odometer: How far have you advanced in life?

offended: If you've been offended by something in a dream, perhaps you've been too sensitive and let certain things bother you. Perhaps there's something eating away at you.

offering: If you're making one, perhaps you are trying to make up for something (i.e., some offense).

office: Are you having trouble leaving the office? Perhaps you feel overworked. This is also a status symbol or signal of the desire for status. Check out the chair in the office because it might speak to your mobility in your job or your life.

officer: This can represent your attitudes regarding authority or your father. It could also reflect your leadership abilities and prospects. So too, this can represent your inner authority either being expressed too much or too little (see also *numbers*).

ogre: If you see an ogre in a dream, perhaps you are criticizing yourself or others too much. Are you being overbearing and aggressive?

oil lamp: This symbolizes knowledge, enlightenment, and awareness. Using it to walk through the darkness could suggest that you are searching for something and/or need guidance.

oily: This can symbolize being slick, fawning, or being overly flattering in general. It can also represent indirectness.

Oil also makes things run more smoothly. Perhaps you need to *grease the wheels* to get things running better? Massage oil might suggest that you need to work with something to get it to work better, or it could reflect your sensual side or lack thereof. It can also suggest the need for more compassion.

Baby oil can be about soothing emotions.

An oil spill could reflect emotional turmoil, or it could represent the fact that you are acting too slick.

Something oily in your mouth that you are trying to spit out may indicate that you experienced something distasteful that you're rejecting.

ointment: Are you in need of healing? Does something in your life or relationships need lubrication so it runs more smoothly?

old: Seeing something old in a dream could be about the need to replace something. Alternatively, you might have a need to take something from the past and integrate it into the present.

olives: These can represent healing and immortality. If you see an olive branch, it could be a peace offering.

Olympics: This could represent your desire to go after what you need or some goal. This may symbolize the spirit of competition and overcoming differences.

om: See *aum*.

omelet: If you see or make an omelet in a dream, think about the phrase "You can't make an omelet without breaking a few eggs," which suggests that you may need to make some sacrifices in order to reach some goal. As food, the omelet could refer to your desire to nourish some aspect of yourself or your life.

omen: This may reflect your fears and anxieties about what's to come. Are you worried that you won't be able to control what's happening?

Is something from your subconscious trying to get your attention? Is there something or someone that you are not paying attention to in your waking life?

See also *premonition* and/or *intuition*.

one eye: If you or someone else only has one eye, are you refusing to see more than one point of view? Do you need to broaden your perspective?

oneirology: Combining the Greek word for dreams (*oneiron*) with the word for *the study of* (*logia*), this is another word for the scientific study of dreams.

This is different than dream interpretation in that oneirology tries to quantify the process of dreaming.

oneiromancy: This refers to divination, prognostication, or precognition based on dreams.

Dreams informed those of ancient Egypt, Assyria, Babylonia, and Sumeria. A dream in the biblical story of Joseph and Mary inspired them to flee to Egypt to avoid their child being killed by Herod, and Paul who was told in a dream to go to Macedonia may have been forms of dream divination that have been respected throughout the ages.

During the medieval period, dreams about certain chapters in the Quran would be about prognostication. During this period, theologians wrote most books on dream interpretations and followed a tightly controlled and theologically correct typology.

In dreams, precognitive information may reflect one's subconscious insight or intuitiveness, or it could reflect synchronicities (i.e., meaningful coincidences).

Whether a form of extrasensory perception (ESP) or not, many people have had what appear to be precognitive dreams—dreams that seem to foretell the future.

See *divination, precognition,* and *extrasensory perception.*

onion: This can represent a number of layers to a problem, or it could reflect the layers you have to get through in order to unveil something. Dig deeper into something or into yourself. Perhaps there's some revelation available to you. Crying from an onion might suggest that something is making you cry or that your crying may not be genuine (see *circle* or *mandala*).

online game: This could be about the escape from daily stresses or the need to challenge yourself. Perhaps you've been playing too much and the images have burned into your dreams.

open house: Are you revealing some part of yourself? Do you need to be more open to others and to yourself? Are you an open book? Are you showing off?

opening: To open something could be about releasing your potential or discovering something new (e.g., a new way of being, a new opportunity, a new experience, a new relationship, a realization, or some self-discovery).

To open something such as a box without knowing what's inside may symbolize your curiosity or something hidden in your subconscious that needs to be expressed.

If you see an opening in a wall, it might suggest you have a new insight (see *door*).

opera: Are you being overly dramatic? Are you just putting on airs?

operation: If you're having an operation, perhaps there's something you need to get out of your system or off your chest.

opium: Perhaps there's an issue or situation you're avoiding. It may be time to take control and deal with whatever you're avoiding (see *morphine*).

opponent: Are you in conflict with yourself? What are you fighting in yourself?

opposite sex: If you dream that you are the opposite sex, perhaps you need to incorporate some personality aspect of this gender into yourself. See also the extended *anima/animus* in the *archetypes* section.

oracle: This could symbolize a prophecy or something that's becoming clearer to you. Do you believe in fate?

orange: This can be about health and prosperity, or you may feel the need to be reenergized or revitalized.

See also *fruit* and/or *orchard.*

orangutan: This simian could represent your wild inner urges. It can also represent power. If you're attacked by one, it might be about something that's emotionally overwhelming or an instinctual aspect affecting you negatively. See *animal terms*.

orb: An orb such as a crystal ball could be about sudden understanding or clarity. It can also represent your subconscious and the messages coming from it.

orchard: This may represent being fruitful. This may speak to your potential for success.

orchestra: This can reflect the relationship between different aspects of yourself, your partner, or colleagues. See also *music*.

orchids: This may be symbolic of gentleness, romance, and sensuality. Something or someone may need special attention and care.

order versus chaos: This is a wedding of opposites that will produce the divine child and open one's soul. See the *archetypes* section.

organ: If you're playing one, it could represent your spiritual aspect. As a body part, it could be about the state of your health or be a metaphor for the penis.

orgasm: This might symbolize a great end to something or a peak experience. It may also represent the need to relieve some

tension, or alternatively, you just may not be getting enough sex.

This can also reflect a physical union that you need or want.

Should there be an actual orgasm while you sleep, perhaps your body is relieving built-up sexual stress (known as *nocturnal emissions* or colloquially as a *wet dream*).

orgy: This may be about repressed desires that have built up and need release. There is the possibility that you're trying to do too much and have spread yourself too thin. This image could also represent excesses.

ornament: What you do to add beauty to your life, to make yourself feel good, or adds color to your existence. It can also be a spiritual gift.

orphan: This might represent isolation and the loss of protection or connection with your origins. This also involves aspects of abandonment, being unwanted or rejected, and not belonging.

An orphanage could represent the need to belong or the lack of belonging. Escaping from an orphanage could be about wanting to get away from certain restrictions.

orthodontist: Are you concerned about how you look?

ostrich: Perhaps you're not facing reality and are in denial and unaccepting. Perhaps you need to get your head out of the sand and deal with what's happening. If it's laying an egg, perhaps you have made a big mistake.

Ouija board: Perhaps your subconscious mind is trying to connect with you. What are the messages?

Maybe you're depending too much on magical thinking or letting something outside of yourself make decisions for you.

ouroboros: A snake biting its own tail can signify the need to be self-reflexive or the need to recreate yourself. It can be a symbol for wholeness and also a metaphor for completion. You may feel you are striving to be complete with yourself or some issue.

In the Hindu philosophy, it shows up as representing the cyclicality of life and change—the Samsāra.

In alchemy it often symbolized recreation and the continuous cycle of creation and destruction and life and death. It represented the eternal unity of all things. To the Gnostics it was the symbol of the soul of the world.

Insight: The ouroboros is the most often used symbol in the work of the ancient alchemists. It represents the world-creating spirit that resides within matter.

Many alchemists used it to represent *mercurius* or quicksilver, the prima materia of the alchemists work. It stands for the beginning and the end of the work (i.e., the one that leads back to the one). It's the symbol of the union of opposites, thus creating the whole. It can represent the cold and fiery, matter and spirit, metallic and liquid, poison and healing drought.

He is also the hermaphrodite of the tarot, the coiniunctio, or incorporation/ integration, of all opposites that makes up the world and the psyche of humankind. It appears as a symbol of the stone in the philosopher's stone.

It has been said that the work of the alchemists was more than the experiments in chemistry, and it was all done to discover both immortality and the process for making gold from lead; however, it's also a depiction of human psychology in all its mystery.

According to Erich Neumann, a student of Carl Jung, the first state of psychological development is called the ouroboric stage, derived from ouroboros, the tail-eating serpent. At this stage is the initial totality and self-containment that occurs prior to the birth of consciousness. Here the ego exists only as a latent potentiality in a state of primary identity with the self or the objective psyche. This state is presumed to exist within the prenatal period and into early infancy.

outbreak: Are you being too negative? Is that running your life and infecting everything you see or do? See also *epidemic*.

outburst: See *explosion or eruption*.

outcast: See the *archetypes* section.

outer space: Being in outer space could be about going beyond your personal or current reality, exploring beyond the self and broadening your perspective (i.e., your view of reality).

Consider the reference "spacing out." Perhaps you need to concentrate or focus more.

There's also the reference *spacey*, which may mean you've got your head in the clouds and need to be more grounded (practical and focused).

outlaw: This suggests rebellion, casting out, or outside convention.

out-of-body experience (OBE): This is a feeling when the other self becomes detached from the normal self. It's like projecting your consciousness outside your body and looking back. Many people have reported the feeling of hovering above everything.

Insight: These OBEs often show up during times of extreme stress, deep pain or grief, or alongside near-death experiences. OBEs may be an evolutionary means for dealing with extreme stress or death itself. Some researchers have begun to wonder whether our consciousness is a function of the brain and the body or something that comes to us from outside. This might explain the feeling of being detached from the body during an OBE.

outside: If you are outside, it could symbolize your desire to be free or open to something new. It may also mean the need to be more expressive and open. Perhaps you just need to take a break and get a breath of fresh air.

ovaries: Perhaps this symbolizes your sense of adequacy or validity if you're a woman.

oven: This could be about warmth and togetherness. An oven can also signify the womb, and something in the oven can be about pregnancy—both the fact or the desire for a child.

overcoat: Are you protecting yourself from something, (perhaps hurt)?

overdose: If you or someone else overdoses, this may suggest that you need to know your limits. Perhaps you're taking on too much and are self-destructing. You could be killing yourself by working yourself too hard.

overeating: This could be about the obsessive need for attention, being nurtured, intimacy, or sex.

overpowered: Are you feeling helpless or powerless when it comes to something or someone (see *domination*)?

overwhelm: Images of floods, deluge, being submerged, impotence, helplessness, or swamps can represent this feeling. When in this state, we tend to project the feeling onto others by blaming. See also *conquer, guilt,* or *water.*

owl: See *bird.*

oyster (or clam or any shellfish): Hard on the outside and soft on the inside. What are you protecting in yourself? Consider the phrase "The world is my oyster."

P

pacifier: This is symbolic of emotional nurturance. If you are trying to pacify someone, are you trying to remain calm too, or should you remain calm during some stressful situation or crisis?

pacing back and forth: The pacing could be about some personal anxiety or the way you're dealing with some stress.

packages or parcels: These can be about unwrapped or unrevealed feelings and/or unrecognized gifts from others (such as their love and support). They can also refer to unrevealed talents or latent skills.

packing: This can be about leaving, being more independent, and/or making a change. If you're packing and unpacking over and over again, it could reflect some chaos in your life or some difficulty in making a decision.

padlock: Are you having trouble meeting your needs? Is something or someone locking you out of some situation or goal?

If the lock is broken, it might reflect your insecurities.

page: Pages can be a summary of what you've done in life or a reflection of where you are headed. Being on the wrong page or being on a page you don't want to be on could reflect the feeling of not being where you want to be. Perhaps you want to be on another page and start anew.

pain: This possibly represents a conflict or problem. It could symbolize something that hurts you.

painting: This could represent creativity, self-expression, and/or intuition. As a decoration, it could also represent making changes in your life: This can also be about the kingdom or palace of the self. It can also be about covering (hiding) something up.

palace: This suggests a sense of importance or privilege. It could also be a statement about specialness and possibly your potential for greatness (see also *castle, king,* or *queen*).

palm reader: See *fortune-teller.*

panic: Are you dreading something? Some part of your life may be in a frenzy. Maybe you're feeling insecure.

Perhaps you feel out of control and helpless about some decision. Do you need to get centered and calm down? Do you need some reassurance?

See also *fear*.

paper: If the paper is blank, it could represent an unexpressed idea or the potential for something (see also *absence*). It could also be symbolic for the need to communicate. If it's crumpled it could signify that you've given up on some idea or to give up on it.

paper stack or stack of paper: This might suggest overwhelming responsibility and the stress that comes with it.

parachute: This could symbolize a rescue from failing. It could also refer to retirement.

paradox: If something in a dream seems to be a contradiction or puzzle, it may be pointing at an inconsistency, dilemma, or mystery in your waking life.

Do you need to do something to gain some certainty and/or understanding about some issue? Perhaps you're in a catch-22 or no-win situation.

See also *non sequitur*.

paralysis: This could be about resistance to change. If paralysis accompanies your dreams, then this might indicate a lack of confidence or fear of not coping. This image may also speak to feeling trapped.

Because the body is wired to shut down the neuromuscular system while you're in REM sleep, it is also possible that you have awakened while still in this stage and feel as though you're paralyzed. This can be very scary.

paranormal: This may represent things that your logic cannot explain. It may also represent parts of yourself (i.e., talents) that you did not know you had but that need to be expressed.

It's also possible that you are letting things outside yourself determine your thoughts or actions. You may need to regain control of your life.

Perhaps you need to transcend the usual responses to your circumstances. See also *supernatural*.

parasite: Parasites may be about being physically drained with a loss of vitality. If they were harmless, perhaps you've become too dependent on others.

Parasites can also suggest that you may be taking advantage of someone or that someone is taking advantage of you.

parched: See *dried up* or *thirst*.

parents: These images can be about power, protection, and/or love or the positive or negative aspects associated with each.

Their deaths in the dream or coming back to you after their deaths in your waking life might represent significant changes happening in your life or that need to happen.

See also *mother* or *father*.

park: Perhaps this represents your public self or your controlled nature. What are you controlling in yourself? If you've parked the car or you're in a car park, has your life or progress on something been put on hold? Are you waiting for something?

If you're parked, perhaps you need to rest awhile and take time out for yourself.

If you're parked in a no parking zone, perhaps you are somewhere you shouldn't be.

If you've parked but cannot find your car, perhaps you've lost your way in life and are searching for direction.

If you're parking someone else's car, maybe you are lacking direction or a goal.

See also *car* or *field*.

parking lot (or car park): If you're in a parking lot, perhaps you need to slow down your life. If you're leaving a parking lot, perhaps you need to get back onto the road of your life after having taken a hiatus.

If you're in a parking structure, perhaps you've been going around in circles.

party: If the party is for you, then perhaps it is acclaim or recognition you are looking for. It could also refer to a political party.

passage: See *opening, tunnel,* or *hallway.*

passenger: You may feel the effects of life without intentionally causing them. You may be depending on another person for your opinions, motivation, or direction in life. Perhaps you need to get into the driver's seat.

passport or driver's license: This represents your identity and freedom of movement. A passport might also indicate your desire to explore something or to have an adventure.

past: You may feel as if you are reliving something from the past. You may hear someone say, "I've done this before. Why am I doing it again?" Or a person may say, "I already know this. Why am I doing this again?" For example, you may have a dream where you're in a classroom or in the military again. Perhaps something has resurfaced that requires that you revisit earlier lessons or confirm that you actually have advanced beyond it.

Perhaps you are about to make the same mistake again (see *déjà vu*).

Are you dwelling on the past and/or avoiding the present? Are you fearing your future (see *future*)?

pastel: Maybe there's some part of your emotions or character you aren't recognizing or dealing with. It can also refer to some ambiguity.

past life: If you're viewing yourself in a past life, perhaps you seek to understand yourself better. Maybe there are previous lessons learned that you need to employ now. See also *reincarnating*.

pastor: See *priest*. Any religious leader will fit here.

pasture: See *field*. Does it refer to being put out to pasture (i.e., that you no longer feel useful or have been laid off)?

If it's a green pasture and you're resting in it, could it refer to the Psalm 23 from the Christian Bible?

paternity: See *test* and *suing*.

path: This can symbolize your life's direction. It's similar to a journey. If you're wandering off the path or have lost your way, perhaps you're being too rigid in the plan for your life.

Perhaps you need to get off the path in order to find your way.

The condition of the path and its difficulty will give you more insight. How far down the path are you? See also *road*.

Paths are also ways to one's inner self or toward some solution to a problem. Sometimes it's a calling to get in touch with your soul or your more real and authentic self. Is it a path to your spiritual self? Is it acting as a guide or map to your deeper self?

The parting of the waters, such as with the story of Moses and the Red Sea, are metaphors for a path into a new life, new beginning, or way of being and the leaving of your problems behind.

patricide: If you are killing yours or someone else's father, it may mean you are rejecting some authority or rule. This can also reflect getting rid of some aspect of yourself. See also *father*.

peace: If you are in or viewing a peaceful landscape, are you not in a good place right now in your waking life? Alternatively, a peaceful sunny landscape might reflect your optimism.

This may be about your mental viewpoint or desire for peace. There may be some inner conflict or emotional issue that seeks some resolution. It may reflect a desire for calmness.

peach: This can be about pleasure. It may also be about virginity and/or lust (see *fruit*). Is everything just *peachy* (i.e., working well for you)? Is someone very special to you or very helpful (i.e., a real peach)?

peak experience: This is a concept developed by Abraham Maslow,[15] and it describes the experience when one perceives reality in an altogether mystical and magical way that is deeply moving, intense, and transforming. In many cases, the experience is like being connected to everything and everyone with no separation (i.e., a feeling of oneness) (see also *ego death*).

pear: This may be about the womb or fertility or about some woman in your life. A pear tree could be about new opportunities. Also consider *a pair* of something (see *fruit*).

pearl: This may represent wisdom or tears, which could indicate loss or sorrow. It could be the transformation of an irritant into something of value.

peek: To peek at something or someone may be to show interest without admitting it. Perhaps you want to surreptitiously take something in or check it out.

Are you being a busybody?

Perhaps you're mistrusting someone, something, or some situation, feeling, or yourself. Perhaps you're afraid of getting too close.

Are you being voyeuristic?

If someone is peeking on you, perhaps you feel invaded as though he or she has threatened your privacy.

pendant: Representing the need to feel loved or connected. If the pendant is like an amulet, do you feel as if you need to be protected? Are you feeling vulnerable to someone or something? See also *amulet*.

penis: See *body*.

pentagram: A five-pointed star or pentagram may represent something magical, and it is often used as part of a spell-casting ritual or a means of divining something or calling something into your awareness.

These shapes can also be symbols of protection. Note the colors of the stars points and look up possible meanings in the colors section. Note that the colors red, green, yellow, blue, and white are typical of a magical pentagram and could be referring to the four elements—earth, air, fire, and water (see also *colors*).

penthouse: This could be about your spiritual self. It could also be about looking at something from another perspective or a higher point of view.

Are you acting as though you're better than everyone else?

people: Look at how you relate to the people in the dream. That may give you some idea of how you are relating to others in general.

Their behaviors and actions are nearly always a reflection of you, your personality, and your behaviors, whether wanted or rejected. They may also just represent you in a psychologically removed position that makes it easier for you to deal with certain negative aspects of yourself.

When you find yourself in a large crowd of people, it can be an indicator of your involvement in an issue or in the society you find yourself in (also see *persona* in the *archetypes* section).

Insight: Notice how you're relating to the person or persons in your dream. The people in your dream are related to you in that they represent parts of yourself—wanted or existing, liked or not, accepted or denied.

In general, people in dreams are extremely important symbols. Even dead people can suggest the influence that they may still

have on you though they're no longer around. Notice what people from your past meant to you then or the circumstances of your parting. What about the present is reflected in that past relationship?

The roles that the people play either in the dream or in real life can also give you clues to what the unconscious is trying to communicate.

Some examples include the following:

1. Policemen might hold some special meaning for you, but they might also represent a sense of what is right or wrong in a situation. They may be a statement of moral authority, or perhaps they symbolize punishment or bearers of bad news.
2. Soldiers might symbolize inner conflict or a conflict in the waking world. How is the soldier handling the conflict?
3. A scientist might represent the creative, rational, and inquisitive side of your nature.
4. A seducer might suggest that you're being seduced into something in your waking life. Though this need not be sexual in nature, you might also look to see if you're feeling unloved somewhere in your life.

Note that the gender of the person in your dream can have great significance not only because of who he or she is in your waking life but because the opposite sex in a dream can have archetypal meanings as well (see *anima/animus* in the *archetype* section).

Sometimes people from the past reveal what's missing in the present (see *ex*).

perfume: This could represent the smell or memory of someone.

It can also be about pleasure and sensuality or indulging yourself.

periscope: It enables you to see over obstacles and to achieve another perspective. The dream may be suggesting that you need to change your perspective on something.

A periscope is also a device that is curved so that you can see over obstacles, so perhaps you need to be less linear in the way you think.

perm: Perhaps you need to change the way you think about something (i.e., change your point of view).

Does it feel as though something has become *permanent* in your waking world?

permission: If you are seeking permission in the dream, it may be about you giving yourself permission to take some action.

Perhaps you are feeling a lack of power or freedom to determine your own future.

This may also be about self-doubt, or you could be seeking approval for what you want.

persecution: Are you feeling picked on or demeaned? Do you need to stand up for yourself? Are you being bullied, or are you bullying?

How do you feel when you're persecuted? Do you feel that it justifies and acknowledges what you are doing in your life, or does it cause you to feel invalidated? What's that about? How does this dream image apply to your waking life?

persistence: If something keeps coming back in your dream (e.g., a bug that keeps annoying after you've swatted it away), this may reflect a trait that you need to reveal about some issue. It could also reflect a trait that you've tried to get rid of, but it keeps coming back.

Perhaps you need to be more persistent about something.

persona: This appears as a consciously created personality or identity fashioned out of part of the collective psyche through socialization, acculturation, and experience.

Jung used the classical term *persona* because it meant the *mask* that the actor wears and expresses as he or she plays the role.

The *persona*, he argued, is a mask for the collective psyche, a mask that *pretends* individuality (i.e., who you pretend to be).

personal myth: We develop a lot of myths about ourselves. For example, any time we say, "I am the way I am because of this or that," we are creating our personal myths, our personal explanations for reality—the stories or narratives that we live by and through.

Of course, most of these behavioral explanations require some form of blaming someone or something other than ourselves. And for many of us, the whole of life is a myth.

Does that mean that your life isn't real or true? Not necessarily. In each personal myth, there is the seed of truth if we had the eye to see it. Mostly we are so busy making up stories about who we are that we can't see the reality beneath the stories.

Myths can also be used to hide the assumed reality of ourselves so as to protect us from what we fear the world is or what we fear we are. There is, of course, nothing wrong with a personal myth, and it'll do until something better comes along. The trouble is that over time we can get bound up in our stories, and then it becomes harder to discover who and what we really are.

But you might take the first step in your own growth and in deciphering your own metaphors for understanding your life. As Jean Houston, a leader for the human potentials movement, said, "Myth does serve as a manner of explanation, but it is also a mode of discovery … it is the stuff of the evolving self that awakens consciousness."

You might ask yourself, "What is my personal myth? Who and what do I think I am and am not, and why?" Jot down a list of adjectives along with their explanations, and then scan them and look for themes. What created reality does all this seem to point to? Is there another reality beneath this?

personality types: Carl Jung theorized that people could be characterized by their preference of general attitude, functions of perception, and functions of judging.

He presented these preferences as dichotomies. For example, the first criterion was extraversion-introversion, which signified the direction of a person's energy expression (i.e., inward or outward).

In the second set of preferences, he listed sensing and intuition as the two methods in which one *perceives* information. Does

345

the individual rely mostly on data from the outside world or information received internally or imaginatively?

Third, people tend to process the information either through logic or emotion (i.e., thinking or feeling).

Isabel Briggs Myers added a fourth dichotomy, specifically that of judging and perceiving, which reflects how the person implements the information processed. In a judging personality, the information is organized into plans that are generally followed, whereas the perceiving type will improvise and explore alternatives.

These four sets of traits can be broadened into sixteen personality types. See the Myers-Briggs reference in the introduction.

personal unconscious: In the personal unconscious are all our perceptions, forgotten or repressed memories, hopes, desires, and emotions. Jung claims that knowledge of the personal unconscious is knowledge of the self and that the unconscious is always working toward wholeness (see *individuation*).

As it is with the conscious mind, the unconscious isn't located in any one place in the architecture of the brain but appears to be spread everywhere. There are some scientists who suspect that at least some of it may not even be of the brain or body,

though the theory is highly speculative and doesn't have any data to support it.

This idea of an unconscious isn't new. It was brought to public awareness through the work of such people as Sigmund Freud and philosophers such as Friedrich Schelling and the poet Samuel Taylor Coleridge. In the midsixteenth century, Paracelsus made mention of it as did William Shakespeare.

pet: This can represent self-love. What about yourself do you care for?

It can also represent responsibility, caring, and affection. In a woman's dream, a pet can refer to her maternal drive. In a child's dream, it could be a reflection of being dependent but also about unconditional love.

Feeding a pet can be about nurturing yourself, or if unfed, it could be about how you're not nurturing yourself.

The type of pet will add more information.

petrol: See *gas or gas station*.

petting: Petting some animal may be about taking in or desiring some attribute of that animal. For example, you may desire the love and loyalty of a dog (see *animals*).

Petting can also be a sexual term, but it can also be about being cared for or caring for yourself.

petrified/not able to move: Perhaps you're in a rut or there is no way out of some situation.

pew: Maybe you need to reflect on something or get in touch with your spiritual side.

Chairs or pews in a church might symbolize your need to stop and reflect on your mistakes before you move on. Perhaps you need to take another look at your decisions.

phantasmagoria: This is a projection of such things as ghosts, apparitions, and demons presented as a nightmarish dream for entertainment.

If you were to see such a projection in a dream, it may reflect your unconscious biases. Are you seeing things? Are your illusions about reality making it difficult to actually see what's real?

This can also be a nightmare (see *nightmares*) coming from your shadow aspect from the unconscious mind (see *shadow* in the *archetypes* section).

These projections were often used by charlatans to dupe their benefactors. Sometimes they would project ghostly images of the dead and pretend that they were communicating with them (see *necromancer* or *séance*).

Are you being duped or taken advantage of?

phantom: This may be about fear and repressed memories. Do you need to face your fears? It can also symbolize the concept of something being illusory, fantastical, mirage-like, or spurious. Are you misapprehending something or someone?

Dreams and daydreams might be experienced as phantomlike or unreal occurrences.

Consider that a phantom might also represent a delusion as in a self-deception or false impression.

See also *ghost* and/or *chimera*.

philosopher's stone: To Carl Jung, this was the symbol of the self, that point where all humankind's disparate parts are integrated into a wholeness. See *self*.

In a dream it could mean your need to balance yourself by accepting both that which you embrace and that which you reject (i.e., your opposite natures, positive and negative aspects, and your feminine and masculine traits). (See *anima/animus* in the *Archetypes* section.)

It is also known as the Lapis (Latin for stone) or by some as the personification of Christ.

philosophical tree: See *tree of life*.

phoenix: This is symbolic of rebirth, renewal, and starting over (see *resurrection*).

It also symbolizes the feminine aspects in opposition to the *dragon's* masculine. In a manner of speaking, this contrast is also present in the yin/yang symbol.

The battle between the masculine and feminine archetypes is a struggle toward wholeness. People must learn to embrace both aspects within themselves in order to be wholly functioning human beings.

phone: If someone is trying to phone you, is there something you need to communicate? If you are deliberately not answering, is there some situation you don't want to get involved with or perhaps some habit that you need to break? See also *texting*.

photocopy: This could be about an inaccurate memory or maybe a memory not directly experienced. It could refer to something unreal as in a facsimile. Are you being unoriginal or copying someone else's work or ideas? Perhaps you need to think for yourself. If you're making copies, perhaps you need to spread some communication.

photographs: This can represent the storage of memories, your self-image, or past experience. It can also reflect a vision or your image of an event or the world in general.

It can also reveal a relationship that may need your attention. Are you manipulating the photo in some way? Are you trying to present a false image?

Perhaps the image is a reflection of an earlier time in your life. This can be a reflection of something happening now that also reminds you of a similar event or issue from the past.

If the images in the photo are moving, are you trying to create a story that may or may not be true? Are you animating an incident and giving meaning to something where there is no meaning (i.e., making up a story where there is none)?

See also *selfie*.

piano: This suggests a quest for harmony. If it's silent or it doesn't make any sound when you play it, perhaps you lack self-confidence. If the piano is out of tune, perhaps there's something in your life that is discordant and needs your attention (see also *music*).

picnic: Having a picnic could be about joy, togetherness, and tranquility or the desire for it. It can also represent the desire for simplicity and naturalness.

Consider the phrase "Sometimes life's no picnic," referring to times when things don't go as well as you would like.

It can also represent an escape from the conventional or routine.

Consider also its romantic symbolism.

pickup truck: This can refer to hard work or burdens that you are carrying. There might also be something that you need to pick up (see *truck*).

picture: Consider also the references *picture-perfect*, *the picture of health*, or *as pretty as a picture*.

If you or someone else is just looking at a picture of you, you may not be seeing yourself for who you really are. (You're only seeing a two-dimensional representation.) Perhaps you need to put yourself out there more and demand to be recognized.

See *photographs* as well.

pie: This could be about a reward for hard work. Are you not getting your fair share (i.e., your piece of the pie)? Pi represents something irrational or never-ending, something that you can't get to the root of (see also *circle* and *squaring the circle*).

piercing: If it is a nose piercing, perhaps you need to focus on some issue.

A tongue piercing might be about some negative remark you or another person made.

A pierced eyebrow may be about a piercing stare but also be about something upsetting that you've seen.

Naval piercings can be about connection with your mother. It could also be about your own maternal instincts.

Ear piercings can be about insults or criticisms.

If you're planning to get a piercing, this could just reflect your fears about that.

pig: This could symbolize being greedy and smart. It could also refer to something or someone who is dirty and unkempt.

pigeon: See *bird* in *animal terms*.

pillar: This is something that holds you up, that supports you. Consider the phrase "pillar of the community."

pillow fight: Perhaps you need to be less self-critical or be more relaxed about some conflict. Perhaps you need to get in touch with your inner child and playful self. Are you pretending to be mad at someone, or are you being passive aggressive? Do you need to be more assertive?

pillow talk: This is an intimate conversation, communication, communion, or a one-on-one chat. It could also be another word for gossip.

pilot: Are you in control of the direction your life is going in? Are you confident in the direction you're going?

pimple: This can represent a character flaw, or you may be too caught up in how you look to others. Are you embarrassed about something?

piñata: This can be an image of celebration or an earned reward. If garbage, junk, or insects come out of the piñata, perhaps you've been misled, or maybe someone has not delivered on what he or she promised.

If you are missing the piñata, you may be having difficulties with success.

Are you feeling battered or abused?

pincushion: This could be about stinging and hurtful remarks. Is someone trying to blame or pin something on you?

pine tree: This tree can be about immortality but also death in that it has been used to make coffins. Consider also how one can pine for someone and long for the person. The pine cone can be about new life and/or fertility. See also *tree.*

pirate: Do you feel plundered as though someone or something has taken something of value from you?

Pisces: This is symbolic of imagination, compassion, and/or sensitivity. Are you ready to stand up for what you believe in regardless of the consequences? People under this sign are also said to be escapist and very fussy.

Are you avoiding something or being too idealistic? Are you feeling demoralized or being overly sensitive?

See also *fish* in *animal terms.*

pissing: See *urination.*

pissy: Are you in a bad mood? Are you being erratic, irritable, unreliable, or impatient?

pit: Are you trapped in a difficult situation? Do you feel trapped in your negative judgments and point of view (see *abyss*)?

pizza: Pizza can be about choices or the nourishing of some aspect of yourself. Are you feeling deprived of something?

See *foods.*

See also *circle* in *shapes* and/or *mandala.*

plains: This possibly represents a clear, smooth path into the future and the fact that your truth may be out there somewhere. It could also be a pun for something simple as in the plain truth or something being plain and simple.

planet: This could be about exploration and/or self-discovery, or perhaps you are trying to escape your earthbound reality. Discovering life on another planet may be a reflection of finding something new in yourself.

If it shows up as a specific planet, see the following examples: *Jupiter, Mars, Mercury, Neptune, Saturn,* and *Venus.* Look up planets in your birth chart online for other planets associated with astrology.

plank: If you are walking the plank, perhaps you are feeling emotionally vulnerable. Something may be about to end.

planting: This can be about new growth or putting down roots. You may want to start something new and stabile.

plants: These can relate to fertility or the potential for growth. Dead plants might suggest that you are not growing or are perhaps at a hiatus in your life.

plate: What's on your plate? What do you have to deal with right now? If you're sharing the plate, then what do you have to compete for? An empty plate might be symbolic of your needs not being met.

playing: This can possibly represent your own playfulness or the need for it.

plum: This may be about something special or great. If it's ripe, it can be a sexual image. See also *fruit.*

If something is not plum, perhaps something is off kilter and not quite right.

plumbing or plumber: This could symbolize an emotional release. It can even indicate a health issue with regard to your internal plumbing (your colon, kidneys, bladder, or circulatory system).

pneuma: This what depth psychologists call our essential nature, our true being. Comprised of both spirit and soul, it manifests itself through the psyche, the ego.

In Greek, it literally means *breath.* It is what animates us.

Jewish and Christian tradition translates this word as *spirit.*

Alchemists thought of the philosopher's stone as harboring the pneumatic—the essence of life.

To the Gnostics, the pneuma is that part of the divine unconscious.

Some religionists and analytical/depth psychologists such as Carl Jung and Alfred Adler toyed with the idea that the pneuma was the Son of God who descended into matter in order to bring healing. This descent, however, may actually be an ascent in that it may come from the unconscious mind into the conscious.

See *anima, psyche,* or *soul.*

podium: Standing before a podium might suggest that there's something important that you need to communicate. It's also an image of prominence and influence.

poem: This can represent idealism, essence of experience, profound feelings, deep communication, self-expression, creativity, and/or the words and music of the soul. Sometimes a meditation can be like poetry.

Note the words of the poem. What might they be telling you? See also *music.*

pointing: Is someone or your unconscious trying to draw your attention to something? This could also be an aggressive symbol or a symbol of an accusation.

poinsettias: See *flowers.*

poison: This can suggest something or someone that will not be good for you. This person or thing can destroy your sense of self, self-image, or reputation. Something in your life may be malignant and killing you.

Poisons given by a witch or sorcerer may represent the negative manipulations of others.

police: Police officers are suggestive of order, discipline, authority, protection, and guilt.

Your own thoughts about the police will affect the meaning of this image.

The police image could be symbolic of the guardians of your values who shows up when you are conflicted with those values or are doing something that's in conflict with your values.

Insight: Because policemen in waking life have varied significance, this image can reflect extremes from positive to negative. Frequently, people will negatively differentiate the white policeman from the general category of policemen. In this case, they may be seen as images of abuse, prejudice, mistrust, and arbitrariness. This wide range of projected meanings can hold true for soldiers, politicians, and government officials as well.

Frequently people project their own troubles and the dark sides of their personalities onto authority figures as a means of not dealing with or having to face their own weaknesses or rejected aspects.

When interpreting all images, you may want to see what about the image plays a role in your own personality.

The ego-self or personality does not like being wrong about anything and will easily project error onto something or someone outside itself. When you see this happening in a dream or in everyday wakefulness, you might look to what degree the projection mirrors your own behavior.

politics: This could be about how you need to govern your life or get in touch with the beliefs and emotions that govern what you do. You may have feelings of anger, disgust, distrust, and confusion attached to this image, so look carefully at it.

pollution: If you see a polluted body of water, you may have difficulty identifying your feelings, or they may seem all mixed up and lack any clarity.

Something may be emotionally toxic. Perhaps you need to clean up your own thoughts or words. A polluted sky may be speaking to limitations placed on you by others or by yourself.

Pollution could also be a metaphor for something corrupted or corruption.

pond: This can be about tranquility. The image of a pond can also suggest that you keep your emotions contained and under control. A shallow pond could be about shallow emotions. You may need to go deeper into your emotional self.

The condition of the pond will give more information (see *muddy*, *deep*, and *clear*).

pool: What is going on inside you? If you are underwater, what have you submerged (e.g., a suppressed feeling, hope, or aspect of yourself)?

This can also represent our sense of unity with all living beings.

Pools can also be about contained emotions as can water towers or even water coolers. (You may keep emotions bottled up inside.) Muddy pools can be about the lack of clarity in a situation or suggest that something or someone has muddied the waters, messed something up, and complicated things (see also *lake*).

If it's the game of pool, you may be pushing your luck or feeling competitive. Do you need to concentrate harder on some situation or problem in your waking life.

Are you behind the eight ball and in trouble? Are you taking a chance on something or taking a risk? If you've run the table, are you trying to dominate something or someone?

If you're playing pool by bar rules, your opponent can place the ball anywhere he or she likes. This might suggest a worry that you'll make some mistake that will cost you.

poop: See *feces*.

pope: This is a father figure or a reference to a code of ethics. This can also be a god figure or a reference to your spiritual aspect. See also *preacher*.

porch: This can represent your social self and how you portray yourself to others. It's your façade (see *mask*). Open porches may be about your openness. Closed porches may reflect your need for privacy or suggest that you have closed yourself off to others.

Have you hidden anything under your porch?

See also *stoop*.

porn: Do you have issues regarding intimacy or control? Are you afraid of exposing some part of yourself? If you are in a porn film, it may be about lust or sexual adventurism.

portal: See *door* or *gate*.

posing: Are you striking a pose? If so, are you trying to be something you're not, or are you showing off?

position: This is where you stand in life. Are you above it all, side by side, and thus equal to others or keeping up? Is something beneath you? Are you close or distant to something or somebody? Are you out in front and leading, or are you in the back and trying to catch up? Or are you dealing with your past?

possession: When you feel possessed in a dream, you probably feel that something else is in control and that you are out of control and helpless. If it's a dream about your possessions, then it may be a dream about your self-worth or your identity. It could also be about your materialistic nature or a comment on society's obsession with having things. Perhaps you need to let go. Are you being too possessive of someone?

Insight: Carl Jung suggested that we are a species carried away or possessed by our unconscious minds and that these unexplored parts of ourselves are at the root of our neuroses and complexes (a core pattern of emotions ordered around a common theme such as power or status).

Our shadow aspects or demons will cause all kinds of mischief in our lives until we deal with them directly.

Being possessed is an archetype in itself. Many years ago people would employ priests, lay mediums, medicine men, or shamans to exorcize an individual's devil that had possessed them. Of course, most of the civilized world no longer believes in demon possession.

We all have our dark side, and left unexplored, it can create complexes, which we all have. We damage ourselves when we claim that we have no complexes because they are the very things that determine our psychological view of the world. Left unattended, they can quite literally take over the whole personality.

When we allow ourselves to be possessed by our unexamined unconscious, we can quite literally become marionettes to our darker sides.

post office: This could be about some important message from your subconscious.

pot: If it's marijuana, are you withdrawing from, avoiding something, or trying to mellow out?

Remember a watched pot never boils. Are you micromanaging something?

pothole: Potholes in a road are often metaphors for the obstacles in life. They can also reflect rough and stressful times.

potion: If ingesting a potion, it could be about some negative influence. Are you trying to change the direction something is taking? If you give it to another person, are you trying to manipulate that individual or the circumstance in some way? See also *medicine*.

powder: If it's white powder, it may be a symbol of something that is a danger to you (physically, psychologically, or emotionally). Powder may also be a drug or a sickness-causing and habit-forming agent.

power: See *electricity* and/or *energy*.

praying: You may be seeking help or emotional support, or you may be looking for guidance or surrendering yourself. If it's an entreaty, perhaps something is missing in life.

Perhaps you need to be thankful for what you have.

Praying can also be about being humble and/or giving up your self-importance to something or someone.

If it is one of giving thanks, perhaps you need to acknowledge someone or yourself.

Alternatively the dream could be telling you to stop praying and do something to get what you want.

Most prayer is for things we want and need (entreaty), such as relief from suffering or for forgiveness, peace, justice, love, or health.

If the dream is suggesting a need for a deeper spiritual connection, consider also *mindfulness* as a means of communion.

preacher: Are you being too preachy? See also *priest*.

precognition: This is often known as second vision or future sight. This falls under the umbrella of ESP. Though there is some evidence for the existence of precognition, it is not at this time considered scientifically convincing.

At least some precognitive dreams may reflect the fact that the subconscious picks up on information not focused upon during wakefulness. This is then downloaded through a dream after which the dreamer becomes sensitive to the information and finally recognizes it during wakefulness, thus giving the impression of precognition.

See *divination, extrasensory perception*, and *oneiromancy* or *premonition*.

pregnancy: This could symbolize what you may be ready to produce or give birth to (e.g., an idea, goal, a plan, or a new way of being). This could also be about a new development. On some occasions it can also speak to a personal pregnancy that isn't obvious as yet or reflect the desire to become pregnant.

If someone else is pregnant, perhaps you are feeling a closer affinity with this person.

Alternatively, you may be practicing sex in a risky way.

pregnancy test: Are you entering into something new (e.g., new training, a new job, a new relationship, or a new phase of life)? Are you feeling prepared or unprepared?

prehistoric: This could symbolize primal urges such as territoriality or fear. It could also refer to an old way of doing things.

premonition: This can be about an intuitive *feeling* or suggest that something is evolving and moving on. Do you worry something negative might happen or that someone may be sneaking behind your back? See also *divination, intuition, omen,* and/or *precognition*.

prescription: Are you trying to find answers to or clarity on something? Are you trying to make something happen? Is there some health issue that needs to be addressed?

presence: If you experience a presence without seeing it, you might try *ghost*. This might also symbolize something hidden in you.

present: Do you need to give something to someone? It could also be about the present moment (i.e., that you need to be here now).

If you're receiving one, perhaps you need to be open to some support from others, some unexpected development, or a new way of thinking.

presentation: If you're giving a presentation, this could be how you are presenting yourself to others. This could be about your self-image.

president (or prime minister): This could be a symbol for authority or power, or it could reflect your biases or judgments about a president. If you're running for president, this could be about your desire for power or control. Do you believe that you could do a better job than someone who is in charge?

pressure cooker: A pressure cooker may be a metaphor for some great pressures or stress that you are experiencing somewhere in your life.

pretending: Are you trying to be something you're not? Are you bluffing or lying to yourself? What are you trying to cover up? Is there something that you need to bring out in the open? See *counterfeit money.*

pretty: If you're pretty in the dream or the focus is on someone pretty, perhaps you need to acknowledge your own beauty. Alternatively, it could be about your desire to be pretty.

prideful: Perhaps you need to stand up for yourself when you are challenged. Are you being too arrogant?

Have you been emotionally hurt in some way?

priest: This can also include a minister, pastor, rabbi, reverend, imam, guru, pope, Rinpoche, cardinal, Lama, Zen master, and others. These religious leaders could represent the spiritual side of yourself. They can also represent a nonsexual relationship or the keeper or interpreter of the Word of God.

He or she is an image of the spiritual teacher and possibly a guide into enlightenment or into your heart.

This image can also have some very strong symbolic meanings, depending on your experiences with priests.

prince: Do you desire to be important or admired for something? Are you looking for a good man to start a relationship?

Are you hoping to be acknowledged for some honor or for some activity?

princess: Are you behaving like a spoiled brat? Are you acting like you're entitled to something, or do you behave in some manner?

Are you being too demanding? Do you have great potential but have a lot more growing to do? Note that both prince and princess can be romance symbols.

principal: This can be an authority or power figure. It may also reflect your leadership skills if you're the principal in the dream.

If you're waiting in the principal's office, perhaps you feel some guilt, or maybe you have low self-esteem.

printer: Perhaps you're trying to get a thought or idea across. If it's broken, this could reflect your frustration or failure to express your ideas adequately. If the ink runs dry, you might be having difficulty expressing something or making your point of view heard.

prism: This might represent different aspects of a situation or problem or the need to see various points of view or take a different approach to something.

It could also refer to your spiritual aspect and suggest that you need to be in tune with this.

Insight: Prisms break up white light (sunlight) into the visual spectrum of red to violet. The rainbow in a dream can indicate better things to come, beauty amongst hardship, or a metaphor for chasing the rainbow (going after the unattainable).

prison: This suggests forced limitations or punishment. It could also mean being controlled by another person. It can also refer to a feeling of claustrophobia (i.e., being shut in).

Is there some part of your personality or your life that you feel trapped in and can't let go of?

prisoner: Are you feeling restricted and confined, or have you lost your sense of freedom in some way? Is there some part of you that isn't getting expressed?

Are you feeling shame or guilt, and consequently, are you punishing yourself? Do you need to stop punishing yourself?

prison guard: Prison guards can be symbolic of something holding you back and restricting your growth and development. Your behaviors may be preventing you from having certain experiences in your life. See also *guard*.

probation: Are you putting something off that you should be doing? Do you need to clean up some past mistakes? Do you feel as though you are on trial or that your integrity or worth is being questioned?

proclamation: This could be reflected in standing on a soapbox or posting something on a fence, wall, or pole. This could be referring to something that you want to or need to say.

It could also be about making a moral or political stand and a way of maintaining your integrity.

professor: See *teacher*.

programming: Are you doing everything by rote? Do you feel as though you don't have any personal control over the direction your life is taking? If you are a programmer, are you controlling or manipulating the outcome of something or the direction it's going in? Should you?

projection: Do you need to make your voice heard? Do you need to project yourself into someone else's world (i.e., step into his or her shoes)?

Insight: Every judgment and belief we see and hear is a projection of our egos and our unexplored unconscious minds.

Dreams are projections from the unconscious psyche and a statement about what is going on in there, especially in regard to what is happening around us.

Given that most of what we perceive going on around us is a projection (i.e., a personal construct of what is going on inside us), it might behoove us to look at who is really responsible for what we experience.

Projection of the unacknowledged shadow in society shows up as war, sexism, racism, bigotry, and destruction of the environment.

prom: If you're at a prom, perhaps this symbolizes the end to something and the beginning of something else. It can also reflect memories of a past prom event or your actual upcoming event.

promise: This could be about your waking life commitments and your integrity in terms of doing what you say you will do.

promoted: This could be about positive self-confidence and self-esteem.

propeller: This is a driving force. What's driving/motivating you? Do you need motivation?

prophecy: See *premonition* and/or *divination*.

prophet: This image could be about the need for guidance or some wisdom. This could also reflect your concerns and worries for the future.

prostitute: This could be about promiscuity and your own sexual value. Have you sold out your values? See also *whore*.

protection: If searching for protection, perhaps you are feeling helpless or vulnerable. Are you being too dependent on others for your well-being or progress in life? Do you need to take charge? Are you putting up a wall between you and others? What are you protecting?

See *Psalm 23*.

pruning: This could be about getting rid of old habits in order to grow. It could also be about getting rid of relationships and beliefs that no longer serve you and may negatively affect your growth.

Psalm 23: This psalm begins as follows:

> The Lord is my shepherd; I shall not want.
> He makes me to lie down in green pastures;
> He leads me beside the still waters.
> He restores my soul;
> He leads me in the paths of righteousness
> For His name's sake.
> Yea, though I walk through the valley of the shadow of death,
> I will fear no evil;
> For You are with me.

If you are reciting Psalm 23 in your dream, it may be acting as a protection poem with a "trust in God" theme.

In your dream it may suggest that you let go of some fear or worry. The idea being that you may need to surrender the part of yourself that's in the way of you achieving some goal.

This kind of image in a dream can also represent a need for healing and/or spiritual nourishment.

King David, who allegedly wrote this poem, likened it to being cared for and feeling protected. This may be lacking somewhere in your life. See also *protection*.

psyche: This refers to your soul, spirit, conscious and unconscious mind, and your whole personality with nothing left out, nothing rejected. It represents the totality of the human mind, the whole of your being.

Jung drew a distinction between psyche and soul in that he saw soul as a functional complex or partial personality and therefore not of the psyche.

In cognitive psychology the word *mind* is used in preference to *psyche*.

Psychology is the study of psyche.

This psyche can be divided into two parts—the conscious and unconscious. So too, the unconscious will compensate for conscious attitude. (When things become too one-sided, the unconscious brings up the opposite so as to encourage balance.) You can see this happening in dreams and especially in nightmares. Some psychologists believe that if this compensating material is ignored for too long, it can manifest itself in disease.

Unconscious material of the psyche can also project itself onto another person. For example, we often have emotional or negative responses to people we don't know for no real reason (unless we make one up to satisfy the lack of reason). These responses are often manifestations of these projections. We often project our own shadow material that we haven't dealt with (stuff we don't like or want in ourselves) onto others. This is how we demonize our enemies, whether imagined or real (see *projection* and *shadow*).

In depth psychology (see *depth psychology*), psyche refers to the forces in humans that influence our thoughts, behaviors, and personalities. According to the Freudian discipline, the psyche is composed of three parts—ego (the I), superego (the upper I) and id (the it).

psychic: This could refer to your need to expand your awareness or point of view or to see beyond the everyday. It may be about looking for the hidden meaning of some event or person's words.

psychoid: This is something that directs the behavior of an individual. This might include archetypal material from the collective unconscious.

psychokinesis: This is where you are able to make objects move with the power of your mind. In a dream, it might suggest that you are being manipulative and/or being too controlling.

Are you being too controlling? Or this could be about being ready to take control of the events in your life.

psychopath: This can be portrayed by any number of crazed image (e.g., Freddy Krueger or Hannibal Lecter).

The dream image may represent a loss of control or suggest that you are disconnected from your core self or from other people in general. It can symbolize that you're being deceived and/or manipulated.

It can also represent a loss of ego control (i.e., that your boundaries or someone's boundaries have become porous or nonexistent).

It can symbolize remorselessness and a total lack of compassion.

psychopomp: These are guides for the soul heading into the afterlife. They can come in the form of dogs, horses, birds, angels, or spirits. They can also take the form of elves or fairies. In many cultures the shaman would perform the duties of the psychopomp. Sometimes this individual would guide souls into the world as well.

Jung suggested that these images were mediators between the unconscious and conscious realms. See also *Cupid, Eros and Logos*, or *sex*.

pub: This place could reflect your social interactions or your need to relax a little more.

public speaking: This could be about your fears of getting up in front of others. It could also mean that you need to express yourself more. Are you feeling exposed and vulnerable?

If no one's listening, perhaps you're feeling ignored. If someone is making a speech, listen carefully. Is he or she talking about you?

If it is a political speech, perhaps it reflects your biases about political speeches or politicians in general.

puddle: This sometimes represents small but messy emotions.

pumpkin: A pumpkin may involve female sexuality. Cinderella's pumpkin could suggest that time is running out.

It is also possible that the pumpkin represents openness or receptivity to new ideas.

punching: This could represent hidden anger or rage. If you are being punched, it could be about being threatened or someone attacking your self-esteem. If

you are punched in the stomach, it could be about some emotional attack. See also *fighting*.

punk: This could be about rebellion. Are you being foolish or behaving inappropriately? Are you feeling inexperienced or just a beginner with something?

If you are being *punked*, perhaps you are feeling betrayed, humiliated, or ripped off.

puppet: This possibly represents the fear of being controlled, manipulated, or powerless. It can represent a lack of free choice. Are you not seeing reality for what it is. Most people are puppets to their own egos.

Perhaps you need to look deeper to find your real self. If you are the puppeteer, then perhaps you desire to have power or control over someone else. See also *possessed*.

purchase: This is symbolic of choosing, getting a better grip, or understanding.

You are trying to get something. It may also reflect buying or accepting and believing in something.

purse, wallet, or handbag: This may symbolize something valued or closely held secrets or desires. It also could represent your identity and sense of self.

The handbag could also be about your identity and/or sense of power and even secrets that you may be hiding.

Losing it means losing personal power, control, and your identity, leaving you confused about your place in your life. Its loss can also represent a feeling of vulnerability and an ability to self-support. It may reflect a loss of independence.

If you find the lost contents, it could be a metaphor that what's inside you is more important than your exterior appearance.

See also *identification* or *id*.

pushing: This can be likened to exerting your will or someone else's will being forced on to you. This could also represent *coercion*.

If pushing back against someone or something, perhaps you are resisting or countering some situation, or maybe you need to do so.

If you're pushing back against a person, what does he or she represent that you may be holding at bay or resisting? For example, a female holding back a male might be about resisting her masculine aspect.

puzzle: You may be trying to work something out or trying to put the pieces together to get the whole picture. Or something may have confused you. Perhaps you don't have all the facts you need to make a decision or judgment.

A crossword puzzle may be about some mental challenge or finding the right words for some situation. A sudoku might reflect a complex problem or be about the numbers themselves (see *numbers*), or if the numbers are symbols, that might suggest some financial numbers aren't lining up. A word jumble might be about being confused.

pyramid: This could be about longevity or something ancient or old. It may also reflect stability or even mystery. It can also be a metaphor for perseverance and sustainability.

python: See *snake* or *boa constrictor*.

quack: Perhaps you need to be cautious about people who present themselves as things they're not or others who are less competent or knowledgeable than they make themselves out to be. Are you pretending to be something you're not?

quagmire: Are you stuck and unable to move on or unable to achieve some goal?

qualifiers: When there are a number of qualifiers in your dream (or in your waking life for that matter), you may be lying to yourself. Such qualifiers include the following: "I'm not a racist, but …" "Not to be offensive …" "Though I don't feel the need to apologize …" "Not to change the subject, but …" "I don't mean to interrupt, but …"

What do you not want to take responsibility for? For what way of being are you trying to excuse yourself?

quarrel: This may be a conflict within yourself or perhaps with something outside yourself (see *fight* and *argue*).

quarry: This could be an emotional hole or negative situation you've dug or are digging yourself into. It could also be symbolic of a hole in your life.

Because there are often riches to be found in the underground, this may be a statement about your subconscious and the wealth to be found there. Alternatively, it could represent something you're searching for, trying to find, or chasing after.

quarter: This might be symbolic of not being whole (see also the *number four*, *quaternity*, and *squaring the circle*).

quaternity: This is the idea posed by Jung that the adding of a fourth to an established three transforms something by adding depth and wholeness. This might be said of the Christian Trinity. Adding the feminine to the Father, Son, and Holy Ghost of the Holy Trinity makes God more whole.

When *four* shows up in a dream in some fashion, it may very well be encouraging you to include what you have rejected so that you may continue to grow.

See also *squaring the circle*.

quartet: You may be looking for support and harmony. See also *four* in *numbers* or *quaternity*.

queen: This can represent one's mother. Her persona as perceived by you will affect the meaning of this image. It can also represent any woman who might reflect aspects of one's mother. See *goddess* and *mother* in *archetypes* section.

Insight: In *Alice through the Looking Glass* by Lewis Carroll, the White Queen may represent the wisdom of the inner mother who encourages Alice to challenge her beliefs and go beyond what she thinks is impossible.

On the other hand, the Red Queen seems to reflect her irrational side and chaotic aspect.

The White Queen seems to rule through finesse while the Red Queen rules through force and intimidation.

Both are probably unexplored aspects of Alice herself.

quest: Are you searching for something? Is there a part of me that has the answer? It could also be about adventure. See also the *archetypes* section and *cup*.

queue: This is possibly about boundaries, limits, and rules. Do you need to be more attentive to some situation? Do you need to be more patient? Do you need to learn to defer gratification? Wait your turn.

query or question: Someone questioning you might relate to some information you should be sharing. It could also be a critique on some belief or point of view.

It can also represent curiosity or the questioning of something believed or some alleged truth. If an answer is in the dream, listen carefully.

It can be about you questioning yourself about some decision. Are you losing confidence in something, or do you doubt yourself?

quicksand: This can represent insecurity, the loss of personal control, being mired in something, and instability. Perhaps you've misjudged the solid ground you thought you were on. It could also reflect your quick temper.

quiet: Silence in the dream may suggest that you need to stop and reflect (i.e., be a little introspective) or that you need some quiet time. Do you need to be quiet about something?

quilt: This could be about warmth and protection. Perhaps you need to stitch together various elements in order to create something whole, complete a project, or work on a relationship.

quintuplets: Five of anything can represent the five senses. See *number five*.

quiver: Are you nervous about something? Perhaps you need to focus on your goals. Consider the phrase "all a quiver," meaning excited.

quota: If you're trying to meet a quota, are you feeling a little overwhelmed and stressed? Perhaps you're worried about meeting someone's expectations or your own expectations.

quote: If you're quoted a price, it may represent the value being placed on something. If it's a quote from what someone else has said, are you trying to sound knowledgeable or support your own statements? Are you repeating someone else's ideas and passing them off as your own?

Are you being too exacting in your communication?

If it's a quotation mark or you're using your fingers to imply quotation marks, are you saying something that might not be true or stating an example that may or may not reflect the whole truth of something? It can also be a symbol for being sarcastic.

Quran: This represents the Islamic faith and laws to live by. It suggests a need to pay greater attention to your spiritual side.

See also *Bible*.

R

rabbit: See *animal terms.*

rabbit hole: Chasing a rabbit down a hole could reflect your obsessions or your poor impulse control.

It can be symbolic of regression or turning inward in order to escape problems. If you go too far, it can lead to depression and an inability to escape.

Down the rabbit hole is a commonly used phrase for entering into something new and strange—either something positive and life-affirming or negative and sinister, such as becoming addicted to a substance.

It can also be about walking into something new without any knowledge of how it will turn out. It can also be about embracing any radically new idea, especially those where there aren't many (or any) people who are willing to go along with you.

Insight: The rabbit hole that one enters may also represent regression—a turning inward sometimes to escape from problems or boredom. You could also want to return to a simpler and more innocent time. Wasn't this what Alice was doing?

The hole can also be a pit and represent the void, a place of emptiness where feelings of being trapped prevail. In facing the void, when falling into it, we fall into the nothing, but we have the potential for everything and the transformation of our imagined limits. Within lies the power for change and liberation. Wasn't this so for Alice?

Going down the rabbit hole is also a euphemism for becoming enlightened with the potential for being liberated from oneself and imposed limits. After all, isn't this what happened to Alice when she went down the hole? It can also refer to letting go of the old ways, recreating your life, and starting anew.

Strangely enough, going down the rabbit hole can be another word for dying (i.e., where one transitions from one state of being to be reborn into another). See also *corridor, death, hallway, hole,* and *tunnel.*

In a dream, going down or into any hole can represent the start of a change—a transformation. Where does it lead? It leads into the underground—the hidden side of the self. This is where the shadow lies, and you can explore the depths of your experience. Here sexual desires and unexpressed potentials lie.

The white rabbit in this story was serving as the archetypal trickster that lured Alice into the hole that lead to the unconscious so that she could explore her naughty side (i.e., her negative or shadow side). It was also an opportunity for her to get in touch with her power.

A third level of awareness was also offered to Alice in her dream. She was able to compensate for her lack of power in her waking world because of her age and the pecking order among her siblings.

In wonderland, she was introduced to many aspects of her nature and was able to confront and perhaps accept them. For Alice, this dream was part of her individuation process, the process toward becoming a fully functional person.

race: This is symbolic of rivalry, competition, or being in a hurry. Consider your prejudices. If you are racing, perhaps you need to slow down.

radar: This could symbolize your intuition. It can represent awareness, as in being on someone's radar.

radio: What ideas are you picking up from other people? What am I ready to say or hear?

radioactive: Are there some emotions that you've been stuffing down inside yourself and not dealing with? Are these about to escape and have negative influences somewhere in your life?

railroad: This is possibly a statement about your life direction. Is it on track? It could also refer to an accepted direction for your life. If you have missed the train, you may be feeling left out of something.

railroad crossing: Has something prevented your forward movement? If you're seeing the crossing sign, it may mean that you need to stop doing something, or it might represent the symbol X (see *X*).

rain: This could symbolize a release of emotion or threat, as in raining on one's parade. Rain can also be a metaphor for tears or a much-needed cleansing (see *water*).

The tears can suggest the need to cry, or they might be something you need to do but that isn't appropriate in your present circumstances. How heavy the rain is will also give information about the intensity of emotion involved.

Watching it through a window might suggest spiritual insights entering your awareness. Rain is also a symbol of renewal and the quenching of some spiritual or psychological thirst (see *thirst*).

Rain can also be symbolic of a cleansing or a washing away of something negative (see *shower*).

rainbow: See *color* words.

random: When something happens randomly in a dream, this may refer to something unplanned, fortuitous, irregular, or odd happening in your life.

rape: This could signal a possible invasion, a violation of the self, or being demeaned in some way. Are you being taken advantage of?

It can also signify helplessness, vulnerability, and the loss of personal power in some situation.

You may have resentful feelings toward the opposite sex. There may be a fear of you or someone close to you being vulnerable to others.

rapid eye movement (REM) sleep: For approximately every ninety minutes during our sleep, we experience what is called REM sleep.

REM is the last stage of sleep where the EEG wave pattern is similar to the waking brain with some of the characteristics of both the alpha and beta states, which are earlier states of sleeping.

As a point of interest, the alpha state is also that same state that people find themselves in when they are meditating, when they're in the zone, or when they're daydreaming.

REM is that time during sleep when we dream and when our eyes move rapidly under their lids as though tracking what they see, though that part of the theory has not been shown to be true.

However, having said that, there are those theories that continue to suggest an eye-brain correlation during REM sleep is due to the discontinuous nature of most dreams and the brain looking around the dream scene and trying to make sense of these discontinuities. We have these same discontinuities when we're awake, only the brain smooths them all out and projects what looks like a linear presentation.

During REM, a normal person's musculoskeletal system (which is your body movement system) is suppressed or shut down. Why? Well, we don't have solid answers for this, but we do have research that points to the reasons.

Some evidence suggests that one of the reasons for dreaming includes both memory consolidation and memory erasure. In the erasure mode, any memory that is not reinforced becomes weakened. Memories with physical reactions are strengthened through repeated physicality. Thus, those memories brought up during sleep would be less likely to be retained if there were no physical reinforcement. This feedback loop is shut down during REM.

So too, when we were all huddled together against the cold in our dark and lonely caves, we wouldn't reenact the day's physicality in our dreams to the annoyance of our neighbors. If that were the case, we'd be punching and strangling them, thinking that we were being attacked by some saber-toothed tiger.

Of course, this theory only holds up for unwanted memories, and some other activity is then responsible for the retention of those memories that are needed for survival.

But don't dismiss the erasure concept too quickly because if our brains could not erase the unwanted (which is enormous when compared to the wanted), we would need bigger brains to hold it all. This is in fact what we see in animals that have huge brain masses compared to their body masses and that experience no REM sleep.

Studies have shown that when someone is deprived of REM sleep for too long, the brain goes almost instantly into REM and resists any further attempt to prevent it. So REM seems to be an adaptation for those creatures with higher-order neural network systems such as humans.

It also gives us many hours of entertainment as we project meaning onto our sleep visions, which may or may not have any inherent meaning. But isn't this pretty much like the rest of our lives where we are continuously projecting meaning onto every object, person, or event?

Basically, both REM and non-REM have what appear to be important, perhaps even vital, functions to our survival and learning. It turns out that non-REM is our internal trainer. It mirrors past experience in a time-compressed manner. It literally helps you in the present to relate to the future.

The REM dream, however, expands time and takes you into the future in order to practice and test various scenarios. This may explain why some dreams seem to be about what's happened during your waking life the day before, while others seem more distant or unrelated to events in our waking life events, perhaps more internal in nature.

It seems to me that the dream interpretation of meaning projection is a pretty nonconfrontational way of looking at what's going on inside of you. And who knows? Higher-level self-awareness may just be the next neural adaptation the evolving human is developing.[*]

rat: See *animal terms.*

reaching out: Do you need help? Do you need to reach out to others? Are you being too reclusive?

Perhaps you need to help someone in need.

reading: This can mean that you're exploring alternate realities or suggest that you want to escape. It could also suggest the need for entertainment or the need to learn.

reality: Thinking that you know something about what is real can be very limiting to living what is real.

rearview mirror: Are you looking at or living in the past? If the mirror is oversized, perhaps you are spending too much time looking at your past. Are you fixating on

some past event or grievance? Are you stuck in some old decision or prejudice?

If you're in a car and trying to drive it by holding on to the rearview mirror, perhaps you're letting the past drive what you do in the present.

rebooting: See *reset button.*

recipe: This is a formulaic pattern without the need to be creative. Note that certain recipes have nostalgic or emotional significance. A recipe is also a form of chemistry and can connect people.

reconciliation: This could be about reuniting or reconnecting parts of the self. See the *archetypes* section.

recurrent dreams: Recurrent dreams, which can continue for weeks, months, or even years, may be treated as any other dream. One may look for parallels between the dream and the thoughts, feelings, behavior, and motives of the dreamer. Understanding the meaning of the recurrent dream sometimes can help the dreamer resolve an issue that he or she has been struggling with for years.

After the issue has been resolved, the dream frequently disappears.

In order to deal with a recurring dream, you have to be ready to accept a change in your behavior or circumstances. There

---

[*] Excerpt from Cole, R. J., *Positive and Negative Dreams … REM and non-REM,* http://thebookofdreamsblog.wordpress.com.

will no doubt be a lot of emotional baggage attached to the behavior or situation that will cause uncomfortable disturbances that many people would shy away from.

But confronting the dream images is necessary in order to deal with whatever it is that is causing them and trying to get your attention through the dream.

Write down each and every dream and look for small changes in details and figure out how the dream and those changes may relate to what's going on in your waking life.

Remember these dreams are trying to teach you something about yourself, and regardless of their content, they come to you in the interest of your health and well-being.

red: See *colors*.

redhead: This could represent a tempestuous and dramatic aspect of your personality.

red riding hood: Are you feeling vulnerable, manipulated, or overwhelmed? Does your life feel like a fairy tale?

In a man's dream, she could represent his anima (see the *archetypes* section). In a woman's dream, it could represent certain aspects of herself consistent with the character in the story.

The story also shows a wolf that could represent the male desire for what seems innocent (or the female). It could also represent the union (or balance) of opposites of the masculine and feminine traits (see the *archetypes* section).

redwood tree: This may be about longevity. It can also be about stateliness, strength, and passion. See also *tree*.

reflection: Should you take time to reflect on something (i.e., to look before you leap)? This could also have a *mirror* meaning.

Insight: One can also be further bewitched by what is reflected in a mirror. Much like Narcissus, who fell in love with his own reflection in a pool, each of us can become captivated by our own ego reflections and lose sight of our deeper selves. Or because a pool of water is like a pool of one's emotions, it might be like looking into your unconscious to see who you are.

Mythology is replete with those who are enchanted by their own reflections and thus cut off from their deeper meaning (e.g., a mythical Greek nymph who was in love with the sound of her own voice or Pygmalion, the sculptor, who fell in love with his own creation).

Alice traveling through the looking glass was an adventure into a little girl's behavior and fantasy, a portal into her imagination.

In short, it was a snapshot or a reflection of her inner life—her fears, confusion, youthful arrogance, and jealousies. Alice desired to see something other than what she had. She was all about engaging boredom and curiosity, and this was reflected in her adventures beyond the mirror.

In the beginning of this book, there was a quote by Carl Gustav Jung, "Who looks outside, dreams. Who looks inside, awakens." This lends credibility to the idea that we can use what we see in others as a means of contributing to our understanding of ourselves. For example, take some time today to notice the faces of others you meet and see if they reflect an image of your own thoughts.

If you or someone else is standing before a mirror and you do not see a reflection, you may have lost your sense of identity. Have you changed yourself so as to please others and now don't know who are?

regret: You may be disappointed in something, someone, or yourself. If you're disappointed in yourself, it could involve negative feelings about yourself. Perhaps you're not expressing or acknowledging these feelings adequately.

rehabilitate: Are you trying to fix something, or do you need to recover from some hurt? You may be ready to begin anew.

rehearsing: Are you getting ready for some new endeavor or some new stage of life? Do you need to prepare yourself for something? Are you having trouble being spontaneous?

reincarnating: Are you dreaming of being reincarnated as someone else? This might suggest that you are unsatisfied with yourself. Perhaps you're not happy with yourself and therefore not being yourself. Are you making major changes in your life? Should you? See also *past life*.

reins: Are you being reined in, restricted, or limited in some way? Are you wanting or losing control of something?

rejection: Perhaps there's something in or some aspect of your life that you want to get rid of. If someone is rejecting you, it could reflect a loss or lack of self-worth.

Are you feeling left out, alienated, and separate from those around you?

Rejection can look like distancing yourself from people or others distancing themselves from you. Sometimes the distancing or rejection can symbolize the rejection of an emotion.

See also *not good enough*.

relationships: Dream relationships can mirror waking world relationships. What you're doing in the dream may reflect what you're doing or need to do in the waking world.

relatives: Family members in a dream can represent issues and feelings associated with them. They all represent some aspect of yourself (see *brother, daughter, father, grandparents, husband, mother, sister, son,* and *wife*).

religion: Dreaming of religion may reflect your faithfulness or an aspect of your spirituality.

If the religion is different than your own, perhaps there is some aspect of that religion that you need to integrate into your own life. Perhaps you need to be more accepting or tolerant of another's religion.

Are you being religious or passionate about something?

Perhaps you are treating something religiously and not deviating from some ritualistic behavior.

See also *Buddha, Christ, Christian, church, Judaism,* and *Muslim*.

remarrying: To remarry someone might signify acceptance of some change in yourself. This may also be symbolic of healing an injury or rift.

remembering dreams: Though you can prime the pump by having a journal by your side and writing whatever you recall when you awake even if it's just a fragment or a word, there is evidence that some people possess high recall of their dreams more often.

In the so-called recallers, two brain areas were more active during rapid eye movement (REM) sleep, which is when our most vivid and memorable dreams occur. These areas were the temporoparietal junction (where the temporal and parietal lobes meet) and the medial prefrontal cortex in the frontal lobes.

This supports the idea that if you wake during the REM phase of sleep, you tend to recall your dreams better. There are some electronic devices that will wake a sleeper after about the first ninety minutes of sleep when REM typically starts. This could help dreamers recall their dreams better.

remodeling: This could refer to the restructuring the house of the self.

remote viewing: This is seeking visual impressions from a distant and unseen target. It is considered extrasensory perception (ESP) and one of the psychic phenomena. Though there have been many experiments conducted to prove or disprove its existence, no definitive evidence has been produced.

renovate: If something is being renovated, this might indicate that something in your life needs some work or needs to be upgraded or repaired.

renunciation: If something is offered and then turned down, there may be something in your life or personality that you need to turn down (e.g., pride, greed, or emotional outbursts).

repetitive action: Some action that you repeat sequentially over and over might symbolize something that you are obsessing over. It could also reflect an addictive behavior.

rescue: To be rescued, to rescue, or to save someone could be about needing or giving counseling or being saved or protected from something.

There may be some part of yourself that you have been ignoring or that needs saving from some negative circumstances. It may also be symbolic of a cry for help. Do you need to ask for help/assistance?

Are you trying to rescue some part of yourself or your life?

reservoir: This could possibly mean repressed emotions or pent-up feelings. If its nearly empty or empty, then you may

have used up most of or all your energy reserves.

reset button: Are you stuck in some situation, or is your life not working? Do you want to start over? This image could also be about getting a second chance or at least trying to make something happen one more time.

resignation: To resign a position might mean there are major changes happening or looming. Perhaps you are giving up on something, someone, or yourself. Do you need to let go of something in your life?

respect: If there are people in the dream for whom you have little or no respect in your waking life or people with whom you don't really get along, it could also be a reflection of the lack of respect that you may be giving yourself.

This self-critique or lack of respect for yourself may be what leads you into some of the messes and questionable choices that plague your well-being.

If there is someone in the dream for which you have a great deal of respect in your waking life, perhaps this person represents something that you are lacking in your waking life and/or want to gain and integrate into yourself.

restaurant: This may represent a search for emotional or sexual satisfaction or nourishment.

It may also represent the sociable side of your personality. What you're ordering might help with the interpretation. The actual restaurant or type of restaurant might also help with the interpretation. See also *café, cafeteria,* or *food.*

Restaurants and eateries can be about decisions or choices you have to make, and sometimes these are overwhelming. They can also represent the need for emotional nourishment.

If an ordered meal never arrives, it could be about disappointment or a lack of support, especially emotional support.

restraint: If you're being held down, are you holding yourself back? Is someone or something making you feel helpless?

résumé: Do you need to reevaluate your abilities and/or your performance to date?

resurrection: Do you need to revisit some part of your life or some part of yourself that you thought was buried and gone?

Do you need to start over or begin anew with something or someone?

See also *reset button.*

This represents the return or reanimation of deceased people, trees, or animals. It can represent new life brought to old ways of being or old ideas as well as novel solutions to old problems. See also *zombie.*

It can also be about the awakening of your spiritual nature or an enlightening experience (see the *archetypes* section under *rebirth/resurrection*).

Insight: In nearly every philosophy or religion, some sort of resurrection follows death. Life itself appears to be in continuous birth, death, and renewal. All cultures have various rituals to celebrate the connection between life and death, and all self-development programs require you let go of your way of being in order to manifest another.

reunion: If you're at a reunion, perhaps you need to revisit or acknowledge something from your past, whether good or bad.

revenge: Maybe you are experiencing some emotional imbalance or harboring some repressed emotions. You may wish to punish someone or even yourself.

Insight: Often this is related to anger. Revenge (vengeance, retribution, retaliation, and/or reprisal) as a means of reducing one's anger is counterproductive in that revenge begets revenge. One need only look at the ethnic battles going on in virtually every country in the world to see the truth of this.

The bottom line is that revenge does not, will not, and cannot restore equity or balance to any relationship. Every attempt to use it only escalates a negative cycle. When punishment is used to bring fairness into the equation, neither the punished or the punisher is ever able to let go and truly move on.

revolution: Perhaps you want to revolt against something or overthrow or replace some idea. Are you avoiding some kind of domination? Are you being too domineering?

Do you need to make major changes in yourself or your life happen?

Perhaps you are experiencing some inner and/or outer emotional turmoil.

rice: Rice can be about comfort food or something nourishing to the soul. Cooking it could be about the way one transforms the unpalatable to the palatable.

Food is often a statement about the need to nourish or be nourished (emotionally, spiritually, or physically).

It's also rather blah and uninteresting, and it could refer to some part of your life or yourself that reflects this.

rich: To be rich in a dream may refer to success and self-confidence.

Rich people around you may suggest that you may need to watch your spending. Given that money can be a metaphor for love, it may suggest that you need to watch the love that you're giving out. Is it not a good investment?

Riches might also refer to someone named Rich or Richard.

rickety: If you are or something is feeling rickety, perhaps you are feeling unsteady or unsure about something. Are you on shaky ground with someone or something? A group or idea can be rickety if it is unstable or unsound.

riddle: A riddle in a dream could be about a test of your patience or an attempt to solve some mystery, tricky question, or something that is perplexing you. Because riddles are also cryptic in nature, you may be too cryptic or vague about your intentions.

Sometimes people who seem to be speaking in riddles are those who are trying to cover up that they don't have the answer to something that they think they should have the answer to, not unlike a politician or bureaucrat.

If a creature is accosting you with a riddle, what kind of creature is it? The answer could give a hint about the aspect of yourself you may not understand.

Insight: Riddle challenges are ancient, coming to us from the Bible and the epic poems of the pre-Christian Sumerians. Some biblical scholars have said that Jesus spoke in riddles when he spoke in parables.

One of the oldest stories involving a riddle and a protecting creature comes to us from ancient Greece in the form of the Sphinx sent by Hera (or possibly Ares) to create anguish for Thebes.

Just outside the city, this creature, which was part lion and part female human, sat and challenged all who approached the gateway to the city with what is arguably the most well-known riddle. When people failed to answer, she would pounce upon them and eat them.

"What goes on four legs in the morning, on two in the afternoon, and on three in the evening?"

Give up? Prepare to be eaten! Here's a hint, the day the Sphinx refers to here is metaphorical.

Here's the answer: A baby crawls on all fours at first but then walks upright on two legs until the person becomes old and feeble, at which point this individual requires a cane (three).

Here's another that came to me shortly after I awoke the other morning: "It can be misplaced but never lost, owned but never held onto. You can't earn it or spend it. It can be buried but never destroyed. It is real but does not exist because it is intangible. It is not a thing but is the essence of all things."

It's the *soul*.

right (as in a direction or side): This may refer to the dominant hand or a statement about something being right or wrong. It is also considered by some to be representative of our conscious mind and rational thought.

Moving from right to left could be something moving from being dominant to less dominant or indicate that something or someone is losing dominance or that there is a change in the dominant narrative of your life.

Right to left could also be symbolic of something conscious becoming unconscious. This could be an attempt to suppress some feeling or memory. It's also symbolic of a conservative.

righteous: Acting in a self-righteous way might be about thinking of yourself as always right. It may be symbolic of being better than, and it had a ring of arrogance too. You may also be compensating for being unethical, vicious, or unscrupulous in some way.

ring: This can represent a wholeness, the cycle of something, a completion, a pledge, or a commitment. It can also represent your core or essential self.

If in the dream you have lost a ring or had it taken from you, perhaps there is something in you that has disappeared or been taken away.

A wedding ring can reflect the condition of a relationship. An heirloom ring can be about family influences on you.

Note that this definition was the foundational theme of the *Lord of the Rings Trilogy*.

One ring to rule them all, One ring to find them. One Ring to bring them all and in the darkness bind them.

—J. R. R. Tolkien (*The Lord of the Rings*)

If the ring is around a neck, consider also the phrase "wring your neck," meaning to kill off something within you.

riot: This might mean a loss of individuality. It might also refer to a loss of personal control or chaos.

river: This can reflect the feelings that flow through you. A river might represent

the events of your life flowing by. Are there any rapids, or is it smooth and tranquil?

If you're crossing a river, you may be making great changes in your life. If you're swimming across, you may feel much emotion as you make the transition (see *drowning*). Do you need to make some changes in your life?

If you're resisting the flow and trying to swim against the current, are you going against your nature or the nature of the environment around you?

Are you exerting effort and struggling where effortlessness is called for?

Going against the current could also be symbolic of going against your own feelings or the prevailing attitudes of others.

Are you letting the outside circumstances of your life determine what you do in it or get in the way of achieving your goals?

Just floating down the river and letting it take you wherever it flows can be about letting go and not resisting. However, in another context, it might suggest that you are not taking control or being responsible for the goals in your life.

Do you just need to let go of your fear of not being accepted and make the changes you seek?

A raging river can reflect an out-of-control aspect to your life. Contaminated rivers can be about some illness, whether you currently recognize it or not.

To swim in one can be about cleansing or washing away some dirtiness or bad behavior.

road: This may represent your life's journey (see *path*). What's happening on this road? Is the road smooth the whole way?

robbery: See *stealing*.

robot: This might suggest automatic responses, armor against hurt, and apathy (see *zombie*).

rock: This suggests stability or being rigid or immovable. To see a rock on your or someone else's head might symbolize that you're being crazy or foolish about some idea (see also *stone*).

rocket: This could be symbolic of your need to break free of restrictions or self-imposed limits.

rock star: See *celebrity* or *famous person*.

Rogers, Carl: He is a psychologist famous for *On Becoming a Person* (Houghton Mifflin, 1961), which outlines the process humans go through in defining themselves through the interactions with their environments and other humans. His theory suggests that each of us develops an internal conceptual pattern or gestalt that literally defines the reality experienced and thus the resulting behaviors toward that reality.

Rogers also believed that we each grow toward a more fully functioning human by being more open to experience versus being defensive and suppressive of experiences that we find troubling.

He suggested that we grow psychologically and emotionally when we live in the moment, trust our own intuitive judgment, allow for greater freedom of choice, and not restrict ourselves to certain beliefs or dogmas.

We also become more fully functioning when we are less conforming and therefore more creative, and as a result, we act more trustworthy and constructively. We then balance personal needs with the needs of others or with those of the environment.

rogue: See *clown*, *fool*, or *jester*. Also see *trickster* in the *archetypes* section.

roller coaster: Suggesting the ups and downs of life.

room: See *house*.

rooster: Roosters can be about pride and arrogance or suggest that you or someone else is showing off too much.

roots: They can represent the entrance to your core self. As they grow down into the earth, perhaps it is a metaphor for looking for your *truth*.

They can also represent your family values and beliefs, as well as family bonds.

Are the roots searching for water that might suggest the need for emotional nurturing? Are you searching for something in your past?

If you're pulling something up from its roots, are you ready to move on with something or go somewhere else?

Consider also the word *grassroots*, referring to the work necessary at the beginning level, or it might symbolize ordinary people as opposed to the leadership or the elite.

rope: These can represent attachments and connections. People can be tied up emotionally or be at the end of their rope and not know what to do next.

It can also be about bondage or domination by someone or by some thought or behavior on your part.

If you are climbing a rope, it can represent ambition and determination. Climbing down a rope can be about loss and disappointment.

rose: This is possibly symbolic of goodness, beauty, and integration.

rough: Are you having a rough time?

roulette: Are you taking chances with something or someone, or do you need to take a chance? Consider the consequences before getting involved or going ahead with your plans.

Consider also that the image of a roulette wheel is very much like a mandala and thus may reflect the Buddhist wheel of life—the teachings that lead to enlightenment. This may also be a metaphor for attempting to understand the purpose of life (see *mandala*).

round table: This is another mandala-like image that can represent wholeness and equality much as it did for King Arthur and his knights. It can signify that you are equal to those around you. See also *mandala*.

rowan tree: One of the most sacred of trees amongst the druids in the Scottish folk tradition. It has been called the witch tree or wiccan tree. It is a tree associated with St. Brighid, patroness of the arts and healing in the Celtic tradition.

A rowan that could morph into a female human warrior was a main character in the book *The Archipelago of Dreams* by R. J. Cole (2010).

rowing: Perhaps you are trying to get somewhere. You may be gliding across your emotions. How you're rowing might give you some insight into how you're dealing with your emotions (see *boat* and/or *ocean*).

royalty: This can represent spiritual strength, power, extravagance, and/or ruthlessness. Are you dominating others? See also *king* or *queen* in the *archetypes* section.

ruby: This could be symbolic of passion and sexual desire. This can also represent emotions in general. See also *red* in *colors*.

ruby slipper: Think of those worn by Dorothy Gale in *The Wizard of Oz*. This might represent the journey one must go on to find spiritual enlightenment. They might also represent finding your way back to your center and to your inner home.

See also *shoe*.

ruins: This may be about some part of you, your life, or a goal (both physically or emotionally) that is in ruins or is falling apart.

Perhaps there's some aspect of yourself that needs to come to an end, or maybe it has come to an end. Maybe you no longer need it. To see a castle in ruins could refer to the fact that your sense of protection is in ruins (see *roof* in *house* and/or *faulty structure*).

Insight: Ruins of any kind are particularly interesting in that they often refer to ways of being that have become useless or a personality trait that is no longer useful and perhaps even damaging.

Aspects of one's life can also be in ruins. If the castle is in ruins, it could mean that your defenses are in shambles and that you're feeling vulnerable. It could also mean that you no longer need some defensive posture and that it's time to let a particular issue go.

In some dreams, one's entire hometown may lie in ruins, suggesting that the old and familiar ways of doing things are coming to an end. Ruined cities can also refer to one's social/community relationships.

If the house or building is burning or falling down, big changes may be happening, or they may be about to happen in one's life.

Structural faults in a building may represent character faults, bodily illness, or even the breakdown of a relationship.

ruler: This could be about managing others, lording over them (see also *king*), or taking the *measure* of people or things (i.e., evaluating them). You may feel you don't measure up to some expectation or standard (of yourself or others).

rules: If you're breaking them, this may reflect your frustrations. Perhaps you need to stand up for yourself. Some people can become rule-oriented and lose creative flexibility in their lives.

runaway bride: Running away may be a symbol for avoidance. Perhaps you are avoiding commitment.

The runaway bride image might also be about some fear associated with the act of having broken up.

See also *running away* and/or *running.*

running: This can indicate rapid movement. It could also refer to an attempt to get somewhere fast or symbolize impatience. Running away could be about avoiding something or someone, while running toward something could be about chasing after that something (e.g., trying to achieve something or become something). Of course, this can be seen both positively and negatively. To administrate something is to *run* it.

Consider also the phrase "to run with it," meaning to proceed with something.

Also think about running at the mouth or a running nose.

running away: This might be a metaphor for avoiding something (i.e., not wanting to deal with or confront something).

rusty: This could reflect deterioration, negligence, or aging. You may not feel as good as you used to. My uncle used to call his old age "the rust years" as opposed to the golden years.

S

sabotage: Something that you may be overlooking could cause a failure. If you are sabotaging something, you may be in conflict with what's right and wrong.

Old ways of thinking may be sabotaging your goal(s). Perhaps you need to change your thinking.

sacred: This can refer to the things that you value and hold close.

sacrifice: Perhaps you are punishing yourself or giving up on some part of yourself. Do you feel like a martyr? Are you letting go of something?

sad: If you feel sad or unhappy, it may suggest that you need to learn from your disappointments and try not to dwell on the negative. The dream may also be a reflection of how you are feeling in your waking life.

Dreaming that someone else is sad may be a projection of your own feelings. Perhaps you are sad about something that happened with this person.

This can also show up as a sad face (see *face* in *body*).

sadism: This may be about repressed anger. You may be punishing yourself for past deeds.

safari: This can be about confronting your instincts. It can represent freedom from confinement and/or civilization.

sage: Whether a plant or a person, this could be a metaphor for wisdom. Also see *wizard*. Mixing sage with other ingredients can have meaning as well. For example, sage with honey mixes sweetness and bitterness (bittersweet).

Sagittarius: This can be a symbol for high ideals, adventurousness, or one's outspokenness. Perhaps you're looking for some adventure or need to be more scrupulous. See also *zodiac*.

sailing: How are you dealing with and navigating life? The image of a sailboat that's gliding smoothly across the water might indicate smooth sailing.

Notice if there's wind or choppy seas. Make note if you are sinking, marooned, or in a calm sea too. This might determine how you are dealing with your emotions. See *boat* and/or *ocean/lake*.

saint: This might represent some message from the spiritual side of your nature (see also *angel*).

sale: This could symbolize an opportunity or a bargain. What is or is not in reach?

salesman or salesperson: This could symbolize someone trying to influence or con you. Perhaps there's something that you need to take into your life or some new way of being or changes that are necessary.

salmon: This fish can represent determination and strength. Perhaps you need to do what is necessary to overcome some obstacle.

salon: This may have something to do with your concern about your looks or the way others see you. Are you trying too hard to impress people or someone in particular?

saloon, bar, pub: Are you trying to overcome life's stresses?

salt: This could be about the salt of the earth. Are you dependable? Do you need to add a little spice to your life?

salt and pepper: This could be about opposite aspects of yourself or suggest that you need more seasoning (i.e., experience with something).

salute: Being saluted could be a metaphor for being recognized or honored in some

way. It could also reflect a salutation such as with the word *hello*.

You may want to be noticed by someone.

same-sex sex: This can show up (especially between women) even if neither is gay. It can reflect a natural closeness that women can feel for one another.

The desire for greater connection and closeness can also show up as same-sex sex in a man's dream. Unless the dreamers also feel attracted to the same sex in their waking lives, this kind of dream doesn't mean that they are gay. See also *sex*.

sanctuary: Perhaps this represents an escape from life's stresses. Are you looking for a little peace and quiet?

sand: Sand can be about a change of attitude because of a shift in perspective.

Sometimes standing on sand can be about a lack of sure-footedness. You may feel you don't have a leg to stand on, or you may feel that your position or point of view is precarious and not very solid. If the sand is wet, it can also be about a loss of a firm footing.

If the sand is dirty or littered, it may refer to the way you're approaching something. You may need to clean it up and approach it differently or organize it differently. Litter can also be about issues that you may need to let go of or throw away. Maybe your ideas are getting lost in the mess.

sandpaper: This could symbolize abrasiveness or something you might want to rub away. It also may be a metaphor for smoothing things over and making hard feelings or rough edges go away.

Santa Claus: To see this guy in your dream might suggest that you need to be more giving, forgiving, and/or accepting.

To dream that you or someone is dressed as Santa Claus may suggest that you need to treat others as you would like to be treated.

A picture with Santa Claus might symbolize your personal memories of the holidays.

Perhaps you're reflecting on the good and bad things about yourself.

This may also represent the archetypal image of the great father or wise old man. He might bring great wisdom along with his toys. Your own associations with Christmas might give you more insight into the dream.

sapphires: This may represent an aspect of the unconscious. It can represent someone born in September. It can be a symbol of divinity and protection.

Satan: This image might represent things in the inner and outer world that you may fear or you think are out of your control. This can represent something or someone adversarial or confrontational as in an attacker or accuser (see *devil* in the *archetypes* section).

Frequently, people invoke this image and project it onto other people in order to justify hurting them.

satori: See *mystical experience.*

Saturn: An image of the planet Saturn or its symbol could refer to its astrological significance. For example, it can be related to challenges that help us grow up (i.e., restrictions, limitations, or delayed gratifications). Saturn can be about developing or the need for discipline.

Saturn in a dream might also refer to the feeling of blueness or depression, being down and hopeless, or being cranky and fretful as with the word *saturnine.*

savage: To see a savage might represent the instinctual part of yourself or your wild side. Perhaps you're being a little harsh with someone or yourself.

saving: See *rescue.*

saw: As a tool, it can symbolize separation. It could also mean to cut something off (to stop) or out.

saxophone: To me, the saxophone is a sexy sound. Perhaps there's something deep inside you that you want and need to express. It may also reflect the desire to have a deeper connection with someone.

scam: See *shady deal.*

scapegoat: Do you feel victimized? Do you feel as if you are not taking responsibility for yourself? Are you looking for something or someone to blame? See also the *archetypes* section.

scar: This indicates a healed wound. Perhaps you need to let old wounds heal.

scarab: This is symbolic of your anxieties about death or a symbol for resurrection and eternal life. See also *scarab* in the *animals* section.

scarecrow: The image of the scarecrow might represent someone who looks scary but is using that exterior as a cover-up to protect a vulnerable interior. Do you think of yourself as being inferior? Do you feel stupid? Is your exterior not matching your interior? Has your self-presentation been tattered?

scared: To dream that you are scared might suggest that you are experiencing feelings of self-doubt, incompetence, or a lack of control in your waking life. Perhaps you are having second thoughts about a decision.

Note that fear can masquerade as anger. Consider something about which you are angry in your waking life. See *fear.*

scarred: Seeing scars or being scarred in a dream might represent painful memories that you are allowing to run your life.

Have you been emotionally hurt in some way?

If you are proud of some scar, perhaps your pride has been hurt, or your sense of self needs bolstering.

Insight: Some native tribesmen scar their bodies as a form of body transformation. This is sometimes done as a rite of passage or for religious or aesthetic reasons. It is also an initiation rite into a group.

Seeing someone with body scarification might be about wanting to stand out or belong to something. It can be symbolic of independence just as tattoos are.

scarf: Are you muffling your or someone else's voice? If the scarf is around your neck, are you separating your mind from your body by relying too much on thoughts than to the feelings sent by the body? Are you in need of some emotional warmth?

scavenger hunt: Is there something missing in your life? What are you hunting for or chasing after?

schematic: This is similar to a map (i.e., the route to some goal, a plan of action, a blueprint for how something will happen). It could also represent your idea of how something works or doesn't work. Are you being too rigid with your plan (see also *map* and *mandala*)?

school: What do you need to learn? This could be about discipline and organization. Dreaming of going back to school may suggest that you are currently dealing with something that you need to learn about or learn how to handle.

If you are in school, these dreams can also reflect something that you need to pay attention to in school right now.

Schools can also be about structure, relationships, past embarrassment, feelings of incompetence or competence, success or failures, rejection and loneliness, or your relationship to authority. Places in a school can refer to particular skills or difficulties. See also *exams* or *class*.

Insight: There may have been some insecurities when you went to school that are coming up again in a new situation. But these dreams can also be about wanting to recapture the freedom and/ or successes felt during this time. Is there something you need to learn from your current circumstances?

science: Something scientific in a dream might be symbolic of understanding, creativity, and rationality. For example, you may want to know why something happened the way it did.

Perhaps you are looking at yourself or someone else analytically.

Some people see science as the enemy of religion. If this is true for you, then you may have a fearful or negative and distrustful association with science or scientists. In reality, the threat could reflect a threatening aspect of yourself. Perhaps your beliefs are being challenged. Perhaps it's time to look at things from a different perspective.

Most people think that science and religion are polar opposites when in fact they are two sides of the same coin. The science side of the coin presents a rational approach to understanding how the universe works whereas religion deals with the emotional, spiritual, and mystical side of the coin.

science fiction or sci-fi: This can be about seeing into the future or represent an escape from present-day reality. You might think that some fact, idea, or belief is just fiction (i.e., fantasy).

scientist: If a mad scientist shows up in a dream, perhaps you have some fearful, negative, and/or distrustful association with science or scientists.

The threat could reflect a threatening aspect of yourself. Perhaps your beliefs are being challenged.

Perhaps you are not looking at some issue rationally.

Maybe you need to experiment with some way of being.

Has your curiosity been piqued? See also *detective or detecting*, *laboratory*, or *science*.

scissors: This could reflect a need to cut something or someone loose (i.e., let the person go).

If you're being cut up or you're cutting something up, perhaps you're being divided amongst too many things, situations, or people and need to focus your energies better.

Alternatively, it could suggest your need to be decisive and in control of some situation.

scolded: Do you have feelings of guilt? Do you feel censored or self-censoring? Do you have feelings of inferiority? Do you have any unresolved anxieties from now or your childhood that may be affecting your life negatively?

score: This could be a reference to attaining or winning something. It also has a sexual meaning.

Are you keeping score of something?

See also *music*.

Scorpio: The symbol for Scorpio or a scorpion in a dream might represent fierce independence, ambition, extremes in relationships, and being unforgiving. This sign may also symbolize determination and self-control. Are you being too intense?

See also *scorpion* in *animals*.

scream: This can be about fear or anger. Something may be pent up inside and screaming to get out

If you're trying to scream but no sound comes out or a weak sound comes out, perhaps you're feeling helpless in some situation. Maybe you're trying to get certain people's attention, but they're not hearing you.

You may be having problems communicating your needs. Perhaps you need to deal with these feelings directly in your waking life.

screw: This may be symbolic of connecting with someone or getting the shaft (i.e., losing). There's also a sexual connotation. See *sex*.

screwdriver: Do you need to or are you working on a connection? Is there something that needs fixing?

sea: This is similar to ocean. It may represent your subconscious and the transition between it and the conscious mind. It's also related to your emotions as are most water symbols. If you find in the dream that you are lost at sea, perhaps you are drifting around in your life without direction? A frozen sea may be about looking for some stability.

A stormy sea can be about stormy emotions, but it can also represent what one feels when watching a choppy sea from the shore. It can clearly produce fear mixed with a sense of power, awe, and mystery. Standing before it can be like confronting the power or the glory of the divine. Is it time to stand up before some power?

The condition of the sea (e.g., what's floating in it, whether it's clear or polluted, whether you're swimming freely or floundering or even drowning) will give much insight to the dream's meaning.

If you're on a boat, the condition of the boat and how it's navigating will also give you information (see *ocean, water, boat, swimming,* and *fish*).

The dream is like a vast sea upon which consciousness sails and each of us are born

as fishermen who must learn the way of the ocean.

Cast the net of thoughts and you catch only what is of the mind, but Self swims within the pools of wonder and is caught only by the heart.

—Hermann Hesse, *Sidartha*

seafood: This could signal a need for nourishing your spiritual side. Fish are often symbols for your inner nature or the unconscious mind. See *fish* in *animal terms.*

seal: As an animal, it might represent the playful side of your nature.

If it's a seal like a wax stamp or an Asian signature device, then it might be a reference to *sealing a deal* or bringing closure to something.

seam: As on a dress or piece of cloth, a seam could suggest that there are two parts of something that you may need to bring together. Perhaps there's something you need to fix.

seamstress: See *tailor.*

séance: This might be about intuition or looking deep within yourself. It may also reflect a need for more insight into yourself or some situation.

Because these often deal with communicating with the dead, it may reflect your need to get in touch with your feelings about someone who has died, a dead relationship, or something that may have died in you.

Trying to contact the dead for information may also reflect your worries about the future.

Perhaps there's something in your subconscious that you need to bring into the light (see also *candle, mystical experience,* and/or *mysticism*).

search: If you're searching, perhaps there's something missing in your life (e.g., love, enlightenment, peacefulness, a job, stability, etc.).

Maybe you're looking to recapture some part of the past. You may have lost something or someone, and you may be looking to recapture it. (This could include such things as motivation, sex appeal, creativity, youth, and/or love.)

searchlight: This could be about concentrating or focusing. It could also be about insight. See also *light*.

sea serpent: This may represent an emotional transformation. If you're keeping it contained, then perhaps you're keeping your emotions contained (see also *snake*).

seasick: This may be about emotions that make you sick or that throw you off balance. Is something dragging you down?

seasons: Suggesting the passage of time and periods of your life. If they're passing quickly, it may be a statement about how fast life is passing, or it could be about some kind of rapid transformation (see *winter, spring, summer,* and *fall*).

seat belt: Do you need to control your emotions? Have you lost control? Are you not being safe with some endeavor or not protecting yourself adequately?

secondhand dreams: Secondhand dreams are always a little difficult because of what the person recounting them adds, leaves out, or emphasizes. So too, dreams about you that other people have are most likely about them and not you. You only represent an aspect of them that is reflected in their lives somehow.

Also note that dreams reveal very personal and intimate aspects of the dreamer and should be treated with respect and only shared with the person's blessing.

secret: Are you withholding something from someone? Keeping something secret can also be about incompleteness and closure. Until the secret is made public, there can be no closure.

It might also reflect a secret that you are withholding from others or not dealing with yourself. It could be a hidden part of yourself.

Secretiveness can also reflect a trust issue. Is there some part of yourself that you don't trust? Is there somewhere you are not being open or trustworthy?

secretary: This can represent the *other woman*. This person could represent the practical, ordered, and businesslike supporter. Where do you need to get organized?

It's also possible that you may feel as though you are being treated as the lesser person in a relationship. Do you feel in partnership with a person?

seed: This can represent a beginning, potential growth, or a goal not yet realized.

self: This is one of the Jungian archetypes signifying the unification of consciousness and unconsciousness in a person and representing the psyche as a whole.

According to Jung, it is the end product of individuation, which in his view is the process of integrating the different aspects of one's personality. He thought of it as the central ordering principle of a human psyche (i.e., the director of the show) (see *archetypes* section as well as *philosopher's stone*).

As the ego is the center of the conscious mind, the self is the center and circumference of the combined conscious and unconscious. See also *mandala*.

The self shows up in dreams, fairy tales, myths, and the figure of the supraordinate personality (i.e., a king, hero, prophet, or savior). It can also reveal itself in the form of a totality symbol (e.g., circle, square, squared circle, sun, or cross). It is the union of opposites.

The symbolic representation of the self is a circle surrounding a dot. The dot represents the ego, and the self is both the circle and the dot. Interestingly, this is also the astronomical symbol for the sun (see *sun*). It is also a simple mandala image.

selfie: If you are taking a picture of yourself, it might suggest you are focusing too much on yourself.

A nude selfie could be about vulnerability, exhibitionism, or self-confidence.

It's also possible that the dream is saying the opposite of what it seems to be saying. For instance, you may feel out of touch with those around you and need to be better connected by focusing more on them than on yourself.

See also *photographs*.

self-injury: Self-harming in a dream can mean that you need to distance yourself from a relationship that is unhealthy. It can also be a desperate cry for help.

If the dream is also reflecting self-harm in your waking life, you need to seek help.

See also *cutting* and/or *suicide*.

self-talk: If you're talking to yourself or about yourself in the dream, is it positive or negative self-talk? Is it uplifting or demeaning? This may be a reflection of what you're doing in your waking life.

selling: When you dream of selling something, it might suggest that you are undergoing changes in your waking life.

Are you experiencing difficulties in letting go or parting with something? Do you need to learn to compromise?

Alternatively, it may be a pun for you *selling* yourself short. (This might be especially true if it is your house that you are selling.)

senility: This may represent declining abilities or suggest that you're wasting your abilities. It can be a symbol of confusion and loss.

serial killer: This could represent a negative habit of self-destructive behavior. See *kill or killing*.

sermon: If listening to or giving a sermon, you may need to receive inspiration or need to inspire others.

Are you lecturing too much? Do you need to listen more?

Perhaps you are trying to or should get in touch with your spiritual side.

Maybe you're being judgmental. Is there a lesson to be learned?

Are you trying to enroll someone into your way of thinking?

See also *lecture*.

serpent: See *snake* in *animal terms*.

servant: Are you being too submissive? Do you need to stand up for yourself or stand up to someone or some circumstance?

If you see a servant in your dream, perhaps you are being too authoritative or commanding, or maybe you need to be if you aren't.

setting someone free: If you're setting someone free from some kind of bondage, perhaps you are trying to get free of some psychological or emotional restriction. You may be wanting to release someone else from this kind of domination.

sewer: If you see a sewer in your dream, this may be symbolic of something that you need to clean up or change. Perhaps there are outdated habits, beliefs, or ideas that you need to let go of.

Sometimes we consciously suppress or unconsciously repress issues that we don't want to deal with. We can flush these into a sewer, but they can back up and overflow with time if we do not handle them.

If you're walking down a sewer or have been thrown into one, you may be feeling disrespected or belittled.

sewing: This can symbolize joining together, repairing, and restoring. Perhaps you should take up a new attitude.

sex: Sex in a dream can speak to the challenges that face you in your life and how you are dealing with them.

Look to see what the setting is, where the sex takes place, and what the drama is surrounding it. Does it involve an affair or exhibitionism?

Frequently, sex in dreams can speak about your relationship with yourself. For example, lust can suggest that you are not fulfilled somewhere in your life.

If the woman is on top during sex, there could be dominance issues. If the woman in the dream morphs into an older woman or even one's mother, these dominance issues may be enhanced.

A longing for a sexual relationship that is not being acknowledged in your waking life may show up in your dreams. The absence of sex in dreams when the circumstances would suggest sexual encounters could signal feelings of inadequacy or low self-esteem.

The absence can show up as withholding, or the rejection may reflect some circumstance you are experiencing in your relationship. If you are rejected, you may feel unattended to (or unloved) in your relationship.

Sometimes sex in a dream or the desire for it in your waking life can reflect the soul's passion to be fully alive and fully expressed. In this case, Aphrodite, the symbol of sexual desire, is mistaken for Eros, the symbol for passion. They can include one another but also operate separately. See also *Eros and Logos* as well as *soul*.

Other symbols for sex could include a sword, a snake, a horse (especially a stallion), or being naked.

Insight: Humans seem to hunger for fulfilling their emotional/spiritual aspects. In this vein, both sex and spirit are metaphors for the desire for oneness, wholeness, or fulfillment.

The act of sex itself is often a doorway into the spirit where one can transcend the limits of the mind and body and where two can become one. This unity is an archetypal drive for wholeness. Thus, sex in dreams can be a part of the spiritual search that lies in all of us.

See also *intimate*.

shack: This could represent an undeveloped part of yourself. Consider the phrase "shacking up," meaning living with someone.

The shack image can also be a symbol for poverty, the need for humbleness, or the fact that you feel humbled.

shadow: Shadow creatures or people (either those hiding in the dark or threatening black figures) in dreams can represent the unaccepted and sometimes rejected parts of yourself.

They often come as dark people or creatures and frequently show up as the same gender

as the dreamer (see *archetypes* section for more information on this image).

Insight: One of the most basic ways of dealing with your shadows (and your darker self) is to call out your shadows and your demons. Do not suppress them because that only gives them power over you. The truth is that you are not your negative aspects. You have negative aspects, but you are not only your negative aspects. It was because the character Harry Potter in J. K. Rowling's series actually named the Voldemort character the one whom everyone else labeled, "He who must not be named"[16] that he was able to exercise some power over this dark side. By naming and thus confronting the negative he was able to separate himself from its influence over him.

shady deal: This can symbolize inappropriate behaviors, lies, disloyalty, betrayal, a lack of trust, scams, or something illegal.

Have you been lying or scamming someone, or have others done this to you?

shaft: This may be an entry to the unconscious. Perhaps it is an invitation to go deeper into yourself (see also *hole*).

shame: This could be about feelings of guilt. Are you feeling insecure about something? Do you feel like you've failed someone or yourself?

shamrock or four-leaf clover: This may be a symbol of protection. Do you need better luck with something?

shampoo: This may be about cleaning up some negative thoughts. It may also be suggesting clearing out old attitudes. It might suggest the need for self-growth as well. See also *hair* in *body* or *washing*.

shapes: If you see a *sphere or ball*, it could be about wholeness or a rounded character. Perhaps the *ball* is in your court, meaning that you have to make the next move. Consider the phrase "having a ball," referring to having a great time. If you see a *square*, it could signal stability, being down-to-earth, or a balance for your nature. If you see a *star*, it can reflect your aspirations or your transcendent aspect of self, and for some, it can be a symbol of the godhead. If you see a *spiral*, it could represent things you may be repeating over and over. Consider a downward spiral, which refers to sinking into failure or depression. A *circle* may represent yourself, wholeness, or your personal identity. It could also indicate completeness or centeredness. Perhaps you have come full circle.

Is your life just going in circles? Consider also the *mandala*. If you see a *triangle*, this can represent one's aspirations, potential.

and truth. Sometimes it can represent your spiritual truth—body, mind, and spirit. Consider also the *trinity*. Like circles, triangles and squares can also represent the mandala. If you see a *crescent*, this may symbolize the feminine aspect of the self (see *anima/animus* in the *archetypes* section). A *cross* can suggest the issues, burdens, and problems we bear. A *diamond* can signify the many directions you can take in life (see also *diamond*).

If you see a *heart*, this could be symbolic of love or caring. It could also be about getting at the root of some issue (e.g., the heart of the matter).

Sometimes the heart is thought of as the source of our compassionate selves. Sometimes it is a euphemism for one's soul and/or emotional self. Sometimes the heart can be seen as representing the soul or the center of your spiritual self. See also *body*.

If you see a *polyhedron*, perhaps something is complex or becoming complex and multifaceted. The number of sides might reflect meaning as well (see *numbers*).

shape-shifter: The shape-shifter may represent someone who may portend or reflect radical changes in your life. When he or she undergoes metamorphosis, it may reflect two conflicting aspects of your life, though a smooth change may suggest that some change is necessary in order to adapt to some new situation.

Unpleasant metamorphosis may suggest that you aren't feeling prepared for the changes.

The presence of a shape-shifter may also represent you or someone else changing your mind too often. Perhaps you won't take a firm stance/position on something. See also *morphing* or *zoomorphism*.

shared dreaming: These are not as unusual as you might think. When someone you are emotionally connected to shares in parts of dreams you have, it can be most mysterious.

It's also possible that you are communicating your worries or anxieties in your waking life and that the other person is picking them up.

If the images are archetypal in nature, meaning that they share similar meanings with all human cultures (e.g., snakes, people, death), the dream may reflect what people are picking up subconsciously from you.

It may also be possible that the experience of shared dreaming is synchronistic in nature (see *mutual dreams, synchronicity,* and/or *telepathy*).

sharing: If you are or someone else is sharing something, perhaps you need to share more.

Perhaps you need to be more giving of your time, money, friendship, caring, or expertise.

shark: Is there a powerful notion threatening you? Is there someone devious and out to get you? Is something threatening coming up from your unconscious?

Sharks can also represent certain people in your life (e.g., a boss, parent, or teacher). See also *animals*.

sharpen: You can make a point or hone something for clarity, such as your communication or a document.

Do you need to be more flexible?

Do you need to improve your skills?

shaving: If you are shaving, perhaps you're having trouble with your self-image or want to clean it up. If you give yourself a close shave, perhaps you feel vulnerable.

sheep: This can be symbolic of docility and conforming behavior. Perhaps you are not expressing your individuality and creativity. If it's a black sheep, perhaps you are being a nonconformist, or you've been banned from some group (see *alien* and *lamb*).

In Christianity, sheep are seen as the followers of Jesus, and he is both a shepherd and a lamb. See *animals*.

shelf: This could be about memories. If it's an old dusty shelf, it could refer to old memories that are perhaps no longer useful.

shepherd: This can reflect both authority and a nurturing quality. It can also be about guidance or the need for direction.

Consider also the religious connotation of the Good Shepherd (see *Jesus*).

shield: This can symbolize defense, defensiveness, protection, and closing off your vulnerability. See also *fence*.

shimmering: See *bathed in light* and/or *sparkling*.

ship: How you are navigating the emotional waters (see *boat* or *cruise ship*).

Insight: Ships upon the sea can be about how we are negotiating and navigating our lives and the struggles lost or overcome.

Depending on the condition of the sea (e.g., choppy, stormy, becalmed, or dried up), ships can be about one's desires being quenched or parched, personal growth or death, or of being rejuvenated or washed away.

See also *floating*.

shipwreck: If you see a shipwreck or you're in one, you might be experiencing some emotional conflict. Though you may be having difficulty expressing your feelings, it may be time to confront them. See also *storm*.

shit: See *feces* or *defecation*.

Shiva: The Hindu god Shiva in your dream might signify struggle and conflict.

Perhaps you are undecided between two choices you have to make. As a symbol for the archetype God, this could refer to your unsuccessful attempts to be perfect. It could also reflect your attitudes and feelings about the divine.

Often this symbol can be about your inner spiritual guide and your need for guidance. This symbol can be both benevolent (as a protecting god) and fearsome (as a punishing god).

The symbol could refer to anything auspicious. Any of the high-level pantheons of gods can represent the archetype of something all-powerful. This may include Vishnu and also the representative of the anima (feminine within the male) Lakshmi, who may also symbolize health and wealth and generosity. Her equivalent in the Western religions might be Sophia, the goddess of wisdom.

Kali is also symbolic of death, rebirth, and the power of the mother. Many of the Hindu pantheon of gods and goddesses reflect both creation and destruction, life and death, nurturance and punishment (see *Great Mother* or *god* and *goddess* in the *archetypes* section).

shock: This could signal a sudden awareness or awakening.

shoe: This may represent a feeling of being well grounded. Changing shoes can be about a change in roles or the need for that change. To lose your shoes might mean that you have lost your footing in life. Wearing no shoes might indicate low self-esteem.

Muddy shoes might suggest a destabilizing event or the fact that you are mucking something up. See *muck*, *mud*, or *muddy*.

If the shoes are undone or untied or if the laces are missing, perhaps you're feeling undone or ungrounded.

See *shoes* in *clothing* for additional meanings.

Insight: In some Arab cultures, throwing shoes is an attack meant to demean the person they're thrown at. Shoes are dirty, thus the implication is that the other person is dirt. It's like throwing dirt upon him or her. Showing others the bottom of your shoe is meant as an insult in these cultures.

shooting: This could be about destroying or killing some aspect or some habit, belief, routine, point of view, or behavior.

This could be a metaphor for aiming at some goal or staying on target with the goal. If you are shooting someone, it could symbolize your aggressive stance with people or someone in particular.

However, if someone is shooting you, perhaps you are experiencing some confrontation in your life. This can include being criticized. For example, sometimes when you are criticized or judged negatively, this can show up as someone shooting or shooting at you in a dream.

Are you feeling victimized? Being shot in the back could be about feeling that someone has betrayed you or that someone is being deceitful (see *guns*, *gunmen*, or *killing*).

shooting stars: In a dream, these may be signs of self-fulfillment and advancement. It may also be symbolic of something new or big changes in your life.

Insight: Shooting stars are often seen as divine signs or messengers from God. Hence, the ancient ritual of asking (praying) for some intervention as it shoots across the sky.

shoplifting: If someone or you are doing this in your dream, then perhaps you feel deprived or unloved. It could also be a reflection of your sense of entitlement (i.e., that you're owed something).

shopping: This may reflect your needs and desires as well as your options and opportunities in life. Sometimes it reflects things missing in your life and your attempt to fill the void. Not finding what you're looking for might suggest that you haven't found your answer.

Shopping for others could be about buying acceptance, though it could also be about the giving of yourself. See also *mall* if that is where you're shopping.

shore: See *beach*.

shovel: This is a symbol for looking into something, investigating, digging into something, and/or seeking knowledge or insight.

Are you unearthing something? If this shovel is used while digging a hole, perhaps you are digging yourself into a hole (e.g., getting into something over your head). It could also be about hard work.

shower: You could be trying to get clean emotionally. You may also want to get rid of guilt or shame. What are trying to clean off?

If you're wearing your clothes while you're showering, it could symbolize that cleaning up your outer self may not change any of your inner aspects. Perhaps you need to come clean or tell the truth about something.

shrapnel: Has your anger and temper caused damaging consequences?

If you're hit by shrapnel, perhaps you are sticking your nose into something that is none of your business. See also *bomb or atom bomb* and *explosion or eruption*.

shredder: Are you trying to hide something? Perhaps something has torn up your life.

shrine: This can represent a sacred place within yourself.

shrink: Perhaps you're getting smaller, which suggests that you're losing self-confidence or becoming less important. Consider also that this can refer to a psychologist or the need for one. Are you analyzing everyone and everything too much or overanalyzing yourself?

shutters: You may be shutting yourself off from some aspect of your life. Or you may be shutting someone or something out of your life. Alternatively, perhaps someone is hiding something from you.

shy: Perhaps you need to be more assertive or confident. It could also suggest that there's a situation that you are avoiding in your waking life.

It often refers to low self-esteem or a lack of self-confidence.

sibling: In a dream, this may be about sibling rivalry, unresolved issues, or insecurities. This can also be representative of some shared or wishful attribute that the sibling reflects.

sickness: There may be some discordance in your life, or there may be a part of yourself that needs to be healed. Perhaps you need to stop feeling sorry for yourself (see *illness*).

sign: What are you searching for? Do you need help or directions to your life or on some project? Are you looking for something to save you? Do you need help? Do you need some direction or guidance? Consider the phrase a "sign of the times." What does the sign say?

If you're signing something, perhaps you are giving your agreement or acceptance to something or someone. Should you do this, or is this a statement that you need to?

significance: Seeing yourself as something or someone significant might suggest you are feeling insignificant and/or unimportant. You may also think that because you're seeing and thinking

significant things, this makes you significant.

This is ego stuff and gets in the way of your personal growth. (You don't need to be significant to be worth anything.)

silence: Are you having difficulty expressing yourself? Do you feel inhibited in speaking up for yourself or speaking your mind?

silent witness: A person in a dream who refuses or can't talk sometimes represents an undeveloped or underdeveloped part of the dreamer. It could also represent an imbalance between ones emotions and intellect. It could also represent that which overpowers and makes you speechless.

silhouette: You may not be looking directly at an issue. You may be seeing only part of it. Perhaps you are seeing or presenting only a half-truth.

silver: See *color.*

sin: If you or someone else is doing something in the dream that you consider a sin, perhaps you are feeling guilty about something. Perhaps you have done something you're not proud of, and it's festering inside you.

If you know the true meaning of sin (i.e., to be separated from God), it could then mean that you have separated yourself from your spiritual self or your head from your heart.

Have you missed the mark or failed to be your best with some endeavor?

singer: What are the attributes of the singer? How do you feel when you hear the song from the singer? These will give you hints about the meaning of the singer.

singing: This can be about happiness and joy, but consider the words of the song because they can also be about the loss and sadness that you fear.

This can be symbolic of inner feelings and can be in contrast to one's outward expression. Singing can also be an expression of your real self and the general tone of your life.

See also *song*.

single: If you are not single but dream that you are, perhaps you are leaning too much on someone else and need to stand up for yourself. Or it could reflect a desire to have some attribute of being single back in your life. Consider the phrase "being singled out."

sink: This can be about cleaning up some aspect of your life or a need to control your emotions. If you have everything that you could possibly want or have overindulged, then the phrase "everything but the kitchen sink" might be apropos.

Maybe you don't have all that you want.

sinking: This can represent despair or overwhelm. Are you feeling overwhelmed? Are you in over your head with something?

See also *drowning*.

sister: This image could represent your feeling self or the less dominant aspect of yourself (see *anima/animus* in the *archetypes* section).

If it's your adult sister, this could represent your rival for your parents' attention. (We tend to carry unresolved rivalries far into adulthood and sometimes throughout life.) If it's an older sister, she could represent the feeling of being dominated or persecuted.

sitting: This can be about some indecision. Perhaps you're waiting for something or need to take a rest or break from something. See also *lotus position*.

skate: Whether ice skates, a skateboard, or in-line skates, it could refer to balance in life.

Are you just skating through life (i.e., just getting by and avoiding the serious issues)? Are you just doing the minimum? This could also be a symbol for a lack of ambition.

This could also reflect your fun-loving aspects. Are you skating on thin ice? Are you overstepping your boundaries?

skeleton: This could symbolize something not fully developed or something in the planning stage. It can also mean death, transformation, or change.

These can also represent skeletons in your closet. Are you hiding something?

Is there some aspect of yourself that you have killed off? See also *skull*.

skiing: To see yourself skiing or someone else skiing could be about freedom. It could also represent something going downhill (i.e., failing or becoming easier).

If you are racing, are you racing for the bottom (i.e., the ultimate achievement or total loss)?

skin: This can represent your connection with the inner and outer world. It could be about protection or a line of defense against hurts. If the skin is thin, perhaps you're being too sensitive about something, or if it's thick, perhaps nothing sensitive is getting through to you (i.e., you're being insensitive).

skinning: Skinning something, someone, or oneself can be about becoming vulnerable. It can also be about shedding one's old way of being to make room for a new way.

Skinning oneself may also be about self-criticism.

skull: This can mean death, or it can represent evil or the secrets of the mind. If it's talking or if something is coming out of its mouth, it might reflect a release of those secrets that you've suppressed.

Eventually, in order to maintain mental health and the sense of free will, one has to learn to deal with these repressed aspects or feelings. See also *skeleton*.

Sometimes, as with any skeleton image, a skull can represent the killing off (ending) of a part of oneself.

skunk: Are you driving people away and turning them off? It can also express fear (especially if you imagine smelling it), a suspicion of something that doesn't seem quite right, a lie. Do you have some unexpressed anger?

sky: Frequently, the sky represents limitless freedom. It can symbolize your potential and possibilities. Consider the phrase "The sky's the limit."

A red-colored sky can signify danger, something coming to an end, or a new dawning. If the sky is falling, this can be about dashed hopes, failed dreams, some failing project, or even pessimism.

slandered: This image can represent being defamed and/or misrepresented. Do you feel as if someone is lying about you? Are you looking for approval?

slaughterhouse: This could represent the sacrificial death of something or martyrdom.

sleeping: If you are sleeping in a dream, perhaps there is something you are unaware of or not paying attention to. You need to wake up (i.e., be more conscious of what's going on around you).

Seeing someone else sleeping can also reflect you and your subconscious. Perhaps you need to be more alert about something. Are you turning a blind eye to something or someone?

slime: This may refer to unclean emotions or feeling untrustworthy (see *feces*).

slipper: This could symbolize a casual stance. See also *shoe*.

slums: This can refer to a feeling, a building, or an area. You could be living in one or just passing through.

Do you feel impoverished? Do you need to clean up your act and your way of behaving?

This could also reflect your outlook on life. Perhaps your ideals are beginning to fall apart. Your negative thinking may be overwhelming you and affecting your self-image.

small: If you or others are small in the dream, perhaps you are not playing up to your potential. Are you tired of being unimportant or being given small tasks? Do you need to stand tall and stand up for yourself? Do you want to play a more major part in some endeavor?

smell: Certain smells can evoke certain memories or emotions. It's possible that the dream is drawing on a similar feeling associated with the smell.

The smell of death in a dream may refer to something rotten in your life or something that has long since ended and from which you should just move on.

See also the different types of tastes that might also translate into the dreams of smells.

A moldy smell might suggest there's something in your life that may no longer be of any use. Perhaps some negative attitude is affecting your well-being and needs to be brought into the light and dealt with. See also *mold*.

It is also possible that certain ambient smells in the room where you're sleeping have been translated into your dream.

smile: If you see smiles in a dream, do you feel happy? Are you looking for something or someone to make you happy?

It's also possible that a smile is symbolic of accepting some aspect of yourself.

It can also symbolize that you are not happy.

smog: This might symbolize negative emotions or something upsetting. See also *fog*.

smoke: Trouble may be brewing. It could mean impending doom or a warning of danger that's yet unseen.

If it is dark smoke, perhaps you're not seeing something clearly. White smoke, however, might suggest that your feelings are clouding your judgment. When electing the pope, white smoke means consensus. Pink smoke may be a metaphor for something obfuscating/hiding your ability to get clear about something or someone who looks harmless but may not be.

smoke and mirrors: Something may be fake, or someone may be trying to fool, deceive, or manipulate you (i.e., create some illusion).

smoking gun: Are you looking for evidence or proof of something? Have you been caught red-handed doing something wrong?

smooth: Do you have to correct a mistake or soothe some ruffled feathers?

smother: See *suffocating*.

smuggling: Do you feel as if you've been denied something? Do you imagine that you have to secretly obtain something that may be rightfully yours? Are you hiding something or trying to get away with something?

snail: See *animal terms*.

snake: See *animal terms* and *ouroboros*.

snake charmer: Perhaps you need to take control of your sexual desires and urges or bring someone who is acting like a snake under control.

sneaky: If you or someone in a dream is acting sneaky, perhaps you are trying to hide something that you are ashamed of or not sure you should be doing. Perhaps you're not being upfront or forthright (i.e., lying).

sniper: Maybe there's some hidden aggression you're not dealing with. You may need to be more open and communicative about some anger (see *gun*).

snitch: Are you feeling insecure? If someone is snitching on you, are you worried about being found out or exposed? Do you need to reveal something?

See also *betrayal*.

sniveling: See *whining*.

snow: This may be about emotional coldness. You may need to warm up and express your inhibitions rather than being controlled by them. It can also mean purity, or if the snow is dirty, it can represent the loss of innocence or an impure act. To *snow* a person is to deceive him or her.

snowflakes: This could reflect inner beauty or your uniqueness. Their melting could reflect a loss of self-esteem and uniqueness.

snow globe: This could mean peace and serenity. However, if you're inside it, then it could mean you're feeling stuck or trapped in your life or some unreality.

snowman: Seeing a snowman in a dream suggests that you might feel emotionally cold and frigid, or you may be acting too coldly or insensitively.

Alternatively, it could also represent your playful side if you're building a snowman.

snowstorm: This could mean you are feeling emotionally cold or left out in the cold if you're outside in it.

soap: What needs cleaning up? Are you feeling dirty and want to clean it off (i.e., get rid of the feeling)?

soap opera: Are you being overly dramatic, unreal, and superficial? Consider the reference "drama queen." Is it all an act with no sincerity?

software: This can represent your personality traits, habits, and behaviors. What are you downloading into yourself? Will this help you to adapt, or will it only corrupt you?

Is something hidden controlling your life? Is some old belief affecting what you want to do in life? Do you need to rewrite your software?

Do you need to be more organized or present your ideas in a way that will be more applicable?

soil: This could refer to something spoiled, tainted, or made dirty. Alternatively, it can represent growth and fertility. See also *dirt*.

soldier/warrior: This could represent things, ideas, or people we may be in conflict with. It can mean a confrontation, challenge, or extreme defensiveness regarding something inside yourself or in the waking world.

Insight: A Celtic warrior can be seen as representing the wild, less organized side of yourself, and a Roman soldier represents the more disciplined side of your character or aspect of yourself.

See also *battle, enemy, medals*, or *military*.

son: In a mother's dream, he could reflect her personal aspirations and/or her relationship with his father. In a father's dream, he could reflect the father when he was that age. A son could also reflect your own potential or lack thereof or even a rivalry.

Sometimes a mother will kill off a son in her dreams as she experiences him becoming more independent in waking life. His death in a dream can even happen when he's about to enter the first day of school.

song: You may be looking at something from a spiritual standpoint. Note the lyrics or even the title of the song because these can inform the message. The song can reveal your feelings as well (see also *singer*).

song lines: These may be symbolic of the intuitive energy lines of your life. Do you need to follow your intuitive aspect? Do you need help in navigating your life right now? See also *navigation*.

Sophia

Sophia: The image of Sophia is sometimes symbolic of one's inner wisdom or gnosis (deep knowledge), especially spiritual wisdom.

She is sometimes the Earth Mother, Gaia, or Athena, and she can also be represented by Isis or the Virgin Mary.

She may represent the inner feminine aspect of males (i.e., his anima). In the realm of God, she represents its feminine aspect. In Catholicism, she is the mediator to God.

As the anima, she is often seen as the soul of a male. For me, she represents a spiritual guide who comes into my dreams from time to time and invites me into new realities. She also comes to me as a spiritual guide or psychopomp (see *psychopomp*).

See the *archetypes* section in the next chapter or *anima/animus*.

sorcerer: This could be about your inner strengths and creative ability. See *wizard* in the *archetypes* section.

sores: If these are on the body, they could represent pent-up negative emotions that need to be released. Where on the body are the sores located? To feel sore may be a symbol for feeling worn out.

sorrow: This could reflect your depression.

sorry: If someone feels sorry, perhaps you feel regretful or remorseful. You may not be able to express this when you are awake, so you may then express these feelings in the dream.

Insight: Many feelings or actions that cannot for various reasons be expressed in one's waking life can find release in one's dreams (e.g., love, lust, sadness, anger, tears, fear, etc.).

soul: Feeling as though you have lost your soul or have no soul to begin with could suggest that you are feeling spiritually lost. You may feel fragmented and less than whole.

If it's leaving your body, it could be a message of self-guilt in that you've compromised your values.

If you have someone else's soul, it could be a problem with self-acceptance or lack thereof. Soul can also refer to the *heart* of something or its essence.

If it is speaking to you, listen to its message. Sometimes the soul seems to act as a trickster, confusing us and seemingly encouraging us to do something that will get us into trouble (i.e., contrary to whatever is the status quo or common sense).

The image of the soul—whether real or just a mysterious yet subjective perspective of the psyche's viewpoint on the world—comes from the deepest part of ourselves and has much to teach. See *animus/anima*, *spirit*, or *trickster* in the *archetypes* section. See also *heart* in this section.

So what is the difference between soul and spirit? Amongst the writings of such psychologists and philosophers as Meister Eckhart, James Hillman, Carl Jung, and Thomas Moore, the soul may be said to represent the everyday in our lives—its emotional ups and downs, imagination, ugliness, brilliance, love, drama, and subjective biases. However, the spirit is not within the understanding or grasp of the human mind.

While soul deals with the everyday, spirit demands a union with God and does this through the ego, which strives to build its edifices toward the heavens.

Ego is that part of the soul that strives to unite with spirit so as to transcend the mess of the everyday. Together soul and spirit represent the whole, what Carl Jung referred to as a fully individuated being (see *ego* or *individuation*).

Soul is often suppressed by the conscious ego, and through this limiting factor, pathologies can arise in the psyche's attempt to correct the denied expression of the soul.

The dream is the small hidden door in the deepest and most intimate sanctum of the soul, which opens to that primeval cosmic night that was soul long before there was conscious ego and will be soul far beyond what a conscious ego could ever reach.

—Carl Jung (1934)

sounds: These have the same impact as they do in one's waking life. Some convey warning, fear, anger, explosiveness, danger, happiness, and/or joy.

Some sounds convey irritation and annoyance. Some are mechanical in nature and may reflect your own routines or automatic activities (see *machine*).

Sounds can remind you of things and events from the past or can herald the future. See musical instruments (e.g., *drums, saxophone,* or *trumpet*).

Is the sound discordant or harmonic (see *music*)? In what way might this sound reflect something in your waking life?

soup: This could be about emotional hunger or satisfaction. Soup can also be about healing (emotional, physical, and spiritual).

south (as a direction): This could be about youth, beginnings, summer, vulnerability, emotions, and spontaneity. As with all directions, one might ask, "Where am I heading?" See also *cross*.

South Pole: This could symbolize endurance and survival skill.

sowing: This can suggest new beginnings. It can be about reaping what you sow. (What goes around comes around.) There's a possibility of a sexual connotation with the phrase "sowing one's seed or oats."

spa: This may be symbolic of the need to pamper yourself. It may also be a metaphoric means for cleansing the self and steaming away old feelings and pains. It is also a means of starting afresh.

space: See *outer space*.

spaceship: This can represent exploring beyond the everyday, beyond your senses. Seeing a spaceship in your dream might symbolize your creative mind. It suggests a spiritual journey into the unknown and could signal self-development and self-awareness or just exploring the unknown.

spaghetti: This could be about some relationship entanglement. As with any food, it could also be about nourishment of your soul.

spanking: Are you working on some childish behaviors? Are you punishing yourself?

spark: This could be an idea, a new beginning, a new love. Perhaps something new is growing into something much bigger.

sparkling: If something is sparkling, perhaps it's a signal to pay attention. Consider the phrase "All that glitters is not gold." Don't be fooled by all the glitter of something. Beneath it all may be commonness or deceit.

It could also be a feeling of joy or happiness or a desire for that feeling. It may also symbolize something of value (see *gold* and also *spark*).

sparrow: See *birds* under *animals*.

speaking in tongues: If you are spiritually inclined, this may speak to your spiritual aspect and thus be encouraging you to reconnect. It's also possible that you long to be someone special or anointed but that this has not been so in your waking life. Therefore, it may show up in your dream

life as a way of compensating for some lack. See also *languages (strange or foreign to you)*.

specters or spectral figures: These could be about hidden knowledge that you may need to flesh out and make more solid. Sometimes these images reflect one's own fears of death. See also *chimera*, *ghost*, and *phantom*.

speed bump: Do you need to slow down? You may be moving too fast in some relationship. You may also have experienced some kind of obstacle in life.

speeding: Do you need to slow down? Are you in a hurry to finish something? There's also the chance that the dream is saying, "Hurry up. You're moving too slowly."

speeding ticket: Are you rushing through some decision or into something? You may need to slow down.

spell: If you're under a spell, someone may have influence over you or may be manipulating you. It might also suggest that you are falling in love. If you're casting the spell, perhaps you're doing the manipulation (see *bewitched*).

Spells can also be like amulets or protective charms (see *amulet*).

spelling: If trying to spell something, perhaps you're trying to understand something difficult. You may need to understand some problem in life.

spending: By spending money, perhaps you may be emotionally exhausted. Are you spending too much time on the wrong things?

If you're being extra careful with your spending, perhaps you are holding your emotions in check.

sphere: This could symbolize completeness or wholeness. If it is a ball, it could represent competition. Consider the phrase "The ball is in your court." See also *shapes*.

spider: See *animal terms*.

spinach: Spinach can sometimes refer to the need to revitalize or be reenergized. It can be about power and strength. Do you remember the cartoon character Popeye?

spinning: Is something spinning in your dream? If so, it could be symbolic for something spinning out of control.

It can also represent confusion. It could also signal that you're spinning in circles and going nowhere in your life or some endeavor.

spiral: This can represent actions and behaviors that repeat over and over in your life. Also consider the phrase "spiraling out of control." Do you feel trapped in ever-diminishing circles?

spirit: This image could reflect the essence of our being or our motivating force. The spirit can come to us in the form of a loved one who has died, or as a ghost. There can also be an impression of the infinite, what is called a numinous feeling, that can give you the sense of something divine and entirely different from all that you experience in your usual waking life. Consider also that the word might be a metaphor for alcohol.

Spirit images in our dreams also remind us of death, endings, transformation, and letting go. They also reflect what needs to happen in order to grow beyond our own self-imposed limits and what is absolutely necessary to evolve sustainably.

Insight: At its very root, the spirit is our connection with nature, what Carl Jung called "the nourishing soil of the soul." I believe that our dissociation with nature has left us disconnected from our experience of spirit (i.e., the divine).

Nature is part of our existence, and to pollute it and destroy it in order to make way for more hamburgers (destroying the rain forests in order to grow more beef), cars, parking lots, and shopping malls is to destroy or sicken part of our own souls.

As Jung once said, "Nature is not matter only, she is also Spirit." I think that when we make our wallets more important, when we make our material objects more important, and when we make ourselves more important, we rob the earth of its spirit, and thus, we steal from ourselves as well.

For a short explanation of the difference between spirit and soul, see also *soul*.

splinter: A splinter in you or another person in the dream can be about the annoyance of some trivial matter that may have upset or hurt you.

If you're having difficulty getting it out, then perhaps you may be having trouble dealing with this vexation, and it may be affecting your progress in some situation or in your life in general.

If you are getting a lot of these splinters, perhaps you're being a little thin-skinned and taking something too personally.

sports car: Are you living in the fast lane? Do you need to slow down? Do you need to get more serious in your life?

spotlight: Are you trying to be the center of attention? Do you feel overlooked?

spring: This can symbolize new beginnings, developments, ideas, and ways of being (see also *birth*).

spy: Are you being a busybody and snooping into others' affairs? Do you feel as though you are being watched?

square: This can refer to stability, being down to earth, or being conventional. A square inside a circle might indicate that you want to make something more stable (i.e., to bring order out of chaos).

As with a circle, the square can also represent the self. See *self*.

squaring of the circle: Essentially, this has become a metaphor for trying to do the impossible.

In all mandalas, a concept called the "squaring of the circle" is represented. (Note that the mandala can be broken down into four sections.) The original chaotic unity is broken down into four elements and are then recombined into a higher unity.

Jung found this *quaternity* in many of the psychic processes that go on toward the achievement of wholeness—a symbol of the union of opposites.

Each of these sections represents oppositions that are constantly doing a dance with one another toward a harmonious balance, and ultimately, they result in a wholeness of the psyche and the actualization of a complete human being.

Thus, these cryptograms, as Jung called them, function to bring order out of chaos. When I held my ego-self as the context, order could not fit within because it was something separate.

It's interesting to note that Jung would always look for the fourth element when his patients told him about three of something from a dream or any other event related to their experience. Like the alchemists of old, he thought that things weren't finished until the quaternity was completed (i.e., the circle squared). See also *mandala* in the *archetypes* section. See also *quaternity*.

The concept of trying to unite the impossible is an age old philosophical exercise originally proposed by ancient mathematicians (geometers) long before the common era, going back as far as 1800 BCE with the Egyptians.

It is impossible to unite exactly the areas of a square and a circle because the circle's area uses an infinite irrational number (pi) for its measurement whereas the square is measured in rational numbers finitely.

This is an example of a yantra. The symbol within the tantric square is the alchemical symbol for the philosopher's stone. See also *yantra*.

stabbing: If you've been stabbed, then perhaps you're struggling with power or feeling betrayed or defensive. Consider the phrase "stabbed in the back." It could also mean a fear of being dominated. To stab someone else could be about your untrusting nature (see *knife*).

A number of people stabbing one another may reflect a culture of domination. If you're bleeding, see *blood*.

If you're stabbed in the gut or in the back, it could be a metaphor for betrayal. You may also feel some loss of resolve, especially if your guts spill out. See also *guts* and *intestines* in *body*.

stack of paper: If you envision a stack of papers piled high on a desk or table, you may be working out your anxiety in a dream and experiencing some overwhelming emotions. Perhaps the stresses of life are demanding too much of you. Are you dealing effectively with the demands?

stag: This is symbolic of male sexuality. Consider the phrase "going stag," referring to going it alone (see also *deer* in *animals*).

stage: See *theater or play*.

stain: If something is stained, it may be symbolic of a mistake that you are trying to correct. The inability to get a stain out could be about a feeling of guilt and/or an unwillingness to forgive (yourself or others).

stairs: See *house*.

stairway to heaven: See *Jacob's ladder*.

stalker or stalking: Most likely, you are being stalked by a negative part of yourself (as you perceive it) trying to make itself known. If the stalker is of the same gender as the dreamer, this could be the shadow archetype making itself known.

This could reflect a problem in your life that you need to recognize, or it may reflect an actual feeling of being stalked. Are you trying to track down something?

Are you being obsessive? Cats also stalk and represent feminine power and energy. See also *chased*, *chasing*, or *shadow* in the *archetypes* section.

stallion: This animal might suggest wildness, sexual prowess, and/or independence.

stand: This could be about independence. Consider the phrase "stand up for yourself" or "stand for something." What do you stand for? What's important to you? What purpose do you give your life to?

standing on water: See *walking on water*.

star: This represents the light within. It can represent intuition, destiny, hopes, and/or wishes. It could also reference a need for acknowledgment or a spiritual awakening. Where are you ready to shine?

If you see a star hovering above an object, especially a circular object (e.g., a mandala-like object), it might represent the godhead. See *godhead*.

If you are seeing shooting stars in a dream, it may be a sign of self-fulfillment and advancement. It may also be symbolic of something new or big changes in your life (see *shooting stars*).

Insight: Generally, stars in one's dream can represent success (i.e., fame, fortune, aspirations, and high ideals). Or you could be putting your fortunes into the hands of the stars. A star can also refer to the dreamer, the star of his or her own life.

star-crossed lovers: See the *archetypes* section.

starvation: This can refer to something within yourself or in your life that you are not attending to.

Some part of you needs nourishing.

Star Wars: The *Star Wars* image may represent an epic battle between good and evil. It may be the force and the dark side of the force, which can represent an inner emotional conflict that threatens to drown or overwhelm your life.

static: This could be about a lack of clarity and understanding, or someone may be opposed to your point of view. Someone may be giving you static instead of being straight with you. Are you creating the static? Negative thoughts about yourself or others could also be symbolized by static.

station: If you're standing at a station, are you at some transitional place in your life? What path do you need to take?

statistic: Are you weighing the positives and negatives about some decision? Are you having doubts?

Do you feel as though you are one of the crowd and unimportant? Do you feel as if you don't stand out?

statue: This could possibly be a rigid representation of something, perhaps yourself. Are you out of touch with some reality? If you know the person the statue represents, is it someone you admire? What about his or her personality do you admire and would like to emulate? See also *idol* or *fetish*.

Statue of Liberty: This image may be about personal freedom, patriotism, and/or independence. It can also represent irony or the lack of freedom.

stealing: This is emblematic of taking something under false pretenses. You may be cheating yourself or others. It could also refer to being cheated out of something.

Look to see what the thief is stealing. Are you cutting corners because of some unmet need? Are you feeling deprived? Is there some goal that is unfulfilled? Are you stealing some time by getting off on your own, or are you procrastinating?

Has someone taken something from you that represents some aspect of yourself (i.e., pride, self-image, or self-confidence)?

steam: This could represent your heated passion or anger about something. It could also be about a steamy relationship. Moving full steam ahead could be a metaphor for pushing forward on some project or toward some goal.

steel: This can represent toughness and determination or the need for it. Perhaps you need to steel yourself against something (i.e., prepare for some hardship).

A steel plate may be a symbol of protection or defensiveness.

Consider also that *steel* may refer to *steal*.

steep: Climbing (or driving up) something steep might be about making progress toward some goal. It can be a metaphor for hard work. If you're slipping or sliding down, you may be on the slippery slope, and you may be headed in the wrong direction.

stepping stones: Maybe you need to slow down and take things one step at a time. Depending on where the stones are going, it could be showing you what your next steps are in some situation.

sterilize: Perhaps you need a cleansing physically, emotionally, or psychologically. Do you feel life lacks anything interesting (i.e., colorless)?

stick: This may express anger or threat. Sticks can also be phallic symbols representing power (see *gun*). Various sticks, such as walking sticks, wands, daggers, and swords, have all been used for channeling magic energy. A stick figure may point out your simplistic nature or suggest that you're treating something in a simplistic way (see also *sword* or *dagger*).

stigmata: You may have been singled out by someone in either a positive or negative way. It can also refer to sacrifices you're making and problems you've endured. So too, it can bring attention to your religious or spiritual beliefs.

stillborn: If a baby in a dream has been born dead, perhaps some new endeavor has died or ended before really beginning. It could signal a loss of innocence as well.

It could also mean that you've lost trust in someone or something. See also *baby*.

sting: Has some remark or action hurt you? Are you trying to set someone up, or is someone trying to set you up?

stitches: This image is symbolic of trying to hold something together that may be falling apart. Being in stitches could be a reference to laughter.

stock market: Are you willing to take risks and roll with the ups and downs of life? Are you in support of something as long as it's going well or in it for the long haul through all its trials? What's your level of commitment?

stolen: If someone has stolen something, perhaps you're suffering some kind of loss, or maybe you're having a crisis of personal identity. Perhaps someone else was acknowledged for something you did. Has someone stolen your heart? Have you fallen in love, or have you lost compassion, caring, or love? See also *stealing*.

stomach: See *abdomen* or *stomach* under *body terms*.

stomachache: See *indigestion*.

stone: This can represent rigidity (as in something carved in stone and can't be changed), emotional coldness, a thing's essence, and death (as in a headstone).

It can also mean stability (as in calling someone a rock).

If you are buried in or carrying heavy stones, is something weighing you down?

A stone is sometimes at the center of some fruit. Consider the phrase "at the heart of the matter."

If people are throwing rocks at you or someone else, are you being punished or feeling guilty?

Insight: For the Celts, stones were a dwelling place of the gods. They were the eternal expressed in the physical world. Some stones are used for healing rituals, such as amethyst for headaches, aquamarine for stomachaches, and citrine for depression.

Henges such as Stonehenge (found on the Salisbury Plain in England) can be metaphors for spiritual enlightenment and mysterious forces.

The Black Stone of Mecca that the Muslims believe was sent down by Allah as a marker for the Ka'abah is also a spiritual image.

Native Americans carved stones called effigies that represented the aspects and power and spirit of the various animals depicted.

Stone megaliths called dolmen (or stone table) in the Briton language (Taol Maen) were used as graves for important Celts from India to Turkey as well as Germany to Ireland.

Some Romans believed that they were Celtic entrances to the otherworld. Tribal peoples all over the world transfer ancestor energy through stones called spirit stones.

stoop: This may be similar to a front porch. This could represent your reputation. See also *porch*.

store: Stores can be about searching for something or a new way of doing something. They can also signify the need to make some significant choices in your life.

storehouse: See *warehouse*.

store window: If the window is filled with things you'd like to have but cannot, perhaps it's referring to your feelings of exclusion. But it may also represent your dreams for a better future.

storm: This might suggest some difficulty in your life. (The ferocity of the storm will give you a clue about how much difficulty.) Did it pass? Did it cause damage or portend damage? How did you weather it?

story: If you are reading or listening to a story, it could be about the narrative of your life (i.e., your biography). It could reflect the drama you are experiencing. Do you need to describe some event?

The type of story (e.g., romance, mystery, history, fable, drama, tragedy, or comedy) could also help decipher this symbol.

This could also be about a mental narrative (i.e., an internal conversation). What's happening with the story?

See also *book*.

straight ahead: If you are looking straight ahead, you may have your sights set on the future, or you may be keeping a practical outlook on life.

stranded: This may a variation of being trapped. Perhaps you are feeling isolated and/or lonely.

Are you seeking help for your escape or trying to handle it on your own?

strange: If you or the dream seems strange, see *odd, surprise, unexpected,* or *unfamiliar surroundings.*

If you're feeling excited about the pace, perhaps you are ready for change.

stranger: This can also be a strange place and can represent an unacknowledged or unfamiliar aspect of yourself. If the stranger is dark and foreboding, see *shadow* under the *archetypes* and/or *alien* or *foreigner.*

As you become more self-aware, parts of yourself that you haven't paid attention to may show up. It may also be possible that you are walking through life oblivious to most of what's going on around you and the dream is suggesting that you wake up and pay more attention.

If people you know are in the dream but seem to be strangers, perhaps they're not who they say they are in your waking life.

strangle: You may be choking off something such as communication or some aspect of yourself. Are you holding back feelings? It could mean that something or someone is threatening to kill your joy in life (see *cage* or *trapped*).

strawberry: This may be about sensuality and sexual desires. This is often a feminine symbol for female sexuality.

stray animal: This might suggest that you are feeling lost, unwanted, or abandoned. Are you feeling disconnected from people? Look for the specific animal in *animals.*

stream: Seeing a stream in your dream could be about your emotions and how they are flowing (e.g., smoothly or with turbulence). It can also reflect how your life is flowing. See also *river* and *water*.

street: It's like a road or path. The name of the street might have some significance as well. If it's the street you lived on as a child, it may have something to do with that time of your life, an earlier and simpler time of life, or a lesson you learned that you may need to revisit.

stress: This could be about the stress you are actually experiencing in your waking life. Stress over time can be unhealthy and can cause breakdowns in your well-being. Pay attention when this emotion invades your dreams (see *emotions*).

strike: This can symbolize stopping an activity. This could also represent a protest or a need to be heard. If going on a strike, perhaps you feel unappreciated. Are you trying to better yourself? Do you need to stand up for yourself?

If it's a strike in baseball, it can represent a missed opportunity.

string: This may be a pun for stringing someone along (i.e., fooling others or being deceitful). This may also be about something binding as a constraint or something that you're sworn to do. Can you hold something together and do what you've said you will do?

A tangled string could be about some issue that needs working out or something you're entangled in from which you need to set yourself free.

If there are strings attached to something or someone, are you attaching unseen or unspoken demands or costs to some endeavor, project, request, or favor?

See also *web*.

stripper: Perhaps you need to be more open with your sexuality. If you're in a strip club, perhaps you have some repressed sexual thoughts that you need to let out or explore.

Perhaps you need to be more at ease with and accepting of your body.

stroke: Are you feeling paralyzed in dealing with some issue? Are you overly stressed out? Do you need to calm down?

Because dreams can sometimes warn of health issues, you may want to look at this image from a health aspect and act accordingly.

struggling: Perhaps you're making something into a bigger problem than it needs to be. You may also be dealing with some internal conflicts and having trouble resolving them.

See also *tied up*.

studying: If you are studying in a dream, do you need to study more or look at something with greater depth?

The dream may also suggest that studying is your path to success with some endeavor.

Do you need to be more open to self-knowledge?

stuffed animals: In dreams, these could represent an immature way of being. Or you may be feeling a need for love and comfort.

You could also be trying to escape from some stressful circumstances. It is also possible that you need to be less serious about something.

Perhaps this represents something from your childhood that is trying to get your attention.

stump: This may be symbolic of an interrupted development. It might also be a reference for "on the stump," such as with political campaigning or being stumped (i.e., confused or without an answer to something).

stun gun: Are you in need of a jolt of energy in your life? Or do you need to stop and think about something before you do it? Have you been stunned by some situation, person, or event?

stunt: Have you pulled some stunt? Are you trying too hard for attention? Are you stooping to some trick to get yourself noticed or cared for (e.g., faking an injury or loss)?

stutter: Are you or someone stuttering in the dream? It could be that you're having difficulty being heard or that you're concerned about something you've said.

submarine: This may be a way of exploring the unconscious or the depth of your feelings. Being underwater may also refer to being emotionally overwhelmed.

subway: This can symbolize transportation or a means of navigation through or to the unconscious mind. Dreaming that you are in the subway suggests that you might be reaching your goal via unconscious methods. You may be exploring hidden aspects of yourself or aspects that you had as a child that still present themselves as an adult.

success: Are you feeling like a failure or hoping for success? Are you seeing someone else's success in a dream but not enjoying it? Are you feeling a little insecure?

sucking: In a dream, sucking could be about the need for nurturance. If others are sucking on you, it could be that you feel drained (see *vampire*).

suffocating: Are you feeling smothered in some relationship (e.g., work, friendship, romantic, family)? Perhaps somebody is holding you back.

If you're causing the suffocation of another, perhaps you are being too dominating and controlling. The person in the dream that you are suffocating may represent some aspect of yourself that is smothering you (see also *strangling* or *trapped*).

sugar: This can sometimes represent the good things you are denying yourself in your waking life.

Sometimes it symbolizes indulging yourself or your need to indulge.

suicide: Are you killing some aspect of yourself, perhaps something you may feel guilty about? This may also be a metaphor for escaping from something in your waking life (see *chase*).

Note: If this seems to be your general mood, then consult a professional as soon as possible, or contact a friend or someone you trust to talk about your mood and thoughts. Just about every city has a suicide hotline, and you can always call the national number, which is as follows:

1-800-273-TALK
1-800-273-8255

Or you can call 911 for support.

suing: If you are being sued or are suing someone, it could suggest that you feel accused of something or that you are afraid of being blamed. Is there some responsibility you have not fulfilled or some dishonest behavior you're not acknowledging? Do you need to apologize for something or assuage some guilt?

The image might also suggest that you are seeking justice or trying to prove that you are right about something.

suit: A suit in a dream could be the formal or officious way that you present yourself to others. It could also represent a more formal commitment to something.

suitcase: Perhaps you need a change of scenery. Is this where you keep your life organized and together? Sometimes this symbol can represent the womb where we carry all our longings, attitudes, and emotions.

It can also be a sign of status or a symbol of independence. It's also a place for hiding something, perhaps a secret (see also *bag* or *luggage*).

sultan: This could be a symbol for a controlling father or father image. It could also represent your leadership abilities (see *king* in the *archetypes* section).

summer: Sometimes this represents midlife, growth, knowledge, expanding the realm of understanding, freedom, leisure, warmth of feeling, and perhaps the peak of life.

summit: This could symbolize ambitions and goals or a new perspective on something. See also *mountain*.

sumo: Are you throwing your weight around? Are you wrestling with some idea or problem?

sun: This often represents vitality and warmth—life's energy. It could also represent the light of God. The sun is also a masculine symbol (see *anime/animus* in the *archetypes* section). It can represent time periods of your life. For example, the morning can represent the early years. The midday can represent the middle years, and sunset can represent the waning years (see *light*).

Frequently in dreams, we are visited by the image of light sometimes as a sunrise piercing the darkness of the night or as a sunset bringing an end to the day.

Some dreamers experience the sun peeking from behind darkened clouds or just the sun brightly shining on the land or through the window of a house. These

may be metaphors for the need for some enlightenment.

In depth psychology, the sun can represent the self in a dream.

The exploding image of the sun might reflect either the destruction of a God image (i.e., destroying the lovingness of God) or the explosive feelings of God's presence in one's life.

Alternatively, the sun exploding can reflect a traumatic end to something or some relationship (i.e., that some aspect of your life is or has ended).

sunburn: This can signal an emotional problem or situation that you should no longer avoid. This can also be a sign of an urgent matter.

sundae: This image could be about pleasure. It could also be a pun referring to Sunday.

sundial: Is it time to do something? Does something seem not quite real?

sunflower: This can represent warmth and abundance and can point to your spiritual guide. Is someone putting on a show, a false front? See also *flowers*.

sunglasses: Perhaps something has dimmed or darkened your perception (i.e., made it harder to see reality or made you see only the negative side to something). See *eye* in *body*.

Alternatively, it could be a protective symbol or one of disguise.

sunscreen: This can be about the rejection of some message. Are you resisting some truth?

sunset: This could symbolize a desire to quit or rest, the end of something, but it could also represent an opening to a new beginning (also see *west* and/or *dusk*).

This might also be considered an image reflecting the primal darkness that you need to overcome or transcend in order to redeem yourself (i.e., to release yourself from the darkened prison of your negative emotions).

sunshine: If sunshine is breaking through a cloud, it could be that you have had a breakthrough or are in need of one. It could also be a metaphor for an aha experience. You may be looking for enlightenment, or you may want to shed some light on something.

sunrise: This might indicate new beginnings whereas a sunset suggests closure and completion. Jung thought this was a symbol for divinity and the unity of self (i.e., the representation of the ultimate wholeness of people).

Because a sunrise is common to all of us, it could be considered archetypal. Man's soul seems to have an irrepressible urge to rise up out of darkness into the light, and this image can reflect that in a dream. It may be that you are spending too much time in the negative darkness of your psyche and need to find healthy ways to bring balance to your life.

superego: This represents the moral self. It includes the values and morals of the society and more importantly, those of one's parents (i.e., whatever the child in you thinks that Mom and Dad will approve or disapprove of). It is your conscience and image of the ideal self.

The familiar self-critical voice is your constant companion in your head, and it most often sounds like your parents and other parent figures. When you fall short of the so-called ideal, you are then punished by the voice of your internal superego. It is where your guilt comes from, though it also rewards you for proper behavior that meets or occasionally exceeds the ideal.

This ideal is actually someone else's expectation and is frequently tainted by the perpetrator's experience of loss, fear, failure, not measuring up, and feelings of betrayal that of course came from the experiences of those who came before. These can include familial experiences or cultural experiences (i.e., centuries-old resentments passed down from generation to generation).

Most of the time these internal voices don't even reflect what's actually happening, so to reconcile the discrepancy, the mind makes something up that will correspond to the predetermined position (i.e., point of view) and then calls it fact.

Often we label our self-criticisms or our criticisms and judgments of others as facts when they actually are not.

superhero: This suggests great ideas and talents, hidden abilities, or the desire for these skills. Sometimes this image is compensating for a lack in your waking life. Maybe you are taking on too much in your life.

Superman: This image may represent the heroic male figure in your life (see *hero* and *anima/animus* in the *archetypes* section), or perhaps you're taking on too much. If you're flying, see *flying.*

supernatural: Perhaps you are letting something beyond your control influence your actions or thoughts. Do you need to take responsibility for your life and actions? See also *paranormal.*

supernatural being: See *chimera, ghost,* or *specters or spectral figures.*

super villain: This may represent the negative aspects of yourself. See *shadow* in the *archetypes* section.

superpower: This can represent positive energy and a sense of confidence. What is the superpower being depicted?

Superwoman or Supergirl: These are heroic female figures (see *anima/animus* and *heroine* in the *archetypes* section).

support: This can be anything supporting (e.g., a support beam, something or someone holding someone or something up, or someone in a supportive role). These may reflect your need for support. Do you need to help someone out, or do you need to ask for help?

suppression: This can be about censorship (of yourself or others) or trying to control someone or some aspect of yourself.

It can also represent intolerance, thought, and emotional control. Do you feel vulnerable? Are you avoiding some feeling?

Perhaps some emotion is overwhelming you.

surfing: This may be symbolic of the ups and downs of life or some emotional relationship. You may want to conquer something that is overwhelming. Also consider the phrase "wipe out," which suggests that all is not going well. If all is calm and you're just riding the light swells, perhaps you are just going with the flow (see *water, ocean,* and *waves*).

surgery: Perhaps you need to remove something negative from your life. Does something need to be fixed or healed? It may also be a metaphor for opening yourself up, or if you're about to go into surgery, it could be a reflection of your concerns.

surprise: Has something caught you off guard? Are you willing or ready to confront something from the subconscious?

Has something unexpected threatened to spoil some goal, desire, or way of being?

Often we tend to try to forget upsetting material; however, the mind never forgets, and a current situation may have triggered this old material so that you can actually deal with it.

This can even be something about yourself that surprises you or something that you didn't know was there (e.g., some talent, ability, or courage).

The surprise may come from a realization that there may be more alternatives than the one you were presented with or the one you took. Is there any sense of betrayal and/or resentment in that?

See also *unexpected.*

surrender: Are you giving something up or letting go? Do you need to let go of some habit or behavior? Are you having second thoughts about something or someone? See *letting go.*

survey: Are you assessing some situation or your abilities? Are you being tested?

survivor: Are you hoping to be able to survive something? Look on the bright side of some situation.

sushi: This might represent raw emotions. It might also suggest that you acknowledge your spiritual side.

suspended: Whether you're suspended from school or your job or you're just hanging from the ceiling, you may feel disconnected, and you may question your future or your identity. It may feel as though your life is on hold.

suspense: Are you uncertain of something? Are you waiting for the answer to something and perhaps experiencing some anxiety about it?

suspicious: This could symbolize your intuition, a hunch about something, or your insecurities. Have you been left in the dark about something, or are you unprepared?

swallowing: What are you holding back? What are you not communicating? Do you need to fess up to something or just swallow your pride? Are you swallowing some untruth or some negative feeling? What are you swallowing in the dream?

swamp: Perhaps this represents the repressed dark aspects of yourself. Do you feel swamped (overwhelmed) at work or in your life? Swamps can also be metaphors for some adverse conditions or suggest that you are trying to attain some goal through some messy means.

Perhaps you are overwhelmed with something. If you're bogged down in the swamp, this might suggest that you find yourself in a difficult or adverse situation.

See also *water*.

swan: See *birds* under *animals*.

SWAT: Something may need careful handling. Some part of yourself may need protection or intervention.

swearing: Is someone verbally abusing you? Are you feeling pushed around? Are you being verbally abusive? Are you not being honest about something? Are you feeling defamed? Do you get angry enough to be in a tirade?

sweater: This can be about warmth, nurturance, and love. As with any clothing, it can also represent a cover-up of some aspect of yourself.

sweating: Are you sweating something out? Are you worried? Could it refer to some overwhelming anxiety or stress? Or do you need to struggle more with something (e.g., work harder at it)? Sweating can also be a cleansing symbol (i.e., getting rid of something unwanted or the need to cool off).

sweeping: Maybe you are clearing the mind or your life of something. Alternatively, are you sweeping something under the rug (i.e., ignoring or denying something that you should be dealing with)?

swimming: This can represent controlled movement through your emotions (e.g., confidence or a lack of confidence in dealing with your emotional events).

Insight: Swimming in the sea can be about survival, and how you're negotiating the waves may say something about how you're dealing with impulses, desires, and strong emotions. Thus, dealing with them may be about letting go of something or suggest that it may be time to just go with the flow instead of resisting.

Treading water can reflect a standstill in life where you don't seem to be going anywhere or achieving anything.

sword: This can be a symbol of great courage, strength, ambition, power, or the love of truth, and if you live by truth, nothing of any lesser value can hurt you. This is the promise of the magic swords—Caledfwich, Caliburnis, or Excalibur—specifically that the bearer will not die from any spilt blood.

It is also a tool to do battle with something and a symbol of social power. It can also represent a threat hanging over you as in the Sword of Damocles. The sword can also be an instrument of magic as in the singing sword.

A wooden sword may suggest that you are being fake or not telling the truth.

A sword may also symbolize cutting or severing something from something else or from yourself (see *knife*). It can also be a phallic symbol such as with a knife or a gun.

Insight: In tarot, the sword is also the symbol for creativity and original thinking. One can "cut to the chase" (i.e., get to the point) or be on the "cutting edge." It represents strength and ethics. It is basically male in energy, though there is a queen of swords that represents sorrow, which a person can overcome by reason and thought. This card also represents profound clarity.

symbols: If you see unknown symbols in the dream, perhaps you are confused or ambivalent about something. If they cover a body or your body, perhaps you are feeling overwhelmed by this ambivalence or confusion.

If the symbols are all over your forehead, you may be letting your thoughts overwhelm you.

sympathy: This may reflect the need to be more sympathetic. It might also symbolize the need for more sympathy.

symphony: This can be about harmony and cooperation or the need for it. It can also refer to the need for something spiritual and/or emotional uplifting. As with every image, your attitude toward symphonies can also give you clues about the meaning.

synchronicity: Synchronicity says that the relationship between ideas and meaning is structured in its own logical way and gives rise to relationships that are not causal in nature (but are not exactly coincidental). These relationships can show up as occurrences that are meaningfully related. See also *insight* under *scarab* in *animals*.

Synchronistic events can reveal an underlying pattern and a conceptual framework that includes (but is also larger than) any of the systems that display the synchronicity.

See also *coincidence*.

synagogue: Perhaps this symbolizes the need for more spirituality in your life, and it may suggest you are looking for a place of refuge. As with any religious symbol, look at your own relationship with it, your own prejudices, and/or judgments regarding it (also see *church*).

syringe (hypodermic, shot): This may be about health issues or worry. It could also represent the need to inoculate (protect) yourself from something or someone. Are you injecting more excitement into some issue or your life? It can also be phallic (see *sword*).

syrup: Are you in a sticky situation? Are things moving too slowly?

syzygy: This can represent the union of opposites (e.g., the masculine and feminine aspects of a person). Symbols for this might be an eclipse, marriage, wedding, and a yin and yang.

It is the union of Logos and Eros as well as the anima and animus. See also the *union of opposites*.

T

table: A table may reflect a place of activity, nourishment, and/or communication.

Emotional memories can be attached to particular tables. For example, where your grandmother served you warm milk and cookies could symbolize love, or the table where your parents forced you to sit and stare at a wall could symbolize something else. This will obviously affect this image's meaning. Note that both these examples could also represent the need for love.

tag or name tag: Tags can be about identity (one's own identity or something that you identify with) or a reputation that one is tagged with. It could also be the punch line of a joke. To name something is to make it real.

tailor: Maybe you're trying to fit in or make yourself look good. Consider the word tailor-made for something that suits you or some situation (see *seam*, *sew*, or *clothing*).

tackle: Tackling or being tackled by someone may be about the obstacles preventing you from achieving a goal. It could also reference tackling or taking on some job or task.

talking trees: This may represent your inner wisdom and spirit guide. Your unconscious may be trying to communicate something to you. Perhaps you need to improve your own communication.

The rustling of oak trees was once thought to be the voice of Zeus. See also *trees* for the meaning of specific trees.

The Tree folk of Inverness, California, by R. J. Cole. These caricatures of trees seemed almost animated. It was as though they could talk with me.

In the Middle Earth of J. R. R. Tolkien's *The Hobbit*, the animated talking trees were called Ents. To many

429

ancient cultures here on regular Earth they were known as oracle trees.

Native Americans had a story of a tree with two faces that alternately spoke to them depending on the time of day, while the ancient Greeks told the story of two philosophers who were arguing beneath an elm when the elm spoke up and joined the conversation.

Talking trees have played an important role in the mythologies and religions of the world and have often shown up in people's dreams.

tangle: Are you caught up in something? To be in a tangle might also suggest confusion, whereas untangling might be about bringing clarity to something.

tank: This can represent aggressiveness and protection of the self. Are you using anger as a defense against hurt or fear?

tarantula: This could be about your dark side. Because spiders can also symbolize the negative feminine, it may also reflect a woman with a sinister influence in your life. See also *spider* in *animals*.

tarot: Perhaps you are or should be open to the idea of exploring your subconscious feelings and/or thoughts.

Of course, the type of card can provide you with more information.

The symbolic meaning of a number of the major arcana cards is reviewed in the *archetypes* section.

There are four basic tarot suits found in the lesser arcana in addition to the archetypal images I've outlined in the *archetypes* section.

From left to right: Wands can be about inspiration, action, taking the initiative, or your spiritual aspects. Cups can be about emotions and your outlook on the future. Swords can be about strength, determination, and dealing with fear. Pentacles (a five-pointed star or a five-sided shape such as a pentagon) can be about finances, worldliness, and/or your connection with the earth.

See also *cards*.

tarp: If you are covering something with a tarp, perhaps you are trying to protect it. You could also be disguising or trying to cover something up in order to hide it.

It can also be about dressing something up or hiding something (i.e., creating a façade or false front).

task: See the *archetypes* section.

taste: Has something left a bad taste in your mouth? Something in the bad taste may reflect some unethical, indecent, or inappropriate behavior.

Taste can also be about your likes and dislikes.

If it's sour, do you resent someone or something? Are you behaving caustically? Maybe you need to be more friendly and cheerful.

Perhaps something has gone wrong with some plan. For example, has something turned sour?

If the taste is salty, could it be referring to the salt of the earth (i.e., being dependable and truthful). Salt in an open wound might refer to a difficulty or painful memory. Tasting the salt of your tears might be about heartache and loss.

Perhaps you need more spice in your life to liven things up.

A sweet taste may be about some indulgence or taking advantage of a good deal. Is someone being too sugary or sugarcoating some message? Perhaps you need to be more direct.

A bitter taste might be about something that is difficult for you to accept or tolerate.

It's also possible that this could refer to some guilt. Perhaps you need to be more agreeable and nicer to people or someone in particular.

tattoo: This may suggest a sense of individuality and uniqueness. You may desire to stand out and be noticed or attended to. Consider also that it may be a symbol for belonging to some group or a rite of passage (see the insight section under *scarred*).

It could also mean that something has left a lasting impression (see *face paint*).

Seeing a big guy with lots of tattoos can be about intimidation.

Taurus: This is sometimes symbolic of being stubborn, persevering, or having a strong will (see *bull* in the *animal* section).

taxi: This could include any of the online transportation networks. See *cab*.

taxidermy: This could be about giving new life to something you thought was dead and gone, or it could be about being stuck in the old and unwilling to let go.

tea: This could be about satisfaction and comfort with some situation. If you are making tea, this might suggest that you need more calmness in your life.

teacher: This figure can be symbolic of seeking some advice or guidance. You may need to learn something new. Your relationship with and judgments about the teacher in the dream will help your determine the meaning.

Teachers are also authority figures just like parents. They can represent all authority or one's own inner authority—the person who determines the course of your life. They can also act as your own censoring aspect if you are scolded (see *scolded*).

They can also reflect your own inner wisdom or suggest that there is something you need to learn.

tea leaves: These could represent a means for looking past the superficial and onto a deeper level.

If you don't believe in divination, then this may reflect a judgment that something is nonsense or fake.

tears: These can sometimes refer to a healing, perhaps an emotional healing.

They can represent compassion and spiritual cleansing, but they can also represent pain (or its release) in your life.

Insight: From a spiritual context, tears can be about letting go of the everyday, hardwired dichotomy of our brains that says we must perceive everything as either/or. (For example, things are either you or not you.)

Dreams with tears, especially when accompanied with numinous images and/or mystical feelings, may suggest the need to empty the mind of its usual perceptions so as to shift it from a dichotomous or me/them view into a more unity oriented or we/us perception.

If you're causing someone to cry in the dream, perhaps you need to rethink your behavior toward that person or people in general (see *rain*).

teasing: Are you not acting appropriately or taking something seriously? Is there something in your own character that you're not happy with and you are teasing someone else in the dream with?

teen: Assuming you are not a teen, are you acting inappropriately? Is there an aspect of yourself that still needs developing?

Does the teen reflect you at around the same age? What was happening then that you still need to deal with or that still seems to be happening now? Are you struggling for your independence?

teddy bear: This could represent trust and the need for emotional comfort. It can also be about loving something that cannot hurt you.

If it's a teddy from your childhood, it could represent innocence and a simpler time with fewer burdens, depending on the overall emotional theme of your childhood.

teeth: Perhaps you are having trouble reaching your goals and/or getting a point across.

Are you giving your power to others? For some cultures this image can portend or reveal sickness in yourself or someone else. The Chinese think of it as a symbol for someone not being truthful. Consider the phrase "There's no teeth in it," meaning there's no power behind it.

See also *teeth* under *body*.

telekinesis: This may represent the act of transporting yourself to other places. It may be symbolic of moving to a higher level of consciousness, another point of view, or a different way of thinking.

Perhaps you need to use all your potential. Or perhaps you aren't using your full potential. See *escape* as well.

telepathy: Do you need to pay more attention to what people are trying to tell you? Perhaps you need to connect more or better with people.

As a dream symbol, it can also potentially relate to a highly spiritual or metaphysical message from your subconscious mind.

Note what you are communicating to another person telepathically (or what the person is saying to you). This might help you say what needs to be said to someone in your waking life.

Depending on the emotions you have attached to this kind of dream image, it might also suggest a fear of exposure and vulnerability.

Another level of dreaming akin to telepathic dreaming would be the experience of shared dreaming or mutual dreaming, where two or more people share roughly the same dream. Again, there are literally thousands of accounts of this phenomenon, but there are no scientific investigations yet. Scientists have documented instances of twins sharing dreams and also dreams shared between therapist and patient. However, all of these have been anecdotal in nature and not as yet been scientifically tested.

No telepathic connection between two or more people has been found to exist through research to date, though this does not mean that it doesn't exist. The absence of evidence is not evidence of absence.

In order to prove or disprove the phenomena of dream telepathy, we need a well-designed and well–executed study that others can replicate.

telephone: This could represent the need to communicate. A broken phone might suggest that some communication has been lost.

An old landline phone might suggest the need to update your ideas or means of communicating. Perhaps you need to modernize your approach to something. See *cell phone*.

telescope: This may be symbolic of an instrument used to look at something more closely. It could also refer to looking at something beyond your normal experience (see *microscope*).

temperature: If the temperature feels *hot*, this could symbolize warm feelings and passion. If it's *very hot*, then perhaps this could symbolize painful feelings. Consider the word hot-blooded. If it's *cold*, you could feel held back by emotions related to fear, shame, or hurt. Consider the references to cold shoulder or cold feet.

An iceberg or ice in general could refer to being cold emotionally and/or sexually. If you are trapped in ice, it may refer to a deadening of feeling or a feeling of being paralyzed and/or frozen in time (i.e., not growing or evolving).

temple: This is a sanctuary of the soul. A church or mosque can represent this as well. This can be about your spiritual self, including your feelings, beliefs, and the forces of your relationship with the outside world.

temporary building: This may represent a temporary situation. See also *mobile home*.

tenacious: See *determined*.

tent: Tents can signal temporary changes from your everyday routine. Perhaps you need to take some time off.

Depending on the overall context of the dream, this can also reflect some insecurity or instability.

This might also mean you should live more frugally or closer to nature.

See also *camping*.

termite: This could represent an attack on your core being.

terrarium: This could be about protecting yourself from others or hiding some aspect of yourself. It's limited, contained, and/or restricted (see *garden* and *fence*).

terror: This could represent extreme fear and loss of trust and an inability to face these emotions.

It could also reflect unresolved fears or doubts that you need to deal with.

434

terrorist: This image could reflect violence created out of frustration, thwarted intention, and an inability to cope. This could also signal extremist views and a lack of human caring (because of extreme attention to the ego-self). See also *bully* and/or *tyrant*.

Insight: Extremists unconsciously project their fears onto a similarly uptight, self-righteous masculine deity with strict rules and uncompromising sternness. But a God that lacks mercy is not an authentic or moral God. This is all too often a flawed God image growing out of a fearful, self-important, and self-serving ego.

In my opinion, religion that lacks compassion is not being practiced authentically or morally. It is simply a collection of inflexible man-made doctrines. In short, people who cannot accept their personal flaws or forgive the flaws of others are but the fearful puppets of their egos.

An authentic morality is not restrictive, exclusive, or judgmental. It is always freeing, accepting, merciful, and compassionate.

test: In general, tests in dreams (and sometimes in our waking life) represent an ordeal or the intention of living up to some standard. It could represent a critique of the self or of some personal value. Or if the test is administered by a medical doctor, it could represent some concern about health.

Are you testing someone's integrity or your own?

If you're dreaming that you're late for class or that you've never attended a class you didn't realize you had or if you didn't study for the final and you find that it's scheduled for this morning, then this image may speak to you feeling disorganized in your everyday life or with respect to some event. This is usually associated with some overwhelming feeling as you will feel there's too much on your plate. You may feel as if you are falling behind as well.

If the image is of a paternity test, it's possible that the test is a statement of what you were after or your expectation for a relationship (i.e., having a baby). Are you trying to accept or reject some responsibility?

It may also reflect an accusation of blame for something or seeking justice (see also *suing*).

If you are failing the test, perhaps you're not living up to your potential or someone else's expectations.

In reality, tests say nothing about who you are really, though they may make a statement about your understanding of something.

See also *class*, *exams*, and/or *school*.

testicles: This image could represent your sense of adequacy or validity if you're a man. If you're covering them with your hands or another object, you may be acting defensively in some situation.

If someone is trying to cut them off, perhaps you are feeling emasculated and disempowered (see also *balls*).

texting: This may suggest your connection with others. Texts may also represent messages from your subconscious.

Perhaps there's something important that you need to communicate.

If you're having trouble sending a text, you may be having some difficulty communicating some thought or feeling. If you keep deleting your texts after you send them, you may be trying to hide something. If you delete them before you send, you may be having doubts about something. See also *phone*.

thanksgiving: If you are giving thanks or if the holiday Thanksgiving shows up in a dream, it is often about acknowledging someone or yourself or accepting some aspect within yourself.

It may also represent being thankful for what you have.

Thanksgiving can represent togetherness, reunion, resolution, a sense of community, and perhaps even the connections you have made in your life.

theater or play: This can represent the play of life. It could symbolize your own thoughts, feelings, hopes, fears, and dreams.

What kind of drama is being played on the stage? Are you or someone being overly dramatic? If you are on the stage, it may represent your desire to be noticed (e.g., wanting to take center stage), or it could represent the drama of one's life. If people are acting out emotions on this stage, it may refer to how you are dealing with public relationships.

Sometimes when you are transitioning from one stage in your life to another, it can be a bit traumatic. Along with the change comes a small crisis of identity. You may ask yourself, "Who am I now?"

Are you overacting or being too showy? Are you being real or acting out some role? See also *actor*.

Are you living your life or the one someone has written for you?

How you are moving on the stage (e.g., from left to right or vice versa) may also have significance (see *right* or *left*).

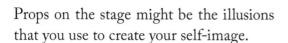

Props on the stage might be the illusions that you use to create your self-image.

The backdrop might be the narrative behind your life that helps to sustain the illusion.

The stage could reflect where you are in life or where you stand on some project. Perhaps you're not being real, or maybe something has been staged (i.e., inauthentic).

Being upstaged could be about being overlooked or made to look less than.

If you are downstage, it could be about being more front and center. It could also be about nearing the downside of something.

Being backstage could be about working behind the scenes or hidden aspects of yourself. It could also suggest deceit.

The set could represent something rigid or fixed, or you may feel the setting needs to be changed in some way. It could also represent a place of some importance to you.

If the curtain comes crashing down, this can be about catastrophic or traumatic endings.

If the curtain has come up but no one shows up on stage, are you feeling deserted, let down, or betrayed?

The lines spoken by an actor could represent your own inner dialogue or the narrative of your life. Are the lines negative or positive? Are they comedic, dramatic, or tragic?

thief: See *stealing*.

thirst: This could refer to an inner need, an unmet satisfaction, or an emotional emptiness or void (see also *hunger, desert,* or *dried up*).

thong: See *naked*.

thread: This can be about one's life path or destiny. It can also be a connection between things such as thoughts, feelings, ideas, or events. Colors of thread can also give meaning. See *colors*.

throne: A throne could represent power, the seat of power as in your own inner power, or your own personal authority over what you are and what you do.

If it's empty, this might suggest that you have not yet taken responsibility for something. The dream from your subconscious may be suggesting that you need to take responsibility.

throwing: Throwing something away can be about changes needed or letting go of something and moving on. See also *letting go*.

throw up: See *letting go* and *vomiting*.

thunder: This can suggest withheld emotions being strongly released as they would in an outburst, especially ones of anger or hate. See also *explosion or eruption* or *lightning*.

ticket: See *boarding pass*.

tidal wave: This can represent a huge release of emotional energy that takes you over (and overwhelms) as in a new love or a tragedy.

Tsunamis fit here as well because they can represent overwhelming emotions, and they can suggest that something in your life has been washed away or that you're inundated with problems and having trouble coping. They can also reflect your level of fear and anxiety (see also *water* and *drowning*).

tie: The tie could be about feeling trapped, or if it only fits loosely, it could be about unfinished business. Basically, the tie can be about one's obligations and relationship bonds. Is something keeping you tied down?

See also *necktie*.

tied up: This possibly represents tangled feelings and/or tension. It could be a tie between you and someone else (e.g., some kind of relationship).

Consider someone's apron strings. Are you dependent on someone else, especially a mother figure?

Perhaps you feel that you're out of control or that you want to do something but have too many other things going on and can't take on anything new.

This can also refer to your need for freedom, especially from emotional or psychological domination. Perhaps you are too controlling, or maybe you're controlling of your own emotions and psychology. Consider also the urge to dominate someone. There can also be an aspect of sexual domination to the dream (see also *domination, knot, struggling,* and *web*).

tiger: See *animals*.

tight or tighten: Are you being too loose or unorganized? Are you too unyielding or rigid? Could this be a euphemism for being drunk?

tightrope: Perhaps you're in a precarious situation and have to negotiate your way through it very carefully. See also *balance*.

time capsule: If you find or dig up a time capsule, you may need to discover some part of your subconscious self. Do you need to look deeper into your feelings and emotions?

time of day: Perhaps this symbolizes the passage of time in general, age, or aging. Daylight might represent your conscious self whereas darkness may represent your unconscious self (see also *clock*).

time passing: This may represent a chronology of events. It may suggest that you're getting older or that events and circumstances will not wait for you to make a decision or take an action.

Are you wasting yours or someone else's time?

Are things evolving, or do you need to let things evolve?

If there's not enough time, perhaps you need to take a break, or maybe you shouldn't take on more than you can handle. Are you too busy?

If it's at a standstill, perhaps this reflects your life. You may feel as if you are not going anywhere in your life or that some project has come to a halt or been obstructed.

timer: If a timer goes off in your dream, are you feeling under some deadline? Have you missed an opportunity? Is time passing you by and leaving you behind?

Perhaps it's time for you to get started on some project or some change.

If you see two timers in the dream, perhaps someone has betrayed you (i.e., two-timed you).

time travel: If you are time-traveling in your dream, perhaps you're trying to escape your present circumstances. Are you hoping to find what you're looking for in life somewhere other than where you are?

Note your feelings about going forward or backward in time.

See also *future* or *past*.

Tinker Bell: If you are seeing the famous animated character Tinker Bell, perhaps you are being childish or inappropriate with some behavior. Do you need to grow up? See also fairy or faery in *animal terms*.

tin man: A tin man may be someone who seems to have no heart, but deep down the person may have a big one. It can represent someone acting without compassion, someone who is unsympathetic, or someone who is unforgiving or unkind. When oiled (given some kind and loving attention), the person may become less rigid and stuck in his or her position. Do you know someone like this?

This can also be an euphemism for a policeman or a male abuser of meth. In short, an image like this can represent a variety of meanings from urban slang.

tires: Flat tires can also be about being emotionally drained and having trouble moving on in life. If they've been stolen, perhaps someone is obstructing your forward progress.

Changing tires could be about reevaluating your goals or getting ready to take a different path.

Titanic: This could be a symbol of overwhelming emotions. It could also reflect your fears of failing to overcome or navigate treacherous emotional waters.

toddler: Seeing or being a toddler in your dream can be about the development of a new sense of self. It can also be about you testing new boundaries, new environments, and/or new ways of being.

toilet: This could be about releasing feelings, letting go, getting rid of something, or flushing away some attitude, behavior, or dependency. Of course, as in many of my dreams, it may just be the body saying that you need to wake up and go to the bathroom.

Toilet dreams can also speak to one's public anxiety and shame, especially if they are dirty. Being filthy may also symbolize your worry that you are messing something up.

Unsuccessfully searching for a toilet could represent the conflict between expressing yourself publically and the fear of actually doing so. Is something eluding you?

A lack of privacy may indicate a fear of public exposure or a need for greater self-expression. Are you feeling vulnerable for some reason?

If the toilet is overflowing, it might be about the loss of emotional control or the fear of losing it (see also *bathroom, defecation, feces,* and *urination*).

toll: Maybe it's the price one pays in order to get ahead or to just stay in place. Is it worth it?

tomato: This is symbolic of happiness and harmony. However, if it's rotten, then it can represent disharmony, unhappiness, and/or dissatisfaction (see *vegetable*).

tombs: Tombs can reflect major changes happening or about to happen in one's life. They can also be about something hidden or buried, or they can represent a feeling of being trapped by some circumstance or behavior (see also *coffin* or *grave*).

tombstone: If you see a tombstone, it's possible that there is a major change happening in your life. It could also mean that you want to bury (reject or hide) something and forget about it (see *grave*).

tongue: This often represents what you say or express. Perhaps you've said too much, said something offensive or dirty, or need to express yourself more.

A cut tongue might have to do with being extremely upset. If you see someone's tongue cut out, you might be extremely upset but can't say anything in your waking life about it.

Sticking a tongue out can be a taunt/insult, or it could have sexual connotations. Forked tongues can be about lying or being hypocritical.

tool: This can be about self-expression or skill. It may also signal that you need to fix something or exercise damage control. It's also slang for someone who is being taken advantage of and/or blindly following.

toolbox: This might be about repairing some situation or relationship (see *hammer, saw,* or *screwdriver*).

tooth: See *teeth* under *body terms.*

tooth fairy: This could be about your need to be rewarded for some hardship.

toothbrush: Seeing or using a toothbrush can suggest that you may be preoccupied with how you look, or it could be a form of protecting yourself.

toothless or loss of teeth: To see yourself or another as being toothless may reflect your difficulty with achieving some goal.

The loss of teeth often reflects a loss of personal power.

top: A spinning top could mean that you're just going around in circles (i.e., not getting ahead).

Being on top alludes to your aspirations and goals. Maybe you're at the top of your game, or you want to be. It could be that you're seeking a higher understanding of something.

top hat: This can represent sophistication, elegance, flamboyancy, being stylish, and/or the desire for status.

topiary: Are you forcing your ideas and points of views on others? If it moves on its own, perhaps you need to let go of your influence, or maybe you are losing it anyway.

topless: Perhaps you're showing off, or you may want to be more vulnerable and open. If it's not voluntary, you may feel exposed and vulnerable in a negative light.

Torah: Perhaps you're in need of guidance. See also *Bible* and/or *Quran.*

torch: Carrying a torch could signify love but also enlightenment and the quest for spirituality.

tornado: This may represent powerful emotions that we may feel helpless against (see *wind*).

torpedo: Perhaps someone has torpedoed or destroyed some project or relationship. Have you been sneakily aggressing on someone or destroying some project? See also *bomb or atom bomb* or *explosion or eruption*.

tortoise: See *turtle*.

torture: If you are being tortured, you may be feeling victimized.

Are you being sadistic toward someone?

Torturing yourself or others could also indicate self-punishment.

Are you experiencing a desire for revenge?

totem or totem pole: This can be a symbol of protection. It can also be a symbol of power, strength, and familial loyalty or affiliation. These were often represented by animals.

Pagan religions often had totems. For example, the Canaanites had the lamb, which became a symbol for Christ when Christianity replaced their religion. For the Jews, Jehovah was represented by a bull. For the Celts in the Book of Kells, St. John was symbolized by an eagle.

Today members of certain service organizations are known as elks or moose.

See the introduction to *animals*.

touchdown: Are you achieving or missing a goal?

touching: Are you trying to communicate to someone? Perhaps you're trying to make an emotional connection. Touching can be about trying to get close or maintaining some kind of relationship.

If you are touched, perhaps you have been emotionally moved by something.

toupee: This may be about some sort of deception. Are you pretending to be what you're not?

If you lose your toupee, you may be losing your mind or your power (see *hair*).

tourists: Tourists can be those who don't belong or outsiders. This could be symbolic of what you're feeling in some situation.

You may be on a tour and thus need or want to explore some hidden or unknown part of yourself.

The presence of tourists can also be about your ability to help with something or help someone, or alternatively, you may need a little help or direction. It can also reflect that you, too, may feel a little lost and vulnerable.

tower: This image often represents the masculine (i.e., the phallus). Climbing it can have sexual connotations but can also be symbolic of wanting to get above it all (i.e., beyond the crowd).

Towers can also be about high hopes and aspirations. If you're looking up at it, it could represent envy or hope for something better. If you're looking down from it, perhaps you feel superior to those you deem below or beneath you.

It could represent an ivory tower and suggest that you are out of touch with reality.

If you're trapped in a tower, see *trapped*.

If you're climbing it, perhaps it signifies a spiritual quest or the need to gain a different perspective.

The kind of tower it is might also add meaning (see *castle*, *Eiffel Tower*, or *water tower*).

towing: Are you experiencing some burden or feeling overworked or overburdened? Are you or others not pulling their own weight (i.e., not working hard enough or doing their fair share)?

toxic: See *poison*.

toy: This could be about your childhood or playful attitudes. Alternatively, it could represent childishness or childish attitudes.

Are you toying with someone's emotions?

If the toy is broken, perhaps you're trying to make the best of a bad situation.

If someone breaks your toy, a person may be causing you to lose the joy in your life.

The type of toy and your relationship with it may also provide information.

traffic: This could be about frustration. You may feel stuck and unable to move forward with something in your life.

Are you just going with the flow? Do you need to break out of the mold?

If you are directing traffic, perhaps you need to start to control the direction something is going in or where your life is heading.

traffic light: Is something else determining how your life is going? Are you free to move on, or are you prevented from moving forward?

A green light can be symbolic of approval whereas a red light can indicate disapproval.

tragedy: You may be experiencing grief, loss, or regret.

trail: See *path*.

train: This could represent your forward movement on a narrow and controlled path. It may represent conformity and suggest that you're going along with the crowd or following the status quo.

You may be living in a rigid, orderly fashion. Perhaps you need to get off the track and explore your own road.

A train wreck can be about chaos and suggest that things are not going according to plan. You may have lost self-confidence and may not know how to get back on track. If the train has hit someone, perhaps you're on the wrong path in your life. If you're the engineer, then you are directing the forward movement of your life, but if you're only a passenger you may be letting someone do it.

A missed train can be about missed opportunities. A train station can be about waiting to get started on your path in life. The tracks in the dream can suggest that your thinking or your goals may be too linear. If you're crossing the tracks, perhaps you're going against the path laid out for you. Consider a person who comes from the wrong side of the tracks.

A toy train can be about the need to control the direction of your life. It can also suggest that you may be too mechanical

and predictable. Playing with a toy train can also symbolize the desire to return to the simpler time of childhood.

See also *derailment* and *train crash* under *crash*.

traitor: If you are accused of being a traitor, perhaps you are dealing with self-guilt. Maybe you've done something that you are not proud of.

Seeing a traitor might mean you feel betrayed in some way.

tramp, bum, or panhandler: This may represent the complainer, that part of you that wants other people and outside circumstances to be responsible for what you have not done in life. Sometimes this image can suggest an attitude as though life owes you something.

trance: This is a state of awareness outside of your normal state of consciousness. It can be associated with meditation, prayer, hypnosis, and some parts of the dream state (see *hypnogogia*).

This can feel like you have been enchanted as though through magic, something mystical, or an out-of-body experience (see *out-of-body experience*).

Seeing yourself or someone else in a trance might suggest that you need to look deeper into yourself for insight into some situation. Perhaps you need to open up more to others.

Are you zoning out (i.e., going unconscious and missing something important)?

transcendence: This is a sense of going beyond the limits of the ordinary and achieving something greater than the usual.

Do you need to transcend your ego-self or some way of being, seeing, or doing?

See also *mystical, noetic,* and *transformative.*

transfiguration: See *bathed in light* and/or *mountaintop.*

transformative: This can represent a feeling that you have changed in character, appearance, form, or nature. See also *morphing, tunnel,* and/or *transition dreams.*

transfusion: Perhaps you need to be revitalized. You may not be feeling motivated, and you may need something to get you started.

transgender: Seeing someone who is male in woman's clothing or morphing from male to female or vice versa could be about the need for change or a desire to integrate different aspects of yourself.

If this image seems to be more about cross-dressing, it might be reflecting your need

to explore your masculine aspect if you're a woman or your feminine aspect if you're a man (see *masculine* and *feminine* in the *archetypes* section and *cross-dressing*).

It may also reflect how you think of yourself or some aspect of yourself. It may also be encouraging you to be more authentic with some aspect of yourself.

It might be about your ambivalence in regards to male/female roles in some relationship. It could also reflect the difficulty you may have in dealing with the issues this image brings up for you. Has your own gender role been damaged or compromised in some way?

This could also be a transition dream. See also *gay, homosexual, lesbian,* and *transformation.*

transition dreams: Whether it's the journey from teen to adult, adult to parent, high school or college to the freedom of no school, unmarried to married, one job to another, work to retirement, or life to death, change dogs our waking life and haunts the images of our dreams.

Death in a dream can symbolize the need for the dreamer to make a conscious choice to change his or her life, perceptions, reactions, and circumstances.

Spiritual visitors to our dreams, such as the Christlike child, often symbolize spiritual truth and may suggest an important transition regarding some aspect of your being or your life.

In dreams we find ourselves standing at doors or gates that beckon us to enter. We run down tunnels, launch ourselves into the air, and fly freely across fields and valleys. We dream of marriages and weddings, of murders and deaths, and of greeting a sunrise or bidding farewell to a sunset. We fall down holes and morph from one thing to another.

If you are morphing into someone else, it could mean that you need to incorporate some aspect of that person into your own character, or you may be in need of a major change in life. Rapid morphing can reflect rapid change in your life—whether it's needed or currently happening. These are all symbolic images of change.

Whether threatening, pending, or ongoing, change is the one constant in all life, and our dreams mirror it all.

translating: If you are translating some language in a dream, is there something you need to understand better? It can also be about your ability to get your ideas across.

transparent: When something is see-through, it may reflect vulnerability. Perhaps you can see through someone's

hidden motives or your own hidden intentions.

Something being transparent can also represent clarity on some issue.

trapped: Perhaps you are having trouble breaking free of the past, old fears, or bad attitudes. This can reflect social pressures, someone restraining your free expression, a lack of opportunity, or a need to create an opportunity.

Perhaps there is something holding you back. You may have done something that you can't figure how to get out of (see *cage* or *suffocating*).

trash: This can signal a prejudiced comment or a feeling about someone or something (e.g., something of no worth or someone of no importance). If you feel this way about yourself or find yourself (or even someone else) in the trash in a dream, you might feel depressed and should probably seek professional guidance.

Sometimes this image can suggest that there is something you need to get rid of, such as some behavior or negative habit (see also *garbage*).

travel: You may feel the need to get out. Perhaps you're feeling closed in or even constricted by some circumstance in your life.

Do you need to move along in life?

Perhaps you feel the need to expand your horizons and live freely in some way. Is there something holding you back? See also *trapped*.

treason: You may feel some conflict between you and society. Are you acting in an unacceptable way?

treasure: Finding or hunting for treasure could be about the wonder or value of life, self-realization, wholeness, integration, spiritual reward, and fulfillment.

Finding treasures in a gutter can be about finding value in the least expected places (see *gutter*).

It may also represent your inner knowledge, wisdom, and spirit.

The loss of treasure can suggest the loss of balance or wholeness.

Insight: Sometimes we lose this sense of balance because we have accepted conventional attitudes or someone else's definition of who/what we are. When we do this, we may not be in harmony with our real selves.

By not looking deeper into ourselves, we can mistakenly identify with only our surface attributes and lose touch with the whole of us.

A buried treasure could suggest that you have buried some valued aspect of yourself. This may be a part of you that you previously rejected and need to find again. This can also be a symbol of some opportunity that you haven't seen until now.

Sometimes when we are emotionally or psychologically wounded, we may bury the most valued parts of ourselves that we wish to protect.

Buried treasure can also point to the valued parts of you that are hidden within and that you need to uncover and bring into the open.

Sometimes treasure can be seen as yin power to a dragon's yang power (i.e., the feminine in contrast to the masculine), and it can also suggest that you need to get in touch with the feminine in order to become more whole.

To find what you treasure most, all you need to do is look within with a pure heart and open your mind without judgment or bias.

If you are hunting for treasure, this could be about what it is you are searching for in life, your own Holy Grail (see *cup*).

The bottom line is that a buried or hidden treasure revealed in a dream can reflect the spiritual you, the soul that is being revealed.

treaty: Perhaps you are trying to negotiate a deal or a pact. Are you trying to sanction some behavior?

A treaty can also be about reconciliation. See also *negotiate*.

trees: These can represent the structure of your inner being, your self-portrait, and how you see yourself psychologically (e.g., your connection with the family and your roots).

Dead roots could signal a disconnection or an unresolved issue with some childhood experience. Dead trees could be about dashed hopes or dreams.

The branches become your aspirations but also your vulnerabilities. Consider the phrase "out on a limb." Dead branches might suggest a loss of your ability to achieve your dreams or to seek satisfaction in some aspect of life. It can also mean the end to a familial line. Bare trees can be about lost vitality.

Trees can represent your personal growth or the stages of your life. Many believe that the roots and trunk represent the divine nature of man, the branches representing the separate parts of this nature. Because of their temporary nature, leaves might correspond to one's personality.

Fallen or missing leaves might indicate a sense of losing your ability to hide your feelings or thoughts. Scars on the trunk might reveal traumatic physical or psychic experiences.

A falling tree can represent a feeling of imbalance. See also *roots* and individual trees such as *hazel, holly, oak, pine, redwood, rowan, willow,* or *yew.*

Insight: To the Hindu, trees often serve as images of the Axis Mundi, the world center. Their sacred tree, the Ashwath Vriksha, a banyan tree, represents eternal life because of its ever-expanding branches.

Throughout history many of the world's religions referenced a cosmic tree with its branches reaching into the sky, its trunk steadfast on the earth, and its roots imbedded into the underworld.

The Celts believed trees to be representations of deities and mediators between the world of the sky and the earth they lived on. Sometimes trees were seen as entrances into the Otherworld. It has been said that the Cornish King Arthur entered Avalon after he died through an opening in a tree.

Druids were said to believe that hollow *oaks* were the haunts of spirits. There is an old English rhyme that says, "Turn your cloakes, for fairy folks are in old oakes," meaning that when you turn your cloak inside out, the fairies could not use their magic and distract you from your journey.

In the Celtic world, one of the most magical trees was the *hawthorn*, which one could find in a witch's garden. It was said to guard the entrance to a fairy portal.

Rowan (mountain ash) and yew were also sacred trees to the Celts. A *hazel* tree was associated with fairies, and in Ireland, it was called the "tree of wrath" or a fairy fort. If you stirred your preserves with a hazel stick, it would prevent the fairies from stealing it.

The *oak* has often figured in my dreams, but it did not always have the same meaning. I have watched many majestic oaks succumb to what is called "sudden oak death" and despair every time that I see the initial signs that yet another oak has fallen prey to this deadly blight. Once the tree is infected, there is no hope.

The phrase "For how the mighty have fallen" comes to mind as I think about what is happening with the oak. Dreams about sadness, loss, hopelessness, and inevitability show up as oaks in my dreams these days, even though in some dreams the oak still represents the majestic, the noble, and the powerful.

In the Celtic tradition, the Welsh word for druid is *derwydd* and translates to "oak man." Trees in general were often seen as entrances to the Otherworld as well.

Trees offer power, strength, patience, steadfastness, and quiet centeredness, and I admire and desire all of these.

But the trees also reveal a darker side, especially when I wander too far into the tangled forest of the unconscious. They can come to me in my dreams in many dark shapes—some recognizable, others amorphous in form. But I have learned that they always come on behalf of my well-being.

Trees play an integral part in the book *The Archipelago of Dreams* (iUniverse, 2011).

I frequently tramped eight or ten miles through the deepest snow to keep an appointment with a beech-tree, or a yellow birch, or an old acquaintance among the pines.

—Henry David Thoreau, 1817–62

tree house: Are you trying to escape from your everyday problems and just climb above it all? The dream of building one could reflect self-development and the attempt to maximize potential.

Insight: Tree dwellings can incorporate both elements of the house and the tree. The tree itself can be a symbol for one's inner structure, the structure of one's life.

The roots can represent the family background and influence. The trunk may represent how one directs his or her energy and growth, while the branches can be about the directions taken in life, members of one's family, or one's many abilities. Whether large or small, canopies can say something about one's ambitions.

The type of tree can say something about your inner attributes. For example, an oak can be about strength, mightiness, protection, and hardiness. Oaks have also been seen as entrances into the underworld, the unconscious, and/or the fantasy world of fairies and elves (i.e., beings that represent realms of the self beyond the ordinary).

The banyan tree might represent shelter or a connection between the earthly and the spiritual. It is said to be the resting place of the god Krishna. In Hong Kong, the banyan are called wishing trees. In many Asian cultures, this tree is symbolic of eternal life.

The redwood tree may also symbolize longevity or continuity. The bay can also represent this concept of longevity and immortality.

Another sacred fig tree worshipped in various Asian cultures is the bodhi tree. This was the tree that Siddhartha Gautama was reported to have been sitting under when he attained enlightenment and became the Buddha.

To sit under any tree may be about seeking refuge from life's struggles.

A Christmas tree might be about family celebrations as well as looming stress and anxiety. It can also symbolic of your spirituality.

tree of life: This can represent the union of one's spiritual and bodily aspects and the need to balance both.

The tree of life links heaven and earth because it is rooted in the ground with its canopy in the sky. Its reach to the sky has often been the symbol of humankind's reach for perfection. Christians sometimes depict Jesus crucified on a tree of knowledge, which can symbolize redemption for Adam and Eve defiling the tree in the garden of Eden. Muslims often pray to Mecca on a carpet with tree symbols, while the Buddhists revere their bodhi tree, which is where the Buddha received enlightenment.

Insight: I've always been fascinated by images of trees and the mythological images of trees of life or what Carl Jung called the *philosophical tree.*

This tree has its head in heaven and its roots in the earth, thus metaphorically representing the binding of the higher and lower aspects of the human psyche (i.e., the spiritual and the mundane or the body and the soul). Many of these trees have visited my dreams over the years.

trellis: This may represent your support system. What condition is it in?

trenches: What are you trying to hide or defend against? Is there something below the surface of your outer being that needs fixing? It's also a metaphor for being in the thick of something, hard work, or vulnerability.

trespassing: Are you not respecting someone's personal boundaries? Is this happening to you, or are you observing someone else doing it to another?

trial: If you're on trial, perhaps you need to be less judgmental or more accepting of yourself. Are you feeling guilty about something? See *judge* and *jury.*

triangle: This suggests one's aspirations, potential, and truth. Sometimes it represents spiritual truth as in its three legs (body, mind, and spirit). If it's pointing upward, it may represent the masculine aspects of the self, but if it's pointing downward, then it may represent the feminine aspects (see *anima/animus* in the *archetypes* section).

Note that a yellow triangle can be a metaphor for a warning, caution, or a need to yield. If it's associated with people, consider a love triangle.

tribe: The tribe aspect might have something to do with being confronted with an unknown situation or idea or a group of people. At that point, you may not be sure how to deal with it.

If you are joining the tribe, are you going along with the crowd? Are you sure you want to join?

trick: This could be about being fooled. It could mean that something isn't true or real.

trick-or-treating: These may be about the rewards you can receive from asking for what you want. Perhaps you need to open the door and share some parts of yourself.

trickster: See the *archetypes* section.

tricycle: Perhaps it's suggesting that you show more of your carefree nature. Three wheels could also speak to the need for greater stability (see the *number three*).

451

trimming: Trimming something may be about growth or cutting back on something.

Trinity: If the Christian Trinity shows up in your dream, perhaps you need to spend some time looking at all the aspects of a problem or situation. You may need to integrate certain aspects of yourself such as your masculine and feminine sides to your nature (e.g., your assertive and compassionate aspects or your decisive and thoughtful aspects).

Simplified, the Christian Trinity refers to the Father, the Son, and the Holy Spirit, which very roughly translates as the creator, the implementer, and the administrator of the Word of God.

The Trinity or anything within a dream that represents the three could also represent the trinity of the soul, body (or mind), and spirit of the human being.

In a trinity of crosses, if one of the crosses seems to be bigger and dominate the others, which aspect of yourself is dominating the others?

Which of the aspects seem dominant or weakest in you? Do you need to become more balanced in your approach? See also the number three in *numbers*.

trinket: Holding on to one might suggest that you need to let go of something.

Maybe you're obsessed with something too trivial.

trip: If you're taking one, are you in the need of a change in scenery? Perhaps you need some relaxation, or perhaps you're ready to explore some other aspects of yourself.

triplets: Having triplets can represent aspects of yourself, some situation, or a decision (i.e., the physical, emotional and spiritual aspects). See also the *number three* and or the *Trinity*.

troll: This represents an inferior self-image. Are you belittling someone or yourself? Are others demeaning you? Do you need to avoid them?

trophy: This could represent recognition for hard work, or perhaps you need to work harder.

trouble: Are you feeling guilty about something?

trough: Drinking from one might suggest that there's some emotional issue you might need to deal with.

trousers: These could be about sexual temptations. Or perhaps you're questioning your role in something if they're on backward. Perhaps you're experiencing a role reversal. It can also symbolize

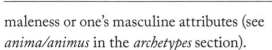
maleness or one's masculine attributes (see *anima/animus* in the *archetypes* section).

trout: See *fish.*

truck: This can suggest that you are overworked or burdened with something. Crashing it suggests you're overburdened and about to burn out.

A truck driving off and leaving you behind could be a metaphor for feeling abandoned.

truck stop: You may need to take a break and reenergize.

trumpet: To hear one might signify a warning or a presence that you need to pay attention to. Perhaps you need to stand out more. Something from the unconscious may be trying to get your attention.

The sound of a trumpet is often felt in the upper body and may be symbolic of your higher self or even your intellectual self.

trunk: This can suggest old memories, hopes, or feelings that you have not dealt with. They could also represent your burdens if you're carrying the trunk around or if it's the trunk of a car.

The trunk of a tree could represent your character and inner sense of well-being. Is it big and strong or thin and fragile? If the trunk is too thin and fragile, perhaps you're being too sensitive.

trust: Trusting someone or something in a dream could be about self-acceptance for all that you are, even the parts you've deemed negative.

You may or may not feel self-confident.

There may be parts of yourself or your personality that you don't trust or need to trust more. Perhaps you've lost faith in yourself and can't see your own worth.

See also *faith.*

truth: Are you telling the truth about something? Do you need to? Are you lying to yourself or others?

Perhaps you are trying to get to the bottom of something (i.e., the truth of something). Are trying to right a wrong?

Are you seeking another reality?

Some say that we don't see objective truth, that we see only subjective truth. The truth that we see and share with others may only be a projection (i.e., a confession of our own biases or repressed material that we are uncomfortable with).

See also *shadow* in the *archetypes* section.

tsunami: This may possibly symbolize overwhelming emotions and instability. See also *water.*

tuba: The sound of a tuba is deep and is often felt in the heart or the center of your body. It may be a metaphor for a visceral experience (i.e., a gut feeling and intuition).

Perhaps you need to get in touch with your center. See also *trumpet*.

tug-of-war: This can represent the need to balance things better or suggest that you are feeling pulled in two different directions. Are you struggling for dominance (to resist being dominated or to dominate)? Is there an inner conflict raging inside of you that hasn't quite played out?

tumbleweed: This could symbolize loneliness or a lack of direction and purpose.

tumor: This can represent a repressed memory or feeling that needs to get out and be recognized before it takes you over. Because dreams sometimes refer to bodily health, you may also consider it to reflect a possible health issue.

tunnel: This can symbolize a pathway into the unconscious. In a dream, tunnels are sometimes reminiscent of the birth trauma. In some dreams I feel almost claustrophobic and in near panic when I find myself going through a tight tubelike space. It can sometimes feel like impending death. See also *paralysis* or *suffocating*.

Sometimes getting through a tunnel represents something such as an idea, a memory, or a hidden emotion trying to work itself to consciousness. See also *transformative*.

Tunnels in dreams can often be about transitioning from one state of being to another. In this way, they represent transition or change. How you're going down the tunnel (e.g., walking, running, crawling, or flying) will add to the meaning of the dream.

You might use contextual clues to see what is trying to work its way out.

turkey: Are you being foolish? If it's sick or has been attacked, perhaps there's been an attack on your pride.

turn: This may represent a departure from the path you're on. Perhaps you need to change the direction of your life or of some goal.

A left turn can be about the unconscious and any repressed thoughts or feelings that you may want to deal with. Left turns might also suggest turning toward your intuitive side.

A right turn can be about conscious reality (e.g., a change toward something more rational).

A turn around could be about success or a need to change direction and reverse course.

Turns can also be events that are either a turn for the better or for the worse. It can also suggest turning toward something (engaging) or away from something (avoiding).

To turn off a path could also be symbolic of avoidance (e.g., avoiding things or people who have presented themselves on your current path). This could be an appropriate avoidance or one generated out of the fear of failing.

Turning can also symbolize exiting (see also *left* and *right* in *directions* and exit).

turtle: This is a symbol of wisdom and longevity. Maybe you need to take something slow. Perhaps you're presenting a hardened exterior and not letting others in.

If you're pulling your head in, perhaps you're hiding from something and not wishing to deal with it.

tutor: See *teacher.*

tuxedo: If you're wearing one, it could represent sophistication, grace, and money. Do you want to amount to something or look as though you do?

TV: This is possibly a symbol of looking at your own inner news (e.g., values, messages, and/or politics). Perhaps the shows you're watching in your dream reflect what's on your mind. If you are on TV, is there something that you want to say (broadcast) to others?

If the screen is blurry or all fuzzy, perhaps you are looking at something all wrong, or maybe you lack clarity on some issue. If there's no sound, perhaps there's something you need to hear but aren't getting it or letting the message in.

twilight: This might represent the end of something. But it also might suggest making room for something new.

See also *death* and/or *dusk.*

twins: This image suggests ambivalence, dualities, or opposites. If they are fighting, it may represent inner conflict.

Is there some specific situation regarding your current circumstances that you're not dealing with or not dealing with adequately? Is there some indecision or hesitation about something?

If you're birthing twins, it may be an image of inspiration or creativity.

Twins can also suggest being a couple or a desire to link with something, someone, or an idea. As an idea, it could represent something being a carbon copy or replica.

See also *doppelganger*.

Twitter: This can reflect a desire to stay connected or in communication. This could also include an excess of desire such as the need to be recognized, accepted, or affirmed. It can also be about gossiping. Are you being appropriate with your communications?

See also *bully*.

Consider also that it may be about shallow interactions and suggest that you need to have more face-to-face interactions.

See also *email*, *iPad*, and/or *memo*.

typhoon: This could be symbolic of sudden change and overwhelming emotional occurrences. Something may be building up in you that can sweep you away if you haven't dealt with it.

typing: This can represent the need to communicate or to express something in yourself. Consider also the reference to a person's type.

Tyrannosaurus rex: Could it be about your biggest fear? Perhaps it is you who is being tyrannical. If you're being chased or attacked, perhaps you are being demeaned or criticized by others (see *dinosaur* as well)

tyrant: Something or someone that may be overpowering. Do you need to dial it back a little? Are you or someone being too over controlling? Are you afraid of something?

See also *bully* or *terrorist*.

U

UFO: This can be symbolic of searching for spiritual purpose, or it can represent the feeling of being alienated from a group or in general (see *alien* and *spaceship*).

ugly: This could be symbolic of something ugly in you, possibly parts of yourself or a thought that repulses you and that you may be repressing.

ultrasound: If you are having an ultrasound procedure, perhaps you are looking into yourself for answers. Are you trying to find a solution to some issue or problem?

umbilical: This could suggest a dependence on others for your needs or an emotional tie. Some psychics and shamans talk about the psychic umbilical (i.e., where you are emotionally or psychically tied to), which is usually tethered to the place of your birth.

umbrella: This could represent something to protect against the elements. For example, difficult feelings or circumstances or anything not wanted from the unconscious may need protecting to your point of view.

unbalanced: Are you acting crazy? Are you treating someone unequally? Are you feeling a little unsteady and unsure of yourself?

Perhaps you need to center yourself and calm down.

Insight: All humans exhibit an inner balancing system designed to maintain an equilibrium within. When too much of any psychic force, whether positive or negative, is exerted either through practice or resistance, its opposite comes to the forefront.

Jung labeled this process *enantiodromia*. It's not unlike the process of yin/yang. When a counterforce is suppressed for long enough, it will eventually make itself known, sometimes in very dark and bizarre ways, such as with neuroses.

Essentially, when any part of the whole personality of a person or group of persons (e.g., a society) is suppressed for a great length of time, the Being will do whatever it takes to bring back balance. Sometimes that takes the form of war, pestilence, and famine. Too much or extreme good can produce evil.

uncertainty: Are you ambivalent about something? Are you confused, anxious, or uneasy about something?

See *confusion* and *anxiety*.

unconscious: We each have a part of our unconscious mind that is both collective and personal. Both inform the way we behave in the world and may even predispose the experiences that we have in it.

The material both of image and effect cannot be directly known though their expression in themes, and the shadows they leave behind in the form of metaphor, can be witnessed by those who are willing (or predisposed) to look.

See also the *archetypes* section, *collective unconscious*, and *personal unconscious*.

under: This may represent who you are beneath the social mask that you wear.

under or underground: This could represent the hidden part of you. Depending on the dreamer's physical orientation in the dream, you may be feeling less than, suppressed, or above others (i.e., feeling superior).

In the underground you may be looking at your unconscious depth that you have been ignoring.

Insight: Celts and other pagan cultures saw the underground as a place akin to the Otherworld or the origin of all beings (Native Americans and Australian Aborigines imagined that the world was born through the underground).

Caves, holes, and man-built underground chambers in the earth were often seen as entrances or transition points to the Otherworld and as a means of contacting the spirit and energy of the underworld. Irish Celts saw caves as a place where the transmigration of the soul took place.

Dreaming of going or living underground may indicate that you are trying to push certain thoughts and issues into your subconscious mind. You really need to confront and explore your unconscious.

Animals such as moles or badgers burrowing underground could represent you digging into your unconscious self in order to get down to the essence of who you are.

undertow: If you are swimming in the ocean and caught in the undertow, perhaps you feel overwhelmed by your emotions (see *drowning*).

Unresolved issues in your subconscious may be pulling you down and making you depressed. Maybe it's time that you deal with these issues head-on.

underwater: You may be submerged in your own emotions right now.

Sometimes breathing underwater is symbolic of returning to the womb, a place free from responsibilities where you feel totally cared for.

Underwater cities can be about suppressed feelings within your subconscious. To see people in that city might signal the need to go deeper into yourself in order to find common ground with other people (see *water*).

If you find pockets of air while trying to swim to the surface, it's possible you may have to consider suggestions for dealing with this overwhelming issue. For example, taking periodic breaks from it may allow you to rise above it and survive.

Insight: Swimming underwater may be about searching the unconscious or the inner self (i.e., the spiritual self), or it could represent the search for the warmth and comfort of the womb. Diving down can be about transcending one's normal boundaries though sinking into the depths. Drowning can be about failure or depression.

underwear: To see yourself in your underwear can be about a loss of self-respect or an aspect of you that is private. If you are standing in your underwear in public, you may be feeling exposed and vulnerable. Perhaps your secrets have been revealed. (This is even more true if you aren't wearing any underwear.)

Seeing others in their underwear could suggest that you are seeing them for who they really are. Perhaps you are experiencing an embarrassing situation.

Underwear can also be about revealing something that's been hidden. You may be ready to expose something.

If the underwear doesn't fit, perhaps there's something about you or the person who's wearing the underwear that doesn't quite fit, doesn't seem quite right, or is inconsistent. Perhaps a part of your persona or self-image (something that you've taken on) seems ill-fitting.

Torn or dirty underwear could be about feelings of inadequacy, or you may be feeling critical about yourself. Perhaps you're feeling sexually inadequate.

undressing: This could be about revealing yourself or discovering something hidden. Do you need to reveal your true feelings or thoughts about something?

To undress others is to get to know who they are (e.g., to understand them better).

unemployed: This can possibly represent a lack of self-worth or feelings of insecurity (i.e., that you aren't good enough or that you need to use your fullest potential). Perhaps you're afraid that you aren't going anywhere in life.

unexpected: Has something startled you in a dream? If so, the unexpected or unforeseen event could represent that you feel blindsided or could suggest that something has opened your eyes to something new.

Have you encountered some consequences that you did intend from a certain action?

Alternatively, perhaps you need to be more intentional in your actions or more predictable.

Unpredictable events can also speak to the abnormal, anomalous, bizarre, odd, or strange.

See also *surprise* or *unfamiliar surroundings*.

unfamiliar surroundings: Do you feel lost, regretful, or apprehensive?

Maybe you're not ready to leave your old life or way of being behind in order to take on something new. However, if the unfamiliar seems to be exciting instead of fearful, perhaps you are ready for a change.

If you are wearing unfamiliar clothing, are you facing a role change?

See also *strange* or *unexpected*.

unfriend: See *defriend*.

unhappy: See *sad*.

unicorn: This animal could symbolize magical consciousness. It can also refer to the union between your spiritual and animal nature. It is also sometimes representative of Jesus, indicating his dual nature of the divine and the human/animal. See also *animals as fantasy creatures*.

uniform: This can represent the need to belong and be part of a group. It can also reflect the need for greater self-discipline or suggest that you are conforming too much or too little. A uniform can also represent your identity or how you see yourself.

A uniform can also be a form of armor (i.e., self-protection) or what you hide behind. We do this with the roles we play in life as well (see also *soldier*).

union of opposites: This is an idea first recorded by the pre-Socratic philosopher Heraclitus (535–475 BCE).

This opposition is required for the existence of anything. For example, hot could not be hot without cold. There is no infinite without the finite. These things remain separate, and yet they define one another, causing a fragmented reality—that is, until they are able to reconcile and unite, thus becoming a whole.

Jung saw this as metaphor for the individuation process and saw its images in dreams such as an eclipse (solar or lunar) or of the marriage of a man and woman. It is the alchemical process in all human beings of "out of one, two and out of two, one." Also known as the Axiom of Maria, which states, "One becomes two, two becomes three, and out of the third comes the one as the fourth."

The concept can be seen across all religions. For example, the Star of David with its star of conjoined upward- and downward-pointing triangles represents the union of heaven and earth, and the Islamic crescent and star represents the union of solar and lunar forces. These are just two examples of the union of opposites.

Taoist yin/yang symbolism represents the union of feminine and masculine aspects.

The cross of Christianity also represents the union of spirit and matter.

See also *enantiodromia, squaring the circle,* and/or *yin/yang.*

universal soul: This can represent the anima mundi (soul of the world) or the Brahman-Atman of the Hindu, the Buddha nature, or the Chinese and Taoist Qi. It is Hegel's spirit/mind or the oversoul popularized by Ralph Waldo Emerson. It is the connection between all peoples and all living things. There are similarities between this concept and the more modern Gaia. Consider the world as an organism and an underlying unified reality, unus mundus, or one source (see also *soul*).

universe: This image could represent limitless possibilities, diversity, or potential. Perhaps you need to look at the big picture. Sometimes this can be a synonym for God or wholeness. See also *universal soul.*

unknown place: The unknown place may be a part of yourself that you are not familiar with or something that you have repressed or hidden but that you may need to explore. It can represent a change in your life or a need for a change. See also *stranger.*

unlock: See *door* in *house.* See also *code.*

unprepared: Perhaps you feel some anxiety and fear associated with some upcoming task. Do you feel a distinct lack of self-confidence or feel that you won't measure up?

untrusting: Are you not trusting yourself? Do you worry that you can't do something or might fail at something? Do you feel insecure?

unwrap: To unwrap something is to reveal some potential. You may be revealing some hidden talents, or if you're wrapping something, then perhaps you are covering up the real you, the real gifts you have to offer.

up: This could symbolize ascending or climbing to a higher attainment. Is something an uphill struggle? Are you moving out of some depression? Or the dream may be compensating for you feeling down.

If you're looking up, perhaps things look more positive.

upended: Has some plan or goal gone awry? See also *upside down*.

upholstering: Are you renewing or updating your self-image, or are you covering up something? Are you hiding something?

upside down: This can reflect confusion. Do you feel as if everything has been turned upside down? This could also be a metaphor for an antithesis (i.e., something in opposition or thinking differently about something or someone).

Are you being illogical?

Perhaps you need to see something from a different perspective.

If a building is turned upside down, the type of building (e.g., your family home, a school, or a museum) might add meaning. See *building, house, library, museum,* or *school.*

Do you need to straighten something up? Perhaps you are seeing something from the wrong perspective.

upstairs: This could be about being in touch with your higher self or some higher understanding (i.e., rational thought and objective thoughts). (See *attic* and *upstairs* under *house.*) You may also hold yourself in high regard.

urinate: This can represent the release of tension or feelings that have been held back. This can symbolize a release of negative memories, thoughts, or feelings. Perhaps you are pissed off about something. If someone is urinating on you or in your house, then perhaps you are feeling burdened by what he or she is dumping on you.

If you are urinating on yourself, are you on the verge of an emotional outburst?

Urinating all over the place or seeing urine all over the place could represent bottled-up emotions that desperately need to get out and be released (see *defecate* or *feces*).

Consider also that this may be a pun for being *pissy*.

used car salesman: This may be about dirty tricks, deceitfulness, and lying. Are you guilty of any of these behaviors, or do you know someone who is? Are you being dishonest with yourself or someone else? Are you manipulating someone or some situation?

Perhaps you need to be more cautious about some situation and not take something at face value. Maybe you should do more research.

This image can also be seen as a trickster archetype (see this in the *archetype* section).

utensils: This could be about lending a hand. A fork could be symbolic of a decision you must make. Consider the reference to a fork in the road. A knife might suggest that you may need to cut something out of your life, and a spoon might indicate that you're being given or are giving special treatment or that you feel entitled or spoiled (i.e., born with a silver spoon in your mouth).

utopia: Perhaps you're striving for perfection or expecting too much from yourself or others. You may be trying to escape the stresses of the everyday.

U-turn: Do you need to make a change in your life (i.e., change directions)? You may also want a do-over but know that you cannot have one.

V

vacant: A vacant piece of property could be about needing your own space, emotional or physical distance, or just time for yourself. Consider a vacant stare where you're not really focusing or seeing anything. Are you refusing to take in reality or another point of view? It's also possible that something may be missing in your life (see *void*).

vacation: Do you need a break? Are you trying to escape something in your waking life?

vaccination: Are you feeling vulnerable and trying to find a way to protect yourself? Do you need to take better care of yourself?

vacuum: This could represent a feeling of emptiness or the experience of a void in your life. Is your energy be sucked up by something or someone? If you're vacuuming, are you trying to make something look good on the surface?

vagina: This could be about sexual attitudes regarding feminine sexuality or reflect some urge. As a birth canal, it could

represent an entry into something new (see *birth* or *rebirth*).

vagrant: This could reflect your escape from social confines and expectations or suggest that you're being antisocial or feeling down and out.

valentine: Perhaps you need to show more love. Who you're giving that love to may tell you more about the dream's meaning. It could also be about a new relationship. Do you need to tell someone that you love him or her?

valley: Sometimes this can mean you are down-to-earth. It can also be a metaphor for being depressed. If it's a valley with no exit, it could be about something ending. A valley can also represent a deeper place where some part of you or your experience is hiding. Are you transitioning through some new way of being?

valve: Do you need to let off some steam and keep a cooler head about something?

vampire: This can represent fears about a sexual relationship and something that consumes your life force. There are people who just by their presence in a room seem to suck the energy out of everyone.

Someone on the surface may look good, but underneath this individual may be sucking up your vitality and self-esteem. See also *bully*.

vandalism: This could be about repressed anger or your passive aggressive tendencies. Perhaps you need to express your frustrations more constructively.

If you are the vandal, it could represent repressed anger. Maybe you feel that you've been treated unjustly or abused in some way.

vanishing: This often represents the loss of awareness or the loss of a loved one (see _disappearing_).

vase: This may symbolize a womb, something contained, or something on display.

vault: This can represent the womb, memories, or unmaterialized wisdom. It could also symbolize something you're hiding or some part of your life that you're trying to keep safe.

vegetable: This can represent spiritual nourishment. Look up the type of vegetable for more information.

vehicles: These can suggest movement and power in that movement. A vehicle can also be a car and represent your personal power, motivating drives, ambition, personal mobility, or the power to direct your life.

veil: This can represent a mystery that's hidden (i.e., a veiled threat). It can also be an image that suggests something hidden within you or something that you are hiding from others or from yourself.

Colored veils are often used in some worship dances or what are sometimes called praise dances. They often reflect the aspects and things hidden behind them (i.e., things not known to you now but hinting at something behind them).

veneer: Putting a veneer onto some piece of furniture might suggest that you are deceiving someone or yourself. Peeling it off might suggest that you can peel off this false front to reveal the genuine you.

See _clothing, fake,_ or _pretending_ as well.

venereal disease: Something may have contaminated your life in some way.

Do you feel victimized in some way?

This might also reflect a fear of having sex.

venom: Dreaming that a snake or someone has injected you with venom might suggest your own repressed anger or hate. You may also be experiencing this anger from others as well.

This can also represent someone's poisonous words.

Your own poisonous self-criticisms can be a result of poor self-esteem.

See also *snake* in *animals*.

vent or ventilate: Ventilation or an image of ventilating may be about releasing what you have pent up inside of you. Hyperventilating might then suggest that you are venting too much or need to let go or release more. See also *breath*.

venue: Venues can be like rooms and can often reflect your own personality traits (i.e., parts of yourself). If it's strange, then perhaps the image is highlighting an unknown, strange, or unacknowledged part of yourself.

Venus: If you see the planet Venus in a dream, it could symbolize a zodiac or astrological aspect (see also *planet*). It is a love symbol that also represents beauty, affection, and social appeal.

If this refers to a goddess, see the *archetypes* section.

veteran: This can possibly refer to a survivor or someone with experience and knowledge. It could also refer to someone or something that represents duty.

victim: This is often symbolic of that part of yourself that you beat up. It can also refer to a loss of personal power. Do you need to take control of your circumstances and/or your life?

You may be acting as though you are not in control of your actions or the circumstances of some part of your life.

video game: This may represent manipulation. If you're one of the characters, perhaps you are being manipulated. Perhaps you feel like you have little or no control over your life or some issue.

It can also be an escapist symbol suggesting that you aren't dealing with some issue. If the dream world is just one big video game, you may be having difficulty dealing with your waking world reality, or you may be rejecting reality in some way.

village: This can be symbolic of the need to be part of a community. It may also encourage you to simplify your life.

villain: This can be a representation of yourself. Perhaps there are parts of yourself that you aren't proud of. See *crime*.

violated: If you're feeling violated or some action in the dream implies a violation or intrusion, it may be symbolic of feelings of being oppressed or controlled in some way.

Has your privacy been violated in some way, or has something been revealed about you that you rather hadn't gotten out?

It may also have something to do with breached personal defenses.

See also *rape* or *intrusion*.

violence: This is probably symbolic of your unexpressed rage.

Perhaps you need more discipline in your waking life? Violence in a dream can also represent forgotten memories of violence early in your life that you now need to confront and deal with in a safe environment.

If you are being violent with others in the dream, perhaps you are struggling with an inner conflict (see also *anger, kill or killing,* and/or *mob*).

Insight: Basically, anger is a fight reaction, a defensive response. Unless you're hiding under some rock, anger will find you, and when it does, it will wreak havoc with your well-being, sense of centeredness, health, and virtually every activity of your life.

When provoked, most of us if not all of us will react angrily. Love, care, and compassion tend to fly out the window at this point, and revenge and violence becomes our focus as a means of reobtaining equanimity. However, it doesn't work. It either makes us cold and indifferent, cut off from ourselves or others, or sickened in heart or in limb. And yet we react anyway.

Violence as a means of righting a wrong doesn't work either because violence only begets violence. It's not a deterrent either.

Note that capital punishment is a violent act and has little or no long range deterring effect on future violence.

Violence in the form of hate perpetuates hate and hurts/damages both the hater and the target. And the damage is not only psychological, emotional, and moral but physical as well because the body's health is negatively affected by anger and hate. The nightmare violence and hate in our dreams over a prolonged period can have this effect as well. [17]

There is nothing more damaging to the human psyche (soul or spirit) than doing or sanctioning violence to another human being regardless of the reason or justification.

violin: This can represent peacefulness and honor, but if it's broken, then it could signal feelings of separation or sadness.

viper: This may suggest hidden fears or someone who is being malicious and poisoning the environment and/or your reputation. Be on your guard. This can also reflect you being self-critical. See *snake* in *animals*.

virgin: This is sometimes symbolic of potential or emotional innocence. If you are not a virgin, it could represent regret or remorse for something. It could also be about wanting to regain your innocence or your loss of innocence.

If you're dreaming that you are losing your virginity, it might represent a desire for closeness or the desire for understanding and expertise in some area of your life. In a man's dream, it could represent his feeling self or his soul.

Virgin Mary: This image is often symbolic of ideal motherhood, spiritual harmony, selfless love, and compassion.

This sometimes represents the divine feminine that shows up as purity in most of the world's religions. Others in this category might include Isis, Sophia, Dianna, and Venus (see also *goddess* in *archetypes* section).

Virgo: This often represents purity or perfection. It's symbolic of a detail-oriented personality. Do you need to pay attention to the details of something or of all things in general? This can also be a symbol of your emotional side and thus may be about being more or less emotional (i.e., releasing or controlling).

virus: This image could suggest a hidden attack. It can reflect hidden anxieties or other feelings that infect you and may keep away from others. The negativity around you can be infectious and cause

anxiety, and your own negativity can be infectious too.

If it's a computer virus, then perhaps someone has attacked you, put you down, or undermined your work or credibility. It could also be a destructive aspect or process in you.

If you have contracted a virus in the dream, perhaps you are experiencing upsetting changes in your waking life. It could reflect an impending or ongoing emotional breakdown.

Vishnu: See *Shiva*.

vision: If your vision is obstructed, are you making an error in judgment?

Insight: Sometimes people have great dreams—powerful and compelling dreams that seem to have a life-changing and mystical quality that can't be ignored. Because of their numinous quality, you may want to look for meaning amongst the images of the *archetypes* section.

These dreams have a very vivid and strong emotional component that can leave you awestruck and reveal greater awareness. After that, you may have to reevaluate a long-held point of view.

Though they often show up in dreams when the great editor (the ego) is sleeping, they can also show up unbidden and sometimes unprovoked in our waking lives.

Often these dreams or visions will last for many years and feel as though they just happened yesterday.

The Talmud, Christian Bible, and the Muslim Quran are rife with this type of dream. Jacob's dream of angels ascending and descending a ladder from heaven, Saul's encounter on the road to Damascus, Mohammad's night journey are all such life-changing dreams.

visiting: Perhaps you need to reconnect with someone or with an aspect of what that person represents?

visitor: A visitor can symbolize that some important information or communication is to be revealed. One can herald a new phase or change to your life. If the visitor is not welcome, you may be resisting this change.

If you are the visitor, perhaps you need to change your perspective on something.

If the visitor comes to your house, perhaps your house is a reflection of you, your body, and where you live. A visitor could reflect a new idea or a health issue.

vitamin: This may signal a concern about health or vitality.

voice: If you're hearing a voice, maybe it's your inner voice or personality trying to be heard.

If you've lost your voice or it is being hushed, then perhaps you or someone else is preventing you from expressing something.

A person's voice can also represent his or her personal power.

voiceless: Perhaps this represents a loss of identity. Maybe it's a loss of personal power.

voice mail: Is there something (communication or advice) you may have overlooked? Do you need to communicate something to someone?

voices: This can suggest messages from your deeper self. Perhaps you need to have a stronger voice in your life so that you can speak up for yourself.

void: This could suggest that something is missing in your life. It may represent a fear of losing something or a fear of failure (see *abyss*). Because a void is the symbol for nothing, it may also be everything, and confronting it may be good for your emotional health.

A void may also be a metaphor for loneliness. Standing at its edge could symbolize insignificance. See also *abyss*.

volcano: This could symbolize erupting emotions. Are you ready to blow?

volume: Perhaps this represents turning up the loudness, and it might also suggest that you are demanding to be heard and noticed.

If you're too loud, then perhaps you are forcing your opinions on others. If the volume is too low, perhaps you're not listening to someone (see also *yelling*).

volunteer: This could be about your willingness to offer yourself, someone asking for your help, or some situation that is calling for assistance.

vomiting: This can be about purging anything poisonous to your well-being. You may want to throw up whatever makes you feel bad about yourself in order to get it out. You may desire to discard some toxic point of view or to purge something from your memory (see also *nausea*).

Sometimes before starting anew, one needs to purge the bad habits of the old.

voodoo: Are you trying to defend against some negativity in others or in yourself?

voting: This suggests choosing and taking a side or a position. Depending on your point of view, it could also represent a feeling of futility.

vow: This may symbolize a promise and perhaps a commitment to be made or reinforced.

voyage: This could represent self-discovery. It may also reflect feelings, depending on the mode of travel (see *boat, ship, car, train,* and *bus*).

voyeur: Perhaps you are afraid of your own desires, or maybe you are scared of getting too close to something or someone.

vulture: This can suggest insight. Perhaps you or someone else is being opportunistic and taking advantage of an unfortunate situation. This can also be a symbol for the end of something, or it can symbolize rebirth if death is also involved.

W

wading: This could be about your control over your emotions.

If the water is muddy, you may not be able to see what you're getting into. Wading can also be about wading into a project or problem. You may just need to dive on in and get started.

How deep the water is may tell you how big the problem is or how little control you have, especially if you sink and the water level is over your head.

wager: Are you taking a risk with something? Should you be more cautious?

wages: Are you indebted to someone, or are you giving more than you're getting? See also *money*.

wagon: Like a truck, this could represent some burdens or difficulties you're experiencing.

If you are jumping on or falling off this wagon, it may reflect a broken promise. If the wagon is empty or abandoned, perhaps you are suffering some loss. See also *truck*.

waitress or waiter: This can often symbolize being of service or resisting being servile.

waiting: This could reflect a control issue. Are you being too passive? Should you be more dominant?

Do you need to take control of some situation? If you are keeping someone else waiting, perhaps you're taking advantage of someone.

How patient are you? If you are impatient, are you being too demanding?

waking: If you can't wake someone up in the dream or you can't wake yourself up, this may be about feeling helpless, frustrated, alone, or isolated from some issue.

waking dream: There are those who believe that the reality we live in is a waking dream, a dream within a dream.

The concept of the waking dream is also used by some psychoanalysts to help people get a better handle on what motivates them by looking closely at what the world presents them and then using that data to better understand what is going on within.

Given that we all project ourselves onto the world we experience, I often use the input from the waking world along with that from the dream world. I also add a note or two in the margins of my dream journal about what's happening in and around the time of a dream in order to add context and broader meaning for the dream.

walkabout: Do you need to reconnect with your source? See *wandering*.

walking: This could be about making steady progress toward some goal. However, if you were riding in a vehicle and then were stopped and had to continue by walking, this might refer to some obstacle that has slowed your forward progress.

Perhaps you are unsure about how to proceed in some situation. If walking on rocks or slippery ground, you may be in an uneasy situation. Perhaps you shouldn't be too overconfident in some situation.

Where you're walking will also add meaning to the dream.

walking on water: Perhaps you need to understand your emotions better. Do you fear drowning emotionally and therefore need to remain on the surface of this part of yourself? For example, do you keep everything on a surface or superficial level?

walking stick: Do you need support? Do you need help? See also *cane*.

wall: This represents a barrier or partition, and it can also reflect defensiveness. Walls can symbolize a way of maintaining emotional control and stability.

A crumbling wall might indicate disintegrating control or a deteriorating sense of safety. It can also mean that you may need to take down the walls you put up between you and others that you previously used to protect yourself.

Building a wall might suggest the need to create some boundaries in your life. Perhaps you are being too loose with the truth or too open, thus making yourself too vulnerable to others. See also *fence*.

wallet: See *purse*.

wand: A wand can symbolize your power, influence, or control over others. However, if someone else is waving the wand, then it could suggest that he or she has power over you. See also *witches, witchcraft, wizard*, or *tarot*.

wandering: Wandering around in a dream could be about you searching for answers or looking for some direction and guidance. It could also suggest that you lack focus and goals (see also *walkabout*).

wanting: This may be a feeling in the dream and thus be about desire. If the feeling is about not wanting, it could be about being independent. Perhaps someone has been looking at you and found you wanting (i.e., judging that you are not meeting expectations).

Insight: Sometimes we want something that is not in our best interest or desire something that we actually oppose. This can set up an inner conflict that we need to resolve before we take action.

war: This could represent violent resolution of conflict. Are there parts of you in conflict? There may be a serious conflict between your instinctual self and the social rules of conduct.

As with any dream, the image can also represent the opposite, and in this case, it can be about the need to reconcile rather than shoot for victory. Most violence in dreams involves self-assertion and societal assertion or the need to dominate. War can also represent the fight between one's inner and outer life.

wardrobe: The wardrobe could reflect a transitional period or a new phase in your life. Because this contains clothing, it could also relate to your self-image or the mask you wear in order to present a certain image to people.

See also *closet*.

warehouse: This may represent a place for storing memories or unwanted things and past experiences. It could also be where you store your potential. Have you put something on hold, or do you feel as though you've been put on hold?

warmth: If you are experiencing warmth in your dream, you may be looking for love, compassion, and/or caring. Perhaps you need to express more of your positive feminine aspects. Are you just warming up to some idea or some person? See also *cold*.

warning: Something may need your attention. There may be something you need to bring to consciousness.

warrior: See *knight, marine,* or *soldier.*

warts: You may need to acknowledge the beauty in someone, something, or even yourself—warts and all.

washing: Washing can be about emotional, psychological, or spiritual cleansing. The washing of hair can be about a change of attitude or getting rid of something or someone negative. See *shampoo*.

wasp: See *animals*.

waste: Are you wasting your time on something? Are you wasting your talents, your potential, or your life? Are you physically wasting away? Are you treating someone or being treated like garbage?

watch: Are you just standing by without engaging? Are you being too passive?

Do you need to be more engaged, more involved in your life?

Do you feel like an outsider?

What were you feeling as you stood there watching? Did you have any thoughts or judgments about what you were seeing? These questions can give you more insight into the dream's meaning.

Think about the phrase "Watch it," which requests that you pay attention to what's going on around you. It could also give you a warning of some danger. If you are a watchman in the dream, perhaps you need to watch out for something. See also *wristwatch*.

water: In its many forms, it is often symbolic of the unconscious.

Water could be reflecting the state of your emotions. If you're entering the water, then you may be wading into strong feelings, and deep water may mean that you are looking deep into your unconscious.

People can drown in their emotions. See *drowning* or *walking on water*.

If you are floating on water, see *floating*.

Hot water could be symbolic for being in trouble or for facing difficult situations (see *trouble*).

Clear water may symbolize feeling safe so that you can deal with your emotions. Dirty water could signal that you don't feel safe with regard to dealing with your emotions.

Muddy or polluted water might be a euphemism for making things more complicated than they are and/or for causing problems where there were none. See also *pollution*.

If you're in over your head and you're in deep water, you may not feel competent enough to handle some situation. See also *drowning, flood, tidal wave, underwater, walking on water*, and the *archetypes* section.

Because water often reflects the state of one's emotions, raging water (as with a raging river) may reflect raging emotions that can be either good or bad, exciting or chaotic and tumultuous.

How deep is the water? How is it contained? How do feel when you're wet? Consider also the phrase "You're all wet," meaning that you don't know what you're talking about.

Insight: Water is one of the four ancient elements—water for emotions, air for the intellectual self, fire for spirit, and earth for the body.

In reality, water is the very basis of life itself, for nothing can grow without it. In fact, it makes up 71 percent of the surface of the world we live on, and it also makes upward of 65 percent of our bodies. Our lungs are 90 percent water. Our brains are 70 percent water, and our blood 80 percent water.

Water plays an integral role in all the earth's systems, including its weather and ability to sustain life.

Water has been used metaphorically as a means of cleansing the soul so that the spirit of God may enter or as a symbol of death and resurrection (a rebirth into something new). It can reflect a way of washing away one state of being to make room for another.

It can represent the inner self, the spiritual self, and the feeling self. It can summarize our coping, our sexuality, our unconscious minds, and the boundary between them and that of our conscious minds. How we interact with all that life throws at us is reflected in the waters of our dreams.

See also *lake, ocean, pool, sea,* or *swamp.*

waterfall: Waterfalls are symbols of letting go and the release of pent-up emotions. They can also be about revitalization, empowerment, and renewal. Being at the bottom of one could indicate that one is overwhelmed or that the dreamer is having difficulty coping with his or her feelings.

If you've voluntarily ducked under the waterfall, especially if on a hot and sweaty day, it could be about relief (either having been relieved or the need for relief). Emotions associated with this image will provide more information about its meaning.

water's edge: This may represent where the conscious and unconscious meet (just as you wake from the dream) or that which is unconscious and trying to come to consciousness (see also *beach*).

watermelons: Watermelons can be about love and desire.

Women on the verge of their period sometimes dream of watermelons (because of the attendant bloating).

It can also be a pregnancy dream. Watermelons are often summer images and can represent leisure activities.

waterslide: Are you being carried away by your emotions? There's also the possibility that you're just going with the flow.

What are you sliding into? Are you moving toward hell, fire, bliss, chaos, or peacefulness?

water tower: This can represent stored or contained emotions. This might also reflect the impulse to contain your feelings of love.

waves: If you are riding the waves as in surfing or bodysurfing, it could mean you are trying to get control over your emotions. If you wipe out, perhaps you've lost it and let your emotions get the better of you.

weak: This may suggest that you are feeling inadequate. Do you need to be more assertive with someone or some aspect of your life? Do you need to stand up for yourself?

weapons: These could be about defending yourself from hurt. If the weapon fails to work, you may be feeling powerless and defenseless. If you are aggressing upon someone, you might want to look at what about yourself you are attacking.

If the weapons aren't working, perhaps you are feeling vulnerable and/or inadequate. This might also suggest that your aggression is turning against you (see also *gun* or *knife*).

weather: When the weather in a dream dominates, it could be about your moods and emotions (e.g., stormy, calm, rainy, windy, sunny, or cold).

Any kind of turbulent weather can be a reflection of feelings you are having. For example, *stormy* can reflect a quarrel you may be having with someone. If the storm comes up suddenly, perhaps you are jumping to anger too quickly.

Note if the weather is changing in the dream because this may be calling for some action of change on your part. See also *environment* and/or *moon*.

web: This could symbolize an entanglement or sticky situation. Are you caught up in something? A web can also represent conspiracy and lies. Consider the phrase "Oh, what a tangled web we weave," referring to the telling of lies or half-truths.

They can represent our relationship entanglements and the sticky circumstances we get ourselves into. Webs can be supportive or negative. Consider the phrase "the web of life." See also *knot* and *tied up*.

Note also that an orb spiderweb is like a mandala and may reflect the various levels of yourself from the superficial ego to the soul in the center.

A web may also refer to the World Wide Web (www) and thus be about communication and connections (see *internet*).

See also *strings*.

Insight: There's a Hindu myth that Maya spun the world of illusion. Medieval spiders spun a protective veil over the holy family just as Charlotte spun her words into a web to protect her pig in E. B. White's book *Charlotte's Web*.

wedding: This could symbolize a union of complementary yet opposite aspects of the self, such as your masculine or feminine aspects.

If you don't know who you're marrying, this may have something to do with something unseen, mysterious, or strange within yourself that is trying to be expressed.

It can also represent other contrasting creative forces, such as rationality and imagination, conscious and unconscious, or body and spirit.

It can also represent the transition from one way of being to another (see *transition dreams*).

See also *runaway bride*.

See *anima/animus* in the *archetypes* section and *marriage*.

wedding dress: Wearing a wedding dress can be about the need to evaluate your personal relationship with someone.

Are you at a wedding but not the bride? Perhaps it reflects your desire to be the one married to someone like the groom.

If wearing the dress at a venue or event where it's inappropriate, perhaps you are feeling unworthy or that your role in something is confused and you're not fitting in.

weeds: Perhaps this represents a growth that is choking out more nourishing growth. Is it actually a flower? Is one man's weed really another man's flower?

weight: This can represent burden or responsibility. Is something weighing you down? Overweight could be about a heavy burden, while underweight may be about taking something too lightly (i.e., not seriously enough).

well: This could suggest a way of getting to your deepest resources of life. It can also represent deep transcendent wisdom. This image could be about contained emotions as well. This can represent a view into your depths. What does it reveal? Also see *water*.

werewolf: This fanciful animal could be symbolic of repressed instincts or uncontrollable instincts. Its bite can cause you to become what you are not. Are others controlling you through their biting remarks (see *possessed*)?

west: This could represent an ending. West is the direction from which darkness comes. It is the unknown, the subconscious, and the place of self-discovery. One might ask of any of the four directions, "Where am I heading?" It is also where the sun sets, and thus, it can signal an end to something.

If the sun is rising in the west instead of the east, it could suggest that instead of something coming to an end, something new may be just beginning. Often endings or even deaths in a dream suggest that there is now room for something new.

I also wonder if this reverse image could be reflecting some inner conflict in your life. Could the dream be suggesting that you take a different perspective on some issue, person, or event?

Moving from west to east might indicate that something is ending while something else is now beginning (see also *dead people*).

wet: Being wet can be about being overwhelmed by emotion. It could also reflect the need for cleansing oneself. Perhaps some idea is all wet (i.e., not true or without merit).

See also *bed* in *house* if you are wetting the bed.

Whac-A-Mole: If you're playing Whac-A-Mole in your dream, perhaps you're experiencing a painful issue, memory, or feeling that keeps coming up no matter how you try to forget it or deal with it.

You may feel as though you've lost control of some situation. You may feel frustrated, and you may also ask yourself, "What's the use in trying?"

whale: This could be about the power of your unconscious. To be swallowed by a whale might suggest being consumed by your shadow self. They can represent the power of the collective unconscious.

Whales can represent our psychological impulses either for good or ill. They can represent huge emotions, urges, or the drive for reproduction.

wheel: This could reflect the ability to meet change. It can also represent the cyclical nature of life. As a wheel of fortune, it can represent the wins and losses. As the steering wheel of a car, it can be about taking the direction of your life into your own hands.

Sometimes wheels begin to make noise, and thus, it becomes the squeaky wheel that gets all the attention. Are you demanding too much attention? If you start the wheel moving, perhaps you're setting things in motion (e.g., starting a new project).

Sometimes wheels can be symbolic of mandalas.

wheelchair: Where do you feel a loss of power? Are you handicapping yourself in some way? The wheelchair can also represent a person who seems disabled. Do you feel unable to motivate yourself? Do you need some help to get going on some project?

whining: If you or someone else is whining, are you or something else being annoying? Are you complaining too much and not taking responsibility for something getting done? Are you unwilling to let something go? Are you trying to get attention?

whip: This could reflect hurtful comments. These should also include the ones you make against others and against yourself.

Are you someone's whipping boy? Are you letting someone walk all over you and blame you for his or her failures? Is someone bullying you, or are you being the bully?

Do you need to whip something or someone into shape?

Do you feel defeated?

Note that this image also has a sexual symbolism. Are you being sadistic or masochistic?

whisper: Hearing a whisper or whispering in a dream might suggest that you need to listen closer to something.

Are you unsure of something or feeling insecure? Is someone talking behind your back?

Are you keeping something hidden?

white person, black person: These may reflect your prejudices and biases. They can also reflect your fears and level of trust.

The black man or woman can represent your shadow nature (see *shadow* in the *archetypes* section).

In a man's dream, a black woman can represent his soul. In a woman's dream, the black man can represent her soul. His or her soul can be black (i.e., dark or negative) and represent the opposite nature. See *anima/animus* in the *archetypes* section.

In certain parts of the world, the white man can be seen as an authority figure or one who dominates others.

whore: If this is a negative image, it may represent a misuse of sexuality, but if it's portrayed in a positive context, it could represent the need for sexual healing. As a prostitute, are you selling yourself short (see also *prostitute*)?

wiccan: See *witches*.

widow: Do you fear a breakup? This image could also be symbolic of isolation.

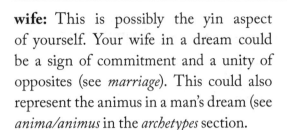

wife: This is possibly the yin aspect of yourself. Your wife in a dream could be a sign of commitment and a unity of opposites (see *marriage*). This could also represent the animus in a man's dream (see *anima/animus* in the *archetypes* section.

Wi-Fi: Perhaps you need to build a means of expressing yourself more readily. Do you need to be more personal in your communication?

wilderness: This could represent the wild, uncultivated, undeveloped self. This could be where your animal self resides. It could express your unchecked or boundless self and symbolize freedom from the restrictions of the ego and society's ego.

The wilderness could also represent your unconscious mind, the primeval part of the mind, or the part of you that fears it is an empty wasteland.

It might also represent the forgotten part(s) of yourself.

willow tree: This could be about sadness (as in a weeping willow). It could also be a tree of mourning and loss. See also *tree*.

win: This may be about achieving some goal. If something is won without any action on your part or if it's won mysteriously, it could be a metaphor for grace (e.g., an unmerited gift). See also *win/lose*.

wind: This may represent what can move you or other hidden influences. It may represent overwhelming emotions if it's very windy.

If the wind is blowing you back but you finally overcome it, this might mean that there are hidden forces holding you back, but persistence will win the day.

The wind could be your own spirit. Native Americans thought of it as a spirit that one could talk to or call upon in need.

It could also indicate a change in your life, either positive or negative (in the case of an ill wind). See *storm*.

The type of wind movement can say something about the dynamics of how your life is moving. If it's blowing hard, it may be about chaos in life, frustrations, or feeling out of control.

Seeing which way the wind is blowing could suggest the need to be expedient. It could also mean you want to take some time to understand a situation before making a decision.

In both the Talmud and Old Testament of the Christian Bible, the wind can be seen as the spirit of God (i.e., divine inspiration). This would be known as the Ruach or Holy Spirit. In this form, the wind would be associated with Sophia, the feminine aspect of God (see *Sophia*).

Once while standing at dusk in the Winnemucca desert in the state of Nevada, I witnessed a moderate wind that came off the mountains and brought with it the sense of the holy and numinous divine.

I've felt that same wind in the Atacama, Mojave, and the Peruvian Andes with all the winds seemingly alive and holy. It's the same wind wherever I go.

Insight: Tibetan and Nepalese Buddhists speak of the Windhorse that flies their prayers up to heaven. (The multicolored prayer flags seen blowing in the wind in most Buddhist areas are called the Windhorse.)

Buddhist Windhorse prayer flags

windmill: This could be symbolic of the power of mind and the state of your emotional being. If tilting at or pushing against a windmill, perhaps you are trying to do something foolish. Are you trying to make a difference and failing?

window: This is possibly an opportunity to see what's happening around you and look closely at what you see through the window. This could be symbolic of your personal outlook on life. Looking in a window is a way of looking within ourselves.

A closed window might indicate closed communication. The window may also be framing something that you need to pay attention to.

A broken window might indicate that you are seeing things wrong.

Windows are also modes of contact, of seeing and being seen. The absence of windows might indicate withdrawal or even hostility to the outside world.

Cleaning a window might be a metaphor for changing your perspective or point of view. A foggy or dirty window might also suggest that you clear your perceptions of someone or something or that you are not seeing something clearly or without prejudice.

wine: Drinking wine could be about celebration or contentment. If it's Communion wine, then it may be about your spiritual aspect.

Christians see it as a symbol for the blood of Christ, that which brings life (see *cup*). If you get drunk on wine, perhaps you are getting your hopes too high, or you are trying to forget something or escape something (see *drunk*). Consider also whine (see *whining*).

wings: Seeing a bird's wings may represent a freer way of living. Perhaps you desire to soar to great heights. Angel wings could be about an angelic quality or the desire for protection from certain stresses.

Wings can also be about escape (see *flying*).

win/lose: The win/lose aspect of a dream may at some level reflect a conflict in your waking life that may be affecting some goal, intention, or stake you have in the outcome. It could also reflect an inner conflict.

winter: This could represent being emotionally cold. It might also represent a quiet period before the development of something new. For some people, there may be an association with certain holidays.

wiping: If wiping something down, perhaps you are wanting to start anew with a clean slate.

wiring: This can represent your energy flow or your connections with others. If the wiring is tangled, it may be about getting your communications crossed.

wishing: This may be akin to praying. See *praying*.

wise old man or woman: See *queen* or *king* in the *archetypes* section.

witchcraft: This can reflect your fear of someone manipulating your reality or controlling you. Witchcraft itself can signify transformations or changes happening or needed in one's life. So too, someone may be trying to manipulate you or your environment.

Witches, witchcraft, wizards, and wands can also reflect a desire for the fantastical and mystical (i.e., a world more exciting than the one you find yourself in). What's missing in your life?

Witch images in a dream can be both positive and negative with both representing feminine power. On the negative side, "stirring the pot" as in the illustration above can be about stirring things up or causing mischief. This image could also refer to bringing different ingredients or aspects together to make a whole. Consider also starting a fire beneath someone to give them the incentive needed to complete a task.

witches: Witches are often representatives of the negative feminine aspects such as heartlessness and temptation. However, images of witches are also good images of enchantment and positive power.

They can be symbols of difficult feelings and old behavior patterns that speak to your relationship with your mother. Your feeling and the action that is taking place will reveal whether the symbol is positive or negative.

In the story *The Wizard of Oz* by L. Frank Baum, the Wicked Witch of the West symbolically represented the negative feminine—in this case, her insensitivity and lack of focus except inwardly, thus creating self-involvement and social rejection. She is the witch of the west and symbolic of darkness and endings. Dorothy needed to face her in order to bring back the light and a new beginning.

Glinda, the Good Witch of the South, represents these new beginnings.

Perhaps you need to face the darker aspects of yourself or some relationship.

Carl Jung thought of witches as part of the *collective unconscious.* Often they are symbols of unlikeable acquaintances and therefore associated with some part of your own personality.

Are you or someone else casting a spell and manipulating someone or something? See also *magic, magician or conjurer,* or *wizard.*

Note also that the witches may represent aspects of yourself. Consider also that a witch can represent one's mother and the magical effect she has on you. (She is both nurturer and punisher.) See *Lakshmi* and *Kali* under *Shiva.*

witness: To witness something might be about being a better observer.

Religiously, it could mean that you need to share yourself more. To be a witness in a court of law could mean that you need to be accountable for some action or that you need to swear that you're telling the truth. Do you need to tell the truth about something?

If there's a judge, lawyer, or part of a jury in the dream, note what the others are doing and saying. This can add even more meaning to the dream.

If you are just an observer in the dream and not participating in any way, you may want to look at your waking life to see if you're being too unattached and unemotional (i.e., disconnected from others).

wizard: This can represent the mastery of power or the desire to gain more power. This can also be seen as an archetype (see *wise old man* under *archetypes*).

He can represent someone who can do amazing things or knows amazing facts. For example, one can say, "He is a computer wizard."

Insight: Wizards are often archetypal figures in that they show up in the dreams of all cultures, though not in the same form, and often share similar meanings.

If one shows up, it can signal the need to exercise some power, hone a skill, be more creative, and consult your inner skills. They are often guides who offer wisdom and insight to some issue or problem.

They can come in the form of prophets, shamans, priests, medicine men, sorcerers, warlocks, sages, father figures, or any respected authority figures. For women, they can take the form of the grandmother or goddess, the Virgin Mary, Sophia, or Fatima.

The wizard can be the magician or magus, representing the divine intermediary whose wisdom can settle worldly disputes.

They are often messengers from our unconscious minds and can represent our untapped potential. If we view them as *astrologers*, they can represent our concerns for the future (see *magic, magician or conjurer*, and/or *witches*).

A wizard can also represent one's father and the power he wields.

wolf: See *animals*.

woman: A woman can represent the feminine aspect of yourself.

In a man's dream, this may reflect his feminine aspect and/or his attitudes or biases about females in general and his mother specifically.

In a woman's dream, the woman may reflect a personality aspect that she wants or rejects (see *animus/anima* in the *archetypes* section).

woods: This image can be symbolic of your unknown or unconscious self. A walk through the woods could be about a return to your spiritual self, your natural self.

If you are lost in the woods, you may feel some anxiety about your direction in life or where some current situation is taking you.

Perhaps you're at the very beginning of something, and nothing looks familiar. See also *forest*.

words: Seeing a jumble of words might signify confusion. To see a word jumble might suggest that you need to work out some problem. A specific word may reflect something in your waking life. What comes to mind when you think of that word?

A word can also be a declaration, and the Word of God can represent a creation or creation itself. Look up the synonyms and antonyms of the word in the dictionary. This may help to decode its meaning.

work: If you're at your job, it may mean that you feel some anxiety about it or that you need to work harder. Perhaps you're procrastinating with some project. If you are working in a former job, that might suggest that a lesson you learned from that time may be useful in the present.

If you're losing your job in the dream, perhaps you feel a little insecure or worried about something. If you're late, perhaps you're feeling stressed or overwhelmed.

workshop: Do you need to develop your skills? Do you need to work on yourself (i.e., self-development)?

world: If it's the end of the world, it could reflect the end to something in your personal world or some new way of experiencing your world or yourself. You may feel that you are under great stress and that you are vulnerable.

If you're saving the world, it could be a reflection of your self-confidence. Consider also the phrase "on top of the world," meaning that you feel great.

worm: If there are worms in your dream, you may feel insignificant or perhaps ineffective. Do you need to assert yourself? See also *maggots*.

worry: This could be a worry from the waking world that has transferred into your dream. You may have some repressed or unexpressed emotions or resentments that are triggering this type of dream. See also *fear*.

worship: Perhaps you're being overly attentive or placing someone on a pedestal.

This image may also represent your spiritual aspect and the need to exercise it.

wound: This might be about hurt feelings. You may need to heal (emotional, psychological, physical, relational, and/or social).

wraith: See *chimera, ghost, phantom,* and *specters or spectral figures*.

wreath: This image can refer to honoring something or someone. It's also a symbol for completeness and wholeness like a circle (see *circle* under *shapes* and *mandala*).

wreck: Any kind of wreck in a dream may represent an obstacle to achieving a goal. Forward progress may be frustrated or put on hold. Does your life feel like a wreck? Do you feel ill as if you're wrecked? See also *crash*.

It might also have something to do with rejection or something that prevents your progress. It can also represent being out of control with your emotions (see also *car*).

wrestle: Are you struggling with something? Are you trying to pin something or someone down? Are you trying to dominate others, or are they trying to dominate you?

wristwatch: Perhaps you're too bound by time and structured. Maybe you need to loosen up a little. If the watch is broken, perhaps you feel like things are at a standstill. Is time running out on something?

writing: This may be about sorting out ideas and thinking about something. Do you hope to leave a mark on the world (see also *ancient writing*)?

X

X: This might suggest something forbidden.

An X on a map might suggest that your goals are in sight, or it could represent a place where you need to uncover (reveal or divulge) something. If it marks the location of a treasure, see *treasure*.

It could also refer to your ex or be symbolic of a cross. If it is a cross, see *cross*.

To draw an X across something is to get rid of it or negate it. Are you crossing something off (i.e., rejecting it)?

A triple X might be about something pornographic.

Xerox: You may feel that something is a copy, not the real thing.

X-rays: This can represent something in the unconscious that's influencing your life. It can refer to seeing inside of something. You may not feel fully protected. In fact, you may feel exposed.

xxoo: This is internet slang for sex. But it can also be a metaphor for kissing and hugging.

Y as a letter or as a Y in the road: This can represent a decision-making time or a path to choose (similar to a fork in the road). It could also be emblematic of a question, perhaps an existential question. You may ask yourself, "Why me?"

yacht: This can represent wealth, luxury, abundance, recreation. Perhaps you're feeling quite relaxed. Alternatively, this image could be about poverty.

yak: This can represent uniqueness or talking too much.

yams: This might be a symbol for sensuality or a statement about your virility. It might be symbolic of something that has been growing in you and that may be ready to harvest.

yantra: This symbolizes an emerging consciousness and cosmic energy. It can represent something mysterious and spiritual (see *mandala*), a map to the unknown, and/or spiritual awakening.

yard: This may be symbolic of how you look to others. If it's well kept, it could refer to your orderliness. If not, then it can reveal the depth of your disorderliness or how out of control your life is (see *backyard* or *ruler*).

yardstick: This can represent both unyielding desire and acceptance. It's also a way to take the measure of something and perhaps evaluate it. If you're being threatened with it, perhaps it refers to punishment or feeling punished. Is someone trying to control you?

yelling: This can signal an emotional release from repressed anger or fear. Perhaps you feel an emotion that is not safe to exhibit in your waking life, but the dream can provide an outlet for it.

If no one seems to hear your scream, perhaps you feel as though your voice is of no importance to others. Do you fear you're not being heard, that what you have to say doesn't matter, or that you aren't taken seriously?

yellow: See *colors*.

yes: When you say yes to anyone in a dream, you are saying yes to yourself. Are you just saying yes in order to be agreeable?

yesterday: This represents the past or the before time. This might also represent something to let go of or suggest that you're too late.

yeti: This creature is part man and part beast. Is something stalking you? Do you need to bring balance to the rational and instinctive sides of your nature?

yew: An evergreen tree can symbolize death, mourning, and resurrection. Alternatively, these trees can be symbolic of eternality (see the insight that follows).

A churchyard yew

Insight: Both druids and early Christians thought of the yew tree as symbolic of reincarnation or resurrection and everlasting life because it was an evergreen.

Interestingly, some yews will give off a toxic gas (taxine) during very hot days. This gas could be hallucinogenic.

Some of these English yews are fifteen meters in diameter and are more than two thousand years old. Because some of these trees would last up to three thousand

years, they were considered symbols of eternity and the transcendence of death. Frequently, these trees are found in or near tombs and churchyards.

In Ireland, it is said to be one of the sacred trees because its branches can sometimes burrow into the earth and become new roots, thus uniting the earth with the heavens.

Staves of yews were used to carve Ogham letters for magical use.

Though yew bark can be toxic to humans and livestock, the ancients used the bark to treat kidney disease, heart problems, and arthritis. Today large concentrations of an alkaloid in yew called taxol are used in the treatment of a variety of cancers.

yield: If you are giving way to something or someone or you see a yield sign, it might suggest that you should sacrifice your own authority for the good of the whole (i.e., be more flexible and less structured).

yin/yang: This is somewhat like anima/animus; however, Jung saw them as unconscious motivators, and the Eastern concept is somewhat broader in scope. This represents the balance and union of the female energy (yin) and the male energy (yang).

Where do you need more balance in your life? What aspect of yourself is too dominant and needs to be more balanced?

Jung saw our spiritual aspect in opposition to our sensual aspect but not separate in that they reside on a continuum. The parts of this pair are often confused with each other because they are so very much like each other in expression.

Jung would have supported the need for balance between these two psychic opposites. See also *enantiodromia*.

Insight: I usually view any imbalance between male and female characters in dreams as an imbalance indicator in waking life.

Symbols where the object is split in half and separated can represent yin/yang imbalances.

In the waking dream, groups with only one or two males or only one or two females tend to underrepresent the yin/yang energies of the underrepresented gender, thus throwing off the balance of the group. This often affects the creativity of the group as it would with the individual (see *anima/animus* in the *archetypes* section).

The owl can represent darkness, the shadow, and the unconscious stirring of fear. The eagle can represent that which uplifts and provides a protecting influence. The soul is both yin and yang integrated into a whole. It's only the ego that separates. The sun is the light within, while the moon is the ruler of darkness. The sun is masculine, while the moon is feminine. Both combine to create a single landscape.

yoga: Perhaps you have found or need to find harmony, balance, and self-discipline. Alternatively, are you stressed and/or overwhelmed, or do you have a need to heal or unify different aspects of yourself?

Are you seeking to transcend the body in order to hear your inner self talking? Alternatively, have you gotten yourself into a position that you can't get out of?

yoke: Do you feel controlled or enslaved by others? Do you feel an unwillingness to conform? It can also represent being tied to another or even tied down. It could reflect your desire to be emancipated or freed.

youth: This can symbolize immaturity. You may also feel full of energy. This could represent a younger version of you.

YouTube: This can be about frivolously wasting time or wanting to increase personal knowledge. Perhaps you need to be open to new experiences.

yo-yo: This image suggests the ups and downs of life. Are you just playing around and not taking something seriously enough?

yurt: This is a type of dwelling often associated with primitive cultures or a desire to get back to nature (see *house*).

Z

Z: This is a comic graphic to represent sleeping. As a letter, it could also represent the end of something. See also *sleeping*.

Zen: This can represent a quest for balance and harmony. It could mean that you are at peace with yourself or that you need to be. See also *yin/yang*.

zenith: This could be about your potential and your need to overcome obstacles in order to achieve your goals. If you dream that you've reached it, perhaps you're at a dead end. See also *mountain*.

zephyr: See *wind*.

zeppelin: See *dirigible*.

zero: This can signify nothing or suggest something of no worth. It can represent the unconscious, the void, the silence, and the feeling of being emptied or depleted.

This can also be about emotional coldness.

It can be the space between sounds or musical notes that allows their individuality to be heard.

It can also represent the point between the conscious and unconscious.

zigzag: This could be about being indecisive or ambivalent. It can also signal avoidance. It could refer to your erratic behavior as well.

zipper: If a zipper is broken, this might indicate something embarrassing or suggest that something private is in danger of being exposed. Of course, this image may also have a sexual connection.

Consider also the phrase "zip it up," demanding that one be quiet or stop talking.

zit: Something may be getting under your skin and becoming a nuisance. This can also be about repressed anger flaring up.

zodiac: This may be about how you connect with the universe. It can also represent the passage of time and be a metaphor for destiny. So too, it can be symbolic of having no control.

The zodiac symbols can also be symbolic of the need for spiritual guidance.

It can represent patterns in behavior or cycles in your life. The specific zodiac sign can give you more information about the behaviors assigned to each (see various zodiac signs).

In some cases, the assigned behavior may be one that you need to either reject or embrace in your life, and the context and emotions of the dream will say which action you must take.

Insight: Not only do signs of the zodiac show up in people's dreams, but there's also what has been called the thirteenth sign of the zodiac. Ophiuchus, the snake god, shows up at around the same time as Sagittarius (see *god* in the *archetypes* section and *snake* in *animals*).

Humankind is always trying to figure out what influences life. This comes from the belief that we are not involved in the creation of our experience of reality. Originally, these were seen as wheels of fortune that combined personality variables ordained by the heavens and the four elements (earth, air, fire, and water).

In our waking lives, we can view these as the rulers of our moods along with the sun, moon, and planets. Fire signs are considered to be energetic and assertive. Water signs are emotional and intuitive. Air signs are logical and objective, and earth signs are practical and down-to-earth.

These symbolic representations may also hold true for the times when they show up in our dreams.

Check out individual zodiac symbols for further information. See also *fortune-teller.*

zombies: These are symbolic of the living dead. They could represent something refusing to die or stay buried (a memory, a fear, a feeling, a thought, or a habit).

They can also reflect rejected parts of yourself that refuses to die.

Something without free will is being controlled by basal emotions. Is something eating at you?

If you're being attacked by zombies, are you feeling overwhelmed by forces that are out of your control? Are there some unresolved issues that you are not dealing with?

Perhaps you have reverted back to an old way of being.

Has something died in you, perhaps a feeling, an ambition, or an idea? See also *death.*

A zombie baby could be about an idea refusing to die or one that has died but still hangs around.

If you are being chased by a zombie, this might mean someone in your waking life is threatening you or your way of life.

It's also possible that this is a resurrection image (see *resurrection*).

zoo: This is a symbol for controlled and ordered wildness. If there are animals in the zoo, see *animal terms*.

It could also mean that things are out of control. After all, one may say, "This place is a zoo." There's also an element of feeling caged.

zookeeper: Are you about to lose control over some part of your life? Are you keeping your natural self caged (see *cage*)?

zoomorphism: If you're changing into some animal, are you becoming less civilized in some part of your life or giving in to your animal nature (i.e., your primal desires or urges)?

See also *morphing*.

Section 2

Archetypes

Stories thrive on archetypal characters. There are the heroes such as Odysseus of Homer's work or Hercules in Greek mythology. There are characters like Puck, Lady Macbeth, Othello, and King Lear along with a whole host of others in the works of Shakespeare who are also archetypal memes.

The white rabbit and the Cheshire cat lead us into our inner realm as all animals do in our dreams.

Music such as Tchaikovsky's *Nutcracker* shows evidence of characters like the trickster and shadow. The psychic archetypes portrayed within this work show up in the form of the trickster-magician Drosselmeyer, the shadow creature portrayed by the mouse king and his minions, and the various goddess images envisioned as the sugar plum and snow fairies.

The nutcracker itself transforms from one state of being to another, becoming human in the process, a nice metaphor for Carl Jung's individuation process and not unlike the transformative performance experienced by Pinocchio, who morphed from being a puppet to becoming a real boy. Both represent the magical development of the human psyche as it transmutes toward wholeness and realness.

As with anything in the imaginal world of the psychic archetypes, they are more metaphor than actual. We can't touch them but only point toward their attributes. They represent the patterns of the psychic function.

The depth psychologist James Hillman said that they were the root of the soul. He went on to say that because of this imaginal description of archetype, we are lead "to envision the basic nature and structure of the soul in an imaginative way and to approach the basic questions of psychology first of all by means of the imagination."[*18]

Imagination is the faculty of imagining or of forming mental images or concepts of what is not actually present to the senses.

A psychologist might say that it is the power of reproducing images stored in the memory under the suggestion of associated images or of recombining former experiences in the creation of new images that aid in the solution of problems or that are directed at a specific goal.

The archetypal imagination of the soul has the ability to create unreal or whimsical imagery as well as the decorative detail that we experience in our poetry, dramas, stories, and other artworks.

On occasion, an archetypal image will visit a dream and deliver a luminous or what has been dubbed a numinous (i.e., holy or sacred) quality to the dream that can stimulate an emotional state and thus bring transformational meaning and purpose to one's life.

To the religious, one might think of the archetypes as different facets of God.

To the scientist, the archetypes might be considered controlling paradigms—the patterns that control our experience of the world. Both the religious person and the scientific person can study the social, emotional, and political effects of archetypes through art, literature, dreams, and myths.

The emotion associated with archetypal images can be of deep sweetness, ecstasy, terror, and/or dread, but it's definitely a wholly other experience of astonishment and wonder.

---

[*] ibid

Whether the experience is real or not or whether one has been visited by some spirit isn't all that important because the effect it has on one's psyche and resulting behavior is what matters.

The archetypes of the symbolic mind roam the primeval forest, the deep inner self, the unconscious, the ancestral underworld of the human psyche.

This part of our psyche leads us, guides us, and informs the essence of our being. It's what the soul draws on to manifest into the world and mingle with our dreams. It is our connection with all other humans, and part of our shared patterns of thought. These archetypes of the unconscious are the universal images in our dreams and myths.

Among their vast number reside the symbols of the shadow, the anima/animus, great wisdom, and the divine. The trickster, the monk, the father and the queen, the devil, demons, and death itself are also characters of this universal inner theater of the mind.

Here dream images of the budding flower, egg, and the phoenix bring forth a message of rebirth and resurrection and the idea that what we are needs to continuously die in order to make room for something new. Everything that grows requires death.

It is in this world that the conflict between opposites is confronted, where Armageddon is played out as the metaphorical reconciliation of the conscious and unconscious mind.

There is no real win here, for it is not about dominance but about balance. It is in these nether regions that people can learn to accept both sides of their nature and become whole again. Until people sit down with both sides of themselves and reconcile the differences, there can be no inner peace and therefore no peace on earth.

Without this ongoing negotiation, humans cannot see or hear one another genuinely because they will only project some unrecognized parts of themselves onto the others with whom they are sharing a dialogue.

> While in the unrecognized shadow of the internal self the world's problems seem to be outside ourselves so we try to manipulate this outside world with limited success. But this results in less not more personal control that then leads to even greater attempts to control others.

Those who reject their shadow either through the rejection of others or in their rejection of themselves shackle their opposite personality (e.g., the extrovert to the introvert, the thinker to the emotional, the sensing to the intuitive). Note that in the evil person the shadow is its good side, its compassionate side.

For some this rejection hinders the expression of the "Oversoul," the Christ, the symbol of the True Self, the Pneuma of humankind.

When we demonize another being we lay on them our shadow self in order to punish or kill them. For many the rejection of the shadow is equal to the rejection of sin. But the sin is not in having a shadow it is in refusing to recognize it and deal with it.

When we call another person arrogant who is it that is being arrogant? When we label another person as being greedy whose greed is it we are rejecting or refusing to see? When we accuse someone as incompetent have we acknowledged our own contribution to that legion of dishonor?

Contrary to the common sense quote that what we don't know won't hurt us, the hidden parts of ourselves (i.e., that which we don't know), *can* hurt us, and others.

Taking a walk into the forest of our unconscious mind is not to be feared and run from for it is a journey toward healing and toward bringing balance to our chaotic lives.[19]

Deep into that darkness peering, long I stood there, wondering, fearing, doubting, dreaming dreams no mortal ever dared to dream before.
—Edgar Allan Poe, "The Raven"

Archetypes Section

Archetypes

This section is an addendum to the preceding dream image dictionary. Though these images may, as do all other images, reflect specific meaning to the dreamer they also have universal meaning to all dreamers.

What is an archetype? Perhaps the following will help with the definition.

Greek: Archetupos; origin, pattern or model

ar·che·type [ahr-ki-tahyp] *noun* (Dictionary.com)

1. The original pattern or model from which all things of the same kind are copied or on which they are based; a model or first form; prototype.
2. In Jungian psychology: an invisible pattern of collectively inherited unconscious ideas, pattern of thought, image, etc., universally present in individual psyches.

• • •

Simply defined, it is a universal symbol for an evolutionary instinctive pattern of behavior, or it's a personality variable expressed in emotional symbols (e.g., the generic version of a personality such as a father figure).

Carl Jung, the Swiss psychiatrist, made famous the idea of universal psychological images in dreams and myths that we can use to interpret dreams.

He suggested five main archetypes—the self, shadow, anima, animus, and persona. They all reside within the collective unconscious, and all affect the personal unconscious and conscious ego and show up as both characters and plots in our dreams.

Each of us are born with these images, events, and patterns, and they inform what we do and what we become as we go through life. It is the pattern beneath the form that is inherited, not the figure. After all, these may be individual or cultural in nature.

Jung believed that all phenomena that are manifest are supported by a unitary reality he called the unus mundus and that it was the archetypes that mediated or organized this unity.

In short, archetypes seem to be innate predispositions that form patterns that mediate our conscious behavior. In other words, they literally coordinate our behaviors and the stories of our lives. These images and patterns can be thought of as the DNA of the human psyche.

The *self* regulates the psyche and facilitates the individuation process (the process toward becoming a fully realized human being).

The *shadow* is that part of us that we would rather not acknowledge. It is our darker nature. It is often a dark creature, frequently of the same gender as the dreamer.

The *anima* is the feminine image, and it encompasses the attributes within the male. It has been said that the soul of a man is feminine.

The *animus* is the masculine image, and it encompasses the attributes within the female. It has been said that the soul of a woman is masculine.

The anima and animus can be thought of as soul images and can act as guides to the soul and offer creative possibilities to the development of the individual.

In the *persona* Jung believed was the face that people presented to others i.e., a mask (see *mask* in previous section). It is said to present a favorable impression to others and to hide the real person or what the person really thinks of themselves.

There are also *archetypal events*, such as birth, death, separation from parents, marriage, initiation, and the union of opposites.

So too, there are *archetypal motifs* or themes, such as the apocalypse, the deluge, and creation, all of which can be found in every culture.

These archetypes show up in all our fairy tales, folklore, and myths. They are literally the foundation and basis of all the world's creation stories (both personal and universal).

From the Australian Aborigine to the urban subcultures of the United States, all are influenced by these patterns, though each shapes and predisposes the forms uniquely to the culture and the experiences of the individual. It may also be possible that they predispose the type of experiences we have.

In-depth Study of the Archetypes

Anima (Female within the Male)

The female in a man's dream might represent the male's feminine aspects, such as caring and feeling, intuition, receptivity, and creativity. This is known as the *anima*. This character can show up in the form of an elf, a goddess, a mermaid, a man's sister, or any female persona.

It should be noted that Jung tended to create a splitting phenomenon when he asserted that archetypes such as the anima, animus, and the shadow were only in a particular gender (the animus in a female's dream only, anima in a male's dream only, and the shadow exclusively male within a male's dream and female within a female's).

She could also come to the dreamer as an image of Mother Earth, a cat, a tiger, a cave, or a ship at sea. Even the sea can be feminine because it can represent the waters of the womb.

The female in a man's dream is often said to be the soul image in a man. Many have said that this can create problems for a man if he projects this image onto a female in the waking world.

Dream analyst Jeremy Taylor doesn't believe that this is true. In fact, he suggested that these designations of exclusivity were "arbitrary" (his word). Taylor considers the Jungian view to be somewhat masculine and probably reflected unconscious gender stereotypes of the day.

Taylor also suggests that contemporary women have archetypal dreams of the feminine that correspond to the inner development of the goddess and deserve to be called the anima. It is also the same for the animus. Taylor recommends that some of the archetypal definitions attributable to Jung be revisited in the light of contemporary sensibilities.

Animus (Male within the Female)

Shown as a man in a woman's dream, it could be represented by her brother or any other male figure.

Its presence in a dream might indicate assertiveness, mental and social power, latent characteristics, and even her contacts with males.

The soul image of a female is reflected in the male within her dreams.

These archetypes have their opposites as well. The positive can reveal inner wisdom as well as spiritual and emotional depth, but the negative side might indicate that the negative aspects of the opposite gender are taking you over.

For example, the male in the female dream may be showing an argumentative, controlling, or excessively critical aspect. Thus, the dream character could serve as a warning.

Note that a moody, irritable, and oversensitive female character could symbolize the negative side of the animus.

Jung suggested that there was a proper balance to the inner gender qualities and that an unbalanced dream could serve as a means of guarding against this by not letting the negative dominate.

I tend to think that there's no good reason for this gender exclusivity given that there's male and female traits in all of us. Ruling out the influence of a female shadow in a male who is trying to resolve his feminine aspect or a female trying to do the same with her masculine aspect seems a bit confusing, even more for those who are homosexual, lesbian, bisexual, or transsexual.

There are also the interactions between males and females in the dream that can show both the positive and negative aspects of gender, and those can also be informing.

Though I'm using standard gender characteristics, remember that we each have both the masculine and feminine in us regardless of our gender. I perceive the feminine aspect to include

- intuition,
- spontaneous creativity,
- receptivity,
- social expressiveness,
- contemplativeness, and
- being inner world-directed.

I perceive the masculine aspect to include

- assertiveness,
- decisiveness,
- physical expression,
- rational creativity,
- mental and social power, and
- being outer world-directed.

Of course, there are the negative aspects as well.

The feminine receptive can become *submissive*, and the contemplative can become *indecisive*. The inner world-directed can become *insensitive to others*, and the spontaneously creative can become *unfocused* and *scattered*.

The masculine assertive can become *aggressive*. The physically expressive can become *violent*. One with mental and social power can become *arrogant* and *overpowering* The outer world-directed can become *aloof* and *insensitive*, and the decisive can become *inflexible* or *rigid*.

apocalypse: This is the archetype of endings—the destruction of worlds. This may represent the central archetype of meaning. It is often the bearer of change or a new worldview, new relationship with the divine, or a redefinition of oneself.

It can show up in one's dreams when what once made sense in the world no longer makes any sense (i.e., when traditional meaning collapses).

Sometimes what has been hidden both in yourself or the collective self of society comes out forcefully. It may want you to hear and deal with it, and it can show up in an apocalyptic form.

It's the ultimate image of the war between good and evil.

See also *apocalypse, end of the world,* and *Armageddon* in the first section.

ascending: Are you ascending to a higher self? This can also represent purification or refinement, becoming more detached, and attaining different and wider perspectives. Ascension is often linked with change and transformation (e.g., leaving things behind, moving on, and becoming something new). In contrast, descending can represent going down into the unconscious.

ascetic or monk: This is the archetype of the true inner self and represents one's inner teacher or the light within.

It is the loner. This person links us with things beyond the personal and unites us. It is also about withdrawal. It involves the monk who lives alone, and it represents the experience to be gained outside the social norms.

The ascetic is an experience of the connection found between all people and one's central or core self. It can be about turning away from the everyday, and it can also represent a certain mindful discipline.

child: This comes in many forms. For example, there's the divine child (see also *Christ*). This figure is innocence and redemptive with godlike qualities. It often comes to you when you need to transform your traditional and conservative way of thinking and acting in order to transcend a situation or evolve your psychological and spiritual experience.

The divine child is also the wonderful child who deals with the efforts of growing up. It is the symbol of perfection, rebirth, and the purity of primal wisdom. This symbol may reflect your own spiritual potential.

This child is always associated with new ideas and emotions coming into our awareness. It is the spirit that is always pushing for increased awareness and consciousness. It is the symbol for the previously unimagined and the antithesis of the conservative.

The creative and the conventional sides of you each want to be heard. But be careful here. Conventional authority resists creative change or change of any kind.

Remember it was the conservative mind that saw a threat in Jesus and ordered him to be killed. It was the conservative element that wanted the colonies to remain loyal to the British Empire, and it was the conservative mind that wanted to only allow whites as citizens in this nation. But the spirit is always pressing to bring new light where there is darkness—to actualize spiritual possibility in our psyches.

Insight: In the state of the divine child, political problems are solved, and creative inventions are discovered.

Conventionalism and conservatism tends to prematurely close off ideas and images of potential and possibility. In essence, this closes off the power of the divine child.

There's also the nature child, who attempts to bond us with the natural world. There's the eternal child, who encourages us to remain young and to see the world through the eyes of a child. There's the magical child, who sees the sacred beauty in everything and embodies the courage to face all difficulties. There's the orphan child, the abandoned child who may not feel that he or she belongs anywhere. Finally, there's the dependent child (i.e., the needy child) where nothing is ever good enough.

All have both healthy and unhealthy aspects to their natures, and all can come to you in dreams in the service of health and wisdom.

Christ: This figure may represent the symbol of the self, soul, oversoul, or the god-man.

Christ is also the cosmic mystery that each of us has been born as—the essence of who we really are. To seek this is to undertake a powerful journey, not unlike that of Muhammad in the Night Journey.

Muhammad and the Night Journey may very well have been a journey for the self, the spirit, to the pneuma. This may be the archetypal journey in the search for the real self as opposed to the body or soul. This may relate to the process of individuation that Carl Jung referenced.

Individuation according to Jung is the process that the individual self goes through to integrate its disparate aspects and become a well-functioning whole (see *wholeness*).

Individuation may be the process whereby a person reconciles the spirit with the ego by standing between them.

In a quote from the book *The Gospel of Mary Magdalene* (and transcribed into the gnostic gospels and translated by Jean-Yves Leloup), Mary Magdalene meets Jesus and has the following exchange:

> "Lord, when someone meets you in a Moment of vision, is it through the soul [psyche] that they see, or is it through the Spirit [Pneuma]?"
>
> The Teacher answered: "It is neither through the soul nor the Spirit, but the nous between the two which sees the vision."

The "nous between the two" may thus be the self-actualized being, the fully integrated and individuated self, and the balance between spirit and ego.

death: This involves how we deal with our disintegration and demise. Symbols of death include a stopped clock, a skeleton, gravestones, a cemetery, an empty abyss, falling leaves, or a dead animal.

This is probably the most difficult of archetypes to deal with as it involves the ultimate letting go. In a dream it can often shed light on your relationship with it and your level of acceptance or rejection of it. Often one's response to the death of someone else provides insight into one's personal relationship with death. The denial of a death in a dream can be a reflection of one's own denial in waking life.

Seeing dead loved ones often means that you are dealing with this death and trying to integrate the new relationship from the once physical reality of the now deceased to that of the memory of them and all the emotions that go with that.

In the American psyche, death is often denied. Hence, our almost pathological resistance to it as evidenced in our dysfunctional health care system. The rejection of death can also reflect the level of fear associated with one's potential end.

The ego (as in the persona that you think you are) cannot imagine its demise and the ultimate disintegration into oblivion. Our reactions to it in both the waking and sleeping dream state can often reveal our ambient level of fear and the degree to which we unconsciously let fear determine the course of our life.

Much of life seems to be about letting go and confronting the emotional fallout that inevitably arises as part of the process of dealing with it.

Older people have a more immediate relationship with death. They observe the loss of physical ability, sexual attraction, and mental acuity, and they also begin to experience a constricted future.

These all have their attached emotions, but even though the process of letting go can speed up in later years, it can also provide an environment where even the most mundane can become precious. After all, there is no time for crap.

Carlos Castaneda, the author of *Journey to Ixtlan*,[20] said, "In a world where death is the hunter, my friend, there is no time for regrets or doubts. There is only time for decisions."

He goes on to say, "Death is the only wise advisor that we have."

Most people in the United States seem to shun the wise advisor concept because it has a rather immature relationship with death in that most have great difficulty letting go of life or in confronting its inevitability. All too often death is denied by the taking of extreme measures to prevent it or by putting off the filling out of a will or even refusing to even talk about it. However, to deny it is to never fully experience it as part of the process of living.

None of this is to say that there is no grief when we are letting go. However, the only way to deal with grief, in my opinion, is to go through the extremely painful process of allowing it, not resisting it or avoiding it. You must grieve when you are grieving, but you have to do it in a way so that you don't become your grief. You don't want to become trapped and defined by it.

The death tarot signifies change, transition, an end, and inevitability. The rose in the death card symbolizes life and new beginnings, while the flag heralds a coming change. The sun reminds that where there is an ending, there is a new beginning.

In addition, some death in dreams is more about the death or end of a circumstance (job, relationship, situation, etc.), not your own personal death or the death of another.

Death in a dream also refers to all endings, our feelings about them, our myths about them, and how our psyches deal with the inevitability. We clearly need to deal with it on a psychological level in order to be reborn (i.e., transformed into something new).

In short, each stage of our life needs to die to the next stage, and if it does not, we become fixated and don't move on.

I think that we dwell in awe and fear at the world's greatest mystery—death. It's that part of life that terrifies most of us because it portends something we can know nothing about.

What is not living? We know it's the opposite of what we have now, but what is the opposite of life really? And why do we even ask the question? Are we afraid of the unknown and what is dark to us? Our unconscious minds are dark to us, but as long as we are alive, we have potential access even though we'd rather not. But death? Now there's a darkness and unknown we can't even begin to fathom. It's a bottomless abyss that goes on forever.

For some, they don't fear death as much as the process of getting there. It can be so frighteningly painful and mostly uncomfortable, or at least that's how it looks. We humans will enter into almost anything if we truly believe there's a pot of gold at the end of it. It may look like something better than what we have, though we're never satisfied with what we have. But not knowing is just too scary.

The promise of no pain and eternal peacefulness seems like a pretty good draw for letting go of life in order to enter some kind of heaven, but the great decider determines whether we wind up there or in the burning cauldrons of hell. However, I'm pretty sure those stories come from the same type of folk that shared the stories for the Brothers Grimm. They were all meant to keep the children in line, whether little or adult children.

These stories seem to reflect the belief that left to their own devices, people won't do the right thing. Of course, that is a pretty cynical view of humanity, one that's usually portrayed by fearful people who don't know who they really are and who we are.

Some folks take solace in the belief that they, body and all, pass into another realm. But the ego parts of us are of the flesh. Our egos reside in that three-pound squishy thing inside our heads that some of us occasionally think with. These decay, shrivel, and turn to dust, and like everything else in life, we can't take these with us. So what continues on?

The soul goes on. But what is that? Have you ever seen it? How often have you been aware of it? Do you actually identify with it? How many of us truly understand that invisible, ephemeral ghost in the machine? After all, aren't we those thinking, feeling, frightened, pain-wracked, memory-filled, squealing things with names and social security numbers?

So what is the soul? Is it a living thing? Well, if it is living within the body, wouldn't it be subject to the same decaying effects after death? Ah, so it's not alive. So is it a spirit? What's that? And why do spirits need us as hosts to visit the world? And if they lose their hosts, where are the spirits then? What does one experience then? Is your consciousness? Was it your consciousness all along? Were you duped by the temporary ego that convinced you that you were actually the ego and not the soul?

This soul thing probably has no fear of death because death isn't part of its life; however, the ego is a jealous thing, and it envies and fears the soul because of its everlasting life. It dreams of being like its opposite and creates a myth of everlasting life. An everlasting life exists, but it's probably not like the life we currently experience; however, the ego doesn't want to hear that, so let's just keep that between us.

Still others see the soul as a transmitter of the spirit into the receiver of the brain, which then allows it to be manifest in the world, making one sort of like a TV with arms and legs. Are we just devices for streaming?[22]

Tell me not, in mournful numbers,
Life is but an empty dream!
For the soul is dead that slumbers,
And things are not what they seem.

Life is real! Life is earnest!
And the grave is not its goal;
Dust thou art, to dust returnest,
Was not spoken of the soul.

—Henry Wadsworth Longfellow, The Psalm of Life

Sometimes death visits our dreams as a healing nightmare.

Emotions that you haven't dealt with or acknowledged (i.e., fears and anxieties, stresses, hurts, and angers) will often show up in your dreams as images of drowning or tidal waves, volcanic eruptions, floods, waterfalls, fires, cliff-hangers, and plunges. They all come to visit so that we can sit down and discuss, confront, and deal with them openly.

Unacknowledged emotional pain will fester and consume the body's energy and vitality and can in some cases lead to the breakdown of the body and/or its psyche.

All the emotional pain experienced in life is most often a function of that part of the psyche called the ego. The ego is designed to avoid all types of pain, and it does this through suppression (shoving it into the unconscious), denial, distraction, or projection. It uses whatever is handy and proven over time to be most effective in short-term avoidance. But as with physical pain, it's eventually necessary to find its cause and deal with it directly. It will not resolve itself without some kind of intervention.

The mind or psyche is doing this all the time through the medium of the dream. For those who remember them or train themselves to remember them, dreams are a gift to aid in their healing.

During sleep and in the process of dying, the ego becomes weakened. While it's awake, it defends mightily against anything that might threaten, and that usually refers to any form of self-reflection; however, the dream, on the other hand, is like a self-reflective apparatus that acts as a mirror to all the stored material the ego has rejected but that still manages to use to inform every action of our lives.

I've also read that the dreams of those who are in the end stages of their lives, who are within days or weeks of dying, will present many emotional scenarios that give them a chance to let go of the pains of the past, forgive, and complete their experience of life.

I've been told that some of these dreams become like visions with many bringing solace to the dreamer by completing and resolving earlier distress. For others, this is an opportunity to explore the truth of the story they've been in.

For many of the dying, when they are not over drugged or when they have had their vision experiences denied by their caretakers as being delusional or nonsensical, the visions can be thought of as a natural process of the ego letting go. It is during this time as the ego grows weaker that these visions and dreams can provide healing to the psyche and through this unfettered healing many have found that long-sought-after peace.[23]

Though medical science once saw the visions as part of the dying brain or delusional experiences that were better denied or controlled with pharmaceuticals, many modern physicians and medical personnel are looking closer at the psychic healing aspect of these dreams. Some are now open to these dreams of the dying, and this has actually helped the staff work with the dying in a more understanding and compassionate way.[23]

Yes, some dreams negatively agitate people. They can bring up past traumas, but sometimes administering something that would calm the anxieties associated with these dreams without cutting off the dreams themselves can assist with this natural healing process.

The ego spends a lifetime defending itself from all kinds of real or perceived threats. Toward the end of its reign, it loosens its grip giving the individual a chance to really heal some of those wounds. We need to find ways to assist and not resist that process.

Some of these ideas come from my experience with the dying, their dreams, and my readings. An eye-opener for me was a book titled *Imagination and Medicine: The Future of Healing in an Age of Neuroscience*[23] and most recently a *New York Times* article by Jan Hoffman titled "Dreams of the Dying."

Sometimes the devil represents temptation or a loss of faith. If you have befriended him perhaps you are being easily persuaded by something or someone and know you shouldn't be.

devil/demon: This can represent our struggle with our basic urges, which often pull us down. The image of a dragon as a demon can also represent this struggle.

The devil can symbolize our fears, negative aspects, limitations, and things we can't control. It can also represent being cunning, cleverness, and deception. If the devil is talking to you, it can suggest you might be worried that certain temptations are becoming hard to resist.

If you're friendly with the devil, perhaps you are talking yourself or allowing someone to talk you into something that you really don't want to do. Dealing with the devil or a demon in any way may reflect your need to deal with an issue of morality. (See *shadow*. Also see *possession* here and in the main encyclopedia.)

If someone you know, even a child of your own, morphs into a demon, he or she may represent a demon in you that has resided there since your own childhood.

Insight: Being possessed is an archetype itself. Many years ago, people would employ priests, shamans, or even lay mediums to exorcize devils that had *possessed* them.

But even now the old version of the primitive possessor demon lives within an unexplored psychic phenomena and acts out behaviors that are contrary to a person's best interest.

One only needs to look at how many so-called fearful *conservatives* will vote for the very issues and people who only mean them harm, directly or indirectly, to see the truth of that statement.

All too often when we deny our complexes, our demons possess us, and we allow another force and energy to take over our lives both internally and externally.

disciple: It is defined from the Latin *discipulus*, meaning learner. This can reflect the need to give authority to another (e.g., to allow someone else to author our lives).

This seems to reinforce the we/them dichotomy and that sense of separateness—the holy and unholy, the less holy and holier.

When heavy into the disciple archetype, one can become quite religious. Of course, this can be destructive as with the Jim Jones debacle, but it can also be a means of getting the ego out of the way.

divine mother: The divine mother is an archetype that Jung suggested was the personification of the feminine. The symbol shows up across all cultures and throughout the ages as Magna Mater (Roman), Cybele (Greek), Isis (Egyptian), Eve (Hebrew), Guanyin (the Chinese Buddhist goddess of mercy), and the Virgin Mary or Sophia (Christian). It is also represented by the church, the nation (the motherland), a forest, and an ocean. Many of the ancient mythological goddesses (e.g., Diana, Hecate, Venus) represented aspects of the Great Mother archetype.

As a woman, she can be seen as one who is sympathetic, caring, and solicitous on one end of the spectrum (as with the Virgin Mary) or as one who is devouring, seductive, and poisonous on the other end (as represented by the Hindu goddess Kali, who devoured her young).

All archetypes that show up in dreams seem to be spiritual demands and reside in each of us. They demand from us that we look closely at our behaviors and the effects they have on our lives and the lives of others. Frequently, they are unconsciously projected onto others, especially if they are absent in the personalities we confront. In the normal mother-child experience, both the archetypal mother and the real mother personality become blended.

But this blend can create a duality or split, and the child will often spend his or her life trying to reconcile this to some degree. For example, should your own mother fail to provide the nurturing aspects of the divine mother, you might seek comfort in other women, many other women, the church, or the motherland. (Note that this is also true for the father archetype.)

In dreams, the symbol of a queen, our own mother, the Virgin Mary, an old woman, or a wise old grandmother may show up and offer guidance. She can also suggest that you continue to feel stuck and therefore dependent on your mother (alive or dead) and that this can continue to affect your independence and maturity in relationships. She can also represent someone (or a memory) who is stifling you.

In many cultures the break with the mother was—and is—communally and ritualistically supported for the health of the child and the community. In the modern Western society, most of us are left to complete this separation alone. This has left many more people stuck with a less mature or incompletely integrated personality.

For both men and women, this insufficient break with the mother causes great difficulty in relationships. As a dream symbol, it most often shows up when a relationship issue is adversely affecting your life.

explorer: This can represent the need to be free and not fenced in or conforming. When heavy into this archetype or when one is ruled by it, one is always on the move, always seeking something that will be fulfilling.

However, one can wind up wandering around aimlessly, trying to find his or her authentic self.

father: This can represent not only one's own father but also God, the male leader, or the progenitor of something. He is the original authority and one's strength in life. A wizard, an old man, a priest, a king, or a wise old man can also represent the father figure. Avoiding this figure might be about denying some aspect of yourself or feeling guilty and not wanting to face up to something.

flying: This is a metaphor for creativity, defying convention, escaping our limited selves, and the desire to be free and independent. This may also reflect a spiritual longing and sometimes shows up in a dream as a vertical ascent. This may reflect the psyche and spirit taking you to new places that you didn't even know existed.

Insight: As a young psychologist, I used to have many dreams in which I attempted to fly. I would struggle to get just a few feet off the ground but would always fall back to earth before the end of the dream. Over time I became more confident and sure of myself, and flying became easier.

The fool comes to us to remind us that no matter how educated or wise we think we are, we are all just beginners. This image points out the fact that we know nothing and that acting as though we do gets in the way of reality.

The zero on the top of the card indicates that it is the point between positive and negative, thus being conditioned to neither.

This fool is unaware of the dangerous cliff he dances near. To us, this seems irrational, but to him, it's all an illusion, a construct of our limited minds. The archetype of the fool thus acts as our true perception of reality by embracing reality totally.

fool (or trickster): This can sometimes be seen as the wise fool or one whose antics can lead to transformation (often as a catalyst), but this is also the least developed part of one's personality.

517

"Everything is possible, Grandpa!" said my youngest granddaughter in response to me saying, "You can't get me!" We were skipping along, and then we leaped onto the low wall framing a neighbor's garden. We walked along it while giggling and trying to be the first to push the other off onto the grass. For a brief moment, I thought about how foolish we must look.

On the way home from dropping her off at school, I thought about the idea of looking foolish and realized that the older I got, the less worried I was about looking foolish. This got me thinking about the image of the trickster, one of the archetypes of the collective unconscious of the human psyche that we don't really talk about, and yet perhaps it's the most important.

We try to ignore this figure because he or she makes us look foolish, which makes us look wrong, and this is not good for the ego.

However, the fool is a symbol of breaking the rules, but with ultimately positive effects. For example, in Greek mythology, Prometheus stole fire from the gods to give to the humans. Jesus trashed the moneylenders at the temple, and Robin Hood stole from the rich to give to the poor.

Buddha gave up his riches and position in life as a prince to live among the common people and to suffer with them.

But the fool's thinking can also be shallow and narrow, and it doesn't rise above its basal needs. The fool can be self-centered, unfeeling, and cynical.

Others see the fool as living in the here and now. It loves life, but it is not attached to living. The fool teaches us detachment, simplicity, and the joy of the moment. Both the young child and the old man share the qualities of the fool in that they are not run by how things look and are thus considered beings connected with the sacred.

Insight: In tarot, the fool is the alpha card, the concept of all-potential, the beginning from which nothing proceeds into everything. He or she often represents bright flashes of insight. For the Buddhists, the fool can represent the beginner, the know-nothing of a free mind.

Mathematically, the fool is represented by zero (i.e., the space between positive and negative). In the field of quantum physics, this is *potentia*—that place between an idea and reality.

The fool disregards prevailing common sense and thus seems foolhardy, foolish, and perhaps even a little dangerous. Often this individual shows up as one who chooses to abandon commonly held beliefs and responds to the world much more spontaneously.

In the Native American culture, the fool archetype is frequently portrayed as a coyote who is often seen as a cocreator of the world. In its sacred role, the fool can be seen as the one who steps out of socially accepted patterns to point to a higher truth, even at the risk of being denounced. By this definition, Jesus could be seen as the archetypal fool, trickster, or coyote.

The fool is the archetype of consciousness, and though it presents itself as weak and unassuming, it is quite capable of creating much havoc and deception through very creative means. In fact, it is frequently the bearer of new ideas.

The fool is a creator and destroyer, but it is neither good nor evil. It creates balance in the universe. It is also stubbornness personified in the face of prevailing reality.

In short, it is the reflection of the human consciousness.

All my life I have been possessed by the need to not look like a fool and to do whatever I could to be helpful to others. This has left me in near continuous conflict. I believe that I entered this life as a fool, thinking that I could be useful, and as Franz Kafka might have said, only a fool can really help.

But in shunning the fool, I was blind to failure, and my life was filled with dissatisfaction. Once I acknowledged that I had failed at being of any true help, I found myself less possessed and a little freer to just be myself, and that's pretty satisfying.

I contend that the fool sees the world—and thus itself—for what it is. It lives in the space of nonsense or no sense, an abstraction where one has not committed to a single vision, a narrow way of being but one open to a much broader reality.

The archetypal pattern of the fool has shown up throughout history in the forms of Buddha, Jesus of Nazareth, and Mohammad, and when visiting your dream, it plays the same role by trying to shake up your rigid self or worldview.

Interestingly enough, the fool or court jester was the only person who could tell the king the truth. In this way, the king could have some balance in his regard of the world about him.

The fool is there to help the dreamers transcend their conditioning and learned behaviors. It is there to assist the dreamers in going beyond their limited images of themselves.

The downside of letting the fool archetype run your waking life is that the funny guy who lives mostly in the moment can become frivolous and boring to others.

In the book *The Archipelago of Dreams*,[24] Robert was helped by a vicious riddle gnome to transcend his limiting self-image by posing three riddles to be solved. Failing to solve these would result in Robert becoming the gnome's lunch. Riddles had always been Robert's nemesis, and this spoke loudly to his sense of personal incompetence.

The Fool/Trickster as an Animal

This figure is seen as the fool, trickster, jester, clown, and shaman in our dreams, but it can show up as an animal as well. It shows up in literature as Brer Rabbit[25] or in *Aesop's Fables* as a fox and in *The Lion King* as the character Rafiki.[26] All represent the essence of the unpredictable, slightly crazy character with gentle wisdom.

Native American Indians have a great tradition of using animals to represent the cunning features of the trickster (e.g., the coyote and raven). These animals are often seen as creators of the world. The raven can also be found in Norse and Siberian myths.

In Lewis Carroll's book *Alice's Adventures in Wonderland*, the white rabbit is a trickster image who lures Alice to explore her unconscious and the naughty (or shadow) sides of her personality. Some dream analysts see this part as the least developed side of ourselves and suggest that its physical appetites rule its actions and decisions.

Spiritual leaders help us to cast off our individual and cultural limits so that we can better see the reality of our existence. Because the archetypal symbolic purpose of the trickster image is to shake up our entrenched belief systems, I have used these three who did just that during the time of their life on earth. Each of them can make us aware of a reality that we did not see before them. We should celebrate what they did and why they did it.

fugitive: This figure avoids and runs from things. He is the ultimate alien and loner. He represents fear, anxiety, and desertion.

God: This is the spirit that lies behind life, creation, and reality. It represents the creative process of the universe and life itself. It is what lies behind. It is the source of our potential and existence. It is also the manifestation of the masculine, the counterpart to the goddess.

Ask yourself if you are taking adequate responsibility for your own potential or projecting it onto something else. Is your God just another representation of your relationship with your father and mother?

Beyond the archetypal meaning, one's views of God can affect any additional meaning they project onto this image.

For example, if one were to believe in *Atheism* which presents a case against the existence of God, wouldn't it need an image of God to present a case against it? Why would you possess the need to refute the existence of something you know doesn't exist? In atheism, there is no belief in any life beyond death. Of course, there is no evidence to support this claim. What would a God image mean to an atheist?

Another point of view is *Deism* and suggests that there is a God but that it is not involved in our everyday lives. It teaches that God is knowable through creation itself. Regarding any phenomenon after death, the deist claims that there's no evidence either way of its existence or nonexistence.

As a deist, to dream of God might suggest the personal need to take control of one's life and not wait for God to intervene on his behalf.

My third example is labeled *Theism* and makes a case for God's continued intervention in the lives of its creation. Theism teaches that God is not knowable. Theists believe in a life after death, though there is no evidence to support this claim either.

To dream of God, the theist might be asking for help (i.e., for some kind of intervention).

goddess: The goddess, the divine feminine, shows up as the mother, the queen, and the wise old woman with the attributes of all. Goddess worship was cyclical, and it often involved the phases of the moon, the harvest of crops, and the movement of wild animals. Our present-day approach is linear in nature where everything changes and moves toward either greater knowledge or chaos.

In the pagan world of the pre-Christian Celts, the goddess was a trinity—maiden, mother, and crone—and she was represented symbolically as the phases of the moon.

The maiden symbolizes youth, emerging sexuality, and the huntress running with her hounds. The mother symbolizes feminine power, fertility, and nurturing. The crone symbolizes wisdom and the compassion that comes from experience, and she is the one who guides us through death.

Goddesses come to us with many names—Anahita, Anat, Aphrodite, Aradia, Arianrhod, Artemis, Astarte, Brighid, Ceres, Demeter, Diana, Eostre, Freya, Gaia, Hera, Ishtar, Isis, Juno, Kaili, Lilith, Ma'at, Mary, Minerva, Ostare, Persephone, Sarasvati, Venus, and Vesta, just to name a few.

Some modern religionists acknowledge that in order for their God to be whole and complete, the trinity of masculine traits assigned to God (Father, Son, and Holy Ghost) needs a fourth, namely that of the feminine, the goddess aspect. See also *quaternity* in the encyclopedic section.

The heroic legend of St. George and the dragon incorporates a number of archetypal elements (e.g., the hero subduing his own shadow and negative masculine in order to reclaim or save the anima or feminine aspect within). This reflects the process of individuation and the reconciliation of opposites in honor of wholeness.

Instead of the female figure in this drawing, other depictions show the figure of Christ being saved from Satan in the form of a dragon, thus representing the archetypal battle between good and evil (the struggle between opposites).

heart: This is seen across many cultures as representing one's life force, soul, or spirit. See also *heart, heart* in *body*, or *heart lines*.

hero or heroine: In mythology, this figure used to be a demigod with great courage and power, and his or her quest is seen as a journey toward great service for humanity (e.g., Jason, Achilles, Perseus, Luke Skywalker, Harry Potter, the princess in the *Frog Prince*). For some scholars, this list could include Buddha, Jesus, and Mohammed. Many see this as a journey toward reconciliation, a connection between the spirit and body of man.

Note that the love hero that rescues the day or the damsel in distress is particularly common across all cultures. This figure shows up frequently when matters of the heart are involved. There is also an antihero in the form of a shadow aspect.

In the fairy tale *Sleeping Beauty*, the kiss that awakens her is often seen as the kiss of life itself, the unleashing of the anima.

You are the hero or heroine in your own life. You brave whatever the world gives you. It is what goes through each developmental phase of life, what dies to make way for what is new. It is a journey of epic proportions. It is your story. This figure points the way to the self.

Negatively, the hero fears vulnerability and being called chicken or cowardly. If overwhelmed by this archetype, one can become arrogant and seemingly always looking for the next fight, the next battle to be won.

initiation: This is a discovery process where the character is brought to a new understanding or sphere of influence, and it is frequently spiritual or mystical in nature.

The characters in *The Wizard of Oz* went through this process in order to discover that they already were what they sought and more.

king: The king is like the hero or the father, but he is the prime authority. He represents all aspects of control, such as taking control or maintaining control. It is perhaps the most powerful aspect of fatherhood, the source and progenitor of us all.

When ruled by this archetype, one can become authoritarian and find it difficult to delegate or include others in the decision-making process.

The lovers represents the inner marriage of opposites (e.g., the anima/animus). It is the process of individuation where the basal self is transformed into spiritual gold.

These dream images often refer to the letting go of the persona (i.e., the protective mask that we wear) and allowing us the freedom to confront our rejected darker sides (our shadows).

The winged Eros is sometimes seen with a bow and arrow and represents the pain of letting go of what we think we have. But until we are able to do this, we cannot become whole and complete human beings, and we will be relegated to lives of separateness.

lover: This figure represents all the forces that bind two people together—the intimacy, dreams, fears, pains, movement toward our wholeness, and all our personal experiences with love.

They can symbolize the union between yourself and others, between yourself and the whole of humanity, between yourself and the environment, or between yourself and the divine.

See the *union of opposites* and *marriage* or *wedding* in the encyclopedia.

magician: This figure can make things happen. A person in this archetypal mode may want to understand the fundamental laws of the universe.

A person steeped in this archetype is a visionary, charismatic leader, shaman, or healer.

When consumed by this archetype, you might become manipulative, and this behavior might have unintended negative consequences.

See also *magician* in the encyclopedia section.

mandala: Any circle (e.g., a Celtic cross, yantra, a bicycle wheel, and even the shape of your typical UFO) represents the wholeness of the personality. Jung believed that these showed up in one's dreams when the person was going through intense personal growth.

Mandalas can also represent the order of one's inner life, the layers of oneself leading to the soul, and the center of oneness.

Usually, our minds are in constant chaos with a maelstrom of issues, fears, and passions creating a continuous imbalance.

The mandala is like a template or blueprint for the mind. It does this by showing us that there is within us a central point to which everything else is related. Both the material within ourselves and the external material interface continuously. The patterns of this interface can help us to understand ourselves and our relationship with the world more clearly.

Interestingly, the mandalas across every culture and throughout recorded history has shown a quaternary pattern that literally squares the circle (i.e., a pattern that brings order to the architecture of the human psyche that the mandala represents).

The mandala seems to show up across all cultures, and the symbolism displays such a commonality that it makes it part of the collective unconscious of the human psyche (see also the *eye* in *body*).

Pencil drawing of a dream mandala
R J Cole, 2015

Sometimes light is paired with the image of a mandala, and the light of creation resides at the center. When I dreamed of the mandala, I experienced it rising from a formless and empty black sea, my unconscious mind, bringing with it a new awareness and leading me to spiritual growth. At the time, the mandala suggested that I needed to look deeper into the darkness of that unknown part of me, for it was in that blackness that a much-needed awareness lay.

The mandala is the psychological expression of the totality of the self.
—C. G. Jung

martyr: The ultimate scapegoat. It may do what it does to be loved or appreciated. It can represent being abused or unrewarded.

The archetype of the caregiver, the one who needs to be always helping others, can often be exploited and become martyred.

mother: This figure can include the Virgin Mary, the sorceress, one's own mother, and the old woman. It can represent what influences our growth and development. Often both the father and the mother have great religious significance.

the Great Mother: This figure can include the queen, goddess, Virgin Mary, Sophia, Mother Earth, Gaia, and Lakshmi. It is often our own experience of the mother figure and how we are related to independence. Mothers can be magical in that they have the power to give and to take away (reward and discipline).

outcast: If you feel different than others in some way, this can lead to feeling like an outcast in one's dreams as well as one's waking life. This may cause people to rebel from that which they feel alienated.

If one cannot live within the prescribed values of a group, this archetype may show up as well. A nonconformist may have this kind of feeling in a dream, especially when he or she is forced to make a stand.

The outcast also represents the archetypal feelings of abandonment and the alienation of being different.

persona: Probably the most important archetype is the persona, that part of each of us that is concerned with how we look to others. It is the part of us that interacts with others. It is the mask that we wear in public—what we want others to see.

States, countries, and even religions have personas. Their symbols, whether they be flags or traditions, animals or anthems, legal codes or architecture or stories of their history are all part of the masks they present to the world. But like with a mask, there is something behind it, and when that is not acknowledged either publically and/or personally, the shadow begins to take over.

possessed: This occurs when you are taken over or controlled by something other than yourself (frequently by a demon or devil). See also the *insight* section in *devil*.

Insight: Carl Jung suggested that we are a species carried away or possessed by our unconscious minds and that these unexplored parts of ourselves are at the root of our neuroses and complexes (a core pattern of emotions ordered around a common theme such as power or status).

Our shadow aspects or demons will cause all kinds of mischief in our lives until we deal with them directly.

Movies like *The Exorcist, Insidious,* and *The Body Snatchers* present examples of possession themes—the loss of personal control and the fear of helplessness.

Zombies can represent the fear of being consumed by fear itself. This was the case for *Jaws* as well. Freddy Krueger, Jack the Ripper, Jekyll and Hyde, and others represent the animals in each of us that we fear we won't be able to control.

queen: This figure can often represent one's mother or someone who acknowledges us.

quest: The characters of the dream or story may be searching for something consciously or unconsciously. It's usually something of great personal value (e.g., Pilgrim's Progress or the search for the golden fleece in Homer's work or the Holy Grail in the tales of King Arthur).

rebel: This figure believes that the rules are meant to be broken. When you are run by this archetype, the main goal can be about overturning what isn't working. Of course, this is not a bad thing in and of itself, but what often happens when in this mode is that revenge and revolution for revolution's sake show up.

When controlled by this archetype, one can cause a lot of damage.

This can be a very disruptive archetype.

Outrageous behavior and irrational radicalism can be a hallmark of someone consumed by this archetype.

When left unmediated, this archetype can drive one toward crime and the dark side.

rebirth/resurrection: This can represent the unknown future and possibility, and it is often symbolized by an egg, a spring, a rising sun, the cross, a budding flower, the phoenix, or the birth canal. It can also show up when the dream takes the dreamer back to his or her childhood (see *childhood* in the encyclopedia section). This can be as difficult to confront as death in that one needs to die to something before there can be a rebirth.

The search for self is also the search for God—what we go through to grow up. To Jung, it was the process of individuation. The self, as used by Jung, meant the ego, what we are aware of, and what we are not, which he considered but a small part of who we are.

Symbols for birth and rebirth (resurrection or eternality) are universal. For example, the endless knot shows up as long life in Chinese myth, all things joined in Tibet, and no beginning/no end in Celtic myth (timelessness).

The same concept shows up in the Eastern Mandala, the circle (the endless cycle), the Möbius strip, the ouroboros (the snake biting its tail, which is a Norse, Egyptian, and alchemical symbol of the one, the integration of opposites, birth/rebirth and immortality), and yin/yang (eternal stasis and balance that gives continuous rise to each other).

The concept of birth and rebirth also shows up when physicists speak of oscillatory or eternal return universes that suggest that the universe cycles through the same events infinitely.

The concept of birth, death, and rebirth shows up in the subatomic realm of quantum mechanics where the dualist quality of particles (e.g., an electron and its antiparticle, the positron) initially annihilate each other in a crazy burst of energy that creates a photon and generates another duality (electron-positron) that annihilates itself and so on.

reconciliation: This is an alchemical process of uniting the disparate parts of ourselves and bringing together opposites in conflict either by overcoming them or integrating them. Both seem to me to be forms of transcending our differences and becoming whole and complete.

There are typically two ways to think of alchemy—the scientific way as a precursor to modern chemistry and the mystical way. Many now believe that this is the core of analytical psychology or depth psychology. I tend toward the mystical. Both seem to have as their goal—the combination of all four elements of the universe (earth, fire, air, and water) to create a fifth (the philosopher's stone).

The stone for the mystical alchemist is the symbol for ultimate state of enlightenment. Here the disparate parts of humankind are separated and then recombined into one.

For example—and this is where mercury comes in—the prima materia of the universe comes as a dichotomy that of masculine and feminine with the masculine represented by sulphur that is hot, dry, and active in opposition to the feminine represented by the argent-vive (mercury) being cold, moist, and receptive. The masculine can also be represented by Sol, the creative force, and the feminine, represented by Luna, the receptive force of wisdom.

Following a certain pattern, the conjunction of these two will produce what Carl Jung termed a "coiniunctio," the ultimate goal of the individuation process. This is the achievement of wholeness by integrating what had once been separate.

The action of mercury in this process participates in both the light and dark worlds of the psyche and thus participates at all levels during the process of transformation.

Thus, the feminine is the catalyst to the reunion of the male and female dichotomy, that which was originally one as symbolically represented by Adam.

Instead of lead transmuted into gold via the philosopher's stone, the mystical way is talking about the psychological process of individuation. It is the transmutation of the conflicted and separated human dichotomy into the wholeness of the illuminated philosopher, the prima materia, the so-called philosopher's stone.

By securing the prima materia (philosophical mercury), the dark matter of this bit of alchemy, the light of the stone can be found. In a way, the light of what we are can be found within (distilled from) the darkness of the unconscious, both personal and collective.

The anima mundi or world soul that Jung so eloquently spoke of is released from its bondage when the union between Sol and Luna takes place.

Perhaps this is the reconciliation that so many Christians speak of. Jung saw within the way of the alchemists the archetypes—the primordial dream symbols that form and inform the myths of humankind. Of course, Jung saw all this as a means for understanding the enigmatic psyche.[27]

regular guy: This can reflect the desire to belong or be included.

Someone heavy into this archetype hates to be left out or to stand out in a crowd.

The good old boy, the everyman, the working stiff, the good neighbor, or the silent majority often represent this archetype.

The danger when totally absorbed by this archetype is that people can lose themselves and can only engage in superficial relationships.

scapegoat: This is the character that gets blamed for everything regardless of his or her guilt.

When the shadow side of ourselves as individuals or as communities and societies becomes too distasteful to deal with, we either repress it into the subconscious or project it out from ourselves onto other people, communities, or societies. See *shadow* in this section and/or *betrayal* in the previous section.

Insight: I once had an administrator I worked with decide that she wanted to nip the culture of blame that permeated the office by electing a scapegoat of the month. Everything that went wrong that month would be blamed on that one person. I was the first goat. It was all very tongue-in-cheek, and it didn't work. (No one volunteered for the next month.) But it was interesting to hear about the number of various things that others blamed on me.

I think this happens in both workplaces and families where someone is designated unconsciously the goat. This is a normal response of the ego, which often projects its failings on the outside world.

self: According to Jung, it is both what we are aware of (i.e., our conscious self), the ego, and a much larger unconscious potential (75 to 85 percent). The unconscious self seems to have no boundaries because it is not ruled by the ego.

Insight: Humankind seems to be constantly in search of the real self, knowing intuitively that we are more than our conscious minds would have us believe. This urge, this quest is the archetypal search for the self that we all seem to be on. It takes the form of the search for God, the meaning of our lives, and some idea about where it's all going. Often it feels as though the journey is everlasting and continues even beyond death itself.

This journey is the process Carl Jung called individuation, the pilgrimage toward wholeness. Jung also saw it as the most important organ of adaptation in that it is the force behind the whole personality.

Self: This can represent the universal and eternal soul. It can symbolize all-potentiality. It is the nous, the fully integrated, individuated, and self-actualized Self.

Sometimes the rejected parts of yourself can be talents or skills that you've rejected or that you have not recognized. Sometimes they can be the undeveloped or underdeveloped parts of yourself.

shadow: This can represent the dark, animalistic, and uncivilized side of the self—all the negative feelings or deeds that we have done, thought, and perhaps repressed. It hides our weaknesses and shortcomings.

In short, the shadow is the disowned self and an artifact of our unwillingness to be fallible and imperfect. It is sometimes called the alter ego or dark twin.

The shadow can be depicted as a shadowy figure who's the same sex as the dreamer, the walking dead, the addict, the pervert, a human, an animal, an alien, or anything threatening.

To Jung, the shadow must be brought to the light and dealt with because the less it is acknowledged, the denser and darker it becomes. In short, what you don't know *can* hurt you.

In early Christian, Jewish, and Islamic belief, dreams were thought to be either good or bad. If they were bad, one should take refuge from them. Bad dreams were considered to come from Satan, and therefore, people were advised not to entertain them.

However, when people think that good and evil come from some place outside them, then a problem arises. If they never confront and forgive the real source of their shadow, it will come to rule them.

532

Note: In the Talmud, good and evil dreams are acknowledged, though evil did have a plus side in that it could lead one to repentance.

The Effects of the Unrecognized Shadow

They are the reason we have certain addictions, failures (both in relationships and careers), negative thoughts, judgments, and self-criticisms.

They are why we can't seem to just make it, why we keep choosing the wrong mate or love interest, or why we continuously make the wrong choices. They represent all those dark impulses and desires—the selfishness, hostility, and greediness we sometimes experience within ourselves.

When we are closed to these darker aspects of ourselves, when we are in wrong relationships with them (i.e., not consciously attentive), our darker sides become dangerous.

Simply put, our shadows will not be denied. They will project themselves into everything and everywhere, demanding to be recognized. Greed, ill will, pride, and all the so-called cardinal sins are but reflections of our shadow selves.

But it is fear that commands the greatest attention, and our greatest nightmares are trying to overcome and come to terms with those fears.

There is also what is called the "projection trap" that some religious people or cultish zealots fall into where some overly sanctimonious individuals and organizations project their own shadow onto others and thus neglect their own evil within themselves.

Because many religious sects and cults are mostly artifacts of the egoistic persona, it is possible for the followers to become superficial in their quest for spiritual balance.

In our waking lives, we can see the shadow most easily by looking at all those people or ideas we most dislike or fear.

The projection of the shadow shows up collectively in the horrors of war, extremism of any kind, sexism, and racism, and it tries to justify exploiting anyone and anything.

In short, the collective or global society has its own shadow. When ignored, it can show up in any number of chaotic ways. I believe this is what we are seeing in the current state of our political system.

For most religions, the devil (Satan) personifies the unrecognized internal shadow, and some form of Armageddon becomes the metaphorical reconciliation between the opposites of the conscious self and the unconscious self (the shadow). But this battle is not to be won in the traditional sense. The battle is about obtaining balance, not the destruction of one or the other. But balance can't be obtained unless you know from where the imbalance comes from.

The oppression of women by males in any culture is an expression and projection of the shadow.

Insight: These shadow energies are inside us, and so long as we continue to not recognize them as coming from ourselves, we will continue to project them onto others.

And to the extent that we think that the problem is outside of us, we will try to control and manipulate the world around us. But this vanity usually results in the feeling of less personal control and leads to even greater attempts to oppress or suppress others.

All this outer-directed energy literally drains our internal energy, and we become ever more frantic, trapped, and bound to the mercy of our circumstances.

The persona's projection of the shadow also tends to prematurely close you off from all other possibilities other than the ones ascribed by you.

You can see this collectively in those religions that purport to have the one and only truth (which applies to the scientific community as well), political organizations that suggest that only they have the answer, or nations that suggest they are the best. Polarization is a hallmark of the unrecognized shadow.

An unrecognized shadow blocks and redirects one's movements through life. When denied, it will play tricks on you. It will urge you to do things that are not in your best interest or in the best interest of others. For the religious, an unrecognized or denied shadow will limit people's experience of God and their ability to do his work.

Between the conception and the creation, between the emotion and the response, falls the Shadow.

—T. S. Elliott, "The Hollow Men" (1925)

The bottom line is that one cannot get rid of the shadow because it is often the very energy one uses to do what is good in the world. Thus, to deny it is to give it power over you. As the old saying goes, "What you resist will persist."

The shadow is also our opposite personality. It can be the extravert to our introvert, the thinker to our emotional side, the sensing aspect to our intuitive nature. We all have a dominant nature that is presented to the world. The shadow is the nondominant side to our personality.

It shows up in literature as well (e.g., Dr. Jekyll and Hyde). It involves the two sides of every personality, which gives the characters complexity and realness in every story.

In the Cinderella story, she is actually the shadow aspect of her sisters because they represent the realm of the conscious ego. As an archetype of the shadow, she finds her opposite in the prince and marries him, thus bringing about the joining into wholeness the two disparate aspects of the psyche.

We also project onto our movies these fears and shadows and how we want to conquer them (see *insight* on *possessed*).

Darkness loses its power during the light of day when we deal with it, understand what it is and where it comes from, and include it as part of who we are. That's when we have free will. Being voluntarily or involuntarily attached to our shadow selves weighs us down.

This attachment, caused by denial, robs us of our self-esteem and satisfaction in life. The cheater or liar can win an acknowledgment, but such victory is blunted because hypocrisy hides in the shadows.

Early in my career, I worked hard to look good, but I felt like a charlatan. When I learned that I should look like myself, the stress of maintaining the lie disappeared. Of course, this is an ongoing process throughout our lives because the ego hates to look bad.

But Where Do These Shadows Come From?

We know where the shadow resides, and some of us know what the shadows look like; however, where did these shadows come from?

Let's start from our early beginnings as individuals. Before we had developed a filter for such things, the criticisms of our parents and others around us often shamed us into thinking that some things in us were bad, wrong, or even broken. "You're too loud, too rambunctious, and don't follow directions," a parent could say. As children, we could interpret this as meaning that there's something wrong with unfettered self-expression, so we learned to bury or temper our expression.

Sometimes we may have been told that we were selfish when we took too much candy or wouldn't share a treasured toy. We were punished, and we learned to either hide this trait or sacrifice ourselves.

I can remember yelling out the answer to a question in class and then being admonished by the teacher for not raising my hand while the other kids laughed at me derisively. Rather than learn that I should take my turn among equals and that a room full of children needed some boundaries to contain the chaos, I learned to not answer questions.

These aren't rational responses, but they are logical from the point of view of the child who is trying to do the right thing but doesn't understand what's behind the rules. Rarely do adults give reasons for the rules.

We learn to separate ourselves from our true selves, and our authentic selves become suppressed to protect us from further trauma. Eventually, we develop an ego ideal and limit our access to our greater selves.

As time goes on, we reject more and more of ourselves in order to fit society's image for how we should be. Genuine self-expression becomes suppressed, and we are left with a constricted range of emotions. This also limits our choices in life, and we become more robotic in nature, eating many of the same foods, wearing the same type of clothes, working the same type of jobs or careers.

Soon life becomes monotonous, and we feel trapped by the personas and masks we've created. Uniqueness is gone, though we try to show that we are still unique by wearing something outlandish, shaving our heads, joining a group, or getting a tattoo.

The pain of what we've hidden is still there beneath the surface of our fake selves, and it literally steals away our joy and significance. Much of what we do or choose is at the effect of these shadows so that we don't have to ever experience their pain again.

Within these shadows is hidden our light, but it can only be seen when we accept the darkness as it is. In short, without the darkness, the light can't shine. If you deny the darkness, you deny the light.

Develop a relationship of give-and-take with your shadow so that it becomes more approachable.

Make peace with your humanness, and turn your pain into something useful to others. Then you will transform yourself.

Because guilt often keeps the shadow stuck, people must acknowledge their guilt in order to free themselves.

There may also be a collective shadow that resides in the collective unconscious (see *collective unconscious* in the encyclopedia section). This material seems to be passed down through the generations as though it were somehow attached to our DNA.

There are also shadow aspects of a culture and society where certain aspects are ignored or actively suppressed through an unwritten and even unacknowledged agreement between members of a society.

These can take the form of natural urges and desires that are suppressed, but these frequently leak out and cause social havoc. They often show up in our dreams as slogans saying the following: "Sex is bad." "Women are less than." "People of color or foreigners are not to be trusted." "Boys must not cry."

If you want to increase your understanding of your own shadow and have not done shadow work before, it is wise to work with a professional (e.g., a depth psychologist or therapist) before attempting this level of personal development.

soul: Not all societies believe in a soul, though many do believe in an inner motivating essence identified as spirit. For a discussion on the experience of soul in dreams, see *soul* in the image encyclopedia.

spirit guide: From this universal center of the human psyche comes an image of the spirit. It is the opposite of matter and may visit dreamers as a wise old man or woman who can guide them through the spiritual world and /or through problem issues in the waking world. Collectively, these are known as spirit guides. In the world of the shaman, these may come as a spirit spouse who assists in the shamanic work through dreams, ritual, or trance.

The ancient Egyptian Magus Hermes Trismegistus believed that all beings possessed the potential to access the infinite wisdom of the spirit, that the individual had the ability to know the whole by becoming like the whole. People could do this by aligning themselves with the divine source of their beings.

The spirit can come to us in the form of a loved one who has died, a ghost, or a numinous feeling, which is something entirely different from what we experience in our usual waking lives.

star-crossed lovers: Think Romeo and Juliet. They were joined in love and parted by fate.

task: This may represent some great or even horrendous duty that needs to be completed in order to save the day (e.g., Frodo's task with the ring from the *Lord of the Rings* or all the tasks set for the Jedi in the *Star Wars* saga).

unus mundus: This is the concept of one world (the interrelation of psyche and body).

water: This is the symbol of life, cleansing, and rebirth. It is often depicted as a living force (see *water* in the encyclopedia section).

wholeness: Human beings seem to have an archetypal drive toward wholeness and a search for the spirit. Frequently, this image shows up as a circle (see *mandala*).

Many dreams can be about this continual search in the attempt to reconcile differences or sex (see *sex*).

wise old man or woman: As women (queen, grandmother, witch, goddess, or your own mother) or as men (king, magician, prophet, wizard, sage, your father, guide, or authority figure), they are full of power and wisdom, deep insight, and unconditional love.

These figures are full of holy power with their quality of wisdom being greater than that of the mother or the father. These can show up as the king, magician, prophet, wizard, sage, doctor, sorceress, or shaman.

There can be both negative and positive aspects to each. These images in our dreams can represent the soul talking to us and sometimes are called the archetype of the spirit. They can also get so bogged down in details that they never act on anything.

wizard: Wizards in dreams are often your inner wisdom or the wisdom of the soul. They can represent your personal power and sometimes even unconditional love. They can come in the guise of prophets, shaman, fathers/grandfathers, or kings, and be metaphors for deep wisdom and holy power. They can represent the spiritual side of yourself.

Sometimes wizards can be power symbols. Depending on what they are doing,
you may not be expressing your power or expressing it inappropriately.

Insight: Each of us tends to express two or three or more of these archetypes in our lives. It's as though our personal souls express themselves through the collective soul by way of the archetypes.

When you were reading the descriptions in this chapter, was there one or more that resonated with you more than others? Is it possible that these archetypal images are expressions of your soul's purpose?

Section 3

Nightmares

Nightmares are a special category of dream, so I gave them their own section. This kind of dream is known as a REM anxiety dream and usually occurs in the latter part of the sleep cycle just before waking (see *REM* in the image encyclopedia).

By virtue of our ancient roots, we are all instinctively disposed to respond immediately to threatening and fearful stimuli. We do this in both our waking lives and in our dreams, often through the intervention of nightmares. In a very real way, nightmares tell us that all is not well in our outer or inner worlds. Though the form of these nightmares may be affected by culture and individual experience, the pattern is often archetypal in nature and demands that we pay attention and focus.

Fundamentally, nightmares are high-anxiety dreams that come in service of our health and well-being with the intent of urgently identifying and dealing with sources of anxiety. One of the most common features of a nightmare is that we are desperately trying to escape some fearful situation in many of them.

I had a nightmare not too long ago—one of those where the narrative takes you right up to the most awful part of the horror and then you wake up. Whew, thank goodness!

Well, not really. Frequently, I try to get back to sleep in order to resolve the outcome and finish the story. In that way, I have some control over the outcome, or at least I get more information on the meaning of the dream. However, letting a dream play all the way out (often a technique used with nightmare treatment), especially when emotional, psychological, and/or physical trauma is involved, should not be done alone. Working with a therapist can be helpful when you are working on all recurring nightmare issues.

If this were a regular nightmare experience, which we all have from time to time, especially when we are stressed, you might want to consider the point where you wake up as the climax of a story and then perhaps ask yourself, "What happens next?" or, "How might the story end?" This might be a good technique for exploring the nightmare further.

Now, I'm not referring to people who are reenacting literal horrors that happened to them in their waking lives (such as for those who are suffering from PTSD). Stay away from those nightmares. The people may need more professional guidance. I'm talking about those that are symbolic of something going on inside you or those that you are reacting to in your daily life. You might ask yourself, "Does this dream remind me of something in my waking life?"

Nightmares can be normal after a trauma, but most of the time, it is material that you've kept hidden (e.g., threats to your self-esteem, the loss of something or someone important, trouble coping with certain stresses, unconscious memories stimulated by some recent event, or scary emotions that you have avoided), and the unconscious mind, which is in the service of your health and well-being, is trying to bring them to consciousness so that you can deal with them appropriately. They literally *demand* attention.

I think that many of us with the standard events of unfinished nightmares want to be able to master them. It's probably why we like such authors as Stephen King. Finishing the nightmare in a psychically satisfying manner is much better than ignoring it. If you do try to ignore it, it'll just come back!

We're not talking night terrors here. In those there are no plots, just a lot of scary chaos. Night terrors—or what are sometimes referred to as "incubus attacks"—happen during stage-four sleep, and the person usually doesn't remember any details, only extreme fear.

Nightmares often have fairly complicated plots. You go from balance or equilibrium to extreme imbalance and then wake up. When you awaken, then the climax dominates the story, and this can truncate the meaning and leave you stuck. If you were to treat the nightmare as a narrative, you would then want the story to return to equilibrium (i.e., resolution). Basically, I'm talking about the process of transformation, the psychic alchemical process of turning something base into something of value.

The kind of intervention to which I'm referring has the advantage of giving you some feedback. If the nightmare has reoccurred but disappears after intervention, then you've been successful. If not, try something else.

Four Nightmare Case Studies

Dark night of the world soul
—Brittany Cole (2005)

1) Walking the Dark Night

I had three nightmares across nine nights of fretful sleep. In one, a character is shot several times as he runs down the road, the last shot bringing him down. I fall with him and reach out to comfort him. Another has me wearing a CPAP mask at a restaurant dining table, feeling shocked, vulnerable, humiliated, and virtually emasculated. In the last dream, I'm threatened and abused by three twenty-foot giants.

What to make of it all?

In the first dream, the character being shot is an expression of myself suffering what William Shakespeare called "slings and arrows of outrageous fortune" (attacks against the psyche in this case). I fear that there will be one too many attacks, and I will not be able to soothe and get up from so many. Watching a friend take several psychic blows that would have left me emotionally bleeding may have triggered this first dream and my inability to come to his defense. (The idea of bringing comfort was disturbing because it spoke to a feeling of cowardice on my part.) There's also a theme running through the world psyche at the moment. Many people are taking the blows, and the collective ego is becoming increasingly more self-critical.

The second dream seems to echo the first, and indeed, it came on the night following the first. This dream seemed to suggest humiliation and a feeling of emasculation. It continued a theme of feeling vulnerable and not being able to protect myself adequately. The mask itself also may have symbolized a fear of being found out, of not being able to successfully hide what I was feeling in my everyday life.

Seven days later the third nightmare interrupted my sleep. In this dream, three imposing and quite frightening giants attacked me and stood threateningly astride me as I fell. I felt that I wouldn't be able to save myself from what was about to happen, and then I awoke. *Are my feelings overwhelming me? Is my negative inner dialogue going to injure me? Who are these three antagonists?* I wondered. Then it hit me that they might represent my three biggest concerns as I grow older—body deterioration (not only reflecting all the aches and pains but the loss of attractiveness to the opposite sex), deteriorating usefulness, and a contracting future.

There's a lot to be learned from one's darker dreams. There's light in our dark nightmares. In this case, there are few if any answers, but knowing in deeper detail about what's going on with me emotionally may give me a starting point to dealing with these emotions.

2) Nightmares and Shadows in the Dark

Again, I had another visit from one of my shadows. He was menacing and swarthy and trying hard to enter the locked car I was in through the cracks around the windows and doors. I was paralyzed with fear and unable to defend myself.

When I awoke, I thought that I had a handle on these dark denizens of my psyche, but when I looked closer, I saw that I was continuing to create dichotomies and conflicts all around me. I was continuing to see things as good or bad, black or white, right or wrong.

Every time I judged the world or myself or when I blamed any part of it for its folly, I was conjuring the shadow.

I saw fear in the dream. I saw fear in the world, and the fear was in me. The world was in me. I shared the inner and outer conflict between what was safe and what was unsafe. I also shared the struggle between fear and love. I had great difficulty loving what I feared and could not add enough outer safety to protect me from the lack of safety. My inner world mirrored the outer world. Love and the experience of security were at a premium because of my propensity to create dichotomies and to separate myself from the essence of what I am.

I'm not alone, of course. You all know what I'm talking about. You may not use a word as strong as fear, but worry, anxiety, concern, nervousness, and discomfort will fit just as well.

Safety is not in keeping the doors locked against the shadow. Building up our armies, carrying guns on our hips, or building walls around our borders will not help us to feel safe. Those will not protect us. The problem is not out there. It is and always has been in here (your head).

I don't feel safe when I don't remember who I really am at my core—the source of my being. At the source or soul level, nothing is threatened from the external world. Fear and its partners (e.g., anxiety and worry) need an external focus (whether the past, the present, trauma, memories) and the experience of the unknown—and everything is unknown. Change is of the external world and is not an aspect of the soul.

Sometimes I wonder if I belong in this world, and this thought always leads me toward uneasiness, a feeling of loneliness and insecurity. I never feel this when I feel loved. When I experience love, both given and received, I feel secure, connected, and part of everything.

Some will say that we need to trust in God's love. I wish I could, but there's enough grief and tragedy around me that I'm not always sure of the steadfastness of this love. I've tried to intellectually believe that all is well because God is with me or to emotionally embrace the concept, but both are faulty because they are open to doubt. No, I think that love has to reside somewhere inside of me that is immutable, unchanging, and independent of circumstances. When I objectify love, when I reduce it to a feeling, or when I layer my images and expectations onto it, I miss the reality of it. Love is always there, though it is not always experienced because we throw up fears that mask it.

I think that many of our nightmares come from the fear of the loss or the absence of love or belonging. When in the presence of love, we feel powerful and in control of our lives, and when it's absent, we become disconnected from one another and from our source and can spiral out of control. The nightmare can then act as a means of highlighting what's going on inside us and point to what we need to do.

> If I love myself I love you. If I love you I love myself.
>
> —Rumi

I always love my wife, but sometimes I don't experience it because I am defending some part of myself or fearing some action on her part that I've misinterpreted as an unloving action. Why is this? Frequently, I am on the alert for betrayal. Betrayal is both a waking and sleeping world shadow that often betrays me—the real me and the loved and loving me. It's my fearful, untrusting, externally focused self that shuts me off from my core self.

So what does it take to experience and manifest the real me? I think that it may be the absence of fear, or at the very least, it may be the absence of not acting in a fearful way. And how might this play out in my response to the waking world?

> Love is the cure, for your pain will keep giving birth to more pain until
> your eyes constantly exhale love as effortlessly as your body yields its scent.
>
> —Rumi

3) Horrible Death Nightmare

There she knelt with a metal stake through her heart. It had impaled her and permanently pinned her to the ground. I held her, trying desperately to comfort her as the life passed out of her. Sadness and great depression overwhelmed me, and then I awoke.

Thus ended the night's dream, a rarely experienced nightmare for these days, though I used to experience many more like this when I was younger.

Leaning over, I peered at the clock and groaned, "It's only three thirty!" I grumbled as I got up and stumbled in the dark toward the kitchen, knowing full well that I wouldn't be able to get back to sleep without brewing a hot cup of my special tea blend that I used when sleep eluded me.

Later in the morning as I walked to the coffee shop, a favored routine after I had walked my youngest granddaughter to school, I reviewed the dream that had troubled and awakened me so early. *What could it possibly mean?* I wondered silently.

The image of the young woman may have represented some part of me that had felt threatened, perhaps some compassionate part or some goal or ambition of mine. To be stabbed through the heart could symbolize some kind of betrayal. *Is that its meaning?* I wondered. Often dreams would come to me with more than one agenda or level of meaning.

Since the untimely death and loss of a close and longtime friend and the grim illness of another, I'd been more than just a little down. And when I'm down, I tend to become quite negative about myself and my life. Then self-criticisms abound. The more I criticize, the more it feels as though I'm eating my heart (i.e., destroying the loving, compassionate, and hopeful side of myself), and I begin to spiral out of control. Once into this emotional spiral, it feels as though I can't free myself, and I begin to feel stuck and unable to snap myself out of it.

The experience of losing a loved one is like being shot through the heart with all the pain and shock that that implies. It's also like suffering a broken heart.

On another level, I'd been experiencing some sustained criticisms from someone outside myself, and these also struck deep.

Combined, the experiences left me on my knees, figuratively speaking, and feeling helpless.

In yet another of the dream messages, I understood that I needed to be more compassionate with myself right now, even though I felt a little helpless in this endeavor.

In the dream there was also the sense that the young woman would die, which could mean that my feelings would eventually pass and/or that change was an inevitable and natural outcome.

As with the death of anyone who's close, we are often faced with the reality of our own mortality—its inevitability, helplessness, and betrayal. It is just part of the mind having to deal with the concept of death, endings, and finality. It's times like these when one is dealing with death that we need to acknowledge that what's going on with us is real and normal and that we need to allow the grief to happen so that we don't get stuck in it.

549

4) Staring into the Abyss

Here's a nightmare from a writer who commented on one of my blogs.

> There I stood at the edge of a cliff high above a dark and forbidding abyss. The earth beneath my feet began to shake and as I peered over the edge I could just make out something huge crawling out of the blackness. In terror I tried to step back fearing that I would lose my footing and fall into the inky dark and the cavernous maw of the creature below. And then I awoke.

Yep, a good old-fashioned nightmare had gripped this man and shaken him to the bone, rattling his soul until he awoke to save himself.

Sound familiar?

Apparently, a lot of us have these dreamtime cliff-hangers that grab our attention from time to time, but what's the message?

Let's look at the images for some clues. The cliff could be about being on the edge of an understanding, a solution, a realization, or an awareness. Perhaps it represents a critical point in life where you can't afford to make any errors or lose your footing. Falling itself in this case could be about failure or at least the fear of it.

We have expectations for ourselves, and others have expectations for us as well. These can put the pressure on us to succeed or at least not to fail. Stuffing these fears as a way of dealing with the pressures can eventually create the kind of nightmare the dreamer experienced.

How you got to the top of the cliff could speak to your ambitions, drive, and the risks you took. In this case, being at the edge might indicate that you are at your limit. If you were to stand tall against the scary creature below, it might suggest that you need to stand up to your fears, or if you cower, it may suggest that you are not standing up to the fear.

Looking down into any abyss can be like staring into the unknown. This in itself can create great anxiety, and the dream reflects that. This dream may reflect an obstacle to your ambitions, but it also can suggest that you may be afraid of taking the plunge or the leap of faith into the unknown that often needs to happen if you want to succeed at something.

But the abyss or void can also represent the depths of your unconscious mind and your uncertainty of what lies beyond what you already know. This unknown can also represent change or the need for change, which may be stalking you in this case.

Clearly, something is stalking this dreamer, and it may very well be a shadow creature, a part of his rejected self that he has pushed down into his subconscious. It is crawling menacingly out of its hiding place and forcing the dreamer to confront and deal with it directly. Is this a manifestation of the dreamer's depression? These shadows can also represent a raw ambition that needs to be confronted and tamed.

In another nightmarish dream shared by a reader, the dreamer was stalked by a mob of people making untrue accusations about him and threatening his well-being. In the dream he tried to reason with the crowd of accusers but found that they were also now part of the mob.

In this dream the person was experiencing an attack on his self-image and his ability to defend himself from a misinformed vision of who he was, and consequently, his very identity was being threatened. In his attempt to defend himself, he became like the mob and began to doubt himself. This led the dreamer to reevaluate how he was responding to the threat that triggered this dream. He also became aware that the mob might represent himself and how his self-critical inner dialogue was threatening his well-being.

Falling Is Often a High–Anxiety Dream

Falling from a great height might reflect that you have climbed too high and might now be threatened by great failure. This kind of nightmare may serve the purpose of bringing to consciousness repressed desires and energies of one's powerful nature. As a male, I was taught to be aggressive, but at the same time, I was told to not be too obvious about this behavior. What tends to happen with this push/pull type of message is that I go in and out of my power. Women, on the other hand, can have a great deal of unexpressed power because society has taught them that it is not feminine to be assertive (i.e., to express their power). This can develop an inner conflict where the dreamer often stands at the edge of a precipice and fears failing.

Being Chased in a Dream

This is a very common nightmare where some unseen but terrifying presence chases a person down. Frequently, it occurs when some part of one's nature wants to be integrated into one's consciousness.

If you want to discover what this presence wants from you, you can imagine turning around and asking it directly what it wants. Some believe that the very act of facing one's scary dream images enhances one's courage.

Positive and Negative in REM and Non-REM Dreams

In the encyclopedia section of the codex, I highlighted the phenomenon of rapid eye movement (REM) sleep.* But research has shown that we don't just dream during REM. We also dream during non-REM (with its four stages leading up to and from REM). In fact, non-REM may outperform REM by more than 2.5 to one. And it turns out that there's a qualitative difference between the types of dreams as well.

About every ninety minutes or so, the brain switches between REM and non-REM sleep. With every new iteration of REM, the time spent in it increases with the longest period showing up just before you waken. If you wake up during this time, you tend to remember your dreams better. It turns out that nightmares also occur during this final stage of REM.

Because nightmares are experienced during REM, they are affected by dysfunctional sleep cycles. People with depression and/or PTSD (post-traumatic stress disorder) tend to have a lot of them, which then truncates the REM cycle, causing even greater dysfunctional sleep patterns. There's a movement in the psychiatric field to find pharmacological ways of diminishing nightmares in those with chronic depression and PTSD.

But nightmares are similar to ancestral dreams and may very well be rehearsals in the struggle to survive. They may be the brain's way of helping an individual confront his or her fears and tensions head-on. During REM sleep, the amygdala (located deep within the medial temporal lobes of the brain), which deals with unpleasant emotions, aggression, and fear and also modulates REM sleep, may be responsible for the negative vibes.

---

* A stage of deep sleep when the eyes can be seen moving rapidly beneath the eyelids.

Along that note, it's interesting that people with depression jump into REM quickly by bypassing the non-REM stages, which are often the positive stages. A dysfunctional amygdala is also implicated. This rapid entrance into REM and the depletion of overall non-REM is a marker for depression and often precedes a depressive episode.[*] Those who are awakened during a non-REM episode report generally positive dreams, while those who are awakened from REM report mostly negative. What's that about?

In the short term, drugs provide a respite for the insomnia of the depressed that is caused by nightmares, but if used over the long term, might they be altering the process that nature uses to resolve and deal with fear? Do we really understand the functions of sleep and dreaming well enough to be interfering in this way? Might not it be better to develop a different way of therapeutically dealing with the darkness other than popping a pill to suppress it?

Perhaps in some of us, it takes the form of chronic depression or chronically unresolved fears, especially those fears that seem to be unattached to any stimulus, what psychologists call "free-floating fears."

There may also be a cultural consequence that shows up in our attitude toward death (and medicine) and our overwhelming need to suppress the negative behaviors in others because of our fears. Why does the United States always seem to be at war with someone? Why does capitalism require continuous growth and happiness? This may be an avoidance of the negative, but it can lead to bubbles that pop, an unsustainable depletion of resources, and unstable societies. With the focus on the avoidance of the negative, we seem to be constantly running from it. It's like a bully that we've inadvertently given power to.

REM dreams tend to be dark and sometimes unpleasant, and the Western culture tends to avoid these emotions. In fact, many believe that it's best to leave them alone. But what is the consequence of this avoidance over time? What is the consequence of suppressing the natural negative?

Both REM and non-REM have what appear to be important, perhaps even vital functions to our survival and learning. It turns out that non-REM is our internal trainer. It mirrors past experience in a time-compressed manner. It literally is helping you in the present to

---

[*] Bypassing non-REM sleep also interrupts the body's cycle of healing, repair, rejuvenation, and/ or immunization, which only further reinforces the depression.

relate to the future base on experience from the past. The REM dream, however, expands time and takes you into the future in order to practice it and to test various scenarios. This may explain why some dreams seem to be about what's happened during your waking life the day before, while others seem more distant or unrelated to events in waking life.

Dreams in both forms seem to be nature's way of preparing us for whatever comes next. Basically, it's an ancient survival tool. The content is different, but the mechanics are pretty much the same.

Whether in positive or nightmarish form, dreams seem to reinforce learning, creativity, and survival skills, provide a window to your emotional self, and open a space for life preparation (i.e., practice). They do this by providing a totally different point of view to that of our waking lives. They are intuitive and visual in contrast to the linear and logical perspective in our waking lives. What seem to be intractable problems in one's waking life can be overcome through the highly creative, free-associating content of dreams.

Nightmares and Recurring Dreams

The unconscious mind seems to *see* everything—every nuance and everything operating at the periphery of our awareness. The dream is the processing of this information, and we can use this information to enlighten our experience of our waking lives.

If the information is critical to your well-being, it may show up in recurring dreams, or if your immediate attention is required, it may come in the form of a nightmare, particularly if you're not in the habit of remembering your dreams. They always come in the service of your well-being.

The nightmare may very well be an evolutionary, instinctive adaptation, and it should not be ignored! Just as you would pay attention to threatening stimuli in your waking life, you should also pay attention to your nightmares. You should look at and interpret them closely to gain insight about the message being communicated.

Many people send me their bad dreams or dreams they keep having night after night (recurring dreams) that speak to events in their waking lives. Most often these are things they either know but lurk in the shadows, things they haven't paid attention to, or things they don't know consciously. These so-called bogeymen are actually unresolved parts of ourselves and can even represent our opposite personalities.

Repetitive Trauma Dreams in Nightmares

The following are included here to show that there is diagnostic value to dreams. It may also be possible to identify mental disorders such as PTSD (also referred to as shell shock and battle fatigue) through the adjunct analysis of dreams. Inasmuch as dreams can also provide information on healing, attention to dream patterns could also be helpful to the therapeutic process.

The recurrence of this kind of dream and extreme anxiety symbolically represented within the context of the dream (e.g., storms at sea, etc.) can also add to the diagnostic pattern.

According to expertpages.com,

> These recurrent images of the trauma intrude upon the victim's sleep in the form of disturbing dreams and nightmares. Unlike normal dreams, which utilize symbolism to conceal from consciousness the dreamer's actual life conflicts and concerns, PTSD dreams are often literal representations of the traumatic event.

> The starkly realistic presentation of the dreamer's traumatic experience reflects the psyche's inability to master, process, and integrate these overwhelming stimuli, through the disguising processes of sublimation and symbol formation.

> They also seem to be acting or feeling as if the traumatic event were recurring This often includes a sense of reliving the experience, illusions, hallucinations and dissociative flashback episodes, including those that occur on awakening or when intoxicated.

> Note: Though alcohol, marijuana, and cocaine tend to suppress dream recall, barbiturates, antipsychotics, sleeping pills, and antianxiety drugs drastically reduce dream recall as well. High stress itself will also make it more difficult to recall as will drugs to reduce that stress.

> In short, the use of dream material in the diagnosis and intervention of PTSD may be negatively affected through the standard use of pharmaceuticals to deal with the symptoms of the trauma.

> Note: In young children, trauma-specific reenactment may occur.

The victim frequently feels a sense of déjà vu as if reliving the experience, sometimes in the form of illusions or hallucinations, frequently when in physiologically altered states of consciousness such as those induced by alcohol, drugs or sleep. Young children may actually reenact the traumatic events in their play behavior, alone or with others.

It has also been found that the intensity of dream material is affected by whether the person who has sustained the trauma had lifelong nightmares (LLNM) prior to the trauma or the person experienced them only after the trauma.[28]

Children's Nightmares

Though nightmares occur for many children, they typically show up with some frequency in children between three and six years old, peaking at around six to ten and then tapering off. Often this is because that's the age when children's imaginations become very active and their normal fears begin to interact with them. It's part of the normal stage of coping development. Somewhere around 50 to 75 percent of children in this age range have nightmare activity.

Children's nightmares generally reflect their fears of the unknown and the seemingly overwhelming emotional environments they find themselves in. These can be normal reflections of their emotional development or their psychic responses to traumas seen or experienced (in real life or in movies and TV).

All dreams, including the unpleasant and frightening ones that we call nightmares, should be treated as real and not put down with the well-intentioned bromide "It's just a dream." This can be insulting to the child and lose the adult some respect. For the child, it's *very* real. The idea that a dream is meaningless because it's not real also begins the process of extinguishing the interest and therefore the psychological and emotional usefulness of dreams, which will ultimately handicap these children throughout their lives.

As with adults, some of the best therapy for dealing with childhood nightmares is to just have someone listen to them talk about these bad dreams.

Beyond the nightmare there is something called a night terror that can cause children to bolt upright and begin screaming with their eyes wide open with fear and panic. This can be very distressing to parents. Though children may remember intense parts of nightmares, they rarely remember anything from night terrors with the exception of some physical impressions such as a sense of heaviness, visual anomalies (e.g., pulsating), or difficulty breathing. About 15 percent of children between three and six years old will have them, and they can last anywhere from five minutes or so up to as long as a half hour. The best way to handle these events is to not wake them and to make them safe. Holding them while they cycle through the experience and then helping them back to sleep is usually the best way to deal with them.

My mother used to hold me and then sing me to sleep with my favorite song, "Over the Rainbow," when these fearsome terrors would show up. I remember that they would often start with the ominous and threatening feeling that there was some dark presence in my room, and when I would reach for the light switch, it wouldn't work. I would wake up screaming and would literally try to scale the walls, sometimes bloodying my fingers in the process. My mother would have to pull me down and put her arms around me while she sat beside me. As she sang, I could see the room pulsating outward and then inward as though it were breathing heavily until everything finally calmed down. Then I would fall back to sleep.

Ideas for Dealing with Nightmares

Many psychologists recommend that we not avoid our fears but face them and what triggers them head-on. It is also recommended that we begin to ferret out the positives in what have become negative events. Noticing the positive can broaden our perspectives.

For those who have suffered tragedy, finding a sense of meaning and purpose to life cannot only greatly affect your daily response to events but actually prolong life.

Viktor Frankl, a twentieth-century psychiatrist, developed a therapy he called Logotherapy, which is still used today to treat people who have suffered trauma. To him, people possessed a leaning toward meaning and wanted to reinforce that as a means of reconnecting or strengthening their connection with their core selves. They do so to move themselves from the experience of being victims of their circumstances to having some meaningful control over those circumstances.[29]

My wife and I set up a cot next to our bed. Whatever child had a nightmare could crawl in there and stay next to us. Playing flashlight tag in the dark can also be an effective way of desensitizing a child as can checking under the bed and in the closet before bedtime. You can also provide a special toy for defense against the darkness during this period.

Relaxing before bedtime (no TV or video games) works wonders for both children and adults who suffer with nightmares. Working on strategies for feeling secure during the day will also help both children and adults prevent recurring nightmares.

We are continuously bathed in fearful images—violent TV shows, news media, and the games we play. The body has natural hormonal responses to fear or threat that can become conditioned to threat stimuli as with any biological system and eventually alter the baseline triggers. Though these reactions are usually short-lived, the endocrine system can become conditioned to continuous fear reactivity. Eventually, this conditioning changes the response pathways and keeps our bodies and minds in a constant state of crisis reactivity. It's as though we are continually running from the saber-toothed tiger. The body was not designed to handle continuous fight-or-flight activity, and after a time the body begins to break down, exhibiting physical abnormalities as well as psychological and emotional dysfunction.

Chronic fear threatens the body's immune system. It can cause cardiovascular damage, cause or exacerbate depression, and retard the formation of long-term memory.[30]

Being in a continuous state of fear affects our rational processing of information, and we succumb to a state of overreacting many times to threats that aren't even there. I believe the gun industry and its handmaiden, the NRA, along with certain politicians, exploit this reaction to their own advantage.

Because all dreams—even nightmares—come to us in the service of our health and well-being, we should pay attention to them, but with that in mind, there is a caveat. When nightmares begin to impair your daily functioning, wake you repeatedly from sleep, and distress your overall mental well-being because of intense, vivid, and disturbing images as they do sometimes with those who are experiencing PTSD (e.g., war veterans as well as rape, assault, and torture victims), some kind of intervention may be needed.

Recent research indicates that the occurrence of frequent nightmares is linked to a reduced tolerance to stress, though it's unclear to me whether the nightmares are causal or the people who have frequent nightmares are already at a high stress level.[31]Various cognitive behavior therapies using such techniques as imagery rehearsal (IRT), where individuals rescripts their nightmares and change them into something less debilitating, relaxation techniques, and systematic desensitization have proven to be somewhat successful as has the use of a certain blood pressure medicine that has proved to reduce nightmares. (Ask your physician about this.)

Sometimes prescribed medications can lead to nightmares, such as certain antidepressants, especially narcotics. They can also be triggered by stressors in one's waking life, such as anxiety, late-night snacks, sleep deprivation, substance abuse, and sleep disorders such as sleep apnea.

Recurrent dreams, those whose themes repeat over and over again for several nights or throughout your life, may speak to issues that haven't been resolved, or these may be just a symbolic means of communication from the unconscious to the conscious. Like everything else in life, we tend to use what works, and the unconscious side of us is no different.

Cultural Treatments

All societies tend to deal with the aftermath of traumatic events through a filter of traditional and local cultural values. Some non-Western societies still use the aid of local wise men, shamans, and diviners, as well as ritual practice, to deal with nightmares. In some parts of the third world, ghosts visiting the dream world can communicate information that is useful in curing what ails the living. Certain rituals are still used to protect and/or cure the dreamer from these visiting nightmares that haunt his or her dreams.

Modern therapists are beginning to respect some of these traditions in their own practices so that they don't compromise the effectiveness of the therapeutic process by ignoring these rituals' usefulness.[32]

A Short List of Nightmare Treatments

The following are treatments for nightmare disorders. Because a detailed description of each of the techniques is beyond the scope of this book, they are presented as a means of bringing awareness to the field of working with nightmares that may have become chronic in nature. For this reason, I provide only a brief description. All therapies should only be undertaken with the assistance of a trained professional.

These are all nonpharmacological therapies used to treat excessive nightmares. The journal article goes into greater detail.[33]

Image Rehearsal Therapy (IRT)

This therapy is the one with the most empirical support.

Jot down a brief description of a recent nightmare. If your most recent nightmare is too upsetting to think about, pick another.

Think of a way to change the nightmare. Some therapists decline to tell their patients what sort of change to make, encouraging them to rely on their intuition to make an appropriate change.

Set aside a few minutes each day to imagine this altered version of the nightmare. Simply paint a mental picture of the altered version.

Cognitive Behavior Therapy

Cognitive behavior therapy (CBT) is a type of psychotherapeutic treatment that helps patients understand the thoughts and feelings that influence behaviors. It's more often used for insomnia.

Lucid Dreaming Therapy

Because of the state of lucidity, the dream self is less fearful of threatening dream images or situations. Because of this, there is less resistance to confrontation with these figures or situations.

A recent study has shown that when lucid dreaming therapy (LDT) is combined with IRT, the control of the dream's content seems to contribute to changes in recurrent post-traumatic nightmares.[34]

Self-Exposure Therapy

This kind of therapy is often used with phobias, panic attacks, social disorders, and PTSD. It's a means of safely facing your fears and imagining ways to deal with them.

Exposure Relaxation and Rescripting Therapy

This is a modified version of image rehearsal therapy with an enhanced exposure component.

Systematic Desensitization

This is a type of behavior therapy with graduated exposure to the nightmare stressors. It has also been called counterconditioning.

Sleep Dynamic Therapy

This requires an in-depth discovery process to explain the nature and complexities of what is causing the sleep disorder.

A Final Word

Of course, there are medications that have proven useful in the treatment of chronic nightmares, but again, you should discuss these with a physician.

Mindfulness training and meditation are also used to reduce the incidence of nightmares.

Endnotes

Introduction

1   Thomas Moore, *Care of the Soul: A Guide for Cultivating Depth and Sacredness in Everyday Life* (New York: Harper Collins, 1992), 291.

2   James Hillman, *The Dream and the Underworld* (New York: Harper & Row, 1979).

3   Elis Gruffudd, *The Chronicle of Elis Gruffudd*, National Library of Wales MS 5276D, edited and translated by Thomas Jones in Etude Celtique, 1947.(referenced as source on The Story of Myrddin Wyllt, http://www.maryjones.us/ctexts/myrddin.html)

4   Chuang Tzu, *The Complete Works of Chuang Tzu*, trans. Burton Watson (New York: Columbia University Press, 1968), 49.

5   R. Evin and T. Nielsen, "Disturbed Dreaming, Post-Traumatic Stress Disorder, and Affect Distress: A Review and Neurocognitive Model," *Psychological Bulletin* 133 (2007): 482–528.

6   Derek and Julia Parker, *Dreaming: Remembering, Interpreting* (New York: Simon & Shuster, 1985), 28.

7   R. J. Cole, *The Dragon's Treasure: A Dreamer's Guide to Inner Discovery through Dream Interpretation* (Bloomington, IN: iUniverse, 2009), 28.

8   Carl G. Jung, et al., *Jung Extracts: Dreams, Vol. 20* (Princeton: Princeton University Press, 1974), 46.

9   Carl G. Jung, *The Collected Works of C.G. Jung, Vol. 16, edited by* Adler, G., Hull, R.F.C., *The Practice of Psychotherapy*, 322. Princeton University Press,1934.

10 As referenced in the Jewish Encyclopedia, http://jewishencyclopedia.com/articles/5311-dreams.

Section 1
Encyclopedia of Images

11 Meister Eckhart, "Sermon IV" from the Christian Classics Ethereal Library, http://www.ccel.org/ccel/eckhart/sermons.vii.html.

12 W. Coe, L. Buckner, M. Howard, and K. Kobayashi, "Hypnosis as Role Enactment: Focus on a Role Specific Skill," *American Journal of Clinical Hypnosis* 15, no. 1 (1972): 41–45.

13 Z. Klemenc-Ketis, "Life Changes in Patients after out-of-Hospital Cardiac Arrest: The Effect of Near-Death Experiences," *International Journal of Behavioral Medicine* 20, no. 1 (March 2013): 7–12.

14 Stephen Menn, *Descartes and Augustine* (Cambridge: University of Cambridge Press, 1998).

15 A. H. Maslow, *Religions, Values, and Peak Experiences* (London: Penguin Books Limited, 1964).

16 J. K. Rowling, *Harry Potter and the Sorcerer's Stone.* London: Bloomsbury Children's, 1997.

17 Joanne Davis et al., "A Comparison of Lifelong and Post Trauma Nightmares in Civilian Trauma Sample," University of Tulsa, *Dreaming* 21, no. 1, March 2011, 70–80.

Section 2
The Archetypes of the Symbolic Mind

18 J. Hillman, *A Blue Fire* (New York: Harper Perennial, 1989), 23.

19 R. J. Cole, excerpt from the Dreaming Wizard, http://thedreamingwizard.com/dream-symbol-archetypes_296.html.

20 Carlos Castaneda, *Journey to Ixtlan: The Lessons of Don Juan* (New York: Pocket Books, 1972).

22 R. J. Cole, excerpt from the https://thebookofdreamsblog.wordpress.com/2016/08/04/life-is-not-an-empty-dream/.

23 S. Aizenstat R. and Bosnak, eds., *Imagination and Medicine: The Future of Healing in an Age of Neuroscience* (New Orleans: Spring Journal Books, 2009).

24 R. J. Cole, *The Archipelago of Dreams: The Island of the Dream Healer* (Bloomington, IN: iUniverse, 2011).

25 J. C. Harris, The Complete Tales of *Uncle Remus* (Norwalk, Connecticut: Easton Press, 2006).

26 *The Lion King*, Walt Disney Pictures, 1994.

27 C. G. Jung, *The Collected Works of C. G. Jung: Alchemical Studies* (Princeton: Princeton University Press, 1970).

Section 3
Nightmares

28 Joanne Davis et al., "A Comparison of Lifelong and Post Trauma Nightmares in Civilian Trauma Sample," University of Tulsa, *Dreaming* 21, no. 1, March 2011,70–80.

29 Joseph B. Fabry, The Pursuit of Meaning: Viktor Frankl, Logotherapy and Life, Purpose Research, LLC, 2013A

30   According to University of Minnesota, http://www.takingcharge.csh.umn.edu/enhance-your-wellbeing/security/facing-fear/impact-fear.

31   M. Blagrove, L. Farmer, and E. Williams, "The Relationship of Nightmare Frequency and Nightmare Distress to Well-Being," *Journal of Sleep Research* 13 (2004): 129–36.

32   G. T. Eagle, "Promoting Peace by Integrating Western and Indigenous Healing in Treating Trauma," *Journal of Peace Psychology* 4 (2004): 271–82.

33   Nisha R. Aurora, MD, Rochelle S. Zak, et al., "Best Practice Guide for the Treatment of Nightmare Disorder in Adults Standards of Practice Committee," *Journal of Clinical Sleep Medicine* 6, no. 4 (2010): 389–401.

34   Gerlinde C. Harb and Janeese A. Brownlow, "Post Traumatic Nightmares and Imagery Rehearsal: The Possible Role of Lucid Dreaming," *Dreaming: The Journal of the Association for the Study of Dreams* 26, no. 3, September 2016. 238–49.

About the Author

R. J. Cole, MS, LEP, is a certified educational psychologist with more than thirty-five years of experience working with adjudicated youth and children with severe emotional disabilities. He is a member of the American Psychological Association and the International Association for the Study of Dreams. Author of the *Archipelago of Dreams* and The Dragon's Treasure, he lives with his wife in California.

CPSIA information can be obtained
at www.ICGtesting.com
Printed in the USA
LVHW101608060220
646086LV00006B/268

FEB 1 3 2020

9 781532 070068